The Social Teaching of the Christian Churches

The
Social Teaching
of the
Christian Churches

Ernst Troeltsch

With an
Introduction by
H. Richard Niebuhr

Translated by
Olive Wyon

Volume 1

The University of Chicago Press
Chicago and London

DEDICATED

IN DEEPEST GRATITUDE AND RESPECT

TO

THE EMINENT PHILOSOPHICAL FACULTY
AT GREIFSWALD

AND

TO THE EMINENT LAW FACULTY
AT BRESLAU

The University of Chicago Press, Chicago 60637
The University of Chicago Press, Ltd., London

88 87 86 85 84 83 82 81   1 2 3 4 5

Library of Congress Cataloging in Publication Data

Troeltsch, Ernst, 1865–1923.
  The social teaching of the Christian churches.

  Translation of Die Soziallehren der christlichen Kirchen und Gruppen.
  Reprint. Originally published: London: Allen & Unwin, 1931.
  Includes index.
  1. Church and social problems—History.
2. Church history. I. Title.
HN31.T752   1981   261.8′3   81-10443
ISBN 0-226-81298-7 (v. 1)   AACR2
ISBN 0-226-81299-5 (v. 2)

INTRODUCTION
BY H. RICHARD NIEBUHR

The Social Teaching of The Christian Churches is a potent book. During the half century that has elapsed since its first publication in German it has influenced the work of scholars in a number of fields—in history and sociology in general, in the history and sociology of religion in particular, in Christian ethics and in jurisprudence. It has been effective, at least indirectly, in qualifying practical decisions made by leaders of churches and states.

It is not an easy book to read for those who approach it with the expectation of finding in it a consistent argument in support of a simple thesis. As the author points out in his Foreword, the con-- clusions he summarizes at the end of the second volume are the actual results of the studies that precede and not propositions he had set out to illuminate and defend. The work is more like a river, flowing toward junction with other streams on their way to the sea, than like a house built according to planned specifications. To read it in the way in which it was written is to accompany the author in his effort to understand a mass of historical data and to seek with him solutions of some intellectual and practical problems. If the concern of the reader is more with the results of the inquiry than with the method of arriving at them, he had best heed Troeltsch's advice and begin at the conclusion; to this I would add the counsel to read also the concluding section of Volume I (Chapter II, section 9, pp. 328 ff.) and the opening pages of Volume II (pp.461 ff.). Yet those who follow this method will miss adventurous participation in a journey of inquiry as well as many enlightening views of special scenes on the way.

The external history of *The Social Teaching* supports the counsel to read it as the report of an inquiry more than as an argument for a set of propositions. The work had its inception, as the author often pointed out, in a book review. Troeltsch had been asked by the editors of a social science journal to review a book entitled *The Co-operation of the Church in the Solution of the Social Problem*. The work had been written by a practical theologian, Nathusius, who was deeply concerned with the human problems attendant on the rise of industrial society. But it was a "miserable book," said Troeltsch. Like many a similar call to action it lacked understanding both of the problem for which the church was to help find a solution

and of the church's resources. Troeltsch found as he considered the
situation that available literature did not supply the basis for such
self-understanding, and so he set about the work of laying that
foundation (See note 510, Volume II, pp. 986 f.). The results of his
studies in the history of the ancient church, Catholicism, and Lutheranism were printed in successive numbers of the *Archiv fuer Sozial-
wissenschaften und Sozialpolitik* during the years 1908 to 1910.
Further inquiries followed; and when (in 1912) the author decided
to publish his studies as the first volume of his collected writings
he added the large sections on Calvinism, the Protestant sects, and
mysticisms, as well as the summary of conclusions. Even so the work
was not completed; the relations of the religious groups to other societies in the modern world, in the nineteenth century particularly,
required further attention; consideration of Augustine had been
omitted from *The Social Teaching*. Hence came further books and
articles such as *Augustine, Christian Antiquity and the Middle Ages*
(1914) and various essays reprinted especially in Volume IV of the
collected writings.

Troeltsch began the inquiry of which a substantial part is set forth
in the present work, with certain interests and in the presence of
certain challenges issuing from his own historical and social situation. He was a complex man and lived in a complex time; hence
the interests and challenges were many but the most important can
be distinguished. His practical, moral concern in the presence of
pluralistic, centrifugal modern civilization is evident throughout his
total work. He lived and thought in the presence of the confusions
and alarms, the hopes and threats that issue from class and party
conflict, church and state tensions, international wars remembered
and impending, from colonial imperialisms and rising nationalisms,
from industrialism growing in extent and in power over the common life, from the spectacular development of the natural and social
sciences, from the radical criticism of modern civilization by Marx
and Nietzsche. Troeltsch, academician though he was by profession,
experienced the need for ethical decision and action in this situation
as the ultimate challenge. But like many another large-minded man
before him—like Plato, above all, but also like his particular heroes,
Leibniz, Kant and Schleiermacher—he realized how interdependent
scientific and moral reasoning were and how much ethical decision
needed to be accompanied, in order to be wise and effective, by
thorough self-knowledge and equally thorough understanding of the
situation in which moral action took place. He realized, and frequently stated, that no amount of study could relieve the responsible

person from the necessity and the risk of decision; yet it was equally clear to him that decisions could be made responsibly only in the light of the fullest understanding possible. The alternation between study and action came to expression in his own life when at a later period he assumed political office in the Weimar republic yet continued his inquiries into the philosophy of history at the University of Berlin. But from the earliest time onward he was deeply concerned with all the great historical social institutions, never with academic inquiry and teaching in separation from them.

His immediate standpoint as he sought answers to his questions and ground for his decisions was in that conjunction of two great social institutions—a theological faculty in a state university. "When I went to the university in 1884," he wrote, "I was very undecided about my vocation. Jurisprudence seemed to me to offer a key to the understanding of history, which I had learned at an early time to conceive as conditioned by the character of the institutions. But that was not a sufficient motivation for the study of law and for the career of an official. Classical philology . . . gripped me; but my experiences with the teachers of that time had clearly shown that Hellenic ideals of life could not be practically realized today. Philosophy in its current state was not attractive. Medicine [his father's profession] interested me only theoretically. So I became a theologian. In theology at that time one had the only available access to both Metaphysics and the extraordinarily exciting historical problems. Metaphysics and history represented the two sets of highly significant problems which challenged me, independently and in their interaction. This led naturally to the study of religion which contains both sets of problems in close relation to each other. But the science of religion was theology. Insofar as the practical career (in the church) was concerned, that could develop as it would. A native, strong religious bent in me seemed to guarantee that that would somehow work out alright." (*Gesammelte Schriften*, Vol. IV, p. 4).

So Troeltsch's standpoint was in theology as the place where man might have in view his relations both to the eternal and unconditioned and to the historical and relative in all their intricate interrelations. Practical and theoretical questions crowd upon a man in that situation; questions about the relations of personal and social faith, of churches to modern society with its political and economic institutions and of religion to the currents of thought flowing through history. Two dogmatic ways of dealing with the flux of history presented themselves, the Marxian and the orthodox Christian, though the latter appeared in many forms. Marxism interpreted religion, law, politics, and ethics as ultimately functions of economic conditions and the class structure; it could try to master the multiplicity of human problems by directing its attack on the economic institutions of society. Orthodoxy believed religious faith to be the basic element in human life and developed accordingly what social strategy it had. Troeltsch saw the truth-value in both approaches but was convinced that life was more pluralistic and more historical than either theory allowed. Religion, he believed, was based on something primal in human nature and in the relation of man to the world of being. Yet such primal religion was actualized only in the great historical religions; for Western man actual religion was the historic faith of Judaism and Christianity. This religion had its social consequences in the formation of religious societies with their internal ethos. But where orthodoxy tended to claim that only one sort of social result ought to follow from the religion, Troeltsch, the historian, instructed by his friend the great sociologist Max Weber, saw that at least three kinds of religious social organization followed on the coming of the Christian faith—the church, the sect, and mysticism.

Moreover, though religion had its independent roots in the human spirit and though the rise of historical religions needed to be understood otherwise than as the Marxists did, it was clear to Troeltsch that religion was not the only independent power in life and history. Man's interests in cultural values and the sociological consequences of these as actualized again in history through the development of particular institutions were not any more explicable in religious than in solely economic terms. States and political systems, scientific thought, family, economics, ethics, art—all had their own roots. But human personal and social life is not carried on in a series of movements along parallel, non-intersecting lines. Societies and institutions based on various interests interact in complex fashion, while through that interaction runs the constant quest for unity or synthesis.

The picture of history Troeltsch so saw and described is manifold and dynamic; hence *The Social Teaching* is like a multi-perspectival painting. In one perspective it is a book about the church, presenting a double rebuttal to the Marxian thesis and to the orthodox; in another it is a book about Western history which uses the story of the churches' social teachings as an illustration of the whole complex process; in still another, it is a prolegomenon to the work of modern social construction or to the effort, as Troeltsch liked to say, of damming the stream of history for a while and of achieving a synthesis of culture, which, of course, again would pass away.

The problems with which Troeltsch the historian, theologian, churchman, and statesman, undertook to deal theoretically and practically have not changed greatly since this book was first published. They have rather increased in intensity. Theology, to be sure, especially in Europe, has turned away from these problems; and with the dominance of greater interest on its part in the absolute rather than relative character of Christianity, in the church's internal life rather than in its relations to the culture, Troeltsch the theologian passed into eclipse. There are signs, however, that the eclipse is passing and that in theology as well as in the sociology of religion and in history Troeltsch's methods and convictions will again become effective.

In the meantime, also, many parts of the book have been subjected to the criticism of historical specialists. The section on Luther has been much attacked and would doubtless be revised today in the light of modern Luther research. The conception of relative natural law has been questioned. The relation of Calvinism and capitalism which Troeltsch took over from Max Weber, though he pointed it in another direction, has been greatly refined in consequence of many later studies and discussions. Doubtless almost every particular section of the book would be written somewhat differently if it were done today. But the picture as a whole of the church in the world remains something more important than one man's vision of the panorama of Western history. As in the case of other books of this kind, every part can be legitimately criticized by specialists, of whom none has the ability to put all the corrected pieces together in any similar, synoptic view of the whole, nor to stimulate equally the labors of scholars and the exercise of responsible churchmanship and statesmanship.

In conclusion a few additional details about the author may be in place. He was born in Augsburg, Germany, in 1866 and died in Berlin in 1923. From 1894 to 1915 he was Professor of Theology at the University in Heidelberg; from 1915 to 1923, Professor of Philosophy at Berlin. After the democratic revolution in Germany he held political offices in the Prussian and national administrations until his death. Many of his important writings have been republished in four large volumes of collected works of which *The Social Teaching* forms the first, and several large essays on the philosophy of history the third. Also published were *The Absoluteness of Christianity; Protestant Christianity and the Church in Modern Period;*

Augustine; and many smaller works. Of the latter, two are available in English translation : his final work, *Christian Thought,* and an early essay, *Protestantism and Progress.* Critical appraisals of Troeltsch's theological thought may be found in H. R. Mackintosh, *Types of Modern Theology;* Baron Friedrich von Huegel, *Essays and Addresses on the Philosophy of Religion;* and S. R. Sleigh, *The Sufficiency of Christianity.*

New Haven, Conn.
April 1960

TRANSLATOR'S PREFACE

FRIEDRICH VON HÜGEL, in his essay on *The Specific Genius of Christianity*, remarks that "it is not easy to furnish a short yet useful account and criticism of Troeltsch's *Soziallehren*, with its nearly thousand pages, its bewildering variety of topics, and the range and delicacy of competence it so strikingly reveals." It is obvious that the translation of this "monumental work," as Baron Von Hügel calls it, would present peculiar difficulties. In addition to the wide range of the author's learning and his extensive use of unusual and technical terms, there was the added difficulty of an extremely involved style.

For the sake of clarity the translator has introduced cross-headings which are not in the German text. Paragraphs have been subdivided, and where it was possible sentences have been broken up into their constituent parts. The present work, however, is an unabridged translation of the famous book published in Germany in the year 1911 under the title: *Die Soziallehren der christlichen Kirchen und Gruppen*. It forms the first volume in the Collected Works of Ernst Troeltsch.

The footnotes occupy a large part of the book. Some of these notes are dissertations or articles rather than "notes," and they often contain most valuable material. In order to free the text from this mass of annotations, however, the longer notes have been placed at the end of the chapters to which they belong. Actual footnotes alone have been left in their original position. A very few notes have been slightly condensed. No references have been omitted, and the numbering of the German edition has been retained. Note 80, which belongs to Chapter II, will be found on page 199, at the end of the Notes belonging to Chapter I.

The translator owes a very great debt of gratitude to several friends who have given most generous help out of the stores of their knowledge and experience. She would offer her cordial thanks to Mrs. Margrieta Beer, M.A.; Mrs. John May, B.A.; Frau Maria Schlüter-Hermkes, D.D.; and Miss Evelyn Underhill. The Rev. A. E. Garvie, M.A., D.D., D.Th., has kindly read the full text of the translation; for this, as well as for other most generous assistance, the translator wishes to render special acknowledgement and gratitude.

OLIVE WYON

LONDON

August 1931

CONTENTS OF VOLUME ONE

CHAPTER II

MEDIAEVAL CATHOLICISM

FOREWORD

In accordance with my own desires and those of others, I have gathered within this volume the fruit of my scattered researches. Apart from my large work on the place of Protestantism in contemporary culture, most of my researches have been gathered into monographs, studies of method, and various sketches, covering a great variety of subjects. Now that they appear in public in collected form, it will be clear that, in spite of the fact that they are drawn from so many sources, they all spring from a unified plan. On this point a few words of explanation are necessary.

The connection of ideas is easy to recognize. Trained in the school of Ritschl, I learned very early that two elements were united in the impressive teaching of this energetic and great scholar: a distinct conception of traditional dogma by means of which modern needs and problems were met, and just as decided a conception of the modern intellectual and religious situation, by means of which it seemed possible to accept and carry forward the teaching of tradition, understood in the Ritschlian sense. The question arose, therefore, quite naturally, first, whether this conception were true to dogmatic tradition in its actual historical sense, and, second, whether the present situation was being interpreted as it actually is. Then it became clear that from both sides a certain process of assimilation had been completed which did not correspond with actual facts and which did not permit the real contrast to appear in its full actuality. Thus I found myself confronted by a double task: to make clear to myself both the ecclesiastical dogmatic tradition of Protestantism in its own historical sense, and the intellectual and practical situation of the present day in its true fundamental tendencies. Hence the double nature of my researches—the analysis of early Protestantism and the analysis of the modern world. All this research, however, was only intended to serve the purpose of solving the systematic problem, in order to think through and formulate the world of Christian thought and life in frank relation to the modern world. This led me to researches in methodology and in the philosophy of religion which are absolutely necessary before a Christian doctrine of thought and life can be built up. In the process, however, I found that the more I studied modern problems the more I found that the balance leaned to the side of ethics. If Christianity is first and foremost a matter of practice, then its main problems lie in the sphere of practical life, and it is from this realm that the most complicated difficulties and contrasts arise in opposition to the world of Christian life. Particularly in relation to social ethics the ethic of the churches is out of date.

When, however, I pursued this line of thought, I was confronted with this further question: What, then, would be the relation of such a new and formative conception of the Christian attitude to life to its own ancient organizations, the churches? Further, could such a new conception, indeed, in any way be grafted on to the old organizations at all and, if this were possible, what kind of social adhesion or relation with a fellowship would be possible in harmony with this new view of life?

It was considerations such as these which led to the researches which are collected in this first volume. They readily became unified when the sociological formulation of the problem was applied to the whole sweep of the history of the Christian Church. This unified point of view illuminated the significance and nature of the varying forms of religious fellowship, the underlying characteristics of the Christian Ethos in its relation to the ethical problems and tasks of secular life, and the inner connection of each formulated dogma to a fellowship group more or less affected by it. At the same time this led me to a peculiar conception of the nature of Christianity, its history and its relation to the general history of civilization. This again led to progress in my whole formulation of the theological problem in general. The results have been summarized in the concluding section. They are genuine results which have been gained from the process of research, not theses which the book was written to support. This is why they are placed at the end and not at the beginning. The reader can, however, lighten his task by referring to the closing section of the book—that is, if he does not prefer to allow the results of the whole study to become clear to him naturally in the course of his reading.

With its nearly one thousand pages this work has become a very substantial volume. Especially in a subject of this kind, it was necessary to support the actual text with a very wide range of illustrations in the form of notes. In order to explain the facts upon which my ideas are based and to relate the explanation to the previous process of research, this annotation became inevitable. About two-thirds of the material had already been published in the *Archives for Social Science and Social Politics*, but the chapters on Calvinism, the Sects, and Mysticism are entirely new. The introductory chapters have been revised and expanded since they were published in the *Archives*, but they were then taken out of their context. This explains why there is no reference to some of the latest works on this subject.

There is one thing which consoles me for the enormous size of this volume, and that is that it enables it to bear the weight and the honour of a double dedication. The Philosophical Faculty at Greifswald, in the year 1903, on the occasion of their Jubilee celebrations, did me the honour of promoting me to the rank of *Doctor philosophias honoris causa*. In the first place this honour was accorded me on account of my inclusive study of Protestantism, which had just appeared. In the present year, 1911, the Faculty of Law at Breslau, on the occasion of its centenary celebrations, gave me the honour of *Doctor juris honoris causa*, in recognition of the work already published in the *Archives*, which is now contained in this book. The present volume is closely connected with its predecessor; indeed, it is only in this volume that actual proofs are provided for many of the statements made in the earlier treatise. I therefore venture upon a double dedication for the following reasons: the massive nature of this work, combined with the fact that both these honours prove how clear a connection exists between philosophy and law and the general subject of this book.

Both these honours also show very clearly that my work recognizes no special theological or Christian methods of research. I am, however, convinced, and believe that this work proves the force of my conviction, that in the process the Christian outlook on life loses nothing of its greatness or its inward significance.

ERNST TROELTSCH

HEIDELBERG

November 1, 1911

INTRODUCTION AND PRELIMINARY
QUESTIONS OF METHOD

THE CHURCHES AND THE SOCIAL PROBLEM

Amid all the social confusion of the present day, with its clamour of conflicting voices, the churches also are making their voice heard. These social conflicts are due in part to the growth of large modern unified States, with their democratic tendencies and their party struggles. They are also the outcome of modern industrialization, the development of the proletariat, and the emancipation of the masses in many lands. These problems do not merely concern politicians, political economists, specialists in social science, and modern independent philosophers of culture; they are also the concern of the churches, whose roots are entwined with traditions of great historical importance and vital energy. At the present time the churches are employing their considerable powers of organization in the endeavour to find a solution for these problems. To a great extent their efforts coincide with those of the various political parties, particularly with the Centre Party, the Conservatives, and the anti-Semitic *Mittelstandpolitik*;* this, however, means that the churches themselves are also strongly influenced in their turn by the political and class interests which these parties represent. To some extent, however, the churches are trying to exercise their influence in a practical way on religious, non-party lines, through movements like the Protestant Social Congress and by the promotion of scientific literature on social questions. They also find a fruitful sphere of activity in the semi-ecclesiastical societies and organizations of the Home Mission Movement and other movements of the same kind. At any rate, since these religious groups have perceived that the modern social situation has brought them face to face with new problems and new duties in the ordering of social life, they have plunged into the study of these questions, both theoretically and practically. Linking their investigations with those contained in the existing scientific literature on the subject, they have attempted to outline or to define a peculiarly Christian doctrine of the State, of social science, and of economics. The more clearly, too, that the churches have discerned the fact that all higher spiritual culture is largely dependent upon the economic basis of life, the more earnestly they have thrown their energies into an endeavour to understand and solve

* That is, the lower middle-class supporters of the Conservative and clerical parties.—TRANSLATOR.

these questions. In this endeavour they have also been aided by
several national political economists, and by several representatives of political science. It is well known that leading government
officials are in the habit of taking an interest in these questions,
and that Bismarck in particular—in strange contrast to the rest of
his political realism and naturalism—favoured social reform, on
his own lines. In itself such a procedure is quite intelligible and
in order, since in point of fact the science of Society cannot create
ultimate values and standards from within, for even economic
science, in regard to the ultimate valuation of the goods which it
handles, and in regard to the complicated social, political, and
moral energies which it presupposes, is obliged to use institutions
outside the borders of its own special faculty.[1] The question,
therefore, is not whether it is permissible to formulate social
doctrines from the standpoint of the churches and of religion in
general; all we have to do is to ask whether these attempts have
achieved something useful and valuable for the modern situation. In order to be able to answer this question, however, we need,
above all, a detailed knowledge of these endeavours and aspirations.

A task of this kind, however, is extremely complicated. To
attempt to estimate what the churches have actually achieved in
practice in social reform and in social science is such a broad
question that only a specialist with a training in politics and in
political economy, who has consecrated all his energies to the
investigation of these problems, would be fit to deal with the
subject. On this point I cannot allow myself to offer an opinion.
There is, however, another aspect of the question which, from the
theoretical point of view, is still more important; I refer to the
theological aspect of the problem. This, then, is the question:
What is the basis of the social teaching of the churches? From the
point of view of their essential nature in principle what is their
attitude towards the modern social problem? And what should
be their attitude?

This question is all the more important since one of the special
advantages of ecclesiastical social science is that it possesses metaphysical convictions based on principle. In this the churches are
one with the Social Democrats, and for that reason the political
party of the Centre, the Conservatives with their "patriarchal"
ideas, and the revolutionary Social Democrats have the strongest
power of influencing other people, whereas Liberalism, which by
its relative tendency is split up into individual peculiarities, practical compromises, and middle-class learning, either does not

[1] See p. 35.

possess this power, or it possesses it no longer, since for the present, at least, its fundamental individualistic idea has become exhausted. A study of the history of doctrine on these lines is preeminently a matter for the theologian and Church historian, or at least for someone who is familiar with these subjects. For at the outset we are faced at once with the fundamental fact that the churches and Christianity, which are pre-eminently historic forces, are at all points conditioned by their past, by the Gospel which, together with the Bible, exerts its influence ever anew, and by the dogmas which concern social life and the whole of civilization. Whether in agreement or opposition, in dependence or in change of meaning, all the modern ecclesiastical social doctrines are determined by this point of view. Since their spiritual power is only produced by this consciousness of an ancient and worldwide religious tradition, their content also can only be understood from this point of view. These modern ecclesiastical social doctrines would have to be studied in the light of the history of the Christian ethic, and, properly speaking, in the light of its fundamental doctrines—if, indeed, there were such a thing as a history of the Christian ethic—which could present the Christian Ethos in its inward connection with the universal history of civilization.[2] Since no history of this kind is in existence, I am forced to open up the subject myself, and to try to answer the question which has here been raised. My object will be to pave the way for the understanding of the social doctrines of the Gospel, of the Early Church, of the Middle Ages, of the post-Reformation confessions, right down to the formation of the new situation in the modern world, in which the old theories no longer suffice, and where, therefore, new theories must be constructed, composed of old and new elements, consciously or unconsciously, whether so avowed or not.

CHRISTIAN SOCIOLOGICAL DEVELOPMENT

The attempt, therefore, must be made to present a clear view of the facts based on the results of this historical study. In order to achieve this result the briefest possible presentation will suffice. Brevity, indeed, will be an advantage, for in a small compass it is possible to indicate the outstanding features of this historical development, which, in any detailed treatment of the subject, would very easily be hidden by the intricate and perplexing process of building up ecclesiastical dogmas, with their particularly confusing details. The moment the problem is

[2] See p. 35.

formulated, however, we are faced by one great difficulty: What, after all, does constitute the "Social" element in relation to the churches and to Christianity?

In face of the confusion which characterizes most of the writings dealing with the problem when it has been thus stated, we need at the outset to clear our minds as to the real content of the term "Social", in order to arrive at a clear formulation of this question. If we examine a typical work of this kind, say, for instance, the book by Nathusius, which has gone into its third edition, on the "Co-operation of the Church in the Solution of the Social Question" of 1904, we find that two elements have been inextricably mingled, and that it is this confusion of thought which obviously causes the obscurities and errors of the book. At one point the writer speaks of a fellowship which issues from the religious idea itself, of the "social character of Christianity" as a whole. On closer consideration, however, this is something quite obvious; it simply means the particular religious group-fellowship which is the outcome of the religious object, representing the sociological effect of the religious phenomenon. This, however, can be paralleled by any other phenomenon we may care to mention, such as the sex-instinct, art, science, the earning of a living, or even any favourite pursuit or passing intention which, in one way or another, produces its own sociological effect, great or small, permanent or temporary, upon the sociological circle which it affects, and the constituent elements of such a group.[3] This has nothing to do with the "Social" element in the usual sense of the word. As a matter of fact, all sociological reflection shows us the vast differences which exist in questions of basis and structure, in their function and in their connection with other groups, between these various sociological phenomena—differences which are affected by the object which produces them. But it is plain that the use of the word "Social" by Nathusius for this human co-operation which proceeds from Christian thought confuses everything. Hastily jumping to conclusions, he deduces from Christianity, on the basis of its "Social" character, a principle of social life in general. Since, according to the author, this social life consists "in the natural relationships of sex, age, etc., in natural economic necessities, in the classification to which they give rise, in property, and in a human commonwealth of nations",

---

[3] On this point compare the various treatises of *Simmel* on sociological questions; they are extremely instructive; the idea which has been expressed above is to be found in *Soziologie der Ueber- und Unterordnung, Band XXIV (1907)* of this *Archiv.*

so also the social principle of Christianity becomes *eo ipso* the principle of all these things. Hence we cannot be surprised that the writer proceeds to say plainly: "That not only does Christianity contain a social spirit, a power which draws men and unites them to each other, but that also, for that very reason, certain principles are established for the natural classification of mankind—relationships of sex and age and of conditions of life, upon whose observance their healthy development depends!"[3a] Nathusius fails to see that possibly the sociological group which proceeds from the Christian view of life might be inwardly and essentially different from those sociological groups which proceed from other aims; merely, for the sake of formal equality, because they are "associating forces" they are forced into one mould, and then the one is deduced from the other.

SECULAR SOCIOLOGICAL DEVELOPMENT

This, however, is far from being the only instance of serious confusion in this process of thought. The second instance appears in the question of the conception of Society, or of the "Social" element, which has thus been cast into the sociological circle of Christian ideas. This conception is anything but natural and obvious, and does not in any way denote the sum-total of the sociological relationships which are present and possible alongside of the sociological group formed by the ideas of Christianity. Nathusius gathers up all other forms of association into a unity, and contrasts this unity with the Christian sociological unity, and then reduces both unities like Reason and Revelation to the same thing, because ultimately, that is in God, they are one. The main characteristic of this argument, however, is the habit of the Christian theologian and apologist of setting everything as a unity over against the absolute nature of Christianity, and then somehow of tracing both unities back to a common source, and thus of smoothing out all difficulties; this is an error which disappears when it is placed in the clear light of dispassionate historical research. This habit of thought, however, contains a more far-reaching error: a vast extension of the general use of the conception of the "Social", which makes any definite and clear formulation of the problem impossible. This is a very frequent misconception among non-theological dogmatic thinkers, the representatives of the conception of Society based on natural science. The "Social" is neither the sum-total of "natural" forms of association contrasted with the association which has been effected

[3a] See p. 307 (Nathusius).

by "supernatural" means, nor the sum-total of human association in general, which, as a universal conception, would include every sociological phenomenon as a particular detail, and by which it would then be explained and understood. If this argument were valid, it would lead to the same confusion of ideas as we see in Nathusius only from the opposite direction. Instead of allowing the idea of the "Social" to be swallowed up in the Christian-sociological ideal, it would mean that the latter would be absorbed into the supposedly clear and unambiguous conception of the "Social" itself. Here the Socialist dogmatist is a warning to the theological dogmatist; a paper like Kautsky's "Programme" Pamphlet: *Social Democracy and the Catholic Church* (2nd ed., 1906) is a good example.[3b]

In the current sense, the idea of the "Social" means a definite, clearly defined section of the general sociological phenomena—that is, the sociological relations which are not regulated by the State, nor by political interest, save in so far as they are indirectly influenced by them. This sociological section is composed of the various questions which arise out of economic life, the sociological tension between various groups with different customs and aims, division of labour, class organization, and some other interests which cannot be directly characterized as political, but which actually have a great influence on the collective life of the State; since the development of the modern constitutional State, however, these interests have definitely separated themselves from it. The "social problem", therefore, really consists in the relation between the political community and these sociological phenomena, which, although they are essentially non-political, are yet of outstanding importance from the political point of view. Thus Lorenz von Stein, for instance, from his observation of the development of France, set the conception of "Society" alongside that of the State, and heralded the social problem of the present day. Rodbertus, the other prophet of the social problem, has defined Society as the "personified total content of the peripheral life-activities, which express themselves in the lower strata of social life, through individual multiplicities, in those sections of social life which the State does not control".[4] It is, however, essential to retain this narrower significance of the words "society" and "social" as they are particularly accentuated by the present situa-

---

[3b] See p. 36.
[4] Cf. *Gothein*, in the article on *Gesellschaft* in *HWB der Staatswissenschaften*. L. von Stein: *Der Sozialismus und Kommunismus des heutigen Frankreichs, 1842*. Dietzel: *Rodbertus, II, 1888, p. 46*.

tion. For it is impossible to speak of Society as the total sum of varying grades of sociological groups, with their mutual complexities and interactions. It is not an entity which can be surveyed scientifically. Because of the infinitude of its groupings and the manifold ways we may choose for the linking up of sociological phenomena, Society is something inconceivable—an abstraction like civilization, or history in general, about which only dilettanti speak as a whole. In truth, all thought of it involves a seizing and relating of some particular factor which interests us, and by means of which the sociological phenomena which are related to it come into the field of vision at the same time. Even the keenest thinker, who is capable of looking at things from the broadest point of view and in abstract terms, if he tries to think about Society as a whole, finds his ideas dispersing in all directions, into the infinitude of sociological classifications which emerge from any other possible point of view.

There is no "natural-science" conception of Society such as there is of mechanics, which will cover all particular phenomena. The conception of Society is an historical conception, and out of an infinite wealth of individual sociological developments it is always only able to seize upon certain phenomena and to study them in their various connections; even when this conception seizes upon those aspects which are most important for life—and in so doing naturally touches an extremely widespread complication of sociological groups—it never exhausts the universal conception of Society in general.[5] This means, however, that in this instance "Society" and the "Social", in the sense of the problem of the present day, is only a specially important and a strongly emphasized part of the general sociological situation; it is a part only, not the whole. The relation of Christianity to social problems, therefore, can only mean the relation to these great questions specially emphasized by the present situation, which, however, have always been present in "Society" in the narrower sense of the word, as it is used by Stein. However inconsistent it may be to class Christianity with all other sociological phenomena which are characterized by the faculty of creating the sociological "association" type, precisely because it

---

[5] It is quite plain that the information which is here used is based upon material gathered from the following works: Simmel: *Probleme der Geschichtsphilosophie*[3], *1907;* Rickert: *Die Grenzen der naturwissenschaftlichen Begriffsbildung, 1902;* Kistiakowski: *Gesellschaft und Einzelwesen, 1899;* Max Weber: *Stammlers "Überwindung" der materialistischen Geschichtsauffassung (Vol. XXIV (1907)* of this *Archiv);* G. *Jellinek: Recht des modernen Staates, I*[1], *1905, pp. 1-9, 24-32.*

possesses this faculty, it is equally inconsistent to use the terms "society" and the "social element" with which Christianity is contrasted to indicate Society as a whole. Indeed, even Stein's conception of Society, which includes everything which does not come under the scope of the modern constitutional State, is still too broad. By "Society" modern science means, and rightly, primarily the social relationships which result from the economic phenomena. That is to say, it is the Society composed of all who labour, who are divided up into various classes and professional groups according to the work they do, which produces and exchanges goods, a Society organized upon the basis of the economic needs of existence, with all its manifold complications.

Both Elements combined in a Fundamental Social Theory

It is true, of course, that a sociological point of view which issues from universal ideas, like the Christian regulation of the connection between the individual and the community, certainly constitutes a general fundamental sociological theory, which in some way or another will exert an influence upon all social relationships. This influence, however, is only intermittent; sometimes it is strong and sometimes it is weak, sometimes it is clear and sometimes it is confused, and it can never be held to be part of the social tissue of relations itself. All that can be done is to attempt to discover the possible influence of this fundamental theory in particular instances, in definite social groups. For all these social groups possess independent instincts of organization; all that we can do, therefore, is to try to discover how far the religious-sociological fundamental theory has been able to penetrate into these motives, and to what extent it has been able to assimilate these groups into itself. Wherever this has taken place it will be found that the process of development has been very different within the various social groups. In particular, the economic form of "Society" based on the division of labour always remains an independent phenomenon, with its own sociological basis, in contrast to the spirit of fellowship which is derived from religious ideas. Further, the question of the inward influence of Christianity upon the sense of personality, and upon ethical mutual relationships, is certainly of immense importance, but in the main it can be neither conceived nor answered. The only method of attempting to find an answer at all is by investigating the concrete effect of its influence in different social groups. In the course of such an investigation, however, it will become evident that great tracts of social life, like that of the economic-

social order, throw a great deal of light upon the general fundamental tendency of Christian sociology, which permit us to draw
certain inferences about the general character, and the effect on
civilization, of Christian-sociological principles. This will be a
valuable deduction, which will be a by-product of our inquiry
into the relation between Christian thought and the "Social".
We must realize, however, that in so doing we are narrowing the
universal by representing it in terms of a particular problem.
The "Social" in an intelligible sense does not mean "Society" in
general, and certainly not the ethical life in general—it is merely
a section; and all the light which is cast on the sociological
effects on civilization of Christianity from the standpoint of
the "Social" only constitutes an illumination which is derived
from a specially important province of culture, but it is not a
revelation of its collective sociological influence upon civilization
as a whole.

This leads, however, to a further important point. In our
modern way of speech the State and Society are conceived as
quite distinct from each other, and the characteristic conception
of Society only arises out of the contrast with the modern, formal
constitutional conception of the State. It is only in the light of
this contrast that the whole conception is given clear and concrete meaning. Now, however, a quite new and special problem
arises when this Society, which is characterized by its separation
and difference from the State, is related to the Church or the
churches. Obviously through this process of contrast it gains a
new meaning. It then becomes a contrast between the sociological
group, which is organized from the viewpoint of the religious idea
of love to God and man, and those sociological forces which have
been organized from an entirely secular point of view.

FUNCTION OF THE RELIGIOUS ETHIC WITHIN THIS THEORY

The modern social problem is thus first of all orientated by the
idea of the State, and by its orientation towards the Church it
becomes the quite different problem of the relation between the
religious forces and the economic social and political forces.
This constitutes the element of truth in the distinction which
doctrinal theologians make between the religious social group
and the opposing unity composed of the non-religious social
groups. But the difference is not that which exists between the
"natural" and the "supernatural"; it is the distinction between
an association which proceeds from a religious aim and the most
important associations which exist for purely temporal ends. It

is neither the general conception of the "natural", nor that of the "Social" which is expressed in the social group with a purely temporal purpose, but both the most powerful and far-reaching sociological formations which exist alongside of the religious social group, and their equal basis in a point of reference which concerns this world, whereas the churches claim that they constitute a religious, that is a supernatural, point of reference. Thus the State again tends to become identified with economic social problems, and the social doctrines of the Church (apart from its own view of its own sociological nature) become the doctrine of its relation both to the State and to Society, which are the most important secular forces confronting the Church.[6]

Thus it is an actual fact of history that from the beginning all the social doctrines of Christianity have been likewise doctrines both of the State and of Society. At the same time, owing to the emphasis of Christian thought upon personality, the Family is always regarded as the basis both of the State and of Society, and is thus bound up with all Christian social doctrine. Once more, therefore, the conception of the "Social" widens out, since in the development of a religious doctrine of fellowship the Family, the State, and the economic order of Society are combined as closely related sociological formations. They do not exhaust the meaning of Society in general, but they are the great objects which the religious structure of Society must seek to assimilate, whereas it can leave the other elements to look after themselves. Christian social doctrine, therefore, is a doctrine of the most important non-religious sociological structures which are erected upon an independent foundation, or, to use its own language, of its relation with the most powerful social forces of the "world". If we admit that the State and Society, together with innumerable other forces, are still the main formative powers of civilization, then the ultimate problem may be stated thus: How can the Church harmonize with these main forces in such a way that together they will form a unity of civilization?

Thus the question of the attitude of the churches towards the social problem also includes their attitude towards the State. It is precisely that modern separation between the idea of politics and of Society (which was only possible because the Church, which had hitherto been supreme, was now set aside and ignored) which makes the modern social doctrines of the churches so extraordinarily difficult, because, in point of fact, they have to deal at the same time both with the State and with the Church,

[6] See p. 36.

and yet under the influence of the catchword "social", in their Christian-social ardour, they only plunge into the isolated "Social" problem. Thus even Nathusius in his theory entirely overlooked the State, as if the State itself had not the most burning interest in the social problem, and as though it would ever allow the churches to solve the question from a point of view which is often essentially different from its own. Thus, on the other hand, in earlier days the churches found it possible to solve the social problem in their own way, because they were able to keep both Society and the State in a position of natural dependence upon themselves, and because both the State and Society willingly and entirely submitted to the power of the Faith, and the State placed itself at the disposal of the Church for the realization of her ideal. This is the point at which there still remains to-day the characteristic difference between the Catholic and Protestant social doctrines; the Catholic Church still demands, even at the present day, dominion over the State, in order to be able to solve the social problem on ecclesiastical lines; the Protestant churches, with their freedom from the State, are uncertain in their aim; sometimes their aim seems to be a Christian State, and sometimes it is that of a purely ecclesiastical social activity exercised alongside of the State. On the other hand, at the present time, to a great extent the State is inclined to look upon the churches as free associations representing private interests, and thus to regard them as part of that "Society" from which the State is differentiated.[7]

The praiseworthy bluntness and almost brutal directness of the statements of Nathusius, however, only reveal a confusion of thought which exists in many other minds, though it may be expressed in a less obvious manner.[7a] Men think that with the "Social", that is the "sociological" nature of the Church, they have already solved "social" problems, that is, the problems which belong to the life of Society and of the State. They think that if they form an organization which expresses the love which flows forth from God and returns to Him once more, they are also meeting the need of the social groups which make up humanity as a whole. However, that cannot be admitted for an instant; indeed, every idea of that kind only obscures the understanding of the real historical significance of the Gospel, and of its historical development, and all the talk we hear so frequently about the "social spirit of Christianity" is full of this ambiguous meaning, even with reference to the problems of the present day. These

[7] See p. 36.   [7a] See p. 37.

ideas are not necessarily false, but they can be interpreted in various ways, and they lead us astray.

GUIDING PRINCIPLES OF THIS SURVEY

We have now indicated the guiding principles of our subject. In the first place we shall have to inquire into the intrinsic sociological idea of Christianity, and its structure and organization. This will always be found to contain an ideal of a universal fundamental theory of human relationships in general, which will extend far beyond the borders of the actual religious community or Church. The problem then will be how far this fundamental theory will be able to penetrate into actual conditions and influence them; in what way also it will feel the reflex influence of these conditions, and to what extent in such a situation an inner life unity can be, or is, actually created.

We shall then have to ask, further: What is the relation between this sociological structure and the "Social"? That is the State, the economic order with its division of labour, and the family? Naturally, in historical fact the latter will always be treated and regulated by the former, but the problems themselves are connected with the following questions. What was the actual influence of the sociological religious fundamental theory upon other social groups? And thus, what has been the actual influence of the churches upon social phenomena? On the other hand, what influences did the religious community on its side receive from the politico-social formations?[8] Finally, to what extent was an inward contact with, and penetration of, social life rendered possible, and how far did it lead to an inward uniformity of the collective life?[9]

In the ancient world that ideal was never attained; in the Middle Ages and in the daughter churches of the Reformation it was realized, at least in ideal and in theory; in the modern world the discord has again become evident.

Thus a direct survey of the Ancient World, of the Middle Ages, of the Reformation, and finally of the Modern World, causes our material to fall into its natural divisions. First of all, however, we must direct our attention to the Gospel and to the Bible itself, and also to the Early Church, for they constitute the permanent basis of our inquiry.

---

[8] A brilliant example of the latter formulation of the question, with special reference to the economic sphere, is *Max Weber's* well-known work *Die Protestantische Ethik und der Geist des Kapitalismus, Jg., 1903/4* of this *Archiv*; for an example of the former, see the article entitled *"Kirchen" und "Sekten" in Nordamerika. Christl. Welt, 1906, pp. 558 ff., 577 ff.*   [9] See p. 37.

NOTES TO INTRODUCTION

[1] (p. 24.) *Schmoller's Grundriss der Volkswirtschaft* illustrates this point with an admirable breadth of understanding and of knowledge; it reveals equally clearly his independence of all standards of judgment, for all that he had at his disposal for this purpose was the historical-psychological causal connection from which he was able to gain either no norms or values at all, or when he did gain any he was forced to use sophistry.

[2] (p. 25.) Histories of the Christian Ethic by *Luthhardt, 1888/93* (orthodox Lutheran) (in the Gospel and ideally the Christian ethic is the penetration of the system of secular callings with the spirit of trust in God and the love of one's neighbours). *Gass, 1881* (a great deal of material and very little order: reconciliation and penetration of the Christian-supernatural and the Human-natural). *Ziegler*, 1886 (Theory of the break-up of Christian Dualism into modern Immanence and Autonomy). Here the Christian ethic is everywhere regarded essentially from the point of view of the assistance of grace granted to sinful weakness or impotence; essentially, therefore, it is concerned with the doctrine of Grace. Therefore the question of the special content of the Christian Ethos, and of the connection of its content with the other norms and values of civilized humanity, is only treated incidentally. This is also true of the consideration of the Christian ethic which *Jodl* gives in his *Geschichte der Ethik, I², 1906*. Along with Stoicism and Platonism the Christian ethic is the type of the spiritually idealistic, metaphysical, and dualistic ethic, which, based upon religious illusions, asserts essentially the aid of grace, and with that an extreme Dualism, which may even develop into asceticism; otherwise, however, in contrast to Stoicism and Platonism, it contains elements of barbarian ignorance; indeed, at its best it is perhaps only a barbarian and popular mythical form of the Stoic-Platonic doctrine. In all these cases there is an insufficient analysis of the fundamental ethical ideas of the Gospel, and therefore also of an adequate analysis of the sociological constitution peculiar to Christianity and its social relations. *Uhlhorn: Die Christliche Liebestätigkeit, I² 1882, II 1884, III 1890*, is a very valuable work; although, naturally, it is not exhaustive, it deals with the connection between Christianity and the general life of society, especially on the economic side. On the whole the standpoint is orthodox Lutheran. The *Geschichte des Pietismus* by *Ritschl* is similar (1880/84/86): in it the writer develops in a classic way the ethic of a modernized form of Lutheranism "open to the world".—The conceptions of the history of civilization developed by *Jakob Burkhardt, Franz Overbeck*, and *Friedrich Nietzsche* are entirely opposed to the views of the writers who have just been mentioned; these three men share a good many ideas, but in many respects also they are very dissimilar. From their point of view the Christian ethic, as in Catholicism, seems to be essentially asceticism; the only difference is that in them the emphasis of Catholicism on the assimilation of the natural sphere of life is absent. In point of fact the whole question of asceticism is one of the main problems connected with this subject. But the purely ascetic interpretation of the Gospel is a misreading of its chief religious ideas, and therefore it underestimates the sociological energies which issue from this leading religious idea; all three thinkers are indeed decidedly hostile to the masses and to the whole idea of the "Social", therefore either they have no interest at all in this aspect of the subject or they simply treat it polemically. If Christianity were pure asceticism, then all we could say about its social doctrines in general would be that logically it has produced monasti-

cism, and that illogically it has produced a semi-monasticism which is adjusted to the life of the world. It is, however, obvious that this statement does not cover the whole subject, and that there must be a good deal more in it than this. Renan also, in his *Origines du Christianisme,* now and again has expressed similar ideas, but he has also recognized the existence of far-reaching ethical and sociological ideas.

3b (p. 28.) Here from the very outset the Church is regarded solely as an economic phenomenon, since, being a sociological phenomenon, she must be essentially an economic phenomenon as well. In contrast with democracy and all forms of non-sacerdotal religion which agree with society as such, the Christian religion, as a degenerate product, is a new social group of a communistic nature. As it extends among the masses, however, it produces a ruling class of its own, the clergy, and the further course of development only serves to consolidate the political and economic dominant position of the clergy; this class then becomes in part a rival, and in part a confederate, of the political and economic ruling class of the day. There is, therefore, no question here of a religious-sociological development issuing from a specifically religious motive; the Church is simply absorbed into the general course of economic and social development, within which at the beginning she represents a communistic class-movement of the poor, concealing her economic-communistic idea beneath the veil of her general religious idea of love. This explains the church policy of the present-day proletariat; it accepts the communistic tendency hidden under the veil of religion, and protects the ideas of religion by the statement that religion is a private matter, and it secures the sympathies of the Catholics by fighting against all exceptional legislation, as, for example, that against the Religious Orders. At the same time the power of the clergy is to be broken through the separation of Church and State, the abolition of religion from the schools, and the fight against the idea of religion by the stress laid on Socialistic science. In this contradictory church policy, which aims at protecting and annihilating religion at one and the same time, the real meaning of the whole is expressed, i.e. that in the Church there is something more than a phenomenon of the economic class struggle, that behind the "ideological religious veil" an independent interest is concealed. This admission, however, is more diplomatic than sincere, and it has no real effect upon the conception of the problem itself, which cannot be solved at all from the point of view of the dogmatic general conception of "Society".

6 (p. 32.) Science and art are excluded from this statement, since, if the sphere of the "social" is rather rigidly limited, they do not belong to it, although they are very important component parts of the sociological system in general, and science in particular plays a vital part in a religion of knowledge and of faith. This must, however, be reserved for the history of dogma and of art. We may, however, point out the interesting parallels that here the relation to the "world"—that is, to the social structure which is not directly conditioned by religion—points to the following secularization in the political and social sphere. In science and in art also it is much restricted.

7 (p. 33.) In this respect it is interesting to note the development of Friedrich Naumann, who by his Christian Socialism was thrown more and more upon the State, through a realistic knowledge of the actual situation, until he came to regard the social problem almost entirely from the point of view of the State; the Church, and Christianity in general, he relegates to the sphere of the purely personal and ethical life (*Wenck: Geschichte der National-Sozialen, 1905*). Catholic social policy, on the contrary, claims first of all that the State should submit to

the point of view of the Church. Cf. *Theod. Meyer: Die christlich-ethischen Sozialprinzipien, 1904.* This implies the "organic", that is, the theocratically unified theory. The distinctive element in the Christian social doctrine lies in this: "That the Christian idea of the social organism excludes naturally and organically all absolutist arbitrary action on the part of the central principle (that is, of the State), whereas the non-Christian idea naturally and essentially includes it." This means opposition to absolutism, not merely in the form of government, but in the principle of the State itself. Similarly, on the other hand, the Conservatives never produce an energetic social policy, because owing to the political passivity of Lutheranism they do not dare to summon the State to reform, quite apart from the fact that their own political interest to a great extent coincides with this passivity. For the assignment of the churches to "Society" as a consequence of the modern conception of the State, see *Troeltsch: Die Trennung von Staat und Kirche, 1907, pp. 23–48.*

7a (p. 33.) As, for example, the Christian Socialism of St. Simon, who proclaimed that the metaphysical-religious basis needed by every positive social system was provided by the Christian idea of fellowship; at the same time he saw clearly that his *nouveau christianisme* would have to be really new—that is, that it would need to recognize the values of life in the world far more openly (*v. Stein: Sozialismus und Kommunismus, p. 174*). Even so, however, the Christian spirit of brotherhood tends to become merged in the very indefinite idea of equality as the social principle in general. The following study will show how contrary to history is this identification of the two.

9 (p. 34.) These, then, are the formulations of the problem in principle, from the point of view of the ethical, theological, or cultural-philosophical interest, whereas the previously named examples of *Max Weber* apply simply and solely to the region of facts, from the standpoint of economic history and of social history. A work like that of *v. Schulze-Gävernitz: Britischer Imperialismus und englischer Freihandel, 1906*, treats both kinds of problem at once. In the present work we are concerned essentially with the second group because this problem forms the real main interest of the social doctrines of the churches, whereas research into the actual position and influence of the Christian forces of thought upon the political and economic sphere only are relevant as presuppositions for the reply to this theoretical question. So far as the concrete side of these problems is concerned, my work only has access in a limited way to original sources, at least so far as the Early and the Mediaeval Church is concerned. Whatever merit it may possess is not due to independent study of the sources, but to its character of independent thought, which seeks to produce out of the study of a given situation a unification of the whole into a theory of the attitude of the religious element to the political-social element. I believe, however, that where questions of fact are concerned I have everywhere based my study upon the best authorities.

THE SOCIAL TEACHING OF
THE CHRISTIAN CHURCHES

CHAPTER I

THE FOUNDATIONS IN THE EARLY CHURCH

1. THE GOSPEL

PRIMITIVE CHRISTIANITY AN INDEPENDENT PHENOMENON

In order to understand the foundation principles of Christianity
as a whole, in its relation to social problems, it is of the utmost
importance to recognize that the preaching of Jesus and the
creation of the Christian Church were not due in any sense to
the impulse of a social movement. To put it quite plainly:
Christianity was not the product of a class struggle of any kind;
it was not shaped, when it did arise, in order to fit into any such
situation; indeed, at no point was it directly concerned with the
social upheavals of the ancient world. The fact, however, remains
that Jesus addressed Himself primarily to the oppressed, and to
the "little ones" of the human family, that He considered wealth
a danger to the soul, and that He opposed the Jewish priestly
aristocracy which represented the dominant ecclesiastical forces of
His day. It is also clear that the Early Church sought and won
her new adherents chiefly among the lower classes in the cities,
and that members of the well-to-do, educated upper classes only
began to enter the Church in the second century, and then
only very gradually; and we are aware that this change did
not take place without a good deal of opposition on the part of
the educated and wealthy sections of Society.

At the same time it is equally clear that in the whole range of
the Early Christian literature—missionary and devotional—both
within and without the New Testament, there is no hint of any
formulation of the "Social" question; the central problem is always
purely religious, dealing with such questions as the salvation of
the soul, monotheism, life after death, purity of worship, the
right kind of congregational organization, the application of
Christian ideals to daily life, and the need for severe self-discipline
in the interests of personal holiness; further, we must admit that
from the beginning no class distinctions were recognized; rather

they were lost sight of in the supreme question of eternal salvation and the appropriation of a spiritual inheritance. It is worthy of special note that Early Christian apologetic contains no arguments dealing either with hopes of improving the existing social situation, or with any attempt to heal social ills; it is based solely upon theology, philosophy, and ethics; further, these ethical considerations always aim at fostering habits of sobriety and industry, that is, they are concerned with the usefulness of the Christian as a citizen. Jesus began His public ministry, it is true, by proclaiming the Kingdom of God as the great hope of Redemption, and this Hope was cherished by the Early Christian Church as a whole; this "Kingdom", however, was never regarded as a perfect social order to be created by the Power of God rather than by the skill of man. The "Hope of the Kingdom" was not an attempt to console those who were suffering from social wrongs by promising them happiness and compensation, perhaps even to the extent of complete revolution, in another existence—an assurance given by the Gospel to the destitute over against the dominant forces of contemporary human society. This Message of the Kingdom was primarily the vision of an ideal ethical and religious situation, of a world entirely controlled by God, in which all the values of pure spirituality would be recognized and appreciated at their true worth. When, later on, the idea of a future redemption receded into the background, giving place to the idea of a redemption already achieved through the Life and Death of Christ, the values of redemption were still purely inward, ethical, and spiritual, leading inevitably and naturally to a sphere of painless bliss. This is the foundation fact from which we have to start.[10]

This point of view is further explained and supported by the fact that parallel religious systems and groups—as, for example, the great mass of so-called Gnosticism, or the Mithraic Mysteries—did not adopt the policy of preaching a social gospel for a certain class, nor did they advocate an attack on social wrongs; they were rather institutions of a higher theology, of mightier "mysteries", of a more certain salvation.[11] Even when we find communistic groups among the Gnostics, particularly the Carpocratians, whose spirit and outlook were far from Christian, we see that their influence was confined to their immediate circle, and that they did not advocate any programme of general social and political reform. From the second century, to a great extent, the transcendental interest was paramount, and the desire to improve social

[10] See p. 165.   [11] See p. 167.

conditions in any practical way had died down. This, however, is not at all surprising. Although, from the time of the Peloponnesian Wars and the Reform Movement of the Gracchi the class struggles of the ancient world were shattering and profound, and although the ideals—socio-political, economic, socialistic, communist, and anarchist—produced by the politics of democracy and by philosophical reflection and literature were widely diffused,[12] in the main the feverish period of these struggles ended with the Hellenistic Empires followed by the Empire of the Caesars. Order and prosperity returned, and social upheaval and oppression, the policy of exploitation which had caused so much misery, coupled with the insecurity of the wage-earners, were all lessened. The iron stability of the Monarchy influenced the whole spirit of social and political order, and all free movement retired into the sphere of personal, interior life, into the domain of ethical and religious reflection.

The reduction of the slave markets as one result of the *Pax Romana* made it possible for a middle class to arise once more. That social righteousness, so long and so ardently desired, lay now in the hands of the Emperor, and the great humanitarian School of the Stoics (which believed that the purest ideal had only been realized in remote antiquity), taught men, on the one hand, to acquiesce in the present condition of society, with all its limitations, while, on the other hand, it influenced Imperial legislation in favour of the most humane reforms.[13] It is true, of course, that the social history of the Imperial period has not yet been studied in much detail, but we know that the process of the dissolution of ancient society was long delayed. The primitive Christian communities, however, had very little to do with the most important socio-historical events of the Imperial period: the disappearance of the peasant class, the reduction of the number of slaves, the development of slavery into serfdom, the transfer of capital to the hands of the owners of large estates, the withdrawal of power from the coast towns into the interior, the complete alteration of military and civil life, with the final reversion to rural life.[14] It is not difficult to understand why these events affected the earliest Christian communities so little, for during the first few centuries the Christians belonged to the lower classes in the towns, and shared in the gradual improvement in social conditions which took place in urban life; again, their real centre lay in the East, where social cleavages were far fewer; thus in their general outlook these communities were rather middle

[12] See p. 168.   [13] See p. 168.   [14] See p. 168.

class than working class, and, in spite of all their hopes of a new world, they were also very anxious for ordered conditions and for civic usefulness.

Further, in the ancient world, in which the peasants were at least theoretically citizens, the struggles for their rights were included in the struggles of the bourgeoisie; there were no factories at that time, in the modern sense of the term, and there was no large body of free wage-earners; hence a great social movement in favour of economic freedom, or even the rise of a new class, would have been quite impossible. The democratic struggles which actually took place were always semi-political, and were concerned with such questions as land distribution and the lessening of financial burdens; all along, the continuance of the lowest class as a slave class was accepted by everyone as inevitable. The idea of emancipation was practically never included in attempts to improve the lot of the slaves. Thus, apart from the peace and order established by the Empire, there was no class-movement for social freedom. The various philosophical theories and political romances certainly indicate, on the ethical and inward side of life, some modification of violent contrasts, but they cannot be held to signify the emergence of a new class. In the last resort, also, we ought not to think of the primitive Christian communities as in any way belonging entirely to one social class. It is true that for a long time the Church membership was mainly composed of slaves, freedmen, and manual labourers, although at the same time, as Overbeck rightly remarks, when we take into consideration the total number of slaves at that time, and recall also the caution which was exercised in receiving slaves into membership, we realize that we must not exaggerate their share in the Early Church; at all events, special provision was made to exclude slaves who were eager to obtain their freedom. From the very outset some of the members came from the upper classes; indeed, it was they who were chiefly responsible for providing the necessary financial support and the places where the Christians could gather for fellowship and worship. During the reign of Domitian, Christianity permeated every section of Society, including the highest Court circles, and Pliny's famous letter speaks distinctly of *multi omnis ordinis*. From the time of Commodus the upper classes took an increasing share in the life of the Christian Church. All this is only natural when we realize that we are here dealing with an essentially religious movement, and it is a clear proof of the error of the view which would have us believe that we are dealing with a "class-movement of the proletariat", or with a religious reshaping of the Socialism of the ancient world.[15]

CHRISTIANITY AND RELIGIOUS MOVEMENTS IN THE GRAECO-ROMAN WORLD

It is, therefore, clear that the rise of Christianity is a religious and not a social phenomenon. For although religion is interwoven with life as a whole, in development and dialectic it has an independent existence. A new era of creative religious experience and sensitiveness to religious influences characterized the close of the ancient world. The way had been prepared for this change by a number of factors, which may be briefly enumerated: the destruction of national religions, which was a natural result of the loss of national independence; the mingling of races, which led naturally to the mingling of various cults; the rise of mystery-religions, with their exclusive emphasis upon the inward life, and their independence of questions of nationality and birth; the fusion of various fragments of religion which had broken away from their national foundation; the philosophical religion of culture with its varied forms of assimilation to the popular religions; the need of a world empire for a world religion, a need which was only partially satisfied by worship of the Emperor; the amazing deepening and spiritualizing of ethical thought during a period of intellectual development which covered four hundred years of unexampled richness in criticism and intensive growth; and, finally, the decline of polytheism (which was connected with all these factors) both in its *Mythus* and in its forms of worship, and the desire for a final form of religion which would offer eternal values to mankind.

The close of the era of antiquity was marked by two outstanding developments: (*a*) the destruction of the popular religions, due to a variety of causes, though in the last resort it was due to the fact that religious thought itself had gradually become more spiritual and more ethical; (*b*) a new and powerful religious movement, due to the mingling of many varied currents of thought.[16] Ultimately, however, this development was the result of an independent development in the religious idea itself. It was out of this situation that Christianity arose; the Church

---

[15] For the social composition of the community cf. *Keim, 164, 319; Overbeck, 188;* especially *Harnack: Mission,*[2] *II, 25 ff.,* and *Bigelmair: Die Beteiligung der Christen am öffentlichen Leben, 1902, pp. 208–226; Knopf: Die soziale Zusammensetzung der ältesten heidenchristlichen Gemeinden, Z. f. Theol. u. Kirche, 1900;* and *Knopf: Nachapost. Zeitalter, pp. 64 ff.* [16] See p. 170.

became the receptacle for the new ideas which grew out of this religious development, and, as far as possible, it linked them up with the fundamental doctrines of Christianity.

If, however, the process which I have just described gives a true picture of the relation of Christianity to the inner religious development of the ancient world, we see at once the reason for its appeal to the lower classes, and its development from them. This attitude, however, cannot be explained as the alleged product of a social process, but simply as one which has arisen out of the nature of a new religious movement. New religious movements of this kind develop along two lines; on the one hand, they proceed from the rarefied atmosphere of cultivated thoughtful circles, and express themselves in criticism and speculation; their actual importance depends upon the depth of the real religious vitality which these forms of criticism and speculation conceal. Platonism and Stoicism, each in its own way, are examples of new religious movements of this kind. Essentially, however, both are systems of reflection and attempts to reach truth through the reason, and therefore they never achieve the specifically religious power of a faith founded on revelation. Conscious of their weakness, they cling in part to the old popular religion, which they merely explain in somewhat different terms, and in part they base their confidence on the power of the abstract arguments which each individual may construct for himself after quiet reflection on the explanations offered by these systems. On the other hand, it is the lower classes which do the really creative work, forming communities on a genuine religious basis. They alone unite imagination and simplicity of feeling with a non-reflective habit of mind, a primitive energy, and an urgent sense of need. On such a foundation alone is it possible to build up an unconditional authoritative faith in a Divine Revelation with simplicity of surrender and unshaken certainty. Only within a fellowship of this kind is there room for those who have a sense of spiritual need, and who have not acquired the habit of intellectual reasoning, which always regards everything from a relative point of view. All great religious movements based on Divine revelation which have created large communities have always issued from circles of this kind. The meaning and capacity for development of the religious movement which arose in this way were always dependent upon the power and depth of the stimulus which had been imparted by such a naïve revelation, and, on the other hand, upon the energy of the religious conviction which gave to this stimulus a divine and absolute authority. Of course, it cannot be claimed that such movements are always characterized by a deep inward energy. But where this *is* the case simplicity is manifestly superior to speculation, for it produces a driving force and imparts a deep spiritual experience without which no religious movement can live. Inevitably, as the movement develops, the early naïve vital religious content always fuses with all the highest religious forces of the intellectual culture of the day; apart from this fusion faith would be broken by the impact of the cultural environment.

From the second century onwards this kind of fusion took place in the history of Christianity. The fact that the connection between faith and thought increased as time went on was a sure sign that the new faith contained a deep religious power, which not only did not break down when it came into touch with intellectual culture, but rather became more fruitful and developed still further. The Christian origins, however, reveal the popular character and outlook of all naïve religion. This is the reason why the new faith bore no trace of the much-discussed "senility" of the Imperial period. Jesus Himself was a man of the people, and His Gospel bears clear traces of the simple peasant and artisan conditions of Galilee. It is only the poor and the humble who easily understand His Gospel; it is difficult for the rich and for the religious leaders because they do not feel their need. In their wisdom they cannot see the wood for the trees, and their hearts are attached to too many other things to be able to offer an unconditional surrender; yet "with God all things are possible"; even a rich man can be saved, and even a scribe may not be far from the Kingdom of God.

The first disciples of Jesus came from religious groups of this humble type, and the first Christian congregation which was based on faith in the Risen Lord belonged to the same class of society; in the case of the latter, however, it is quite evident that the members possessed a moderate amount of this world's goods.[17] Even Paul, the man who transformed this faith in Jesus into a missionary world religion, and who made the worship of Christ the foundation of a new Church and of a new form of the worship of God, was essentially both an organizer and a creative, mystical soul; in fact, in spite of his intellectual powers his bent was mainly contemplative. In any case, his whole outlook was entirely independent of the spirit of purely scientific inquiry, balanced criticism, and the higher world culture of the epoch. He was "an unliterary person in the unliterary class of the Imperial period, but as a spiritually gifted man he rose out of his class and regarded the

[17] See p. 170.

surrounding world of contemporary culture with a supreme sense of power. All his scattered attempts at systematization reveal the limitation of his powers; the secret of his greatness lay in the realm of formless religion".

Similarly, the whole of the Early Christian literature was popular in character; it was propagated in secret, and was characterized by all the peculiarities of a popular tradition. Written in the vernacular, and at all points adapted to the need and the imagination of the people, for a long time it was neither noticed nor influenced by the educated classes. Its legendary character too, which was combined with a good and sound tradition, reveals the peculiarity of a popular tradition. After the creative outburst which produced the Gospels, the Pauline epistles and the Johannine literature—itself coming very near to the mystery wisdom of the educated classes—the standard of Early Christian literature sank to a very low level, revealing the poverty-stricken condition of a merely popular literature. With the Apologists, however, Christian literature began its upward development into the literary upper classes, into their world of speech and thought. On their part, however, the Apologists emphasize the fact that the Christians are simple and ignorant people, and out of that, in the style of the Cynics, they make a *captatio benevolentiae*; this shows very plainly that the appeal of Christianity to the lower classes had nothing to do with a "class" movement, or with a Chiliastic Socialism. Poverty and simplicity are the foundation of truth; but an artificial and polished age neither sees nor believes this fact; Rousseau brought this out very clearly with reference to "natural" truth.[18]

INDIRECT CONNECTION BETWEEN CHRISTIANITY AND SOCIAL HISTORY

It may, indeed, be asserted that the whole great religious crisis of the ancient world was itself a result of the social struggles of the period, and that obviously it was the collapse of the national states in the East and in the West which paved the way for this whole process. We may also conclude that the disastrous effect of the great social conflicts which lasted for centuries, and the indescribable misery which they caused, opened the minds of men to thoughts of religious redemption. Further, the renuncia-

[18] This point of view is strongly emphasized by Overbeck: *Ueber die Anfänge der patristischen Literatur*, Hist. *Zeitschrift*, *1882, pp. 417–472*, and Deissmann: *Bibelstudien, 1895, Neue Bibelstudien, 1897, Das Neue Testament und die Schriftdenkmäler der römischen Kaiserzeit (Jahrbuch des Freien deutschen Hochstiftes, 1905)*.

tion of individual activity in social matters, and submission to the
world domination of the Empire, drove the individual into his
own inner life, and forced him to concentrate his energies on the
effort to elevate private and personal morality; it also gave social
ideals a transcendent turn; meanwhile both individuals, and
groups composed of individuals on a voluntary basis, found
comfort in religious exaltation as a compensation for the hopeless-
ness of the temporal outlook. The failure of so many great plans
owing to the pettiness and selfishness of the masses, and the
criminal, unbridled licence of their leaders, aroused a sense of
sin and weakness, and the violent changes in the destinies of men,
combined with the decline of political systems which seemed to
have an almost religious character and which seemed to have
been built for eternity, aroused the desire for eternal values in a
higher sphere [19]

These struggles, however, had little in common with the
modern struggles for freedom, whether of an enslaved peasantry
or of the "wage-slaves" of the modern proletariat. It was the
destruction of the ancient *Polis*, however, and the extinction of
ancient freedom in a bureaucratic sovereign state, involving the
destruction of many treasured ideals, and a great deal of oppression, which more and more caused men's thoughts to turn with
longing towards more spiritual aims. Both in the East and in the
West this was certainly the case. Social distinctions ceased to have
any meaning for the different classes when they found an interior
union on the basis of religion. Indeed, it is absolutely certain that
the great religious crisis which marked the close of the ancient
world was a result of vast social crises, in which it had become
plain that the social ideal could not be realized by human thought
and effort; then men were willing to submit to the order established by the Roman Empire; henceforth the conduct of external
affairs was left to the rulers, while men sought and cultivated
individual and spiritual freedom. This applies to the later development of Platonism and Stoicism; it applies to countless new
religious movements, and in particular it applies to the establishment of Christianity as well as to the preparation for it within
Judaism. Although, in the main, it was the upper classes who were
specially open to these influences, the lower classes also were influenced by the uprooting of institutions, by uncertainty about
the ancient faith, and by the ethical and religious teaching of the
mystagogues, and thus their latent energies sought passionately
for new religious life. In the upper classes the ground was prepared

[19] See p. 171.

to receive a new spiritual and universal human view of the universe; in the lower classes the soil was ready to receive the seed of a new spiritual and universal cult.

At the same time, however, the influence of these social and historical developments was only indirect. Only those who see in all spiritual movements merely the influence of social movements, and especially those who imagine that all religion is merely the reflection of social conditions in transcendental terms, will see in them a direct cause of the religious crisis. In reality, however, all impartial religious research reveals the fact that, to some extent at least, religious thought is independent; it has its own inner dialectic and its own power of development; it is therefore precisely during these periods of a total bankruptcy of human hope and effort that it is able to step in and fill the vacant space with its own ideas and its own sentiment.

This dialectic developed independently amid the criticism of the Greek period of Enlightenment, the new speculative mono-theistic movements which it provoked in reply, as well as amid the syncretistic Oriental religions which were divorced from their own environment. When it was fully developed it caused the desire for ethical and religious renewal to increase in depth and urgency under the Empire. Then, as the religious idea gained a firmer foothold within human life, it produced a great variety of independent results, which led increasingly to a movement away from materialism and awakened a longing for the purely mystical and religious values of life. The real achievement of Christianity in the ancient world was undoubtedly the concentration and co-ordination of all these efforts and aspirations. In this, however, it was only continuing the mighty religious process which had already begun, by giving it a new centre in a genuine, strong, and popular religious movement, with a new system of worship and a new revelation of God.

This result, however, was due only indirectly to the course of social development; its most genuine and essential elements were simply the result of its own religious thought. This comes out very clearly in the new hope offered by Christianity; it does not offer simply a transformed social ideal, expressed in transcendental terms, the promise of a world in which equality, freedom, pain-lessness, and satisfaction shall reign, effected by a Divine and miraculous intervention when human effort has proved unable to achieve this end[20]; the Christian ideal means rather the entire renunciation of the material social ideal of all political and

[20] See p. 171.

economic values, and the turning towards the religious treasures of peace of heart, love of humanity, fellowship with God, which are open to all because they are not subject to any difficulties of leadership or organization. This means an entire transformation of values; there is here no idea of calling in Divine power to establish an organization which men are unable to effect in their own strength. Manifestly this was the case in Stoicism and in the "Saviour-religions"; this, however, is also the meaning of the Christian hope of the "Kingdom of God". The whole conception of Eudaemonism, or the fundamental ethical principle of happiness, which implies that moral excellence and political and economic well-being coincide, has been altered. Rückert's lines might well serve as a motto for the new age which was beginning:

> Pluck happiness
> And give to each a share;
> To me give bliss
> And let who will
> Have happiness.

Bliss itself is conceived increasingly as the state of the future life, and thus it becomes increasingly possible to do without earthly happiness. The value of the present life was further depreciated by the idea that man is by nature totally corrupt, and also that this life is inextricably bound by the chains of material things.

Thus, by its own inherent energy the religious idea itself neutralized secular distinctions; and with this depreciation of political and economic values the barriers between races and classes and peoples were also removed. It was then, of course, quite natural that this religious idea should develop a great attraction for all who were suffering from these restrictions. It was also quite natural that Christianity should primarily seek and find its disciples among those who were feeling the weight of this oppression most acutely. Further, we must not forget the simple fact that a popular movement, which, from the very outset, was steeped in the ideas and feelings of the lower classes, naturally was only able to spread amongst them, and that it found difficulty in gaining an entry into the upper classes of Society; thus for a long time, in the main, it found most acceptance among the lower orders; in its apologetic, therefore, it turned this necessity into a virtue. From the beginning, however, attempts were made to reach like-minded souls in the upper classes, of whom there were very many, and in the end these efforts were most successful. Another quite obvious point, which was very important, is this: a religion which sets its adherents in absolute opposition to the State religion, and to the social and civic customs with which it is connected, can only now and again, quite exceptionally, win its adherents among those circles which, by their wealth and education, are most closely connected with these institutions. It was for the same reason that the Austrian *Los-von-Rom* movement, for example, was most successful among the lower classes; they were less closely bound up with the dominant religious system. In so far as this was the case, it is obvious that the religious movement was strongly, though indirectly, influenced by the social situation. The religious community has to do something for its members beyond the mere preaching of salvation; it has to try to provide men with shelter and assistance during the period of their earthly struggle. Thus the influence of the social situation becomes direct as soon as the Christian community is able to give help on these lines. But the more the Christian community becomes a society within a society, or a state within the State, the more strongly it becomes conscious of the fact that it is bound up with concrete social problems, and it then turns its attention and its power of organization to these matters. All this, however, is simply the result of the new religious idea, it is not its starting-point.

If this is so, however, it is a great mistake to treat all the ideas which underlie the preaching of Jesus as though they were primarily connected with the "Social" problem. The message of Jesus is obviously purely religious; it issues directly from a very definite idea of God, and of the Divine Will in relation to man. To Jesus the whole meaning of life is religious; His life and His teaching are wholly determined by His thought of God. At the same time we must also remember that late Judaism shared the prevalent religious tendency of the ancient world; that is to say, here also political and social disintegration had shaken men's faith in finite ideals, and had caused them to look with longing towards the horizon of the infinite.[21] Once this is realized, however, it is quite permissible to study the connection between the sociological problem and these religious ideals; we may then inquire how the relation between the individual and Society in general is shaped from this religious standpoint, and how the sociological result which follows every fresh revelation of truth is affected by this religious idea. This certainly brings us up sharply against some very important points; it is essential to note that

[21] Cf. *Bousset: Die Religion des Judentums im neutestamentlichen Zeitalter.*

their peculiar significance is due precisely to the fact that they have been produced by the religious idea.[22]

THE GOSPEL ETHIC

Amidst all the uncertainties of tradition the fundamental idea underlying the preaching of Jesus is easy to discern. It deals with the proclamation of the great final Judgment of the coming of the "Kingdom of God", by which is meant that state of life in which God will have supreme control, when His Will will be done on earth, as it is now being done only in heaven; in this "Kingdom" sin, suffering, and pain will have been overcome, and the true spiritual values, combined with single-eyed devotion to the Will of God, will shine out in the glory that is their due. That is why sinful men who acknowledge their sinfulness, and those who have learned the lessons of submission and humility through their experience of sorrow and poverty, will enter the Kingdom of God before the self-satisfied and the righteous as well as before the rich and the great ones of the earth.

Further, the message of Jesus also deals with the formation of the community based on the Hope of the Kingdom, which, in the meantime, possesses both the pledge of the Kingdom and the preparation for its coming in Jesus Himself. This community is to be founded by the missionary efforts of the narrower circle of the immediate disciples and followers of Jesus; they therefore are entrusted with the special duties which devolve upon the heralds of the Kingdom. With their help the Kingdom is preached everywhere. Jesus does not speculate about the nature of the Kingdom of God; it simply includes all ethical and religious ideals, among which freedom from suffering is certainly one aspect of the message. All attempts at a closer analysis are incomplete and uncertain. All that can be said about "times and seasons" is that the Kingdom is to come "soon"; the actual date Jesus left entirely in the Hands of God, and from the study of the tradition it is quite impossible to discover with any certainty what He taught about the manner of its coming. The Kingdom of God means the rule of God upon earth, to be followed, later on, by the end of the world and the Judgment. These events, however, are so closely connected, and preparation for the coming Kingdom

[22] For the following cf. *Holtzmann: Neutestamentliche Theologie; Wernle: Anfänge;* and the *Reichgotteshoffnung, 1903; Wrede: Predigt Jesu vom Reiche Gottes (Vorträge und Studien, 1907)*; above all *Jülicher: Gleichnisreden, II, 1899; A. Harnack: Sprüche und Reden Jesu. Die zweite Quelle des Matthäus und Lukas, 1907;* so far as the ethic of the Gospel is concerned, here also I adhere to the point of view expressed in *Grundprobleme der Ethik, Z. f. Theol. u. Kirche, 1902.*

is also so vital for the Final Judgment, that nothing definite is taught about either the difference or the relationship between these two conceptions. All the emphasis is laid on preparing for the Kingdom of God, and this preparation is so thorough that the community which is "looking out for the Kingdom of God" can already in anticipation be described as the "Kingdom of God". There is no desire to organize a special group of chosen souls; the way that leads to salvation, and the rock upon which men ought to build, is to be made plain to as many as possible.

This demand for "preparation" includes both the ethic of Jesus and the idea of God which determines His ethic; at this point it is unnecessary to discuss the question of the element of novelty in His teaching contrasted with His Jewish environment.

His fundamental moral demand, briefly expressed, is the sanctification of the individual in all his moral activity for the sake of God, or that "purity of heart" which, when the Kingdom has actually come, will enable a man to "see God". The moral commandments themselves are conceived from the point of view of ordinary practice and general human interest, but they are illuminated by the fact that as they are obeyed with devotion and inner simplicity, all that is done takes place under the Eye of God, which penetrates every disguise and tests human motives to the utmost; thus the will is given to God in absolute obedience, in order that it may attain the real and true life, its real spiritual eternal value in the sight of God. Hence the ethic of the Gospel is marked by emphasis on purity of intention and a greatly intensified reverence for all moral commands, without any allowance for conflicting motives or for expediency. Above all, it connects this moral conduct with its supreme object—a personal relation with God and the supreme value of the soul, "for what is a man profited if he shall gain the whole world and lose his own soul?"

We need not here discuss the question of the connection of these ideas with the Jewish Law, with the ordinary popular ideas of ethical behaviour, and with the popular expectations of reward and merit, and also with the various critical outbreaks against ideas of this kind. The main point is this: that this ethical ideal is absolutely steeped in a twofold idea—(1) the religious idea of the Presence of God, which is conceived as a searching and penetrating gaze and as a "fascination" which draws man to Himself; and (2) with the thought of the infinite and eternal value of the soul to be attained through self-renunciation for the sake of God. These ideas are more easily understood by the soul which is bowed down with a sense of sin and guilt than by a "righteous" man. The poor man, who is not so deeply involved in the cares of this world as the rich man, makes these truths his own more speedily. These are truths which open a way of deliverance to the poor and the despised. For the poor and humble there is comfort in the knowledge that God does not judge of a man's worth by the commonly accepted standards of ordinary life.

This completes the summary of the chief characteristics of the Gospel ethic. We might search it in vain for a detailed list of particular moral requirements. The moral demands seemed so entirely natural to Jewish life that, quite naturally, they were also regarded as universally relevant. Here the Gospel ethic is neither complete nor systematic. But it would be wrong to infer from this that the Gospel ethic is purely subjective, and that it merely amounts to a demand for an independent exercise of conscience. For "reward in heaven" is spoken of quite simply and naturally, although there is no idea of any tangible "reward"; the real reward is the Kingdom of God itself, the goal of a religious consummation. It is also clear that among the various demands which the general consciousness recognizes as valid, distinctions are made which force moral instruction to concentrate on certain definite points, so that the ethic of the Gospel deals not merely with the will and its intention, or with the inner constraint of conscience, but also with certain definite concrete demands.

This concrete and extremely characteristic tendency of the Gospel ethic is due to the fact that the Idea of God is set in the very centre of all moral purpose. This is the God who tries the heart and the reins, whose eyes pierce the inmost depths of the heart, revealing the most subtle self-deception; the God who is also a living and active Will, as the Prophets of old proclaimed Him. This is the God who draws into the fulfilment of His own creative Will the soul that is utterly surrendered to Him. All the virtues, therefore, are thoroughly systematized from the fundamental religious point of view: union with the Will and the Being of God, and co-operation with the work of God. In the sight of God the highest position is that of those in whom consecrated self-sacrifice and self-surrender to God through obedience have been expressed most clearly. So far as character formation is concerned the virtues of complete sincerity and integrity alone make it possible for the soul to attain union with the All-Knowing and All-Holy; this, of course, involves thoroughly conscientious behaviour in daily life. Stress is also laid on humility, which helps man to realize his littleness in the presence of God, and therefore forbids too much being made of men's sins against each other, and on self-denial, which demands the sacrifice of love of self, love of pleasure and comfort, and of all human preferences, to the severity of the moral claims involved in union with God. Christ requires men to be indifferent to material happiness and to money, to practise sexual self-restraint, to have a mind that values the unseen and eternal more than the seen and temporal, and finally to develop a personality which in its central aim is thoroughly harmonious and unified.

Here the Gospel is extremely radical. It is not ascetic, but it is very severe; no doubt about the possibility of its practical realization is permitted; yet this austerity in no way destroys the innocent joy of life. The same applies to the question of relationship with other people; all moral achievements of this kind are regarded from the point of view of participation in the work of God, of the revelation within us of the true spirit of God Himself, which we have received from Him, the awakening of the sense of the true knowledge of God through the revelation of His Being in our own behaviour. Since God is active, creative Love, who maketh His sun to rise upon the evil and upon the good, so men who are consecrated to God ought to manifest their love to friend and foe, to the good and to the bad, overcoming hostility and defiance by a generous love which will break down all barriers and awaken love in return. All this implies the need for gentleness, readiness to forgive others, willingness to serve, warmth of feeling in personal relations, magnanimity, modesty, and forbearance. Here, too, there is no asceticism, which aims at self-depreciation for the sake of the mortification of the "natural man" in the abstract (which is, properly speaking, required as a provision for the future), but only a severity which makes almost superhuman demands, and an idealism which is certain that it can break down the dull resistance of the masses and of utilitarian reason. Other social relations are not mentioned. All the other virtues, however, the demand for self-control and self-cultivation, and also the claim for equity and justice, and things of that kind, pale in importance before these main demands, and they are only touched upon now and then, and in a casual manner. It is expected that they will naturally fall into line with the main tendency, which lies in the double commandment to love God, that is, to give oneself to Him in obedience to His commands, and to love one's neighbour, that is, that in intercourse with him we are to reveal to him or to arouse in him the Divine spirit of Love.[23]

[23] See p. 171.

SOCIOLOGICAL CHARACTERISTICS OF THE GOSPEL ETHIC

These ideas determine the form of the sociological structure. Its first outstanding characteristic is an unlimited, unqualified individualism. The standard of this individualism is wholly self-contained, determined simply by its own sense of that which will further its consecration to God. It is bound to go all lengths in obedience to the demands of the Gospel. Its basis and its justification lie in the fact that man is called to fellowship with God, or, as it is here expressed, to be the child of God, and in the eternal value of the soul which this filial relation confers. The individual as a child of God may regard himself as infinitely precious, but he reaches this goal only through self-abnegation in unconditional obedience to the Holy Will of God.

It is clear that an individualism of this kind is entirely radical, and that it transcends all natural barriers and differences, through the ideal of the religious value of the soul. It is also clear that such an individualism is only possible at all upon this religious basis. It is only fellowship with God which gives value to the individual, and it is only in common relationship with God, in a realm of supernatural values, that natural differences disappear. Where this kind of individualism prevails all earthly differences are swallowed up in the Divine power and love which reduce all other distinctions to nothing. Henceforth the only distinctions which remain are those which characterize creative personalities of infinite worth, each one of whom must trade with his "pound" to the best of his ability, and in no way whatever may make compromise with the differences and interests of the world. Whether, indeed, in practice this ideal will be generally accepted is another question. Sin and the world oppose a heavy weight of obstruction, and in face of stern conflict with a hostile world it is true that "many are called and few are chosen". In face of these difficulties, however, which His absolute religious individualism encounters, Jesus comforts Himself with the knowledge that things that are impossible with men are possible with God. From the very outset this was not an ideal for the masses. Faced by the extreme tension of these demands, we must also remember that they were formulated in the expectation of the final Judgment of the imminent End of the World. However little these demands may have been due to this expectation, we must realize that their radicalism and their indifference towards questions of practicability can only be understood from this point of view. The feeling is that the sphere in which they are to be realized will not last long and has no intrinsic value of its own. This absolute religious individualism, however, which removes all distinctions by concentrating entirely upon differences in character in individuals, each of whom has his own value, also contains within itself a strong idea of fellowship; this idea is based just as clearly upon the specifically religious fundamental idea. This cannot be explained simply by pointing out that the altruistic commandments are bound up with the commands to consecrate the self to God—commands which have to be obeyed to the uttermost limits in self-purification and self-denial. In the last resort the idea of fellowship springs from the fact that those who are being purified for the sake of God meet in Him; and since the dominating thought of God is not that of a peaceful happiness into which souls are gathered but that of a creative will, so those who are united in God must be inspired by the Will and the Spirit of God, and must actively fulfil the loving Will of God. Therefore for the children of God there is no law and no pressure, no war and no conflict, but only an urgent love and a conquest of evil by good, demands which the Sermon on the Mount illustrates by giving extreme instances. Since, as we have seen, absolute individualism springs from the religious idea of pure-hearted self-surrender to Him who seeks men's souls and to the Fatherly Will which calls them to the vocation of being His children, so from this same fundamental idea this absolute individualism leads to just as absolute a fellowship of love among those who are united in God; from this springs an active realization of the love of God even towards strangers and enemies, because only through the revelation of absolute love can a true understanding of God be awakened and the way opened to Him. Everywhere this is the background and meaning of the Gospel emphasis on brotherhood and the love of one's neighbour. It is not simply kindness and gentleness in general, but the union of those who are united in God, and the revelation and awakening of the understanding of the real values of life through the manifestation of love, the melting down of earthly smallness and worldliness in the Fire of the Divine Love, which nothing worldly can resist. But this fellowship only extends as far as the religious message is known. Where this is so it is absolute; where it is absent it seeks and woos; but the way to salvation is narrow, and few there be that find it, and amongst these few those who suffer enter most easily. There is no thought here of a humanitarian ideal in itself. When the effort to establish this fellowship fails the Gospel can only exhort to suffering and patience, until the Judgment will set things right.

Here again, in order to understand Jesus' exhortations, we have to remember that this restoration is not thought of as taking place after a long life in the world, but after a short period of time.

Thus out of an absolute individualism there arises a universalism which is equally absolute. Both these aspects of the Gospel are based entirely upon religion; their support is the thought of the Holy Divine Will of Love, and they mutually aid each other quite logically; we cannot here pursue any farther the particular question of the extent to which Jesus really abrogated the Jewish position of privilege. The interesting point for us is simply the fact that absolute individualism and universalism spring directly out of the religious idea, and that this fact has, sociologically, a double aspect. Both require each other. For individualism only becomes absolute through the ethical surrender of the individual to God, and being filled with God; and on the other hand, in possession of the Absolute, individual differences merge into an unlimited love whose prototype is the Father-God Himself, to whom souls are drawn and in whom they are united. This lesson must be learnt by all who desire to save their souls at the Judgment and have their part in the Kingdom of God; and those who do this are His brothers and sisters, and therefore the firstborn of the coming Kingdom of God.[24]

We can here set aside the question of the significance for this individual preparation for the return of Christ which the certainty of the forgiveness of sins and of the gracious Will of God already has in the preaching of Jesus in producing this spirit of courage and joyfulness. Sociologically, its significance is primarily only that of a strengthening of motive and of a triumph over unavoidable hindrances and obscurities which arise in the effort to realize the ideal. Secondly, however, it tinges both the individualism and the universalism with a feeling which is closely connected with its religious root. Thus the emphasis falls not only on the individual's sense of his dignity in being united with God, but also on his sinful weakness and creaturely infirmity, the sense of the need for trust in God and the help of God, and the confidence in His mercy as the source of all that is good. The spirit of universalism also becomes more than a mere unity in God and common relationship to God—it becomes a unity in a common sense of need, through mutual readiness to forgive, through a common sense of sin and of the fight against evil. The individual, in spite of his sense of personal worth, still remains an "unprofitable servant", needing forgiveness, and in expectation of a settlement

24 See p. 172.

of accounts with God must in brotherly love destroy all human debit accounts, all calculations between man and man. The Idea of God bears both the features of a fatherly loving-kindness which calls all to the highest dignity of life, and also of a perfection which maintains souls always in humility, and yet ever encourages them through the forgiveness of sins. It does not, therefore, represent itself as an inevitable idea, but as authority and revelation. The Hebrew God of Will, in His aloofness from mankind, only makes Himself known in living revelation in the Law and in the Prophets, and in the authority with which Jesus interprets both. In this way the idea of authority is introduced into the sociological structure. The whole system of thought which has just been described arises out of faith in an authority of this kind, and the securing of this authority as its essential source will be a permanent task of the whole structure. At all these points this structure differs from that system (to which otherwise it is so closely related) which will be described later; the religious-ethical and sociological thought of the later Stoics.

Otherwise this sociological structure is a completely free fellowship of thought and knowledge. Its members mingle everywhere with the children of this world, and continue to take part in the national form of worship. They only prepare themselves inwardly for the coming of the Kingdom, coupled with their right behaviour towards one another. Jesus did not organize a Church. He simply asked for helpers who would spread the message by preaching; these assistants were to be men who would leave all and sacrifice everything for His sake and for the Cause. That is one of the main differences between His work and that of the Essenes, with which it is often compared by people who seem to think that it is the special task of the historian to be cleverer than his sources, and to consider everything more probable and more possible than what they say. This is also the reason why the sociological thought of the Gospel has been able to react again and again against ecclesiastical tyranny.

THE GOSPEL ETHIC AND GENERAL SOCIAL VALUES

From this point of view it is easy to forecast what form the Christian attitude will take towards social problems which belong to an entirely different group of interests.[25] These problems belong to the world and will perish with the world. As the world itself is a mixture of good and evil, so the whole social order,

[25] On this point cf. *Jacoby: Neutestamentliche Ethik, 1899*, in which, however, the significance for the future of the Kingdom of God is distinctly underestimated.

with its pleasure and its labour, has its good points. On the other hand, it is also full of danger; its bad side is manifest in its tendency to distract the hearts of men from the one thing needful. Jesus does not preach asceticism; in His teaching there is no trace of contempt for the life of the senses or for pleasure as such, nor does He glorify poverty for its own sake. But He teaches quite plainly that food and work are only of value in so far as they are necessary to life; otherwise they have no ethical value. This point of view is characteristic of popular Oriental feeling with its depreciation of the claims of a higher civilization; it is also the expression of that religious radicalism which cannot see any ethical value at all in anything which is not directly connected with religion.

The ethic of Jesus is heroic rather than ascetic. The heroic aspect is softened only by the gentler elements of trust in the Fatherly Love of God and faith in the forgiveness of sins, but not by any compromise with the claims of the life of the world and the "nature of things". From this point of view we can see plainly the attitude of Jesus towards the State, Society, labour, and the possession of property. There is no thought of the State at all. Jewish nationalism and all its expectations are ignored entirely, even though Israel appears as the germ of the new world that is to be. In the thought of Jesus the Kingdom of God is the rule of God and not the rule of the Jewish people. Jesus makes it perfectly plain that the Roman Empire exists, and has a right to exist, because God permits it; but while He admits this He also adds the injunction: "Render to God the things that are God's."

Jesus' outlook on economic questions is very simple. All that men have to do is to live by the day, trusting their Heavenly Father to provide "for the morrow; for the morrow shall take thought for the things of itself". He also lays down that self-sacrificing love which shares all it has with others (this, of course, assumes the necessity of labour and of earning a living) is the highest proof of true piety. The renunciation of all possessions, however, is the condition of closer membership in the actual missionary group of His disciples.[26]

Thus the only economic doctrine of the Gospel is this: God allows everyone to earn his living by means of work; if distress should arise, then love can help; wealth, however, must be feared on account of its danger for the health of the soul. This is the reason why it is so difficult to reconcile this point of view with the vast social problem created by the tension between increase in

[26] See p. 174.

population and the difficulty of supplying the bare necessities of life. The love which religion requires also proved the simplest way of overcoming distress. Further, all questions of property are considered solely from the standpoint of the consumer, whose practice must remain modest if it is to remain healthy, and who fills up all the bare spaces created by poverty with the exercise of a thoughtful generosity.

It is, however, undeniable that the message of Jesus, in its sympathy with poverty and suffering, does apply more particularly to the poor. The reason for this, however, lies in the assumption, which is here taken for granted, that the Word finds a speedier entrance into the good ground of an "honest and good heart" among the poor. Another reason is that Divine Goodness and Justice are manifested in the fact that it is precisely those who are apparently most backward, and the disinherited, who find it easier to enter into the way of salvation than those who, in the eyes of the world, are more privileged. In this bias towards the poor there may possibly be an attempt to vindicate Divine Providence: for want and distress, which men cannot understand, in the sight of God prove to be a way to salvation. Yet there is here no idea of compensating poverty with some reward in the future life, but rather the thought of the privilege of suffering for the sake of the knowledge of God and of the true values of life.

The message of Jesus, however, is not restricted to the poor, but it is addressed to everyone. When Naumann, overwhelmed with all these reflections and under the direct influence of contact with Palestine itself, exclaims: "His heart was full of love to the poor, hatred of oppression, and joy in the development of the 'little ones', only the way in which He obeyed the dictates of His Heart was more remote from the humane activity of our own day than we thought", we can scarcely agree with him. In the teaching of Jesus there is no trace of a struggle against oppression; the only conflict which He waged was that against false religious leaders, the "blind leaders of the blind"; while love of the poor and joy in the awakening of the "little ones" of Society cannot be interpreted as the desire to improve their material condition, but rather as the active expression of His own principle and fundamental feeling of love, combined with the sense that there was the most receptive soil for His message. But all the problems and difficulties connected with pauperism, such as the question as to whether grave ethical dangers and serious hindrances to spiritual development are not actually caused by poverty, and the lack

[27] *Naumann: Asia, p. 115.*

of mental and material progress, lie beyond the horizon of the Gospel.

On the question of the family, however, Jesus' teaching is more intimate and detailed in character. Starting from the ethical conception of the family, in the pure and chaste sense of later Judaism, Jesus drew upon it for symbols of the highest attributes of God, for the name of the final religious goal, for the original description of the earliest group of His disciples, and for material for most of His parables; indeed, the idea of the family may be regarded as one of the most fundamental features of His feeling for human life. The value which each individual possesses within the monogamous family (the sense of being "a person"), and the intimacy of the family bond, are in fact also inwardly connected with the religious individualism and universalism of His teaching, and the stress He lays on the qualities of the heart is connected with the undogmatic intuitive character of His faith in God. Hence His insistence on the indissolubility of the marriage bond, and on the limitation of sex intercourse to married people, even for men. The new sociological idea had a most direct and profound influence upon the vital centre of all social life, upon the family. On the other hand, Jesus reminds His hearers that sex will not exist at all in the Kingdom of Heaven; that situations may arise in which it may be necessary to renounce the joys of family life in response to some imperious spiritual demand, and that the missionary vocation may require men to "have made themselves eunuchs for the Kingdom of Heaven's sake".[28]

It is therefore clear that the message of Jesus is not a programme of social reform. It is rather the summons to prepare for the coming of the Kingdom of God; this preparation, however, is to take place quietly within the framework of the present world-order, in a purely religious fellowship of love, with an earnest endeavour to conquer self and cultivate the Christian virtues. Even the Kingdom of God itself is not (for its part at least) the new social order founded by God. It creates a new order upon earth, but it is an order which is not concerned with the State, with Society, or with the family at all. How this will work out in detail is God's affair; man's duty is simply to prepare for it. It is, of course, true that Jesus promises that the poor and the suffering shall have their tears wiped away and all their desires satisfied; but after all this is only natural in a message addressed to the poor; it is not the chief point. The centre of His Message was the glory of God's final victory, and the conquest of demons.

[28] Cf. *Marianne Weber: Ehefrau und Mutter in der Rechtsentwickelung, 1907, pp. 180 ff.*

We can, of course, foresee that as soon as a message of this kind creates a permanent community a social order will inevitably arise out of this programme, and that the sociological structure, which at first was conceived solely in religious terms, will be transformed into a social organization within life as a whole. The command to love one another at least is bound to influence a small and intimate community on the economic side as well, which will lead it to make an attempt to realize this idea in practical life, that is, so long as external hindrances do not oppose it and make it impossible. The spirit of love, indeed, will be exercised in all kinds of conceivable circumstances, but so long as the command to love one another is not checked by the pressure of adverse conditions it feels impelled to obey the inward impulse to organize the life of its own community in obedience to the economic principles which this commandment contains.

During the time of Jesus' life on earth there was no sign of an organized community. A visible community was only formed after His death. Then, however, the Primitive Church at once tried to put His teaching on love into practice. The new social order, however, was confined to the Christian community; it was not a popular programme of social reform in general. Within the Church itself, however, which was small, and whose members all belonged to the same social class, the only communism which was possible was one which differed from all other forms of communism and can only be described as the religious Communism of Love. That is to say, it was a communism which regarded the pooling of possessions as a proof of love and of the religious spirit of sacrifice. It was a communism composed solely of consumers, a communism based upon the assumption that its members will continue to earn their living by private enterprise, in order to be able to practise generosity and sacrifice. Above all, it has no theory of equality at all, whether it be the absolute equality of sharing possessions, or the relative equality of the contribution of the various members to the life of the whole according to merit and service. All that matters is that all the members shall sacrifice something and that they all have to live; how this is carried out in practice does not matter. There was also no attempt at any organization on business lines such as a joint group of producers would have desired. Finally, of course, there was no hostility to that which forms the real hindrance to a true communism—opposition to the institution of the family, which is so closely connected with all private enterprise. On the other hand, it seems likely that its members were unwilling to swear in a court of law, and that they avoided lawsuits and participation in official life. This should be our interpretation of the well-known account of primitive Christian Communism in the Book of the Acts; it seems highly probable that this description fits the facts. The fact that it could not last, or at least that it could not be extended when the Church went out to win the world for Christ, is not difficult to understand. We have only to think of its internal organization, which would, of course, be possible in a small group composed of like-minded people, but which was much too loosely knit and insecurely based for world-wide propaganda. The fact that it was merged immediately in the wider work, without even a struggle for the principle, is only a further sign that this communism was a by-product of Christianity and not a fundamental idea. The fundamental idea was solely that of the salvation of souls.[29]

One of the permanent results of the teaching of Jesus, however, was this idea of a Communism of Love. In later ages, during times of special need, there arose again and again the tendency to repeat the same, or at least similar, experiments within the Church, in other forms. The theoretical expositions of the later Fathers of the Church proclaim it in many ways as the genuine fundamental doctrine of Christianity; free and common to all like light, air, and earth, like the fact that we all come from God and to Him we all return; earthly possessions should be for the use of all, through the love which shares and keeps nothing back. When, at a later date, men again tried to construct a purely abstract theory out of Jesus' exhortations on social questions—that is, when men tried to reduce the absolute readiness of Love to sacrifice, into a theory—this always led quite logically to a fresh attempt to realize the Communism of Love. The monastic system, the mediaeval communistic movements, the Anabaptists, modern fanatics and idealists, have all followed this clue. This idea contains a revolutionary element, although it has no desire for revolution.[30] The Church herself has felt and recognized the logical force of this idea. We shall see that when she evolved her own doctrine of Natural Law she eluded the logical result of this

[29] Cf. *Pfleiderer: Urchristentum, 1902, I, 22 f.*
[30] This line of development is followed by *Nathanael Schmidt: The Prophet of Nazareth* (New York, 1905); I only know this book, however, from a very interesting account of it in a review by *Wernle: Theol. Lit. Ztg., 1907, 603 ff.* Worthy of note also is the remark that everywhere this imitation of Christ runs parallel with the lessening of emphasis upon the dogma of the God-Man. In fact the latter dogma removes the ethic of Jesus out of the region of comparison altogether, pointing rather to obedience to the Church, which Christ founded as the organ of His Will.

idea by admitting its existence in the Primitive State and denying its applicability to contemporary life. So far as the present day was concerned, however, even from the time of Paul, the Church developed in a very different direction and, indeed, along the lines of socially conservative theory.[31]

The dominant element of all this system of thought, however, was, on the face of it, not this social result, but the ideal conception of the sociological structure in general which arose out of the religious idea. This conception was destined for a vast historic mission, whose importance is not affected by the conclusions drawn from it whether they be socially conservative or revolutionary.

Once this idea has developed to its full extent it will inevitably alter the fundamental sociological theory wherever the relation of man with man is concerned. It will affect social and political questions, and in one way or another it will breathe a peculiar spirit into the existing world-order. Also from the very outset it is plain that the effort to settle and adjust political and social problems will be far from easy or simple.

Before this idea could become influential, however, the religious-sociological idea itself needed to be much more stable and fully developed than it was in the Gospel, where it was dimly perceived as a sublime and stern, but loosely defined, ideal about the seriousness of preparation for the coming of the Kingdom of God, and which later on no Christian religious organization has ever been able to take over and carry forward, as it was first preached in the Gospel in heroic greatness and childlike freedom.

PARALLEL DEVELOPMENTS WITHIN STOICISM

The question is simply this: Was this idea peculiar to the Christian Gospel, or were there similar movements in existence at the same time? It is quite clear that similar ideas were present among the later Stoics, especially those of Rome, and a glance in that direction will be of great assistance, not merely in the analysis of the idea, but also for our understanding of its further historical development. The doctrine of the Stoics was, primarily, a religious-metaphysical doctrine, which arose out of the religious process of transformation which took place in late antiquity, and here also we have to do with a general sociological structure which has arisen out of a centre of religious thought. Its philosophical monotheism also led to a religious relation with humanity which was clearly opposed to the popular conception of religion in the ancient world. Its leading idea is the conception of God as of the

[31] See p. 175.

"First Cause" or the universal Law of Nature, which is pervaded by the Logos or the ordering force; the universe is controlled by this Divine principle of order, which appoints individuals to their several positions within nature and within Society: in man this becomes the Law of Reason which knows God and is therefore one with God. Thus the Law of Nature (an idea which was destined to play an extraordinary part in Christian theory) requires, on the one hand, conformity with the harmonious course of Nature, and the share of the individual within the social system, and, on the other hand, a spirit of inner elevation above all these considerations, and the moral and religious freedom of the dignity of reason which is united with God, and is therefore far above being disturbed by any concrete external happenings in the world of time and sense. It is the duty of the will to learn to discern this Law of Nature, and through this knowledge to achieve the control of the external desires of sense, and also the inward dignity and purity of harmony between the will of man and the ordering of Providence, and thus through knowledge to attain the personality which is hidden in God. All this leads to a theory of individualism expressed in terms of the idea of religious and ethical personality, and also to its inevitably correlated idea of an equally (logical) universalism, which recognizes that all men are equally called to the same knowledge of God and which, in their common surrender to the Divine Law of Nature, unites them by an ethical bond.

Social Influence of Stoicism

The whole conception forms a complete analogy with the sociological thought of Christianity. It also produced a similar effect upon social problems. Here also this is most easily discerned at the most vulnerable point in social life: the question of the family and of sex ethics. The moral freedom and equality of women, children, and slaves are proclaimed on the basis of the fact that they also are all equally called to the knowledge of God: and, since marriage is a relationship between moral personalities, from the husband also there is demanded a complete personal surrender to the wife, and, together with this, chastity both before and after marriage. This also led to a new attitude towards slavery and to fresh ideas on the question of emancipation, while poor relief and the beginnings of public works of charity were organized. Indeed, a social ideal was erected which demanded moral freedom and equality for all, and a communistic freedom from pain or sorrow, in which men might live without force, or war, or law, or a civil order, and in the perfection of the moral temper. Of course, there was no idea of seeing these ideals put into practice. The Stoics regarded them as part of the Golden Age in the past and irrevocably lost; only a new era in world-history could usher in a fresh beginning. In strange contrast with the fundamental idea of a pantheistic harmony the actualization of the ideal is not simply expected to be realized by the will of humanity, but it is regarded as being hindered by weakness and sin; humanity is below the normal level, and at the present time it is only possible for individuals to rise above it and in a private group. None the less, a distinct effort was made, wherever it was possible, to fit these humanitarian ideas into the existing system of laws. The Stoics' conception of the world immanence of Natural Law (the Law of Nature), the new interpretation of the popular religion, the fact that the Stoics belonged to the upper and ruling class, made it possible for them to have a reforming influence upon the world which was impossible for Christian Dualism with its exclusiveness. The Roman jurists of the Imperial period were steeped in the ideas of the Stoics, which they tried to unite with positive Law. The legal system has, therefore, to a great extent, carried those principles into practice, and, above all, the theory of the jurists undertook to guide the positive legal enactments back to the general Divine Law of Nature, and out of the Natural Law, as a special application, the idea of Natural Law was founded, on which all ordinances of positive law are ultimately based, and in accordance with which the State and Society develop by conforming as far as possible. Cicero stands out with special significance in connection with this subject. Conceptions of the richest significance for the future have been created out of this idea of Natural Law. The communistic Primitive State, corresponding to the ideal or to the Law of Nature, and the positive law of the State and of Society which at least relatively corresponds to that ideal—these were conceptions which later on were to render the most important services to Christian theology.

STOICISM AND CHRISTIANITY

The close connection between these ideas and those of Christianity is obvious, especially when, as among the Roman Stoics, and particularly in Seneca and Epictetus, the Divine Universal Law assumes the character of a kindly Providence and religious feeling develops into the sense of personal fellowship with God. On the sociological side, in particular, the inferences which are drawn from this faith in God are very similar to those of Jesus. Thus it is easy to understand how students of the ethic of Stoicism believed they had found in Christianity the philosophical religion they were seeking, while Christians, on the contrary, thought they had found among them some ideas borrowed from the Bible, or a point of support in general natural knowledge. In Epictetus, however, the traces of Christian influence are less evident. In the case of Seneca the Stoic doctrine of the government of the world and the Theodicy is combined with the dualistic psychology of Plato and the belief in the growth in the similarity of reason to God. In both, observation of actual life softens the Stoic rigorism and the Stoic self-righteousness through fellow-feeling with the infirmities and sins of men.

In spite of all this, however, the differences between Stoicism and Christianity are also very evident. In spite of the Theism of Stoicism the elements of primitive and underlying Pantheism re-appear continually. This Pantheism denies (or ignores) the reality of the Will of God which is opposed to the world and to sin, which leads to the conflict with evil and to the formation of a community; this leads very easily to a change of meaning in its main ideas— the moral laws of nature may become utilitarian laws of a secular and temporary kind, and the affinity between man and God may be turned into an affinity with Nature.

Finally, the fact that these conceptions can bear one meaning only from this aspect also shuts out every other new religious formation from the popular religion; especially noticeable is their lack of any proclamation of a coming Kingdom of God or of world renewal. Instead of that their attention was directed towards a Golden Age which has disappeared for ever, which could not maintain itself for long even in a new world era; the unity and beauty of a world conceived in the pantheistic sense are not too deeply prejudiced by human weakness. Above all, however, this faith is essentially that of the upper classes, who, in spite of all their concentration on the desire for spiritual "goods" in virtue, are still bound up with all the existing institutions: in the Stoic ideal, therefore, the hope of the future seems to be connected with the selection of particular individuals for intensive cultivation and moral knowledge. It fostered the aristocratic self-sufficient spirit of a ruling class which has been recently enlightened and ethically deepened. Christianity, on the contrary, was a movement of the lower classes, who are able to hope for and expect something quite fresh, and who, in their Myths and their Hero, have at their disposal energies of a very different kind which can exert a proper influence by mass-psychology. Stoicism represents the religious and ethical response to the kingdom of this world, and the ethical preservation and reform of the existing social order; Christianity stands for a spiritual revolution, for the creation of a new type of community and of a new future from the lower ranks of society.

The difference between Stoicism and the Pauline and ecclesiastical doctrines was certainly far greater. For Paulinism, with its doctrine of sin and redemption, and its offer of the help of love and grace through the marvellous powers of Christ-Mysticism, set ideas in motion which were quite foreign to the doctrine of the Stoics, and which were able to build up a community which gave every promise of being permanent. When the Christian community became independent and began to penetrate into the upper classes, more and more it began to weave the ideas of Stoicism into its own ethic and sociology; the Christian Church did this when it felt the necessity for placing its new and unique treasure upon a basis of general scientific knowledge.[32]

EMERGENCE OF A NEW IDEAL OF HUMANITY

When we gather up all these impressions and look at the phenomena presented by the Gospel, Stoicism, and by the other religious phenomena of late antiquity of a similar nature (which research must yet illuminate further for us), the main thing we notice is the transformation of life-values and the emergence of a new ideal of humanity, arising out of the destruction of the militaristic and polytheistic nationalist and conquering states. The emphasis on the independence of personality in individuals and the universal idea of humanity is due to Monotheism. The ideal of a humanity based on spiritual freedom and fellowship, in which tyranny, law, war, and force are unknown, was due to the development of a purified and deepened faith in God, which arose over against the polytheistic cults which sanctioned the existing social order with its basis of force. Although these new ideas were very similar, they gained acceptance in very different ways and their course of development was very varied. Finally, however, the underlying unity asserted itself and a new sociological and socio-political ideal arose. This ideal, which was the result of all these efforts and aspirations, maintained its intensity and independence over against the purely secular institutions which had arisen out of the struggle for existence and their legal modifications, even after they had lost their polytheistic sanction.

[32] See p. 175.

Both these ideals—on the one hand, that of equality and union of all men through the possession of the Divine Reason, and, on the other, that of the elevation of the souls of men and their fusion in the Love of God—represent an ideal of humanity which is based upon purely religious ideas, which is separated by a deep gulf from the old naturalistic ideals or from the ideals which only limit and modify natural instincts; and yet this ideal feels constrained to make repeated attempts to bridge this gulf. In their idealism both Christianity and Stoicism reduce the value of the natural basis of life, and both are concerned with the attempt to restore its significance. Thus in both a rich Ethos is working its way up, full of difficulties and tensions, which has remained an abiding possession of the European type of humanity, but which also is always in permanent conflict with the realistic demands of the natural instincts, with the needs of material existence, and with political and legal authority. In increasing measure, however, the leading part in this development was taken by the organization which grew out of the Gospel.[32a]

2. PAUL

The Pauline Ethic

As in all other particulars, so also in the question with which we are especially concerned in this book, the organization of a world-wide Church, independent of Judaism, founded on the worship of Christ and going out into the world to win the world to Him, meant a very material change in the sphere of thought. The fundamental happening, the emergence of the mystical faith in the Exalted and Risen Lord, whose Presence fills the Church, and the redemption and deliverance of those who believe in Him and are rooted in Him which this involved, can be taken for granted[33]; we are here dealing only with the sociological and social results of this process. These results are certainly considerable.

[32a] On this point see *Weinel: Stellung des Urchristentums, pp. 34 ff., 41*. Similarly, only from the opposite point of view, *Jodl* describes the Platonist, Stoic, Neoplatonist, and Christian ethic as metaphysical (that is, religious and monotheistic); everything else he includes under the head of empirical ethics in accord with nature.

[33] Cf. *Wrede: Paulus, 1905; Jülicher: Jesus und Paulus, 1907; Wernle: Anfänge.* To my friend *Deissmann* I owe the opinion that the central happening in Primitive Christianity was the rise of a Christ-cult out of faith in Christ, and that only then there arose a new religious community because there was already a new cult. Here I only state the sociological consequences.

The loosely knit group of Christian believers, waiting in Jerusalem "for the promise of the Father" and preparing for the coming of the Kingdom of God, has undergone a great transformation. Through its faith in Jesus as the Risen Lord, through the identification of Jesus with the Messiah and (in close connection with that) with the universal redeeming Divine principle, through the new worship of Christ and its mystical idea of Redemption, through Baptism and the Lord's Supper as the means of becoming one with the present Exalted Christ, it has become an independent religious community, which, in ideal at least, is strictly exclusive and bound together in unity. It is a new cult. The religious community is the Body of Christ, into which men are incorporated through Baptism, and through which they are fed and nourished by the Supper of the Lord. The historical problems which are connected with this development, as, for instance, the extent to which the example of the synagogue or the' influence of the mystery cults may have been operative, may likewise be taken for granted[33a]; the fundamental point is the growth of an independent religious community possessing the essential ideas of the Gospel and equipped with its powers, which then develops its own dialectic over against the synagogue and mystery cults. At the same time the main elements of the Gospel ethic are preserved, but as the ethics of a new religious community they receive a new shade of meaning. Purity of heart becomes sanctification, and the believer who is planted in Christ through Baptism develops a spirit of great hostility to the world, which, however, may still include everything which is "just, pure, lovely, of good report", everything in which there is "any virtue or any praise". Love of one's neighbour becomes brotherly love and the principle of love in general, in praise of which Paul sang his famous hymn. With the emphasis on the Church the principle of love seems to come very much to the fore, and in the Gospel of John love constitutes the whole content of the Christian ethic. This, however, is a false impression; this love rests upon a religious individualistic foundation, and religious individualism is and remains the root idea.

On the other hand, the sociological structure, as can be well understood, experiences greater changes. The very general idea of individuality, and the very free and wavering idea of fellowship which characterized the Gospel, have been intensified and

[33a] For the former, cf. *K. Rieker: Staat und Kirche* in *Festschrift für Emil Friedberg, 1908;* for the latter *A. Dieterich: Eine Mithrasliturgie, 1903.* All these questions are still very obscure.

appreciably narrowed. In the Pneuma-Christ, pervading all things and identical with the Spirit of God, the sociological idea receives an incalculably efficient presentation for worship of its point of reference as well as a closer dogmatic organic connection among the social relations themselves. The infinite worth of the individual is now related not merely to the process of self-sanctification in obedience to the fatherly Will of God, but to Christ, in whom the believer lives and moves. Christ imparts His own life, mystically, to those who trust Him: it is He who works through Baptism and the Lord's Supper, forming the true higher life in the believer; Christ, indeed, in His exalted pneumatic Being, is none other than the redeeming Spirit of God Himself, who overcomes the demons, the law, and sin. Filial relationship with God, which was the inclusive content of the absolute religious individualism of the Gospel, becomes the state of being "in Christ". Along the same lines the fellowship of the children of God in brotherly love becomes brotherhood not in God but in Christ; in the general union of all believers through life in the actual mystical life-substance of Christ they become members of the Body of Christ. Further, the universalism which revealed love as the Divine attitude towards the world, and which was aroused by this revelation, remains the same within the Church; it is expressed in missionary effort for the conversion of souls; the aim of this missionary work is to draw in the whole world, which is lost without Christ, into redeeming participation in the death and resurrection of the Pneuma-Christ, before the Advent of Christ and the Final Judgment; this process of conversion is brought about by a much more complicated process than merely by proclaiming that love is the attitude of God towards man. This is only natural, since here we are dealing no more with a message to one's fellow countrymen who share the same presuppositions as was the case with Jesus, and no longer simply with the Will of God and the Kingdom of God, but with the doctrine of salvation through Christ.

With this concrete setting, and with the practical development of the fundamental sociological idea which is included in it and results from it, a further important peculiarity emerges, which, indeed, is an integral part of the Gospel, and to which Jesus alluded now and again. It only became significant, however, when a definite group for worship was being formed in which the members were mutually dependent upon one another. This idea is the peculiar conception of equality and inequality which belongs to the Christian religious-sociological idea. Every system of that kind which is both individualistic and universal naturally contains, in some way or another, the idea of equality, and places all individuals upon the level of an equal right to the highest and ultimate life-values, or at least of a common vocation to and destiny for these values. This seems to belong to the idea of an absolute value in general. At this point, however, we immediately perceive the peculiar effect of the religious starting-point upon the whole sociological idea. Since Christian individualism is only founded and completed in God, and since Christian universalism is based solely on the all-embracing love of God which leads to the love of one's neighbour, so this idea of equality is definitely limited to the religious sphere. It is an equality which exists purely in the Presence of God, and in Him, based solely on the religious relation to God as the centre of the whole. At first, it is true, this equality is in no way an equality of mankind in its claim on God, but it is an equality in which all men feel that they "have sinned and come short of the glory of God", a negative equality over against the infinite holiness of God. When the idea of an equal sense of the need of all for redemption through Christ becomes the ruling idea of the missionary message, then this first and most important characteristic of equality stands out clearly: in the presence of a common sinfulness and need all human differences disappear in the Presence of God. The levelling process starts from an equal unworthiness and not from equal claim on God. This "negative" equality is, however, only the basis for the surrender to that salvation through grace which is given in Christ, the Church and its Sacraments, which mediates absolute salvation to all believers. Those, however, who share in the Absolute and the Divine are by this very fact equal in their possession of the Absolute, since here there is no "more" and no "less". This equality of grace is, however, always a peculiar kind of equality. It is not based on a common claim or right of nature, but on the impartation of the Divine Love through grace which, wherever it gives itself at all, can only give itself as a whole, and which of itself alone, apart from all external social institutions, imparts equality in principle, in spite of all human differences in rank, talent, or ethical achievement. It is thus an equality which is only expressed in the common participation of all in common worship. The Supper of the Lord is at the same time the festival of the brotherhood. Even slaves can lead in public worship. Quite naturally and purely inwardly equality is imparted through the worship of Christ, and it needs no other assurance than the participation of all in the religious gift of salvation. For this gift is the One and infinite Love of God which can never be exhausted however much it is shared, which can never be lessened by being imparted, and which must always give itself to others as something which is essentially a unity and a whole.[34] Its external influence, its organization and distribution, consists therefore solely in a common worship which knows no differences in the sight of God, and in love which knows no superiority in the feeling of one's own unworthiness, and which shares everything with the feeling that one has first received everything.

One extraordinarily important point in relation to the idea of equality, however, still remains an open question. All are equal in distance from God, and all are equal before God and in God through grace. But have all men the same destiny and the same rights to be redeemed out of this equality of unworthiness and need into the equality of the possession of grace? Further, is the transition from the one kind of equality to the other destined for all alike? And, if it is not achieved, does the reason for this lie solely in the will and guilt of man, or is it founded in the Will and Being of God? This is the most important point in the whole idea of equality, and in the Pauline Gospel a characteristic uncertainty creeps in which is of the greatest importance for the whole future development of the idea. It is this element of uncertainty which has given rise to the great and famous problems of predestination on the one hand, and of the universal Divine Will of Love on the other. These questions have not merely produced extremely difficult theological problems; they have also become basic coefficients of sociological and therefore of social thought which have lasted for centuries. We are here dealing not simply with an accidental Pauline doctrine which, through the placing of the Pauline letters on the Canon of Scripture, became destined, historically, to be part of the Christian world of thought. Rather, the Pauline doctrine itself is only the working out of the element of will which is contained in the whole Divine thought of the Gospel, which was always specially strongly emphasized in the Jewish idea of God and which gave it the authority of an infinite omnipotence which transcended all that was creaturely. With all His holy and loving fatherly Will, He still remains that Will whose holiness is posited by His own Will, and whose Love is an act of fathomless mercy. This, however, is not merely an accidental element of the Semitic idea of God, which has been retained in

[34] Cf. *Simmel: Die Religion (Die Gesellschaft, Frankfurt, Bd. II), p. 47.* This small work contains much that is fine, but also much that is arbitrary upon the sociology of religion.

the teaching of Jesus and of Paul, and has not yet been completely absorbed in the moral law and into universal love. One only needs to think of the further history of the idea and of its philosophical development from Augustine to Descartes in order to notice that it contains within itself an essential and fundamental religious and metaphysical problem, which is bound to recur in every sociological system of thought which results from religious ideas. Are holiness and love the norm for God Himself? Or do they only have value through His inscrutable Will? Or, to express it in another way: Are laws of thought and values valid in themselves, or because of the will that posits them? Is the universally valid valid because it is universal? Or does its universality result from its being posited by a will which is not subject to universal validity? These are the problems which lie beneath all theories of perception and of metaphysics, and which result from every attempt to think through the idea of God in a deeper way from the dialectic of religious thought.[35] Paul indeed knows nothing of these far-reaching ideas; in this particular, as in so many others, his thinking is instinctive and intuitive; but in spite of his helpless mode of argument, which clings closely to the rabbinic method of exposition, his religious genius finds a solution which corresponds to the whole. God's goodness is grace and fathomless mercy, equally in creation and in redemption. Therefore there can be no claim of the creature for an equal share for all in salvation; it is God's own affair to call one and not to call another, to leave some longer in error than others. In this the predestinarian Will of God is expressed. But while this will sets before itself the goal of goodness and of grace, the unequal distribution of the calling will presumably relate only to the distribution of destinies in relation with the history of salvation, it will only mean an "earlier" or a "later", a longer or shorter period of being given over to error and sin; finally, all will be gathered home, and God will be all in all. This is how in his own mind he accounts for the destiny of his people, for the apparent rejection of Israel.

It is a way out of the problem; whether it is a solution of the problem or not does not concern us now. Here our interest is only in the extraordinary significance of these ideas for the sociology of Christian thought, and for the idea of equality contained therein. The idea of predestination cuts the nerve of the absolute and abstract idea of equality, the equal vocation of all to the ultimate values, the right of all to the highest goal. In spite of the equality

[35] Cf. *Kahl: Die Lehre vom Primat des Willens bei Augustin, Duns Scotus und Descartes, 1886,* and my article on *Predestination* in the *Christliche Welt, 1907.*

of all in their sinful unworthiness and in their possession of grace, however, the real equality in itself, the equal claim of all to an equal share in the highest life-value through equal working out of vocation and destiny, is invalidated. Even if in the end the final aim of the loving Will of God for all men is realized, there still remains the fact of the inscrutable Will of God distributing to individuals very differently along the way to this aim—making things easier for one and harder for another, holding one soul at a distance for a long time and bringing another swiftly to the goal. In spite of the illumination of this world with an absolute religious ethical value, there is still an element of the irrational in the participation in this absolute value, and this element must be referred back to the inscrutable Will of God. This has the following effect upon the sociological idea: that there does not exist an unlimited equal claim on salvation or the Absolute, to be realized by all in the same way, and that one must be satisfied with equality of distance from God and equality of love to God, wherever the latter has taken root. All the rest must be left in the Hands of God.

From the time of Paul, to a greater or less degree, these ideas have been operative all through Christendom, and it is clear in what striking contrast the Christian idea of equality stands out against all other ideas of equality which emerge in the cultural life of Europe. Above all, it is the contrast with all equality-ideas of a rationalistic or Natural Law order which, on the ground of the common validity of reason, make the claim that reason belongs to all and therewith that all equally share in the value of reason. This presupposes that precisely on account of the universal validity of reason it can be completely realized in each individual. It is, however, also not difficult to understand that Christianity, along with all the radical equalizing of men in the sight of God and with all the penetration of this idea in the whole life of the soul, and in all personal relations of men to one another, is yet at the same time very cautious towards any attempt to carry over this equality into the sphere of secular relationships and institutions, which have nothing to do with the real religious basis of this equality. In the great differentiations of national and social life it will be inclined in the first instance to regard them as something foreign to the religious interest, and here also it will tend, in so far as they do not rest openly upon a sinful foundation, to see in them Divine ordinances which are to be accepted without questioning their basis. This tendency will be doubly great at a time when, as in primitive Christianity, religious propaganda and work absorb all their energies, and in a situation in which all political and social conditions are fixed and unchangeable for the general consciousness as they were in the Roman Empire, in a missionary activity where every appearance of political illegality and danger must be carefully avoided.

Christianity will always instinctively fight shy of all ideas of equality, in spite of its close relationship with them, and it will at this point always have its main difficulty in its interpretation of the conception of the righteousness of God which it will be forced to characterize as the equal destiny of all to the same end, and which, on the other hand, it will be unable to maintain. In this lies its contrast with the rationalist ideal of the Stoics, which infers or deduces, at least for the Primitive State, the principle of abstract equality from the possession of reason by all. On the other hand, however, with its emphasis upon equality in weakness, and of a radical distance of all from God, as also with its reference of all salvation to the gracious Will of God, it is far removed from every theoretically aristocratic way of thinking, from the basic doctrine of the rule and privileged position of the few on the ground of natural talent and historic selection. The sociological theory springing from the religious idea is indeed entirely different in its fundamental structure from that which results from rationalism or from naturalism, however often it meets the others in both directions. *Si duo faciunt idem, non est idem.*

Here we come to a further important point, where once more the doctrines of Paul, drawing upon the basic ideas of the Gospel, just on account of their formulation are particularly influential and characteristic. I refer to the question of the inequalities of human life in ordinary affairs—the fact that men are limited partly by the amount of general capacity they possess and by their natural disposition, partly by the social and political situation. From what we have already seen it is clear that there is no idea of removing these inequalities. At the same time, however, they are not treated merely in a negative fashion, but they are taken up positively into the sociological basic idea of the worth of personality and of the unconditioned fellowship of love, and they are turned into sources of peculiar ethical value. The earthly inequality is worked into the religious equality as a material from which the religious equality receives a special stimulus for its activity. In this connection Paul uses the well-known ancient metaphor of the organism and the relation between its nobler and its baser parts, but in so doing he means something much more than a mere "organic" social idea. He makes the inequalities corresponding to the religious basic idea into the occasion and material for the activity of love. The mutual service of all to each other with the gifts which have been given to them by God, the overcoming of evil with good, and the strengthening of the good in the fight against evil, self-giving, and humility towards one another, also ruling and administration, the care of the strong for the weak, and the lifting up of the weak by the strong—all this causes a mutual give-and-take, in which the fundamentally Christian virtues of self-surrender and humility, of love and responsibility for others, are manifested. So the whole closely knit inward connection of a system, which is organically united and all-penetrating, and at all points conditioning itself, here finds expression. Thus every kind of work and capacity, even the least, is honoured, and all those who possess greatness or wealth find that it involves a duty towards others. All the humility required does not mean any depreciation of personality, neither does the exercise of active love, of care for others and authority over them, involve any superiority, because in this sociological system it is never merely a question of men dealing with men as men, but it means rather that it is always the Divine in the one dealing with the Divine in the other. For in these services all men are only God's stewards, and what they do is not done by men but by God or by Christ. That this point of view contains a certain quietism cannot be denied; nowhere is there any talk of improving living conditions, but only of enduring them and making them inwardly fruitful. At the same time, mingled with this quietism there is the expectation of the End of the world, and from this point of view as a permanent arrangement there is the possibility of a more far-reaching reform. Also there remains in such a system, alongside of all adjustment and surrender, the aim which, by using the differences between men in order to reach equality of inward spiritual values (so that at first the revolutionary power of an idea of equality is hidden), is at least working towards the goal; this cannot fail to have a strong effect upon self-consciousness even before the goal is reached. In actual fact, in Christ there is already "neither Jew nor Greek, bond nor free, Barbarian nor Scythian, male nor female". At the same time, the enthusiasm is still great enough to make this inner equality sufficient, and to believe in good faith in the possibility of establishing this kind of equality. The realistic question, whether there are not grades and kinds of poverty which make it impossible to rise to this kind of equality, and whether external uplifting is not necessary, is still remote from this conviction of the omnipotence of good-will.

Out of all this, however, there has now been created an extraordinarily important sociological type. This is the type of Christian patriarchalism founded upon the religious recognition of and the religious overcoming of earthly inequality.[35a] There was a certain preparation for this in late Judaism, but it receives its special colour from the warmth of the Christian idea of love, through the inclusion of all in the Body of Christ. One has only to compare the Book of the Wisdom of Jesus the son of Sirach with the Epistles of Paul to note both the similarities and the differences. It only attained its full development certainly in the Middle Ages, and then acquired its specific character with which we shall deal later on. At this stage it is hindered from working itself out fully by the complicated character and far-reaching atomizing of the life of later antiquity—above all, by the urban character of the local churches and the relative insignificance of the social differences within them. But its basic idea of the willing acceptance of given inequalities, and of making them fruitful for the ethical values of personal relationships, is given. All action is the service of God and is a responsible office, authority as well as obedience. As stewards of God the great must care for the small, and as servants of God the little ones must submit to those who bear authority; and, since in so doing both meet in the service of God, inner religious equality is affirmed and the ethical possession is enlarged by the exercise of the tender virtues of responsibility for and of trustful surrender to each other. It is undeniable that this ideal is perceived dimly by Paul, and only by means of this ideal does he desire to alter given conditions from within outwards, without touching their external aspect at all.

Thus the general sociological structure, by means of an internal process, gradually assumed the form of a compact social system, with its various grades of authority and subordination, which are an inherent element in any sociological system.[35b]

The principle of radical individualism and universalism was actually unorganized; it simply included personalities who are all equal; all are alike infinitely precious, and all are included with the same intensity because the spirit of this principle pene-

---

[35a] This dualistic basis and tendency is excellently described by *F. J. Stahl* in *Der Christliche Staat, 1858, pp. 11–13*.
[35b] Cf. the dissertation which has already been mentioned by *Simmel: Soziologie der Ueber- und Unterordnungs (Archiv, Band XXIV, 1907)* as well as my own treatise on *Politische Ethik und Christentum, 1904*.

trates into the very centre of men's souls. Since, however, this system, when it comes to be realized in practice, cannot dwell merely in the region of those high ideals, it evolved in the Spirit-Christ an authority which held it together, a settlement of the main lines of its thought, and a vividly suggestive operative personal example. There then emerge clearly the natural differences between the two poles of individualism and universalism, which bring with them different capacities, positions, and services into the whole, as well as distinctions which are due to other causes. These differentiations, however, are closely related to the religious idea of fellowship itself, inasmuch as they are turned into means for the development of religious-ethical values. For, on the one hand, they maintain that solidarity due to a religious motive, common responsibility, and care for others towards those who for the time being are in a subordinate position; and, on the other hand, they maintain resignation, love, and the duty of obedience as a religious motive towards those who for the time being are their superiors. Thus there arises a continual movement, and alongside of it also a spirit which transcends all differences and all movement in the Divine life in which all share. A sociological type of this kind is only possible upon a religious basis because here alone is it possible to allow individual differences to sink into oblivion in a common spirit of devotion to the Divine Will which produces these differences, and which makes this community the organ of its aim of unity. Individuals do not enter the whole simply with a part of their being (as they do in most other sociological systems), but because they are wholly and entirely—even with their special characteristics—willed by the unified Will of God, they also enter into the common life with the whole of their being, with their own position, and with their particular characteristics. They are not absorbed into it and lost in it, but rather they make it into a means of specific ethical values, a means for the restoration of the whole.

THE PAULINE ETHIC AND GENERAL SOCIAL VALUES

Thus already we are led from the general religious-sociological idea to social problems.[35c] The sociological idea, while retaining the external form, desires to transform the whole spiritually from within. But it is impossible to leave it at that, at a purely inward change. When the local churches begin to form their own groups for life and worship they are obliged externally to lay down

[35c] Here also see *Jacoby: Neutestamentliche Ethik* and *Weinel: Stellung des Urchristentums.*

limits towards the life of the State and of the Society around them, and within their borders, in so far as they have the power to do so, they must put their own social situation in order. That process took place even in the time of Paul, and in this respect also he indicated important lines of future development. Paul's ideas were quite distinct from the ideals of the Gospel, and, at least for the Early Church, they determined the immediate path of duty; owing to the fact that Paul's Epistles were placed upon the Canon of Scripture, his ideas have also had a varied dogmatic effect upon later ages. The childlikeness, breadth, and height of the Gospel are already being expressed in the concrete and practical realm, and austere radicalism has already given way to compromise, with the necessity for being on terms of understanding with the general life of the world. In spite of all attempts at understanding, however, the modern idea that in order to build up a world on sound spiritual and moral lines a corresponding foundation of material and social conditions is needed is still remote. They are only external adjustments but not inner connections. The ideology of good-will feels itself for more than a thousand years almighty, completely autonomous, and self-sufficient. Where the natural basis does not submit and fit into this theory it is destroyed by renunciation. The positive relation with social organizations remains merely a search for points of contact which will offer themselves naturally.

Thus when the Christian Church began to carry its message into the Roman Empire it proved just as impossible to ignore the existence of the State as it had proved impossible to apply the principles of the communism of love to large corporate groups and associations, which had to be organized and adapted to their social environment. In reality the Pauline world church, in opposition to the revolutionary conclusions revealed in the Apocalypse, did not merely recognize the State as permitted by God, but prized it as an institution which at least cared for justice, order, and external morality. In this respect already Paul drew upon the Stoic doctrine of the moral law which is written in the heart, and ascribed also to the heathen a knowledge of goodness which is outwardly expressed in their State and in their legal system. The Empire wields the sword according to the Will of God and by the order of God. But together with the order of the State there is recognized that which is inevitably bound up with it, the whole order of Society: the distribution of property, divisions of class and rank, in fact, the whole social organization. Christians, indeed, are not to make use of the State authorities,[35d] and they are advised to keep away from all trades and callings which are tainted with heathenism, and to avoid all social life which brings them into contact with heathen forms of worship. But on the whole the Christians are to respect the existing régime and to turn it to good account, since their citizenship is not on earth but in Heaven. They must prove themselves good and industrious citizens, and above all each man must labour to gain his own living, for the sake of general order, and that he may be able to share with those who have need.

It is evident that the situation has changed. The religious community is no longer in the simple rural surroundings of Galilee, with its Oriental freedom from economic needs and its casual system of justice, but in the urban world of slaves and lesser citizens with its more complicated domestic economy and a stricter system of justice.[36] This restriction to town-life naturally influences the ethical ideas until they adjust themselves to this situation, and the radical endeavour to apply the Sermon on the Mount naturally recedes into the background. It is only natural that the conservative attitude should be applied to the institution of the family, which is assumed as the basis of the whole of this ordered life. Marriage is used as the figure of the most important leading idea of Paul, that of the union of Christ with His Church. The existing patriarchalism, with the predominance of the husband, is accepted as the natural order, and submission to it is demanded as an ethical duty, while at the same time the husband also is urged most strongly to preserve his purity before marriage, and monogamous fidelity as well as personal self-giving in love to wife and child are expected of him. The wife and the child, like the slave, are regarded as equal to the husband and the freeman in the religious and moral realm, and this actually, even if not in the eyes of the law, deepens and spiritualizes the whole of family life. Questions of mixed marriages are already being treated with great care and caution, and reveal a great desire to uphold the ideal of marriage. Even though Paul himself, speaking personally, cannot hide his own misgivings about the sex-life, and at least desires it to be kept within very strict limits, in order to avoid finding the sex instinct too strong a competitor with the religious interest—all this has nothing to do with the value set on

[35d] Paul refers Christians who disagree to the judgment of the community or of arbitrators; this constitutes the beginning of an independent system of law, and the position of the Sermon on the Mount (i.e. that all litigation is to be avoided) is—most characteristically—altogether forgotten. *H. Weinel: Stellung des Urchristentums, pp. 32 and 36.*   [36] See p. 176.

the family as a social institution; it is simply the natural ascetic result of a predominant religious aim. Later, however, it was to become very strong and powerful, and it was then destined to place many hindrances in the way of the nobler result of the Christian idea of the personalizing, individualizing, and deepening of the family ideal.

CONSERVATIVE AND REVOLUTIONARY TENDENCIES WITHIN THE CHURCH

Thus for many centuries the conservative attitude of Christianity towards political and social life was decided by this doctrine of Paul. It is a most remarkable thing that the entirely revolutionary and radical principle of unlimited individualism and universalism should adopt such a thoroughly conservative attitude to social questions. In spite of this, however, it actually exercised a revolutionary influence. For the conservative attitude was not founded on love and esteem for the existing institutions, but upon a mixture of contempt, submission, and relative recognition. That is why, in spite of all its submissiveness, Christianity did destroy the Roman State by alienating souls from its ideals, and it has a disintegrating effect upon all undiluted nationalism and upon every form of exclusively earthly authority. But because its individualism and its universalism proceed from the religious idea and are related to religious values, such a conservative attitude is thoroughly possible.

In reality Christianity seems to influence social life in two ways: Either, on the one hand, it develops an idealistic anarchism and the communism of love, which combines radical indifference or hostility towards the rest of the social order with the effort to actualize this ideal of love in a small group; or, on the other hand, it develops along social-conservative lines into an attitude of submission to God and His Will, so far as the world is concerned, combined with a strong independence of an organized community which manages its own affairs, which, as its range of influence increases, finds that it cannot ignore secular institutions, but that it must do its utmost to utilize them for its own purposes. The first ideal is the source of ever-renewed radical social plans for smaller or larger groups of people, while the second ideal produces the conservative principles of patience and suffering within the world, whose ordinances are permitted by God, whose possibilities Christians use for their own ends, and whose continuance they endure, because inwardly they are unaffected by them. The third possibility, that of using the ordinances of Society positively, as preliminary phases for the attainment of the highest religious-ethical goal, lies still entirely beyond the vision of the Early Church. Not yet does she think of trying to understand spiritual and ethical values in constant relationship with, and in dependence upon, the natural basis of life; neither did this idea occur to the Middle Ages, nor to the religious-metaphysical ethic of the ancient world; the empirical ethic of Aristotle alone takes these relationships into account.

From this point of view, above all, the whole problem of economics and of property is regarded essentially from the standpoint of the consumer, and it is regulated accordingly in the direction of frugality. The idea that wealth and property are a means of unlimited power of production, and that they are there-fore the means of providing a healthy basis of life for an increasing population, is peculiar to the modern world; it arose only when the relationship between ethico-spiritual values and economic organization was perceived. At times, indeed, these ideas have gone beyond the ideological extreme and have developed into historical materialism; and even to-day the relationship of both causalities is still a difficult problem. If, however, the dependence of the ideological superstructure upon economic conditions is less evident, then the State and the Law seem much less closely connected with the economic basis of life, and their chief use seems to be merely that of the preservation of the peace, of public order and discipline. Since at the same time the State lost its religious-polytheistic sanctity, it naturally lost also a great deal of ethical importance, and it came to be regarded by the Christians only in its most external and superficial aspects. This is why it was possible for the Pauline churches and for primitive Christianity to adopt a social conservative attitude, and yet at the same time to remain inwardly deeply separated from the whole life of Society around them, patiently enduring the conditions in which they found themselves, and cleverly using them for their own ends, while at the same time, in contrast with the life of Society, they build up an entirely new and quite different community life. The principle which Paulinism here lays down, on the threshold of the great development of the future, is the duty of the recogni-tion and use of social phenomena as organizations and institu-tions—which did not come into existence without God's per-mission and which contain an element of good—mingled with a spirit of inner detachment and independence, since, after all, these things belong to a perishing world and are everywhere steeped in paganism. This, however, suggested a positive relationship which was capable of further development, and one which, as will be seen later, was increasingly produced by the Early Church; but, however widely the Christian communities might have been extended, this attitude could never have become a programme of social reform, nor even possibly of a Christian civilization. When later on something of that kind did take place, entirely new circumstances and ideas had produced a new situation.

The socially conservative development of Christian thought which is proved as an established fact mainly by Paul's Epistles, and which then received a lasting authority through the inclusion of these letters in the Sacred Canon, contains at the same time and in some degree, however, the radical elements of Christian thought. These radical elements are directed purely towards spiritual renewal, the development of religious personality, and the fellowship of such personalities among themselves; combined with these ideas, is an other-worldly goal of ethico-religious perfection, which finds in the organizations of this present world useful points of support; these are regarded as merely provisional arrangements which have to be endured, and from which the Christian holds himself inwardly entirely aloof. Thus for a long time the conservative and revolutionary elements in Christian thought were united to and conditioned by each other in a classic manner, which constituted the general Christian standard. This turn of mind, moreover, was in no way influenced merely by the expectation of the End of the World, even though it was encouraged by it; it remained on in the ancient world even after the thought of an imminent Judgment had entirely disappeared; indeed, it continued right on into the Middle Ages and into Protestantism.

At this point, therefore, on the very threshold of the whole historical development, it is necessary to raise this question: Does this combination of conservative and radical elements correspond to the inner essence of Christian thought, or is it an accidental element due to the personal attitude of Paul himself and to the needs of the most primitive churches? Is it an essential characteristic of all the Christian social doctrines which has developed out of the central thought of Christianity, and thus already from the very beginning casts a clear light on the developments of the future? May it be that the two forms of social influence which have just been indicated, which are apparently diametrically opposed to each other, are not after all two equally possible applications existing side by side, but that perhaps they really belong to each other and are united in the fundamental idea from which they sprang? This seems all the more probable when we remember that the love-communism of the small primitive Christian community did not interfere with the world in which it was set, and also that apocalyptic fanaticism was not an expression of social or political reform, but of hatred of paganism and the hope of some miraculous act of God, and that, on the other hand, Pauline conservatism had no inward interest in the values and standards of the present world, but that it only endured and used them as ordained and permitted by God. Although both these tendencies may at times diverge very widely, they might perhaps still be united in an inward relationship, and form a united stream of development[36a] for the sake of the great ends to be realized.

It is my belief that, without danger of a forced construction, we are right in saying that the Pauline turn of thought in relation to social matters corresponds to the spirit and meaning of the Gospel, and that in this respect it presents the classical example of the union of fundamental ideas right down to the beginning of the modern era. A religious doctrine like that of Christian monotheism, which takes religion out of the sphere of existing conditions and the existing order and turns it purely into an ethical religion of redemption, will possess and reveal the radicalism of an ethical and universal ideal in face of all existing conditions. But, on the other hand, just because it is a religious faith which believes that the whole world and its order is being guided by God, in spite of devils and demons, just because it means submission to the Will of God who predestinates and allows all kinds of human differences to exist, it can never be a principle of revolution. So far it will always have a conservative trait of adaptation and submission towards the existing social order and social institutions, the conditions of power and their variations. A theoretic revolutionary tendency will only be possible in the sphere of abstract rationalism which, from the point of view of the individual and his generally reasonable point of view, restores the rational element, and only recognizes the Divine element in the universality of reason, but not in the irrational course of things which cannot be controlled by the individual. Therefore modern rationalism alone provides the sphere for a revolutionary principle in theory and practice which will construct Society according to the claims of reason.[36b]

On the other hand, however, that spirit of Christian submission and adaptation to circumstances will always stop short at the

[36a] See p. 176.   [36b] See p. 177.

borders of the values of the inner life, of the religious-ethical world of ideals, and of the ecclesiastical organization which supports these ideals. In actual fact it will exercise a very profound transforming influence, and will venture on the most searching interference with the social order; it will do this sometimes by indifference to existing conditions, sometimes by submitting existing conditions to the only valid test, the test of its own ideals and of its transcendent values; thus, without any deliberately revolutionary intent, it will succeed in destroying and breaking down evil institutions and in inaugurating new ones.[36c] A purely and unconditionally conservative doctrine can therefore never be produced by it. Its monotheism and universalism, its belief in Redemption and its ethico-personal inwardness, contain a radicalism and a striving after unity which will always either ignore all merely temporary conditions or set them aside, and beyond all national and other forms of unity it will press forward towards an ideal religious unity which will be spiritual, inward, and living.

SIMPLE SOCIAL CONDITIONS FAVOURABLE TO CHRISTIANITY

It is, however, clear that Christianity has a distinct leaning towards comparatively simple conditions of living, in which immediate contact with God's gifts in Nature determines the way of earning a living and thus the possibility of maintaining life, and keeps vivid the feelings of dependence and gratitude towards the gifts of God in Nature. It also has a leaning towards little groups and corporations which are closely bound together in personal relationships, in which the formal legal and economic tendency of a dehumanized and abstract organization of the common life has not yet forced purely personal relationships and decisions into the sphere of isolated instances. This, however, is a new element in Christianity which has not yet been interpreted by what had gone before, and in itself has nothing to do with the conservatism of Christianity. It is caused by the fact that an ethic which is so deeply personal, and which lays so much stress upon the inward spirit, while it replaces law by love and trust, is much easier to carry out in these simpler conditions of life than in a complicated civilization which is founded upon legal political and economic abstract forms—above all, upon law and upon impersonal institutions and necessities. This explains why it was that the Early Church met with a greater response among the artisan and middle-class group, in which something

[36c] See p. 178.

remained of that more primitive group-ethic of trust and confidence than among the upper classes. The Pauline churches
were essentially small communities, remote from the great legal
organization of a giant State; it would, indeed, be impossible to
imagine their existence in any other setting. This is also why in
the central period of the Middle Ages, and also in Lutheranism,
an attempt was made to preserve these simpler conditions. This
was due to a socially conservative attitude only in so far as it was
connected with a striving after simpler conditions which, under
some circumstances, happened to coincide with the preservation
of older and less developed conditions. In this instance, however,
this was not due to a spirit of submission to and adaptation to
existing conditions, but to a desire to discover a general situation
in which it would be easier to carry the Gospel ethic into practice
with less compromise. Indeed, much of later monasticism tended
in this direction—not, however, monasticism as a whole; since,
in a small group, in a simple relationship with Nature, in a
personal dealing with all circumstances, and in freedom from
possessions, it actually realized the ideal which all the agitation
of a complicated social order either rendered altogether impossible,
or at least meant that it could only be realized to a very limited
extent.[36d]

Forecast of Future Developments

Later history only serves to illustrate this curious blend of
conservative and revolutionary elements which can be discerned
from a close study of St. Paul's Epistles, in which, however, the
conservative rather than the revolutionary elements are emphasized. In reality, in spite of all its conservatism, Christianity
became a principle which contained immense spiritual energies
of a revolutionary nature, which, once its ecclesiastical and
theocratic powers were combined, also led to revolutionary
changes in very concrete matters, in the realm of Law and of
institutions. Christianity shattered the ancient world, both in its
spirit and in its outward form; in the Gregorian revolution it
destroyed the Territorial Church system, and the rights of states
and peoples; at the Reformation it revolutionized the Church, and
created new politico-ecclesiastical forms; through all this, however, Christianity always either tolerated the existing social order,
while inwardly it undermined it, or by its comparative conservatism it supported and glorified it. It only became revolutionary in principle when its ideal (which as will be shown

[36d] See p. 178.

presently had become fused with the Natural Law of the Stoics) broke through the limits which it had prescribed for its conception of Natural Law and assimilated its rationalistic results. On the other hand, it was only conservative in principle when it gave a religious sanction to the existing order purely for political reasons, while, for the time, it obscured or discarded its ethical radicalism.

Characteristically, however, this blend of conservative and radical elements was based precisely upon that circumstance upon which so much emphasis has been laid all along—that Christianity neither sought nor found an inward connection and historical continuity between the general political, economic, and social situation and the values of personal religion; its radical ideology always insisted either that everything creative must proceed from within, or that everything depends upon obedience to an external authority; sometimes, therefore, it ignored and sometimes it rejected the conditions which formed the substructure of the spiritual and ethical world; in both instances, however, it tolerated and therefore conserved this lower realm, either because it had been instituted by God after all, or because it was necessary for Christianity to accept the conditions sin has caused.

This being so, social reform took the shape of philanthropy, which aided individuals and allowed conditions to remain as they were; this ideal could, of course, only be carried out successfully within a limited sphere and in an economic situation in which the general conditions were comparatively tolerable.[36e] This principle, which allowed existing conditions and the challenge of the ideal merely to co-exist alongside of one another, or this combination of the conservative and radical elements in Christianity, was not overthrown until the time of Calvin, when modern economic forms of industry and modern political life were sanctioned in the belief that they would lead to the development of a "holy community", of a Christian social order; Calvinism also realized that spiritual values are conditioned by the material, external setting within which they are placed. Hence Calvinism developed a radical policy which affected the general conditions of political and economic life, and gradually overcame the old passive Christian conservative attitude; at the same time, however, the predestinarian conception of God, which was such a marked feature of Calvinism, still continued to exercise its influence in the Pauline sense, upon the idea of the need to

[36e] This constitutes the whole difference between charity and a social policy.

recognize and utilize for ethical purposes the various differences due to natural causes.[36f] The social theories and the social policies of the modern churches have followed the path opened up by Calvinism, for the study of modern conditions and of the modern point of view in theoretical social science, politics, and economics, has forced them to recognize that the ethico-religious values of the Christian idea of personality and love are just as closely bound up with the general assumption of the economic-legal-political substructure as are all other spiritual and ethical values in general.

The immense importance which was implicit in the earliest development of sociological ideas and of a Christian point of view in social questions, within the earliest church of Gentile converts, forced us, even at this early stage of the Pauline mission, to let our eyes travel down the centuries. In so doing we have anticipated much with which this book will deal; the vast significance of this development in history brings out all the more clearly the contrast between this development and the little Pauline churches themselves. At that stage they still lacked not merely the greatness and the importance, but also the full clarity of the principle, and the solidarity of a body out of which alone first the clearness of the principle, and its relation to opposing forces and to its surroundings, could be established. At first they were still mainly occupied in defining the relation between the social revolutionary and social conservative tendency, and of the radical ethic of holiness and love with its heavenly goal, against the natural claims of social existence; in settling these problems they were also busy working out the problem of the development of the life of the Church itself, for which faith in the mystical presence of Christ within the Church and of the Spirit "shed abroad" by Him, was not sufficient for the stability of their life as a social body.

3. EARLY CATHOLICISM

CHURCH ORGANIZATION

The sociological idea of the Gospel was based on that faith in God which arose out of the Jewish Bible and the Jewish national life, intensified and illuminated by the proclamation of the Kingdom of God, and on the incarnation of this idea in the

---

[36f] For the moment I will only call attention to the two books by Choisy: *La théocratie à Genève au temps de Calvin* and *L'état chrétien calviniste à Genève au temps de Théodore de Bèze.*

personality of Jesus Himself. When, however, in accord with its essential nature, this new faith had severed its connection with Judaism and Jesus was no longer with His disciples, it then felt the need for something to take the place of this outward relationship; it needed an independent centre of organization which would incarnate the idea at any given point of time with reference to its relation to the actual setting in which it found itself. Both aspects of the Christian faith—its individualism and its universalism—needed this independent organization in order that they might find fresh and vital forms of expression, which would provide it with an ever new standard and also keep it firmly anchored to the religious foundation. Perhaps it would be more true to say that it was only because the Christian community found a rallying-point of this kind that it was able to develop and permanently maintain these logical results of its own thought. This rallying-point was its faith in the Exalted Pneuma-Christ, whose living presence permeated the whole of life. This conviction was the driving force and organizing power of the new community; it created its only new article of faith, faith in the Christ who is identical with the Spirit of God.

It created the new cult (which alone made it possible to form a new religious community at all), which consisted of the worship of God in Christ, implying the two sacraments: (1) of baptism, which meant being planted "into Christ"; and (2) of the Eucharist, in which the believer is fed and nourished by the Exalted Christ. It created the new ethic, which meant that all believers in Christ were united into one body against the world; this ethic also taught that individual believers must die unto sin and live unto righteousness, repeating in their own history the dying and the resurrection of Christ by rising again to a new life in the spirit—a life of endeavour after personal holiness for the love of God, and of brotherly love.

At the same time, however, the development of dogma, cultus, and ethic was still very free, simple, undefined, and receptive of new impressions. This fact comes out very clearly in the whole idea of the Exalted Christ Himself, which, freed from its historical limitations, is now able to be used very freely to develop all kinds of new applications and new meanings. Its special influence, therefore, was manifested in its "enthusiastic" spiritual influence which produced achievements of religious awakening and devotion, of theological interpretation and understanding of the Scriptures, of missionary activity and of organizing ability, of love and sacrifice, of self-conquest and transformation of character, which seemed to transcend the ordinary achievements of humanity in a remarkable way. In the popular miracle-psychology of the ancient world all these phenomena were regarded as miracles.

The Pneuma-Christ constitutes the objective presence of the sociological point of reference. It is, therefore, quite clear why it was that, from that time forward, the main problems of theology centred round the question of the interpretation of the Pneuma-Christ, of His identity with and difference between Himself and God. Thus the first fundamental doctrine became that of the Father and the Logos, from which (through a process of development into which we cannot enter here) there issued finally the doctrine of the Trinity. It is, however, also easy to see that this Pneuma-Christ, and the various spiritual effects which He produced, could not suffice permanently as the incorporation and presence of the sociological point of reference. The "enthusiasm" which it produced led, in some instances, to an hysterical confusion, and also to an inevitable weakening of actual faith in Christ, which was a grave menace to the new Faith. Further, the Idea of God which was incorporated in this Christ-mysticism was also menaced by the competition of externally similar syncretistic cults and speculations; indeed, it was in still more imminent danger of being stifled and evaporated since it had only come into existence itself by means of theological interpretations, which, in many respects, seemed to be closely related with the ideas of those cults; for neither in the Jewish Bible nor in the Gospel narrative did it possess a sufficiently strong basis for the stability of its peculiar religious content. From the sociological point of view in particular, the Christian community felt the need for establishing the sociological point of reference upon a firmer basis, and of providing it with a more objective point of view, a more practical method of definition (and one which would be actually carried out) with a more coherent lucidity and with a more logical certainty of interpretation.

It was out of this need that there arose that peculiar form of the Christian priesthood, the episcopate, with which the new Christian Bible or the New Testament was closely connected, the emphasis on a genuine tradition, secured by the bishops, and the development of the sacramental idea, which ascribed a miraculous power to the new ceremonies, and which ordained that the Sacrament was only valid within a properly constituted Christian community through the hands of the regular clergy. This constitutes the development of Early Catholicism, which, after Pauline Christianity, was the second great development of the Christian Faith. We cannot here enter into the question of the extent to which this development was affected by the thought and practice of Jewish and pagan ritual. The chief point is this: that the sociological situation did actually require some development of that kind, and that in this main concern, in spite of everything, a certain continuity can be clearly traced. The episcopate meant that the endowment with the Spirit was clearly defined within fixed limits; it formed the channel through which the miraculous powers, the authority, and the power of celebrating the Sacrament, could be conveyed to the official ministry which had been called forth by the needs of the organization; such an emphasis in fact was suggested by the actual authority of the Christian tradition and of its close relation with the original founders of the new religion. In a concrete way the episcopate was substituted for the earlier faith in the Exalted Christ and the Spirit; it is the successor of Christ and of the Apostles, the Bearer of the Spirit, the extension or eternalizing of the Incarnation, a visible and tangible proof of the Divine Truth and Power, the concrete presence of the sociological point of reference.[37] Accordingly, it also reacts upon the conception of Christ by transforming the idea of the incarnation of a Spirit working freely in the hearts of men into that of Christ as the Great High Priest and celebrant, the source of all the sacerdotal energies of grace.[38] Throughout the whole course of this development, however, it is quite clear that the driving force of the organization and of the development as a whole was religious; it was not in any way due to any attempt at social reorganization or reform. The office of the diaconate, which was dedicated to works of charity, was made subordinate to the episcopal office, as a clear token that all Christian philanthropy proceeds from the religious idea itself and is at its disposal.[39]

[37] This is one of the leading ideas in the famous and instructive book by *Loisy: L'évangile et l'église, 1902.*

[38] This subject is handled in an extremely interesting manner by *Thalhofer: Handbuch der katholischen Liturgik², 1894.*

[39] From the point of view of thought this institution of assistance was from the first the outflow of the supernatural idea of the Body of Christ or of the *Ecclesia,* which in the Presence of Christ and the Spirit everywhere bears the objective signs of an institutional body, as *Sohm: Kirchenrecht, I, 1892, p. 20,* rightly points out. In a passage quoted by Sohm from *De aleatoribus* these words occur: *pecuniam tuam adsidente Christo, spectantibus angelis et martyribus praesentibus super mensam dominicam sparge.* This gives the right meaning to the phrase of Harnack: "In the form of an altar a table served to express at one and the same time the love of God and the love of our neighbour" (*p. 39*). On the office of deacon, see *Uhlhorn, I, 154–159.*

The Episcopal Church of sacrament and tradition has, therefore, become the second fundamental dogma.

This represents, however, a further extraordinary limitation of the original sociological idea of absolute religious individualism and universalism. The religious community is now no longer bound merely to the worship of Christ, to baptism and the Supper of the Lord, but to the Church, to tradition, to the bishop, and to the use of the sacramental means of grace through the legally appointed bishop. Even in Jesus the original ideal was not supported solely by a purely independent experience of God, but by an authoritative tradition and by the force of His own authority. The episcopate only meant that those forms of authority were transformed into powers which were also capable of organizing and extending the sociological idea, since both in its starting-point and in its foundation the Divine idea and the Divine power are firmly established in the ministry and in the sacraments. For that very reason this new Christian priesthood constituted a peculiar phenomenon. It was explicitly stated that its authority was not based upon the human element in the priest, but upon the indwelling Divine power which he has received through tradition and consecration; only in so far as his actions flow from this source are they Divine; in so far as they are human their value is merely incidental or useful from the point of view of expediency. This Divine element, however, does not belong to some special priestly order as such, nor is it imparted to each individual through some wonderful Divine call; it resides in the presence of the Spirit of Christ, which, properly speaking, is only securely "canalized" through ordination and Apostolic Succession. The institution of the priesthood does not remove the general religious equality and freedom, the pure community character of all Christian religious fellowship, and it does not place certain human beings in a superior position over other human beings; it is only the chosen and regular vehicle of the Christ-Spirit, the organ of the presentation of truth and of redeeming sacramental grace. In submitting to it one is only submitting to God, and, indeed, not to special illuminations which are given only to the priest, but to the general truth and power which come to the community as a whole, but which is only tangibly localized in the priest. It only means the incorporation of universal religious truth in concrete form, and it only represents that in so far as it is active in making that truth known. Since the position of the priesthood is established by ecclesiastical law, it distinguishes quite logically between the *jus divinum*, which refers only to this position of the priest

through which salvation is received and mediated, and its immediate consequences, and the *jus humanum*, which refers to all the
other activity of the Church, which, so far as organization is concerned, under certain circumstances is far more important; that
is, it is a free and purely human activity capable of change with
a defined goal. To the extent in which Catholicism emphasizes
this aspect of the priesthood it can describe itself as a "religious
and non-political" Catholicism; it separates the Divine element
from the merely human. The whole value of the institution as an
organization, however, lies in the fact that it is so difficult to
distinguish the Divine and the human elements from each other,
and that this combination of elements makes it very easy to
invest a human order and centralization with the character of
Divine authority. The whole attempt to make this distinction is a
fiction; it permits the free purely religious spirit and the severe
methods by which it is realized to blend with each other, and
while it emphasizes the original spiritual and inward idea, it yet
binds it up indissolubly with the strictly clerical-sacramental
organization. This is the real secularization of the Church in
which the central point of religion is materialized and external-
ized, and delivered up into the hands of the secular art of organization. This secularization affected the other spheres of life,
science, and art, and the life of the State and of Society, far less.
So far as these spheres of life were concerned, Christian thought
retained its original religious and supernatural character in relation with them, and, after the sociological results of the sacramental
priesthood had been completed, to some extent in monasticism,
and partly later on in the lay religion of the declining Middle
Ages, there issued from them violent forms of reaction. When that
took place, however, characteristically this always involved profound agitation and difficulty for the sociology of the religious
community itself.

In any case, however, here at the very beginning the most
urgent need—that of giving the sociological point of reference a
concrete form—has been met by this institution of the new priesthood, and all other organizations which serve the same end are
made subordinate to it. Moreover, it is only the centre or focus
for all development of that kind, but it is in no sense the only one.
As a certain definite idea of God formed the centre of the whole
system, the need to make this idea quite clear, with its resultant
influence on doctrine, became a main concern of the Church.
The work of fixing, proving, and developing the traditional
doctrine became a matter for the clergy, and that is the reason

why the conception of God, the sociological point of reference of the whole, is formulated as a conception of truth of the most rigid kind, which completely corresponded to the conception of truth of the philosophical formal scholastic doctrines, but which was based upon authority and revelation. The ministry possesses a truth of the highest order, uniform in meaning and entirely comprehensive as the centre of its life, and this exclusive conception of truth, which demands that all shall be subject to it and to its dogma, then becomes the driving force in all its work of unification and centralization; later it becomes the reason for the claim of the Church to have the supreme authority over the spiritual life and everything which pertains to it. A situation in which different churches can exist side by side will only become possible when a different conception of truth prevails; this was, indeed, the case in pre-Catholic Christianity, whose great variety was connected with a conception of truth which involved an individualistic "enthusiasm".[40] From the point of view of Church History it is still more important to note that the spiritual energies to which the new knowledge of God gave rise were not left entirely to the purely inward influence of thought, but that as miraculous processes they were connected with the miracle of sacramental celebrations in particular. The mystery religions are drawn into Christianity, above all, in order to concentrate the redeeming power of the new knowledge of God in definite objective processes, and thus to remove them from the sphere of a fitful, merely human subjectivity. Even these rites which had originally been free were also put under the control of the clergy. The sociological significance of this fact, however, is extraordinary; it meant that the sacraments were now not merely the highest and central point of the cultus, but that, above all, they had become the main channel through which salvation is imparted to the souls of men. Outside the Sacrament there is no salvation and, since—with negligible exceptions—there is no sacrament without a priest, so there is no salvation outside the Church. The Church possesses not merely the sole truth, but also and chiefly the sole power of imparting salvation through the sacraments which link the world of sense and the super-sensible world. The Gospel, which was a completely non-sacramental and purely ethical Gospel, has thus assimilated a complex of ideas which was also alien to its basis in Judaism, but which is fundamentally inherent in all natural religion, and which from the point of view of Christ-mysticism could very well be utilized as a means of restoring real substantial

[40] See p. 179.

union with God.[40a] This also strengthened the religious-socio-logical connection, which was indeed entirely opposed to the original fundamental idea; in any case, however, it replaces its indefiniteness and looseness by a connection which cannot be broken. So long as all participated in faith in the priesthood, the sacraments, and the unity of religious knowledge it was indissoluble, and all that was weak and uncertain was finally absorbed by it.

Once the Church had been organized on these lines, she became an independent body, and it was only natural that her conception of her own nature should lead her to form her own juridical constitution. Accordingly, she gradually founded her own system of law, the law of the Church, in which, from her own standpoint, without any consideration for the State (which until then had been the only possible source of law), she evolved her own peculiar conception of the legal relation between Society and the individual, between the Church and the world. Thus the specific sociological idea which had arisen out of concern for the salvation of the soul now created for itself a new specific legal system. Out of the original naïve and concrete non-conceptual manner of thinking, which centred round the sense-image of the Church and of the presence of Christ in the Church, and then, later on, in the actual union of the churches amongst themselves, in their common possession of truth and salvation, the structure which it had all unconsciously contained stood out in conceptual clearness and was juridically expressed. The legal subjectivity of the whole body and of the individual congregation, the sphere of authority of the bishops in the first and the second respect, the representation of this legal subjectivity, the rights of individuals over against this objective law, ecclesiastical possession of property, religious institutions of charity, the ecclesiastical control of sections of life which could be reached (above all, in the law of marriage), decisions affecting disputes of Christians amongst themselves and the care of morals—all this became increasingly the subject of an ecclesiastical-juridical system of thought.[41]

[40a] Cf. *Heitmüller: Taufe und Abendmahl bei Paulus, 1903.* For the fundamental significance of sacramentalism for Catholic Christendom see my article *Der Ehrhardsche Reformkatholizismus. Chr. Welt, 1902, Nr. 20.*

[41] *Gass: Gesch. d. Ethik, I, 71 f., 229 f.* Attempts at the formulation of an ecclesiastical marriage law already under Calixtus; rejection of the death penalty and attempts to substitute legal proceedings by the Church; *Bigelmair, 92–94,* Constantine then granted legal validity to the episcopal sentences; *Weinel: Stellung u.s.w., pp. 35–37.*

From this, however, there arose a stable organism, firmly united in an organized ecclesiastical system, which was finally recognized by the State, which was then slowly and painfully forced to compromise with the law of the State, which was entirely different; in the Early Church, however, this system did not extend its influence beyond its own borders and affect the social order in general.

With great delicacy of feeling Gierke has analysed the sociological meaning of this ecclesiastical law in contrast with the general group-ideas of the Ancient World and of the Germanic tribes, and has examined the significance of the ecclesiastical conception of law for the development of the idea of fellowship in general. In the Ancient World the sociological ideal starts instinctively from the point of view of the city-state, of a community of citizens and of the ruling classes. Over all is enthroned the law; and the objective value of the law means that neither Society as a whole, nor the individual, has any legal claim apart from that which is based upon participation in the law as a whole. The legal group-fellowship itself arises from a central tendency of human natural disposition. All religion is an affair of the State and itself comes under the law. All associations are either identical with the State, or they are merely groups formed rather casually for certain definite ends, to which, under certain circumstances, Roman law deliberately granted a fictitious juristic personality (*persona ficta*). In contrast to all this the Church presents an entirely different sociological idea, and also an entirely different idea of law. "While a group-unity whose origin, nature, and destiny were transcendent was also called to be the 'subject' of an earthly sphere of law, there entered into the process of development of the theory of what constitutes a community an element which had previously been unknown. Just as the antique theory regarded the State, so Christian theology regarded the Church, as the living organism, as an independent and united whole. Only here the organic way of thinking received a new religious and mystical content. It utilized the figure of a body informed with a soul in a sense far beyond that which similar conceptions of ancient philosophy had ever reached. Here especially there was added to the whole, at its transcendent Centre, a living spiritual unity, while each member retained a value of its own, a special personality. Here the relation of the whole to its parts, and of the parts to one another, was conceived as an entirely reciprocal relationship; the principles of unity and of multiplicity were here regarded as equally real and equally necessary elements of the all-embracing Divine Being".[42] Since this Divine Being became tangible in the episcopate, "the Church appeared as a *corpus mysticum* which, on the one hand, in a mystical manner was inspired, directed, and bound together by God in a living unity, while, on the other hand, as a body which was so constituted that she also formed an external 'subject' of unity, she entered into the temporal realm with the claim to have a legal right to exercise her sovereignty over it." Thus from within the Church appears as an organism which is partly an institution for faith, partly a fellowship of believers, while from without she appears to be the ruler of a sphere of law which is independent of the State and cannot be touched by the State. It is obvious that here the mutual relationship of Christian individualism and universalism is struggling to find a legal embodiment; Gierke lays stress on the fact that these ideas resemble the Germanic ideas of social unity, which "assert, alongside of the rights of individuals as 'subjects', distinguished from one another in their peculiarity, the rights which belong to a community, which has arisen out of an association of individuals; in this case the community itself is also regarded as a 'subject' in the eyes of the law". Within the Early Church, however, this was all confined to the Church's own theory of her nature, and it did not colour the legal and sociological thought of the State, but the birth of these ideas gave rise to developments of the widest significance for all political and sociological thought, as well as for concrete institutions.[43] The deep inner inconsistency of a law which takes its rise from a transcendental source to be the fundamental characteristic of all law, capable of being enforced, is only the result emerging in the sphere of law of the general inconsistency between a purely religious society of inward life and its being made objectively tangible in dogma, sacrament, and ministry, and thus it only emphasizes the difficult problem which occurs again and again in the formation of a purely religious society.[44]

The important element in this development, however, was not merely the stabilization of the outward sociological form of the Church by means of an authority which from every point of view

[42] Cf. *Gierke: Genossenschaftsrecht, III, 108 ff.;* also the interesting section in *Harnack: Mission, I, 206–234,* where the Christians describe themselves as a "new nation and the third race".

[43] *Gierke: III, 110 f.;* the formulae for the Germanic idea of corporation, *III. i. f.*

[44] *Sohm's Kirchenrecht,* with its thesis that "Kirchenrecht" is a contradiction in terms, serves for the further discussion of this subject. Until now, however, he has not yet proved that it is possible to have a Church and an organized religious fellowship without some kind of Church order.

appeared purely supernatural, the very incarnation of miracle in priesthood, Bible and Sacrament, in tradition and law, forming the point of departure for the supernaturalism of the Church as a whole; the progress made within the Church as a whole in organization and classification was equally important. The rise of the clergy as a body of men entrusted with the leadership and government of the Church meant, that, owing to the need of the organization itself, the clergy as a class were always striving to perfect their own organization; the old charismatic gifts and free offering of service were logically transformed into a hierarchical sacerdotal system,[44a] which placed the bishops and the clergy in a special category by themselves, which was contrasted with the rest of the community called the laity. These developments formed the basis of the theocratic organization of the Church, in which the ideas of a universal priesthood and of an abstract religious equality were isolated, and produced far-reaching and essential differences. But this aristocracy differed from every other by the fact that it simply represented an attempt to render visible and concrete the redeeming energies contained within the Church as a whole; this emphasis was necessary lest these energies should become stifled and obscured by over-emphasis upon human effort; accordingly, it is always fundamentally referred back to the whole. On that account either the laity becomes a semblance or it leads to the restriction and depreciation of the clergy. Hence the contrast between the priesthood and the laity and the consequent power of the priesthood was made ethically fruitful along the same lines of religious patriarchalism, which we have already seen to be operative in differences of other kinds: the priest is regarded as the father of the congregation and the servant of the servants of God. Just as the germ of the patriarchal idea was contained in the religious reverence for personality and the resultant overcoming of accidental differences, so this system of theocratic authority contained the germ of a ladder-like organization of the whole of Society, which in the Middle Ages was destined to come into close touch with feudalism. In the Early Church neither of these tendencies had yet begun to develop. The element of patriarchalism was expressed merely in a conservative acceptance of the existing situation, while the hierarchical idea simply led to a more closely knit organization within the Church itself. Moreover, the bishops of the primitive period were still simple handicraftsmen, traders, and, under certain circum-

[44a] Cf. Harnack: "Über den Ursprung des Lektorats und der anderen niederen Weihen (Texte und Untersuchungen, III, 5).

stances, even slaves. The priestly office was only an honorary post, alongside of which a man earned his living as a citizen. Only gradually did the intellectual and well-to-do people press into the ministry, like Cyprian, for instance, and it was only after the Church had received the legal right to hold property, and after the imperial privileges of the post-Constantine period, that the bishops became a ruling class.

THE CHURCH AND THE WORLD

What then, we may ask, was the attitude of this Christian-social organism to the social institutions of the "world"? Before this question can be answered, however, we must realize the changes and further developments in the ethical thought and sentiment of the Christian churches which had meanwhile taken place. These changes were the crux of the whole problem. It is most important to note the very characteristic idea which was expressed by the fact that the term "the world" came to be regarded as a synonym for all those social institutions of life outside the Church; it was this idea which determined the attitude of the Christian Church towards them.

The more the Christian movement closed its ranks and became an organized and unified body, the more it tended to regard the rest of life as the "world". In the eyes of Jesus the ordinary life of humanity, in spite of its sin, was full of traces of the Divine goodness, and He recognized the naïve and natural accents of piety in children, sinners, and Samaritans; to Him the dividing-line was not drawn between the world and the Church, but between the present and the future; even in the thought of Paul, however, the Kingdom of Christ, or the Church, already stands out in complete contrast to the kingdom of the first Adam, of the flesh, of sin, of the law, and of the devil. With the idea of the sacerdotal and sacramental Church as the *civitas Dei*,[44b] around which the angels play, and in which the Christ-God sits enthroned, the opposite idea of the "world" as the kingdom of Satan, in which there is nothing but perdition and impotence, was intensified. In this idea of the contrast between the Church and the world the sociological aspect of Christian thought was brought to a clear and settled issue, which became increasingly important for the social doctrines of Christianity. It was at this point that primitive

[44b] The expression *civitas Dei* is not primarily Augustinian; Paul had already described the Christian community as a πολίτευμα ἐν οὐρανοῖς, and in Hermas, too, πολις is the expression for Christianity in contrast with the city of this world; *Weinel: Stellung u.s.w., p. 52.*

Christian apologetic became aggressive, since in order to maintain the unique redemptive power of the Christian faith all the forces of the world for good must be either denied or depreciated. All further developments in thought and in organization were determined by this point of view. Deliverance from the world comes to be regarded as a completely sacramental miracle, whether it be through baptism or through repentance, and the ethic of the Church becomes the ethic of the morality of grace, of the supernatural impartation of moral power, which cannot be derived from the world but only from the miracle of the Divine-human Church. Further, all the content of moral conduct is now placed in the sharpest contrast to secular conduct, and that element which, in Jesus, was a kind of heroism which regarded the natural conditions of ordinary human life with unforced detachment, developed into asceticism; this was due to the influence of various motives, in which, however, this idea of the gulf between the world and the Kingdom of God predominated. This asceticism was suspicious of Nature and hostile towards it, and it also fell under the spell of Platonism, which taught that the world of sense, with its phantasmagoria of delusive appearances, was entirely opposed to the Idea of the Good. Above all, however—and this is the most important point for us to note in this connection—the world with all its ordinances came to be regarded as a solid and unchangeable mass of evil, a system which could only be accepted or rejected *en bloc*. Monasticism, which became the ideal rule of life for the clergy, decided to reject it, while the great mass of the workers felt they must accept it; in accepting the "world", however, they also submitted to the consequences produced by the Fall. From that time forward, when Christians wished to take part in secular life, the argument which was always employed was this: these secular institutions are the result of sin; by participation in this social order the Christian submits to the results of the sin of humanity in general. He cannot alter these things; all he can do is to submit to them; in his heart he is still opposed to them, and he himself has at least no inner pleasure in or attraction to these things which he is forced to use, although they are due to sin alone. Throughout the whole history of the Primitive Church this was the accepted point of view, and even at a later stage the Church fell back on this argument when she felt it necessary to do so. As we study the question of the social attitude and activity of the Church the significance of this development of thought will become plain.

ASCETICISM

As we have already seen, asceticism in its particular Christian and ecclesiastical form, which was the strongest force in the Early Church, had developed naturally out of that contrast between the world and the Church. Nothing, indeed, would be more erroneous than to seek to explain the rise of this mighty and serious phenomenon simply by the need for the establishment of a contrast of this kind. But the special form and influence of ecclesiastical asceticism was certainly very closely connected with it. In itself asceticism is based on something much broader and more universal; indeed, it can be interpreted in a variety of ways which need to be satisfactorily ascertained. There is an "asceticism" which is simply the result of a religious idea which has come into its own and then developed its whole depth of meaning. Where communion with God and life in God are sought there the sense of mortality, of nothingness, or at least of the vanity of all earthly values, arises, and religion develops into redemption. With the final period of the ancient world the religious movements of the time introduced—even on the intellectual side—the belief in redemption and the depreciation of secular life. This meant, however, a real dualism, faith in a principle in the world which was opposed to God; it was not an inevitable conclusion. It was transcendental, but it did not deny the value of the world.[45] The Gospel and the teaching of Jesus were of this kind. The Hope of the Kingdom of God which Jesus proclaimed, and the radicalism of His ethical and religious demand, simply destroyed the power of worldly interests by the demand for trust in God and simplicity of life; otherwise, however, Jesus accepted the Jewish faith in the Creation, and with that He unquestioningly accepted the world and its simple and innocent joys. The fact that the mind of Jesus and of the most primitive period of the Church was full of the hope that the ideal would very soon be realized in a marvellous way also helped to lessen the value of the short remaining span of the world; this depreciation, however, did not take the form of denial of the world, of the senses, or of nature; it was rather an attitude of indifference towards an order which, in any case, is about to pass away. It was rather a radical super-

---

[45] Cf. *Siebeck: Lehrbuch der Religionsphilosophie, 1893, pp. 1–31, 101–156.* A positivist like Bender sees in every form of metaphysic (that is, in every assertion of a reality which differs from direct experience and can only be conceived through the intellect) the germ of dualism and therefore of asceticism; cf. *Metaphysik und Asketik (Archiv. f. Gesch. d. Philos., VI, 1888).*

naturalism, a heroism which was not concerned with the conditions of ordinary life, rather than asceticism in the more literal
sense.[46]

It was only when mysticism and an acosmistic pantheism
entered in that faith in redemption really became asceticism, for
which reason also the monastic life was described as the philo-
sophic life. "Asceticism", however, did not rise only out of the
central religious aim, but also out of the ethical rigorism of the
Gospel. The purely spiritual ethic which dispenses with law and
authority could only be carried out in practice in very simple
social conditions, and it assumed a situation in which small
groups of people were living in close touch with each other.
When Christianity became involved in larger and more complicated social conditions, Christians found it advisable either to
remain aloof from them altogether, or to establish special groups
of their own in which such practice was possible. That also was
scarcely asceticism; it only meant holding aloof from the dangers
and complications of the life round them, but it easily developed
into asceticism, especially in monastic circles.[46a]

Genuine asceticism, however, very easily fell into a mistake
which was closely related to its own ideas; this development had
a great effect upon the whole conception of asceticism. The
confusion of thought arose in this way. Since the characteristics
of the evangelical ethic were self-denial and the severity of its
demands, it seemed, inversely, as though everything which was
difficult, self-denying, and contrary to nature were a service to
God demanded by the Gospel. A similar confusion of thought is
evident when the exercises which were meant to aid in religious
concentration, and the preservation of morality, were made an
end in themselves, and were used to satisfy the desire to attract
attention and appear singular, as nearly always happens in
groups which practise an overstrained piety. While the self-
denial of the evangelical ethic had a positive aim—the love of
God and the love of humanity—and thus produced the inner

[46] Here the researches of *Jacoby: Neutestamentliche Ethik* contain much useful
material.
[46a] See above, p. 86, and *Harnack: Das Mönchtum, seine Ideale und seine Geschichte,
1907, p. 10*: "The imitation of Christ in which the desire for the Kingdom of
God and His righteousness is realized, includes the casting aside of all that
can hinder. Monasticism, however, tried to do further justice to the command
'deny thyself' by applying renunciation wholesale, without consideration of
the nature or the calling of the individual in particular." The latter, however,
produces categories in which only Lutheranism was able to solve the problem,
or believed that it had solved it.

values of union with God or the filial relationship with God, here self-denial became an end in itself, a good work, a penance, an achievement, which is all the more valuable the more it opposes natural feelings and the more difficult it is to struggle against them. The good works of mortification and humiliation arose out of a certain association of ideas, all of which were connected with the depreciation of the value of personality through an exaggerated emphasis upon the doctrine of Original Sin, coupled with the lowering of the evangelical standard to a system of quantitative merit and a detailed eschatology of punishment and reward. Exaggeration of this kind, and a tendency to reduce a spiritual religion to the popular level, are phenomena which are inseparably connected with every form of idealism, and it was therefore only natural that they should appear in connection with primitive Christian idealism; as the "good works" of mortification and humiliation they served the ends of the salvation of the soul and of deliverance from the final judgment. Mortification—as well as the ideal of "virginity"—became the most peculiar and the most frequent form of Christian asceticism, which found its permanent source of nourishment in the increasing emphasis upon the doctrine of Original Sin, and in an ever more highly developed system of eschatology. It contained an element of passivity, of pure negation and ethical aimlessness, which constituted a hindrance to the true Christian ethic and was in opposition to its fundamental tendencies. On the other hand, however, since an asceticism of this kind presupposes an extraordinary effort of the will and of enthusiasm, it is always, or at least very frequently, one of the strongest means of vivifying and stimulating Christian movements of thought; and, since it was not based upon a system of acosmism, nor indeed upon any system at all, but was only an extraordinary effort of the will and an eschatological and eudaemonistic guarantee, so, without any theory at all, it was able to unite with all positive tendencies of deliberate charity or useful occupation. Under some circumstances it was able to exercise the most varied effects, hindering and furthering, in accordance with principle or against principle; it could be exercised in all forms and degrees, in mere self-discipline and in the monastic life, and also in the wildest eccentricities.[46b]

On the other hand, another source of genuine asceticism is to be found in conscious and willed dualism; it appears in the East with the so-called Gnostic movements whose origin is still very obscure, and in the West with Neo-Platonism and Pythagoreanism.

[46b] See p. 179.

Here it developed into the opposition between sense and spirit, into the fight against the realm of sense and matter as such; the denial of the material world is expressed sometimes by the severest abstinence, sometimes by a libertine ignoring of material conditions altogether.[47] Paul's doctrine of the flesh and the spirit seems already to contain some admixture of this element, and his conception of the thought of redemption is also influenced by it: in his doctrine he offers not merely a future redemption in the Kingdom of God, but a redemption that has already been achieved in the overcoming of the flesh through the Death of Christ. Paul did not deduce asceticism from that doctrine, however; in his mind, too, the sinfulness of the flesh is determined by the Fall—that is, by the will of the creature.

With Gnosticism, however, dualistic asceticism penetrated into Christianity, and in its wake came the whole technique of frenzied and ecstatic movements. Behind and beneath these religious desires for redemption and the speculative dualism a more universal reason was the decline of an overripe and static civilization, whose delight in life and vitality had been drained out of it, and which in dull dissatisfaction with itself was seeking for something new; it desired to go beyond itself, and therefore grasped eagerly at all new movements. This is, indeed, a solemn and affecting spectacle for all who have gazed with admiration at the splendid development of this civilization, and who feel that a similar fate threatens every fully developed form of civilization. This mood, however, was not really asceticism; it was satiety, exhaustion, and fatigue, and those who were influenced by it only dabbled in the ascetic doctrines and cults which appeared in the hope of finding something new and higher.[48]

Further (and this seems particularly strange to us) there was an extraordinary increase of the belief in demons, a phenomenon which was due to a great variety of causes; in the main, however, it may be ascribed to the decline of faith in the old religions which characterized the Imperial age, and to the religious unrest which this produced. The whole world was believed to be full of demons. The atmosphere swarmed with them. These "spirits" were no longer conceived as morally indifferent; they were now regarded

---

[47] Cf. *Anz: Zur Frage nach dem Ursprung des Gnostizismus* (*Texte und Untersuchungen, XV, 4*). *Rohde: Psyche,*[2] *1898.* The research into these questions is only now becoming active. Here especially the eschatological ideas of late antiquity ought to be studied, in order to see how far they led to asceticism. We need to remember, however, that in itself eschatology does not mean asceticism.

[48] See p. 179.

as dangerous and wicked, and contact with them must be avoided at all costs. This fear gave rise to a host of precautions and methods of repelling the demons, which robbed life of all spontaneity. In this situation Christian thinkers only needed to identify matter with evil spirits and world principles, or the pagan world with the dominion of Satan, in order to be able to argue the need for detachment from the whole world of matter and of sense; prudence suggests doing too much rather than too little, and thus detachment from the sense life leads to an asceticism, which, however, is not really based upon the metaphysical dualism of spirit and matter. In all this there may be a basis of theoretical monotheism and a conviction of the unity of the world principle, but the reawakened and vigorous elements of polytheism were able to gain a footing within the whole religious outlook because they were linked up with the general ideas of good and evil through the belief in good and evil demons; and since polytheism developed into the fear of demons, it was able to further the growth of asceticism in spite of a theoretical belief in the goodness of the world.[49]

Finally, we may perhaps also discover another reason for the growth of asceticism in the neuropathic weakening of vitality, due to a certain weariness and slackness of the sex instinct, caused by ignorance of the laws of sex. In any case, this fact caused a great deal of trouble during the Imperial age, and on purely social and ideal grounds it is difficult to explain why the ideal of chastity should increase to such a great extent. The explanation can scarcely be solely in the natural desire of strong religious feeling to thrust out of its way the rival interest of eroticism, whether through severe discipline of the sex instinct or through the fusion of erotic and religious excitement, nor by the effort to neutralize the sex life by the strength of its own feeling.[50] It looks rather as though the real reason for the immense appeal of this ascetic ideal lay in the fact that the civilized world of that day was suffering from a nervous disease which sought purification and support in religious ideas. In any case, the stress laid on the "purity" of the "virgin" state opened the door to asceticism, and at the same time there was a great outburst of similar ideas—men sang the praises of vegetarianism and simplicity of life, of the natural state, and of the hermit life. When this ideal of celibacy began to appeal to the healthy and the strong, it produced a system of physical self-torture whose one aim was the repression

[49] Cf. Weinel: Geist und Geister im nachapostolischen Zeitalter, 1899.
[50] See p. 179.

of the sex instinct. This, of course, became combined with all the abnormalities of the perverted sex instinct.

The life of the Christian Church then became involved in all these problems. The Gospel of Jesus and the teaching of Paul had not encouraged asceticism, but they had encouraged an attitude of indifference towards the natural conditions of existence, only permitting them to be recognized to a limited extent. The prevailing eschatological outlook also called for a heroism which far transcended preoccupation with the concerns of everyday life, and likewise impelled Christians to live under conditions of great simplicity and intimacy. From that standpoint the Church found it impossible to regard Nature, the world, and the sense life as essentially and metaphysically evil and at enmity with God—a tendency which the Old Testament, with its belief in the Creation, its nature poetry, and its healthy Jewish proverb morality, which the Church called in as a triumphant witness in the struggle against Gnosticism, helped to strengthen. It was in that tendency that the increasing adaptation to the world which accompanied the growth of the Church found its justification, and it was in it that the doctrine of a Divine germ of reason contained also in the ordinances of the world maintained its logical connection with its origin.

Now, however, the standard which permitted this degree of recognition of the world had become extremely uncertain; the tendency was to assign very little value to it at all, and in any case any acknowledgment of secular values as having any use or worth in themselves was completely excluded; even from the most favourable point of view they were simply ordinances given with the rest of creation, set up by the Will of God, and therefore simply to be accepted. Under these circumstances all positive interest in them was forbidden, and the reduction of them to a minimum easily leads to complete negation; then one is sure of having reached the absolute minimum. In addition, there were all the other influences which have already been mentioned, especially the belief in demons, which, in spite of a theoretical belief in monotheism and faith in the goodness of the world, still can admit *per accidens* that the world is so largely under the power of sin and the devil that it leads to a practical attitude of negation. The sense of uncertainty was further increased by the following elements in the situation—speculative dualism, weariness of civilization, the hermit life, celibacy, the mood of martyrdom, and the controversy about treatment of those who had avoided martyrdom; all this made the Christian attitude towards the

"world" a very perplexing matter, and those who could do so
sought to escape the problem by flight from the world altogether.
Even the Pauline exhortation so often quoted by the Fathers—
"Let each man abide in that calling wherein he was called"—
merely inculcated submission to the order of this world, but no
inner appreciation of it, and the more Christians became involved in the actual life and work of the great world around them,
the more acute the problem became. Thus the attitude of the
leaders of the Church towards the "world" has become hesitating
and uncertain. They are doubtful about its origin, and this leads
them to advocate a semi-ascetic position; this position implies
a minimum of justification for the "world", but the misgivings
with which even this "minimum" is regarded sometimes leads to
genuine and whole-hearted asceticism, while at other times,
under the pressure of practical circumstances, this "minimum"
is considerably enlarged.[51]

Into all this confusion and uncertainty the Church, which had
now begun to feel its sociological unity, brought a certain unity
and stability. The effect was both to restrict and to define more
clearly asceticism on the one hand and the idea of the "world"
on the other. The Church pointed out that the "world" in itself
is not evil; it has only become so through the Fall, and it is only
under the power of the demons so long as it is sinful. It is certainly
everywhere steeped in sin, and forms a coherent system of sin, a
sociological counterpart of the Church. The only Divine element
within it is the spirit of order and of law, which assures the *pax
terrena* and thus the peaceful work of the Christians. Christians
themselves, however, do not live directly within the world, but
only through the medium of the Church. They are, first of all,
members of the Church, and it is only as such that they live at
the same time in the world, since the Church, while it is still in
the flesh, is *ecclesia militans*. Thus the Church permits its members a
minimum of participation in the life of the world, and takes from
them the responsibility for their own decision. She regulates this
minimum herself, and at the same time secures the ascetic spirit
by the very demands she makes on the laity in their relation
to the Church. These requirements are summed up in the humility
which renounces all self-will, opens the heart to the inflow of
sacramental grace (which alone gives the power to achieve any
good), and in the love which sets the unity of the Church above
all else. For the great majority of the faithful this way of life makes
it possible to preserve the ascetic spirit without a sense of strain.[52]

[51] See p. 180.   [52] See p. 180.

There is, however, a higher degree of perfection, in which complete asceticism, poverty, and celibacy can be partially or wholly attained. This is a special *Charisma*, which indeed should always characterize the priest, and which is supported by laws for the regulation of the lives of the clergy.

This expedient of a dual and yet equally binding morality is, however, no mere renunciation of the real fundamental ideal of asceticism. Rather it corresponds to a dual tendency, which, from the very beginning, was always present in Christian thought: this dual tendency includes, on the one hand, the spirit which sees the goodness of God expressed in this world as it now is, and, on the other, that aspiration and desire which long to rise above this world into the freedom of the children of God and into spiritual unity in Him as its final and supreme End. But in the special form which it here assumed it was limited by all the forces of the situation at that time, and especially by the opposition of the Church—as an institution which alone contains salvation and redemption—to the world which has been handed over to the Evil One. In itself, however, this opposition was not due to the influence of asceticism; it was due, first of all, to the fact that the Church claimed that she alone possessed the Truth, together with the miraculous power which went with it; it was, therefore, an effect of the supernatural claim with which the Church had secured her position against the world. This supernaturalism then provided a great opportunity for the development of asceticism, which was encouraged by the influence of Paul's teaching on sex questions, and by the Jewish practice of fasting and the Jewish doctrine of almsgiving. In the mind of Jesus grateful enjoyment of the innocent pleasures of this world and the severity of His high ideal had existed side by side, without difficulty or strain. In the Church, however, in the far more complicated life of the world, both these elements drifted farther and farther away from one another. The natural assumption of the heroism of the Gospel, the expectation of the End, receded; that indifference to the values of civilization which was quite intelligible in the enthusiasm of the founding of a religion, and in the rural simplicity of Galilee, could not be maintained. Thus everything came to be regarded from the standpoint of the contrast between the Church and the world. The religious reference in particular, of all moral commands towards fellowship with God which could only be won through obedience, developed very largely into asceticism, or the breaking of the natural will simply for the sake of destroying it and for the merit which was thus acquired. From that time forward the Church was only able to unite these two elements by proclaiming a double standard of morals, by making a clear distinction between an ethic which was semi-ascetic and an ethic which was asceticism pure and simple.[53]

Ethic of Early Catholicism

Under these influences the whole ethic of the Church became entirely changed. It lost the certainty of aim which was contained in the twofold idea of self-consecration for the love of God and the brethren, and it was broken up into varied combinations of particular scriptural commands, unscrupulous borrowings from the ethics of Stoicism and of Cynicism, ascetic regulations and regulations of church order; it confused worship and ethical behaviour, and connected good works, fasting, and almsgiving with the idea of merit and the assurance of personal salvation. The Christian nature of morality seemed to lie no longer in the direct specific content of the Ethos, but in the supernatural character of Christian behaviour, which is due to grace alone; and the difference between it and heathen morality seems to consist no longer in opposition to the order of the State and the spirit of eudaemonism, but in opposition to the use of natural powers. From the time of the Pelagian controversy the whole question centres round this formal difference. Augustine's own famous doctrine (continually repeated in the Middle Ages) of the content of the Christian moral law was this: that it consists in directing all activity towards the ultimate goal of union with God, and then expresses itself in contemplative purity of heart and in active brotherly love. This doctrine had already introduced strange and confusing motives into Christian ethics: (1) by the place given to contemplation, and (2) by the distinction drawn between the contemplative and the active life; thus these ideas of Augustine did nothing to encourage the formation of a system of Christian ethics. The Christian ethic consisted, in fact, rather in an extremely varied mass of regulations in which the Christian element depends mainly on achievements effected by grace but tinged with asceticism.[53a] The Church was, however, already so firmly united as a sociological organism, and it contained the fundamental ethical ideas so clearly within its structure, that this uncertainty in the realm of ethics could not endanger it. It did not actually need a system of ethics at all, and instinctively and unconsciously it imparted to its ethical teaching those funda-

[53] See p. 181.
[53a] Cf. *Gass: Gesch. der Ethik, I, 174; Liebner; Hugo v. St. Victor, 1832, pp. 466 ff.*

mental impulses which in another form were really the fundamental commandment of love to God and love to the brethren;
the form alone had been altered by the influences of asceticism,
ecclesiasticism, the idea of merit, and other-worldliness. In so doing
both these fundamental requirements of Christianity have replaced their original simple religious aim of a filial relationship
with God, and the fellowship of love with one another, by the
more complicated intention directed towards the Church and
asceticism. Self-consecration in free obedience of conscience, with
the goal of the infinite value of the soul, heart purity, and the love
of God, become humility and meekness towards the Church,
which involves the sacrifice of one's own will and of one's own
knowledge, and is ethically most valuable when the renunciation
is most difficult. Brotherly love, with the aim of the universal
fellowship of love, becomes the collective consciousness of the
Church, which has the right to claim every sacrifice of the individual will, and without which a man is like a withered leaf
fallen from the parent stem. It is precisely in obedience to the
Church, and in sacrifice for the unity of the Church, that the
destruction of the ego and self-sacrifice for others is exercised,
good works are acquired, and future salvation is assured. That
which a man renounces he gives to the Church, and by means of
services of this kind, controlled by the Church, he secures salvation in the other world, and this again is mediated by the Church.
This also leads to a change of emphasis among the fundamental
elements of the sociological idea of the Gospel. Whereas this
sociological idea arose in a radical religious individualism, which
developed its universalism through the meeting of individuals in
God, and by the fact that those who are united to God then turn
back to the world in order to reveal the Divine spirit of love to
the brethren, now the chief emphasis is laid on the authority of
the Church, charity consists in submission to the Church, and in
doing good works for the brethren. Ascetic meritorious love
swallows up individualism; love becomes the chief and fundamental virtue, based upon humility, which, with its strong psychological tendency towards inwardness and introspection, maintains
the fundamental Christian individualism, and indeed, from this
source, permits it continually to break out anew. Among other
things, monasticism and contemplation were the salvation of
Christian individualism, in the only form in which it was then
possible to preserve it.[54]

Out of all the confusion of the "ethic" of the Church, which, in

[54] See p. 182.

the main, cannot in any way be compared with the scientific systems of Greek morality, the two ancient fundamental commandments have again reasserted their power, summing up in themselves the essence of the whole, only in a sense altered by ecclesiasticism and asceticism. In so doing they also determine the sociological fundamental theory in which man is related to man, absorbing into it the hierarchical organization of laity, clergy, and monks, and, together with Christian patriarchalism, they shape life as far as it was possible to them, that is, life in the home and in the Church. The Church was still too small and inwardly too remote from the world to desire to carry this out into the public and common life.

The Church and Social Problems

Although, therefore, the Church now actually controlled social problems from the point of view of these fundamental ideas, she could only do it directly for herself and in the circle within reach of her influence. Since from the time of the Antonines the number of her members had enormously increased, she had to do within her community that which she had no power to do outside. For herself and within her own sphere she had to attack social problems. Since, however, all these institutions belonged to the State, to its legal system, to its ordering of property, and to its social structure, the Church found directly that all its contact with the world outside forced it to consider its relation to the State. The Church did not regard the State merely as the power which ordered that Christians should be persecuted—the Christians ascribed persecutions either to individual emperors or to the people and their misunderstanding of the Christians—to the Church the State was before all else the support of those institutions, and so in the long run it was impossible to hold a purely negative or even a merely indifferent attitude towards it. But a clear and settled attitude to the State was the latest development of all. Public life and the State offered in the beginning the fewest direct contacts with the social formation of the churches, and for a long time the Christians did all that was possible to keep out of the way in order to avoid friction. It was only when, from the third century onwards, the social changes in the Christian churches rendered this attitude impossible, that gradually a more clearly defined position with reference to the State had to be adopted. In the Christian Empire, moreover, this became absolutely necessary. So the social influence of the Church was felt first of all at its most accessible point—the family, which the

Church henceforth regarded as the basis of all social and political order; then its social influence was felt in the economic realm and in Society, with which the life of the family is inextricably mingled; and finally in the State, which maintains the stability of the whole.

If we are to understand these social achievements and theories of the Early Church, however, we must keep always clearly before us the following points, some of which have already been mentioned. The first point of importance is the decline of millenarianism and the transformation of the idea of the Kingdom of God. Even in the apostolic age the idea of the Kingdom of God had become merged with that of the Church, and the idea of the coming of the Kingdom was replaced by the exaltation of the Church, the shattering of the earthen vessel, and the freeing of the gleaming treasure from all that concealed its glory. Otherwise the idea of the Kingdom of God was replaced by "eschatology", Heaven, Hell, and Purgatory, immortality and the future life, a contrast with the teaching of the Gospel, which is of the highest significance. But even this final "end" was continually deferred, until at last the Thousand Year Reign of Christ was applied to the Church.[55] The effect of this change was certainly a closer connection between the Church and the world, but most emphatically it did not mean that the Church really acknowledged the world as the embodiment of independent ethical values. Rather, precisely to the extent in which the indifference to the world which was felt by all who cherished the hope of the imminence of the coming of the Kingdom receded, it was replaced by the spirit of an ascetic condemnation of the world. Thus the effect of the decline of the Hope of the Kingdom was twofold. The Kingdom which the Early Church had expected was, indeed, an ideal state of life upon earth, not an eschatology of heaven and hell, and to this extent it led inevitably to a certain regard for life in the world. This expectation might foster indifference towards the present world, but its effect was not directly ascetic. When, however, the hope of the Kingdom was replaced by an "eschatology", naturally the result was a closer identification with the

[55] For the very early identification of the Church with the Kingdom of God, cf. *Wernle: Reichgotteshoffnung nach den ältesten Dokumenten.*—Hippolytus thinks the world will last about 300 and Lactantius 200 years; *Bigelmair, S.15.* With the exclusion of Montanism (which meant the revival of eschatology and of a correspondingly strict separation from the world) this tendency became confirmed. *Augustine: De civitate Dei, XX, 9. 2*, identifies the 1,000 years' kingdom with the Church, gives also about 600 years, and indeed later, in the year 1000, the end of the world was expected.

permanent life of the world; at the same time this abstract eschatology, with its mere rewards and penalties and their entirely other-worldly character, led to a decided increase in the depreciation of the world as a whole; the Church now felt itself to be opposed, not only to the pagan world, but to the world in general. It was only at this point that there arose that direct contrast between this world and the other which produced the spirit which was concerned mainly with a future salvation, with the desire to pile up "merits" and "good works"; this meant that men soon decided that the best way to pile up "good works" was through the practice of asceticism. Thus it was precisely this eschatology which produced asceticism; its influence in this direction was far stronger than that of the hope of the Kingdom of God. The aims of the asceticism of the West, and the early Middle Ages in particular, were purely eschatological and eudaemonistic.[55a] The fundamental attitude of the Gospel towards the "world" was retained, but the influence of the hope in the coming of the Kingdom was replaced by asceticism; this encouraged the growth of asceticism, for at that time it was not realized that this tendency was opposed to the spirit of the Gospel. The need for modification and adaptation was met by the double standard of morality.

The second point is the conviction that existing conditions are static and immutable. They seem to constitute a system in which each part depends on the others, and which can only be thus or not at all.[56] It is the absolutist habit of mind, which can only think of the Church and the "world" in terms of "absolutes". This way of thinking also reveals the peculiar sentiment of the Ancient World itself, which had done with the Empire and had outlived its impulses in life and education; yet, in spite of the enormous change in its social, economic, administrative, and legal structure, it still could not imagine any other future than the continuation of the Roman Empire and its officials. Rome is eternal. Further, the Ancient World only regarded politics and economics as part of ethics or of positive law, and it had no power of thinking independently on economic and social problems.

The third point is the increasing complexity of the social and economic situation of the members of the Church. Questions of property and profession may have been comparatively easy to settle so long as they only concerned a small middle class, but

[55a] This was the average reason for asceticism in the Gallic and the Frankish Church. See *Hauck: KG Deutschlands, I 265, II 766; Harnack: Mönchtum, 38.*
[56] See p. 182.

with the entrance of the wealthy and educated classes, i.e. from the third and fourth centuries, these questions became far more difficult. There were now Christians who held public official positions, who served in the army, who had luxurious tastes, who possessed scientific interests, men whose lives were woven into the very fabric of the whole of the life of the State and of Society. There were speculators, monopoly owners, holders of large estates, officers, officials, nobles and scholars, artists and technicians. It was all the more difficult to regulate the life of these complicated masses because the principles which were contained in the canonical Scriptures referred to far simpler conditions. It is not surprising that inconsequences and sophistries arose.

Finally, we must not forget the immense influence exercised by the growing worldliness of the Church; the Church was largely "secularized" by the world in the really bad sense of the word. The earnestness of the genuine early Christians was followed by the externalism of the nominal Christians, who really remained just what they were before. However, at this point we can leave them out of account. They did not affect the theory and ideal of the Church so much as its practice.

PROBLEM OF PROPERTY

The first social problem with which the Church had to deal was the problem of property. It was an extremely difficult problem, and it was only solved amid much hesitation and uncertainty.[57] From the outset we can ignore all statements which ascribe private property to sin, and which describe Paradise as the home of communism; the very people who say these things urge the Church to acquiesce for the present in the social order which has been produced by sin. The only purpose served by such statements was to establish the duty of charity on a firmer basis, since charity, to some extent at least, restores the Primitive State. In all this, however, there was no idea of doing away with private property, and the special reference which it had at this point to the Primitive State will be explained in another connection. Also the frequent exhortations to regard property[58] as nothing, and all the talk about community of possessions which are gifts of God like light and air, were equally only a challenge to energetic charitable activity. In all these discussions the possession of private

[57] See p. 183.
[58] A familiar phrase originating in Acts iv. 32 (the account of the "having all things in common").

property itself was always assumed. The problem, therefore, was not that of private property in itself and the economic order which was based upon it, but the measure and the range of the duty of love. There was no economic problem of property, but there was an ethico-religious problem, which fluctuated between the radicalism of the claims of love and the natural claims of the necessity of earning a living. At first, however, in the small and poor churches the situation was simple. There was plenty of want and distress, and the practice of charity naturally had to be extended as far as possible. Then, too, the necessary minimum of existence was quite clear: "Having food and raiment let us be therewith content" (1 Tim. vi. 8). The few people who were well-to-do had their hands full in looking after the welfare of others and in sacrificing themselves for the churches, as the letters of Paul show clearly.

But as the churches increased in number, and there was a greater variety in the economic conditions within them, the matter became much more difficult. Now arises the problem of "the rich". Jesus' radical commandment of love was now emphasized in an abstract manner; the instructions to missionaries were turned into universal dogmas, and the story of the Rich Young Ruler was made the basis of the system. The ascetic basis was quickened by the spirit of love, and the coarsening of the Gospel morality of spirit and temper into the morality of good works exalts individual deeds of sacrifice. The renunciation of possessions now becomes the main demand, whether it be from obedience to the commandment of love, which urges that no one ought to possess anything for himself so long as others are in want, or whether the ascetic idea is pre-eminent, that every joy in possession is self-love and love of the world and a hindrance to the love of God, or whether the sin-expiating power of almsgiving is emphasized.[58a] All along, however, private property itself remains untouched, but it is limited to the absolutely necessary minimum of existence; all that is superfluous must be given away. Possessions and earthly goods are, as all the Fathers emphasize, from God; but they were originally destined for all, and it is only due to sin and greed that they have been drawn into the present oppressive state of affairs in which there are such glaring differences between those who have and those who have not. The balance ought to be redressed, as far as possible, by love and

---

[58a] Cf. *Seipel, 195–244.* For the expiatory power of charitable deeds, which also requires a spiritual effort, and is only applied to the smaller sins of everyday life, see *Seipel, 219–229.*

sacrifice.[58b] Quite naturally a great many obvious difficulties arose in connection with this problem. For different positions in life the existence minimum which is permitted is different. Clement is even inclined to permit a certain amount of luxury within the limits of the natural life, while Tertullian will not hear of such a thing.[59] It was also clearly perceived that not a great deal was gained merely by giving away, that it only impoverished the well-to-do without really helping others, that property was not merely a means of consumption, but that it was also a means of production to many other people, that the very fact of active charity assumed the existence of private property, that indiscriminate giving produced pride and self-righteousness in the givers and the begging habit in those who received, but that the heart of the problem was the spirit of love and inward detachment from possessions, and that this energy of love was neither gained nor exercised by mere charity. Considerations of this kind became increasingly prominent as the number of churches increased, and their life was more and more drawn into connection with the general economic situation. On the other hand, however, it was felt likewise that this contact with the world introduced a spirit of compromise into the Church which weakened the radicalism of the commandment of love with its emphasis upon the "one thing needful", and especially that it pierced the growing spirit of asceticism at its most vital and effective point. So this spirit of compromise was attacked by a bold radicalism which was all the more purely ascetic in motive, the less reason there was to think that in a great society gifts of love would really remove all distress. Monasticism went forward until it established an actual system of community of possessions, and at least the duty of giving away was preached to the laity with increased energy. The great leaders of the fourth century were all under the influence of this monastic ideal, but they were also able to treat the laity, who were under the influence of the natural life, more easily. Thus there arose a twofold solution of the problem: on the one hand, there was an ethic of compromise, with relative standards, which permitted private property and "riches"; which sanctions it as a means of social prosperity, and only requires that superfluous possessions shall be shared, and an inner spirit of detachment from all pleasure in property. That means that those who have possessions

[58b] Hence for the present day the only profit which can be said to be allowed by God is that which has been gained in decent and honest callings; hence also the criticism of the various callings which will be described later.

[59] See p. 184.

must limit them to the necessary existence minimum, and that they must hold the rest in trust for purposes of charity. Finally, for Christians and non-Christians the question of property is outwardly and actually just the same. The Church also acquires Church property in land, slaves, money, and payment in kind, and thus acquires special property and the privileges of the former temple property. Confronted with this the Fathers only emphasized the fact that the inward attitude of the Christian towards possessions ought to be different, and then stressed the duty of regarding possessions as a gift of God which ought to be used for purposes of charity. Above all, in a society constructed upon the census and on distinctions based on wealth the Fathers lay stress on the true and real classification of human beings according to the only effective "riches", the riches of virtue and piety; they also point out that the true order of rank is independent of the social differences revealed by the census, which determined the right of being elected to city councils, and the possibility of belonging to the senate and the official classes. Here the Christians appropriated for their own use similar powerful phrases of the Stoics. That this "having property as though one had it not" might lead just as easily to "having Christianity as though one had it not" is obvious. All the more strongly, therefore, the other solution was emphasized—the way of monasticism. Here the difficulty was removed by doing away with private property altogether; the real motive for this, however, was no longer love but asceticism: but in the love exercised within the monastic community, and in intercession for those who are living in the world, love still comes into her own. Thus the principle of a double morality, by means of which the Church solved the problem of the relationship between the world and the ethic of the Gospel, was also the solution of the problem of property.

PROBLEM OF WORK

Closely related to the problem of property was that of production. (We must always remember that the question of property was always regarded as a means of consumption.) Here the simplest ideas prevailed. The amount of private property which was considered to be absolutely necessary for the minimum of existence, and for purposes of charity, is gained by work, which in those early days naturally meant manual labour.[60] From the very outset, therefore, work was emphatically encouraged. It was prized also as an education in sobriety and industry, and as a

[60] See p. 184.

means of protection against certain dangers. Those who did not
want to work were sent about their business, and work was found
for the unemployed. Labour was also regarded as useful for the
purposes of asceticism and the discipline of the body; the monastic
ethic in particular stressed this aspect; moreover, the Church
Fathers also liked to proclaim this duty very often. From another
point of view, however, work was also regarded as the consequence of the Fall and as the punishment of sin. We must not
expect to find here the love of work and its products; that assumes
a far more positive appreciation of the world than the early
Christians possessed, and it cannot be conceived without pleasure
in possessions.[60a] Therefore the saying that "Christianity has
dignified labour" ought not to be exaggerated. The appreciation
of labour was only natural since so many of the early Christians
belonged to the lower classes, in which the aristocratic words of
Aristotle about the mechanics were always as little understood as
our lower classes would understand the opinions of the "Junker"
on labour and trade; also the Cynics had already directly preached
the ethical value of work. The standpoint of the early Christians,
to whom manual labour was perfectly natural, was followed by
the demand that work should not be despised by the educated
Christians and by emphasis on the duty of charity towards the
working classes. Again and again the limited ancient political
ideal of the city-state appears, which assumes that a decent human
being lives on an income derived from land or business, and that
he has a great deal of leisure. The Christians, however, certainly
did increase the sense of the duty of labour. "If a man will not
work neither shall he eat" was strictly enforced. The refusal to
encourage beggars or the abuse of charity increased this attitude;
the man who would not work lost his right to receive relief. The
monks also were made to work; it remains to be proved how far
the same could be said of capitalists and large-property owners.
Here also the true ideal of labour was realized only in monasticism.
On this point an expression of Augustine is characteristic. He
demands work from the monks who come from the peasant and
labouring classes with the argument: If even a senator or a landowner who is unused to work must work in the cloister, how much
more is it the duty of peasants and labourers who are accustomed
to work. Above all, we must never forget that economic views
were very little developed in the Ancient World, and that among
the Christians they were quite naïve. Christians who have lost

[60a] See, however, the esteem in which the arts were held by Origen, *Seipel*, *159*;
here it is obvious that Greek culture has had its own influence.

their positions and their means of livelihood are answered in the following strain by Tertullian: "Hunger can have no terror for him who is ready to die with Christ." Against the objection that the giving away of goods in alms may endanger the existence of the family and the children Cyprian retorts: "God is the best guardian and steward for the children"; and this becomes a standing theme of Christian morality. It is Cyprian, too, who attributes economic distress to over-population and preaches celibacy as a cure; when the world was young the commandment at the Creation to increase was the right one, but for the old age of the world the command is the evangelical counsel of chastity. Augustine comforts a merchant who feels that he cannot conduct his business according to strictly moral principles with profit by saying that God, who has already nourished him while he was acting unrighteously, will much more support him when he is dealing righteously. The misgivings which people expressed in Constantinople, that after a "communistic" pooling of income and all has been spent there will be nothing left, were silenced by Chrysostom with the assurance that "the Lord will provide". With people of this kind it is no use looking for penetrating ideas on economic questions. The whole of modern political economy, and the modern pride in mastering the world in the technical and economic sphere, would have been just as unintelligible to them as anxiety about economic and social crises. They lived in an entirely different world. Yet this naïveté of theory in economic matters does not mean ignorance in practical affairs. The Church, which acquired great wealth in capital, slaves and land, whose bishops finally played a great part as large landowners, whose assistance was enlisted by the State—which was no longer equal to its responsibilities—for police work, the care of the poor, and the control of the population, possessed, on the practical side, an extraordinary intelligence in economic matters. Only its effect upon theory was either nil, or, at most, merely incidental.

THE CHURCH AND SOCIAL DISTINCTIONS: CLASSES AND CALLINGS

It is, therefore, not surprising that the Christians did not indulge in any criticism of the economic ideas which underlay the social life of the world around them; indeed, they do not appear to have felt that there was anything to observe or to criticize.[61] They seem to have accepted unquestioningly the whole social structure, with its professional and labour organization, its distribution of wealth

[61] See p. 185.

and property, and its social classification as part of the life of the
State; in the pre-Diocletian period, indeed, this organization varied
greatly; to a great extent it was still subject to free competition,
and it was only gradually regulated by the social policy of the
Emperor. As we have already seen, during the peace of the
Imperial period there never were any great social movements,
with an equally constructive criticism of social conditions, in
spite of the suppression of ancient capitalism by a bureaucratic
government, the decline in the slave markets, and the growth
of a mixed lower middle class composed of slaves, freedmen,
and free men. Indeed, it was only thus that it was possible for
a movement like Christianity to arise which was essentially
philanthropic but not social. Within their own circle and in
religious matters the Christians did away with social distinctions;
in every other sphere they allowed them to remain. The main
point is this: The Early Church seems to have been familiar with
the idea of variety in business and trade, and with differences of
rank and class, but it had no idea of a "calling", in the sense in
which that word was used in the central period of the Middle
Ages and by the early Protestants. The reason for this is obvious.
An ethic which starts from the point of view of an original equality,
and which holds that the differences that do exist are due to sin,
and which at its best regards the division of labour as a Divine
arrangement adapted to the needs of fallen humanity, is inherently unable to see any value in "callings" at all. At the beginning,
during the period when the Church appealed mainly to the lower
middle class, its eschatological outlook and the spirit of other-
worldliness had also prevented the development of this feeling.
At the outset the Jewish artisan point of view, the emphasis on
the absolutism of the Divine Government of the world, as well as
on predestination, had strongly emphasized the fact that external
inequality could exist alongside of an interior equality, while at
the same time work was held in high esteem. As the Church
strengthened her position, however, more and more clearly
religious equality stood out as an essentially attractive element in
Christian doctrine; it became fused with the Stoic ideal of
Reason, and it asserted that at least in the Primitive State entire
equality had prevailed. This, however, had the effect of decreasing
the social distinctions in the contemporary social order, although
it did not remove them. On the other hand, however, the social
order of the Imperial period did not provide a basis for the development of this conception; this was only given at a later stage by
the feudal society of the Middle Ages, and then, above all, by the

industrial town with its closely knit political and economic unity. Apart from the river-civilization of Egypt and Mesopotamia, the social life of the Imperial period was based upon the town with its democratic form of organization, upon the equal right of citizenship for all, upon a comparative freedom in trade and emigration (which, however, steadily decreased), upon differences in wealth and position, which determined the question of admission into the ranks of the upper classes, upon the industrial work of the lower classes, carried out by slaves or freedmen who were provisionally placed in charge; the latter were not permitted, however, to form independent municipal organizations similar to those which were afterwards developed by working men in the Middle Ages. The town still held the ideal of the "private gentleman and capitalist", and this class was obliged to remain part of the city proletariat. Above all, this social order of the Ancient World was determined by the fact that it was predominantly a coastal civilization, which only created towns as its centres of organization for military and commercial reasons. The social order of the Middle Ages, on the other hand, was based upon a continental or inland civilization, which produced a vastly more intensive and more richly differentiated agrarian, and then industrial, civilization with a stable organization. Thus, in the early days, even from the point of view of Society itself, there existed no stimulus which might eventually give birth to the idea of a stable, well-organized system of "callings" and of the division of labour. Until the time of Constantine all the leaders of the Church take this point of view; they regard all callings with complete indifference, as "fate" or "destiny", and they merely criticize them without attempting to make concrete constructive suggestions. From the third and fourth centuries onward, however, the social order of the Ancient World developed in the direction of settled organization; military and official positions became hereditary; compulsory associations of labourers were formed within the food-producing industries, and some of these corporations resembled the later institutions of feudal times. This development took place alongside of the gradual relapse into an economy based on agriculture, the growth of an inland civilization, the decrease in the value of money, and the State system of regulation which tried to grapple with these difficulties. It may be that this development gave rise to the idea which often appears in the writings of the Fathers of the fourth century—that is, of a necessary social organization which would be mutually complementary. This idea, however, was always entirely obliterated by their habit of harping upon the equality of the Primitive State, and their insistence on the restoration of equality by love and sacrifice, which, if it cannot be done in the world, must be carried out in the monastic life. The increasing esteem in which monasticism was held was due to the very fact that it seemed impossible to regard this social order—with all its difficulty, friction, conflict, and reaction—as a system of "callings" ordained by God and destined to contribute its part to the supreme religious meaning of life. On the other hand, we shall see that the Middle Ages only succeeded in fitting monasticism—that high explosive of all social systems—into its social order to the extent in which it made the monastic life one among several suitable "callings". Once this fact has been clearly perceived we have gained a very important clue to the understanding of the difference between primitive, mediaeval, and modern Christianity.

At first, under the influence of the eschatological outlook and the Pauline conservative attitude, the duty of the Christian was summed up in obedience to the exhortation, "Let every man abide in the same calling wherein he was called" (1 Cor. vii. 20), in which he was to maintain the Christian virtues. Thus Christians took part in all the general conditions of life and industry, and avoided only those callings which were impossible for them as Christians; those who had lost their work for this reason were cared for by the Church. In those stern early days, however, this principle of excluding all unsuitable employments cut very deeply into life. All offices and callings were barred which had any connection with idol-worship, or with the worship of the Emperor, or those which had anything to do with bloodshed or with capital punishment, or those which would bring Christians into contact with pagan immorality. This meant that Christians were debarred from taking service under the State or the municipality; they could not serve as judges or as officers in the army; any kind of military service, indeed, was impossible. The drama, art, and rhetoric were also forbidden. At first, however, these restrictions did not affect the Early Church very harshly, owing to the class from which its members were drawn. It was far more deeply affected by the exclusion from all technical occupations, from all arts and crafts which had any connection with idolatrous emblems or with pagan-worship: "Carpenters, stucco-workers, cabinet-makers, thatchers, goldleaf-beaters, painters, workers in bronze, and engravers—all these are forbidden to take any part whatever in any work which is necessary for temple service." That, of course, included all dealers in meat, flowers, and other things used in temple-worship. Magicians and astrologers are tabooed. A Christian could not be a school teacher nor a teacher of science, since those professions were connected with idolatry through the books they had to use and in other ways. The effect of all this on social life was very evident. The Christians were proud of this opposition between their way of life and that of paganism, and they laid stress on the fact that they were able to cause stagnation in trade. The pagans were aware of the danger; the famous report of Pliny emphasizes the economic desolation, and Celsus complains that if such principles prevail the Emperor will soon have no army and no officials, and that the Empire will perish. Origen's reply to this complaint is highly characteristic: "If all Romans would accept the Faith they would conquer their enemies by prayer and supplication, or rather they would no longer have any enemies at all, for the Divine power would preserve them." "There is no one who fights better for the King than we. It is true that we do not go with him into battle, even when he desires it, but we fight for him by forming an army of our own, an army of piety, through our prayers to the Godhead." "Once all men have become Christians, then even the barbarians will be inclined towards peace."

In such a situation, of course, it is clear that the question of social reform could not arise. The Church had no idea that the Christian criticism of Society ought to lead to an organic reform. The leaders of the Church believed that God would prevent Society from going to pieces. From the Christian point of view it was sufficient to renounce the forbidden professions and occupations; the rest of the social order could go on as usual. Indeed, the Christians had already gained a position which entitled them to be regarded, in the opinion of the writer of the *Epistle to Diognetus*, as "the soul" of the world. Characteristically this writer adds: "Christians are not differentiated from the rest of mankind by locality, language, or customs. . . . They dwell in cities of Greeks and of non-Greeks as their respective lot is cast, following the native customs in dress and food and the rest of life." The dominant idea is not that of a "calling", but of the lot which falls to each individual. The point on which most emphasis is laid is the "admirable and well-known system of the organization of the Christian community".[61a]

[61a] *ad Diognetum, 5, 4*: Κατοικοῦντες δε πόλεις ῾Ελληνίδας τε καὶ βαρβάρους, ὡς ἕκαστος ἐκληρώθη, καὶ τοῖς ἐγχωρίοις ἔθεσιν ἀκολουθοῦντες ἐν τῇ ἐσθῆτι καὶ διαίτῃ καὶ τῷ λοιπῷ βίῳ θαυμαστὴν καὶ ὁμολογουμένως παράδοξον ἐνδείκνυνται τὴν κατάστασιν τῆς ἑαυτῶν πολιτείας.

From the third century onwards the situation grew more difficult, for the Christians became more numerous in the higher ranks of Society and in the more eminent professions, in the army and in official circles. In several passages in the Christian writings there are indignant protests against participation in these things; on the other hand, we also find attempts to compromise—arguments designed to quiet uneasy consciences: "After all", they suggest, "these occupations are necessary for the social system, and therefore people ought to stay in them." Practically there were many ways of evading and softening these rules, and probably also a good deal of connivance on the part of the authorities, who saved the Christians from taking part in pagan worship, or made things easier for them. In the provinces there were even Christian *Flamens* of the Emperor-worship, who managed to evade participation in the cult itself, and yet enjoyed the social importance of their position. These difficulties, however, only occurred during the time of transition—that is, between the time when the Church had become a force, and its recognition by the State. From the time of Constantine these difficulties disappeared; friction between Christians and pagans ceased, and all offices in the State were thrown open.[62]

The Church was now able to assert that all these occupations formed an integral part of the social order; by participating in them, therefore, Christians were upholding the order of the State, of the *pax terrena*; and since the external difficulties caused by the taint of idol-worship had disappeared, Christians were now free to take part in the army, and in official and economic life in general. In all this, however, there was no idea of social reform. The only practices which were still forbidden were rough games, licentious drama, and pagan art; these the Church desired to see forbidden by law. The laws against the exposure of children, and against sins connected with marriage and sex, were also made more severe. The social system as a whole, however, was accepted as it was, or, rather, it was still entrusted to the care of the State, to which, it was felt, it naturally belongs. While the pre-Constantine Church was hostile to the State, and did not envisage or demand any social reform, holding itself entirely aloof from "this

[62] *Harnack: Militia, 71 ff., Bigelmair, 171.*—Lactantius still proclaims that the office of a judge is forbidden to a Christian owing to the power of a judge to inflict the death penalty. *Bigelmair, 123.* I do not know when these scruples disappeared. Cf. also *Ziegler: Gesch. d. christl. Ethik, p. 233.* In any case in the Donatist controversy the Church herself demanded the punishment of death for certain heretics. *Gass, I, 228.* With regard to the oath the position was similar.

fleeting world", and only taking part in it so far as it was possible from the Christian point of view, the post-Constantine Church had just as little idea of social reform because the reasons for holding aloof from social life had disappeared and the existing Imperial system seemed as immutable as ever. The process of secularization was in full swing, but it would not be right to regard this process simply as a mere participation in the life of the world and fusion with its spirit. Practically, of course, that was what it did mean for the masses, but genuine Christians and the religious leaders still regarded the world with all its institutions of property, labour, force, violence, and law as the result of sin. In participating in the life of the world the Christian submits to the consequences of sin, and within the secular organization he remains in the position to which he is called. The question is always whether a certain calling is permitted or not, or whether it ought to be modified or restricted in certain directions. The various occupations themselves, however, were hardly ever regarded as having a positive value of their own, or any inner connection with religious values. Inwardly, the Church still remained separate from the world; on her part within her own sphere she removed the consequences of sin by the exercise of love and gentleness; and the more difficult this task became for a Church which, as it spread, tended to become more and more identified with the world, the higher rose the value of monasticism, in which alone it was possible to redress the balance by a rigid practice of Christian principles.

The idea of a Christian civilization, of a spirit which should penetrate, mould, and renew the common life, was entirely absent; for that very reason also there was no idea that the Church might initiate any social reform. This, however, was not due simply to the thought of the Church: it was also due to the life of the day as a whole. The post-Diocletian Emperors did what they could, but they were able to do nothing more than conserve. The increasing financial difficulties of the State, and the continually increasing return to an economy based on agriculture, combined with the many disasters and catastrophes which took place, made it impossible to think of anything save actual preservation. The social policy of the Church consisted simply in supporting the State in this endeavour, and in placing her organization at the disposal of the State. Even if the Church had wished to do differently it would have been quite impossible. Further, the old customs had an immense tenacity, as is shown by the fact that the Church never once succeeded permanently in removing free divorce; i.e. divorce without a legal sentence, only on the basis of a mutual agreement. Thus in her attitude towards the social and economic organizations of the day the Church was divided between submission to the conditions imposed by sin and insistence on the monastic communistic ideal of love. Only incidentally do ideas appear now and again which were to dominate the thought of the later Middle Ages, namely, that the mutual integration of callings and groups of workers is willed by God, and that therefore they are to be regarded as the normal Divine order. The same Chrysostom who utters these ideas would like, however, to turn Constantinople and Antioch into a communistic fellowship of love like the monastic life; at the same time he calms the fears of his wealthy hearers by assuring them that in the present situation it will not be possible to carry out these ideas[62a] in practice. In this thought, and in that of almost all the other Fathers of the Church, their realistic reflections on the actual state of the world are constantly mingled with the Stoic-Christian idea of the equality of the Primitive State.

PROBLEM OF TRADE

One particularly difficult question in social life was that of trade.[63] Since most Christians lived in cities, that is, in conditions which assumed the existence and the use of money, they could not dream of doing away with trade. They therefore accepted it entirely; even the monasteries sold the products of their labour, and right into the fourth century the clergy lived on the proceeds of trade and business; later on Church property was administered on these lines, and it even enjoyed immunity from taxation. Trade was, however, certainly surrounded by strong precautions. From the ascetic point of view it was suspect since it assumed pleasure in possessions and in gain, and from the point of view of the principle of love it was suspect because it meant taking from one to give to another, and enriching oneself at the expense of others. The practices connected with trade on a larger scale such

---

[62a] See p. 185.

[63] Cf. Brentano: *Wirtschaftl. Lehren; Funk: Kirchengesch. Absch.*, II, 60 ff., *Zins und Wucher im christlichen Altertum* (*Tübinger Theol. Quartalschrift, 1875*), *Zins und Wucher, 1868, Seipel, 162–182; Ratzinger: Volkswirtschaft, 222–269; Endemann: Die Nationalökonomischen Grundsätze der kanonistischen Lehre (Jahrb. für National-ökonomie und Statistik, 1863); Bigelmair, 306–321.* The subject has been treated by many writers; that is why here I only call attention to some of the main points. *Brentano* allows himself to be too much influenced by the authors whose sympathies are with monasticism. See also *Max Weber: Agrargeschichte (Altertum), p. 120.*

as monopolies, forestalling the market, money-lending and usury, calculation and exploitation of the turn of the market, and the various tendencies to seek one's own advantage and to dishonesty increased moral misgivings. In theological theory, therefore, trade was considered the most reactionary form of earning a living, ethically lower in the scale than agriculture and manual labour, and it was safeguarded by the precautionary regulation that in fixing the price all that might be asked was the costs of production plus the additional amount necessary for a moderate profit. After the reign of Diocletian prices and taxes were regulated, and the doctrine of an objective, just, and fixed price was developed; this seems to have been due less to theological theory than to the practical course of actual events. All that the theologians cared about was to prevent profits exceeding the sum that was necessary for a man to gain a living. Priests, however, were forbidden to engage in trade, so far as it became possible to support them out of Church funds. All that this amounts to, however, is an acknowledgment of retail business. Wholesale business was still regarded with suspicion, and the Church forbade the business connected with it which involved credit and interest; it supported its theory by appealing to the Jewish law (which only permitted interest to be taken from aliens)[63a] and to the Gospel; its main objection, however, was based on the feeling that usury was an exploitation of distress which injured the spirit of love. In all these expressions of opinion we see the point of view of love and comradeship, which considers the taking of interest within an intimate group an indecent and unloving practice, a point of view which is usual "among brethren" in groups which are undeveloped from the economic point of view. There is still no hint of the theoretical scholastic argument of Aristotelian economics about the unproductiveness of money.[63b] We can also understand the heated opposition of the great Church leaders to usury when we remember how harsh was the system of usury and of the collection of debts during a period when Society was relapsing from an economic system based on money into one based on agriculture. At that time, in fact, the system of usury was a lucrative method of extorting money out of those who had got into difficulties and of monopolistic exploitation; it was not the stimulation of a process of production through productive capital. Ideas of that kind were naturally alien to the

[63a] See above, p. 87.
[63b] Sommerlad (p. 136) believes that in Gregory of Nazianzen there is an allusion to this.

thought of the Church. Practically, these theological inhibitions had very little effect; as long as the economic system based on money lasted it resisted them quite successfully; it was always possible to meet the anti-capitalistic theological arguments with all kinds of Scriptural and other suitable reasons; it was not in vain that the Bible had said, "All things are yours". All the same, however, in principle these doctrines were quite important: they meant that Christianity only permitted its followers to earn sufficient to maintain life at a very moderate level of comfort; the early Christians had no idea of an unlimited and increasing productiveness, which leads to a general rise in the standard of living. They regarded the world as ruined by sin, and yet good at the same time; but the good in it is merely the satisfaction of the minimum of the external needs of life, by using the ordinances permitted by God; and this "minimum" fluctuates between a moderate self-indulgence and an ascetic severity.

THE CHURCH AND THE FAMILY

Hitherto, after an initial period of hesitation and restraint, as it penetrated into the higher ranks of Society, to an increasing extent the Church had accepted the existing conditions, and had only attempted to regulate them at ethically doubtful points; in any case, neither before nor after did it attempt to transform the social system; the attitude of the Church towards the inmost heart of the system, the family,[64] was, however, entirely different. At this point the moulding of conditions was so closely bound up with the contemporary value and conception of the life of the individual that here the realization of the ideal meant that the Church had to intervene and transform hostile circumstances. The family with its patriarchal dominion of man and its compulsory matrimonial right was, indeed, still regarded as a consequence of the Fall, like all law and all compulsion which had replaced the complete inner freedom of the Primitive State. Others, however, argued that the manner of Eve's creation proves that the subjection of women is in the natural order of things; however, the overlordship of man was only established when the curse was pronounced and Adam and Eve were driven out of Paradise. Here, however, adaptation to the ideals of the world is strictly limited. From the very beginning the Church set before its members a high and strict ideal; it required them to observe the ideal of monogamy, of chastity before marriage (for both husband and wife), of conjugal fidelity, to exercise an ethical

[64] See p. 185.

and religious discipline in the care of children, to reject all regulation of the birth-rate by the exposure of children or by artificial sterilization; and after the Church was established by the State, as far as possible this ideal was made a general principle of Society, partly by the influence of the Church upon ecclesiastical law, penitential order and discipline, and partly by its influence upon the law of the State. According to the religious philosophy of the Church, which was based upon that of the Bible, the monogamous family is the basis of Society and of the State, which has itself been formed by the expansion of the family; among pagans the idea of the family had become most confused and perverted by its false views of sex, and it was radically purified by the Christians in order to serve as the foundation of a purer and better order of life; it was, indeed, only able to submit to the external forms of the existing marriage law amid continual conflict. The question has often been discussed: How far can the alterations in Roman matrimonial law during the Byzantine period be attributed to Christian influence? There was "a perpetual struggle between the highest ideals of Christianity—permission only of complete marriage and that only as an indissoluble union—and the motives of the secular legal system, which, indeed, was interested in the stabilization of the family, but which also had to take into account the ingrained habits of the socially dominant classes". Among these customs was the Roman habit of concubinage, which was always monogamous and quite public, and the contract character of a legitimate marriage, which also implied that it could be easily dissolved. Constantine forbade married men to have extra-matrimonial connections, and made concubinage difficult by making invalid all gifts and legacies from the man to his companion and to his children. His Christian successors attempted now and again to make it more difficult to dissolve a marriage by limiting the reasons for divorce, and by confining women more closely to their homes they tried to ensure the greater purity of marriage. The effort to gain recognition for the families of slaves was successful; at the same time their growth was furthered by the transformation of slaves, on economic grounds, into serfs and *coloni*; they were also allowed to expand, and it was ordered that families of slaves were not to be separated from each other in an arbitrary manner.

The Justinian legislation, then, was a compromise, largely controlled by economic and State interests; its main points may be thus summarized: the permission of concubinage, with the nearest approximation to legitimate marriage; the removal of inequality of rank as a hindrance to marriage; divorce made difficult, with the strongest possible emphasis on the only reason for divorce allowed by the Church, that of adultery, and thus in principle the destruction of the freedom of contract in matters of marriage; decree for the protection of slave marriages, while slave children who are set free receive the inheritance rights of legitimate children; limitation of the *patria potestas* in favour of the power of holding property of the children of the house, and the capacity of the wife for the guardianship of her children; and a better right of inheritance for the wife towards her husband, and of the children in relation to their mother. The Church, however, did not succeed in carrying through the strict doctrine of divorce, nor the rejection of concubinage.

Alongside of this influence of Christian thought upon the idea of the Family there were, however, the quite different ideas of Christian asceticism and the ideal of celibacy. This dual character of the Christian sex ethic was already apparent in the thought of Paul, and under the influence of asceticism and monasticism it led to a grotesque exaltation of sexual restraint, which again led to the well-known ideas about the danger inherent in the female sex and to a low estimate of women—these ideas certainly arose out of the overstrained imagination of monasticism, and not out of the thought of Christianity.

We must not forget the other side of the question, however, for the state of virginity and the establishment of convents for women gave a value and a position to the unmarried woman, which gave women an influence and scope in spiritual matters, which again worked out to the advantage of the position and understanding of women. In any case, this development had an immense influence, sometimes it seemed as though the "virgin state" constituted the very heart of Christianity. St. Methodius of Olympus, in his "psalm of the Virgins", transforms Plato's *Symposion*—the great song in praise of the love of men and the metaphysical significance of Beauty—into a conversation of self-denying virgins about Divine things. Later monasticism penetrated into every part of life, and as far as possible it controlled the lives of the clergy. The Augustan legal penalties against being unmarried were removed in its favour. We may conjecture with some certainty that the terrifying and sudden increase of monasticism (as, for instance, in Egypt) must have been due to reasons which were not all ideal, and it is clear that that was not due to the spirit of the Gospel.[65]

[65] For the economic reasons, see *Uhlhorn, I, 234*; it is the flight from oppressive taxation, forcible serfdom, and the inherited guild compulsion into freedom.

This phenomenon, however, was of general significance for the early Christian Church in that it shows that its real spirit was renunciation of the world, and not world reform, and that this renunciation is simply the Gospel spirit of indifference to the world in another form. It is, however, equally important to recognize that alongside of this ascetic element marriage which has been consecrated by religion is regarded as completely justified, and is not considered as something merely incidental; it belongs to the Divine Order of creation. As the Christian ethic developed further its characteristic element was not the ascetic view of sex, but the fact that the sex ethic split into two parts, one of which was ascetic and one of which consecrated the natural instincts. In this respect the development of the sex ethic was typical of the whole ethic of the Early Christian Church. It is not a concession of original and essential asceticism to Nature, but only in such a division of fundamental instincts could the Christian Ethos, by embracing the conditions of life in the great world, live freely according to its inmost nature. The heroism which admits the natural basis of life, but which is willing to enter into life maimed for the sake of the supernatural end which will shortly appear, was only possible during the period of the earliest struggles and the earliest hopes, in small groups which lived apart from the world. In the complicated conditions of the social life of the great world these two aspects of the sex ethic diverged; the one adapted itself to the life of the world, the other became asceticism.

THE CHURCH AND SLAVERY

Closely connected with the question of the Family is that of slavery—at least, so far as domestic slavery is concerned.[66] Here, in the sphere of close personal relations, the Christianized and spiritualized patriarchalism of Paul is dominant; the responsibility of the master for the physical and spiritual welfare of his slaves, while the slave is exhorted to love and obey his master, since he serves God and not man. To this extent, at least inwardly, the nature of the slave relationship was neutralized by the claims of the ideal. Outwardly, however, slavery was merely part of the general law of property and of the order of the State, which Christianity accepted and did not try to alter; indeed, by its moral guarantees it really strengthened it. This applies very clearly to slave labourers, whose lot, however, was already being humanized in the natural course of events by the merging of slavery into the colonate or serfdom. In the opinion of Christian

[66] See p. 186.

thinkers this right to possess slaves was due, like all law, to the
Fall, and since then it has been an institution which God has
permitted to exist. It was due originally to excessive human greed
—above all, to the curse of Noah on the irreverent Shem. "The
State is based upon the original misdeeds of humanity, and the
particular institution of slavery is founded upon the same basis of
error. Thus, it is true that it is only human laws which make
distinction between slaves and freemen, but, like all the other
contrasts which make up the State, the institution of slavery is a
rod of discipline in the Hands of God, and in this sense namely,
the law of the State, which keeps the slave in bonds, is also appointed by God; thus it may not be transgressed so long as it
does not demand from the slave anything which displeases God."
To that St. Augustine with his predestinarian views adds the
argument of the natural inequality of mankind.

Thus the Christians changed nothing whatever in the laws
affecting slaves. They protected slave marriages, urged non-
Christians to set their slaves free, or to let them buy their freedom
because they thought that the religious welfare of the slaves
was imperilled; they themselves encouraged the manumission of
slaves as a "good work" involving self-denial and the renunciation
of one's possessions; later on, however, the majority of the slaves
were set free for economic reasons. The Church granted the
principle of religious equality to its fullest extent to slaves; later,
when the process of secularization had begun, and merely secular
standards of social value were erected, this ideal was modified;
it was then felt to be too great a menace to the stability of the
general social order, and Gregory the Great revoked the previous
laws which had permitted slaves to hold office in the Church. As
a legal institution, however, even with all its barbarous penalties,
slavery still existed. The Christian Church allowed it to endure,
without question, right on into the Middle Ages—it was only
largely modified by the process of economic evolution—yet the
Church was fully conscious of the inconsistency between this
institution and the inner freedom and equality which was the
Christian ideal. This forms a most typical illustration of the
attitude of Christians towards the world; they renounced the
world, and yet they compromised with it, and they did not, and
could not, dream of making any changes in the social system.

THE CHURCH AND THE PRACTICE OF CHARITY

At the same time, however, the Church was conscious of the
harm and suffering caused by this social system, and she was not

at all willing to adapt herself to it—with all the suffering it caused
—without protest. Her reaction in this particular, however, did
not take the shape of social reform, or of organic change: it was
simply and solely the work of charity.[67] That was her way of
healing social wounds, and in point of fact it constitutes a brilliant
chapter in her history. In the early centuries it was directed in-
wards towards creating a haven of vital mutual aid within the
pagan environment. Later on, in times of great distress and
misery, which affected the masses of the people, the Church lifted
the burden from the State on to her own shoulders, often creating
her own centres of social service and charity.

"It is the aim of the Church to give parental care to the orphan,
to be a husband to the widow, to help those who are ready for
marriage to make a home, to give work to the unemployed, to
show practical compassion to those who cannot work, to give
shelter to the stranger, food to the hungry, drink to the thirsty,
to see that the sick are visited, and that help is forthcoming for
the prisoners." In addition, there was the help given in times of
public calamity, the burial of the dead, and the help given to the
churches amongst themselves. In the early days all this took
place through the Church itself, when bishop and almoner knew
everyone personally, and were thus in a position to centralize
their work, and yet at the same time to treat everyone as an
individual. Church discipline was a help against abuses, and
distress which the Church could not touch was met by an extraordinary exercise of private charity. In the post-Constantine
period this charitable activity broadened out to meet the growing
social need and the rapidly increasing number of Church members,
by the erection of institutions, hostels for travellers, and hospitals,
by undertaking to feed and control masses of people living in the
towns—by turning the ecclesiastical power of jurisdiction and
right of giving asylum to the use of protecting the suffering,
alongside of which the activity of the cloister and an infinitely
varied private philanthropy were exercised. In this book, however, we are not so much concerned with these particular
illustrations as with the spirit and temper of the whole and its
relation to the whole world situation. Here there are three points
to which I would call your attention.

(1) The aim of this charity was not the healing of social wrongs,
nor the endeavour to remove poverty, but the revelation and
awakening of the spirit of love, of that love which Christ imparts
and in which He makes known to us the attitude of God Himself.

[67] See p. 186.

Above all else, the Church desires to show love and to awaken the response of love. The relief of distress which she actually achieves is the result of this spirit, not her first intention, but this happy effect itself is a proof of the Divine origin of this new principle of love. Poverty is still highly honoured, as a method by which we reach the knowledge of God; indeed, it is often voluntarily induced by giving away all one's possessions. At the same time, the relief of distress extends no farther than securing the minimum of existence. The spirit of restraint and simplicity of life are not to be given up; rather this spirit ought to be encouraged both in those who give and in those who receive. Both almsgiving and the method of charity ought to be regulated by this standard. It is only the emphasis laid on the religious nature of this love as the revelation of a spirit, combined with the exaltation of poverty, which explains the fact that this charitable activity very soon, and quite naturally—as the earlier ethic of love shrank into one of "good works"—was able to merge itself in ascetic achievements, whose aim was no longer the welfare of others but the salvation of one's own soul. At first, however, love pressed forward and conquered distress, and the new religion of love was extolled because by means of this love it naturally overcame social distress and suffering, and still more that beyond the sufferings themselves it conquered the spirit in which these sufferings were felt to be too oppressive. Then, however, it immediately became a branch of asceticism and self-denial.

(2) The relief of distress which was thus the result of love was deliberately restricted to philanthropy, to voluntary contributions for parish relief, and to the free exercise of private charity. The aim was a new spirit, not a new social order. In the post-Constantine period certainly the Church permitted her institutions, her legal system, and her bishops to receive privileges from the State, and she placed at the disposal of the State authorities, and then of the legal administration, her own methods of charity and discipline, her authority and her registers, but she did not seek to urge the spirit of social responsibility upon the administration; preferring to use it for her own ends, merely requiring from the State support for her own charitable activity. In so doing, however, she renounced the one method by which permanent reforms might have been secured. That, however, was not an accidental short-sightedness and lack of insight on the part of Christian thought, but it arose in principle out of its attitude towards the world. The Church still felt that in spite of the presence of so much that is good in the world, which is permitted by God, the

world still remains the realm of sin and of Satan, the place of
pilgrimage and of preparation for Heaven; thus there is no need
to think of a positive improvement of this world at all—indeed,
the fundamental spirit of religion is more secure if such questions
are entirely ignored. The services which the Christian State
renders to the Church do not affect this principle one whit.
The question whether, with such principles, it will ever be
possible to overcome social distress, even to the extent of securing
a minimum of existence, is one which the Church, with her
confidence in God and her own absolute self-assurance, will not
allow to be broached at all.

In the earlier centuries, when better economic conditions prevailed, the Church did, indeed, succeed in overcoming distress and
want; in the mass misery of the later period the Church often
struggled to overcome it with immense resources, but in vain;
then the Church came to the conclusion that all this misery was a
punishment from God and a sign of the imminent end of the
world.

(3) The third point is this: That a social reform of this kind,
based on love alone—in so far as it wished to be social reform at
all—was only possible, both practically and spiritually, in small
and intimate communities, with the pressure of external opposition to hold them together, in which, to some extent at least, its
members were drawn from the same social class. When all this
ceased, and in the absence of external opposition the Church
became co-extensive with the whole of Society and bore in her
bosom the differences of all, then the work of charity became a
different thing altogether. Relationship between the brethren
became abstract and general, and giving became impersonal—
to the Church, to institutions. Charity became depersonalized;
the bishops allowed it to be carried out by their officials on the
basis of the registers; in the hands of wealthy bishops and landowners it often resembled the old Roman liberality. On the other
hand, private almsgiving was frittered away in indiscriminate
charity. In this atmosphere the whole practice of charity was
changed from being a means of help to others into a practice of
ascetic self-denial, into "good works" which acquire merit for
oneself and for others, into penances for sin, and into a means of
mitigating the fires of purgatory. This tendency was encouraged
not only by the fact that the original impulse of charity had turned
into asceticism, but also by the fact that the very real, even
though restricted, social interest which this original impulse
contained found it impossible to realize its ideals in these enor-

mous and unwieldy Christian communities and under impersonal mass conditions. The aim and meaning of charity became warped, and in spite of an ever-renewed emphasis on the spirit of love, and in spite of some magnificent achievements, Christian philanthropy lost its earlier spirit, which was closely connected with the original motive of overcoming social distress, of equalizing the distribution of wealth, and of the increase of the spirit of fellowship within the Church itself. Thus hospitals, convents, and episcopal works of charity lasted on into the Middle Ages as very important agencies of civilization; at the same time, however, they were also ascetic institutions, for which it was worth while making sacrifices, since such actions are also the means of acquiring personal merit and of thus ensuring personal salvation. The idea of equalizing social conditions within the Church itself for love's sake has entirely disappeared. This, however, only shows that the social significance and power of achievement of this Christian philanthropy in general were extremely limited. In spite of the fact that in its own way this philanthropy was absolutely necessary and important, it did not provide any solution of the social problem in general; indeed, it only desired to offer such a solution to a very limited extent, because it only regarded the social problem itself as the healing of the most external distress and suffering by assuring a minimum of existence; beyond this the Church simply exhorted mankind to submit to the sufferings of this sinful world and accept all the trials of this "our earthly pilgrimage". The Church was also careful to point out that that "minimum" was not even a right or a claim, but a gift of love, to be received in love and humility. The main point was the creation of loving relationships in the spirit of love, not the giving of material help.

The result of this teaching in the softening and spiritualizing of human relationships was, in the nature of the case, very extensive and important, but it did not effect any organic reform. That was prevented by its conception of the State and the world. To what extent the assertion which is frequently made, that the "softening of the hard Roman Conception of property" was a result of this Christian influence, is true or not, I am not in a position to say. Wherever I have read this assertion it has never been supported by evidence. From the legal point of view it seems much more probable that this statement is not in accordance with the facts. From the ethical point of view the attitude of the Early Church was rather one of misgiving about the right to hold property at all, combined with the religious duty of charity, than a sense of the common responsibility of Society for its members, and thus a restriction of the individual's right to hold property in the interest of the whole. This latter viewpoint assumes that already there is in existence an interest in the development of Society as a whole, but it was precisely that element which was absent from the thought of the Early Church.

RISE OF A NEW CLASS

In its philanthropy the Church undertook the immense task of trying to heal the social evils of a social order whose problems were constantly increasing in difficulty. The activity of the Church, however, did not constitute an interference with this social order; it had no vision of an organic reorganization of Society on a new basis. In this respect the one result produced by Christianity was its own actual reality as a Church. As such it meant the creation of a new class within the social order, and it thus introduced an important element into the organization of the State, which was becoming more and more divided up into classes. From the time of Constantine the bishops and the clergy under them were recognized publicly and legally as a special class, and succeeding Emperors granted them increasingly more and more privileges as a class, so that the highest rank of the episcopate was on the same level as the highest dignitaries in the State and the leading politicians. The fact that these offices were not hereditary meant that the State, through its influence upon appointments, could exercise a continual control over this powerful class, and could even utilize it for its own ends. The prestige and privileged position of this class were heightened by various causes: special class privileges, the right to acquire property, the bestowal of grants and immunities, the oversight of the property belonging to pagan temples and to heretics, the right to accept legacies, the reversion of the private fortune of priests to the Church if there were no direct heirs, and the immense zeal in giving which was displayed by sinners and by those who desired to earn Heaven. An immense system of "dead hand" came into being, and, above all, the Church had acquired an immense amount of landed property. But although the development of this new class meant a great deal to the State, which was developing increasingly upon "class" lines, and although it brought to the State new forces for its use as well as some dangerous and uncertain elements, and although this development of this special class was most important for the coming mediaeval period (that is, for the transformation of an ancient democracy and of the bureaucratic idea of a world-state into the monarchical system, with its ranks and classes, and its social system based on agriculture), to the Early Church itself, so far as the introduction of Christian ethical ideas into social life was concerned, it did not mean a great deal. Outside the charitable activity led by the bishop, carried out by numerous officials, combining the care of the poor in their own homes with that in institutions, the clergy had not very much scope. The bishop was supposed to feed daily with the poor, and he did so very often, the clergy too were to be poor and without ostentation, an example of self-sacrifice to others, and in a great many instances they lived up to this ideal. Church property was to be used for the poor and for public ends. But the influence of Christian ideas on the Imperial legislation was quite insignificant. In this direction the new class achieved nothing (and perhaps it did not wish to achieve anything), beyond the extirpation of pagans and heretics and the gaining of privileges for the Church. Everything else the Church regarded as her own affair, and here she continued the old tradition of alienation from the State and from the existing social order. She brought with her from the old co-operative situation the habit of a far-reaching exercise of arbitration by the bishops in civil disputes and an ecclesiastical handling of criminal cases. On the ground of parity the former was officially conceded both to the Christian and to the Jewish Patriarchs; one could demand from the State the enforcement of episcopal awards of arbitration and bring a great number of legal affairs before the episcopal courts, until Arcadius and Honorius abolished this competitive legislation. The principles upon which this verdict was based would have given us an insight into the Christian-Social outlook of that period, but unfortunately I have been unable to find out anything about them. The chief point, however, is that this competitive legislative activity was not a social reform but a relic of the continuance of the Church as a state within the State, which meant a continued aloofness from the State and from Society in general, and it was for this reason that the Emperors felt obliged to do away with it. Criminal legislation had been administered on similar lines, but here the State was far less inclined to make concessions. Even where criminal charges against the clergy were involved, the Church only succeeded for a brief period in reserving them for her own courts. All that the Church was able to do was to gain certain privileges for the legal treatment of the higher clergy, and an indirect influence by the development of the institution of mediation and by influencing the execution of the penalty and the exercise of mercy; she also brought strong pressure to bear upon the judges by threatening them with ecclesiastical punishments. All this affected the practice of the law in many directions; Christian ideas modified it in many ways; it also served to protect persons who were marked out by the Church as meritorious, either on account of their orthodoxy or their partisanship, against the law and power of the world; it called forth, therefore, also the harshest inhibitions from the Emperors. In spite of all this, however, the Church did not exert a humanizing and softening influence upon the legal system as a whole; on the contrary, in the Christian era it became increasingly cruel and hard; the collapse of the social order demanded harsher methods, and the visible influence of Christianity upon the law consisted merely in the introduction of dogmatic intolerance and religious persecution into the legal administration.

The social position accorded to the bishops had one result, however, which was far more important than the others which have been previously mentioned. They were given public judicial authority in all matters which concerned the care of the poor, and social welfare as a whole. To a State which was itself no longer able to deal with the problem of social distress, the bishops seemed the most suitable persons, since they had the ancient practice of the Church in these things behind them and were also in possession of vast wealth in ecclesiastical property.

"The bishop was recognized by the State as the patron of the poor and the wretched. Thus, in a situation characterized by the lack of any State system for the care of the poor, by harsh and cruel legislation (especially in the law of punishment), by the utter wretchedness of the masses, by ceaseless wars, and from the fifth century onwards by the increasingly frequent and terrible Barbarian invasions, the Church and the bishops were able to make the most beneficent use of the splendid privileges which were granted to them by the State."

Thus, for instance, the right of sanctuary lay in the hands of the Church; it was transferred from the pagan temples and the Imperial statues to the Christian churches, and it was bound up with the episcopal right of mediation. This right, however, was now only enjoyed by orthodox Christians, and in many ways it became an ecclesiastical means of power to be used against the State authorities, who therefore tried to restrict it in various ways; in particular, it was prevented from being used too much for the protection of the economically weak, like debtors and slaves; thus the ecclesiastical right of sanctuary was really less humane than the pagan law.

The Church also waged war on the traffic in girls, and against excesses in the conduct of brothels; she strove to suppress the custom of the exposure of children and undertook the care of foundlings; the Church also supervised the control of punishment in the prisons, especially in ransoming prisoners of war; in this case, however, the Church was unable to prevent those who were thus set free from being forced to work on great estates which were unable to find sufficient labour. It was part of the duty of the Church also to ease the lot of the slaves, and it did this by obtaining the right which decreed that the freeing of a slave both before the praetor as well as before the bishop could lead legally to full Roman citizenship. The Church exhorted the faithful to free their slaves as a "good work" of asceticism, and undertook to protect those who were set free from being enslaved once more. The Church was, however, unable to free her own slaves, because they were part of Church property and as such were inalienable, an inconsistency characteristic of the whole situation. This inconsistency also suggests that the ecclesiastical system of land ownership can scarcely have been administered on the lines of Christian "model farms". Rather everything suggests that this property was administered according to the principles of production of those days, without any special reference to Christian considerations. The only Christian "model farms" were the monasteries, which, however, had broken with the principles of the world altogether.

The social function of the new class was, therefore, very important, and under the protection and privileges of the State it gave Christian ideas a very fair opportunity of exercising their influence. In the main, however, it was only a corrective and a softening of existing conditions: it merely modified some of the worst features of the existing social order, while the ecclesiastical love of power and the exclusiveness of Christianity added fresh severities. The Church was simply another institution alongside of the world and of the State. The very fact that by the isolation of the clergy as a special class the Church was a distinct social phenomenon, was due to this idea of detachment from the world; it meant that the Church and the clergy had secured a position alongside of the world, but it did not mean that the clergy were able to dominate and influence civilization as a whole.

This is why, on the other hand, in spite of all their service to the whole, so much emphasis is laid upon the contrast between the clergy and the world; that, too, is the reason for the constantly renewed and explicitly stated command to the clergy to take no

part in State business or in official public work. This also is why
clerical celibacy was required for purely ascetic reasons, and not
from any idea of making men more able to dominate in the
political and social sphere, and this also accounts for the fact that
monasticism was recommended as the nursery for the higher
clergy, in contrast to the secular clergy who were drawn from the
ranks of the aristocracy. Although this politico-social attitude of
the clergy provided an important basic element for mediaeval
ideas, there was still no trace of the characteristically mediaeval
idea that from their position of influence they might claim
their right to the spiritual leadership of civilization as a
whole.[67a]

THE CHURCH AND SCIENCE

In contrast to this widespread detachment of the Church from
the world we must, however, admit that at one point there was
an almost complete fusion of the Church and the world. It is,
however, characteristic of the whole situation that this did not
take place within the sphere of social life, but in a purely intellectual realm—in that of science. This fusion with science introduced into the Church the social theories of ancient speculation,
and, in so doing, indirectly it had an extremely powerful influence
upon her own social outlook. It is, indeed, not difficult to understand why this fusion took place—science was the element which
had the least connection with the existing order, and in the
system of the division of labour it had produced the fewest fixed
forms and embodiments of its own theories; it was, indeed, the
one element which had almost entirely outgrown the conditions of
life in the ancient world. If we look into the question more closely,
however, here also we discover that fundamentally the Church
has the same attitude towards the world as elsewhere; in the
sphere of science, however, far more than in the social sphere,
tendencies from late antiquity were present which exerted an
influence far beyond the ancient world and its previous way of
life. The Church had left the strongly rhetorical system of education and culture untouched, contenting herself with a few pre-
caution . In questions that affected the general world outlook,
howeve:, she exercised a severe discrimination. Christian writers,
scholars, and teachers only appropriated for their own use those
elements in the religious and ethical philosophy of late antiquity
which had an affinity with Christianity and a similar outlook
on the world. The culminating act in this process, which was so

[67a] See p. 187.

significant for world history, was the fusion of Christianity with Platonism and with the religious element in Stoicism.

Platonism provided Christianity with its unique Gospel of Redemption, with a universal theoretical foundation of mysticism : in the great process by which the world comes forth from God and returns to God, through the Logos or the knowledge of God, Christian redemption is assigned the significance of being regarded as the completion of this process.

To the Christian ethic, which was clumsy both in its terminology and its conceptions, and concerned only with obvious happenings, Stoicism gave both a theoretical foundation and a terminology: the moral Natural Law as the dominion of the Divine Reason over passion and desire in man, and the unification of mankind in the common possession of the Divine Reason—that constitutes the heart and the positive content of the Christian ethic, which is innate in man, then formulated in the Decalogue, and which has finally been proclaimed afresh in the teaching of Christ; all that had to be added was only the special "Evangelical Counsels" or the higher Christian virtues, as well as the Christian system of the means of grace, and the reinvigoration by grace of a will which is either weak or wholly corrupt.

The world-principle of the Logos, who became man in Christ and founded the Church, and on the other hand the moral Law of Nature, which was given with the Logos, contained in the Law of Moses and in the universal moral teaching of Jesus, forms the support for the doctrine of perfection which aims at the future life; those are the two fundamental conceptions and cardinal points of all scientific theology and ethics, in which it differs from the more Biblical and popular Christianity of the lower strata of Society, which attached itself especially to the religious myth, and on a large scale accepted the ancient faith of the people.[67b]

The acceptance of ancient science did not, however, go farther than this. Empiricism was passionately rejected, and natural science was ignored. The *Physiologus* and *Topographia Christiana* of Cosmas Indicopleustes are examples of a view of Nature which is a mixture of Biblical ideas and fantastic fairy-tales. History and criticism likewise were left out of account. Their view of history was represented by monkish legends with their grotesque miracles, by the primeval Scriptural history embroidered with additions from secular historians, with the four world-empires

[67b] For the difference between these two sections of the population see my article, *Der Begriff des Glaubens*. *Z. f. Religion und Geisteskultur, 1907.*

of the Book of Daniel which began with Nimrod and lasted to the present time.

In this opposition to the empirical exact sciences Christianity joined forces with the specific tendency of declining antiquity, and helped to hasten the decline of critical and purely positive knowledge. In the scientifically educated upper classes its religious ideas were fused with Stoicism and Platonism, i.e. with the dualistic, mystical, and ethical-humanitarian forces, and there arose a Christian philosophy and a Christian rhetoric and sophism; in the lower classes the myth continued to flourish, mingled with elements of the ancient popular religion and its forms of worship.[68]

A more detailed study of this question belongs to the history of dogma. For our subject in particular the first and most important point is only the assimilation of Stoicism into Christian thought—the acceptance of the "Stoic Natural Law, or the Divine Law, or the Law of Nature". For this acceptance of Stoicism was not merely the means of fixing and defining the ethical conceptions in general within Christianity, but it was also the means of placing the world, that is, the State, the law, and the system of social functions, in the right relation to the existence of the Church and the community of the redeemed.

Up to this point nearly everything which has been described had to do with the interior order of the Church, with social organization as an essential part of its own life, and the conception of the State and of the world only emerged to the extent in which both of them affected the inner life of the Church; now, however, we have to deal with the relation of the Church to the State as a whole and on its external side. It is precisely in this development, however, that we shall see the extraordinary significance of the ethic of Stoicism, its conception of Nature and of its law. Harmonizing already with the thought of Paul, the Apologists and the Alexandrians took this conception and made it the foundation of the Christian ethic in close connection with the Logos idea. From the time of the Fathers of the fourth century this idea comes more and more to the front, together with the doctrine of the corruption of the Natural Law by the Fall, as we have already seen. Above all, it was this idea which finally made it possible for the Church to come to terms with the State, and it also provided her with a theoretical reply to the question of her relation with the world. The service which Neo-Platonism rendered to theology was rendered to ethics, and above all to social philo-

[68] See p. 187.

sophy, by Stoicism. Not until the later Middle Ages shall we see
the Neo-Platonist categories expand in social theory also beyond
the categories of the Stoics.[69]

CHRISTIANITY AND THE STATE

Thus we have now arrived at the last of the great social
problems of Christianity; the relation of Christianity to the State.

In studying the relation between Church and State it is
possible to go along two lines. We can inquire how far the fundamental theory of sociological behaviour and feeling, as Christianity has evolved it in reference to the religious object, has
possibly, consciously or unconsciously, also been carried over into
the other sociological types? To what extent Christian individualism has awakened the sentiments of freedom, equality, and self-
respect in the State, in Society, in the community, and in the
family? And also how far its universalism of love has also introduced Christian patriarchal sentiments into other relationships?
To what extent humility and love may have coloured human
relations in general?

So far as the pre-Constantine Church is concerned it is, of
course, impossible to give more than a negative reply. All that
can be said is that the old sociological fundamental theories
which had grown up in the city-state and in a militarist atmosphere were broken up by it and that the ancient conception
of the State was destroyed.

So far as the post-Constantine Church is concerned the reply
to these questions would entail a far greater knowledge of her
legal and social history than I have at present at my disposal.
With the increasing connection between the Church and the
State we might, indeed, expect to find traces of an influence of
this kind. It seems to me, however, that in this respect the influence
of Christianity was extraordinarily slight. The institutions and
the intellectual culture rooted in the old ideas were too ancient,
too independent, too radically remote, to be able to assimilate
new impulses, while the Church, on the other hand, was still too
much concerned with the next world, still too much agitated by
the heat of conflict and victory, still inwardly too detached to be
able to weave ideas of that kind into the inner structure of the
State. On the contrary, we might rather speak of the strong
sociological influence on the Church and its institutions exerted
by the Roman corporation law, and by the continued effect of
the ancient *jus sacrum*. On the other hand, we might attribute the

[69] See p. 188.

increasing religious glorification of the Crown and of its officials, the whole Byzantine influence, less to ecclesiastical than to old pagan Oriental influences; and when the Western Empire fell, and churches and bishops often took over the functions of the State, this was only due to actual necessity and an expression of authority, but it was not an inward approximation of the life of the State to that of the Church. Moreover, in all this there was no trace of a tendency to political individualism, even though from the point of view of science and aesthetics, and perhaps also in family life, the individual and personal element was more strongly developed; this was, indeed, in harmony with the whole late Hellenic development, which the Church absorbed into her own life.[70]

Thus in the Early Church we can only look for a theoretical adjustment of the relationship between the Church and the Kingdom of God on the one hand, and the State and the world on the other, as of two inwardly essentially separate magnitudes which, owing to the existence of this essential separation, are prevented from mutual interpenetration.[71] As we have already seen clearly at various points, this problem had now become a peculiar dual problem: on the one hand, there is a widespread acceptance of the world and its institutions, in accordance with the fundamental principles laid down by Paul, and, on the other, the rejection of the world and of the State, on principle, as the fruit of sin and of the demonic realm. The ruling idea which lies behind this is that the State, and the social order in general, actually constitute the "world". The conception of a sinful, lost world over against a Church which alone can offer redemption became more and more the governing idea in the State and the social order; this tendency was increased by the growing necessity for a practical understanding between Church and State. After science had been partly rejected and partly Christianized, and the private forms of life had been Christianized and the heathen laws had been abrogated, the substance of the "world" became the idea of the State pure and simple. The "world", in the sense in which the word is used in late Judaism and primitive Christianity, and then later in the whole of the Ancient Church, is, indeed, not a cosmological conception at all; it is a conception composed of political, social, and historic elements. It means paganism, the Gentiles, the world outside Judaism, which by deterioration and wickedness has become a kingdom of demons, and this idea was intensified in the great Empire of the Caesars

[70] See p. 191.   [71] See p. 191.

with its Emperor-worship. Wherever this worship took place the writer of the Christian Apocalypse also saw the throne of Satan, the Lord of this world. Since, then, the infant Church had to do mainly with the Roman Empire, the Caesars became the rulers and representatives of the "world".

Christianity described herself as a βασιλεία, and therefore her counterpart, the world, was also conceived as a βασιλεία, which is plainly manifested in the Emperor, in the Imperial Law, and in the worship of the Emperor. The world becomes a "kingdom", and it is thus the sum of the existing laws and ordinances. For a kingdom is the support of law and order; and law and order covers the whole order of Society. The problem of the attitude towards the laws is the problem of the attitude towards the world. The world is αἰὼν οὗτος or *saeculum*, i.e. it is that period in history which precedes the Return of Christ. This idea has nothing to do with the metaphysical-cosmological conception of the world, of the *mundus* or κοσμος, although the expressions are used rather loosely. The Early Church rejected the Gnostic doctrines, which taught that the world and its sin had their origin in matter and the world of sense; the doctrine of the Old Testament was retained—that the Creation was good, but that the "world" is the result of the Fall, of the corruption of the will, and a Satanic delusion. The State also sprang from this source, and thus it comes under the uniform and essentially unchangeable principle of the "world", together with all the institutions of marriage, labour, property, slavery, law, and war; all the later changes, which the Christians, of course, also observed—the shifting of the world empire from the East to Rome, then the break-up of the ancient Roman tradition and the orientalizing of the Empire from the time of Severus,* the new constitution and administration of Diocletian—all this did not alter their theory. Even when Christianity was recognized by the State it made no difference so far as the State was regarded simply as the State, and not as a servant, to be directed, hallowed, and purified by the Church, as the body of which the Church is the soul. That which applies to the "world" applies equally to the State: in both there is a mingling of good and evil.[72]

This dualistic attitude towards the "world", therefore, was always the same, and was held by the same people; it is not divided up among different teachers, but it is peculiar to them all, only the emphasis varies in its component parts. Nothing will be rightly understood if that fact is overlooked, and if shades of

* I.e. Septimus and Alexander.—TRANSLATOR.   [72] See p. 191.

opinion are taken to imply differences in theory; this applies with peculiar force to the great theologians of the Christian Empire, and to their attempts to formulate fresh theories. Indeed, this statement also applies to the fundamental statements of Paul, who urges the believer to walk through this world as "a stranger and a pilgrim", and yet teaches that "the powers that be" are ordained by God for a good purpose. After the first sanguinary encounters with the power of the State, in the Apocalypse there is an outbreak of fanatical hatred of the State in which Jewish apocalyptic and a Messianic hatred of paganism are combined, and this hatred of the State broke out now and again in various forms; but it disappeared after Montanism. The main development proceeded along the lines laid down by Paul. Then, however, the dualistic tendency which this point of view contains came out very clearly: on the one hand, acquiescence in the existing order; on the other, the sternest opposition to the State, which reveals its demonic origin in the worship of the Emperor, in the refusal to allow Christians to form their own associations, and in its cruel condemnation of the Christians. The emphasis varies with the fluctuations between peace and persecution; it was also affected by the temperament and outlook of the Christian leaders, but the dualism was there all the time: it was maintained even during the hardest times of savage persecution, with their glorious martyrdoms, which, in spite of all that Christianity had in common with many tendencies of the later period in the Ancient World, revealed a unique spirit of heroism and creative faith. Christians regarded their sufferings either as trials and penalties, or as a stimulus to faith and courage; for either purpose God uses the State as His instrument; but while they held this view they did not give up the one idea, namely that, on the whole, the order of the State is good, and that it comes from God. When the State finally gave up the struggle and absorbed the Church into its own organization, the unjust laws and those tainted with idol-worship were abrogated, and the Church then was able to recognize the goodness of the order of the State more fully. But, just as the leaders of thought in the Church had never allowed the idea of the goodness of the State to disappear in times of persecution, neither did they permit the evil and sinful aspect of the State to be overlooked in the brilliant period which had just begun to dawn.

This dualistic viewpoint was a discord, which, in some way or another, had to be resolved. From the practical point of view, of course, it is quite intelligible. It expressed (*a*) the original indifference of the Gospel towards the world; (*b*) the enhancement of the opposition between the Gospel and the world, for purposes of apologetic, till it became a contrast between a sinful and lost humanity on the one hand, and a redeemed and holy humanity upon the other; (*c*) lastly, the ascetic-dualistic point of view which changed this contrast between the world and the Gospel into a contrast between the physical world of the senses on the one hand, and the super-sensual, other-worldly spiritual realm on the other.

Another very important aspect of this question ought to be taken into account, i.e. the compromise with the world, which was practically forced upon the Church by its size and its numerical increase, as well as by the way in which it became interwoven with the common life. To some extent this compromise was justified by that element within the underlying principle which held the world to be a Divine creation, and which always maintained that a minimum of the secular conditions of life was necessary as a basis and means for the actual ethical and religious values. Everything will depend on the form this "minimum" will take and on its range of influence. This was the question which divided Christianity into two great camps; the main line of development, and the official doctrine of the Church extended this "minimum" more and more, without giving up the "supernaturalism" of the Church theory; monasticism restricted this "minimum" as far as it was humanly possible to do so; it definitely renounced its share in the life of the great world, and it also allowed a lower degree of secular morality to exist at the same time. The inconsistency was intelligible, but it was intolerable, and the Church leaders, though they may have been one-sided, would not have been the keen and great thinkers that they were if they had not attempted to find a theoretical solution of the problem.

Since the State, with its laws, constitutes and represents the whole social system, the problem became one of the nature of the "laws". In the earlier literature this problem was settled by reference to the two statements of Scripture: "The powers that be are ordained by God" for the maintenance of the civil order, but that when conflict does arise, "We must obey God rather than men". These propositions, however, did not solve the whole problem. Firstly, because they were purely dogmatic statements, without any general foundation in theory, clearly connected with religious thought; and, secondly, because in all instances which went beyond a mere clash with the laws which supported pagan worship, or which forbade Christian associations, they were inconclusive.

In spite of the Pauline formulae, however, the Christian writer and "prophet" Hermas placed the laws of the City of God and those of the city of this world in sharpest opposition: "Wilt thou, on account of thy fields and of thy other property, abjure thy law and live according to the law of this city? (i.e. this world). See thou that it be not thy ruin to deny thy law. . . . Since thou art dwelling in a foreign land do not strive to obtain more than is necessary, and just what is sufficient and make thyself ready, in order that when the lord of this city banishes thee, on account of thy opposition to his laws, thou mayest leave this city, and travel to thine own, where thou canst live according to thine own, without suffering ill-treatment in great joy." The Epistle to the Hebrews also makes a very clear distinction between the city of God and the city of this world.[72a]

INFLUENCE OF STOICISM ON THE DOCTRINE OF THE STATE

As soon as the worst struggles were over and Christianity had to adjust its organization to the legal social system in general, the need was felt for a general theory of the basis and validity of the "laws" which the Christians could accept. In this connection it was the Apologists who, in addition to fusing the ethics of Christianity and of Stoicism, were also the first, at least to some extent, to bring the laws of the City of God into harmony with the laws of the city of this world.[72b] The Stoic idea of Natural Law, which the Apologists regarded as identical with the Christian moral law, provided the way out of the difficulty. As we have already seen, the Stoics, and the jurists whom they influenced, regarded positive justice and law as the result of that Natural Law and natural justice which issues from the Divine nature and from Providence, and the validity of the laws was based upon the degree in which they contained the impress of this Natural Law. Since to educated Christians this Law of Nature seemed to be part of the order of creation, the content of the Decalogue, and an integral part of the Christian moral law, and also of the Logos who was incarnate in Christ, this "Natural Law" also seemed to them to be a directly Christian doctrine. Once this was granted, however, it was clear that both a general founda-

[72a] Hermas, Sim. i., Hebr. II, 16. The description of the world and of the Church as a πόλις or civitas also means two forms of legislation, or even two different customs. Cf. Weinel: Stellung, pp. 52 and 63. [72b] See p. 192.

tion and criterion by which to test the validity of the "laws"
had been established. Whereas, in the earlier days, the Church
had thought of law almost exclusively in terms of the Law of
Moses, and possibly also of the new Law of Christ, while the
laws of the State were left to their own devices, now both in
theory and in practice, it was regarded as a Christian duty to
undertake the criticism of the laws of the State, with the result that
these laws were accorded a limited extent of recognition, and
were thus fused with the Christian law, while those which appeared to be tainted by sin and the demons were, in part at least,
rejected.

After the Apologists had given a somewhat hesitating lead,
the great thinker Origen spoke out clearly and plainly on this
subject. He found that the pagan controversialist Celsus had
reproached the Christians for adopting the ideas of the Natural
Law of the Stoics and incorporating them into the legal system of
the States; Celsus also summoned the Christians to submit to this
law, expressing his fear that their hostility to the world will lead
to the desolation and impoverishment of the State. Origen
accepted the idea of Celsus in its entirety; then, however, he
emphasized the incongruity between the existing positive laws and
the rule of Natural Law and natural justice. So far as the laws of
the State agree with the latter they are good and Divine; so far
as they do not, they are not Divine and they ought not to be
obeyed. "One may only obey the laws of the State when they
agree with the Divine Law; when, however, the written law of
the State commands something other than the Divine and Natural
Law, then we must ignore the commands of the State and obey
the command of God alone." The prohibition of the Christian
"associations" and the summons to idol-worship are contrary to
the Divine and Natural Law, and resemble the laws of the
Scythians and the Barbarians rather than the laws of justice. In
the last statement the assumption is characteristically expressed
that Roman Law must correspond to the Natural Law, and that
the Roman laws against the Christians are really Barbarian
and unworthy of the Romans. This way of thinking inaugurated
a method of testing, limiting, and establishing the laws, which
was gradually followed by all the Fathers of the Church. In connection with Cicero, Lactantius ardently defended the same
doctrine, and all the Western Doctors as well as the Justinian
Code took the same point of view. In the period after Constantine,
when the State was Christianized, this point of view became
general, and the final acceptance of the State was based upon

the ethico-juridical theory that its laws proceed from the Divine Law of Nature, which is identical with the Decalogue.[73]

This, however, seems to simply that too much had been conceded, for this view seems to lead to the deification of the State. Of course, that was not the view of the Doctors of the Church. To the extent in which the Church accepted the State and the social order in actual practice she was also forced to feel, and to maintain very fully, her inner hostility to this Law of Nature, which was fundamentally opposed to the social ideal of the Church in slavery, trade, force, and harsh laws, as we have already seen in particular instances. And the Church did take this line with great decision. The ancient protest, however, was couched in new terms; here also the Church followed the example of the Stoics, who, for their part, in spite of their theory that the existing laws are based upon the Natural Law, were likewise unable to conceal the contrast between the existing order and their humane social ideal, and who therefore had sought and found a way out of this difficulty. They found their solution in isolating the primitive period, or the Golden Age, from all the ages which follow. In the Primitive State the Law of Nature prevailed completely, and there was no slavery, no force, no contrast between rich and poor; some attained an actual perfection of freedom and equality, and others a rather childlike and innocent normal ethical standard which still needed to be developed. It is only selfishness, envy, violence, and bad laws which have produced the present situation, in which the Law of Nature is only expressed in a clouded and disfigured form. Despairing of carrying through their social ideal in the present, they placed the Golden Age in the past, and only laid upon the present age the responsibility of adapting the actual laws as far as possible to the Law of Nature.

With one accord the Christian Doctors now adopted these ideas, and combined them with their Scriptural ideas of a period of primitive perfection; the line of division between the two strands of thought, however, remained quite clear; the Scriptural doctrine of the Primitive State presented one pair of human beings only, but the ecclesiastical doctrine of the absolute and complete Law of Nature which was present in the Primitive State assumes, like the Stoics, the existence of several human beings; and the Church was only able to combine these two ideas by teaching that if it had not been for the Fall humanity would have developed along these lines. The lack of logical cohesion also appears in the fact that the Stoic ideal of the Primitive State was characterized

[73] See p. 193.

mainly by freedom, equality, and absence of force, whereas the ecclesiastical doctrine of the Primitive State (when it simply follows its own impulses) emphasizes mainly religious perfection, the love of God, humility, and the state of grace. For the Fathers, however, the idea was so releasing and illuminating that they, nevertheless, adopted it with great vigour. All social institutions which, from their point of view, were intolerable were due to Original Sin; the patriarchal dominion of the male, private property, slavery, and finally the State (which constitutes the essence of the whole)—all are due to sin. The stories of the Curse of Adam, of the Expulsion from the Garden of Eden, of the Patriarchs, and of Cain, Ham, and Nimrod were naïvely incorporated into the Stoic philosophy of history. The Roman Empire is regarded as the successor of the Babylonian Empire, and as the support of the existing laws it will endure until the Return of Christ.[74]

At this point, however, it looked as though too little had been granted where formerly too much had been conceded. Christian thinkers felt that they ought not to lay too much stress upon the influence of original Reason in the development of the laws, in spite of the absolute opposition between existing conditions and the original equality and freedom. Out of this difficulty, however, a third decisive idea was evolved, which then completed the argument: the element of Natural Law in the present order is not merely the effect of a Reason whose clarity has been dimmed, but it is the transformation of the Law of Nature, which, according to the Divine Will, took place after the Fall. Once lawlessness, inequality, avarice, and violence have penetrated into Society the Law of Nature can only become evident in the form of an order of law and compulsion, and thus react against corruption. It is precisely the legal and compulsory character of the laws which protect property, organize and control the masses according to an idea of law, which emphasize inequality by the existence of a slave class, which chastise Barbarians and the enemies of civilization by means of war, which under these conditions constitutes the essence of the Law of Nature. It is at once a result of sin and a remedy for sin. It ensures order, and the *pax terrena*, by the only reasonable methods which are still practicable, and, in accordance with this aim, the positive law can be regulated, at least according to this secondary form of the Law of Nature. All the institutions of property, slavery, patriarchalism, the State, and the Army may, and must, exist as an expression of the Divine Reason; in

[74] See p. 194.

harmony with its intention, however, they may only be used as a means of preserving public order and as a remedy for sin.

This argument enshrines the important idea of a relative Natural Law, corresponding to the conditions of the general sinfulness of humanity, which exist alongside of the absolute Natural Laws of the Primitive State. This is the general doctrine taught by the Fathers, naturally with varying shades of meaning. Augustine also expressed this idea, and it was at the basis of his thought, although, for reasons which will be explained directly, he emphasized it less than some other ideas; here also, as well as in his doctrines of original sin and of predestination, he was to some extent an isolated theologian. But with the Isidorian Decretals, and the explicit statements of Gregory the Great, the doctrine was transmitted to the Middle Ages as a fundamental doctrine. At this point the doctrine of the Church was so closely related with that of the Stoics that we may almost infer that there was some direct connection between the two. The Stoics, with their similar assumptions, encountered exactly the same difficulty of regarding the existing State as the expression of the Law of Nature, and yet of being obliged to distinguish this present Law of Nature from the perfect Law of the Primitive State. After Cicero had already suggested that submission to ordered government was a remedy against lawlessness and wickedness, Seneca developed the implications of this idea in detail, and he exalted this reaction of the Law of Nature against sin as a method of progress. Among the jurists traces of this way of thinking appear even in the *corpus juris* itself. Whether in this instance the Church Fathers also borrowed from this source we cannot say with any certainty, for lack of explicit evidence. After they had adopted the Stoic presuppositions the discovery of this latter doctrine would have been almost inevitable, and that the inference could be drawn independently seems to be proved by the fact that it appears in Irenaeus. In any case, the Fathers gave their own special impress to this idea by emphasizing the theory that these institutions of the relative order of Nature were not merely remedial in character, but that they were also a direct punishment for sin.

The advantage of this point of view was that it enabled the Church to justify the harsher aspects of the positive law which exceeded the purpose of acting as a remedy for sin; indeed, this argument was used to defend the perversions of this Natural Law in general, which had always been a difficulty to the rationalism of the Stoics. Under certain circumstances this led them towards a strongly realistic conception of positive law, and of the historic life of the State, which it had been far more difficult to rationalize. But however far St. Augustine, for instance, went in this direction, the basis of Natural Law itself was not, on that account, discarded.[75]

THEOCRATIC CONCEPTION OF IMPERIAL AUTHORITY

In all this, however, there is still one question which has not been answered; although it was of no practical importance at first, it gained increasing significance as time went on. This is the problem of the nature and the right of the authority from which the laws of the State proceed, and, thus, of the now dominant relative Natural Law. In point of fact this authority was, of course, the Emperor. But the ethical interpretation, basis, and limitation of this Imperial authority was an open question. In the days of the Early Church it was regarded as sufficient to refuse to worship the Emperor, or to obey laws which were contrary to the Will of God, while in everything else the Christians did all they possibly could to compensate for this by honouring him highly as the authority appointed by God, against which the only permissible form of disobedience was that of suffering and passive resistance. If, however, the "laws" could be traced back to the Law of Nature, then the authority which enacts the laws must also derive its power from the same source. In actual fact the Stoics and the jurists took this line of argument; they affirmed the democratic origin of the Imperial authority through the transference of the popular rights to the *Princeps*, and regarded the Imperial power as justifiable to the extent in which it maintained the intention of this transmission of authority, i.e. care for the common weal. This idea of the derivation of the Imperial authority from the Law of Nature through a free and equal people was handed down, by tacit consent, from one generation to another, and it was even accepted by the Justinian Code, and was echoed by the Fathers of the Church, whose sympathies were Roman. This introduced into the ecclesiastical literature of Natural Law sporadic elements of the democratic, "social contract" idea, as the basis of the power of the State, at first, however, without any practical significance. For they were merely commonplaces of Roman thought, learnéd reminiscences from philosophical and juridical literature; at first there was no kind of inward connection between this democratic idea of Natural Law and the entirely inward and purely religious permanent Christian idea of personality; this connection was only achieved at all by

[75] See p. 195.

radical Calvinism. At this point, in the question of the validity
of the Imperial authority, the idea of Natural Law, even that of
the purely relative Natural Law, was thus not developed to its
logical conclusion by the Fathers. The reason for this lay doubtless in the ancient religious feeling which accepted the life of this
world as God's ordering and appointment, and always regarded
the Imperial authority quite simply and unquestioningly as
permitted by God, and therefore as an established fact. In this
refusal to agree to rationalize Natural Law there is a trace of the
conception of God as an arbitrary power who ordains the powers
that be just as He chooses. This idea was strengthened by studying
the way in which the kings were appointed in the Old Testament;
another factor was their repugnance to the logical result of the
idea of the Law of Nature, i.e. that if an Emperor disobeys the
Law of Nature it would be right to depose him. That, they felt,
would be nothing less than rebellion against the actual order
which God has willed and established. Even godless Emperors
must be tolerated, not indeed because their authority is based
upon Natural Law, but as the punishment of God for sin. Thus
at this point the old rationalism of Natural Law asserts itself
against the old religious irrationalism, and its result is the Divine
Right of Kings.

The authority of the Emperor comes from God—even under
pagan rule—and still more that of the Christian Emperors.
Augustine, therefore, the Father of the Church who has laid
most emphasis upon sin and its punishment, and who also taught
predestinarian irrationalism, accepted the view of the State as the
result of Natural Law, it is true; but he defined it more narrowly
than the other Fathers—he wished to allow scope for the argument
that godless Emperors are due to an "act of God", and serve as a
punishment for sin; he also argued that the ruling authority
should be rejected, on ethical grounds, in so far as it does not
allow itself to be guided by the Divine *justitia*. Thus in his legislation Justinian proclaimed the Divine Right of Kings as well as
the idea of the democratic transference of authority to the Emperor, which was based on Natural Law. From this early Christian
viewpoint, however, the "Divine Right of Kings" means that an
Emperor can be Emperor either "by the grace of" or "by the
wrath of" God, just as the people deserve to have a good or a
bad Emperor. Thus this theory of Natural Law which enabled the
Fathers to accept the social system of the ancient world and to
weld it into a unity, broke down on the question of Imperial
authority, the *potestas temporalis*. At this point the jurists also were

uncertain; on the one hand, they argued that the Imperial authority was derived from the will of the people, while, on the other hand, they defended the theory of the purest absolutism. If we are to understand the idea of the Fathers of the Church on "Divine Right", we must not forget the influence of this absolutist theory. The Emperors administer the laws, it is true, or they should do so, according to the standard of relative Natural Law, but for their part they do not base their authority upon that fact, but upon the fact that their position is a Divine appointment. Therefore the problem of the recognition of the State is not the same as that of the Imperial authority itself, and the "Natural Law" theory of the State differs from that of the validity of the Imperial authority.

The question of the authority of the Christian Emperors, indeed, bristles with an extraordinary number of problems. For since the Imperial authority is derived directly from God, it has a special duty in its relation to the world or the State, on the one hand, and to the Church or the "organ of salvation", on the other. But its peculiar position does not mean that the Imperial power is unlimited; it means that it ought not to be limited from below, i.e. from the standpoint of Natural Law. Undoubtedly, however, it may and must be limited from above, by the same God who gave it its power; that, however, means that the Imperial authority must be limited or directed by the institution in which God is incarnate—that is, by the Church. In all secular matters both the laity and the clergy must obey the Emperor, but in all spiritual things, in questions of dogma, of the law of the Church, of ecclesiastical property, of ecclesiastical legislation, the law of God is paramount. Indeed, the secular Imperial power is only considered as divinely justified to the extent in which it is purified and hallowed by service to the Church and submission to her authority. The Imperial power secured protection and privileges for the Church, but in the actual relationships of the State there was no idea of a Christian State or of social reform. Since the Imperial authority gave the Church freedom for full and unfettered activity, the Church herself consecrated, hallowed, and spiritualized the whole great structure of secular aims, by the love of God which is inwardly detached from the world, and yet tolerates it outwardly. Only thus can the Church give to the elements of Natural Law within the State a divine strength and depth; making the secular *justitia* of the legal system into the perfect *justitia* of a piety which uses the world both for renunciation and for the exercise of love. The Imperial authority, however, must give the Church the opportunity of exercising this influence; it must place itself at the disposal of God. This is the theocratic idea as it was first formulated by the Church, which was the result of the sociological development of the religious community, and which was now extended into the sphere of political and social life. The latter theory, as is well known, was worked out pre-eminently by Augustine in his great work. But it is less often recognized that he assumed and maintained the former theory as well. The unadjusted conflict between these two points of view also explains the ambiguous character of the work of this great man, which (for that very reason) also transmitted dualistic tendencies to the future. Theocracy and Natural Law mutually hallow the State; what one cannot do the other can, and in any case the Emperor holds his office first and foremost in virtue of his Divine Right and his position of theocratic dependence. The State, however, still remains an epitome of the "world".[76]

THE CHURCH AND HER DUALISTIC THEORY IN THE SOCIAL REALM

The Church, therefore, had at her disposal two entirely different theories to guide her in her attitude towards social and political problems; the theory of relative Natural Law and the theory of theocratic absolutism. With the aid of the theory of relative Natural Law she learned, on the one hand, how to tolerate the actual social situation—which in itself was opposed to her fundamental principles, but which the very fact of her sense of sin and her orientation towards the future life led her to depreciate—and, on the other hand, how to regulate it according to her theories of Natural Law. The theocratic absolutist theory enabled the Church to adopt the position that the Emperor and the State might act freely in earthly matters, but that in everything which concerned religion and the Church, the Church must have the upper hand. These theories are the clearest proof of the impotence of the attitude of early Christianity towards all social problems. From the sociological point of view the fundamental ideas of an individualism and a human fellowship based wholly upon man's relation with God may have had an immense and incalculable influence. More and more, however, the attitude of the Church towards social problems coincided with that of the State, as the support and the substance of the whole life of Society. Over against that, however, there was the aloofness of the Church from the world, and its opposition to unredeemed humanity; in these

[76] See p. 196.

circumstances all that the Church could attempt to do was to Christianize the State and the world indirectly, by ascribing their origin to the Law of Nature, which was identical with the Law of Moses and the Law of Christ, but which, owing to the Fall, was now only a relative Natural Law. All that this "Christianization" amounted to in the end was that everything was left outwardly exactly as it had been before.

The other solution was that the theocracy of the ecclesiastical social organization also dominated and controlled the temporal power of the Empire. This meant in practice that the Church secured her own unity and stability with the help of the State, that above all she used the authority of the State to make her own power supreme within her own sphere, but that the social life itself was left to the care of the Emperor. Only by means of this theocratic principle did the Church attain a unity in doctrine and in Church order which she would never have attained without Constantine—a unity which was enforced by the power of the State, and not by the inherent logic of the ideas contained in the doctrine of the Church. By means of this principle the Church built up her constitution, acquired property, and gained her legal power which she used to complete and correct the legislation of the State. In all this she was simply attending to her own immediate interests; social life in general was left in the hands of the Emperor and the law. Within the ancient world the Church never achieved, never desired to achieve, and never could have wished to achieve the development of a uniform Christian civilization. This was due to two factors: (a) to the influence of the attitude of detachment from the world which prevailed in the Early Church; and (b) to the overwhelming influence exerted by the presence of two parallel independent social structures—the World Empire and the Universal Church. The "Holy Roman Empire", which was influenced by the theocratic idea and yet erected upon the basis of relative Natural Law, was the result of all these inconsistencies, and therefore it neither was, nor desired to be, an inner unity.

But in these ideas which it had evolved out of its own experience the ancient world was able to transmit to the future those elements which the Middle Ages was to use in the development of a uniform Christian civilization. Executive powers, which do not possess the vigour and the wealth of the legal organization of the ruling power, but which are young and which have grown up with the Church itself, will adapt themselves more easily to theocracy, and thus the whole, at least theoretically, can be conceived and felt from the point of view of theocracy. On the other hand, in the presence of new, less stable, and less developed social conditions it was easier to attribute their origin to the Law of Nature, and the relative Natural Law could more easily be drawn into touch with the Christian moral law, and thus social life could be more simply and completely conceived as Christian and regulated in a Christian way. On the one hand, Theocracy will strike its roots far more deeply, while, on the other hand, the Christian Natural Law will be able to push upwards with greater vigour. Indeed, the fiction of a Christian Natural Law, which makes it possible to regard the State and Society as though both were ordered by one Christian law, will be the means through which it will become possible to speak of a Christian unity of civilization at all, and it is this alone which makes men able to believe in such a possibility. This Christian Law of Nature also will likewise provide the daughter churches of Western Catholicism, Lutheranism and Calvinism, with the means of regarding and shaping themselves as a Christian unity of civilization. The Christian theory of Natural Law—in which the pure Natural Law of the Primitive State, the entirely opposite relative Natural Law of the fallen State, the positive law, which often included the greatest abominations, and that true goodness which, in spite of all these ideas of Natural Law, is the only source of the supreme power of the theocracy, were in continual conflict—as a scientific theory it is wretchedly confused, but as a practical doctrine it is of the highest importance for the history of civilization and of social evolution—it is the real ecclesiastical doctrine of civilization, and as such it is at least as important as the doctrine of the Trinity, or other fundamental doctrines.[77]

The Christian relative Natural Law was the final result of a process created by the Church through the following stages: first of all she gradually modified that indifference towards the natural basis of life which characterized the Gospel, owing to the great enthusiasm and heroism with which it lived only for eternity; then the Church tolerated the natural basis unchanged as she found it, as the product of relative Natural Law; and finally, from the time of the Middle Ages, with the changes in the general conditions of life, she regarded the natural basis of life as instituted by Providence for the purpose of the Christian Church. The sociological, purely ethical, and religious fundamental relationships of the Gospel then become an integral part of the life of the Church, embodied in obedience to the Church

[77] See p. 197.

and in the sense of the unity of the Church, while the social and political elements are embodied and assimilated by means of the Christian theory of the Natural Law of the Church. In this Natural Law, however, there still remains the root idea of Stoic rationalism—that is, that God is related to the universe as the soul is to the body, and the rational equality of all beings endowed with reason; from this root rationalistic reactions will arise, until, in the seventeenth century, when they have developed their full power, they will destroy the ecclesiastical civilization itself. The unity of civilization was only possible on a basis of theocracy and the Christian Law of Nature.

CONCLUDING SUMMARY

This, however, is an anticipation. But it is a necessary digression, in order that we may realize clearly the significance of the conceptions which have been gained through the struggles which I have described. The sociological energy of Christianity was narrowed down to the Church; social and political life was accepted by the Church, and in the future it will also become plastic in its hands. This result seems, however, to suggest that the early ideal of the Gospel, the anarchy of the faith which is responsible to God alone, of the infinite worth of the free soul, and of the "shedding abroad" of the Love of God in the love of the brethren, had disappeared, or at least that it had been hidden and silenced.

This primitive ideal of the Gospel, however, was not dead; it lived on in ideas and in institutions, although it had certainly become greatly changed in the process.

It lived on in the Church itself, in the ideas of sanctification and of brotherly love, which were bound up with sacerdotal and sacramental ideas, and yet were always capable of a vital release. These ideas were also effective within the limits of the ecclesiastical organization, and they manifested a continual tendency to cut themselves free from it. The Church, as the living extension of the Incarnation, had, indeed, replaced or enlarged the New Testament, but it had not discarded it. Also the spirit of inner detachment from the world, which had never been given up, in spite of all the ideas of Theocracy and Natural Law, kept alive the feeling that the sociological ideals of the pure religious faith were felt to represent something which differed from the world entirely.

The primitive ideal of the Gospel lived on in the idea of the Primitive State and of the absolute Natural Law, which kept continually before the minds of men the ideal of freedom, of union with God, of equality, and of love to God and in God. It is true that in this ideal of the Primitive State the idea of equality has been drawn from the Stoics, and that it is conceived in an abstract and rationalistic way, and fused with the idea of righteousness. This is the reason why time after time this ideal of the Primitive State gave birth to theories of Natural Law, of communism, and of Socialism, in a religious guise, and why with the emancipation of the modern Law of Nature, the latter expects that the idea of primitive man as the Church conceives him will support these ideas.

But in addition to these Stoic-rationalist ideas this doctrine of the Primitive State contained in the concrete religious ideal of primitive man so much that is religious that for a long time the influence of this Stoic admixture was not too dangerous. Further, it was precisely the predestinarian Doctors of the Church who, with an intelligent instinct, emphasized, over against the rationalism of a general equality, the difference between human beings both in the Primitive State and in their essential disposition—an anticipation of the opposing tendencies which were destined to break away from each other at a later time.[78]

Finally, the primitive ideal of the Gospel lived on in monasticism. In its origin monasticism is a very complex phenomenon, but in its practical effect it was simply the sanctuary into which the early one-sided Christian ideal had fled for refuge. Just as the primitive Gospel ideal with its heroism had taken little account of the natural basis of life and ignored the values of civilization altogether, so monasticism with its asceticism reduced the value of the natural life and denied the values of civilization altogether. As the Gospel ideal could only be fully realized in a really intimate group of individuals, and found its first natural expression in the small group of the early disciples, so monasticism reproduced these conditions by artificial methods. But although monasticism represented the complete ideal, so far as it could still be felt and realized, in a splendid and overwhelming manner, it had no desire to make those who could not embrace this state feel that they could not be Christians. The relation between the Church, the laity, and monasticism was still undefined. But monasticism assumed the main responsibility. It took charge of all real Christian Social work, so far as there was, and could be, any such work at all, and thus prepared the way for its future incorporation into a complete Christian civilization. Experienced in the discipline

[78] See p. 198.

and the "cure" of souls, and also concerned about the salvation of ordinary people, the monks laid the foundation of that individual pastoral care which replaced the catechumenate of the Church, which had become formal and superfluous. They also created the beginnings of Christian schools—a phase of service which the Church, in her detachment from the world, had entirely overlooked. For the grammar and rhetoric schools of the Roman world they substituted schools of an entirely religious character, which, imitated later on by parish and cathedral schools, also educated lay people. The monks made the scientific labour of thought about Divine things a means of spiritual discipline and of union with God, together with the virtues of asceticism. Thus, in their development of the ascetic and transcendental features of Stoicism, Cynicism, and Platonism they were both true Christians and true philosophers. The laity, therefore, could find in the monastic literature that true knowledge which they could not find in the unrest of the world. The monks lived a life of strenuous labour, while as great communistic productive organizations they still held all things in common. They gave the laity, when necessary, training in labour, exhortation to work, and works of mercy. The idea of free labour, and the demand that a "livelihood" should be based upon labour, was first clearly recognized in the monasteries, and from them it first spread into the world. Thus precisely through their asceticism, and by the seclusion of their small groups, the monasteries were the essential supporters and radiating centres of that which we may now call Christian civilization, of a knowledge, labour, and charity which are based upon and bound up with a most intimate love of God. In spite of all their eccentricities and crudities, in their organization by the great Fathers of monasticism they formed the advance-guard of "Christian civilization", and from this point of view they became increasingly important.[79]

Only now is the picture complete. In the Bible, in the absolute Law of Nature, and in monasticism the old sociological ideals lie ready to exert a new spiritual influence upon the whole of life. In the Church, through the concentration of the Divine power in priest and sacrament, these ideals have been ecclesiastically united, and the creation of the Church is the real great sociological achievement of this period, whose inner fundamental theory does not penetrate too deeply into the common life; so far its influence was mainly felt in family life. Through the ideas of theocracy and relative Natural Law social problems have also

[79] See p. 199.

been mastered, in that, although the State and Society remain outwardly and legally just the same, in their hearts men are quite remote from and hostile to them, without however feeling urged to alter them, and using their institutions for future salvation and for the general security of life. These are the social doctrines of the Ancient Church; they also contain both the germ of the new social doctrines of the Middle Ages, which will be quite different, and also the germ of ideas, which will lead to the disintegration of these same social doctrines at the beginning of the modern period.

NOTES TO CHAPTER I

[10] (p. 40.) On this point in general compare *Uhlhorn: Christliche Liebes-tätigkeit in der alten Kirche*[2], *1882*; *Harnack: Dogmengeschichte*[3], and *Harnack: Mission und Ausbreitung des Christentums in den ersten drei Jahrhunderten*[2], *1906*; the latter contains the best material known to me for the social history of Christianity. See also *Möller von Schubert: Lehrbuch der Kirchengeschichte, I*[2], *1904*; *Duchesne: Histoire ancienne de l'église, 1907*; *Weizsäcker: Das apostolische Zeitalter*[3], *1902*; *Knopf: Das nachapostolische Zeitalter, 1905*; *Th. Keim: Rom und das Christentum, 1881*; *Gierke: Das deutsche Genossenschaftsrecht, III, 1887*, in which the Christian idea of a "corporation" is excellently developed. Cf. also the address of *Adolf Harnack* at the Protestant Social Congress in 1894: *Die ev.-soziale Aufgabe im Lichte der Kirche (Reden und Aufsätze, 1904)*.—The whole question is excellently handled by *P. Wendland* in his book *Die hellenistisch-römische Kultur, 1907*, in which, however, the social history is deliberately left out of account.

In all these books the underlying idea is that they are dealing primarily with a religious movement. There are, however, also books which claim that Christianity is a purely social movement. *Pöhlmann: Gesch. d. antiken Sozialismus und Kommunismus, 1893-1901*, wished originally to describe Christianity as the result of ancient Socialism. He tried to prove that in its hope of the Kingdom of God it placed at the disposal of the philosophically resigned and actually suppressed Socialism of the Imperial period the psychological motives and energies which would have gone beyond the powers of purely politico-social and philosophical endeavours (*II, 583-617*). With this suggestion, however, he let the matter rest, and did not undertake to carry the subject out in further detail, possibly because he found that it was less easy to prove this than he had expected. His theory is based upon a misconception of the idea of the Kingdom of God, which has nothing whatever to do with any politico-social renewal; upon this point more will be said shortly. *Kautsky* naturally also makes the same assumption in his contribution to the *Geschichte des Sozialismus in Einzeldarstellungen, I, i, 1895, pp. 16-40*. Following the theory of "historical materialism", he can only see in Christianity a communistic movement which arose out of the social conditions of the Roman Empire, a reaction against the poverty and misery of the masses, which was caused by the squeezing of the citizens out of the possession of land and manual labour, by the competition of plantation and factory work based on slave-labour, a situation which is openly expressed in the feeding of this ragged, *déclassé*, unemployed proletariat by the State. Elements of an "enthusiastic" nature sought a way out of this misery caused by ancient Capitalism through miracle; Christ the Redeemer was to introduce the ideal communistic society by means of a Divine renewal of the world, for which the Apocalypse in particular serves as a proof, which, however, bears no communistic features at all; its main characteristic being hatred against the sinful world and the Roman Empire. Out of this Chiliastic "enthusiasm", which, however, soon faded, there proceeded even for the life of this world a practical communistic effect. This resulted in the Christian proletariat of the cities, which for that reason remained connected with the life of the towns, and which in the economic state which it had reached could not renounce private property; it was a communism based purely on consumption and on sharing one's possessions suggested by the example of the State, in its feeding of the starving and unemployed. The means of production were changed into means of enjoyment and distributed to the poor. Hence the thoroughly inconsistent character of this communism, which was based upon private property, which for that reason was a failure, and only continued to exist in theory in the declamations of the Fathers of the Church, among whom Chrysostom is singled out for mention. Christianity thus feels obliged to allow the social order to remain unchanged; it only enlarges it by the addition of a new ruling class, the clergy with their ecclesiastical possessions in landed property, a development which it is not difficult to understand when we realize how weak was the democracy which was based upon an "enthusiasm" of this kind. It is the Imperialism of the bishops. When the hierarchy is formed the Catholic Church arises, and thus "out of a communistic institution the most gigantic machine for exploitation which the world has ever seen comes into being" (*p. 34*). In the states formed by the migrations of the Germanic tribes, with the disappearance of a money economy the widespread misery of the Ancient World came to an end, and the Church, through her connection with the feudal system and the manorial estates, became a purely political institution, the central point for the ruling class. Then the charity of the ancient communism disappeared; all that remained was merely the pleasure in giving away that which cannot be eaten, which is found in all social systems based upon a natural economy. When, in the later Middle Ages, modern Capitalism arose, which produced afresh the problem of mass misery and want, the communist movement also arose anew, this time, however, not among a mass of wretched unemployed proletarians, but among free wage-earners who are indispensable to production. The Church then ceased to represent Socialism at all; the only relics of the ancient communism and its charity remained in the monasteries, with the conservatism which usually characterizes such institutions.

Kautsky's argument is a gross misunderstanding of the independent position of religious thought; apart from this, however, his work is not without a value of its own, since it points to aspects of the question which had hitherto been unnoticed. One particularly important point is the difference between the Early Church, which lived under conditions based upon a money economy, and the Mediaeval Church, when Society was based upon a natural economy; this is very significant, although the importance lies elsewhere than at the point suggested by *Kautsky*. This point will be developed farther on.—*Kalthoff: Die Entstehung des Christentums, 1905,* takes a similar line, excepting that his attitude towards religion is different. These are his presuppositions: (*a*) the complete autonomy of the religious consciousness of the present day, whose dependence on history is severed in the most radical way by pointing out, either that Jesus never existed at all, or that if he did exist he was merely one obscure Jewish enthusiast among many similar enthusiasts; as a liberal theologian he is simply developing to its logical conclusion the tendency of *Biedermann's* intellectual dogmatism; (*b*) the impossibility of disentangling any kind of kernel of truth from the miracle stories of the Bible, and the impossibility of understanding Paul's transformation of Jesus into the God-Man, whereas this is all intelligible if it is a free poetical interpretation of the second century; (*c*) the modern collectivist, anti-individualistic, and sociological historical method, which does not admit that such movements can begin with one or even with several individuals, but requires an interpretation from the point of view of mass social movements. Thus the rise of Christianity is explained from the Stoic philosophy, the communistic clubs of late antiquity and the Messianic enthusiasm of the Jews, which blended together created in Jesus a mythical hero and concocted the Biblical literature as primitive history. The speculations dealing with suffering and death reflect the sufferings and victory of the Christian community. The whole work is based upon entirely arbitrary, partially untrue, assumptions, and in its positive section it is a pure work of the imagination.

Above all, however, it is quite possible to gain a true estimate of the real sources as relatively accurate traditions. The one point which has not yet been cleared up is the rise of the Pauline Christology, which, however, is in reality not a product of the formation of the Church but its manifest presupposition. There can be no doubt that it arose as a fact out of the conversion of Paul, however one may try to explain it further through other influences from the non-Christian world.

Overbeck's Studien zur Geschichte der alten Kirche, 1875, forms a contrast, refreshingly clear, to all such attempts to interpret "social" history. This book deals with "the relation of the Early Church to slavery under the Roman Empire"; this is the point at which a tendency towards social reform and a connection with it would most easily show itself. Overbeck shows how, on the contrary, from the very beginning slavery was regarded (along with the State, Society, economics, and the family) as part of the sinful world-order which cannot be altered. Slaves with non-Christian masters may only become members of the Christian Church with the consent of their masters; this rule was made in order to hinder slaves who were politically minded and eager for emancipation from pressing into the Christian community (*pp. 188 and 202*). Indeed, slavery as one of the traditional methods of holding property was even made more sure by Christianity, and the Church itself later actually owned slaves and was unable to set them free. The overcoming of slavery was due to purely inward religious causes, i.e. to the fact that both master and slave equally belong to Christ; from the religious point of view both have equal rights, and in the early days slaves were permitted to hold office in the Church. It was only the Gnostic sects which displayed communistic tendencies, and for that very reason they were opposed with great vigour. More details are given about this subject farther on. But the fact that the Church recognized slavery in this way, and that when she was free to act on her own initiative she intensified rather than modified these conditions, together with her acceptance of slavery as an essential part of the social order, constitutes a very striking refutation of the opposite point of view.

[11] (p. 40.) Cf. *Wendland; Ziebarth: Das griechische Vereinswesen, 1896.* The religious form of this system of associations, which flourished particularly in the Hellenistic and Imperial period, was due to the fact that Greek thought could only think of an association in the form of a community gathered round some permanent form of worship; although this religious form was often an entirely external affair, in themselves these groups did not denote in any way a religious movement. The associations formed for genuine religious ends which arose during a time of denationalization, and with the increase of the means of communication, were destined to serve the purpose partly of gatherings of fellow-countrymen in a foreign land, partly for the reception of new cults; their social significance develops in so far as they create a group of a family kind, and produce the abolition of class-distinctions through sharing in a common worship; in an age of increasing individualism, therefore, they were sought for this reason; but, exactly as in the Christian community, they allowed social distinctions to exist outside the meetings for worship; *Ziebarth* also points out that it was mainly the upper classes which took part in these associations for worship (*p. 210*). Hence there is no question of the existence of "communistic clubs", which according to *Kalthoff* were the soil from which Christianity

sprang into being; therefore even *K.* has to admit that in them "social and religious motives operated in fullest harmony" (*p. 83*). But *Kalthoff* regards the synagogue as "communistic" and John the Baptist is "communistic"!! We ought also to remember the decree of the Emperor against all political or politically suspicious associations which was administered with great severity, and the way in which the Christians were continually trying to prove the political innocence of their associations; cf. *Neumann: Der römische Staat und die allg. Kirche, I, 1890.*

[12] (p. 41.) Cf. *Pöhlmann's* work. This valuable book must, however, so *Max Weber* tells me, be used with caution. It is based too much on modern socialistic categories, although in the period with which the writer is dealing the necessary presupposition, i.e. a new class which is struggling to rise in the social scale, does not exist at all. There is no industrial system and there are no factories. Only the Carthaginians, and, after their example, the Romans, organized an industrial system, and along with that the slave barracks. This does not mean, however, that there was a factory system, because such a system would have been impossible to work with slaves and there were no free manual labourers; thus there was no basis for a socialistic movement. The conflicts which do take place happen rather within the ruling class, and are rather democratic than socialistic, due of course to economic motives. The same groups always opposed each other, with the aim of dividing power and property afresh. *P.* overestimates the meaning of the political romances, and does not enter into the practical side of things in sufficient detail. Even when *Eduard Meyer* speaks of "factory" in his much more accurate study of the question, the political economists have questioned this use of the term, although the latter have had to admit to the historians that the range of Society affected by a money economy and by a system of free labour was much greater than until then the political economists had been disposed to admit.

[13] (p. 41.) *Wendland; Mommsen: Römische Geschichte, Band V; L. Hahn: Rom und Romanismus im griechisch-römischen Osten, 1906;* all that *Pöhlmann* can say about this is to point to the romantic social philosophy of the educated classes which looked back to the Golden Age and the primeval times; then he adds: "Does not the question then arise quite naturally: If even among the educated circles of Roman Society there was such a capacity for dreaming of Utopias, to what heights of fantasy must the revolutionary ideology of the proletariat have risen" (*II, 606*). This is a very insecure line of argument, seeing that a proletariat of this kind cannot even be produced; according to *pp. 616 ff.*, this proletariat is supposed to be composed of the Christians, whose ideas of the Millennium correspond with Zeno's social State of Humanity, which is supposed to form part of the "religious phenomena of the Socialism of the Ancient World". The original Christian sources, however, know nothing of all this.

[14] (p. 41.) For the social history of the Imperial period cf. *Max Weber: "Agrargeschichte" (Altertum)* in *HWB. der Staatswissenschaften* and *"Wahrheit" (Stuttgart, 1896), pp. 57–77, "on the social causes of the decay of the civilization of the Ancient World"; Eduard Meyer: Die wirtschaftliche Entwickelung des Altertums, 1895; Die Sklaverei im Altertum, 1897,* and *Bevölkerung des Altertums* in *HWB. d. Staatsw.; U. Wilcken: Griechische Ostraka aus Aegypten und Nubien, I, 1899, pp. 664–704.* Of a very different character from these works *Uhlhorn: Liebestätigkeit, pp. 93–113, 213–238. Weber* describes the rise and decline of a capitalistic plantation system of large estates based upon slave-labour, and the slave prison (*ergastulum*), which withdrew from the coast to the interior, causing the civilization based on money (which was not very strong in any case) to decline; through its competition it

created an unemployed *Hungerproletariat* of freemen: all this belongs to the development in the West, and through the withdrawal of trade it meant also for Greece the growth of a proletariat of this kind. Among the slaves of the large estates who were herded together at night in the *ergastulum* there would have been little possibility of Christianity being able to effect an entrance; only when, owing to the lack of slaves, the system of the colonate was introduced, and these serfs were again allowed to own property and to have a family life of their own, did Christianity make progress among them. "This is parallel to the victorious development of Christianity; in the slave barracks Christianity could only have found an entrance with difficulty, but the unfree African peasants of the time of Augustine were already supporters of a sect-movement" (*Wahrheit, 68*). Hence the Christian slaves must have belonged chiefly to the smaller class of domestic slaves, or to the category of those who carried on a business in the name of their masters and with their money, who remained slaves in the eyes of the law, it is true, but who both economically and personally enjoyed a considerable amount of independence. One well-known example is that of Calixtus, who conducted a banking business for his master, and who in spite of his rascally ways in business managed to become a bishop and then Pope; this was only another kind of middle class. It is, however, difficult to say what was the situation so far as the free *Hungerproletariat* (*Kautsky's "Lumpenproletariat"*) and its relation to Christianity were concerned. We ought to find traces of this situation in the reports of the charity of the Early Church; here, in fact, we do find exhortations to support those who are unable to work, and to find work for those who are out of work (*Harnack: Mission, I, 150 ff.*). We must also remember the statement that about the year 250 Rome had to feed and care for about 1,500 persons every year (*H., I, 136*). But in any case this provision of work was not a central concern of the Church, and it can scarcely have been successful on a large scale, so that we can only come to the conclusion that the number of actual members of the proletariat who belonged to the Christian community was not so very great; and never do we find anywhere the least trace of any encouragement of revolutionary ideas among a particular class. Further, all this only concerns the West. Also, until the close of the second century the Church in Rome was essentially Greek, and thus it had very little to do with distressed Italian peasants and manual labourers. In the East the situation was considerably different, and it was in the East that the larger number of the Christian churches and groups was to be found, as well as their literature and their thought. Here a money economy was predominant; this obliterated the great difference between the village and the town, and there was an extensive lower middle class of free workmen alongside of a not too extensive system of domestic slavery. It seems probable that the larger number of the Christians were to be found in this middle class, which therefore lived in social conditions where a money economy prevailed, and which was mainly urban, although the villages were not ignored. The reports of the large sums of money which were given for the purposes of Christian philanthropy lead us to conclude that similar conditions also to some extent prevailed in the West (*Harnack, I, 127–172*); what part was played alongside of that by the natural support of charity through hospitality, finding work within the community for those who needed it, through gifts in kind at the love-feasts (*Uhlhorn, I, 138*), cannot be ascertained; in any case, they were not the main concern. Thus for a hundred years Christianity moved in circles which were still scarcely affected by the great social upheaval. The final result of the upheaval as a whole (which may be described as the destruction of the peasant class by the ancient city civilization, and the destruction of this city civilization in its turn by the sinking of capital in the system of large estates) meant, however, the return, very largely, to a natural economy, and to the stable primitive forms of social organization which are connected with it, as well as the return to feudalism, through which, in the West, the Empire passes on into the mediaeval natural economy, and in the East there arises a state strongly conditioned by a natural economy, and also constituted as an exclusive body of officials belonging to an hereditary caste. Obviously the Christian Church was not produced by this process: at the most it was aided by the sense of a material decline, and of the need of masses of people who were in distress. When Christianity rose out of the lower middle class, and the masses, into the upper classes, it then felt the effect of these upheavals, and then it supported the State and the system of government, and as a thoroughly conservative power it also took up the task of meeting the widespread misery and want, with which it was far beyond the power of the State to deal. This, however, did not take place until the third century. Cf. the conclusions which *Harnack* draws from his statistical researches (*Mission, II, 276–287*). "Christianity was a religion of the towns: the larger the town, the greater—probably also relatively—was the number of the Christians. At the same time Christianity had also penetrated already into a large number of provinces (about 300): We know this for a certainty in relation to the majority of the provinces of Asia Minor, also with reference to Armenia, Syria, and Egypt, and parts of Palestine and North Africa" (*p. 278*): "Above all, the great difference between the East and the West sections of the Empire is most evident. If, however, we distinguish between Greeks and Latins the percentage is still greater. The explanation is simple enough: from the days of the apostles there had been a Greek Christianity, but a Latin one, worth the name, only existed probably from the days of Marcus Aurelius" (*p. 282*). At the same time, everywhere the Christian communities are supporters of Hellenism; "it was, however, not the Egyptian Hellenism, but that of Asia Minor, with its connection with Persian civilization, which took the lead" (*p. 283*). This also proves that here primarily we are not dealing with the Italian "*Lumpenproletariat*."—There are many interesting details in *Uhlhorn's* book, but his point of view, i.e. that slave labour suppressed free labour and produced pauperism, which Christianity tried to overcome by charity and by teaching the dignity of labour, that, however, it was unable to do this and failed, and therefore followed the line of asceticism, does not apply to the early centuries, when an improvement had set in. It was only in the fourth century that the State went bankrupt, and the masses fell into such great misery.

[16] (p. 43.) Cf. *E. Meyer: Volkswirtsch. Entw., p. 52.* "The (religious) movement begins in the middle of the first century of Christianity, during the period when the decay of ancient civilization both in the East and in the West was being prepared, which then also receives its definite form through the development of the princedom (*Prinzipat*)."

[17] (p. 45.) The so-called Ebionite passages in Luke, which seem to glorify poverty in itself, are no proof against this contention. For, on the one hand, they assume (as the whole general attitude of the Gospels shows very plainly, as well as the intention of the evangelist himself) the ethico-religious effect of poverty in producing a better religious disposition, while, on the other hand, they are in keeping with the author's tendency to lay stress upon sickness, weakness, want, and poverty in order to exalt the religion of Redemption. This would not be at all surprising if the tradition upon which the author has drawn did glorify

poverty in itself. The tendency is near enough. But Jesus' proclamation of the infinite worth of the soul, seems, without a doubt, to render quite remote any idea of a value in poverty in itself, and a need to be compensated for it. Cf. *Holtzmann: Lehrbuch der neutestamentlichen Theologie, 1827, I, 448–454*, who sees in these passages essentially the reflex of later popular development, which quite naturally regarded the Kingdom of God as compensation for earthly suffering and a reward for renunciation. That, however, is a very natural result, and deterioration, of the thought, not its starting-point. The Apocalypse of John simply preaches hatred against the Roman Empire and against the worship of the Caesars, and pays no attention to social inequalities. The Epistle of James, dating from the beginning of the second century, declaims against rich men (*II*), but they are members of the Church! The severer passage (*V, 1–6*) is directed against rich men in general, but the whole general attitude ought to be judged in the same way as the Ebionite passages. This is the spirit of people with a narrow outlook. It is like treating the doctrines of social democracy in a small way, as though they simply mean a "division of property" and "revenge on the wealthy"; in both cases very big people have accepted the opinion of the lesser folk, and then have thought that they had grasped the meaning of the principle; this makes the task of criticism easier. It is worthy of note that the Gospel of John in all its weighty development of religious thought knows nothing of all this. On this question the essentially religious idea stands in direct opposition to the "spirit of small minds". We notice the same thing in St. Paul. *Weinel: Die Stellung des Urchristentums zum Staat, 1907, pp. 12–17*, overestimates the "socio-radical undercurrent", and since he infers it from the exhortations to quietness and self-restraint, reveals what the real spirit is by this very remark.

[19] (p. 47.) *S. Jodl: Geschichte der Ethik², I, 97, 113 ff.* and *Zeller: Geschichte d. griech. Philos, III², pp. 360 ff.* After all, these motives chiefly affected the cultured upper class, which was forced out of political life. We must assume that the lower classes were less fatigued and resigned, in spite of the influence of all the moral homilies and diatribes of the Cynics and Stoics. They suffered most of all from economic pressure. There is no sufficient material to indicate their outlook and temper, at least the documents which might be gathered from existing inscriptions and papyri have not been collected and studied.

[20] (p. 48.) That is what *Pöhlmann (II, 533)* thinks, who sees in Christianity "with the excessive Chiliastic ideas of revolution" the most powerful revolutionary ideology. The fact that *Pöhlmann* considers that this ideology was "particularly widespread" in Rome shows how inaccurate he is in such matters. But Chiliasm, or the Kingdom of God, has nothing to do with ideal social conditions. Cf. *Wernle: Die Anfänge unserer Religion², 1904, pp. 38–49, 260–266.* P. could only support his theory by referring to those "Ebionite" passages, already mentioned, of which Early Church literature provides many parallels. I have already dealt with this question. How unjustifiable it is to speak of "a social revolution coming down from above, or from God", we learn from the simple circumstance that to a great extent poverty was artificially introduced through the giving away of one's possessions, simply in order to satisfy the religious thirst for self-sacrifice and self-conquest. The dominant idea in the estimate of poverty did not lie in any expected humiliation of the wealthy, but very soon it lay in the ascetic-religious way of thinking, which is the very opposite of Socialism.

[23] (p. 54.) In these conceptions we have the fundamental principles of the history of the Christian ethic. The moral demands themselves are later on

recognized as self-evident, and assumed to be known to everyone; as with Jesus the Jewish ethic, so later on the individualistic-humanitarian morality of late antiquity was simply taken for granted (*Harnack: Mission, I, 180*). All the Christian tables of virtues and vices, the isolated discussions of casuistry, and incidental discussions of demands are therefore more or less accidental; also the later attempts to cram virtues into the Platonic or Aristotelian list of virtues, or into the categories of the Stoics or of Cicero, are merely scientific artificialities. Claims and ideals were conceived out of the universal consciousness, quite opposing schools like those of the Hedonists were sharply opposed as something so completely wrong that their ideas ought not to be taken seriously. No attempt was made to construct a really scientific derivation of ethical ideas from the fundamental principles of Christianity; such attempts were considered superfluous. All that does appear are mere questions of detail, such as those of the connection between the natural powers and the morality of grace, or of a way of life which is either more ascetic or more in touch with the general life of the world, and, while these discussions are usually supported by quotations from Scripture, they are actually entirely incidental, and possess no guiding principle. This is the reason why most histories of Christian ethics give the impression of an infinite confusion.

In point of fact, however, instinctively there is a principle of selection among the presupposed moral judgments, and this principle is already revealed in the dual tendencies of the Gospel here mentioned. The introduction of asceticism, which makes self-denial an end in itself; the preponderance of purely sacerdotal authority, which turns the commands of the Church into a law, and obedience into an ascetic act of humility; the relation between the equivalent reward and the penalties of purgatory, which makes action not a means of union with God but a means of guaranteeing one's future destiny; and, finally, the casuistry which weaves a complicated web of commandments—all this, indeed, produces an atmosphere of uncertainty which is extremely bewildering, but which in its turn is triumphantly broken through by all interior souls. The Jewish Decalogue was only adopted as a summary of Christian ethics quite late in the history of the Church, and the "Evangelical Counsels" were placed alongside it as the really new Christian element. This constitutes a final and complete obscuration of the real facts of the case.

²⁴ (p. 57.) In this particular I do not think I can quite agree with *Harnack's* interpretation of the fundamental position. H. (*Reden, I, 28 f.*) analyses the Gospel and finds here three essential elements: (1) Trust in God, (2) belief in Redemption, (3) love of one's neighbour. The first may lead occasionally to Quietism, the second either to a holy indifference towards the world or to a radical improvement of the world, the third is the social motive. But in my opinion we cannot thus separate the elements, and simply place them side by side like this. In any case, trust in God and faith in Redemption are inseparably connected; this means that man can give himself quietly and unconditionally to the highest interest, to that of the soul's salvation, because God cares sufficiently for his temporal needs, and does not wish him to have any anxiety about temporal matters; suffering too, which very specially belongs to the temporal realm, should be accepted in the same trustful spirit as an experience of real value and for one's eternal good; on the other hand, the emphasis upon a quiet and steadfast trust in God, in the midst of the work and order of a stable world, is only the specifically Lutheran interpretation of this idea. The belief in Redemption which is contained in and conditioned by faith in God, which is the root principle of that which I call absolute religious individualism,

does not stand merely alongside of, or even in contrast to, the love of one's neighbour. It is quite clearly a motive springing out of the fundamental religious idea, as a manifestation of the perfect Divine temper, the awakening of the understanding of the true nature of God, as the fulfilment of the Will of God, in its most distinctive way—in which fulfilment, indeed, the soul frees itself from the world and abandons itself to God. It is true that the Gospel makes no distinction between "bodily and spiritual distress", and that "the needy and the wretched are to be assisted with all the powers of love" (*p. 30*). But even material help issues from the collective unity of all in God, and is a proof of the Perfection of God who lets His Sun shine on the just and on the unjust. Certainly such brotherly love could not possibly be claimed without a real spirit of love, but this spirit of love is attached more to the thought of God as active Fatherly love, and not to the thought of the help and assistance in itself. Otherwise it would be impossible to explain the emphasis laid on manifestations of pure love and the renunciation of all politico-social reform claims. To some extent love always implies self-conquest; or at least it expresses itself in the proclamation of the Message of Christ, or the endeavour to reveal or awaken the true knowledge of God in other souls; love is desired for the sake of God and not for the sake of man. This holds true of the life and times of Jesus, and of all the period which immediately followed. *H*. says on *p. 30*: "The world saw a new drama; whereas until now religion had always been either in close touch with earthly things and had willingly accompanied every circumstance of life, or it had set its face against all this and had striven to nest in the clouds, she was now faced with a new task: she had to learn to consider earthly things—both need and want as well as good fortune—as something of little account, and yet she was to be ready to help every kind of distress; the Christian believer is to gaze courageously towards Heaven, and yet with heart and mouth and hand to work for his brother here on earth." It seems to me that there is something wrong about this "and yet". The sentence on *p. 32*: "Where the Christian sees clearly that a certain economic situation has become full of pain and distress to mankind there he must seek a remedy; for he is a disciple of Him who was a Saviour", was never true of the Early Church, as the history of slavery shows very plainly. Its dangerous effect on character, and the pain and misery it caused, was well known in the Early Church, and even in Christian households it was by no means always avoided. The fact is that the idealism of the Church, coupled with her belief that the world, just as it is, cannot be altered, prevented her from ever perceiving that ethico-religious values are connected with, and to some extent determined by, the natural basis of life. If I cannot agree with *H*. on all these points, I can agree with the following statement by *Schmoller* (*Grundriss, I, 79*): "It is certain that these one-sided phenomena were the necessary accompaniment of that moral idealism which gripped the Western nations, leavened them with its ideas, and lifted them to a high stage of civilization. Out of this Christian surrender to God, these hopes of immortality and everlasting bliss, there arose a trust in God and a power of self-conquest which reached heights of actual moral heroism—a purity of soul, a selflessness, and a self-sacrifice for ideal ends became possible which had never been known before. The idea of brotherly love, of the love of one's neighbour, and of humanity began to permeate all the circumstances of life, modifying the hard conception of property, producing a victory of the interests of Society and of humanity over all selfish personal, class, and national interests, and a spirit of concern for the poor and the weak for which one searches antiquity in vain." In this passage the sociological principle itself, and its social application and influence, are rightly distinguished; the inward difficulty, however, which opposed the latter is not sufficiently emphasized in this passage. On the other hand, in my opinion the incorrectness in *Harnack's* conception seems to lie in this: that he makes no distinction between the two, but that from the beginning both are merged into one. The following are in agreement with my analysis: *Augustine's* interpretation of the Christian idea of love in the first chapter of his *Doctrina Christiana*; Clement of Alexandria, in his προτρεπτικός; *Uhlhorn, pp. 51–66.* On one point, however, I do not agree with *Uhlhorn*; he misunderstands the eschatological nature of the Kingdom of God, and speaks of making the world an instrument for the Kingdom of God, conceived as a redeemed humanity united in the love of God. These ideas are Lutheran and modern accretions; the whole of the following inquiry will show how little an idea of that kind represents the spirit of the Early Church.

[26] (p. 59.) It is a mistake to found the economic doctrine of the Gospel upon the story of the Rich Young Ruler, and certain familiar words which are connected with it concerning rich people. This is what *L. Brentano: Die wirtschaftlichen Lehren des christlichen Altertums (Sitzungsberichte der phil.-hist. Klasse der Münchener Akademie, 1902)* has done, and he was certainly able to claim the support of the Fathers. But these Fathers were already influenced by the need to dogmatize about the words of the Bible, and also by the idea of ascetic poverty, which had gained a position of great importance in the fight against the world. In their embarrassment the word of Jesus offered a very easy way out of their difficulty because it seemed to distinguish between ordinary obedience and higher perfection, and in this way it exactly seemed to answer to both needs, i.e. of life in the world and of ascetic renunciation. The words about the spiritual danger of riches are quite clear when we understand the fundamental point of view of Jesus, and they contain no negation of property, nor indeed any asceticism at all. In any case, the story of the Rich Young Ruler, however, whose genuineness can neither be proved nor disproved, cannot be made to serve as the basis of a doctrine. Jesus' attitude towards the question of possessions is clear enough, namely, to seek first the Kingdom of God and not to be anxious for the morrow. But the young man wants to do something special, so Jesus invites him to take part in His missionary work, and to sell all and give to the poor. We can only raise objections to this story if we believe that Jesus taught the doctrine that there was never any need for any special heroic efforts, but that the ideal was one dead level of the same duty for all. But this abstract kind of teaching was quite remote from Jesus. Its principle is preserved if such an effort constitutes no special merit. All the self-sacrifice of the disciples, and the challenge to prove for themselves whether their strength is equal to the demands of the Gospel (Luke xiv. 33), is a sign that this idea of special achievements was not far from the mind of Jesus; it was, indeed, quite natural to Him. Further, it is quite possible that this story has been influenced either wholly or in its form by later ascetic ideas. In any case, it is not the key to the economic teaching of the Gospel, but only the key to that of the later Church, which, owing to the fact that it had to fight with much more highly developed economic conditions, felt the difficulty and the contrast far more strongly. For her, however, the first part, that it was enough to keep the commandments, was quite as important as the second. Without the recognition of the fact that Jesus did summon His disciples in the narrower sense, or the missionaries and messengers of the Kingdom of God, to tasks which were harder than those which are laid on the mass of His

followers, the whole Gospel cannot be understood—it would indeed seem to have lost all logical meaning.

[31] (p. 64.) It is a remarkable fact that the communistic socialistic statements of the teachers of the Church only appear forcibly in the post-Constantine period. *Harnack* rightly lays stress upon this point (*Reden, II, 41 f.*), and it also comes out very clearly in the collection of passages made by *L. Brentano: Die wirtschaftlichen Lehre des christlichen Altertums*, to which he had already alluded in his rectorial address, *Ethik und Volkswirtschaft in der Geschichte, 1901. Brentano* himself does not notice this, and therefore, on this ground (i.e. of the expressions of opinion by the later Doctors of the Church) he speaks of a "strongly socialistic tendency which is evident in the Christian teaching of property" (*p. 183*). *Kautsky* and *Pöhlmann*, in addition to their misunderstanding of the idea of the Kingdom of God and of the Apocalypse, have appealed to these later Doctors, and especially to *Homily XI* in the *Acta apost.* of *St. Chrysostom*, as the proof of the communistic character of Christianity. This sermon, which certainly is very remarkable, is, however, based upon the story of Ananias and Sapphira; it is, therefore, quite natural that this text should give the whole sermon a communistic flavour. It is, however, a striking phenomenon. The explanation lies, as *Uhlhorn* shows us (*I, 265 ff.*), partly in the fact that the economic situation was growing steadily worse, partly in the doctrine of the Primitive State, which the later Fathers had formulated, and which will be expounded below, partly, and above all, from monasticism, as indeed Chrysostom himself suggests: "Thus to-day men live in the monasteries in the way in which in other days the (Jerusalem) believers used to live" (*Brentano, 158*). The Church gave no practical expression to these ideas at all, as is emphasized by *Harnack* (*Reden, 43*), *Overbeck: Sklaverei, 229,* and *Uhlhorn, I, 293,* but rather the contrary. *Brentano's* treatment of the subject betrays an absence of all understanding of the spirit of the Early Church; indeed, his one desire seems to be to prove that the ideas of Early Christianity are of no use for a Liberal Capitalistic economic policy, which was otherwise quite evident.

[32] (p. 68.) Cf. *Wendland; Zeller: Gesch. d. griech. Philos., III³, 1,* and *III³, 2; Overbeck: Stellung der Alten Kirche u.s.w.; Keim: pp. 31–55, 308–328; Bonhöffer: Die Ethik des Stoikers Epiktet, 1894; Zahn: Der Stoiker Epiktet und sein Verhältniss zum Christentum, 1895; Baur: Drei Abhandlungen zur Geschichte der alten Philosophie und ihres Verhältnisses zum Christentum, 1876; Jodl, I, 584–587, 82–108.* The universal social ethic belongs to the Stoics alone, and this is the reason why it is so extremely important for Christianity, as will be shown later on. The ethical system and school of the Cynics, which in so many ways are closely allied to it, do indeed manifest a striking likeness to it; but the lack of a social system of ethics founded on the religious idea of the Unity of God and the Love of God, means that it is unable to rise far above the average level; it tends rather in the direction of a pure individualism, with insistence on the importance of inner possessions, that is, to asceticism. Otherwise the ancient schools of philosophy possessed no social or ethical importance at all. The social philosophy of Aristotle with its conception of Natural Law, where the idea of the State is based merely upon Reason, with its adherence to the old ideal of the concrete city-state of antiquity, and its merely philosophical regulation of the concrete historical State, is many centuries away from Christian thought, and only later did it gain some significance through fusion with the Stoics' conception of Natural Law. Platonism, which from the second century became a renewed force, was indeed of the highest significance for Christian thought; this, however, was only due to its religious mysticism and its dualistic

metaphysic, not to its social philosophy. The latter is always connected with the city-state by the true Platonist in a specifically Hellenistic and aristocratic manner, and its communism does not arise out of love to God and in God, but out of the intellectual desire for unity, and it has, therefore, no inner relationship with the Christian ideas of a universal communism of love. The interest of the new Pythagoreanism and Platonism, however, unlike Platonism with its interest in patriotism and social reform, based on contact with a concrete Hellenism, was overwhelmingly religious; its main concern was with mysticism, asceticism, the problem of immortality, the attainment of personal salvation through an inward new birth, and the renewed inspiration of the cultus, in which Divine revelations are granted to the believer. In the sphere of social ethics and politics they adapted themselves to the Empire, proclaimed the necessity for an ethical renewal of the existing order, and general goodwill; the real centre of their thought, however, was not that of a humanity in the ethical service of God, but a mystical fellowship in worship, conceived in a very aristocratic and intellectual way. Genuine Neo-Platonism, moreover, places political and socio-ethical interests which were always closely connected in the ancient world, far behind a completely subjective form of religious life, whose highest point is reached in the experience of ecstasy; its conception of God certainly contains some of the essential elements of mysticism, but of social ethics it has no trace. This, of course, is of great significance for the theory of religious knowledge and for metaphysics, for the monastic system, and for the attitude of the Church to the world, but not for the idea of a universal social ethic. This is why all the later attempts to realize the vision contained in the *politeia* of Plato deal only with the relationship between the Church and the world, but not with the general social ethic of Christianity. *Zeller, III, 142 f., 146–189, 605; Vossler: Die göttliche Komödie, I, 2, 1907*, in his study of Dante's Christian social ethics and politics, and of the historical elements which form their setting, comes to quite similar results, in so far as the Hellenistic-Roman social Roman doctrine and ethic are concerned. For the extraordinary importance of Cicero for the Christian ethic see also the excellent book by *Thamin: St. Ambroise et la morale chrétienne au 4ème siècle, 1895*. "Il est un de ses ancêtres moraux, et, à sa manière, lui aussi un père de l'église" (*p. 172*). The same writer, on Seneca (*p. 178*): "Jérôme le compta donc au nombre des écrivains ecclési-astiques, et pendant douze siècles ce fut une tradition incontestée". Curiously enough Epictetus plays almost the same part.

[36] (p. 81.) *Kautsky* is right in his observation that a communism which retains the idea of private property necessarily immediately feels the results of this fact. This is really the reason why primitive Christian communism did not last. Further, however, we must admit (what *Kautsky* himself, owing to his conception of Christianity as a socialistic movement, cannot see) that the conservative religious attitude, which accepts the world-order as natural, and also the possession of private property as an integral part of it, and therefore the refusal of all revolution, is forced to give up communism. The latter would only have been possible to carry through if it had gone very much farther than it did in those primitive days, and then it would have had to give up private property altogether. But no one thought of such a thing, for that would have meant a new order and a total revolution.

[36a] (p. 85.) When this was already written Harnack's instructive discussion of the first section of my contribution, in the *Prussian Yearbook* for *March 1908*, came into my hands. Speaking of the problem contained in the second section he says: "On the one hand, there broods over the growing development of the

Christian community a kind of 'communism of love' which has arisen spontaneously out of the radicalism of love to God and man; on the other hand, it was almost impossible to imagine that this communism of love could ever be realized, or, if it were realized, it would not endure. People were not ready to alter conditions. The consequence was that unconsciously the Christian community adapted itself to a long process of transformation within the framework of existing conditions, or, rather, it set in motion a general process of moral development, which slowly permeated its social environment. Naturally the first institution to benefit was the family, then all social intercourse through trade, in daily life, and Society, through the virtues of faithfulness and trust, purity and peace, support and help. . . . At first, of course, all this was confined to the Christian congregations in their life amongst themselves, but these communities grew larger and larger, and there are several instances of their care for those who were not believers. The position which was gained was, from the social point of view—and realization—the most favourable that can be imagined; the ideal of 'love-communism' brooded over the life of Christian communities, preventing them from settling down in complacency, and yet it was far too high—with some insignificant exceptions —to be realized in practice; in the communities themselves strong moral demands for the purification of private life, marriage, the family, and all social intercourse were operative, but these demands were related to real conditions. From the very beginning the new religion was, or very soon became in the Gentile Church, a conservative power in relation to social conditions. . . . Apart from her nebulous ideal of the communism of love, Christianity neither possessed nor evolved any social programme peculiar to herself; . . . all she did possess was an absolute authority, while she also introduced various improvements, a higher morality, a more inward attitude towards life, and an actual achievement of helpfulness which probably was far ahead of anything of the same kind that existed in the Empire at that time" (*pp. 457 ff.*). All this, of course, is quite true. But, on the one hand, this statement seems to me to underestimate the remoteness of the new community towards the world as well as its fundamental idealism, while, on the other hand, I believe that in this actual historical content there are in principle deeper depths and deeper consequences, which still need to be specially formulated. Behind this "long transformation within the existing world order" there was a peculiar acceptance of it. Thus at the very outset we are confronted with the problem of the relationship between the revolutionary and the conservative elements in Christian thought, a problem which recurs continually throughout the history of Christianity.

[36b] (p. 85.) For the latter see *J. Burkhardt's* teaching on the crises and revolutions of world history, and the special character of the modern crises: *Weltgeschichtliche Betrachtungen, 1905, pp. 132–137, 193 f., 198, 200, 128.*—For the relatively conservative character of the Christian ethic see my *Politische Ethik und Christentum, 1904*, in which, however, the opposite aspect is emphasized. Both tendencies are also noted by *Stahl*, who is still an acute and instructive thinker for the present day. Cf. *Der christliche Staat, p. 8:* "The Christian disposition, that combination of reverence, humility, surrender and freedom, independence and frankness, which is quite remote from all slavishness of spirit." In his opinion most scope is allowed for this spirit under a constitutional monarchy: "It is precisely that, even when in a less perfect form, which must constitute the fundamental relationship of a genuine republic." "Historically also the institution of the constitutional state, as well as the production of this

political temper, have arisen out of Christianity. The Germanic races have received from the Catholic Church the high sense of the consecration of the government which comes from God, and the Christian-religious movement of the English Puritans and Independents arises out of the idea of the liberty and self-government of a Christian nation."

[36c] (p. 86.) In our works on Church History this necessary revolutionary effect of the universalistic-transcendental religious idea on the whole existing order in the State, in Society, and in civilization is not sufficiently stressed. Here also the extremely thoughtful phenomenology of history (mentioned above) by *J. Burkhardt* sees very clearly into the question. The teaching on the six ways in which the State, religion, and civilization mutually condition each other is a mine of apt observation. For the revolutionary character of Christianity and of universal religion in general, see *pp. 137–145.* "Judaism and Primitive Christianity based Society upon religion, just as Islam did at a later date" (*p. 138*). This led these religions into sharp conflict with the civilization which was based upon the State. That the radical opposition still exists at the present day (in which many only see, with *Burkhardt*, the "complicity" of the religious ecclesiastical authorities with the conservative power-interests, which are menaced by abstract rationalism and the free development of civilization) can be seen in the following ways: in the constant struggle of the Roman Catholic Church with the State and with modern civilization, which is not due merely to reactionary motives or to the need for centralization; in the clash between religious cosmopolitanism and the Peace Movement with political interests, in the hostility of ethical policy and its "humanitarianism" to the lack of principle which characterizes all politics which are simply moved by the desire for power, in the suspicion of revolutionary tendencies which is cherished by the conservatives whenever a Christian social policy is outlined, and, in Calvinistic countries, the frequent interference of congregations and ministers by inserting socio-ethical demands into political programmes.

[36d] (p. 87.) With this cf. the extremely able book of *Simmel: Die Philosophie des Geldes*[2], *1908*, which contrasts the intellectual-ethical correlatives of a natural economy (*Naturalwirtschaft*) and of a money economy (*Geldwirtschaft*) with each other in a most instructive manner, and which has opened my eyes to these connections also in the different formations and crises of the Christian ethic. It seems to me of great importance that this tendency of the Christian ethic towards simpler and less stereotyped conditions of life should be separated from the later complications of ecclesiastical and politico-social-conservative interests. The conservatism of the Early Church and of the Middle Ages had nothing to do with this tendency as it did not try to conserve these conditions, but only taught obedience and submission to the existing authorities created by God, which were also, in some way, also due to sin. The conservatism of the modern churches, however, is directed towards conserving politico-social conditions of power. One of the most suspicious elements in the social ethic of the conservative "Christianity" of the present day is the fact that its representatives will not face the glaring inconsistency between their views and the hard facts of the present economic situation. On the other hand, when a political programme of peasants and of manual labourers appeals to the ethical standards of Christianity understood in the patriarchal sense, it is certainly justified in doing so; but this is a very different matter from submission to the conservative principle of obedience to all the powers and authorities created by and permitted by God. *Stahl* also did not venture to claim this tendency to revert to simpler and more patriarchal conditions for politico-social conservatism, but

only for "the conservative tendency in the purest sense" (*p. 16*). *Max Weber* has pointed out to me in conversation the fact of the continuance of the more primitive and personal group-morality in the lower middle classes of the Ancient World, among whom the Early Church met with the greatest response. Long ago scholars noted that the early Christian communities lived, to a great extent, within the same social framework as their contemporaries. The Christians adopted the customary rules of the tribe or association, thus showing how closely their own ethic was connected with that primitive group-ethic with its emphasis on the individual.

⁴⁰ (p. 95.) The fact that the ecclesiastical organization, and its relation to other social groups, is conditioned by the conception of truth, is the point of view from which my treatise, *Die Trennung von Staat und Kirche, 1907*, endeavours to illuminate the problem. For this reason I hold it to be an error to regard Catholicism too exclusively as the heir of the Roman idea of Empire; its need for centralization and its exclusiveness are due primarily to its conceptions of truth and of the Sacraments, and are only connected with the Empire to the extent that the Empire also required a unified form of religion as its correlate. For the same reason I hold it to be an error to derive its dogmatism and intellectualism (which are only connected with its unity, and not with the intelligibility of the doctrine) from "Hellenization" and an admixture of Greek metaphysics. In the main it is explained by the development of the idea of unity, even in the sphere of doctrine. The spirit of real Greek science appeared very seldom in the history of dogma, and when it did it was always condemned.

⁴⁶ᵇ (p. 104.) Cf. *Zöckler: Kritische Geschichte der Askese, 1863*, essentially a collection of material on pagan, Jewish, Catholic, and Protestant asceticism, as well as a statement about the theological theories of asceticism, but for that very reason most instructive. On the other hand, however, the book almost entirely lacks all psychological insight. On that latter point see *James: Varieties of Religious Experience, 1902*, for some fine observations. One-sided and fantastic stimulation of religious feeling, with lack of stress on the ethical side and a lack of objectivity due to lack of scientific training, tends to produce in certain individuals a mass of psychopathic phenomena. But even in individuals who are highly trained on the ethical and scientific side the tendency to melancholy will produce that feeling of distance from God as well as union with all kinds of forcible methods which we see in Origen and in Pascal. Further, such abnormalities do not exclude the growth of real and valuable religious elements which can become detached from the soil in which they arose. See *Hellpach: Zur Formenkunde der Beziehungen zwischen Religiosität und Abnormität, Z. f. Religionspsychologie, 1907.*

⁴⁸ (p. 105.) Cf. *J. Burkhardt: Die Zeit Konstantins des Grossen, 1853*. A description of this kind can certainly only be applied to the upper classes, as I have already suggested. But even among the lower classes it disturbed their confidence in the previous order of things and the old standards of life. To what extent asceticism, which, indeed, in its achievements does constitute in itself an enormous development in force, strengthened the natural energy of these lower classes which was already directed towards the transcendent realm, is difficult to say, but it is worth considering.

⁵⁰ (p. 106.) How little virginity in itself, however, signifies a negative ascetic attitude to life is shown by the Apostle Paul, in whom the tendency towards celibacy is an isolated trait, and can be clearly explained as an aversion to the competition of the passions of sex. The restraint required in other forms of

religion before taking part in religious rites is due partly to the same reason, and partly to the idea of uncleanness, due to the physiological process.

[51] (p. 108.) The transition from the Gospel to asceticism takes place easily when that which only has sense and significance in connection with fellowship with God is practised for its own sake, and, so to speak, laid up as a provision in order to be ready to stand before God. Thus the destruction of self-will, of the love of self and the world, readiness to serve, humility, and love, are practised in matters that are quite indifferent, in order to be used a little more easily in the real and only valid connection. Along this line the transition of the Gospel from heroism to asceticism develops psychologically, and once this has taken place it gathers into itself all the other motives for asceticism which belonged to the time. As proof of this see the meaning of the word "asceticism" and its change in meaning cf. *Gass, I, 104*; it means (first of all) practice in virtue, and forms, for instance, in *Clement* the condition of the higher Gnostic perfection; ascetics are then the martyrs as "developed and strong to suffer, setters forth of the Imitation of Christ". From this point it developed in a direct line towards monasticism. "It was just as possible to regard asceticism as a means of fostering moral activity as also to give to it a meaning in itself, to turn it into a merit. The difference between the two was so finely drawn that it was impossible to prevent the one merging into the other." From that time forward, and not till then, did the word have its modern sense of "mortification" and despising of the world, denial of the world and flight from the world, while even to-day Catholic ecclesiastical language uses it first of all in the sense of practice in virtue and the means of virtue. It has even been used in this sense by Protestant ethics.

[52] (p. 108.) Augustine's explanation of this point is characteristic (*De doctrina christiana, I, 3 ff.*): he distinguishes between *frui* and *uti*, which became a fundamental element of all the later teaching of Catholic ethics. To "enjoy" anything means to "love" anything; but the Christian should love no one but God in the true sense of the word. For the world there remains over the *usus*. It is like the ship in which one returns to one's home. If we were to take such pleasure in the comforts and pleasantness of the journey, or of the means of travel, that we were to give ourselves up to enjoyment, instead of to the mere use of the vessel we would lose sight of the goal of the journey. We must use the world, but not enjoy it, in order that we may see the invisible in God through the visible and created world, i.e. from the things of time and space we must reap a harvest of the unseen and the eternal. This is most characteristic. It is not asceticism in the actual sense of the word, but the replacing of the value of the good things of this world by pressing them into the service of the supernatural. But real asceticism, the mortification of Nature and the annihilation of the natural will, very easily slip into it. The whole of primitive Christian thought and that of the Middle Ages regarding the world sways hither and thither between these ideas—a clear sign that the fundamental idea is not asceticism but the supernatural outlook, the exaltation of a specifically religious life-aim, in fellowship with God, above all worldly interests. Asceticism only steps in as a means to protect the spiritual life from the over-vigorous competition of worldly ends, and it certainly achieves its object, although instead of limiting the Christian's interest in the things of this world it treats them as non-existent. It is the *via tutior*, which is also closely connected with the point of view which leaves out of account the ethic of sentiment and replaces it with the new law and the acquisition of merit. In the 'atter instance great ideas are reduced to the average level, with its

interest in the rewards and penalties of the future life, much of which belongs to Greek eschatology, and has nothing to do with the Kingdom of God; cf. *A. Dieterich: Nekyia, 1893*, and *G. Anrich: Clemens und Origenes als Begründer der Lehre vom Fegfeuer (Theol. Abhh., Festgabe für Holtzmann, 1902)*. Very frequently, however, this means that asceticism becomes an end in itself; but when this is really the case there is always a way out through that radical monasticism, which is suspect to the Church, or through that pantheistic mysticism which is alien to Christian thought. Again and again the Church has refused to admit these by-paths. In this she is completely logical; though she has always done it instinctively, and, in fact, not from the standpoint of a principle which she clearly perceives.

[53] (p. 110.) For the double standard of morality see *Uhlhorn, I, 200 ff.* In my opinion we ought not to regard this from the customary Protestant point of view simply as a departure from the most primitive and genuine Christian morality. For this primitive Christian ethic, with its indifference to the world, with its insistence on the attainment of perfection, had, indeed, from the beginning no theory about the rejection of the world, but, on the other hand, it had no desire to penetrate or to transform the world. Montanism means the rigid adherence to this old attitude of indifference to the world and to the eschatological hope. As the Church expanded and penetrated into the general system of the world's life the force of circumstances finally made all this impossible. *Uhlhorn* says: "Now the Church was faced by the great task of penetrating the whole of the surrounding life of the world—of the nation, the state, science, art and social conditions—with the Christian spirit, and of transforming it from within outwards. She failed to achieve this task, and was turned aside into false paths" (*p. 201*), into the path of laxity on the one hand and into that of asceticism on the other. This task, however, she never stated to herself, and, indeed, she could not formulate it, with the conception of the world which was hers from the very beginning, and which lay at the root of all her thinking. In view of the prevalence of the conception of the world which has just been described there was no other possible solution than that of the division of the task. *Uhlhorn's* ideal is based upon a different conception of the world, which is peculiar to Lutheranism, and especially to "world-transforming" Lutheranism. At bottom it contains the modern attitude to the world, which was only brought into being and completed by the later Middle Ages and the Renaissance. The whole problem of asceticism is altogether much more subtle and complicated than Protestant ethical teachers usually recognize. Further, the idea of a double standard of morals has its parallel and its precedent in Stoicism, whose rigorism also necessitated a higher and a lower morality, a morality of perfection and one of mediocrity. This parallel has not passed unnoticed. The παιδαγωγός of *Clement (III, ii)* and the *De Officiis Ministrorum* of Ambrose, *I, 36–37*, with direct reference to the Stoics, accepted the distinction. To this belongs also Nietzsche's famous doctrine of "slave morality". It is very remarkable that Nietzsche, who in reference to his own system of morals is very conscious that it is the consequence of the proposition *God is dead*, will not allow that the other system of morals is the consequence of the proposition *God is alive*. In truth, the Gospel ethic should be interpreted throughout in the light of its religious motive, which Jesus inherited from Judaism; we can, however, scarcely imagine that his primary motive in this ethic was the elevation of the depressed classes. If there is anything which is characteristic of Jesus it is the natural pre-eminence in Him of the religious element. Humiliation in itself, and for its own sake, is, however, only an

ascetic action, and its setting is far more complicated than Nietzsche admits.

[54] (p. 111.) The only systematic attempt (of which I have any knowledge) to develop the ethical idea from the principle is in this passage from the *Collationes* of *Cassian* quoted by *Ziegler* (*Gesch. d. christl. Ethik, p. 208*): "Principium nostrae salutis sapientiaeque secundum scripturas timor domini est [i.e. above all religion] de timore domini nascitur compunctio salutaris. de compunctione cordis procedit abrenuntiatio, id est nuditas et contemptus omnium facultatum. de nuditate humilitas procreatur, de humilitate mortificatio voluntatum generatur. mortificatione voluntatum extirpantur atque marcescunt universa vitia. expulsione vitiorum virtutes fructificant atque succrescunt. pullulatione virtutum *puritas cordis* acquiritur. puritate cordis apostolicae *caritatis* perfectio possidetur." As *Ziegler* rightly remarks, this is, indeed, primarily the ethic of the cloister. Nevertheless, in its inner connection it is the fundamental type of morality in general; the only monastic element is the looking to the Church to create humility and to exercise charity. Otherwise, it is noteworthy that it is exactly those fundamental commandments of purity of heart and brotherly love which I singled out in my analysis of the Gospel which here also emerge as the leading qualities; it is also very clear that the changed purpose of both is formulated from the point of view of asceticism instead of from that of communion with God; mortification of the will also implies the destruction of evil, and the end is love and communion with God. That love is produced from the task of self-development is, indeed, only possible because silently and naturally the Gospel conception of God is still assumed, because the task of self-development at bottom is still dimly interpreted as self-surrender to the creative Divine activity. Certainly the main idea of God which lies behind all this is very obscure, and therefore even love tends to be regarded rather as asceticism, a "good work", or a "merit". Instead of love, therefore, it is better to use the expression "charity", which has become the customary term in Catholicism. The emphasis on *puritas cordis* and *caritas* amid the varied lists of virtues and vices became fixed for the whole of scholasticism. Cf. *Ziegler* with reference to Augustine (*p. 230*), to Hrabanus Maurus (*p. 253*), to Albertus Magnus (*p. 387*), to the mystics (*p. 389*), The *Theologia Germanica* (*406*), *Thomas à Kempis* (*407*), and *Meister Eckhardt* (*p. 39 ff.*). The combinations fluctuate between humility and charity, detachment and love. The relation of these ideas to the Gospel source is quite clear, as well as the fact that the changes introduced by asceticism, ecclesiasticism, and the doctrine of merit are due to an altered conception of God. The mystical analysis in particular approaches the Gospel very closely, even up to the frontiers of mysticism itself and its acosmic background, which are quite remote from the Hebrew idea of a God of Will.

[55] (p. 114.) *Overbeck, pp. 197–201*, rightly points this out. *Harnack*, in his *Militia christiana, 1905, pp. 50 ff.*, gives it as his opinion that the predominance of the eschatological outlook gave the Church "a quietistic and conservative tendency; after this had declined, while at the same time during the period of the Antonines the Church expanded greatly (which also meant that the Church grew into the conditions of the fourth century), then only did the Church become conscious of her opposition to the State, the social order, and public life in general, as a matter of conscience". "Now there arose with full force the sense of responsibility: What ought to be our attitude as Christians to the world around us? We have grown into this world against our own will, because, believing that it would soon come to an end, we have not sought to make

any changes in it." This can, however, only be explained (as *Harnack's* own description of the relation of Christians to military service shows) by saying that when the Christians began to press into callings which were dubious from the Christian point of view, they began to feel the contrast very clearly, and also expressed it in literary form. In all this, however, it was always only a question of withdrawal from the world, never of a reform of the world; and in the end Christians learnt to tolerate these conditions by regarding them as part of the life of the world, and indissolubly bound up with the existence of the State. Scruples about military service disappear, and the Synod of Arles (*314*) decides to excommunicate deserters from the Army, while Tertullian and Origen had still absolutely forbidden Christians to serve in the Army at all; and even they, in spite of their assertion that the shedding of blood by soldiers is absolutely unchristian, would have tolerated it if it had not been for the fact that military service brought the soldiers into connection with the worship of the Emperor. Thus the non-eschatological Church is still more quietistic and conservative than the one in which the eschatological idea predominated. This is due to her theoretical view of the world and the State, and the closer the Church drew to the State the more conservative became her conclusions, while radicals took refuge in monasticism. The eternal nature of Rome: *Bigelmair, 77, Cumont, l'éternité des empereurs romains (Revue de l'hist. et de littérature religieuse, 1896)*. Lactantius prays for Rome: *"Roma est civitas, quae adhuc sustentat omnia, precandusque nobis et adorandus est deus coeli, ne citius quam putamus tyrannus ille abominabilis veniat, qui tantum facimus moliatur et lumen illud effodiat"* (quoted from *Bigelmair, p. 81*). The *imperium* is for Barnabas, Irenaeus, and Hippolytus the fourth empire in the Vision of Daniel, which will endure until the return of Christ—a philosophy of history which lingered on to the time of the Reformation. Only when Christ returns can it be said with Commodian: *"luget in aeternum, qui se jactabat aeterna"*, ibid., *87*. Even the severe enemy of the world, Tertullian, can only say: *"Christianus nullius est hostis nedum imperatoris, quem sciens a deo suo constitui necesse est, ut salvum velit cum toto Romano imperio, quo usque saeculum stabit, tamdiu enim stabit,"* ibid., *88*. The great Fathers of the fourth century take the eternal character of the Empire for granted just as much; cf. *Uhlhorn, 221 ff*. Ambrose says that the nail of the True Cross which the Empress Helena introduces into the crown is "the good nail which holds the Roman Empire together". In spite of all the incursions of the Barbarians no one believes that the Roman Empire will ever fall. "The idea that the Barbarians could ever make an end of the Roman Empire and the Roman civilization could never be even conceived by any Roman, not even by any Christian Roman." Augustine, Orosius, and Salvian regarded all these calamities as punishments sent by God, which were to cleanse and purify the Empire. For the idea of the eternity of Rome even among the Franks, see *Hauck: K. G. Deutschland, I, 171, 231*, passage from *Beda, p. 429: "Quamdiu stat Colisäus, stat et Roma; quando cadet Colisäus, cadet et Roma; quando cadet Roma, cadet et mundus."*

⁵⁷ (p. 115.) Cf. *Brentano: Wirtschaftliche Lehren; Harnack: Missionsgeschichte, I, 130 ff., 253; Uhlhorn: Liebestätigkeit, I, 120–128, 288–299; F. X. Funk: Kirchengeschichtliche Abhandlungen und Untersuchungen, II, 1899; Klemens von Alexandrien über Familie und Eigentum, 45–60, Handel und Gewerbe im christlichen Altertum, 60–77;* the subject is very fully treated by *J. Seipel: Die wirtschaftsethischen Lehren der Kirchenväter (Theol. Studien der Leo-Gesellschaft, 18), Vienna, 1907;* further, in *Ratzinger: Die Volkswirtschaft in ihren sittlichen Grundlagen, 1881; R. W. and A. J. Carlyle: A History of Medieval Political Theory in the West, I, 1903,* the chapter entitled "*Theory of Property*", *132–146; Gass: Gesch. d. Ethik, I, 94 ff. and 223 ff.*

The only work which deals with the problem directly is—as is well known—that of *Clement: Can a Rich Man be saved?* It is an allegorical account of the story of the Rich Young Ruler, which suggests that it is not necessary to renounce possessions but the spirit which clings to possessions; otherwise wealth ought to be used fully for the purposes of charity. It is most favourable towards wealth, and at the same time it is one of the most sensible works from the economic point of view, and it is also filled with a spirit of very fine and tender piety. For the present day Christians have always refused to adopt communistic principles. *Lactantius* reproaches Plato (who in other respects comes so close to the truth), saying: "Communism in possessions is an offence against righteousness; but the collective possession of wives and children would mean the breaking down of all restraint; moreover, to place them at the disposal of the State would be the greatest misfortune that could happen" (*Bigelmair, 89*). The restriction of communism to the primitive period, and the fact that family life was rigidly preserved, is entirely overlooked by *Brentano* in his insistence upon the communistic character of the Christian doctrine of property.—The work of *Sommerlad: Das Wirtschaftsprogramm der Kirche des Mittelalters, 1903*, is scarcely any use at all, in spite of its appeal to good authorities. In this book, in solemn earnest, economic theories are attributed to the Fathers; to each one is assigned a special theory (or system), and each of these supposed peculiarities is placed in a circumstantial setting. The passages which are here collected are very valuable, but the construction which is put on them has no value at all. The only useful point is the emphasis upon the communistic theories of the Primitive State which were in vogue from the fourth century. *Sommerlad* explains them as a reaction against the despotism of the State, the exclusiveness of Society, and the development of a monopoly of wealth, also to the influence of Plato. The former is possible; instead of the latter the emphasis should be placed upon the Natural Law of the Stoics, which was accepted and absorbed from the time of the Apologists.

[59] (p. 117.) On the question of luxury, see details in *Bigelmair, 231–244*; here very different conditions were allowed according to the social class; upon the whole a fair amount of simple comfort was permitted; this fact throws a good deal of light upon the "existence minimum" and the question of private property, quite apart from the fact that the tone of the exhortations shows that these ideals were not carried out very far into practice. How natural it seemed to possess property is revealed by the fact that Tertullian, who was so austere a man, counsels against Christian women marrying pagans, in order that the husband, by threatening to denounce his wife, may not cause her to renounce her property (*Bigelmair, 251*). All insight into practical details reveals the way in which property was taken for granted; it was only in eloquent speech about love that it took a secondary place.

[60] (p. 118.) On Christianity and work, cf. *Harnack: Mission, I, 134, 156; Uhlhorn: Liebestätigkeit, I, 76–79, 129–131; Seipel, 123–133; Simon Weber: Evangelium und Arbeit, Freiburg, 1898; E. Meyer: Sklaverei, 37; Overbeck, 226.* An example from Tertullian in *Funk, II, 66*, from Chrysostom in *Brentano, 157*, from Augustine in *Funk, II, 70*. All that *Uhlhorn* has to say about the "dignifying" of labour is this: "The ancient Fathers say very little, indeed, remarkably little, about work. Whenever the subject is mentioned, however, then we feel immediately that in the pagan world it had been regarded quite differently . . . certainly the deeper moral estimate of labour, the conception of vocation, the connection of the earthly calling with the heavenly one, had not yet dawned upon the Church. . . . The general duty of work, the significance of labour in

a calling for the exercise of the Christian life and the furtherance of the Kingdom of God, is never expressed anywhere. Hence also the apostolic constitutions can only tell the rich who do not need to earn their bread that they must visit believers and hold edifying conversations with them!" All this, however, only means that the later Lutheran doctrine of the ethic of work and of the "calling" was unknown to the Early Church. These ideas were unknown because they arose out of another kind of spirit.

⁶¹ (p. 120.) On this point see *Harnack: Missionsgeschichte, I, 251-261*, and also his *Militia christiana; Seipel, 146-161*, and *Bigelmair*. The latter work represents an immense amount of industry, and contains a mass of instructive material. For the social and vocational organization of the society of the Imperial period see *Seipel, 1-48*, which in the main is a résumé of *Marquardt's Die römische Staatsverwaltung* and *Das Privatleben der Römer (Handbuch der römischen Altertumer²)*. For the general character of ancient society, and the ways in which it differed from Germanic-mediaeval society, see the great article by *Max Weber: Agrargeschichte (Altertum²)* in *HWB. der Staatswissenschaften, 3rd edition*, especially *p. 67*, which is to be followed by one equally important on the "colonate" system. For the rise of the idea of a "calling" see the remarks of the same writer in *Prot. Ethik u.s.w., Archiv xx, pp. 35-40*. There are many passages from the Fathers upon which the opinion which has been formulated above is based in *Sommerlad*, who certainly lays a true emphasis upon the special points in the social doctrines of the fourth century, but who does not realize that these are due to the development of the Stoic idea of the Law of Nature.

⁶²ᵃ (p. 127.) *Seipel, 107-109, 131*, the system of callings based upon inequality and the need of supplementation. Similar passages from Basil are quoted by *Sommerlad, 131 ff.*, Theodoret, *167 ff*. In addition, the passages collected by *Seipel* from Basil, Chrysostom, Ambrose, Augustine, show that there was everywhere in the background the thought of an original equality, and the idea that differences in possessions were due to the fact of sin, that therefore the ideal is the love-communism of monasticism, that, however, men were quite conscious of the fact that in real life, and within its legal system, such ideals could not be realized in practice. Thus the ideal of "perfection" is not a communistic society for production, but a poverty which gives everything away and depends upon the support of others, in order to be able to serve them in monastic and ecclesiastical ways. Thus Augustine's communistic experiments became the ideal of the life of poverty of the clergy, leading to the toleration of the general situation, with the proviso that a generous charity should be exercised. This, however, does not provide a fruitful soil for the idea of the "calling" (*Seipel, 190-119*).

⁶⁴ (p. 129.) Cf. *Marianne Weber: Ehefrau und Mutter, 186-197*, which in parts I follow literally. There is no idea here, however, of an independent ecclesiastical marriage law. *Zscharnak: Der Dienst der Frau in den ersten Jahrhunderten der Kirche, 1902; Donaldson: Woman, her position in Ancient Greece and Rome, and among the early Christians, London, 1907*. For the derivation of the patriarchal form of law from the Fall, see *Overbeck: Sklaverei, p. 198*, according to Chrysostom, from the variety of Nature according to Augustine, *p. 200*.—For the position of women the "Widow-office" and its development was characteristic. Originally widows were regarded as female presbyters, who took their share in the official work of the Church, and who were entrusted with the work of religious instruction as well as with the administration of poor relief. As the idea of the ministry developed, however, widows became less

important than the deaconesses, and as asceticism increased the "holy virgins" came to the fore. Then women lost their place in the government of the Church altogether, and the deaconess became a lower official in the service of the Church. No woman is allowed to take any part in the function of offering the Mass which mediates salvation; here we may apply the word of the Lord (apocryphal) : "The weak is saved by the strong" (*Uhlhorn, I, 159–171*).

⁶⁶ (p. 132.) On this point cf. *Uhlhorn, I, 184–189, 362–375; Seipel, 30–32;* and the dissertation by *Overbeck*, to whom I owe a great deal for the whole conception and for the indication of passages in the Fathers. The right point of view, several source passages, and a stronger emphasis upon the inner transformation of the relationship than that given by *Overbeck*, are found in *Carlyle, I, 111–125*: "Natural equality and slavery." For passages from Chrysostom see *Overbeck (198)* from Augustine *(200)*. This also throws a light upon the "communism" of Chrysostom; it was, indeed, simply a proposal to try to abolish the misery of the poor in Constantinople by pooling possessions, and a pious desire aroused by the experiment in the Acts of the Apostles. On this question, and on similar Antiochene sermons, *Seipel (98–105)* is very useful.

⁶⁷ (p. 134.) *Harnack: Mission, 127–171; Ratzinger: Geschichte der Armenpflege, 1868,* and especially *Uhlhorn's* masterpiece. Apart from *Uhlhorn's* strongly apologetic tendency my own view differs from *Uhlhorn's* conception in the question of the significance of the "world" for Primitive Christianity and for the Primitive Church. *Uhlhorn* reads into the Gospel the Lutheran ideas about the ethic of the "calling" and of the service of God in the social division of labour, and he suggests that the Catholic ascetic attitude towards the world, and with that also the practice of charity, arose out of asceticism, the misunderstanding of the nature of work and of possessions, and the transformation of the spiritual ethic of the Gospel into an ethic of "works". He himself says, however, that this morality was only present in germ in the Gospel, and that it was only gradually developed. "This heavenly calling includes the earthly calling, for even in one's earthly calling everyone ought to exercise his or her work for the Kingdom of God, in order to further the purposes of the Kingdom of God, doing his part to help to solve the great problem which was placed before man at the Creation, of dominating the earth" (*p. 77*). "To the extent in which the other human group-forms (after that of the family) gradually become permeated with the Christian spirit, they also in their own circles develop the practice of charity. The State, the civil community, the corporations all take their share in the solution of the common task" (*p. 65*). Thus *Uhlhorn* argues; only his own work shows that this Christian penetration and domination of the world was not attained, and not sought after, even from the very beginning. Of the early days he says: "The task of fleeing from the world is the primary one; the duty of penetrating the life of the world with this new life only occurred gradually to the Christians." But that which did come gradually to pass was in reality something quite different. Somewhat later it is said: "The tendency towards renunciation of the world was still stronger than that of acceptance of the world" (*p. 127*). And in another place: "The Church was now also confronted with the great task of penetrating the life by which she was surrounded—in the State, science, art, and social conditions—with the Christian spirit, and of transforming them from within. She failed to achieve this, and this led her into false paths" (*p. 201*). Speaking of the period of Constantine: "A real penetration of the life of the people with the leaven of the Gospel . . . did not even take place approximately, and therefore Christianity was obliged to work in the other direction in a dis-

integrating way" (*p. 218*). Finally: "It was impossible for the life of Christianity to penetrate the life of the Ancient World. It was only the Germanic world which was able to become really Christian" (*p. 342*). In all these statements the fundamental relation between the Gospel and the world (that is, the social conditions) is wrongly conceived, and the Kingdom of God is regarded as a new ethical order within the life of the world. This is quite wrong. But even though it may seem as though the Church failed to penetrate the life of paganism, and only thus became forced into the Catholic-ascetic direction, this also is an error. *Uhlhorn* has nowhere proved that the Church ever had the intention of moulding the life of the pagan world which would have made it possible to say that she had failed. In reality she never failed because she never set out to do this at all; she had not the least intention of doing so. She only failed to believe that it was possible to rid the Christianized world of poverty and misery, at least to a minimum extent; this being so, she withdrew into small monastic groups. *Uhlhorn* recognizes this latter circumstance very clearly. Cf. *p. 34*.

67a (p. 142.) On all these points see *Edgar Löning: Gesch. d. deutschen Kirchenrechtes, I, 1878.* The first volume gives an excellent and most instructive account of the development of the Church after Constantine. Chapters ii–iv are particularly striking. For the influence upon the law of the State, cf. *p. 316.* Cf. also the summary of the social significance of the episcopate (*p. 362*): "The powerful position which the bishops gained during the fourth and fifth centuries was based upon ecclesiastical and secular foundations. The religious and ecclesiastical influence which the bishop exercised within his own territory over the faithful as the representative of the power of the Church was supported and increased by the great wealth of the Church, which he administered almost without let or hindrance, and by means of which he held all the clergy and a large section of the poorer people in the towns in dependence upon himself; his power was also increased by the important legal public powers with which he had gradually been entrusted by the State." If we place the picture sketched by *Löning* in connection with the general situation which had developed, and with its main ideas, we see still more clearly the fact that all this only meant a very limited contact with the life of the world, and that in no wise does it represent a Christian unity of civilization. We cannot even speak of the "mediaeval subordination of the State to the Church" as having been realized even in germ. All that we can say is that here the Emperor was used for some special ecclesiastical ends of power, but there was no question of Christianizing the collective life. More will be said on this subject below in connection with the relation between Church and State.—For the way in which bishops and clergy exercised the office of public poor relief and charity, the life of poverty led by bishops and clergy, the use of the fortune of the Church as the property of the poor, but also the gradual way in which aristocratic ways of living stole into the episcopate, and the division of the wealth of the Church into shares for the bishop, the clergy, the poor, and for the building of churches, as the beginning of the end of the system of poor relief as it was carried on in the Primitive Church, see *Ratzinger: Armenpflege, 61–140.* R. emphasizes rightly that this conception was characteristic of the Primitive Church, and that with the change by which the fortune of the Church was used solely for ecclesiastical purposes, after the new law of property of the Pseudo-Isidorian Decretals, this whole social function of the episcopate ceased, and has never been revived even in the present day.

68 (p. 144.) Cf. *Harnack: Lehrbuch der Dogmengeschichte.* For the Christianizing of the literary professions and forms, see *E. Hatch: On the Influence of Greek Ideas and Usages on the Christian Church, 1888;* v. *Schubert: Kirchengeschichte, I, 806.* For the growth and minglings of the various myths, see *Usener: Religionsgeschichtliche Untersuchungen, I, 1889; Bernoulli: Die Heiligen der Merowinger, 1900; Lucius: Heiligenlegenden, 1905.* Monographs on the subject of the attitude of the period towards natural science and critical history would be very desirable; they would throw a great deal of light upon the whole spiritual and intellectual situation.—In this connection it seems to me not quite accurate to describe the acceptance of "science" as "secularization"; nor can we regard the fact of entering into the life of the State as "secularization" either. The only kind of science which was accepted was that which was already spiritual and idealistic in tendency as well as religious and ethical. The real secularization only belongs to the acceptance of the art of rhetoric, and all that this involved of artificial and tawdry declamation. It was, indeed, a decaying form of culture with a terrible hypertrophy of formal acuteness and rhetoric. For this very reason it is scarcely accurate to describe Gnosticism as acute secularization, as *Overbeck* and *Harnack* have done. The aspects of Gnosticism which approach Christianity are also dualistic and ascetic. In all this there is only an endeavour on the part of the historical and mythical elements in particular to gain universal foundations and conceptions—that is, to reach science. In itself, however, the habit of scientific thought does not necessarily involve secularization as *Overbeck* thinks it does.—For that very reason, therefore, it is also erroneous to speak (as *Thamin* and others do) of the Christian ethic and Gnosticism as being overpowered by "the ancient world". The "ancient world" which was accepted was no longer the ancient world of earlier days; it was the ancient world which had become spiritually idealistic and dualistic.

[69] (p. 145.) Unfortunately there is no monograph on this subject; see my review of *Seeberg's Dogmengeschichte, Gött. Gel. Anzeigen, 1901, pp. 22–26.* In the Early Church the matter was at first concealed behind the idea of the Logos, then it was treated rather incidentally as the presupposition of ethics, especially among the Latins in connection with Cicero. But these relations are of the highest importance for what follows. *Gierke, III, 124.* The subject was only developed into a fundamental dogma by scholasticism. That is why it escaped the notice of the historians of dogma of the Early Church. Cf. *Hergenröther: Katholische Kirche und christlicher Staat, 1872, pp. 13 ff.*

The equation is finally completed by Philo. Cf. *Hirzel: "Ἀγραφος νομος"* (*Abhh. der philol.-hist. Klasse der Sächsischen Akademie, 1903, Bd. XX, pp. 16–17*). The doctrine of the *a.v.* is said to have been formulated by Philo, partly under the influence of his faith and partly under the influence of philosophy: "The wise men of ancient history, the patriarchs and fathers of the race, present in their lives unwritten laws, of which Moses wrote later for the imitation of those who came after. In them the law was fulfilled and it became personal. They themselves, however, needed a norm by which they could direct their actions, and this was provided for them by Nature. This norm also is once described by Philo as an unwritten law. . . . *A.v.* is to him a law which is not written upon stone or upon paper, but which stands out in a living way in action and in life, whether in outstanding individual representatives of the same, of the Patriarchs or heroes, or finally of the Supreme Being, of the Universe or of the Godhead."

Heinrici thus summarizes the content of the books *De Abrahamo, De Josepho, De vita Mosis, De decalogo*: "In both these earlier treatises the element which shaped the lives of these patriarchs is worked out; their lives represent the incarnation of the unwritten law, of the inspired and reasonable law, in which human nature appears in its completeness, and which formed the presupposition for the codified law of later days. Abraham is represented as the type of right knowledge, Joseph as the type of the statesman . . . (a treatise which has been lost) describes Isaac as the type of the autodidact, who develops his nature (φύσις) symmetrically, and Jacob as the type of the ascetic, which here means as a hero of self-denying and successful active energy. The main theme however . . . is the life of Moses, in which the hero appears as the perfect lawgiver, who is also praised as king, priest, and prophet at the same time. The work *De decalogo* according to its introduction, belonged to the series of the νόμοι ἄγραφοι. It glorifies the eternal moral truth, which is imparted by God directly to His interpreter as the basis of all further legislation" (*Theol. Litzg., 1903, col. 77*). Every reader of the two sole ethical treatises of the Primitive Church, the παιδαγωγός of Clement of Alexandria and the *De Officiis Ministrorum* of Ambrose, knows how naturally both follow this line of thought. That Philo was explicitly imitated by Ambrose and the school of Alexandria is confirmed by *Thamin* also in his *St. Ambroise et la morale chrétienne au 4ème siècle, 1895*. The equation between the Law of Nature and the Mosaic-Christian law is restored partly through the identity of the Logos which is operative in them, partly through the well-known doctrine of the borrowing of Greek wisdom from the East.—For Paul, see *Quimbach: Die Lehre des h. Paulus von der natürlichen Gotteserkenntnis und dem natürlichen Sittengesetz; Freiburg, 1906 (Strassburger Theol. Studien, VII, 4)*; *Q.* rightly emphasizes the fact that here already the Natural Law is regarded as identical with the Decalogue.—*Waldstein: Der Einfluss des Stoizismus auf die älteste christliche Lehrbildung (Theol. Stud. u. Krit., 1880)*, considers that the acceptance of the ethical doctrines of the Stoics was confined to Justin and Clement (there certainly very thoroughly), whereby the Logos means the Stoic Law of Nature, according to the word of Chrysippus: "διόπερ τέλος γίνεται τὸ ἀκολούθως τῇ φύσει ζῆν, ὅπερ ἐστὶ κατά γε τὴν αὐτοῦ καὶ κατὰ τὴν τῶν ὅλων, οὐδὲν ἐνεργοῦντας ὧν ἀπαγορεύειν εἴωθεν ὁ νόμος ὁ κοινός, δοπερ ἐστὶν ὁ ὀρθὸς λόγος διὰ πάντων ἐρχόμενος, ὁ αὐτὸς ὢν τῷ Διὶ καθηγημόνι τούτῳ τῆς τῶν ὅλων διοικήσεως ὄντι" (*p. 636*). But in reality the matter went much farther than this; it is everywhere the natural accompaniment of the Logos conception, or an assumption which is everywhere assumed as quite obvious. I note certain passages. *Justin Apol., II, 8:* "Στωικοὶ κἂν τὸν ἠθικὸν λόγον κόσμιοι γεγόνασιν"; *Apol., II, 10:* "ὅσα γὰρ καλῶς ἀεὶ ἐφθέγξαντο καὶ εὗρον οἱ φιλοσοφήσαντες ἢ νομοθετήσαντες, κατὰ λόγου μέρος . . . ἐστι πονηθέντα αὐτοῖς· ἐπειδὴ δὲ οὐ πάντα τὰ τοῦ λόγου ἐγνώρισαν, ὅς ἐστιν ὁ Χριστός, καὶ ἐναντία ἑαυτοῖς πολλάκις εἶπον." *Dialog. II:* "αἰώνιός τε ἡμῖν νόμος καὶ τελευταῖος Χριστὸς ἐδόθη." *Clement: Al. Pad., I, 2, 6:* "ἡμεῖς δὲ ἅμα νοήματι (sc. θεοῦ) νήπιοι γεγόναμεν, τὴν ἀρίστην, καὶ βεβαιοτάτην τάξιν παρὰ τῆς αὐτοῦ εὐταξίας παραλαμβάνοντες, ἢ πρῶτον μὲν ἀμφὶ τὸν κόσμον καὶ τὸν οὐρανὸν, τὰς δὲ ἡλιακὰς περιδινήσεις κυκλεῖται καὶ τῶν λοιπῶν ἄστρων τὰς φορὰς ἀσχολεῖται διὰ τὸν ἄνθρωπον, ἔπειτα δὲ περὶ τὸν ἄνθρωπον αὐτόν, περὶ ὃν ἡ πᾶσα σπουδὴ καταγίνεται· καὶ τοῦτον ἐργονήγουμένη μέγιστον ψυχὴν μὲν αὐτου φρονήσεικαὶ σωφροσύνῃ κατήθυνεν, τὸ δὲ σῶμα κάλλει καὶ εὐρυθμίᾳ, συνεκέρασατο, περὶ δὲ τὰς πράξεις τῆς ἀνθρωπότητος τό τε ἐν αὐτοῖς κατορθοῦν καὶ τὸ εὔτακτον ἐνέπνευσε τὸ ἑαυτῆς." (This is Natural Law, Providence, Logos, Ethic all at once.) Also *Padag. I, 7, 60. Origen, v.* passages which will be quoted later on.—*Irenaeus* (Harvey), *IV, 27, 3:* "Quare igitur patribus non disposuit Dominus testamentum? Quia 'lex non est posita justis', justi autem patres virtutem decalogi habentes in cordibu et animabus suis . . . propter quod non fuit necesse admoneri eos correptoriis litteris, quia habebant in semetipsis justitiam legis. Cum autem haec justitia et dilectio . . . cessisset in oblivionem et extincta in Aegypto, necessario Deus . . . semetipsum ostendebat per vocem." *IV, 9, 2* and *IV, 24, 1*, the immutability of the Divine Law, according to which also the Law of Christ must be identical with that of Moses and of Nature, only divested of its legal form and with an emphasis upon freedom.—*Tatian, 28:* "Διὰ τοῦτο καὶ τῆς παρ᾽ ὑμῖν κατέγνων νομοθεσίας. Μίαν μὲν γὰρ ἐχρῆν εἶναι καὶ κοινὴν ἁπάντων τὴν πολιτείαν." *Tertullian: De virg. rel., I:* "Sic et justitia (nam idem Deus justitiae et creaturae) prima fuit in rudimentis, natura Deum metuens. Dehinc per legem et prophetas promovit in infantiam, dehinc per evangelium efferbuit in juventutem, nunc per paracletum componitur in maturitatem. De test. anim. 5: Magistra natura, anima discipula. Quicquid aut illa edocuit aut ista perdidicit, a Deo traditum est, magistro scilicet ipsius magistrae."—*Lactantius: Just., VI, 8:* "Suscipienda igitur Dei lex est, quae nos ad hoc iter dirigat, illa sancta, illa caelestis, quam Marcus Tullius in libro de re publica tertio paene divina voce depinxit: 'est quidem vera lex recta ratio, naturae congruens, diffusa in omnis, constans, sempiterna, quae vocet ad officium jubendo, vetando a fraude deteneat, quae tamen neque probos frustra jubet aut vetat nec improbos jubendo aut vetando movet. Huic legi nec abrogari fas est neque derogari aliquid ex hac licet neque tota abrogari potest, nec vero aut per senatum aut per populum solvi hac lege possumus . . . sed et omnes gentes et omni tempore una lex et sempiterna et immutabilis continebit unusque erit quasi magister et imperator omnium Deus. . . .' Quis sacramentum Dei sciens tam significanter enarrare legem dei posset quam illam homo longe a veritatis notitia remotus expressit? Ego vero eos, qui vera imprudentes loquuntur, sic habendos puto, tamquam divinent spiritu aliquo instincti. . . . quod (that is, the full exposition) quia facere ille non poterat nobis faciendum est, quibus ipsa lex tradita est ab illo uno magistro et imperatore omnium Deo. Hujus caput primum est ipsum Deum nosse. . . . Dixi quid debeatur deo, dicam nunc quid homini tribuendum sit."—*Ambrose: De officiis, I, 84;* "naturam imitemur," *I, 124,* "ne quid contra naturam, ne quid turpe atque indecorum sentiamus"; *I, 223,* "decorum est secundum naturam vivere, secundum naturam degere, et turpe est quid sit contra naturam"; *I, 229,* "appetitus rationi subjectus est lege naturae ipsius"; *III, 31,* "Justus legem habet mentis suae et aequitatis ac justitiae suae normam"; *III, 19,* "haec utique lex naturae est, quae nos ad omnem stringit humanitatem, ut alter alteri tamquam unius partes corporis invicem deferamus"; *III, 25,* Agreement between morality and utility according to the Law of Nature, likewise *III, 28* and *III, 24. II, 80:* "unde igitur haec vel Tullius vel Panaetius aut ipse Aristoteles transtulerint, apertum est satis," follows a reference to the Old Testament; likewise *II, 6. Epist., 53, 10:* "Non fuit necessaria lex per Moysen, denique subintravit . . . in locum naturalis legis intraverit. Itaque si illa suum servasset locum, haec lex scripta nequaquam esset ingressa"; likewise *53, 2:* "Ea igitur lex non scribitur sed innascitur, nec aliqua percipitur lectione sed profluo quodam fonte in singulis exprimitur et humanis ingeniis hauritur".—*Ambrosiaster: Com. in Ep. ad Rom., 3, 20:* "haec ergo est lex naturalis, quae per Moysen partim reformata partim firmata."—*Hieronymus: Commentary on Isa., 24, 6:* "Audeant Judaei, qui se solos legem accepisse domini gloriantur, quod universae primum gentes totusque orbis naturalem acceperit legem et idcirco postea lex data sit per Moysen, quia prima lex dissipata est," with an appeal to Paul, Rom. ii. 14. From *Augustine: Jodl, I, 596,* gives a number of passages: "Lex vero aeterna est ratio divina aut voluntas Dei, ordinem naturalem conservari jubens, perturbari vetans." *Contra Faustum, 22, 7.* According to *Gierke, III, 128,* I add finally: *Isidorus Hisp. Orig., V, 2:* "Omnes quidem leges aut divinae sunt aut humanae; divina natura, humanae moribus constant,"and from the *Glossa ordinaria:* "Jus naturale dicitur, quod in lege Mosaica vel in Evangelio continetur."—Most emphasis, however, ought perhaps to be laid upon the fact that Lactantius, Ambrose, and Augustine in their works base their teaching in a most outspoken way upon Cicero. The first part of *De civitate* proceeds with the aid of the expositions of Cicero, and the *officiis* of Ambrose are, to some extent, a literal reshaping of those of Cicero. This fact is due to the assumption that the Christian ethic and the Natural Law and Natural Right are identical.

⁷⁰ (p. 146.) Cf. *Gierke: Genossenschaftsrecht, III, 122–186;* for the changed aspect of the fundamental sociological feelings, see some excellent remarks in the section *Vertus nouvelles* in *Thamin's* book, *pp. 250–278.* See also the famous passage in *Lactantius, V, 15 and 16* about equality, which is the essence of that righteousness which the pagan moralists, even including Cicero, had conceived in a mistaken way. To the Christians this has been revealed. But even *Lactantius* does not draw practical conclusions from the fact of equality: "Dicet aliquis nonne sunt apud vos alii pauperes, alii divites, alii servi, alii domini? nonne aliquid inter singulos interest? nihil nec alia causa est cur nobis invicem fratrum nomen impertiamus, nisi quia pares nos esse credimus, nam cum omnia humana non corpore sed spiritu metiamur, tametsi corporum diversa sit condicio, nobis tamen servi non sunt, sed eos et habemus et dicimus spiritu fratres, religione conservos, divitiae quoque non faciunt insignes, nisi quod possunt bonis operibus facere clariores . . . cum igitur et liberi servis et divites pauperibus humilitate animi pares simus, apud deum tamen virtute discernimur: tanto quisque sublimor est, quanto justior . . . si non tantum quasi parem, sed etiam quasi minorem se gesserit, utique multo altiorem dignitatis gradum Deo judice consequetur, nam profecto in hac vita saeculari brevia et caduca sunt omnia." Here the important step has been taken of interpreting righteousness as equality, but the idea of equality is still confined purely to the religious sphere, in which its rationalism naturally finds its own level, and makes its own limits.

⁷¹ (p. 146.) Cf. *Neumann: Der römische Staat und die allgemeine Kirche, I, 1900; Gierke, III, 122–128; Harnack: Mission, I, 206–227; Bigelmair, 76–124; Hergenröther: Katholische Kirche und christlicher Staat, 1872; Weinel: Stellung des Christentums, etc.* The first volume of the work by *R. W. and A. J. Carlyle,* entitled *A History of Medieval Political Theory in the West,* is of especial importance for this subject. In it I found a confirmation of everything which I had already arrived at independently; this work, however, is supported by a mass of authorities greater than were accessible to me in my own researches. *J. Carlyle* accomplished this with the help of a staff of theological assistants. The orientation of his work is to this extent different that he is concerned merely with laying bare the foundations of the mediaeval period, whereas my main concern is with the relation between its social life and groups, and the fundamental ideas and starting-point of Christianity.

⁷² (p. 147.) This is simply and characteristically expressed in the Acts of the Scillitan Martyrs, in which the Christian Speratus, when he is summoned to swear by the genius of the Emperor, replies: "ἐγὼ τὴν βασιλείαν τοῦ νῦν αἰῶνος οὐ γινώσκω"; the *saeculum* and the Empire are coupled together in a passage of Tertullian which is often quoted: "Et Caesares credidissent super Christo, si aut Caesares non essent necessarii saeculo, aut si Christiani potuissent

esse Caesares" (*Neumann, 149*). When the latter idea came in the earlier idea
still remained in existence. The same Tertullian says in the same Apology,
which certainly was deliberately friendly: "The Christians place the Emperor
under God, but only under Him; after Him the Emperor is supreme, and he is
superior to all the pagan deities. He has been chosen by God, and owes his
greatness to Him" (*Neumann, 150*). The idea which lies behind this is that the
greatness of the Emperor consists in presiding over the empire of sin, to which
also he gives a secular order. The question of the attitude of Christians to the
"world" is, therefore, identical with that of their attitude to the "laws" of the
Empire (*Neumann 115 and 168*). But even when the laws of the Empire had been
purified as a whole they still bore the character of the *terrena civitas*: "Invenimus
ergo in terrena civitate duas formas: unam suam praesentiam demonstrantem,
alteram coelesti civitati significandae sua praesentia servientem. Parit autem
cives terrenae civitatis peccato vitiata natura, coelestis vero civitatis cives a
peccato naturam liberans gratia. . . . Ibi humanus usus ostenditur, hic divinum
beneficium commendatur" (*Augustine: De civ. Dei, XV, 2*). This is the double
character of all States, of that of Israel first of all and then of the Roman-
Christian one, which in its first form belongs to the general type (which is
the same everywhere) of the *civitas terrena*. The latter is expressed in an explicit
manner, *De civ. Dei, XVIII, 2, i*: "Societas [i.e. the civitas terrena] igitur
usquequaque mortalium diffusa per terras et in locorum quantislibet diversita-
tibus, unius tamen ejusdemque naturae quaedam communione devincta . . .
adversus se ipsam plerumque dividitur et pars partem, quae praevalet, opprimit
. . . sed inter plurima regna terrarum, in quae terrenae utilitatis vel cupiditatis
est divisa societas (quam civitatem mundi hujus universali vocabulo nuncu-
pamus) dua regna cernimus longe caeteris provenisse clariora, Assyriorum
primum deinde Romanorum. . . . Nam quo modo illud prius, hic posterius,
eo modo illud in Oriente [i.e. Nimrod] hoc in occidente surrexit. denique in
illius fine hujus initium confestim fuit. Regna caetera ceterosque reges velut
appendices istorum dixerim." This means that the "world" is practically
identical with the Roman State. The same is true of the Roman jurists down
to Justinian. "The Roman lawyers, indeed, usually deal with the matter only
from the point of view of the Roman commonwealth . . . and, after all, the
Empire was to the Roman much the same as the world. The principles which
belonged to it were at least the principles of the civilized world, and their
application to the conditions of the world at large was natural and easy"
(*Carlyle, 70*).

72b (p. 150.) Cf. *Weinel, p. 61:* "In reality it is only the Apologists who speak
in this way (relating the νόμοι on both sides to each other), and frequently
they consider the 'lawgivers' to be the philosophers quite as much as the
States. There are, however, sufficient descriptive passages. Only the Apologists
in particular are inclined to regard both the legislation of the State and
philosophy as elements and preparatory stages for Christian laws or the Law
of God.They certainly consider these laws of the State both elementary and
ineffective (*Justin, I, 12*); above all, they differ too much from each other
and are often actually opposed to each other, for even 'harmful things' are
actually commanded by law (*II, 9*). Indeed, in part it was the demons which
gave these laws, as indeed pre-Christian idealists like Heraclitus and the
Stoics were constantly persecuted by the authorities (*II, 8*)." The Apologists
mean that the scientifically educated upper classes are now receiving the Word,
and therefore, as is easy to be understood, neither the old hostility nor the
indefiniteness of the Pauline principle is possible any longer.

⁷³ (p. 152.) The passages from Origen form the starting-point both for *Neumann, pp. 234 ff.*, and for *Carlyle, 103 ff. Contra Celsum, V, 37*: "Δύο τοίνυν νόμων προκειμένων γενικῶς, καὶ τοῦ μὲν ὄντος τῆς φύσεως νόμου, ὃν θεός ἂν νομοθετήσαι, ἑτέρου δὲ τοῦ ταῖς πόλεσι γραπτοῦ· καλον, ὅπου μὲν μὴ ἐναντιοῦται ὁ γραπὸς λόγος νόμῳ τῷ θεοῦ, μὴ λιπεῖν τοὺς πολίτας προφάσει ξένων λόγων· ἔνθα δὲ τὰ ἐναντία τῷ γραπτῷ νόμῳ προςτάσσει ὁ τῆς φύσεως τουτέστι του θεοῦ, ὅρα εἰ μὴ ὁ λόγος ἐρεῖ μακρὰν μὲν χαίρειν εἰπεῖν τοῖς γεγραμμένοις." The same contrast, which is entirely usual among Greek political thinkers (*v. Hirzel: Ἄγραφος νόμος, p. 91*: ἧνικα ἡ φύσις διεθεσμοθέτει τοῖς ἀνθρώποις μόνη, πρίν τους γραπτοὺς εἰςφοιτῆσαι νόμους), recurs in Origen, manifestly as a technical doctrine, frequently; *Contra Celsum, VIII, 26* and *VIII, 75. Neumann* adds a very characteristic passage from the *Commentary on the Epistle to the Romans, IX, 26 and 27*, which Origen himself mentions *c. C. VIII, 65*. Referring to *Romans xiii. 1-2*, he says: "Non est enim, inquit [Paul], potestas nisi a Deo, dicet fortasse aliquis: quid ergo? et illa potestas, quae servos dei persequitur . . . a deo est? ad haec breviter respondemus." The gift of God, the laws, are to be used, not abused. "Erit autem justum judicium Dei erga eos, qui acceptam potestatem secundum suas impietates et non secundum divinas temperant leges. . . . Non hic [Paul] de illis potestatibus dicit, quae persecutiones inferunt fidei: ibi enim dicendum est, 'deo oportet obtemporare magis quam hominibus, sed de istis communibus dicit'." In Origen the idea had a very strong polemical aspect, but one feels at the same time the possibility of a conservative interpretation. In peace between Church and State this emerges ever more plainly; in the West, then, the influence of Cicero and the jurists becomes increasingly evident. The State is here regarded as derived from the social impulse of Natural Law, and its law from the Divine Law of Nature, whereby, of course, the difficulty of the opposition between the Positive Law and the Natural Law constantly appears. On this point see below for further observations. The famous passage from Lactantius in which Cicero's idea of Natural Law is exalted (*Inst., VI, 8*), has already been indicated: "Nec vero aut per senatum aut per populum solvi hac lege possumus neque est quaerendus explanator aut interpres Sextus Aelius nec erit alia lex Romae alia Athenis, alia nunc, alia posthac." Also *VI, 10*: "Deus . . . animal nos esse voluit sociale . . . causa coeundi ipsa potius humanitas . . . natura hominum societatis ac communionis appetens (*VI, 11*), conservanda igitur est humanitas [Nature as the founder of the fellowship of the State and of its laws] . . . discordia igitur ac dissensio non est secundum hominis rationem verumque illud est Ciceronis, quod ait hominem naturae oboedientem homini nocere non posse." This is the nature of the true *jus* and the true *justitia. Epitome Inst., 53*: "Si enim nos idem Deus fecit et universos ad justitiam vitamque aeternam pari condicione generavit, fraterna utique necessitudine cohaeremus." It is, however, the error of the philosophers and the jurists that they measure this *societas juris* only by its earthly use and not its heavenly purpose. The same criticism, half agreement and half improvement, is exercised by *Inst., 3, 8*, on the conception of the *naturae convenienter vivere*. Likewise *Augustine: De civ., XIX, 12*: "Homo fertur quodam modo naturae suae legibus ad ineundam societatem pacemque cum hominibus quantum in ipso est, omnibus obtenendam." *De bono conjugali, I*: "Unusquisque homo humani generis pars est et sociale quiddam est natura magnumque habet et naturale bonum." *De civ., XIX, 5*: "Quod autem socialem vitam volunt esse sapientis, nos multo amplius approbamus." *De lib. arb., 6*: "Nihil est in lege temporali justum, quod ex lege aeterna non derivetur." *De vera religione, 31*: "Conditor

legum temporalium, si vir bonus est et sapiens, illam ipsam consulit aeternam, de qua nulli animae judicare datum est, ut secundum ejus immutabiles regulas quid sit pro tempore jubendum vetandumve discernat." *Contra Faustum, 22, 7*: "Lex vero aeterna est ratio divina aut voluntas Dei ordinem naturalem conservari jubens perturbari vetans." Property rights are valid through the law of the Empire, but ultimately they come from God, from whom these rights are derived, mediated through princes. *Reuter: Augustinische Studien, 1887, p. 382. De civ., II, 21, 2. A.* accepts Cicero's definition of the State's "populum non omnem coetum multitudinis, sed coetum juris consensu et utilitatis communione sociatum esse" as a summary, then (*19, 21*), he refers to this again, and, although he accepts the idea, he denies that according to him pagan Rome was a real State, since with its paganism and its horrors real *justitia* was lacking, but this is only the condemnation of the Positive Law, which is opposed to Nature. In other passages he estimates the Natural-Law content of the Roman laws, which still exists in spite of all, much more highly. He gives his own definition, *19, 24*: "Populus est coetus multitudinis rationalis, rerum quas diligit concordi communione sociatus." Here *justitia* is omitted because he considered that that was too absolute, but the *ratio* idea was left because this can be regarded as more or less; for the *populus* is "tanto utique melior, quanto in melioribus, tantoque deterior quanto in deterioribus concor." Thus he is willing even to call the pagan State of Rome a State "quamdiu manet qualiscunque rationalis multitudinis coetus". The interesting passage, *De diversis quaestionibus, 31*, merges entirely into the usual teaching of the Fathers with regard to the Law of Nature: "Justitia est habitus animi communi utilitate conservata suam cuique tribuens dignitatem. Ejus initium est ab natura profectum. deinde quaedam in consuetudinem ex utilitatis ratione venerunt: postea res et ab natura profectas et a consuetudine probatas legum metus et religio sanxit. Natura jus est, quod non opinio genuit, sed quaedam innata vis inseruit ut religionem pietatem, gratiam, vindicationem, observantiam, veritatem." Thus the elements of truth in pagan religion, morality, and law are referred back to Nature. The written law is derived from the unwritten sphere: "Quod genus pactum est, par, lex, judicatum."—The sources of all that are contained in the Greek doctrine of the νομος ἀγραφος, *v. Hirzel*, and above all in the teaching of Cicero, Seneca, and the Roman jurists who were influenced by the Stoics; on this subject, see *Carlyle, I, 1–78; K. Hildenbrand: Geschichte und System der Rechts- und Staatsphilosophie, I, 1860; M. Voigt: Die Lehre vom jus naturale der Römer, 1856; Zielinsky: Cicero im Wandel der Jahrhunderte, 1897*. While the State was pagan, however, the Fathers found it much more difficult to prove that the Positive Law was derived from the Law of Nature; this produced many inconsistencies in the expression of their views on this subject, especially in Augustine. After the State had become Christian, however, this doctrine made a very conservative attitude possible. With the Code of Justinian and the definitions of Isidore of Seville, the doctrine passed into the Middle Ages; for Justinian, see *Carlyle, I, 71–79*, passages from Ambrose, Ambrosiaster, Hilarius, and especially Isidore, *ibid., I, 104–110*: "St. Isidore has obviously reproduced, with certain changes of detail, the theory of the tripartite character of law (*jus naturale*) as the pure, primitive Law of Nature, *jus civile* as the special form of the Law of Nature in the positive law, which we have already seen in the works of Ulpian, and in the Institutes of Justinian. With this work the conception passes into the common stock of mediaeval tradition" (*110*).

[74] (p. 153.) The doctrine of the pure Law of Nature of the Primitive State, with freedom and equality even to the extent of affecting the intimacies of

family life, is the general doctrine of the later Fathers, which became prominent when the argument which held that the existing State was derived from the Law of Nature necessitated stress being laid upon the contrast between this condition of affairs and the pure Law of Nature in the Primitive State. There are illustrative passages in *Overbeck: Sklaverei, 198–201; Uhlhorn: Liebestätigkeit, I, 292 f.; Carlyle, I, 111–146; Sommerlad, 95–170;* in great detail according to Theodoret, *pp. 165 ff.* It is always questions about property, slavery, the authority of the family and of the State which lead to this point. For the teaching of the Stoics, which also underlies these ideas, see *Hirzel, 84–91; Pöhlmann: Gesch. d. antiken Kommunismus, II, 607–614,* and especially *Carlyle, I, 1–32,* on Cicero and Seneca. Cicero maintains the view that the Primitive State was a state of complete equality and perfection from which the present system with its slavery, property, power, and the law of the State has only arisen out of a gradual process of deterioration. In the opinion of Seneca the Primitive State was not so much perfect as capable of becoming perfect, but in any case it was characterized by innocence and childlike happiness and had no element of compulsion in it. In the course of development sin appeared, but alongside of it there arose the order of the State, which is derived from the Law of Nature, opposes sin, and is a remedy against sin and a means of attaining a better condition. The theory of the Roman lawyers on this question, which was of extreme importance for the thought of the Fathers, is of great interest. They derive positive law first of all simply from the *jus naturale,* but, confronted with the problem of the reasonableness of the prevailing laws, especially those governing slavery, and perhaps also those about property, they came to the opinion that reason did not predominate in them, and that indeed reason (and with that the *jus naturale*) can only have been supreme in a better Primitive State, together with the natural equality of all human beings endowed with reason. Therefore they make a clear distinction between the pure and absolute *jus naturale* and the obscured, relative Natural Law, or the *jus gentium,* which forms part of the order in which conditions have deteriorated. Positive law, or *jus civile,* is then the positive form of the clouded law of reason in empirical law. This theory, then, simply passed on into the *Corpus Justinianeum* and into the literature of the Fathers; cf. the previous note. *Carlyle, I, 33–79. Inst., II, i, ii*: "Palam est autem vetustius esse naturale jus, quod cum ipso genere humano rerum natura prodidit; civilia enim jura tunc demum coeperunt, cum et civitates condi et magistratus creari et leges scribi coeperunt." *Inst. I, 2, 2*: "Jus gentium omni humano generi commune est. Nam usu exigente et humanis necessitatibus gentes humanae quaedam sibi constituerunt: bella enim orta sunt et captivitates secutae et servitutes, quae sunt juri naturali contrariae. Jure enim naturali ab initio omnes homines liberi nascebantur. Ex hoc jure gentium et omnes paene contractus introducti sunt ut emptio, venditio, locatio, conductio, societas, depositum, mutuum et alii innumerabiles."

[75] (p. 155.) *Irenaeus adv. haer. (Harvey), V, 24* with reference to the story of the Temptation: The Devil lies, the riches of this world do not belong to him but to God, who allowed them to arise after the Fall, in order to create within lawless and selfish humanity at least a certain remedy for sin. Likewise *Lactantius: Inst. Epit., 54*: the Fall has destroyed the "societas inter se hominum", the "vinculum necessitudinis". Then men formed laws "pro utilitate communi, ut se interim tutos ab injuriis facerent". This is the theory which is common to Ambrose, Augustine, Gregory the Great, and Isidore (*Carlyle, I, 130*). Augustine especially is to be understood in this sense, as also *Reuter: Aug. Studien, 138* emphasizes. *Reuter* points out in detail that for Augustine the State was, it is

true, according to the absolute standard, a product of sin which is opposed to the Primitive State, but that according to the relative standard the State does still possess a certain value of reason, and in this relative value there is a reaction of reason conditioned in its form by sin. *De civ.*, *19, 21* in connection with Cicero: Domination and lack of freedom do not exclude reasonable righteousness, "ideo justum esse, quod talibus hominibus sit utilis servitus et pro utilitate eorum fieri, cum recte fit, id est cum improbis aufertur injuriarum licentia"; slavery is the result of the change which was caused by the Fall and likewise a penalty, "verum et poenalis servitus ea lege ordinatur, quae naturalem ordinem conservari jubet perturbari vetat: quia si contra eam legem non esset factum, nihil esset poenali servitute coercendum". Hence slaves ought to serve willingly, "donec transeat iniquitas et evacuetur omnis principatus et potestas humana et sit Deus omnia in omnibus". Quite rightly *Reuter* points out that the overestimate of the well-known description of the State as *grande latrocinium, IV, 4,* is really a general argument that the State is derived from sin: "*A.* believes that the State would resemble a *latrocinium* if *justitia* were not in some way or another operative within it; in one passage [*IV, 4*] he calls that which is not a State, a State, while in another place [the definition according to Cicero, *19, 21,* which has already been mentioned] he proves positively that the State only exists where the physical power is at least comparatively controlled by *justitia*, which is itself only relative [in comparison with the *justitiae veritas*]" (*139*). All this would never have been questioned if regard had been paid to Augustine in connection with the Christian and Stoic-juridical doctrines of Natural Law. Also in connection with Augustine one has to remember that his experiences of the State under Honorius could scarcely incline him to err in the direction of exalting the Natural-Law aspect of the State too highly, that *De civitate* is a polemical work directed against the heathen, with the greatest possible depreciation of their State, and that the anti-Donatist writings against the Donatist rejection of the intervention of the State emphasize more strongly the positive aspect of Augustine's doctrine of the State; there, however, he is thinking certainly of the Christian State, which strengthens the natural elements of righteousness within the State by the energy of true Christian righteousness.—I add some passages from *Carlyle*: *Gregory the Great, Exp. moralis in Job. xxi. 15*: "Omnes homines natura aequales sumus, sed accessit dispensatorio ordine, ut quibusdam praelati videamur . . . variante meritorum ordine [i.e. with the Fall] alios aliis dispensatio occulta postponit."—*Isidore Sententiae, 47*: "Propter peccatum primi hominis humano generi poena divinitus illata est servitutis, ita ut quibus aspicit non congruere libertatem, his misericordius irroget servitutem . . . aequus Deus ideo discrevit hominibus vitam, alios servos constituens alios dominos, ut licentia male agendi servorum potestate dominiantium restringatur. . . . Inde et in gentibus principes regesque electi sunt, ut terrore suo populos a malo coercerent atque ad recte vivendum legibus subderent." Only now do we see clearly why it was that there could be no idea of social reform at all.—For corresponding expressions in Cicero and especially plainly in Seneca, see *Carlyle, I, 12* and *25.* Also the juridical distinction between the *jus gentium* and the *jus naturale* has the same meaning (*ibid., 60*).—From the point of view of Dante's doctrine of the State *Vossler* also has recognized this character of Augustine's doctrine of the State, and has described it as the starting-point of a positive estimate: "The same State which through its origin is a sinful organization becomes in its aim an organization against sin" (*Göttliche Komödie, I, 378*).

⁷⁶ (p. 158.) Cf. *Carlyle, I, 63–78, 147–193,* to whom I owe the decisive point

of view that in the theory of the Fathers the Emperor was outside and apart from the point of view of the Natural-Law construction of the State; this was not the case in the theory of the philosophical jurists. Hence *Reuter* also treats the question of the relation of the authority of the Christian Emperors to the Church as a particular problem, quite apart from the general problems of the State. *Aug. Studien, pp. 141–152. Reuter* is only wrong, however, when he argues that this constitutes the basis of the theory of the "Christian State", and that from this point of view also only the "Natural Law" estimate of the State is suggested. The latter has nothing to do with the Christian character of the State, which consisted only in the dominant position which the Emperor gave to the Church, which, then, from its own standpoint effected the Christianization of the State, i.e. the transformation of its outlook. It is thus true to say that "the State only became a true State to the extent in which it became Christian"—that is, to the extent in which the Emperor became serviceable to the Church. The ideal of the true State was then precisely no longer measured by the Law of Nature, but by the believing community. At this point Augustine, with his high ideal of the state of grace and of the Love of God, as well as with his extreme view of the corruption wrought by sin, never inwardly adopted the theories of Natural Law as thoroughly as the other Fathers of the Church. But even in their arguments there remains the hiatus between the Stoic and the Christian ideas, which, although they were akin to each other, were still different. In view of Augustine's pessimism about the actual State the former elements are not fully effective. The latter can only find room to breathe (while the "world" is left to the care of the State) by demanding a privileged position and the sole supremacy of the Church; but a Christian State, and even an economic programme, this is not—as *Sommerlad (pp. 213–216)* seems to think, although he rightly emphasizes the illogical nature of Augustine's theories of the Law of Nature. This was only developed from that by the Middle Ages. The argument that Augustine's theocratic doctrine was a reaction against the Natural-Law-equalitarian-ascetic reaction which is supposed to have been the meaning of the social doctrines of the fourth century against the feudal development of Society, and that this means that the secular realm is once more brought under the control of the spiritual authority through the power of the Church, is a great exaggeration, but it contains in my opinion a germ of truth.—See *Carlyle, I, 64,* for the doctrine of the jurists about the democratic origin of the Imperial authority, also in the *Corpus Justinianeum, p. 169;* the absolutist doctrine, *pp. 69 ff.*—Henceforward my presentation of the subject merges into the well-known representations of the theocratic domination of the Church over the State, which, however, often give a wrong colour to the doctrine of the Fathers on the State, because they speak of the State simply as a product of sin, which is not the straightforward view of the Fathers themselves at all. Also we must not forget the difference between the East—where theocracy meant that the Church was made a department of the State—and the West—where the Church, on the contrary, claims the subordination of the State, or, rather, of the reigning prince.

⁷⁷ (p. 160.) The importance of the doctrine of the relation of the *Lex naturae* to the *Lex Christi* has always naturally been stressed as a fundamental dogma. It is perfectly correlated to the general distinction between Reason and Revelation, and only directs this distinction towards the side of the construction of a practical structure of Society as a whole; cf. the article on *Gesetz* by *Wirthmüller* in the Catholic "*Kirchenlexikon²*" by *Wetzer and Welte; Lehmkuhl: Theologia moralis, I, 39–139; Ottiger: Theologia fundamentalis, I, 37–147; Cathrein:*

Moralphilosophie[3], *1899* (*I, 313*, on Augustine and the Ancient World; *I, 483*, on Isidore of Seville), and the clear popular work of the Jesuit *Theodor Meyer: Die christlich-ethischen Sozialprinzipien und die Arbeiterfrage, 1904* (the social question illustrated by *Stimmen aus Maria Laach, Heft I*); here the difference between the absolute and the relative Law of Nature is clearly unfolded (*p. 40*), and characterized as the fundamental condition of an ecclesiastical cultural and social doctrine, "of the moral organism of Society", "the religious and Natural Law guarantee" (*p. 67*), whereby "religious" here means theocratic. *Gierke* also, in his magnificent work, has clearly recognized the importance of these conceptions, and in his no less fine book on *Althusius* he has described the process of the severance of the ancient Stoic-juridical elements and their development into a position of independence, and with that then their transition into the modern liberal Law of Nature. Protestant theologians, however, are almost all practically blind on this subject. They regard the Christian nature of the State and of Society as something which is so obvious that they have no idea of or eye for the toilsome and devious ways along which the Early Church, the Mediaeval Church, and their own Protestant forefathers had to travel before they could secure these ideas on a firm basis. All they can talk about is the "hallowing and permeation of the world with the ideals of Christ", which they suppose to be the meaning of the Gospel and of the Pauline doctrine of faith: they then explain the fact that this "social-cultural" tendency came to grief, partly (with *Uhlhorn*) owing to the condition of the pagan world, which had become rigid and impervious to influence, partly (with the generality of writers) from the fact that the Gospel ideal was destroyed by the Catholic emphasis upon a holiness consisting in "works", asceticism and the exaltation of the Church, or even by the corruption of the pure conception of faith by spiritual and mystical idealism, and by a realistic doctrine of Redemption, which was very close to the ideas of the ancient mystery cults. Also, with their antithesis of faith and law, in the conception of law the whole idea of a definite content and a concrete tendency of the Christian ethos has been lost so entirely that for them the whole of the Christian ethos is exhausted in denunciation of good works, and in the right definition of the grace which imparts moral energy, but, on the side of content, it is entirely indefinite. That even the historians of dogma are to a very great extent uncertain on the whole doctrine of the Law of Nature, because they do not understand the part it plays in solving the problem of the "world" and of "social life", I have shown in my study of *Seeberg's Dogmengeschichte. Gött. Gelehrte Anzeigen, 1903.*

[78] (p. 162.) This doctrine of equality, even for the Primitive State, was, however, not accepted without question. Even in the Primitive State Augustine accepts the idea that there were differences of disposition and of talents, which produced conditions of voluntary subordination in right proportion (passages in *Overbeck, 200; Quaest. in genesin, 53*) with the ethical effects of these conditions of authority and subordination. In the fallen State this subordination becomes compulsory and often twisted, because brute-force often controls reason, which in itself is stronger and better for the work of government. *Carlyle, I, 127* quotes a passage from *Gregory: Ep. V, 59*, where the same is asserted, and the sinless angels are adduced as examples: "Quia vero creatura in una eademque aequalitate gubernari vel vivere non potest, caelestium militarium exemplar nos instruit, quia, dum sunt angeli et sunt archangeli, liquet, quia non aequalas sunt, sed in potestate et ordine sicut nostris differt alter ab altero. Si ergo inter hos, qui sine peccato sunt, ista constat esse distinctio, quis hominum abnuat huic se libenter dispositioni submittere, cui novit etiam angelos obedire."

Here the Pauline patriarchalism emerges against the entirely unchristian idea of an abstract equality. Since the idea of equality is so important, the whole subject is worthy of further research being given to it.

⁷⁹ (p. 163.) Cf. the excellent study by *von Schubert: Lehrbuch d. KG.*², I, 785–813, also *Uhlhorn, I, 332–354.* The Lutheran here confesses: "Even although at first in small groups, detached from the life of the rest of the world, the New Testament idea of labour was here first realized. Men work because God has commanded it, everyone does his part in the common task, work and prayer are combined, work and rest alternate, and the aim of this labour is not merely the selfish aim of gaining something for oneself, but it is the unselfish aim of earning something in order to be able to serve others with it" (*p. 347*). One only ought to add that these callings consisted solely in spiritual and scientific activity, and the simplest form of handwork, and that their profits were supplemented by the generosity of the supporters and friends of the monasteries, and kept at the level of a strictly low minimum of necessity for existence. The other callings which are absolutely necessary for the general life of the world are here absent, and are exercised by others. Violent contrasts between the Christians who do business in the world and the ascetics described in the Gallic Church (*Hauck: K.G. Deutschlands*³, *1904, I, 53–90*) ; here also it is clear that the ascetics come in from the outside, and that the congregations themselves do not spontaneously produce exclusive asceticism, but that, once they are present, the ascetics know how to prove quite logically that their path is the only right one. On the duty of work and the dignity of labour in the monasteries, and the influence which this had on the conception of work in general, see *Ratzinger: Armenpflege, pp. 99–102.*—For the importance of monasticism for the creation of Christian schools, see the same book; on this point I have also received information from *Herr von Schubert* in private conversation.

⁸⁰ (p. 202.) This difference between the Middle Ages and the Early Church is generally known and recognized; see *Hauck: K.G. Deutschlands, I, 116; Uhlhorn: Liebestätigkeit, II, 5:* "To the Ancient World as a whole, and apart from individual Christian personalities, Christianity was at bottom always something external The pagan past, the cultural life of the ancient peoples which was permeated and steeped in paganism, proved impenetrable for the Christian spirit. Only the Germanic peoples became in reality Christian peoples. Seized by Christianity while they were still young, they grew up with it, and all their civilization was mediated to them through the Church; and as they themselves had a stronger hold on Christianity than the Greeks and Romans who had grown old in paganism, so also Christianity in all its forms of expression dominated them to a degree which was never attained either in Rome or in Byzantium." *P. 7:* "Actually the awakening which began at Cluny in the tenth century constitutes the turning-point for the decisive victory of Christianity." *Harnack: Wesen des Christentums, p. 153:* "What has the Roman Catholic Church achieved? She has educated the Latin and Germanic peoples, in another sense it is true, from the way in which this was effected by the Oriental Church for the Greeks, the Slavs, and the Orientals. Their original disposition, elementary and historical conditions among those peoples, may have made this process easier, and may have helped to accelerate it, but the achievement of the Church is no less meritorious. She brought a Christian civilization to the youthful nations (whence?), and she did not merely bring it to them and then leave them at the lowest stage of development; she gave them the power of developing this gift, and for nearly a thousand years she herself guided and controlled this development and progress."

Sell: Katholizismus und Protestantismus in Geschichte, Religion, Politik, und Kultur, 1908, p. 36: "The progress of the mediaeval stage of Catholicism consists in this, that here Christianity did not form an alliance with a civilization which is already made, as in the Early Church, but that Catholic Christianity became the basis of the whole of Western civilization, since it penetrated into the spiritual substance of the Germanic Latin peoples everywhere with transforming effect." *Ehrhard: Der Katholizismus und das 20. Jahrhundert, 1902, p. 24:* "Out of this combination of the new Germanic-Roman Empire, with its specific natural and cultural disposition, with the spirit of the Latin Church, a new era was born, which had an influence upon actual events which cannot be estimated, so vast was its range. This wealth of facts, however, was controlled by a series of inner factors and elements which constitute the characteristic signs of the Christian Middle Age: (1) The union of the Papacy and the Empire as the two highest representatives of Christendom, and the universalism of the Middle Ages which was determined by this fact. (2) The mutual penetration of the political system of the State and of the life of the Catholic Church, and the synergism between Church and State which this produces. (3) The sole supremacy of the Christian and ecclesiastical spirit in all realms of the higher life of civilization." *P. 35:* "It is to the immortal credit of Gregory the Seventh that he took up the cudgels on behalf of the liberty of the Church, and therefore prepared the way for the complete release of the energies which were bound up within the Church. . . . There now developed the flowering time of the Christian civilization of the Middle Ages, which lasted for two centuries, and which bore ripe fruit of abiding value within all spheres of the higher life of culture." The inner difficulties which were caused within this process by the nature of the Christianity of the Early Church are very largely underestimated in these works. *Von Eicken: Geschichte und System der Mittelalterlichen Weltanschauung, 1887,* makes these difficulties the main theme of his book. His view, that the overcoming of these difficulties was due to the reception of the Roman idea of a world empire, through the ascetic-hierarchical Church, which alone through a political sovereignty could force the world for its good, I cannot accept as true. Of this more anon. I would only remark here that all the universal tendencies of the Church, and all the tendencies in the direction of subduing the world, proceed from the dogmatic conception of truth, and from the influence of the sacraments, in which alone is there salvation, as also *Hauck* shows: *I, 552 ff., II, 110, 502, 535; von Schubert: K.G., I, 726, 730.* It is the sociology of the religious idea which here predominates, the dialectic of thought and not of historical accident, which here *von Eicken* uses in striking contrast with his otherwise purely dialectic construction. But it is precisely at this point that there is no accident. So far as the law and ideal of the Roman Empire is accepted, it takes place as an integral part of the completely independent ecclesiastical tendency of evolution.—For the Catholic unity of civilization as the work of the Middle Ages, see also *Mausbach: Christentum und Weltmoral, 1905,* where this ideal of Catholicism according to St. Thomas is pertinently described, while the problem which it contains for Christian thought itself is characteristically treated in a superficial way. My treatment of the subject will show, above all, that this Catholic unity of civilization, regarded from the historical or from the systematic point of view, is not the obvious "flowering" of the Christian idea.

CHAPTER II

MEDIAEVAL CATHOLICISM

1. THE PROBLEM

THE MEDIAEVAL PRINCIPLE OF UNITY

In the Ancient World the sociological connection of Christian thought was worked out in the sacerdotal and sacramental organization of the Church—an organization which was endowed with grace and with miraculous power. It thus united in one social organism both the absolute individualism and the universalism of the Gospel. Within this social organism each individual, by submission to the institution which imparted grace, could obtain a share in eternal salvation. The spirit of individualism was, however, considerably restricted, both by the action of the authorities who guaranteed salvation, and by hierarchical organizations within the body of the Church, as well as by the patriarchal teaching on submission and adaptation to the existing institutions within the world.

It is impossible to ascertain in detail to what extent, from this point, men evolved a fundamental sociological theory, and an ideal which could be applied to all the conditions of human life.

In any case, the Church did not attempt to regulate the conditions and institutions in the world outside her own borders from the point of view of an ideal of this kind. On the whole, she accepted the conditions of the world, and adjusted herself to them by means of the theory of relative Natural Law. To those who could not accept this compromise monasticism offered a safety-valve, which, however, for that very reason had no clear and logical relation with the Church; indeed, only too often it simply disturbed the conscience of the Church. Thus the attitude of the Church towards the State and towards Society was peculiar. It contained a variety of elements: the recognition of Natural Law, theocratic subjugation and exploitation, the support of the State, whose powers were not equal to its task, by the Church, and the rejection of the State and of Society in general, which worked itself out in the theory of the sinfulness of all the institutions of relative Natural Law and in the practice of renunciation of the world. Neither in theory nor in practice was there any inwardly uniform Christian civilization; the whole idea was foreign to the Ancient World.

The vital difference between the Middle Ages and the period

of the Primitive Church was this: The Church of the mediaeval period did know this ideal, both in practice, and, still more, in theory, and, as an ideal, with some adjustments to modern requirements, its theory is still operative to-day in all the social teaching of contemporary Catholicism.[80]

This ideal of a Christian unity of civilization, however, was also carried forward into early Protestantism, which to a large extent maintained it by the same methods with which the mediaeval period had learned to establish it and to carry it into practice. Even in modern Protestantism, which is so entirely different, this ideal is still retained as a natural fundamental theory which only needs to be placed upon a new basis.

The problem can be stated quite simply. It is this: How was this ideal evolved during the Middle Ages, out of the tradition of the Primitive Church, out of the new situation, and out of the new intellectual movements? And what form did it now assume?

The significance of this question is underestimated by all those who already ascribe to the Primitive Church, or to Christianity in general, this striving after a unity of Christian civilization. The whole of our inquiry up to this point, however, proves that this assumption is unwarranted.

Rather, it is clear that in Stoicism and in Platonism, and still more in Christianity, a theory of social life and of civilization, founded upon the values of free personality in union with God, and of universal human fellowship, was only established with the greatest difficulty. Christianity in particular had created, it is true, a powerful, purely religious organization which was also hostile towards the world; within herself she was able to arrange conditions of life fairly well in accordance with Christian principles, but so far as the world outside was concerned she was unable to find any connection or point of contact.

After all, it is not so simple to build up a civilization and a society upon the supernatural values of the love of God and of the brethren. The self-denial and renunciation of the world which are connected with the former, and the renunciation of the claim on justice and force which are connected with the latter, are not principles of civilization, but radical and universal religious and ethical ideas, which are only absorbed with difficulty into the aims of the secular structure, and into the protective measures which the struggle for existence has produced.

The social ideals of Platonism and of Stoicism remained pure Utopias, and, in spite of all their affinities with Christian ideas,

[80] See p. 199.

they were really much closer to the popular and civic life of the Ancient World; their idealistic theories only had the effect of making clear the difference of their outlook from the ordinary course of the life of the world.

When Christianity was in a condition to establish its ideal State, the Church, upon a purely religious basis, it was still only with difficulty that it was able to reconcile that which was possible upon this basis with the rest of the life of Society.

The Middle Ages, however, witnessed the expansion of the Church to a comprehensive, unifying, and reconciling social whole, which included both the sociological circle of religion itself and the politico-social organizations. In its own way, therefore, it realized in practice the ideal of the Republic of Plato, conceived as an individual State—that is, the rule of wise and God-fearing men over a unified Society, built up organically in ranks, and also the ideal of the Stoics, whose universal commonwealth was to embrace the whole of mankind, without distinction, in one universal ethical kingdom.

The programme which the declining Ancient World had upheld in Platonism, Stoicism, and Christianity as a new ideal of humanity, and which, in the combination of these three tendencies, it had only been able to realize in a very limited manner, now overcame the obstacles which confronted it, and, to some extent at least, it achieved a relative realization. Thus the problem presented by the Middle Ages is one of great historical significance; it is also of importance for all modern historical social doctrines, which, in general, have a closer connection with mediaeval ideas than with those of the Primitive Church.

Here, however, it is quite impossible to survey the whole of this rich and infinitely varied period of the Middle Ages from this point of view. All that concerns us is to indicate the main points in the result of this history, which in the form of Thomism was taken over by the future, and came to be regarded as the classical doctrine. The necessity of explaining Thomism, however, leads us back to the general conditions of the Middle Ages; for it was these conditions alone which, silently and surely, determined the doctrine of St. Thomas (d. 1274), and indeed made it possible. For it is perfectly plain that St. Thomas is related to the whole problem in the way which we indicated in the introduction—a conclusion which the rest of the inquiry has only confirmed.

The Christian social doctrines presuppose, first of all, a definite conception of the Christian religious community, in which the religious idea works itself out directly in a sociological form.

So far as the social doctrines in the narrower sense are concerned, this question then arises: How far is this fellowship (which is regarded as so comprehensive and so penetrating) actually realized in practice? Does it succeed in bringing under the sway of the sociological fundamental theory which it has produced and realized, all the other forms of social life? Or is it only able to come to a working agreement with them, as with foreign phenomena lying outside its own sphere?

The fact that the Thomist social philosophy undertakes the former task presupposes, in the first place, an enormous development of the sociological organism of Christian thought, and, in the second place, the possibility of dominating the whole from the point of view of the sociological fundamental theory which it has developed. This, however, assumes that a universal Christian civilization, in harmony with the Church, is already in existence, which alone makes it possible to incorporate particular social formations into the spirit of the whole.

The problem, then, is this: How did St. Thomas come to accept such an assumption? And only when that has been answered can we put the further question: How did he actually develop his social doctrines from these principles? The weak point in most of the works which deal with this subject is the lack of any sense that the existence of this assumption constitutes the real problem; most writers plunge into the subject at once, and begin to expound the Thomist doctrines themselves.[80a] Yet the most real, the most difficult, and also the most instructive problem lies in the question of how this assumption came into existence. In it are focused all the special conditions of the Middle Ages: all the political, social, and economic movements, those also which affect Church history or the history of religion, in addition to intellectual and scientific movements; it is only because these various currents were thus pooled together that that assumption could be created. Its practical realization, even though it may be only approximate, is therefore also bound up with the continuance or restoration of these conditions, and all attempts to carry out the social doctrines of Catholicism without this foundation will lead either to impossibilities, or to important alterations in the doctrines themselves.[81]

The task of our inquiry, therefore, will be to show how, under the new conditions, the sociological development of the Christian

[80a] See p. 383.
[81] On this point in general, cf. Sell: Katholizismus und Protestantismus, pp. 159–193, is. in my opinion, too optimistic.

system itself was achieved, how as a result the characteristic alienation between the Church and the world disappeared, making room for a mutual inward penetration, and how from that development there sprang the ideal of an all-embracing international ecclesiastical civilization.

From that standpoint alone will it be possible to present the social doctrines of Thomism in their main features. The post-Thomist doctrines of the later Middle Ages reveal the decay of mediaeval society and of its social doctrine, and prepare the way for modern conditions; in that respect, however, they go beyond the limits of our subject. They belong to the history of the rise of modern society and of its theories. For that reason we will deal only with that opposition to the official ecclesiastical social philosophy which sets up essentially Christian ideas of a narrower kind over against the widespread official teaching of the world of society, which form a basis for the sects of the later Middle Ages and of the Reformation period. It will become clear that these sects and their social ethic develop a type of Christian social doctrine which is peculiar to themselves, alongside of the ecclesiastical type and its social doctrines. In contrast with the lowering of the Christian standard in the ecclesiastical unity of civilization, in them there emerges the radicalism of the Christian social ethic, and the tendency to form small groups in which it is possible to carry this radicalism into practice.

This, however, throws an important light upon Christian social doctrine as a whole. The Thomist ecclesiastical unity of civilization is only one of its possibilities of development; alongside of it there stands the other radical possibility, which is connected with the Gospel, with absolute Natural Law, and with monasticism. These tendencies, which in the Primitive Church were mingled and obscure, now diverge in different directions.

SOCIAL THEORY INFLUENCED BY HISTORICAL EVENTS

From the outset, however, one point must be kept in mind. We are dealing, it is true, with the history of the social philosophy of the Church, with a doctrine, with an idea. But history of this kind does not, on that account, need to be treated purely as a process of dialectic. However largely original ideas may have their own dialectic consequence and development, whose evolution has been caused partly by the inner impulse to formulate the content of their thought, partly by the necessity of answering new and urgent problems which arise in practical life, still the fundamental ideas in the great fruitful systems of life are not simple and uniform; rather, to a great extent, they themselves are already the result of a complex. On the other hand, in the unending and involved interplay of various forces, as Eduard Meyer so aptly puts it,[82] everywhere we have to take into account the element of accident and surprise, i.e. the clash of independent causal sequences, which have no inner connection with each other. Both these elements are strongly marked in the history which we are studying in this book. Already it has been clearly shown that Christian thought, with its inclusion of supernatural and natural, with its rich conception of God which combines the ideas of the Creation and world-optimism with Redemption and world-pessimism, is itself a complex structure, containing many elements of tension; this fact will emerge anew, with fresh significance, in our study of the development of mediaeval thought. Likewise the interpenetration of the sacred and the secular, which was possible in the Middle Ages, cannot be explained as the result of intellectual dialectic impulses of development, but out of the actual pressure of events; for no dialectic exists, which, from the standpoint of Christian thought, would itself have been in a position to lay down a programme of this kind; here we have to do with the effect of the possibilities and necessities, which the actual course of affairs in the development of social life outside the Church brought into the ecclesiastical organization.

This ideal must have grown up out of universal changes, which, perfected in silence, were looked upon as quite natural and obvious; and that is the reason why that which was impossible in the Early Church now became possible, and that which did not even exist as an ideal in the mind of the Primitive Church now became a goal of aspiration and desire. Finally, in spite of the development of a unity of civilization under conditions yet to be described which were peculiarly favourable to it, the question still remains: To what extent, in this situation, was Christian thought only able to utilize favourable circumstances for its realization? Or how far was the unity achieved because Christian thought, for its part, was adapting itself to the newer influences?

Above all, we must be on our guard against a tendency of the theologians—upon whose otherwise excellent and sometimes brilliant researches, together with the researches of jurists, secular historians, and political economists, the following study has for the most part been based—the tendency to discover everywhere either deformations of or deviations from the Gospel,

[82] Cf. Eduard Meyer: *Zur Theorie und Methodik der Geschichte, 1902, pp. 17 ff.*

or to discern everywhere foreshadowings of and preparations for the Reformation solution of the problem. Ranke's deep and suggestive saying, that "every historical epoch has its own direct significance in the sight of God", might aptly be applied to this question; it might, indeed, be extended in this direction, in order to include the idea that each epoch is in the direct Presence of God, both in its greatness and its truth, and in its unfaithfulness to its better self. Mediaeval religion and its social doctrines are neither a perversion of the "essence of Christianity", nor a phase of development serving other ends of Christian thought, but an expression of the religious consciousness corresponding to the general social structure, with its own advantages and truths, and its own faulty and terrible side. Mediaeval religion, and its corresponding form of social philosophy, should be understood first of all as they are in themselves; we ought only to consider their connection with tradition in so far as they drew from it, for their own need, the necessary historical nourishment and stimulus.

The religious life, even that of Christianity, in each of its great forms is something new and different, and must first of all be understood as an independent phenomenon. The further problem of connecting this phenomenon with a united and universal ideal is one which lies beyond the borders of pure history.[83]

2. EARLY SOCIAL DEVELOPMENTS AS THE BASIS FOR THE MEDIAEVAL UNITY OF CIVILIZATION

DEVELOPMENT OF THE ECCLESIASTICAL INSTITUTION

The first question with which we have to deal is the development of the Church itself. This is always the primary concern of Christianity; only after this has been entirely and satisfactorily established can social questions be considered. In this respect the essential foundations of Catholicism had already been firmly established in the Ancient World; at the same time, however, the settlement of these fundamental problems still contained some open questions for the future. The Christian congregations which were held together by their common opposition to the State and to the world, and which also represented a minority, had been until then firmly knit together by the pressure of the hostile majority. When, however, these communities passed into the

[83] Cf. my discussion with *Loisy* and *Harnack: Was heisst Wesen des Christentums? Christl. Welt, 1893,* and with *Rickert: Moderne Geschichtsphilosophie. Theol. Rundschau, 1901.*

period of equality, and then into that of increasing privilege by
the State, while they also increased extraordinarily in numbers,
the imperfections, laxities, and inconsistencies of the organization,
which until then had been functioning most admirably, became
apparent. They were unable to prevent the State, in its own
interest, from trying to unify the Church in matters of law and
doctrine, supported by the Church's own legislation.

The support of the whole system, the episcopate, needed a
stronger unity which would make schism and division on questions
of doctrine and worship impossible. The episcopate needed a
strong organization of its own, over against the clergy who were
under the sway of the bishop. Above all, the need was felt for a
higher unity of administration, above the episcopate itself, an
administrative unity which all would recognize, and which
would be the source of the authority of the episcopate. It was felt
that the system of calling the bishops together in general synods
would not meet the case, since the right to call these synods lay
in the hands of the Emperor, and the competence of a synod,
whether it was universal or local, whether its resolutions were
carried out in practice or not, whether the bishops agreed among
themselves or not, was dependent upon its success, the interplay
of forces, upon caprice and accident. Friction began to arise
between the episcopal and aristocratic elements, and the congregational and democratic elements, which had supplemented each
other so well during the period of the struggling Early Church
with its community life. This friction increased as the episcopal
dignity became a coveted office,[84] with official powers and a
force which counted in the State, and was subject to the influence
of the State. The uncertainties which surrounded the election of
bishops, combined with the conflicting influences which arose
from the general body of the faithful, from neighbouring bishops,
the State, and the great Princes of the Church, endangered the
stability of the institution, and opened the gates to the intervention
of alien powers and interests. Even the parochial clergy, who were
under the bishop, both in election and in the determination of the
sphere of their office, were divided among these different influences.[85] The religious communities, which had constituted a very
small group, with apparent suddenness became a very large one,

[84] See p. 383.
[85] On this last point, *Löning: Gesch. des deutschen Kirchenrechtes, I, pp. 131 and 158.*
Other obscurities were due to the lack of clarity in the relation between the
aristocratic and democratic elements in the problem of Church property. It developed out of the property belonging to a corporation into that which belonged
to an institution—a development which the Imperial legislation tacitly sanctioned.

and in the process they became strongly secularized. They then ceased to exercise mutual control, and also slipped away from the control of the bishops; and the ecclesiastical discipline, which only reached open sinners, was an entirely inadequate method of spiritual control and authority.[86]

Further, the fraternities and monasteries which were organized during this period, with their strong tendencies towards separation and independence, were a dangerous explosive, and a serious rival of the priesthood. That is the real reason why the special aim of the ecclesiastical institution, the maintenance of unity of doctrine and the unity of the sacramental powers, was not achieved by the Church, in spite of most vigorous support from the State. The Arian, Nestorian, and Monophysite Churches broke away, and secured their independence by adhesion or submission to foreign States. The Donatist peasant rising believed only in the sacramental power of "pure" priests, and not in its character *indelebilis*: this was the beginning of the great series of sect-movements, with their hostility to the Church, which were to cause extraordinary difficulties in later days.

The great princes of the Church quarrelled violently among themselves, and their dogmatic controversies were the cause of ecclesiastical and political conflicts.

Theological dilettantism and political statecraft often led the Emperors to interfere in these conflicts. Thus, just as the Church was becoming established and recognized, the sociological tendency towards unity which was implicit in the episcopate was split up and impeded, in spite of the powerful assistance of the State. On the other hand, in the process of adjusting the Church to the State, the political aim of making the Church one of the powers which maintain and support the State, was only very partially realized. Particularly in the West, ecclesiastical conflicts and the ecclesiastical powers, incommensurable in contrast to the State, had a directly disintegrating and disturbing effect. The Church was a new sociological structure, whose own nature and logical development were still incomplete, and whose relationship to the rest of the sociological formations and groups, neither for itself nor for these groups, had yet become clear.

Why, then, was this development arrested? And why was the situation so confused and obscure? It was not due merely to the natural immaturity of a new movement, nor to the weakening of public spirit which takes place whenever a minority is changed into a majority, and which—owing to the nominal and compul-

[86] See p. 383.

sory Christianity of the masses—in actual fact had a particularly paralysing effect. This arrested development was due to hindrances which were implicit in the thought and substance of Christianity itself, in all its previous history. The new relation of the Church to the State, that is to the Imperial power, in spite of the extraordinary access of strength in which it resulted, had also a bewildering and hampering effect. The Church received from the hand of the State the unity of her doctrine and of her constitution; at the same time, however, this very authority continually mingled foreign political opinions, interests, and powers with the life of the Church. The Imperial absolutism, which at first the Church accepted as a matter of course, and which effected the consolidation of the Church and of its dogmas, acted at the same time as a disturbing element, both in the unity and exclusiveness of the Church and in her religious interests. The general theory of the Doctors of the Church about the State did not help to clear men's minds; in fact, it only increased the confusion. The institution of the State as an institution of relative Natural Law, and the absolute Imperial power in the service of the theocratic doctrine of salvation, supported by the bishops, which the Emperors in the case of spiritual interests were to subordinate to the structure of relative Natural Law: all that, indeed, gave a positive value to the State, but the relation between Church and State was still obscure. The relationship between them only became clear when the Church was sufficiently able really to dominate and guide the Empire, and when she had a concrete idea of the way in which, with the aid of the Imperial authority, the secular life could actually be woven in detail into the whole scheme of eternal salvation.

At this period, however, something was lacking on all hands. The episcopate did not present that united front to which the Empire could have submitted; the Emperor did not dream of giving up the old Roman idea of the State in favour of a spiritual kingdom of priests. Further, in spite of the stability of the ancient State and its remoteness from the ecclesiastical authorities, with their ascetic and spiritual outlook, in all secular matters the bishops were still prepared to submit unquestioningly to the Emperor as to the authority appointed by God. Where, however, they were to define the border-line between the spiritual and the temporal was hard to say, and there was no court to which this question could be referred.

Religious interests still seemed to be exhausted in fighting against heretics, in the compulsory Christianizing of the heathen, and in gaining privileges for the Church. Ecclesiastical ethics were not ready to claim a subordination of the life of Society as a whole, and in detail, under the standard laid down by the Church; the social order was considered too stable and unalterable for that to happen, the ascetic and religious spirit was still inwardly too remote from the world, and the world, as it was, was in no way prepared for such a change.

Along the following lines, however, it certainly seemed as though the way were being prepared for such an incorporation of social life into the Church: the bishops had begun to take a large share in political and social activity, and in civic and penal legislation; the bishops and the clergy possessed certain rights in the administration of public affairs, and during political upheavals they developed social welfare work, in order to meet the needs of their dioceses.

These developments, however, were the product of necessity, and were contradictory in principle, dictated more by the interest of the communes and of the provinces than by that of the Church. They were hotly opposed by the ascetics, who regarded such things as a secularization of the episcopal office; indeed, very often they were supported by the bishops more from secular than from religious motives; on the other hand, the unique legal position of the clergy, the continuation of their juridical activity, the delegation of charitable activity to them, in the sense in which the State regarded such matters, meant that the Church still occupied her old unique position within the State—in which, to some extent, the State allowed the Church to have an independent existence, while it also used the Church for its own ends. This meant, of course, that, instead of a union between the Church and the world, both were openly and obviously separated. The separation continued along the line which it had hitherto followed, and was definitely limited in both directions, in order that the Church should not be too closely involved in conformity with the world.

When Church and State became allies there were surprises on both sides. The State hoped to include the Church among its supporters, and it found itself confronted with the sovereign authority of a purely spiritual power. With the help of the State the Church hoped to come to a satisfactory conclusion on the question of unity, and in admitting the influence of the State she admitted a disturbing element, a foreign body, which, under certain circumstances, was useful, and in others disintegrating, but which in any case was always an alien influence.

In this situation Chrysostom, Leo I, Gelasius, and Augustine might well demand the theocratic subordination of the Emperor to the priesthood, according to the pattern of the Old Testament, and in so doing foreshadow the "Programme of the Middle Ages"; but in the East this programme was never realized, and in the West it was only realized after the lapse of five hundred years. Between the time of Augustine and of Gregory the Seventh there must lie something more than the mere dissolution of the Empire and the paralysis caused by the influx of barbarism. Otherwise its realization would not have been so long delayed, and the new character of the Church, particularly in relation to social matters, would not have arisen out of the mere disintegration of ecclesiastical unity. The element which arose between these two periods must contain within itself the reasons which caused the nebulous programme of Augustine to develop into a vital reality. In the Early Church this programme was, indeed, not merely still unrealized, but at that time there were also no means at all by which it could have been realized, nor was there any tangible hope for the future; the aloofness of the Church from the world, and the independence of the State, firmly based on a primitive legal and administrative technique, made the very idea of such a fusion impossible.

The theory of the *Lex naturae* made it possible to accept the State in a general way; this meant, however, the State as distinct from the Church, and alongside of all its asserted identity with the *Lex Mosis*, or with the Decalogue, it still contained no concrete suggestion of the way in which the Church, on her side, should order in a practical way the secular situation in property, trade, law, social and political organization, and intellectual life. At the most everything is adapted to fit a parallelism, with incidental exceptions, and as soon as the parallels part asunder wisdom and theory fail.[87]

The sociological consolidation of the unified sacerdotal Church was connected with the formation of a new relationship with the State, in which the State appropriated spiritual aims and standards and inwardly united its own organization with that of the Church; the outcome of this was that either directly or indirectly the general social life was placed under the control of the standards of the Church. This is what took place, after severe conflicts, both in the East and in the West; each time, however, the course of events differed greatly. In the actual course of these concrete struggles and developments a considerable part of the new

[87] See p. 383.

element which ushered in the so-called mediaeval period must have been established. It would, of course, also be quite possible to imagine that the diametrically opposite course was pursued, and that the Church took up her theocratic position, forcing the State to submit to her without further argument. The State, however, was still decidedly the stronger partner, and, on the other hand, the Church was still much too reserved, too restricted to her merely spiritual office, for such a thing even to be imagined; all that happened was that now and again the hierarchy indulged in visionary hopes, which swiftly faded away when the submission of the priesthood in all secular matters to the authority of the State was secured. Thus the quickest way out of all this tension and difficulty was the development of a Christian State Church. In the East this arose directly out of an inner process of development; the peculiar reasons which helped to bring this about in the West, and which gave it its special character, will be dealt with in their own place.

ARRESTED DEVELOPMENT IN THE EAST

In the East, after much strife and conflict, a position of stable unity was attained, in which the Empire itself was transformed into a spiritual dignity, gathering up into itself the religious purpose of the Church; in return, however, it made the Church a department of the State.

The old orientalized and feudalized Roman State, with its Hellenistic culture and literature, remained, but it absorbed into itself the spiritual system, and forced both to agree with each other by the authority of the State. If by the Middle Ages we mean that unity of civilization which combined the sacred and the secular, the natural and the supernatural, the State and the Church (characteristics which also belonged to the culture of the Islamic States, and for similar reasons), then the Eastern Roman Empire is genuinely mediaeval, and those who say that the East had no mediaeval period have very peculiar opinions.[87a] In the East this mediaeval period has lasted down to the present day, and we see before our very eyes the strangest combinations, in which this mediaevalism is mingled with the most modern political and economic plans and aspirations. This Eastern Mediaeval period was, however, very different from its counterpart in the West. The point of divergence lies in the fact that the theocratically and spiritually moulded Roman-Hellenistic State still remained the old State, with its ancient laws and its ancient culture; it only

[87a] See p. 384.

compromised with Christian thought, but never inwardly became united with it. The old alienation of ancient enemies still remained in spite of all apparent softening, and the whole system remained a parallelism whose component parts could only be kept in right relation with each other by the Empire, which was spiritually interested and qualified for the task. The process of uniformity confined itself to the common regulation of both by the spiritual and temporal Imperial power; and inner mutual interpenetration did not take place. The political authority of the State had to be satisfied with an undisturbed parallelism; it did not need to effect an inward intellectual penetration; the necessity for this would only have been felt by the Church if she had been supreme. This is why the Byzantine East lacks the deep inner conflicts of the Middle Ages in the West, and the development of phenomena like the Renaissance and the Reformation. To a great extent these movements arose out of the efforts to achieve an inward fusion which were constantly being attempted by the Middle Ages in the West; the Ancient World, which always remained a vital force, never effected any Renaissance in the East, and in the East the attempt to deepen and renew the religious life always led simply to a revival of asceticism, even in so modern a form as the asceticism of Dostoevsky and Tolstoy.[88] The East never provided a fruitful soil for movements like the Reformation.

DEVELOPMENT IN THE WEST

Why, then, was the course of development so different in the West? In the West the final result of this development was an entirely different relationship to the State, and thus to social life in general; that is, the hierarchical theocratic unity of civilization. As has already been pointed out, this conception could not have been directly deduced from the religious thought of the Church as such. What, then, were the events, which, in spite of this fact, contributed to this development?

These events were the great fundamental events of the Church History of the West: (1) The division of the Church of the Imperial period into Germanic-Roman Territorial Churches,* in which, for five hundred years, the continuity of

[88] On this point cf. *Karl Neumann: Die Weltstellung des byzantinischen Reiches, 1895,* and especially *Byzantinische Kultur und Renaissancekultur, 1903.* Unfortunately the history of the Russian Church is too little known to make it possible to follow up the interesting parallels and differences which certainly must exist in connection with the development in the West.

* The term *Landeskirche* will be thus rendered throughout this book.—
TRANSLATOR.

the previous development seemed to have almost entirely disappeared. The Frankish Territorial Church became the channel of the main line of development, reaching its highest point in the Carolingian Empire, continued by Otto and his successors, and developing, under the Salian emperors, into the Universal Catholic Church. That, too, was a State Church system, but it was quite different from that of the East, since it was based, not upon the strength of the State, but upon the inward permeation of the sacred and the secular, which first gave to the State its power and its civilizing mission; therefore also the result for the Church differed greatly from Byzantinism. (2) The formulation of the idea of the Papacy, and of the ecclesiastical universalism supported by it, in close connection with a new wave of international asceticism, animated by the spirit of detachment from the world, and by an ecclesiastical science supported by the Religious Orders. Since the German Monarchy was forced to give up its Territorial Church religious ideas by the universal Empire, and was led to care for the whole of Christendom, it again enthroned the Papal idea, and the Papacy now had within her grasp the inheritance which five hundred years of the influence of the Territorial Church in Church and State, both in the spiritual and the temporal realm, had laid at her feet.

The Germanic-Roman Territorial Church was something quite different from the Byzantine State Church, and the first reason for the difference between them must lie here. The significance of these events must now be made clear in detail.

3. THE TERRITORIAL CHURCH PERIOD OF THE EARLY MIDDLE AGES

The rise of the Germanic-Roman States, alongside of which stand the Celtic, and, later, the Slavonic and the Hungarian States, meant first of all that the Imperial Church completely disappeared, and that the Canon Law of the ancient united Church was discarded, apparently for ever. It was only in the Anglo-Saxon Church that the Canon Law was retained in its integrity, together with the Roman order of worship, and the connection with the centre through the Roman Bishop. All the other States— above all, the Kingdom of the Franks, which united Central Europe and gave to it a common basis of civilization—administered the Church purely as a Territorial Church, and incorporated its organism into the body of the new State; the idea of the

United Church was only retained in a conventional respect for the Pope, and in the sense of the collective consciousness of Christendom. In these lands there arose a Church order which differed completely from that of the Early Church; its fundamental idea was that of the rights of property and of possession enjoyed by the sovereign Princes over whatever Church might happen to be under their jurisdiction. It was only thus that the development of ecclesiastical vassalage and of ecclesiastical land-tenure became possible, which gave the Church completely into the hands of the lords of the manor and of the feudal lords, at whose head was the King.

The reasons for the emergence of this theory of the Territorial Church, which was something quite new, are still obscure.

The system of the independent Church (*Eigenkirche*) was undoubtedly connected with the old pre-Christian form of worship. The Territorial Church principle was enormously strengthened in the course of time by the independent Church. It seems possible that this principle may have arisen in the Arian churches, which were excluded from the Orthodox Church; thus when national conflict arose they were forced to adopt a "territorial" or "national" Church organization; in so doing they were perhaps related to the traditions of the ancient pre-Christian popular cults. If these suppositions were justified they would illuminate the situation in a very characteristic way. The purely universal religious ethic which arose within the heathen State was unable to find any inward relationship with the life of the world, but the after-effects of the Germanic popular worship, in which, as in all paganism, religious and natural social elements are generally related, involved a natural connection with both these aspects.[88a] In the same way that Byzantine State Christianity was connected with the traditional religion of the Roman State, so also the Western Territorial Church system would then be connected with the previous paganism. That, however, would also explain the difference between the State Church system in the East and the Territorial Church system of the West. In the East a strong State, with an ancient tradition of civilization, incorporated the Church into itself; in the West, on the other hand, the life of a new State was built up with the help of the Church. In an entirely naïve and orthodox way the Church regarded the claims of Church and

[88a] Cf. the important work by *U. Stutz: Die Eigenkirche.* My colleague, *Herr von Schubert*, drew my attention to the Arian churches; he is about to publish a very illuminating essay on this subject. He believes that he can prove the dependence of the Frankish Church upon Arian example.

State as identical; the ecclesiastical organization was also in accord with the general legal and economic conditions of the State. Sufficiently civilized to give to the young State its intellectual basis, its forms of organization and its moral foundations, the Gallic-Germanic clergy, who were solely occupied with questions of adaptation and who were subject to the new law and property conditions, were still too much bound, both intellectually and materially, even to dream of an independent ecclesiastical civilization.

Thus there arose the Territorial Church or the *Landeskirche*.

In any case, there can be no doubt about the novelty of the principle. The remains of the old Church of the Empire (*Reichskirche*) could not resist this development, as they were being pushed back into an ever-diminishing territory; the greater part of her domains fell into the hands of the Eastern Empire and of the Islamic States, while in her centre, the Papacy, she was overwhelmed with her own territorial anxieties.

It is true that from the side of the Anglo-Saxon Church the reform and the ecclesiastical organizations of Boniface, which the Frankish sovereigns used for their own purposes, had restored the connection with Rome, effected the victory of the Italian Benedictine monastic rule over that of the Scottish and Columban rule, and endeavoured to obtain the closest possible approximation to the Canon Law; but while the Frankish rulers utilized this reform in their Church, which was actually most demoralized, they put a stop to the "universal Church" tendencies, and only made use of them for the intellectual quickening and the stabilization of the organization of their own Territorial Church.

When, however, in the time of Charlemagne, all the northern parts of the previous Roman Empire and the new mission territories were united on the one hand, then the Territorial Church (*Landeskirche*) became the Church of the Empire (*Reichskirche*), but it was an Imperial Church in the sense of the Frankish Territorial Church. It was a Territorial Church which now included the Pope. The Emperor governed the Church, and used it as the essential support of the organization and education of his peoples, while he directed in this sense the interior, legal, and land-owning development of the Church and also used them for public ends.

It is to this policy of Charlemagne that we can trace, even after the division of the Carolingian Empire, throughout Central Europe, this fundamental tendency of ecclesiasticism. The resumption of the Carolingian idea of the State by the Saxon

Imperial House meant, indeed, that those who bore spiritual and secular dignities could no longer remain in the position of mere officials; dignitaries of both kinds had to be allowed to become princes. Now, however, it was supported firmly by the spiritual aristocracy, which, owing to the fact that it was not hereditary, was dependent upon the influence of the Crown, and was also responsible for the civilization and political unity of the Empire. In England, Alfred the Great worked on similar lines to those laid down by Charlemagne. This was the state of affairs until the great Gregorian conflict broke out over the question of the severance of the Church from the State, and the renewal of the Universal Church and the Canon Law. Where the effects of the struggle did not extend, as in the remote Scandinavian lands, everything remained as it was before.

THE CHURCH AND CIVILIZATION

This is as far as we can go with the great story; its details belong to the history of the Church, of law and of economics.[89] For our present inquiry the vital point is this: That these five hundred years of the development of the idea of the Territorial Church placed the religious forces of organization and thought at the service of the State and its tasks of civilization.

The fact that Christianity was forced to develop this kind of civilizing activity was neither the result of inner compulsion nor the outcome of religious thought. Rather it was due to the force of circumstances and to the compulsion of an uncivilized State, which had to utilize for its own ends the ecclesiastical organization, and the vital tradition of ancient civilization which it contained; only thus was the State able to build up a civilization of its own. Thus Christianity drew into the realm of ideas governed by the Church and religion those tracts of life which were not directly connected with the Church. In particular, it was the genius of Charlemagne which opened up this path for Christianity, and, in so doing, essentially and permanently determined the peculiar basis of mediaeval Christendom.

It is, however, scarcely possible to ascribe the whole of this result solely to the mere personal genius of Charlemagne. The underlying basis of the work of Charlemagne contained an altogether different idea of the State from the idea of the State which the Church Fathers had taken over from late antiquity. While the Fathers held that the State was both the result of and the discipline for sin, but was otherwise absolutist in character, they

[89] See p. 384.

were only occasionally inclined to use this absolutism in order to gain ecclesiastical privilege; in the Carolingian State, however, in spite of all its outward literary continuance of the patriotic doctrine of the State, there were also present traces of the influence of the Germanic idea of the monarchy.

The Divine Right of Kings appears in a much greater degree in all their proclamations and theories; further, the monarchy, both in the struggle to realize its own existence and in the exercise of its authority, was dependent on the co-cperation of the people and of the nobles, and was therefore bound to observe the law, that is, to preserve the welfare and the security of the masses, and to serve them in a loyal paternal spirit. The basic idea is the King's obligation to care for the good of the whole, from which also is deduced the right to depose a monarch when he acts unworthily and disloyally, as well as the duty of caring for the common weal and of common activity for common ends. This leads to the introduction of a new element into the idea of the State, whose effect is seen first of all in the Carolingian type, in an extension of the royal power over all his subjects, which also makes it possible for the Church to extend its works of charity. Later this same conception has the opposite effect, making it possible for us to understand why kings had to submit to a purely ecclesiastical law.

The Christianizing of the Germanic monarchy makes the King, where he conceives his tasks ideally, the representative of righteousness and of care for all his compatriots, to whom he renders loyalty for loyalty. Upon this new foundation also is based the doctrine of the Divine Right of Kings, which had been taken over from the ancient doctrine of the State, and which now received a new meaning. Not merely the passive reception of the Divine appointment to power, but the purpose of this authority, is the basis of the Divine Right of Kings. The sovereign is the representative of God in his endeavour to realize a Christian order of life.[90]

Such a Christianizing of the Germanic monarchy would indeed have been impossible if Christianity had really been essentially ascetic from the beginning, if the Gospel writings, as well as the early Christian and the Early Church literature, had actually only perpetuated and manifested an ascetic tradition, if the incompatibility between Christianity and royalty in the Early Church had merely consisted in the hostility of Christianity to the world. In reality, however, the Christian ethic had been formed on two planes, and the ecclesiastical tradition contained within itself a large section of the inheritance from the civilization of the ancient

[90] See p. 386.

world, so that the so-called "Renaissances" in the times of the Emperors Charlemagne and Otto I and II, and the later strong development of elements of ancient civilization, formed a natural element in every renewal of ecclesiastical literature and art. We shall return to this subject later.

In the first instance, it is characteristic of the situation that before the acceptance of the Burgundian and Cluniac reform movement, the monastic system was definitely placed at the service of civilization—that is, it served the interests of education and of science. This is particularly true of Charlemagne. The Benedictine Rule, in the interest of the monks, laid great stress upon the importance of scientific and agricultural work, and Charlemagne placed these forces at the service of the State and of Society. Further, the new tendency was made easier by the fact that in the Roman Imperial Church the episcopate had already taken on a series of public duties, and that in the time of disruption the preservation of civic order and of civilizing activities fell chiefly into its hands.

Thus there lay in the Church the possibility of being used for the civilizing aims of the State and of Society, even when it had no inner spontaneous impulse in this direction. The Church was drawn into this kind of activity by the need of the semi-civilized State, and she continued to exercise it because it increased her own position of power and influence, because her own position as a landowner made it essential, and because the Germanic Christians had no sense of any inward inconsistency between the ancient civilization of the State and the ideal of Society within the Church. So far as my knowledge extends, no one ever doubted the possibility of an inner reconciliation between secular and spiritual tasks. If scruples arose, monasticism was there to act as a channel for the sense of the need of asceticism, alongside of the activity of the Church both as a landowner and in the domain of science. The Christian State and the Christian Society, without any theory, seemed to have reached a mutual understanding quite naturally, just as previously their separation had also seemed natural.

In this connection there was a special importance, as we have already seen, in the territorial development of the bishoprics and monasteries themselves. In part this was due to asceticism itself, which ordained that in order to win a heavenly reward, and to expiate earthly sins and deeds of violence, extraordinarily large gifts should be given to the Church, and most of these gifts happened to be gifts of land.[91] Further, the general economic and

[91] Cf. *Uhlhorn, II, 43–54.*

social situation, which, after the land had gradually been absorbed by free occupation and by clearing, caused the rise of the system of large estates, in which small landowners placed themselves under the protection of the large landowners, owing to the loss of freedom caused by feudal tenure, and the system of land-tenure known as *precarium*.

Now, however, the Church took a large share in this growth of large estates, since, owing to her more merciful treatment, and also to the fact that she possessed numerous "immunities" or charters of privilege, she was preferred by the small landowners who gave her themselves and their land. The position of rural economics which had no large business system, made it necessary for large landowners to have their property administered by tenant-farmers, villeins, and serfs, in small individual holdings; this created a complicated social and legal system which forced the landowner to make legal and social provision for all these varied grades and conditions.[92] As a matter of course, therefore, the charitable activity of the Church was forced to undertake the care of tenant-farmers and vassals, whereas the specially organized charity of the Early Church was the work of the congregation, while other charitable needs which were not met by general welfare work were met by the hospital, and later on by the work of the religious communities.

Both for the property of the Crown, and, above all, for the estates of the Church, Charlemagne explicitly decreed this social policy and welfare work, which was certainly still in a very elementary state, and this became the usual practice among all bishops and abbots of goodwill. Once again, however, this whole social transformation itself was based upon the practice of a purely agricultural economic system.[93]

Under the Merovingians the economic system based on money ends, and with the extension of the Empire from the old civic culture of Gaul into the German agricultural territories the urban character of the Early Church, which up till that time had stamped its essential character upon her, disappears. The bishops now own large estates, and the rural parish has come into exist-ence, in which the priest is endowed with full sacerdotal rights, and possesses a certain amount of landed property. The country parish, in addition to its special vocation to educate the people, in the sphere of morals is gradually drawn very deeply into the interests of the general life around it, by its economic relation-ships. In this way the development of Church property made the

[92] Cf. *Uhlhorn, II, 57–60.*　　　　　　　　　　[93] Cf. *Lamprecht, II, 90 ff.*

Church a social force, and through her dependence upon others she became interested in the situation as a whole.

While the economic system based upon agriculture, with the increasing lack of free land, produced the socage farm with its technique of management, its compulsory service, and payment of taxes, ecclesiastical property also was forced into this system, and owing to its considerable size it immediately took a leading position. This had a still more important result. On account of the lack of actual cash the salaries of the officials had to be paid in grants of land, and out of this fact there arose the hereditary character of the office, the whole system of feudal tenure. Since ecclesiastical property, however, was naturally not hereditary, the Kings saw in this fact the one and only method by which—through constant grants of land to the Church—a race of non-hereditary officials could be created, which would thus prevent the division of the Empire into hereditary territorial dominions. So it came about quite naturally that the clergy became the real officials of the Empire and the main support of the royal power. Thus from this side also the clergy were drawn into the general political and social welfare interests; they were invested with public authority, and at the same time their own desires in the direction of the acquisition of land were furthered. Bound up with that development, however, was the complete disappearance of the canonical idea from Church property, in accordance with which Church lands were regarded as the institutional property of the Church; such lands now became the property of the ruler upon whose land the Church stood, and they were only granted in the form of a fief. Thus kings and dukes became the supreme owners of Church property, and those who held the land became territorial lords (great landowners) like other feudal lords; this whole situation drew the Church herself into all the interests of the Empire and of Society.

Finally, we must not forget the missionary activity which characterized the whole of this period, and which only reached its height in the Crusades. The mission of the Early Church was free preaching within a homogeneous social system supported by the Roman Empire, and it gathered the fruits of the interior religious development of antiquity. The mission of the Middle Ages, like that of modern times, was everywhere a political and a civilizing agency. The foundation of new bishoprics was always an act of the State, and at the same time a Germanization, which the ecclesiastical organization utilized for the purposes of political administration and of culture and education. The Crusades produced spiritual and semi-spiritual dominions, which, at least in theory, were supposed to be Christian States, and orders of Chivalry placed at the disposal of Christendom special organs for social purposes of all kinds.[94]

The total effect of these events was an interpenetration of Church and State, of the spiritual and the temporal, of the ascetic and the socio-political aspects of life, which gave the Church of the Middle Ages a quite different character from that of the Early Church. All that differentiates this social policy of the mediaeval Church from a modern social policy based on ethics is the fact that it lacks entirely that deeper and more comprehensive reflection upon the nature of political, economic, and social processes; and also the whole idea of the dependence of spiritual and ethical values upon the soundness of their economic and social substructure, and therefore of prophylactic politics, is entirely undeveloped. Christian idealism has only that in common with the Stoic and Platonic elements which have been fused with it. There could not yet exist a deeper understanding of this kind in a world ruled by mediaeval ideas. Even the empiricism and realism of the Aristotelian doctrine of the State and of ethics, which in spite of its ideological and moral character, as we shall see presently, invests the Thomist doctrine of the State and of Society with at least a certain regard for a rational policy of welfare, has not yet begun to exercise its influence.

4. THE REACTION IN FAVOUR OF THE UNIVERSAL CHURCH AND THE CATHOLIC UNITY OF CIVILIZATION

REACTION IN FAVOUR OF PAPAL SUPREMACY

From the tenth century onwards, however, the conception of the Universal Church arose once more in opposition to this Territorial Church system, which was centralized in the German Church—the Church which was the strongest, the most well organized, and the most fully endowed of this kind. This idea of a Universal Church was closely related to a revival of ascetic idealism, coupled with a renewed assertion of the Latin world against the predominance of the German Church. Another aspect of this movement was the revival of the Canon Law over against that of the Territorial Church, and of the canonical

[94] For the new methods now adopted by the missionary leaders, see the whole work of *Hauck*; for the Crusades regarded as a mission, see *Uhlhorn, II, 93 ff.*

conception of Church property, in opposition to that of the independent Church (*Eigenkirche*).

A detailed description of the process by which these elements came together and finally formed a unity, belongs to the sphere of Church History. At this point our one aim is to lay emphasis upon those aspects of the situation which are particularly relevant to the subject of this book. The movement in favour of a Universal Church began with Latin asceticism. When the Carolingian dominions were broken up into large estates the Church was to a great extent disorganized and despoiled; this prepared the way for an ecclesiastical revolt against the civil authority; in this the tradition of the Primitive Church was more living, and the unifying and organizing impulse stronger than in the German Church. In the nature of things the revival was ascetic in character; this aspect was doubtless intensified by the current expectation of the expiration of the Thousand Years' Reign in the year 1000. The ecclesiastical demands themselves, however, were not on that account directed towards the de-secularization of the Church; on the contrary, they were concerned with such questions as the full restitution of ecclesiastical property to churches and monasteries, the right of the Church to an unhindered administration of Church property, the strict carrying out of the Canon Law in the election of bishops and abbots, as well as in the handling of Church property. All this pointed towards the independence of the Church of the civil authorities, and at the same time to the continuation of her territorial and princely rights; towards a stricter, at first more personal, and then more organized, holding together of the reformed monasteries among themselves; towards uniformity in the Church and opposition to the exploitation of the episcopate for the purposes of Imperial politics.

The urge towards unity in the Canon Law, which was the first element in the whole movement, then led gradually to union with the Papacy, which alone could provide a basis of unity and support against the political bishops; that had become all the more necessary since by this time the Pseudo-Isidorian Decretals formed part of the Canon Law. During the confusion of the post-Carolingian period the clergy had already sought to secure their position against the Metropolitans of the Territorial Church, and against the ruling princes, by proclaiming the universal episcopate of the Pope, based upon the False Decretals. It is only now that this idea reappears which was to form the coping-stone of the sociological structure of the Church; it arose at first for the same reasons as had produced it in the ninth century, and the Cluniac party sought to introduce its own members into the Pontificate. Finally the German Emperors themselves helped to precipitate events; they thought that they were only in full control of their Church if they had the Pope under their thumb; and, in addition, by their politics in Upper Italy they were always forced into contact with the Pope.[95]

Further, since they themselves shared in the ascetic tendencies towards reform, and expected support from a strongly spiritually-minded Pope for their own ethico-reforming Church policy, they helped to enthrone the new movement for a Universal Church, without expecting the ecclesiastical system of feoffment, upon which the German Empire was based, to be shattered.

RESULTS OF THIS REACTION

With Gregory the Seventh, however, the radical consequences of the new system came to light: namely, the centralization of the Church in the Papacy, the strict enactment of the provisions of the Canon Law with regard to celibacy,[96] and the election and administration of the episcopal office, and the theoretical sub-ordination of the Royal and Imperial authority to the Church in all religious questions, with the further proviso, that it is for the Church to decide what are the problems which concern salvation. We cannot pursue this subject any further; it was a vast struggle, full of warring elements and affected by a number of casual events.[97] In the main it was a purely ideological reaction, vitally connected both with international asceticism and with specifically Christian universal ideas, which, however, were certainly not national.

The essential outcome of the whole movement, therefore, was its doctrinal result. It is in this, the conclusion of the whole matter, that the theory of the sociological consolidation of the Church is finally completed and established. It is upon this consolidated theory that the ultimate Catholic position towards all social problems is based.

The fact that the ecclesiastical claims were only realized in a very limited way, that alongside of the crude hierarchical tendency there appeared in the Italian communes successful demo-

[95] See p. 387.
[96] The celibacy of the clergy was required not only for ascetic reasons but for economic ones as well; it saved Church funds from bearing the financial burden of the support of priests' wives and children. *Hauck, III, 528*.
[97] On the subject of the Gregorian Reform, see the detailed presentation of the subject by *Mirbt: Die Publizistik im Zeitalters Gregor VII, 1894*.

cratic and heretical movements, that the ascetic current in the development of the feudal system flowed back strongly towards the civilization of chivalry, that after the high-water mark of the hierarchical world of thought had been reached (that is, after the period of Innocent) very soon the old hostility between the territorial churches and the universal Church broke out once more between papal and episcopal ideas—all this does not in any way alter the fact that the result of the Gregorian struggle is, and remains for all future time, the logical result of the sociological conception of the sacramental sacerdotal Church and of the redemptive institution.

This becomes evident in the doctrinal developments of the twelfth and thirteenth centuries. Until this period the two fundamental dogmas in which all the dogmatic theology of that day consisted were the dogma of Church, Canon and tradition, and the Christological-Trinitarian dogma. To these were now added three new dogmas, which were specifically mediaeval: (1) the dogma of the universal episcopate of the Pope, (2) the dogma of the supremacy of the spiritual power over the temporal, and (3) the dogma of the impartation of grace through the Seven Sacraments. It is of course true that, actually, in the Middle Ages the third dogma alone was officially formulated; but the two former dogmas, which were only finally settled by the Vatican, may still be described as implicit dogmas; in practice they were as effective as though they had been already formulated. The detailed history of their development belongs to the history of dogma, which also in this respect must lay special stress, above all, upon the conclusions and commentaries of St. Thomas[98]; here, however, it is only their sociological significance which interests us.

PAPAL SUPREMACY

The first demand of the Reform, coupled with internationalism and the spiritual rigorism of asceticism, was directed towards the systematic practice of the Canon Law, towards a strict and absolute independence of the spiritual functions. This could only be attained by emphasis upon the centre of the Church, by the exaltation of the Papacy, which alone could guarantee and carry out a system of equal and balanced rights. Further, this central-ization could only find a satisfactory logical basis if the authority of the Pope over the whole Church, and especially over the bishops, were dogmatically established and recognized as an

[98] See p. 387.

article of faith and of *Jus divinum*. That, again, was only possible through the theory of the "Primacy of the Pope", or of the supreme "priestly, teaching, and pastoral office of the Pope", according to which he alone is the direct ruler of the Church; and the bishops may only exercise their office as derived from the papal office, and upon the foundation of the juridical supervision and appointment of the Pope. In its final logical form this argument develops into the doctrine of the universal episcopate of the Pope, in which the bishops rank merely as his representatives, and by which the Pope alone hands over all these powers to the bishops and their clergy in the rite of consecration.

This is the dogma of Gregory VII. It is at the same time the actual logical completion of the theory, which, however, was limited in various ways. It alone also produced, logically, the dogma of the infallibility of the decisions *ex cathedra* in questions of faith and morals, in which the unity of the organism of the Church was finally summarized. Closely connected with this dogmatic development was the movement to secure the Papacy, both politically and juridically, by the new form of Papal election. The power of electing a Pope was placed in the hands of the cardinals, and the election was thus freed from Imperial and local influences, while the elective body of cardinals then developed into the organ of government for the whole Church. Another element in this development was the fact that the Pope was granted the right to summon General Councils, whose decisions could not be made effective until he had confirmed them by his own authority. Above all, however, one of the most important aspects of this movement was the development of the Canon Law into the universal law of Christendom, laid down and administered by the Pope; its influence was felt wherever direct or indirect religious interests were concerned. In this we see absolutely clearly the completion of the sociological idea of the Church.

At first the unity and basis of the religious social structure was founded upon the mystical Christ; then, properly speaking, the mystical Christ was localized in the Christian sacerdotalism of the bishops; then under the bishops unity had to be restored by arranging that their spiritual powers should emanate from and be permanently controlled by a common source. The religious source of truth and life, from which the sociological principle of cohesion proceeds, is narrowed down more and more, until, in the end, the Pope, as the Vicar of Christ and the successor of the Prince of the Apostles, St. Peter, constitutes the real conservation of the source of truth and life. An organism which is founded upon the miracle of absolute Truth and of sacramental redemptive powers stands in need of the clear, permanent, and sure concentration and definition of the miracle which it produces, over against all that is changeable, uncertain, and merely human. Thus the Pope sums up in himself the whole conception of miracle and becomes the central miracle of Christendom; his miraculous power then radiates forth from him again in a precise and regular way through the different degrees of the hierarchy down to the most obscure village *curé*. The concentration of the hierarchy in the Papacy is the dogma which completes the sociological tendency towards unity, as it was bound to develop and become complete once the process had begun by which the Church and the Christian priesthood were conceived as the Body of Christ.

This full logical conclusion, however, was only drawn by considerable sections of the literature dealing with dogma and with Church order, and it was only the distinctive doctrine of the Curia; it arose, however, at the same time as the Pseudo-Isidorian Decretals (which, indeed, belonged to the Canon Law emphasized by the Reform) and the Gregorian conception of the Church, and policy; since that time it has always possessed the right and the authority of a logical argument. Traces still remained, however, of earlier and different stages in the development of the dogma, and frequently a vacillating theory hindered the acceptation of the final conclusions. The starting-point of the whole, priestly ordination by the ancient local bishop based upon Apostolic Succession, is still connected merely with the simple priest; the bishop himself has been promoted, over the heads of his diocesan clergy, to the court from which the spiritual power emanates to the priest. The bishop, however, has no real power to impart sacramental grace; his authority is based upon the sacerdotal consecration which he received simply as a priest, and on the authority for teaching and jurisdiction imparted to him by his consecration. He exercises this power by permission of, and under the control and dominion of, the Pope. It is only the extreme doctrine of the Curia which teaches that the episcopal office really emanates from the authority of the Pope, whereas the modified theory tries to balance the independence of the episcopal office by emphasizing its dependence upon the absolute monarch. The Pope, on the other hand, receives his miraculous power, which involves everything else, neither through sacramental ordination like the priests, nor through consecration like the bishops, but solely through constitutional election. This fact accounts for the retention of certain inequalities and possibilities of important differences in practice, but the general custom was moving more and more in the direction of the absolute universal episcopate of the Pope, and the ideal had been clearly formulated already in the Gregorian struggles. From the standpoint of the whole it is the true ideal, for it was the logical consequence of the sociological consolidation of the Christian organism.[99]

The Church independent of the State

But the result of this ideal and practice soon went far beyond this first and real claim of the Reform into a wider sphere, into the secular realm, into the temporal sphere. The claim for Papal supremacy in the Church developed into the claim for the freedom of the Church from the State, and for its supremacy over the State, a claim which Gregory VII summed up as "righteousness". The more the uniform supremacy of the Pope and of the Canon Law was checked by the admixture of secular power in the nomination of bishops and abbots, and by the whole politico-social rôle of the episcopate as an organic integral part of the order of the State, all the more the closely knit unity of the Church demanded the elimination of every alien element; obviously this could only be secured by authority over the State. "Righteousness" requires the supremacy of the true ruler, of the spiritual authority, in order that in principle all interference with the true ruler may be excluded. In principle, however, such a possibility is only excluded if the State is theoretically subordinate to the Church, as an organ to be appointed by her for the control of secular affairs, for the organization of secular conditions and values, in relation to the absolute spiritual purpose of life, which is supported by the hierarchy.

The dogma of the universal episcopate required as its complement the dogma of theocracy. The interference of foreign powers could not be excluded with any certainty by returning to a mere parallelism, as many religious souls in the reform movement— especially Peter Damiani—expected, and as again, later on, was demanded by the Franciscans and by Dante. The conception of a merely independent spiritual Church devoted to poverty, whose one aim is to fulfil her spiritual function alongside of the State, which serves her voluntarily and out of Christian love, was neither practical nor possible. A thousand times over experience had proved that in such a situation friction was bound to occur. The full freedom and independence of the Church was only reached when the temporal powers were subordinate to the

[99] See p. 388.

Church, conditioned by her in their very nature, and directed by her in all matters pertaining to salvation. Since, however, ultimately, in some way or another, everything can be brought into contact with salvation, and since it is the Church which determines in what such a relation with "salvation" consists, the whole idea of the freedom of the Church means her authority over the State and over temporal matters. Thus, in the great struggle the harsh Augustinian views of the State were re-emphasized, as well as Augustine's doctrine (developed in his writings against the Donatists), that the State ought to place its services at the disposal of the Church, and that the sin-tainted State is hallowed by this service. In the heat of conflict, however, these opinions were radically intensified. The sinfulness of the State, which was emphasized by Augustine, who also always admitted the presence of a germ of the Law of Nature in this institution, was far more strongly emphasized, and his theocratic programme, which was only used to help to get rid of heretics, was immensely broadened ; it was claimed that the authority of the Church ought to control the whole temporal realm, that princes should be held in fief by the authority of the Church, and that the Church ought to direct and control the whole life of the State and of Society. Even when men did not go so far as this, when the idea was maintained that the State had an independent basis in God and in the Law of Nature, even then it was claimed that the State ought to be subordinate to the Church at least in all matters pertaining to salvation, while leaving it otherwise independent. In this modified form, which—regarded from the point of view of the whole—was quite logical, St. Thomas fixed the doctrine. Since, however, the Church always determines when a question "pertains to salvation" and how it is to be decided, in practice the result is the same. The latter theory, which indeed was related to the theory of the State current in the Early Church, and which maintained the "Natural Law" element in the State, became supreme. It, however, also implies a theocracy, even if in a somewhat modified form. We can see in this also simply the logical result of the sociological idea of a religious community based upon absolute truths and life-values. To the peoples of the ancient world the State coincided with religion, and the natural sociological associations of the family, of the race, of the city, and of the Empire, constituted at the same time religious objects and associations for worship. If the religious life cut itself adrift from these natural forms of association, and if instead it established itself upon an organization for worship, upon the values of thought, feeling, and temper, it had then to produce its own organization, and this organization, in the nature of the case, was obliged to regard itself as the superior authority, which regulated and penetrated the natural forms of association from the standpoint of its own ideas. This was the significance of the Republic of Plato and of the Stoics' Commonwealth of mankind, and, to a much greater extent, it was the meaning of the Christian community.

A religious community of this kind will reject the State and her social associations so long as it does not feel certain of being able to permeate them; but as soon as it is forced to recognize the State, whether from interior or exterior causes, it will desire to penetrate and dominate it, as well as all natural associations, with its supreme ideal of a society or commonwealth founded upon ultimate absolute values. Such a result is inevitable; ideals of this kind will always demand a position of at least spiritual and intellectual supremacy; even to-day we see the same process at work even among those who claim most definitely to be spiritually-minded. But wherever the religious fellowship is incarnated in the priesthood and in the organism of the Papal Church, there this dominion will become the dominion of the sacerdotal Church over the State, of the Pope over kings, and over the social groups which are subject to them. This is the inevitable and logical result.

The theocracy of the central period of the Middle Ages came to this conclusion with the full consciousness of its inner necessity, and upheld it by its terrible ecclesiastical methods of domination, which even to-day call forth the horror of the reader, and which modern Catholic Church order, with its predominant spiritual tendency, likes to ignore, regarding it as uncivilized mediaeval crudeness which has long been overcome.

This, however, must be said: Whatever we may think of the methods by which this theory is put into practice, the idea itself has naturally remained supremely effective down to the present day. All attempts to revert from this theocracy to the position of a parallelism have either been united with a revived eschatology, as among the Spiritual Franciscans, or they have been idealistic speculations, which wholly misunderstand what are the warring factors, like Dante's romantic doctrine of the State; in any case, in both instances they were ineffective.[100]

DEVELOPMENT OF SACRAMENTAL DOCTRINE

The third question is that of the method by which such an ecclesiastical domination can be maintained over the minds of

[100] See p. 389.

men. If these methods are to arise organically out of the nature of the Church, they must be rooted in the sacramentalism of the Church; for at bottom it is upon this fact that the whole priesthood is based. The priest alone, by the appointment of Christ, has in his hands the power of the sacramental impartation of grace, and thus of the redemptive miraculous element of the Church, without which there is no deliverance from original sin or from purgatory.

From this point of view, also, it was essential to develop the methods of spiritual and ethical control. Although the priesthood was designed in the first place to secure the religious idea and tradition which affects and determines the whole structure, yet, even in the Early Church, far more important than this guarantee or than the teaching office, was the sacramental power, which, indeed, had become also in dogma the priestly power, or *potestas ordinis*, in the narrowest and most real sense of the word. Sacramental grace is the life of the organism, and is the most essential element in the miraculous power which circulates through the Church; in it the presence of the redeeming, sanctifying, empowering, and saving mystical Christ is poured into the souls of men. It is only through sacramental grace that the Love of God creates that which produces the whole Christian social structure: the supreme value of each individual soul, and the union of all in the love of Christ. As time went on, the more the securing of orthodoxy in doctrine became a matter for the highest courts, all the more peremptory became the need to surround and include the whole life of the faithful with sacramental grace. The great main dogma, therefore, is the development of the doctrine of the Seven Sacraments, which surround and support human beings from birth until death, with which is linked the idea of the grace imparted by these sacraments and its relation to natural qualities and energies.

The story of the formation of these doctrines in detail belongs to the history of dogma; here also St. Thomas set the standard. Our task here is simply to point out the decisive sociological point of view, namely, the close connection between the third great ecclesiastical power, the right of jurisdiction, and the sacraments. That has remained the vital point until the present day; it was this which enabled the sociological structure of the mediaeval Church, as the supporter of the unity of civilization, to realize this ideal of unity. The great weapon of Gregory was exclusion from the sacraments, or excommunication; that of his successors, interdict, and the proclamation of a Crusade. If, however, in sharp contrast with the period of the Primitive Church, excommunication brings with it at the same time the civic consequences of exclusion from Society and the complete loss of legal rights, this only shows that in the intervening period ecclesiastical and social conditions have become very closely interpenetrated and entangled. In theory the Church holds fast the ancient spiritual attitude, since she contents herself with a spiritual judgment; but she expects from the secular powers the civil punishment of any person who is no longer fit for ordinary society. That is not, as is so often asserted, hypocrisy, but it is the naïve conviction which arose out of the union of the spiritual and the temporal spheres—the opinion, namely, that the sinner and the heretic may, indeed, find a spiritual forgiveness, but that at the same time he may be a danger to civil society and to the community, and that as such he ought to be punished by the civil authority. We shall find the same opinion among the Reformers. Indeed, when these weapons were used in an extreme manner, they aroused misgivings, dim or passionate, against this mingling of the spiritual and temporal realms. When, however, these weapons became blunted, they had already fulfilled their purpose, and in their place a much finer method could be used—not that of exclusion from the sacraments, but that of a sacrament whose effect was bound up with the exercise of jurisdiction over the consciences and the conduct of men. This is the infinitely important Sacrament of Penance, which, by its conditional character, was skilfully united with one aspect of the other sacraments. This sacrament became the great support of the spiritual domination of the world. Out of it there develops the whole Christian ethic of the Church—as self-examination and direction of conscience, as absolution, and as the key to the whole system of satisfactions and merits, as the unification of all ethical problems and inconsistencies by the authority of the Church, which removes the responsibility for the unification of the duties of life from the individual, and takes it on to its own shoulders. Again, through this sacrament the ethic of the Church develops out of a mere theory into a practical power, which punishes, counsels, and purifies consciences great and small, noble and mean, and which, above all, leads towards the realization of the true value of life, the rescuing of the soul out of the sinful world. In all this the close inward connection between the dogma of the sacrament, and the two dogmas of the unity and of the authority of the Church, which have already been mentioned, is quite clear. It has also been quite clearly recognized and expressed in theory.

The historical God-Man, who unites in His own Person both natures, the human and the Divine, has founded the Church as a reflection of Himself, as a Divine-human organism. On account of its Divine character this organism must be absolutely uniform, and must dominate the natural realm, just as in the God-Man the Divine Nature dominates the human nature. Thus He stands out in the worship of the Church as the sacramental Christ, who, each time that the Sacrament is celebrated, operates afresh the union of the Divine and the human, making the sacrificing priest the one who effects this unity; thus also He comes to each individual, through the vehicle of the Sacrament, through the senses and yet in a supersensual way, in order to place the natural under the direction of the Divine, and to impart the Divine in a marvellous manner to the natural and the material. The sacraments are the extension of the Incarnation, a repetition of the spiritual process through which Divine grace enters into human life. This method of controlling human life by Divine grace can never be a merely magical process. In order to be in line with Christian thought in general it ought also to work out along ethical lines; this leads to the growth of the Sacrament of Penance, which is conceived in an entirely juridical and ethical spirit. From the doctrinal point of view this sacrament occupies a secondary position, since it has no *materia sacramenti* of its own; in practice, however, together with the Mass, it becomes the main sacrament.

The unity and autonomy of the Church, the penetration of humanity with sacramental grace, coupled with the control of conscience—all these elements are most intimately and vitally related to each other, and they complete the sociological structure.[100a] In this closely knit organization the new principle of a Universal Church meant a revolution in the previous organization of the State, and the separation of Church and State. But although here and there a few idealists wished to see the Church return to her original (Apostolic) poverty, and take up a really detached position alongside of the State, which would serve the Church freely and willingly while retaining its own entire independence, this separation of the Church from the State did not mean the separation of the State from the Church.

The whole feudal development of Church property is retained; the Church still takes an organic part in the life of the State, and in the administration of justice; no longer, however, in the service of a theocratic royalism, but in the service of an hierarchical theocracy and of an ecclesiastically controlled civilization.

[100a] See p. 390.

DEVELOPMENT OF THE ECCLESIASTICAL
UNITY OF CIVILIZATION

In place of the Carolingian type there arises the Gregorian.[101]

This means the introduction of a civilization directed by the Church, who imbibed her ideas and her standards from the highly developed civilization of France, which was then far ahead of other countries. In itself, indeed, the Gregorian ideal is mainly juridical and diplomatic. It is, however, also an ethical ideal, since it is based upon the assumption that the dominion of the Truth will bring about the moral renewal of the world. The papal Universal Church then became a civilizing, spiritual, and uniform principle, gathering up into itself the French theology of the Bernhardines and of the Victorines of Normandy and of Abelard, together with the later development of the Mendicant Orders and their spiritual and scientific activity. The combination of Italian jurisprudence and French theology, philosophy, and poetry, created the spirit of the ecclesiastical universal civilization. We cannot here take up the question of the source of this magnificent development of the French-Norman spirit and of its predominant position in Western civilization. Above all, the Universal Church preserved the fruits of the Territorial Church system in its influence over the spiritual and the temporal realms, placing them under the guidance of the autonomous Church, of her powerfully developed jurisdiction, and of her philosophical and theological, as well as of her juridical and political thought. Thus that which antiquity did not possess, the unity of an ecclesiastical and Christian civilization, was attained, and the ecclesiastical ideal exerted an influence which penetrated into the very foundations of Society and of its various individual groups. In the last resort, therefore, this unity of civilization was based upon the power of the religious, sacerdotal, sacramental, and ascetic idea in general; it was, however, maintained both in theory and in practice as a civilization of authority and of compulsion, since at all points it was controlled by the Church, and all opposition in the realms of custom, politics, and thought was suppressed by ecclesiastical discipline, and its power of inflicting punishment.

The more the great Church controversy aroused scepticism in certain directions, encouraging individualism and provoking hostility which issued in heretical and fanatical movements, all the more sharply did the Church forge the terrible weapon of her

---

[101] Cf. *Hauck: IV, chapter I*, in which, namely, the continuance and the influence of the Carolingian type under new exponents are emphasized.

law against heretics. By means of this law, which was in line with the development which had now fused the elements into one, she transformed exclusion from the Church into an annihilation of civil, or also even of physical, existence.[102]

After all, however, this unified civilization upon which all the social ideas of Catholicism are based, has not yet been adequately interpreted, nor has the original source of the social conceptions which proceed from it been sufficiently explained by this glimpse into the why and the wherefore of that interpenetration of sacred and secular ideas which was not attained until the Middle Ages. The formation of a political ecclesiastical civilization in the five hundred years of the Germanic Territorial Church period, during which the State, which was only half civilized, became penetrated by the civilization of the Church, while the latter was forced by the need of the State into unforeseen developments; and the preservation of these results by the Catholic unity of a compulsory civilization by a new current of asceticism: possibly this constitutes the heart of the matter, but it is not the only aspect of the problem. There still remains the question of the precise nature of that asceticism to which the theocracy assigned such an exalted position; for it must prove itself to be something very different from the suspicious and indifferent attitude of the Primitive Church towards the world if it was to be capable of supporting a theocratic civilization of this kind.

Then there is a further question: Why and how did it then become possible to carry out in practice the Christian moral standard in the State, in Society, in trade, in economic and family life, in a way which was impossible for the Early Church with her views about the sinful, and therefore tainted, origin of the "world" and all its institutions? That it became possible in theory can only be explained on the assumption that to some extent it must previously have become possible in fact; and the reasons which made this actual realization possible must then give to the Catholic social ideal of civilization a permanent character and a permanent relation with definite actual social and economic conditions. In particular, there is still one final question to consider: In what way did the reconciliation between other-worldly and this worldly aims take place in theory, as an expression of the late mediaeval consciousness, so that the theory itself could be formulated? This reconciliation, which, because it was first of all brought about by facts, had all the more urgent need of a theoretical interpretation, and this led to an important develop-

[102] See p. 391.

ment and unification of the Christian world of thought. This last question leads us then directly to the main point of our inquiry, to the presentation of the social philosophy of Thomism, and of its general theological ethical principles. But we must first answer the two previous questions.

5. THE SIGNIFICANCE OF ASCETICISM IN THE SYSTEM OF MEDIAEVAL LIFE

THE ASCETIC IDEA

The international ecclesiastical civilization was brought into being on a flood-tide of asceticism, and the theocratic universal Church took this asceticism under her own control.

For this reason this ecclesiastical civilization has been regarded by some thinkers as a civilization based upon pure asceticism. This view, however, raises the further question: If this were so, how could this asceticism have been transformed into a system of world dominion and a world civilization? It has been suggested that perhaps this change took place because asceticism, in spite of its own preoccupation with other-worldly aims, did realize that salvation was incarnate in the sacramental Church of this present world, and that therefore it felt obliged to establish the dominion of the Divine Society which was the channel of redemption to humanity. The fact that it went farther, and accepted and fostered secular elements of culture, is explained by saying that this hap-pened partly in the interest of the supremacy of the Church, partly in an inconsistent adjustment to the nature of things, which, it realized, could not be destroyed.[103] It is, however, impossible that a really pure asceticism could have achieved such a complete change, if it had actually been the dominant ideal and an end in itself. Wherever and whenever the ascetic ideal actually did predominate, it always had the effect of breaking up the ecclesi-astical unity of civilization and the theocratic world supremacy. The contradictory opinions of Peter Damiani and of St. Bernard, the opposition of Arnold of Brescia, and the development of the Waldensians and the Franciscans illustrate this fact very clearly.

From that point of view it would also be impossible to under-stand the development of agriculture and of territorial dominion, of art and science, simply from the Religious Orders, and from

[103] See p. 393.

the stimulus which they gave to these things; above all, there is no logical connection between this view and the social doctrines of the Middle Ages, which incorporate the Family, the State, and economics quite positively into the *Corpus Christianum*. Asceticism cannot have been the unique and only recognized ideal of perfection, and therefore the essence and the principle of mediaeval Catholicism, in opposition to which everything else was a compromise which was contrary to its own principles. Even from the point of view of the whole historical nature of Christian asceticism this was impossible.

Asceticism is an extremely complex phenomenon, and its relation to the fundamental thought of Christianity is a very complicated question.

The Gospel gave rise to two tendencies, which led, not in the direction of actual asceticism certainly, but of a decided otherworldliness and an attitude of marked detachment on the part of the Christian community towards the forms of a fully developed secular life. The first of the influences which led in this direction was the central position assigned to love to God and man as the supreme end of life, both in ethics and religion, to which all else is subordinate, and alongside of which the institutions of this world —with the possible exception of the Family—only receive scant attention, now and again, as matters of slight importance. The second influence was the rigorism of the ethic of love and of intention, which renounces law and violence, and which tries, whenever it is at all possible, to achieve everything through personal influence and by an inner victory over evil. It can be easily understood that the combination of these two influences made it difficult for Christianity to become part of the life of the great world. This difficulty was only increased by the attitude of the early Apologists, who laid down a hard and fast line of absolute demarcation between the Church, with its supernatural life, and the world, which was sunk in the corruption of original sin, and was outside the realm of grace. The tension was further heightened when the Church came into touch with the upper classes in Society, and their connection with civilization. This fact, together with the incursion of all the ascetic ideas of the period and the development of methods of religious concentration and revival, led to the rise of asceticism and then of monasticism. But, in spite of the belief in original sin, devils, and demons, the idea of the original goodness of the world and of creation still remained, and from this fundamental position it was possible, quite logically, to accept the doctrine that social institutions are based upon a Divine Law of Nature which is identical with the Law of Moses.

The result of all this, however, was that Christianity broke up into a host of almost entirely incompatible tendencies: there was the way of ecclesiastical organization, of the monastic effort to preserve the austere and exalted supernatural ideal, and finally, there was the way of life in the world which was in accordance with the *Lex naturae*—a way of life which, on the one hand, was obscured by Original Sin, and, on the other, was appointed by God as a remedy for sin.

This variety of tendencies continued to exist side by side until the period with which we are now concerned; the situation was not in the least altered by the mighty currents of asceticism which arose out of the Papal theocracy, and the widespread unity of Christian civilization which it had produced through the Religious Orders. Asceticism always remained simply one element among others; it never became the logical expression of Christian morality,[104] nor the sole exponent of a theological metaphysical system. From the theological point of view the main ideas were a combination of the Old Testament conception of the Creation, coupled with the ideas of the Stoics and Aristotle; even the increasing influence of Neo-Platonism, which took place after the period of Augustine, only introduced the idea of a system of stages; it was not a theory of Dualism.

Under the circumstances it is clear that it was not the secularizing influence of the hierarchy, nor a concession to nature, but a quite logical development, which caused the ascetic, the secular, and the theocratic elements to become bound together in a Cosmos of mutual recognition and mutual help, and that within this Cosmos, asceticism, in its peculiarly Western form, leaves room for the values and forms of the world. At the same time the great significance of asceticism remains, as a method of intensifying all religious movements, and as a source of power in periods of revival; in the nature of the case, in particular instances this often led to exaggerations and to sweeping assertions about the supremacy of asceticism.

On the whole, however, asceticism was still only regarded as the organized method of revival, proceeding from certain definite centres; indeed, no religious system or cult has ever dispensed entirely with ascetic methods of revival and intensification of the religious life. It is only the modern world which seems to have lost sight of this fact; indeed, for the moment it has almost no under-

[104] On this point more information will be given immediately.

standing of this phenomenon at all. This lack of insight is due to
the influence of the idea of Immanence, and to the predominance
of an ethic which is confined solely to this world. In spite of the
influence of asceticism in raising a universal and transcendent
form of religious experience to a great pitch of austerity, energy,
and eccentricity, it still remained—so far as the whole Church
and the official ecclesiastical theory were concerned—simply one
method among others. To sum up: asceticism is a vital method of
reawakening the essential religious spirit; in every fresh assault
upon the Faith it is quickened into fresh life; its history presents
the ever-recurring features of decline and renewal; but it is not
the main controlling factor in religion as a whole.[105]

The ecclesiastical civilization was shaped far more by the
independent logical evolution of the sociological idea of the
Church (always, of course, combined with asceticism), which
made mankind submit, not to asceticism, but to the sacraments and
to the priesthood. Another important element in this ecclesiastical
civilization, closely related to the Christian influence upon the
world, was the inheritance of ancient civilization which lived on
in the *Lex naturae* as part of the cultural wealth of the Church
and as the basis of all secular social doctrines, and which after
the Crusades underwent an extraordinary expansion. The fact
remains that even for the Middle Ages the great fundamental
development was this: That alongside of the building up of
the Church there was a process of *rapprochement* and fusion
with the monotheistic religions and the ethical teaching of the
Ancient World which enabled Christianity to develop still
further, to work out the theoretical content of its intellectual
system, and to develop that side of its life which came into actual
contact with the world. In this respect, however, the Mediaeval
Church, contrasted with the Ancient World, brought in an actual
and theoretical new element. Asceticism, which in the Ancient
World was a dangerous element, and a menace both to the Church
and to the world of thought, was subdued by the Church, and
practically incorporated into the cosmos of ecclesiastical activity,
while in theory it made it possible to secure a harmonious relationship between the piety of mediaeval Christian life in the world,
and the piety of monasticism.

---

[105] The ascetic movements of the Middle Ages are exact parallels of the
Methodist Revival Movements, Holiness or Fellowship Movements, or of the
practices of new cults and devotions like the Devotion to the Sacred Heart,
the devotion to the Virgin of Lourdes, and similar movements, which are being
practised at the present day.

MONASTICISM ABSORBED BY THE CHURCH

In order to form this cosmos the first necessity was to incorporate asceticism and monasticism into the life of the Church, in a subordinate position. However hard monasticism might struggle for a certain measure of independence, and however undefined had been its relationship with the Early Church, in the Mediaeval Church it was organized first of all under the bishops, and then, when the Religious Orders came into existence, under the Papacy; every other kind of asceticism either was, or then became, heretical. Friction between the secular and regular clergy no longer took the form of struggles about questions of principle; they were concerned simply with questions of certain rights within the ecclesiastical sphere of jurisdiction. In this change, however, the very idea of monasticism had been altered. Explicitly it is not an end in itself, but one method used by the Church for the common purpose of the Church. The Church was attracted by monasticism because it discerned in it an incomparable method of renewal and of power. The monachism of the clergy also meant, above all, that the clergy were being provided with the strongest incentive for an effective life and for independence of the world. At the same time it is made quite clear that salvation is not attained by monasticism and asceticism, but solely and only through the Church and the sacraments. On the other hand, however, monasticism also is drawn to the Church. For the work of revival and reform can only be effected in connection with the international power of the Church, and the domination of the monasteries by the civil authorities could only be broken with the help of the Church; and, indeed, both the monk's energy in virtue and the religious content of the ascetic achievement are dependent on the impartation of grace through the sacraments; this, again, is only possible through the Church.[106]

Further, in studying the question of the combination of the monastic life and the monastic ideal with the ordinary "life in the world", we must take into account the Catholic idea of the organism with its vicarious offerings and integrations, the whole mediaeval sociological atmosphere of a graded system of class and rank with its services, which, though they vary in value, are all necessary for the whole.

Later this idea will be examined in detail; here it only needs to be emphasized in so far as it is this which makes it both possible and necessary for an individual or for a group to offer a vicarious

[106] See p. 394.

oblation for the rest. In the organism the services of the individual parts are gathered up into the whole; then from this centre their influence again flows out into the individual members. The idea of vicarious repentance and vicarious achievement is really a living category of religious thought; the vicarious offering of Christ both as a punishment and as a source of merit is only a special instance of the general conception; the spiritual treasury of the Church, into which those surplus offerings are poured, to be shared out again as indulgences, is the living, present, concrete manifestation of this idea.

In this way there arose the conception of the ecclesiastical ranks, which rise from the laity through the Religious Orders to the priesthood, and which also indirectly incorporate the lay organizations into the system of the *Corpus Christianum*.

Thus the duty of those who live "in the world" towards the whole is that of preserving and procreating the race—a task in which ascetics cannot share, while they for their part have the duty of showing forth the ideal in an intensified form, and of rendering service for others through intercession, penitence, and the acquisition of merit. This is the reason for the enormous gifts and endowments to monasteries; men wanted to make certain of their own part in the oblation offered by monasticism. And on the other hand, in the arrangements for a semi-monasticism in the Tertiary orders (through fellowships and guilds), asceticism permits a limited kind of asceticism, adjusted to the needs of those who are living in the world under ordinary conditions. Asceticism also permits all kinds of adjustments and arrangements, which only have meaning on the assumption that, in principle, the life of the world is also necessary to the whole.[107]

The unity of the "Ideal of Perfection" demanded by Protestant and modern individualism is quite foreign to the spirit of this "organic" way of thought. Since the different services of the estates are differentiated and yet come together in the unity of the whole, so also the variety of Christian perfection in manner and in method and the mutual completion of these differences is, in this atmosphere, a quite natural and obvious idea. Only at this stage does there appear the often noticed similarity of the Church, or rather of the ecclesiastically controlled *Corpus Christianum*, with the Platonic State[108]; the different services, rendered by groups and estates according to their own nature, are summed up in the idea of the whole.

[107] Cf. *Uhlhorn: Liebestätigkeit*, II, *98 ff.*, *120 ff.*   [108] See p. 395.

These ideas and the atmosphere in which they grew were alien to the Gospel, and meanwhile its radical individualism had been strongly suppressed by the ecclesiastical idea of unity; but as soon as the Church came into contact with the great world its religious supernaturalism and its rigorism also created certain difficult problems.

Along its own lines, then, the mediaeval period solved the problem raised by the Gospel, in that it ensured the supernatural through asceticism, while at the same time it appointed to people living in the world a life which only approximated to asceticism, and united both classes as complementary elements in the organism of the Church. Thus the Thomist theory also teaches that perfection is in itself the same for all Christians, since for all it depends upon the strength imparted by the sacraments, and consists for all in the love of God and man. Different methods might be used by different classes for attaining perfection, in particular, the ascetics, the *Status Monasticus*, possessed specially effective and excellent methods—but nevertheless under certain circumstances a layman might reach higher degrees of perfection than a monk. To this conception modern Catholic theologians add that lay folk both may be, and have been, canonized; whatever goes beyond this doctrine is a one-sided, exaggerated, self-glorification of monasticism, and there is certainly no lack of this exaggerated emphasis.[109]

Thus asceticism is distinguished from the other factors in the *Corpus Christianum*, and incorporated into a richer whole. But that would have been impossible if asceticism had not already contained within its own nature that potentiality, if it really had consisted solely of penitence, mortification, supernatural contemplation, with a complete denial of secular life. Very often asceticism is simply a denial of secular life and nothing else; when it takes that line it leads into a blind alley, and excludes all possibility of contact and union with the rest of life. Also it cannot be denied that a system of grace-morality, which is produced by means of continual miracles in opposition to the natural powers, seems to need a supernatural sphere of action which is contrary to nature; it is at this point, in fact, that asceticism seems to be the logical outcome of the mediaeval system, and quite frequently it feels that this is so in reality.

The elements which constitute asceticism are, however, not exhausted by mortification, contemplation, and penitence. Alongside of it there are various other elements which transform it

[109] See p. 395.

from an end in itself into a method: it is a method of revival, a method of controlling and subduing sensuality, a hardening process in preparation for the ecclesiastical vocation, a way of practice in virtue and in the cultivation of the religious temper, a way of heroism and of special excellence; especially it is always the accompanying phenomenon of religious excitement, or the special endowment of energy for the vocation of the popular evangelist and the missionary. The ethic of grace is, however, no mere miracle, as will be shown directly in more detail, but the continuation, purification, and elevation of nature, to which it is not directly opposed. At this point in particular, in contrast with all kinds of eccentricities, the Thomist theory has pronounced a very balanced judgment. Under these circumstances it is comprehensible that a complex phenomenon of that kind, in spite of all its real or apparent negative tendencies, still bears within itself possibilities of recognition of the world and of positive work in the world. Neither in theory nor in practice has asceticism been evolved in a logical sense; it has simply grown up out of the most divergent and contradictory ideas, and, while these ideas have been to some extent fused with each other, the system contains within itself very varied possibilities.

In any case, as Harnack has shown very finely, this was the case in Western asceticism. Augustine, a lover of asceticism and a herald of mystical contemplation, still, in exhortations which are constantly quoted, commanded the use of the material in the interest of the spiritual; his Platonism discerned in the life of this world, so far as it was not under the yoke of original sin, the radiance of the heavenly world, and again and again this idea was applied until the Platonism of the Renaissance.

In a more robust and matter-of-fact way Gregory the Great prized the merits of monasticism, but with them he also combined the system of supplementary vicarious offerings which was so extremely useful in practice. The Benedictine Rule prescribed manual labour and scientific activity. Charlemagne, as we have already seen, deliberately restricted monasticism, and made it particularly useful for the purposes of education and culture. The asceticism of the early Middle Ages was based primarily upon eschatological and eudaemonistic ideas, as a way of repentance for one's own sin, or for the sin of others, and the acquisition of merit, and thus at bottom it only unburdens and satisfies the conscience of the secular estate.

From the tenth century onwards, moreover, the great international revival movements and the rise of the new Religious

Orders introduced an extraordinary increase of a spirituality of a more emotional type whose main examples are St. Bernard and the Victorines. Contemplation on the Platonist pattern, and a passionate love of Christ, reawakened by Augustinian influences and filled with an affecting glow and tenderness, enrich the whole religious emotional life and raise its temperature. This, however, is essentially a renewal of the religious idea in general, which feels itself to be at the service of the Church and of the brethren.

Contemplation is incomplete without charity, and the Love of God loves in Him both the ego and all that is highest and greatest in the world. Franciscan mysticism especially represents, on the one hand, the highest degree of asceticism, which, however, it desires to make a method of serving the cause of home missions, of the people, and of the masses, while, on the other hand, it is combined with a peculiar religious glorification of Nature and an individualism of feeling. Thus the individualizing art of the pre-Renaissance period was able to come into touch with it. Finally, Dante's great poem, which reveals the poet as a mystic and as an admirer of monasticism, in spite of all its deep inner tension, unites with that, in the most natural way, the humanistic and ancient elements of admiration for the world, and the prizing of secular political achievements. In so far, however, as the ascetic revival-movements strayed into the path of real dualism and asceticism, they split off from the Church as heresy, whose roots—from the Catharist to the Franciscan heresy—lay in the reaction against the secularization of the Church.

Briefly summarized therefore: In itself asceticism is not merely mortification and dualistic contemplation, but positive work for the whole, a method of service at the disposal of the *Corpus Christ-ianum*, while in its release of religious feeling it forms at the same time an emotional and artistic transfiguration of the world.

This asceticism did not hinder the formation of a unified civilization and did not desire to hinder it, and where it did break through it, it did so only for itself and in a single case, but not for the whole. Indeed, the manifold creations of a semi-monasticism showed that asceticism sought to adjust and accommodate itself, and in so doing it confessed that it was only relatively necessary. Its great movements helped to float the vessel, but they did not provide the crew.[110]

[110] See p. 397.

6. RELATIVE APPROXIMATION OF THE ACTUAL FORMS OF SOCIAL LIFE TO THE ECCLESIASTICAL IDEAL

SOCIAL HISTORY OF THE MIDDLE AGES

An asceticism of the kind which has just been described, combined with the ideal of love to God and man which it had re-awakened, could only exist in harmonious co-operation with the life of the world, if the world, for its part, would, or, indeed, could submit unequivocally to the ideals of the Gospel. This was impossible during the period in which the Early Church arose; the Early Church, therefore, never conceived the idea of a Christian unity of civilization. The life of the world in which it was placed was too independent, too settled, and, above all, too complicated, too much under the dominance of the law and the State, and its economic conditions were too complicated, for such an ideal to have been either conceived or realized. At every point the path was blocked by the spirit of the ancient Polis and of the bureaucratic Hellenistic State. The fact that the Middle Ages created a unity of civilization, at least as an ideal, was due not merely to the development of the Church and of asceticism, but also to the life of the world itself, which in its new form fitted in to the whole more easily than it had done hitherto. For even now the Church did not think in terms of social reform and social politics, or of shaping the connection between the economic-legal substructure and the ethico-spiritual superstructure in harmony with her ideas, which it would have been her task to create, in spite of the opposing forces within the actual situation. In this respect the Church herself, and the Church in particular, was full of the most unpractical idealism.[111] She seemed to think that if the spiritual government of the world were functioning properly, and if faith and love were functioning properly, and if faith and love were strong and healthy, then all difficulties would solve themselves. It is true that the Carolingian State and the Territorial Church system of the early Middle Ages had fused both these elements with each other. But the only person who had a vision of social reform was Charlemagne, and he was only able to take this view because the actual situation forced his State and the Church into a position of co-operation; and, moreover, because the situation itself made that kind of fusion possible. Again, both Church and State became inextricably involved in each other's fortunes simply

---

[111] Cf. *Hauck: KG. D., II, 222*; the beginnings during the time of Charlemagne, however, *II, 277 ff.*

through the force of the circumstances which made this union possible. Therefore, when the Papal theocracy took over the supreme power from Kings and Emperors, it was simply entering into their inheritance. This all happened without further reflection, and without any deeper interference with life. The fact that the Church and the secular realm there co-operated harmoniously does not mean that the Church had consciously embarked upon a policy of social reform; it was simply the actual result of certain given circumstances. The real and the ultimate reason, therefore, for the possibility of an interior union, must have lain in the legal, economic, and social conditions of the Roman-Germanic peoples themselves, who either accepted the Ethos of the Church without question or were ready to do so. However foreign and hostile the militaristic feudal spirit, with its warlike conception of honour, its emphasis on brute force, and all the coarseness and insecurity for life with which it was combined, may seem to the Christian spirit, still, on the other hand, there must have been something in these conditions which made it possible to effect such a change more readily than in either the ancient or the modern world. If we try to distinguish the unique element of the Middle Ages, as contrasted with ancient and modern times, it will then become clear why it was easier to accomplish this change, and therefore to make it possible to establish a relative Christian unity of civilization.

In the decaying Roman Empire, in spite of all its political upheavals, the main hindrance was still the continuance of the ancient idea of the State, the domination of a law which formally controlled all human relationships, the administration of a rationalizing bureaucracy, and, finally, the influence of a money economy which, although its force was exhausted, still made itself felt in its secularizing effects. This was a hindrance which continued even after the ancient pagan religious system had been destroyed. The Middle Ages, on the other hand, had no conception of the State at all in either the ancient or the modern sense of the word. Mediaeval economic life was based on agriculture; there was, therefore, no official class, or, rather, its officials were paid in landed property; officials thus became landowners who clung to the ownership of their land as a matter of private right. The military organization in particular, since it was impossible to use the old military levies for wars in distant lands, and for longer periods, was bound up with this system of feoffment and the sharing of immunities (or special charters of privilege). It was, however, only the great feudal lords, or the military levies which they had created, who were affected by this system. This explains why the military class, and, later on, the knightly class, became quite distinct from the peasant and bourgeois sections of the population. Thus there arose two main classes within the State; the Church and the clergy formed the third class, in so far as the clergy, represented by their leaders, did not enter into the ranks of the feudal lords.

The numerous gifts to, and classifications of ordinary freemen, due to economic, social, and other similar reasons, had a similar effect, so that the ancient popular community of nobles and free peasants was transformed into the artificially restricted and most complicated, almost chaotic, system of feudal tenure, which was controlled by the authority of King and Emperor, and also by that of the Church, as supreme ruler and supreme feudal lord. In this system the Church claimed the princes as her feudal tenants, and absorbed the whole system into her hierarchically graded organization. On the other hand, under these various suzerainties, there were sections of the population which were bound to the Crown lands and the demesnes. These groups, however, were very different from the slaves of the Ancient World; they were simply bound to the soil, and to the various degrees of service which that entailed. The tendency towards personal freedom, however, increasingly developed, and the relationship of absolute submission gradually changed into one of mutual service and obligation, of personal contract and of loyalty. Under these circumstances there was no conception of the State as such, no common and uniform dependence upon a central power, no all-dominating sovereignty; no equal exercise of a public civil law; no abstract basis of association in formal and legal rules. At any rate, in so far as anything of that sort did exist at all, it was related only to the Church, and not in any way to the State. The dominant sentiment in human relationships was not obedience to authority, but contract, reverence, loyalty, faith—all of which were elements of feeling; the spirit of feudalism penetrated even into the serf-relationship; not even the army was based upon abstract law and obedience, but upon the good will and loyalty of the troops.

The groups which thus came into being then became united among themselves to all other groups belonging to the same class of Society; this led to the organization of corporations, which ranged from the groups composed of the knights and nobles, down to those composed of free peasants, serfs, workmen attached to the court, and manual labourers; and later it extended to the city industries. All these corporations possessed a law of their own, apart from the law of the State; to a great extent, indeed, they exercised their own right of jurisdiction in harmony with this law. Further, in these corporations or guilds there was a spirit of solidarity and of personal understanding and helpfulness, which, in spite of its traditional severity, was equally opposed to all legal formalism and appealed chiefly to the element of feeling. Finally, law in the narrower sense, civil and penal law, corresponded to this general spirit. Dispersed among many legal authorities, found by the assessors according to use and equity, to a great extent using a symbolism entirely opposed to the whole idea of abstract law, above all with no knowledge of the spirit of the Roman idea of property, or of abstract trade and money laws, this law was itself the expression of a society which had not yet been legally organized on a basis of formal rights and general equality. The Church alone had a written law and a formal process; this, however, was due to the special Divine character of the Church, and was strongly influenced by her standards.

This whole state of affairs was connected with the return to an economic system based on agriculture, for which the way had already been prepared by the period of late antiquity, and which was ultimately completed by the continental civilization of the Middle Ages. It was a return to simpler conditions of life, in which both personal relationships and the remains of the ancient socialistic collective life were predominant. The spirit of the ancient city-state had been broken. The only vestiges which remained were the Stoic and Platonist elements which were preserved by the sacerdotal class, and those were the very elements which had already caused its destruction.

The agrarian character of this civilization, however, involved small and scattered settlements, the exclusion of the right of free change of domicile, as each region had to have its own lord, and each lord his own land, and ultimately every workman and manual labourer was obliged to have his own piece of soil; those who lost this were *déclassés*. This meant, however, that great importance attached to personal relationships, which developed a sense of solidarity in the ordering of life, and a widespread community feeling, expressed in mutual help and interdependence, in which all the people living in one place became a kind of united body, based on a spirit of mutual protection and mutual service. The elements which were lacking were the mobilization of life and of intelligence, independence of the direct gift of Nature, and confidence in a rationalism which regulates and creates social conditions. In this situation everything seemed to be the gift of nature, the obvious way of life, and thus the result of the Divine ordering, whether as a good gift or as a penalty and judgment. The pilgrim, the traveller, the vagabond depend upon charity and hospitality, which thus seemed to supplement completely the normal arrangements of life by means of special demonstrations of charity. For a long time, even after the towns had come into existence, and had drawn to themselves masses of people from agrarian serfdom, there still prevailed in them, so far as it was possible, patriarchal authority and subordination, comradeship and mutual contract, that is, a spirit of mutual loyalty and respect, which was very different from the spirit of law in both the Ancient and the Modern World.

In the Ancient World the city-state practically destroyed agricultural life and absorbed everything into itself; but the mediaeval industrial town long remained semi-agrarian in character; at a later stage we shall see the special significance of the mediaeval town in the development of the ethico-religious ideal.

Above all, the intellectual and ethical fundamental elements of the social type produced by a money economy were lacking. As yet there was no money economy worth the name. In the North, at least, it was very restricted until well into the urban period, and during the period when Catholic social ideals were being developed it was merely subordinate to a natural economy. That intellectual and moral type was also lacking which usually begins to make its own characteristic mark upon the minds of men, even when the money economy has not reached the stage of unrestricted calculating capitalism, or the spirit of gain for the sake of gain. Where this spirit predominates it makes all values abstract, exchangeable, and measurable; it mobilizes property and, in a way of which no one hitherto had dreamed, advancing beyond the merely natural dependence of life, it groups together the economic values and the possibilities which they contain. The economic system based on money depersonalizes values, makes property abstract and individualistic, creates a rational law of trade and possessions, raises men above natural conditions of life, unites its fortunes with forethought, intelligence, and calculation, replaces the idea of Providence and the spirit of mutual help and solidarity of those who are bound together in loyalty to one another, by products which are at all times ready for use; it produces great differences in possessions and in needs, and leads from the simple standpoint of the consumer to an active production of artificial values and conditions. It is the cause of the development of formal abstract law, of an abstract, impersonal way of thinking, of rationalism and relativism. As a result it leads to a restless and changing social differentiation which is based not upon the unchanging land, but upon accidental accumulations of money which can change anything into anything else. The personal relationships depending on nature and on social groups are dissolved; the individual gains an abstract freedom and independence, and, on the other hand, deteriorates into unknown forms of dependence which seem to be the powers of superior common sense and the sum of attractive possibilities. The individual makes up for the loss of concrete individuality, that is, of an originality which is infinitely differentiated and secured by corporate relations, by abstract individualism; that is, by the assertion of individual powers, from which it builds up rationally unions, group fellowships, institutions, and enterprises, and to which it makes conditions rationally serviceable. These results came about very slowly and gradually after the rise of the money economy which began after the Crusades and was connected with the town industries.

During the period when the ecclesiastical social doctrines were being developed this spirit and type of capitalism did not exist at all. The society of that day inhabited regions which had been recently cleared; the population was sparse, the death-rate high; means of communication were primitive, and life itself was insecure. The social system was intelligently organized on an individualistic basis in direct dependence upon Nature, in associations which were based partly upon brute force, quite rationalistically conceived, and also upon the sentiments of inward reverence and loyalty. Science and literature were limited to the smallest groups. Popular thinking was dominated by phantasy and symbolism. The need for unity in life and thought was extremely slight, and was in large measure satisfied by the idea of the unity of the Church and of Christendom, and also by the Christian view of the world, with its teaching on the Creation and the End of the world, and its central point in the institution of grace, the Church. Both in the spiritual and in the temporal realm the social fabric was held together by habit and custom, by reverence and faith, agreement and loyalty, by many of the customs involved in the holding of property in common, and by a mutual helpfulness, which, owing to the defective means of communication, and in the absence of a money-economy traffic in goods, is the natural basis for the existence of the individual group.[112]

[112] See p. 398.

Mediaeval Society and the Christian Ethic

This whole social structure, with its personal relationships open to everyone, with its graded system of estates and corporations, with its emphasis on the existing conditions of authority and their utilization for mutual service, with its emancipation of the individual within his appointed sphere, with its lack of abstract formal justice, with its exclusive groups and its fine shades of feeling in the sense of solidarity, with its fairly equal range of material need (which means at bottom that a man's wealth is proportionate to the number of people for whom he is responsible, and that power and position or prestige are dependent upon the possession of land and tenants), with its confidence in the spirit of mutual agreement, loyalty, and reverence, with its tendency to humanize even the serf-relationship: this prepared a comparatively favourable soil for the realization of the ethical ideals of Christendom as they had been formulated under the guidance of the Church.

Even when art and science began to develop in closest contact with the Church, for a long time they both remained closely connected with the Church; in fact, there were no independent secular values of civilization at all which might have felt and claimed a Divine right to exist apart from the Church and her ideals. The only sovereignty that existed was that of the Church; there was no sovereignty of the State, nor of economic production, nor of science or art. The "other-worldly" ideal of the Gospel had to contend against worldliness, love of pleasure, coarseness, and violence, but it had no rivals in the realm of the spirit; nor did it come into conflict with any order of secular civilization containing its own law and authority which had an existence apart from the Church. Since civilized life was still so little developed, and was also constantly being broken up by almost uncontrollable impulses of passion and of unrestrained violence, it was quite possible to unite with it the pessimism of the Middle Ages, with its emphasis on sin and the sense of transitory existence, which formed the illusion of the sole supremacy of the religious values of life, and which was strengthened by every means imagination could devise. Man's relation to the world was conceived in terms of "duty". The whole outlook and conditions of life which existed at that time were not unfavourable to the growth of the new ecclesiastical social ideals. The conception of "duty", the inwardness of an ethic which had no place for abstract law, but was primarily concerned with the cultivation of a right spirit in personal relationships, and the ideal Christian anarchism of a spiritual ethic; indeed, the whole Christian emphasis on the moral value of an "inner" disposition and a spirit of love which finds expression in mutual help and service, and in a fight against the worship of mammon: all these elements took root in comparatively favourable soil.

Above all, the conditions of property and possessions were also favourable to this ethical system. As the Church itself was a great communistic institution, full of the spirit of solidarity and care for all, so every smaller group bore the same stamp of mutual love and loyalty and service. The charity of the Church, particularly that of the Religious Orders, was mainly needed for the service of the *déclassés*, the sick, and the abnormal. On the other hand, the presence of such needy folk was considered normal and desirable, since they provided an opportunity for the exercise of charity; far from being hindered and set aside by a rational social policy they formed a normal Christian "class" of their own, which was regarded as necessary for the whole. In any case, in theory and in ideal it is permissible to regard the matter in this way. Thus we can understand how it became possible to regard the secular life, as well as the ascetic life, as coming under the control of Christian standards; although in the ascetic life the conditions were more secure and favourable, yet it was possible for the secular life to be controlled by the Christian ethic. The only difference involved was one of degree, and that did not hinder the unity of civilization.[113]

From another point of view, however, this social structure was closely connected with the warlike spirit of feudalism and with the feudal principle of honour; thus at this point it came into conflict with the Christian doctrine of non-resistance, of Christian humility, and, above all, with the Christian idea of love. Here, too, there existed in reality a deep inward hostility towards the universal religious ethic of humanity. In these circumstances it seemed as though the Christian ideal could only be realized within a limited group; it was then that the cloister appeared to present the only conditions within which the Christian ethic could be practised without compromise. The attacks on the secularization of the Church, the attempts to make the incumbents of collegiate churches submit to the rule of the canons, and the ever-renewed assaults of asceticism, were all directed simply against the absorption of the ecclesiastical dignitaries themselves into the feudal system. This undercurrent of coarseness and violence, however, coupled with the world's conception of

[113] See p. 399.

honour, constituted a foil for the ecclesiastical and ethical system, which impelled it to a vigorous assertion of its existence, and prevented it from degenerating into mere hypocrisy or sentimentality. The Church also undertook to transmute the feudal spirit itself into something ethical, in the ecclesiastical sense of the word, by making the order of knighthood a semi-spiritual dignity, and by consecrating its militarism to ideal ends—the defence of widows, orphans, and the oppressed; by transforming the idea of honour into an obligation towards God and man, and into a virile loyalty to Christ and the Saints; and by directing the cult of women into the service of the Mother of God. In so doing the Church incorporated the military system and the use of force, by diverting it into Christian channels, into the ecclesiastical system of morals. This is the peculiar significance of the Crusades, which were organized by the Church with the aim of diverting into Christian channels the military element, together with all the social difficulty and conflict of the feudal world; from this point of view the Crusades were just as useful for external purposes as was asceticism for the inner life of the Church. The ethic of love could not do without the ethic of force, but, so far as it could, it placed it at the disposal of the service of love and of faith.

Although, in spite of this, a strong secular lay civilization, governed by the ideals of chivalry, came into being, this lay civilization was then either replaced by the bourgeois town civilization, or very greatly restricted. Finally, with the aid of the Mendicant Orders who helped the lower classes, this bourgeois civilization (just as in the case of chivalry, only with far greater effect and influence on history) was also guided into religious channels, which meant that the development of knightly civilization did not lead to a break between it and the ecclesiastical civilization.[114]

ETHICAL SIGNIFICANCE OF THE MEDIAEVAL TOWN

We have now reached the point at which we ought to turn to the consideration of the ethical and spiritual significance of the mediaeval town. The ownership of the land which had grown up out of the loss of ancient popular freedom, out of the military organization, and out of the political needs of the monarchy, had never fully met the requirements of the Christian way of life, in spite of the fact that much of its organization was conceived in the Christian spirit. The reason for this lay mainly in the great

[114] See p. 399.

differences of social position, in the feudal system itself, and in its use of violence. Only when the city, which arose out of the decay of the system of territorial dominion and its residue, gathered into one the varied population which was made up of every conceivable kind of element, was the sphere prepared, within which the great advantages of mediaeval society could be cleansed from the coarseness and violence of feudalism.

The one vital need of city life—essentially an industrial association—is peace, with which is combined freedom, and the sharing of each individual citizen in the life of the city as a whole, with freedom to work without disturbance and a right to acquire property by personal effort and labour. All these characteristics suggest a certain parallelism between the city and the claims of the Christian ethic. The town represented a non-military, peaceful community of labour, needing the military element solely as a means of protection, and devoid as yet of capitalistic and city features. As such it was a picture of the Christian Society. This parallelism is exemplified by St. Thomas, as we shall see later when we study this question in greater detail.

From the standpoint of political and economic history, the period of town civilization, which begins with the twelfth century, is regarded mainly as a preparation and foundation for the modern world. At the same time, this period which is characterized by its great cathedrals and their intensive Church life; its religiously consecrated guilds and corporations; its social and political efforts for the spiritual and material welfare of its citizens; its Christian parochial schools and its charitable institutions; its peace and its public spirit, has a direct significance for the history of ethics and of religious life, and it constitutes the high-water mark of the development of the mediaeval spirit.

At first the main economic features of agrarian and rural society were retained, together with all that was in harmony with the ethic of the Church; while those persistent stumbling-blocks, militaristic feudalism and widely separated social grades based on the distribution of property, were absent.

In contradistinction to the ancient Polis, in which aristocratic landowners lived together, which developed its own political and commercial policy, and educated its citizens on the basis of slave labour, as men of independent means (whether large or small) and State pensioners, the mediaeval inland industrial town was a firmly established fellowship of labour and of peace, in which a modest amount of property of equal value was held by the citizens. The mediaeval town, with its strong sense of solidarity, thus proved to be far better adapted to the spread of the Christian ethic than the ancient Polis.

It was the city also which first produced that intensity and elasticity of intellectual life without which a vigorous development of the Christian world of thought is impossible; this is the reason why, from the very beginning, Christianity was a religion of the city. But the mediaeval industrial town was still very closely connected with the conditions of the simpler agrarian life, and as a town of free labour and fellowship it was so far removed from the spirit of the ancient city-state that the ideal of a secular life controlled by the Christian ethic thus took root more easily in the town. The later development of city life, however, did sever this relationship with Christian thought, especially in the Italian cities.[114a]

To sum up: It was thus at first actually due to pure coincidence that the social, economic, and political conditions of mediaeval life made a comparatively thorough and direct Christianization of civilization possible.

Naturally, however, this practical coincidence did not exclude thoughtful examination of the facts. In theory the various elements were reconciled, and ideal rules for the regulation of ideal conditions were deduced from them. Only thus was the foundation laid, and the ecclesiastical unity of civilization achieved. This world of ideas became the permanent foundation of Catholic social doctrine.

This subject, therefore, needs special treatment. It leads us to the consideration of Thomism, whose doctrines have already been considered essentially in connection with particular questions of mediaeval dogma and asceticism. We have now to deal with the theoretical design of the unity of civilization as it is developed in the teaching of the great Saint, and as a result of which he has become the standard theologian of Catholicism.

[114a] *Max Weber* has drawn my attention to this aspect of the significance of the town. See also *Lamprecht: DG, III; Bücher: Entstehung der Volkswirtschaft; Schmoller: Grundriss, 254–276;* and in particular the great article by *Max Weber* entitled *Agrargeschichte (Altertum) HWB der Staatswissenschaften*[3], in which the difference between the town in classical antiquity and in the Middle Ages is treated in a most illuminating way.—*Arnold: Recht und Wirtschaft in geschichtlicher Ansicht, 1863,* says on *p. 83:* "At the outset the towns were nothing more than artificial hot-houses of the Church." But even here there were serious class conflicts; cf. *Kautsky: Sozialismus, 40–103.*

7. THE ILLUMINATION OF THE THEORY OF THE ECCLESIAS-
TICAL UNITY OF CIVILIZATION BY THE THOMIST ETHIC

CHARACTER OF THE THOMIST ETHIC

The ecclesiastical unity of civilization was developed, both
in theory and in practice, under the influence of theological
ethics.

It coincided with the strongly developed, essentially Romance
theology and ecclesiastical philosophy of the High Middle Ages,
and, since this kind of theology chiefly set itself the task of reconciliation, unification, and systematization, so, above all, on its side,
ethics strove to reconcile natural and supernatural morality, the
Natural and the Divine Law, the natural powers of free-will and
the supernatural powers of grace.

Since (as was the case in classical Antiquity) politics, economics,
and social doctrine thus remain under the dominion of ethics,
this ethic proves that neither in theory nor in practice has it any
conception of the possibility of the independent development of
all these sciences and tracts of human life from within, out of
their own sense of inner necessity and fundamental psychological
aptitude. This ought scarcely to be regarded as an imperfection
in theory—it is due rather to the extraordinary lack of practical
development which these questions had experienced in comparison
with the modern world; this lack of practical experience is
revealed in this fact: when these questions are discussed the
moral judgment which is passed upon them is always based
solely upon a comparison with a purely ideal standard. A
social order which had reached a higher practical stage of
development would not have allowed itself to be so completely
dominated by ethics.

Thus everything depended upon the character of the reconciliation, and it was only natural that this should be effected first of
all with the help of that equation which had already been formulated by the Early Church—the equation, that is, of the Natural
Law of the Stoics with the Mosaic-Christian Law of Revelation,
as well as with the aid of the distinction—also under the influence
of the Stoics—between an absolute and a relative Law of Nature.
This equation worked out in two ways: on the one hand the State
was regarded as something Divine, while on the other it was held
to be the result of sin. The former view was the one which predominated during the early Middle Ages, in connection with the
Germanic Territorial Church system and the Carolingian idea

of the State. The Christianized Germanic monarchy did not consider itself to be the result of sin, although it was still firmly believed that the absolute Law of Nature—of equality and of communism—had characterized the primitive state of man. In the Gregorian conflicts, however, the other aspect of Christian Natural Law was emphasized—the conception of the State as both the result of sin and a remedy for sin. For that very reason, then, the State had to be placed under the direction of the ecclesiastical authority and system of thought, by which it needed to be purified, consecrated, and controlled if it was to lose the stain of its sinful origin. Since, at the same time, the Roman absolutist conception of the authority of the State had disappeared and the Germanic idea prevailed, by which the elected sovereign was laid under a strict obligation to perform his righteous duties, from this idea it then became possible to draw the conclusion that unrighteous kings might be deposed, and that the power to appoint and control kings should be in the hands of the Pope.[115] Once the uniformity of an ecclesiastically controlled *respublica Christiana* had thus been established, the problem then arose, not merely of incorporating the State and Society in the Church externally by legal and diplomatic methods, but also of proving this incorporation intellectually and dialectically, and thus of creating a uniform Christian ethic.

Along with the development of dogma and metaphysics which were drawn into new problems by Arabic-Jewish Aristotelianism, which had to fight against heresy, and which had to place ecclesiastical science at the disposal of the ecclesiastical unity of civilization, this led also to a fresh revival and elaboration of the social philosophy and ethics which were a combination of Early Christian and Stoic elements. Even in the Early Church, behind the influences of Platonism and Stoicism, Christian thinkers had discerned that the purely positive miracle of the Church was due to the presence of universal, interior, inevitable, spiritual laws. This vision led the Early Church to an intensive universal breadth, and also to the extension of her influence over tracts of social life which were remote from the Gospel. At this period in her history these methods of making Christianity universal were once more required and were quickened into new life.

The Church is the universal principle, and strives to appropriate everything that will enable it to represent Christianity as universal truth and as an ethic which is applicable in all circumstances.

The fundamental happening in the Early Church, the fusion

115 See p. 400.

of the positive, historical, Christian elements with the universal intellectual necessities and laws of Platonism and Stoicism, now produced fresh forms of life. The main tendency which this process of truth revealed, that is, that of bringing the whole of life into organic connection with religious thought, now achieved a success, which the Early Church, with its mere toleration of the Law of Nature and its institutions, could not have attained. Primarily, in this the Church was only reaping the harvest of the results of the universal change in the general situation, but, at the same time, in the combination of the ideas of Augustine, Gregory the Great, Dionysius the Areopagite, Aristotle, and the Jewish and Arabic philosophers, it developed ideas which were completely new, and which went far beyond the early equation.

Content of the Thomist Ethic

Here we are concerned with the elucidation of these facts by the content of the Thomist ethic.[116]

The principles of this ethic lie, like those of knowledge, in the metaphysical sphere; this is, of course, obvious in connection with such a purely religious habit of mind; it was recognized as such in exactly the same way by Stoicism and Platonism. The Aristotelian doctrine also, which was now assimilated by mediaeval thought, in spite of its empiricism took its share in those statements of idealistic and religious speculation, and especially added to the metaphysical ethic of reason the reference that in all the laws of reason we have to do with the gradual realization of the dominating aim of reason in particular spheres of Reality. Thus, according to the argument of all competent judges, the principle of ethics lies first of all in the eternal, Divine, world-wide, and natural Law of Reason, which governs the whole cosmos, and which in the different spheres of Reality realizes their special purpose, according to the manner, which, for the time being, is fitted for them, which in each lower sphere prepares the way for the succeeding higher sphere; in the sphere of human life this becomes the reasonable law of freedom, which has to regulate in a rational way the senses, the affections, and the passions towards the end of reason.

The ethical dualism which the Stoics had already developed in their later systems of the opposition between the Natural Law and the emotions is here sharply formulated. At the same time, however, after the manner of Aristotle, it is nevertheless qualified in so far as the upward development of Reason out of the natural

[116] See p. 400.

impulses and affections, or the insight which regulates the content of the soul, relates itself to the rational end by means of reason and of order, and makes it the material for morality.

Looked at from the human side, this impulse towards the goal of reason is represented as virtue; from the Godward side it presents itself as the Law of Reason imparted to nature, which also as freedom is the effect of the Divine Law in man; thus the Aristotelian doctrine of virtue and of the end, and the Stoic doctrine of the Law of Nature and of Reason, are united and fused into one.

With that synthesis, too, there is foreshadowed the Christian idea of grace, which actualizes itself in the form of freedom; it is still only the Divine Law of Reason, that is, God Himself, who works in freedom. In the Primitive State this Natural Law prevailed in complete clarity, and although if it had continued the natural inequality of mankind would have made itself felt, introducing all kinds of conditions of authority and subordination, yet it would not have developed any legal position of authority, but only voluntary service, nor private property, but community of property in the spirit of love. The sexual nature of humanity, too, might have existed without libido solely at the service of the purpose of reason, as the completion of humanity to the number willed by God. The bringing forth of children would have been without pain, and patriarchal male domination would not have controlled the family; labour would have been free from wearing toil and anxiety, and the earth free from suffering and death.[117] When by sin man fell from this Primitive State, he still retained a considerable amount of this practical reason, or the knowledge of Natural Law in its main principles.

This knowledge, however, became more and more dim, so that the application of the Natural Law (the development of inferences from it, and their consolidation into a positive human law which necessarily varies in form because it is obliged to adapt itself to variations in period and in circumstances), became more and more difficult. Thus a new Divine revelation of the Natural Law became all the more desirable the more that men learned to feel their need of it, and were thus prepared to receive it.

On the other hand, after the Fall the Natural Law assumed a new form, as the *poena* and *remedium peccati*; and the organization of legal authority, of private property, of slavery, the connections of the sex-life with the passions of lust, and the strict patriarchal law of the family, are represented, on the one hand, as humiliating

[117] See p. 401.

penalties which remind mankind of the Fall, and, on the other, as the *bonum naturae*, the reasonable end of the welfare of all, in the only possible and beneficial form, as institutions which act as a discipline for sin.[118]

Within all these institutions there is, however, an extraordinarily strong element of Natural Law; it is this element which gives them their obligatory character; it is this element which perpetually regulates them by continually referring them back to their necessary standard of reason. That has been the case all the more since the new revelation of the Natural Law in the Decalogue threw a fresh light upon the Natural Law, illuminating reason afresh about its first principles. Thus, in spite of the doctrine of original sin, there is a very strong impression that all secular, social institutions are, or may become, rational, and, above all, that in both, the Divine and the Christian elements in these institutions can be plainly discerned. Thus through this rationalizing process they are actually made to agree, as far as possible, with the main ideas of a Christian patriarchalism; later on, this point will be expounded in detail.

The acceptance of the idea of the rationality of these institutions, and confidence in the possibility of making them rational, is much more pronounced than in the theories of the Early Church, which, outwardly, sounded very similar. Indeed, in reality those theories were dealing with social institutions which, owing to their immaturity and to their special peculiarities, were much easier to adapt to the ecclesiastical Ethos than were those of late antiquity. This closer approximation of the Natural Law to the Christian ideal was not merely a theoretical process, however, it was direct and practical; theoretically it expressed itself above all in the fact that the equation of Natural Law with the Decalogue was carried out far more logically and systematically. The Decalogue is held to be directly the logically developed compendium of the Natural Law, the doctrine of duty towards God and man which belongs to the Natural Law; the duty to one's neighbour, especially, is developed logically, in the true fashion of a social philosopher, from the family outwards to the universal relationships of Society.

The binding power of the Decalogue consists in its derivation from the logical necessity of Natural Law, whereas the other commandments of the Old Testament which are not founded on Natural Law are purely positive Divine Law. This *rapprochement* between the institutions of Natural Law and Christian morality

[118] See p. 402.

becomes all the more significant when we remember that, through the catechetical tradition, and, above all, in preparation for confession, the Decalogue gradually became the formula of the Christian moral law in general, and that from the theoretical point of view it was regarded as the germ and the seed of the New Testament law of morals, repeated and confirmed by Christ, and made the foundation of His own moral code.[119]

So it became possible to regard natural social institutions as though they had been directly derived from the Christian moral law, and thus it seemed as though the tension of the Early Church between the world and that which transcends the world, between social life and the Church, had been directly overcome. Since the actual conditions are supposed to have arisen out of the Natural Law, the Decalogue, and examples from the Old Testament and from the Ancient World, they dovetail into the Bible idea of revelation in so far as the conditions of the fallen State do not cause a painful but irrevocable loss of the ideal. Thus Society in general and in theory is subordinated to the Christian standard of life, and reason becomes the complement of revelation. In the identification of Natural Law with the Decalogue both are reconciled. Without further argument the social philosophy which is derived from the conjunction of the two is Christian.

In reality, however, this theory does not hold good at every point. This is prevented, primarily, by the fact that the difference between the absolute and the ideal Natural Law of the Primitive State and the relative Natural Law of the fallen State can never be overlooked, which means that the whole of the present situation, essentially, falls short of this ideal. The main hindrance, however, is the fundamental fact that the real Christian moral law does assume a moral aim, which is quite different from the aim of Natural Law, that, in reality, it is not merged with the Decalogue at all, but that, regarding the Decalogue merely as "germ and seed", it can only be called Christian in a very mystical and spiritualized sense, by reference to the real moral law of the New Testament.

THOMIST DOCTRINE OF NATURE AND SUPERNATURE

The decisive element is the peculiarly mediaeval conception of Christianity as of something supernatural, or, rather, as the full development of the consequences involved in the idea of the supernatural. This supernatural element does not consist merely in the miracle of the God-Man, of the Church and of the Sacra-

[119] See p. 403.

ments, in the great miracle of man's redemption from a world corrupted by original sin. No longer, as in the Ancient Church, has it an essentially apologetic significance. The supernatural now develops as an independent, logical, religious, and ethical principle. The creature, even the perfect creature, is merely natural—its laws and aims are only natural. God alone is supernatural. The essence of Christian supernaturalism, therefore, consists in raising the creature above the limitations of its nature to God's own supernature, to participation in the Divine nature.

Natural religion and ethics are the knowledge of God and obedience to the Law of God. But supernatural religion, the supernatural aim and the supernatural law—in short, supernature—means the Vision of God given through grace, as He sees Himself. This is a pure gift of grace transcending all the barriers of Nature. The mediation which is necessary here is thus no longer, as in the Early Church, a mediation between two kinds (respectively absolute and relative) of the one sole Natural Law, but between Natural Law and supernature in general. The earlier problem makes way for the later, and in the last resort all ethics and all social philosophy in particular are now concerned with the mediation between nature, perfect or imperfect, and supernature.[119a]

The Decalogue, in reality, is not yet the Christian ethic; and the Natural Law, which is regarded as identical with the Decalogue, stands precisely as near to and as far from the specifically Christian ethic, the *Nova Lex*, as does the Decalogue. It is an introductory and preparatory stage, and if in it the Natural Law is deduced from and supported by Scripture, it is none the less only indirectly Christianized. "Biblical" now means "revealed", but for all that it is not directly Christian; for the Bible, in the thought of St. Thomas, represents a universal historical process of development with its varying stages.

The Decalogue is retained in the new Law of Christ as the preparatory phase for and introduction to Christian morality, and as an instruction in the exterior application of the new motives springing from this ethic. The formula for the specifically Christian moral law, however, is the Augustinian formula of the Love of God, as the absolute, the highest, the entirely simple moral end—an end which contains the claim of the Love of God

[119a] *Denifle: Die katholische Kirche und das Ziel der Menschheit, 1906,* is very characteristic on this point, especially with reference to the doctrine of Society, essentially based upon St. Thomas; see also *Mausbach: Christentum und Weltmoral, 1905.*

in the stricter sense (through self-sanctification, self-denial, and contemplation), and the demand of the love of our neighbour (through the active relating of all to God, the common binding together of all in God, and the most intimate mutual self-sacrifice for God). We have thus a love of self in God, which does not love the natural self but the self united to God; and a brotherly love in God, which loves not the natural fellow-man but the brother in God. These formulas recur again and again in scholasticism.

This real Christian ethic only becomes possible through the infused energies of sacramental grace; it has its peculiar expression in the *Ecclesia militans* and *triumphans*, is active in the higher morality of asceticism and charity, and confers its own reward, the *visio beatifica Dei*, with which God's grace crowns in man His own perfected work of redemption and exaltation.

This ethic is a mystical interpretation of the evangelical message, and forms an unmistakably strong contrast to the "this-world" ethic of the Natural Law, of Aristotle, of the Decalogue, and of natural prosperity; but this cannot fail to be the case, given the entire fundamental character of the Christian ethic, and this was very evident in the life of mediaeval Society in the relation between Church and State, between laymen, monks, and priests, and was still operative within the ethical demands made upon even the simplest layman.

Even although, in a certain sense, the love of God belongs to Natural Law, and is developed from the Aristotelian emphasis upon the theoretical virtues, that is still not sufficient for the expression of the full Christian Ethos; it only leads towards it, but, apart from the fact that its light has been dimmed by Original Sin, it is still not the same as the real and perfect Christian love of God; it is only the natural love of God practised in one's own strength; it is not yet the supernatural love of God, which can only be infused by the sacraments.

Theoretically, again, this finds its best and most characteristic expression in the doctrine of the Primitive State, which is only now clearly formulated; this constitutes one of the greatest progressive achievements of mediaeval thought in comparison with patristic theology. At this point a fundamental distinction is made between the "connatural" perfection of man within the bounds of his reasonable nature, and a perfection which "exceeded" nature, even in the Primitive State by a pure miracle of grace, even without priest and sacrament, granted directly by God Himself. The absolute Natural Law, and the fullest exercise of practical reason, could only have realized reasonable ends, only a *bonum naturae*, only a natural love of God, only a natural love of man, and thus only a natural reward. To this merely connatural Law of Nature there is now added—in the opinion of many, prepared by it—the supernatural perfection of grace, of a mystical communion with God, a mystical brotherly love and a supernatural heavenly reward. The *similitudo Dei* is added to the mere *imago Dei*, which God did not need to grant to human nature as such, but which is the pure gift of God's grace and of "supernature".[120] This *similitudo*, therefore, forms the main point of interest in the doctrine of the Primitive State; the absolute Natural Law which had controlled this doctrine in the Early Church as well as in Stoicism, now takes a secondary position. The unhappiness caused by the Fall, therefore, is not so much the loss of absolute Natural Law and of the forms of life which correspond to it, as loss of the mystical miracle of grace, after the loss of which the knowledge of the mere Natural Law which still exists is useless for the attainment of supernatural salvation. As a punishment, indeed, it has become dim, and the sense of guilt renders it uncertain; therefore reason is no longer able to dominate the senses, the natural instincts, and the passions of man. Natural Law now becomes relative, but the difference that this makes, however painful, is still not the decisive fact; the decisive element is the loss of that miracle of grace.

The same change emerges just as clearly in the doctrine of Redemption as in the doctrine of the Primitive State. Through redeeming grace the original and inherited taint of sin must be forgiven, and the injury and corruption of the natural energies of men which this sin has caused must be expiated and healed. The main point, however, is this: through the sacraments Redemption further renews that mystical miracle of the grace of "supernature", and in the imparted virtues and *Habitus* (or "the fixed habit created by grace")* it again confers that miraculous morality of supernature which exceeds the limits of Natural Law, of the natural love of God, and of natural happiness. In the doctrine of Redemption we are no longer concerned with the effort to do all that is possible to restore the absolute Natural Law by means of the Church, but with a mystical blessedness and love, which in the future life finds fulfilment in union with God, and the unity of the love of souls in God; it then has nothing more to do with Natural Law, which, whether in absolute or in relative form, still always remains bound to material reality, to the senses, and to that which is natural and finite.

* Translator.   [120] See p. 405.

The opposition between the world and the Kingdom of God, which became, quite logically, the settled form of the early Christian Ethos, was retained, but its outlook had entirely changed since the period of the Early Church; and although, in essence, it may be expressing the ideas of Augustine, yet it presents its view of this opposition between the world and the Church quite differently from Augustine. No longer is this opposition held to consist in the antagonism between an ecclesiastical ethic, which is identical with the absolute Natural Law of the Stoics, and the relative Natural Law of the Roman order of Society, in which the Christian position is partly one of adaptation to the unchangeable order of Society, and partly one of mastering it, so far as possible, within the Church.

The opposition is rather one between two stages of purpose, between mystical supernature and its blessedness in the future state, on the one hand, and Natural Law in general, on the other hand; the difference between the absolute Natural Law of the Primitive State and the relative Natural Law of the state of sin has become comparatively unimportant; both these ideas are summed up in the term "Nature", and are therefore opposed to Supernature.

The end of the intramundane ethic of Natural Law with the rational purpose of the organization, unity, and welfare of humanity in all intellectual and material matters, is set over against the end of the supramundane ethic, of the Christian moral law, within which everything aims at the sacramentally effected union with and in the Divine substance of life.

That is why the Decalogue stands for the substance of the Natural Law, and, as the revelation to a particular people, it must submit to the law of Christianity and be baptized into Christianity in order to gain a Christian significance.

The rather more ethical and practical Stoic-Christian idea of the free personality in God, and of the humanitarian idea of a unity of mankind, free from law and force, united by ties of a common humanity and mutual service, has been replaced by the combination of the sacramental idea of miracle with Neo-Platonic and Christian mysticism.

The opposition which has to be overcome is no longer primarily that of a particular society, at enmity within itself, based on law, force, and selfishness, against the universal Kingdom of Love of the children of God; it is now the opposition between Nature, working out its Law of Reason, and the peculiarly Christian purpose of the sacramental and mystical miracle of Grace, between the natural Christian social system, of life in the world, which arises out of the former, and the fellowship of mystical love and happiness which results from the latter. The task of reconciliation is now a double one: to reconcile not only absolute and relative Natural Law, but, above all, nature and supernature.

The new formulation of the contrast is more comprehensive and more theoretical. Thus it makes a new solution possible, based more fully on a definite theory, which, while it recognizes the value of the life of the world, at the same time distinctly defines the limits of its claim. That, indeed, became inevitable with the idea of a unified civilization, and on its side it also served as a basis for this idea.

In this development, therefore, we perceive the really new element in the mediaeval theory, and it was only natural that this new element should give Christian ethics an impetus in a new direction. We must remember, however, that if this impetus caused a greater recognition of the life of the world, this was not due merely to a logical development in theory, but it was effected by the actual relative Christianization of the life of the world.

Aristotelianism, with the help of which this further development took place, was explicitly rejected by the University of Paris, and then by the Popes, in exactly the same way as Modernism is rejected to-day. That it was finally accepted was due to the fact that its acceptance solved problems of practical life and of theoretical thought, while it remained subordinate to the supreme religious fundamental idea.

The difficulty was surmounted no longer by the mere acceptance of secular institutions as expressions of relative Natural Law —in which case, indeed, the ethic of the Church, which was identified with absolute Natural Law, could not have found any real inward relationship with these institutions—rather, the difficulty was overcome by the conception of a system of degrees. As the main contradiction consisted in the difference between nature and grace, the opposition was removed by the acceptance of a relationship of degrees, which, in the development of reason leads upwards from Nature, or from the Law of Nature, to Grace. The Aristotelian idea of development which permeates the whole of this system—the idea, that is, which regards potentialities as being shaped by the directive power of reason—is applied also to this relationship.

The development of the instinctive reason, or of Natural Law, created the preparatory stage, to which the miraculous grace of mystical morality could be added, even in the Primitive State. In precisely the same way, in the fallen State, also (under the influence of relative Natural Law and the relative insight of reason), the instinctive reason created the dispositions and the preparatory stages, upon which the superstructure of the ethic of grace could be erected, together with the necessary apparatus of penance and absolution for the healing of the corruption of nature by sin.

Absolute and relative Natural Law are both ultimately subordinate to the miracle of grace, for which they serve both as a basis and as a preparatory stage. The difference between the two is relatively insignificant compared with that which exists between nature and grace in general. Absolute and relative Natural Law approximate very closely to each other as an expression of reason which corresponds to varying situations, and in so doing they consecrate the natural social groupings as the expression of the Divine Reason.

Reason itself, however, is also subordinate to Grace, as the preparatory condition and temper which enables man to receive it. At this point the Aristotelian idea of evolution merges into the Neo-Platonic idea of the ascent of the soul from the political virtues to those which are contemplative and theoretical, and from these to the mystical Vision of God; the latter process, however, is only possible through the miracle of the ethic of Grace.

Thus the substructure of reason, composed of natural, social, and ethical elements, becames an integral part of the whole; it is justified as the expression of the same Divine Reason which is revealed in the Decalogue, yet at the same time, as mere reason, it is subordinated to the sacramental, ecclesiastical, miraculous realm with its higher morality.

The morality of reason and the natural-social world is the preparation for grace, with which it is united through the common procession of both from God, through the Divinely ordered continuous ascent from reason and nature to Grace; in this process, however, the corruption of reason and of the natural-social system in the fallen State does not go so far as to obliterate the element of reason altogether; it leaves, indeed, sufficient strength to order, dispose, and prepare the hearts of men for the reception of Grace.

Along these lines, then, the social order is rationalized and Christianized—while at the same time, as a means and a presupposition, it is incorporated into the higher absolute aims of mystical morality. The early equation provided by Stoicism is maintained by treating and handling the social organism as the product of the Divine Reason, which is identified with the Decalogue. The new equation, however, rises higher and is more far-reaching in its scope, since it regards the social structure itself as a lower degree of the ethic of grace. To the early equation provided by Stoicism is now added that which has been evolved with the aid of Neo-Platonism, and the transition from the first to the second is effected with the help of the Aristotelian teaching of an ascending series of ends, of a continual building up upon the degree which has already been attained, which then becomes the "potentiality" for a new "actuality". The ethic and order of reason, which corresponds to the Decalogue and to the Natural Law, is the "potentiality" through which the "act" of grace and the "Habitus"* of the supernatural virtues created by it is alone rightly formed and directed. Catholic civilization is based on the relative Natural Law of the fallen State moulded by the ethic of grace. Thus this ethic, so long as it speaks of the instinctive reason and the social order created by Natural Law, can bear a character which emphasizes as far as possible public spirit, love, and freedom; nevertheless, at the same time it is entirely rational and intra-mundane, and, entirely in the manner of Aristotle and the Arabian philosophers, it makes spiritual and physical happiness the object of morality, and its central point of organization; then, however, this whole ethic of Natural Law is incorporated into an organism which imposes upon it the realization of the absolute religious end, as a means and an assumption—which are only justified if everywhere they are used with reference to the service of the absolute end.

The Early Church utilized the ethical, social, and philosophical universal ideas of the Stoics, and over against them it placed the miraculous community of the Church as the restoration of the completed ethic of reason, although still broken by sin. The Thomist ethic utilizes the ethical, social, and philosophical conceptions of Aristotle and of Neo-Platonism; it confronts the Aristotelian philosophy, however, with a combination of ecclesiastical supernaturalism and Neo-Platonism, in which the Church appears, in principle, as a sphere which transcends reason, a mystical sphere conferred by the Divine interposition of grace.

Inconsistencies within the Thomist Ethic

Although this structure may appear very comprehensive, and although it is a great advance on the doctrines of the Early

---

* The fixed habit created by grace—Translator.

Church, to a great extent the inconsistencies of the Early Church have still been retained. They are, however, maintained at a deeper level. This fact ought always to be kept in mind, in order to combat the tendency to assign a higher Christian value to this civilization than it actually possessed. Directly, its Christian character was influenced only by the dominion of the ethic of grace and of the organism of grace, but the dominated material of the life of the world was nowhere directly Christianized. The real method of Christianizing the life of the world in general was the belief in the Divinity and Scriptural character of the Natural Law, possessing its own logic, and this influence was still to some extent indirect. Until the present day, therefore, the fundamental basis of the Catholic ethic still remains formally, alongside of the ecclesiastical theocracy, the principle of the scripturally acknowledged rational Natural Law, whose content is a conception of the Natural Law which is in harmony with the patriarchalism of the Old Testament and the conservatism of Aristotle; it thus regards the social reality of the Middle Ages, in its main features, as the expression of reason.

The true Christian ethic, on the other hand, moves on the plane of the sacramental ethic of grace, and intervenes on the natural plane only through the all-embracing theocracy of the Church. Therefore the actual rules for life in the world still do not issue directly from the Christian Ethos, but from the Natural Law, from Aristotle, the Decalogue, and the Old Testament. Here, too, there is still no direct idea of Christian social reform or social transformation; all that it amounts to is this: that the Natural Law, and the Old Testament conceptions of law, have been subordinated to Christian ideas, and that they naturally regulate the secular social institutions in an indirectly Christian sense, by exposing them to the influence of the Christian ethic. The opposition has been diminished, but it has not been destroyed. The Christian unity of civilization owes its unity not directly to Christian ideas, but to the ideas of the Natural Law, of Aristotle, and of the Old Testament, dominated and appropriated by Christian thought, in which in theory the Natural Law approximates very closely to Christian thought, and in practice sets its own stamp upon an order of Society which is receptive towards Christian thought. Within this social order, however, the Christian standard of life still occupies a very uncertain and precarious position. For that which distinguishes the natural order from the Christian order, and which makes it merely a preparatory stage, is the fact that—in addition to the natural power of action and

the "natural", "this-world" relation to spiritual and social ends—
the Natural Law of fallen humanity is dominated by that fundamental quality in man which entered in with sin, that *Superbia*
which refuses to accept situations and circumstances, which will
not submit to God or to Law; *Superbia* is the source of all conflict,
and of all the institutions of law and property which attempt to
suppress conflict.

Alongside of the Neo-Platonic distinction between the secular
plane and the plane of mystical religion and ethics, there remains,
therefore, the ancient contrast between the struggle for existence
and its institutions, and the Christian ethic of love and freedom.
The contrast has been retained, but it has been forced into the
background by the more important question of the relation
between Nature and Supernature, and in so far as it is immanent
within that nature in its present state it is at the same time
subordinated to the process of the gradual ascent from the natural
to the supernatural. To this extent it has changed from simul-
taneity into succession.[121]

It cannot be denied, however, that this introduction of the
ideas of a successive process and a progressive ascent—which
means the acceptance of Aristotle and its organic connection
with Neo-Platonism—is a matter of extraordinary importance for
the whole Christian ethic. It makes it possible, on the one hand,
to keep a firm hold on the radical religious ethic as the goal to
aim at, since it is transformed into mysticism, and, on the other
hand, to draw into the Christian ethic all other ethical values,
in so far as they entered into the ken of the Middle Ages, that is,
the whole natural basis of life, as a lower degree and preparatory
stage.

Thus the radical principles of the true Christian ethic to a very
large extent became relative; in the idea of a development leading
upwards from the natural values of reason to the specific values of
ethics and of religion, the radical Christian standpoint itself,
however, was preserved. This is a relativism without which a
Christian unity of civilization would be impossible; and, in so far
as a universal world-dominating Church is not possible without a
unity of civilization, a relativism of this kind belongs to the nature
of the Church itself. As a power which dominates the civilized
world, the Church must make room for the natural basis and for
the ethical values of this world; this she does by allowing a relative value to these things, and only then leading up from these
relative values to those which are absolute. Since, however, the

[121] See p. 406.

absolute ideals are united with the recognition of the relative ideals which lead up to them, they themselves finally become relative too, and are thus robbed of their exclusiveness. They enter into various combinations with secular ideals, and in so doing they themselves become secularized in theory; they are drawn into the stream of becoming, and changed into mere approximate values to the Absolute. The pure realization of the Absolute has to be entrusted to a particular class—that of the ascetics—who actualize it vicariously for the rest, and maintain its power and influence, so that from this ascetic class the primitive Christian energy once more radiates fresh vitality into all merely relative approximations to the Christian standard.

The Absolute is preserved only in the conception of the actual ultimate ideal, and in the presence of the ecclesiastical institution of grace itself, which, as the objective incarnation of supernatural miraculous powers, at all times ensures their presence and their influence, apart from the measure of subjective realization of the supernatural ideal in individual believers. The Church signifies the permanent presence of the Absolute, and therefore dispenses individuals from the need to realize it subjectively; an approximate standard is sufficient for them, which the purification of Purgatory will complete.

Morality thus becomes complicated and relative, a teleological evolutionary morality, which is a hierarchy of ends, all of which harmonize with each other. But, since the Church herself represents the Absolute, she also produces ethical uniformity, since by her own authority she determines the different degrees of good and evil in men's actions, and by her system of casuistry she relieves the individual of the responsibility for unifying this complicated Ethos. Thus, indirectly, this morality which was in itself free and teleological, became legal and authoritative through the interpretation of the Church; it was at this point, therefore, that the whole popular heteronomy of belief in the acquisition of merit was able to work its way into the thought of the Church, but in the real fundamental ideas of St. Thomas this belief has no place at all. From this point of view the casuistry and legalism of the Catholic ethic is the result of its complicated character, in which uniformity can only be maintained by authoritative pronouncements. The Church is, however, empowered to do this as the possessor of absolute energies, aims, and truths. She, and she only, is the incarnation of the Absolute and of unity.[121a]

[121a] See p. 407.

THOMIST IDEA OF DEVELOPMENT

The reconciliation which has now been attained is relative in character. This relativism, however, has been attained without the loss of the absolute aim, by means of the idea of a spiritual and ethical development. Out of the contradictory dual morality of the Early Church there has arisen a unified moral development. It looks as though the compromise which has been attained were closely akin to the modern idea of evolution. But this assumption is unwarranted; the supposed "evolution" is not an actual real development; it is not a whole, working itself out continuously from an inward sense of necessity, which as a whole, with its stages of actualization and its aim, is deeply rooted in the hidden Divine source of life. This evolution is simply an architectonic classified system of ends, in which every time a new phase begins the process is initiated by a special Divine act of creation, and the continuity in connection with the preceding stage is only an external preparation and reconciliation, which the Divine Architect of the world has ordained, in order that one phase may be connected with another without too great a hiatus.

Thus in the ascending system of Ends of Reality in general each new phase is based, properly speaking, upon a natural, miraculous intervention of God; above all, the highest phase of the ecclesiastical-sacramental ethic of grace, which finally links mankind together, is based upon a supernatural, unique miracle, proceeding purely from the gift of grace, a miracle which has nothing to do with the being and conception of man and of the world. In this sense, very finely and thoughtfully, St. Thomas, in opposition to Averroistic monism, has maintained the uniqueness of the particular stages of Reality, the uniqueness and the individual particular existence of the human spirit, and the possibility of a continued development of the spirit beyond the border-line of death. Following out this train of thought, however, he also affirmed the whole mystical supernatural ethic of grace, and made it the foundation of the realization of the absolute goal of life.

To him, the mystical "end" of life does not lie in the being and conception of man as in Neo-Platonism, but he only arrives at the being and conception which develops itself naturally, by means of an arbitrary miracle of grace. The transitions between these inwardly disconnected phases are carefully, but quite externally, reconciled, since the highest point of the preceding phase is always advanced as close as possible to the beginning of the next phase, and the leap from the one to the other is made as small as possible.[121b] It is particularly difficult to do this in connection with the stage of natural disposition and preparation for the phase of miracle or grace; here the emphasis shifts continually from one extreme to the other, from the idea of kinship to the idea of contrast. It is at this point that there arise all the intricate discussions about freedom and the power of grace, sin and the ethic of grace, into which it is not necessary to enter here in any further detail.

Since the distance between each stage has been decreased, the intellectual need for unity and for continuity of thought is satisfied; above all, however, that particular need is satisfied with which we are concerned in this inquiry, the need to incorporate and approximate the life of Society within the world to the ultimate values and principles of the living sociological organism of the religious life. Since the sociological organism of the religious life itself becomes the Papal Theocracy, which, directly or indirectly, becomes the all-inclusive determining sociological fundamental form of human existence, covering the whole of life, the life of the world is woven into this whole along two lines; first of all, it is reduced to an emphasis on the Stoic-Christian idea of a freedom of outlook and a human community of love, which blends, very ingeniously, both Conservatism and Radicalism into the whole conception of Natural Law; then, finally (and chiefly) this Natural Law, as it develops, points beyond itself to an absolute supernatural aim of life, which is introduced with the mystical-sacramental miraculous grace of the Church, in which alone are brought to fruition both the natural love of God and the natural love of humanity.[122]

These are the fundamental ideas upon which the ethic of Thomism is based; from this point of view it becomes possible, even dialectically, to justify the indispensable estimate of a right valuation of secular society, viewed in relation to a unity of civilization. The aspect of the question which belongs to the history of Doctrine—that is, the question of how, in detail, this doctrine was formed, by influences from French ecclesiastical philosophy, from Jewish and Arabian philosophy, from Aristotle and from the Fathers—need not be discussed here. The decisive point to note, however, is this: that St. Thomas, in welding together all these influences into a coherent system, was one of the greatest thinkers in Catholicism, but also that, with his strictly papal ideas, he succeeded in connecting very closely this ethic and this idea of culture with the Universal united Church and the Supremacy of the Pope. It is obvious that the connection is thoroughly logical. The ingenious system of an ethic which is based entirely upon a plane of miraculous energies and revelation can only be held together by a central miracle of authority and Divine objectivity. It is also clear that an authority of this kind must be constituted in strict legal form, with the ability to formulate the Divine authority quite clearly, so that it has the right as well as the necessity to subdue the world by force to this possession of truth, and to this knowledge of the aim of life, in so far, that is, as it does not submit voluntarily to this central authority. Voluntary submission is, however, to be expected, as a rule, in view of the progressive and ascending character of the Natural Law.

Like the whole of scholasticism this way of thinking is essentially architectonic; the unity is ascribed to the wisdom of the Divine Architect of the world, who thus orders it according to His Will; all that is left to human thought is reverence for the great creative and miraculous intervention of God, and the thoughtful recognition of the reconciliations which God has introduced. Its rational tendency lies in the idea of continuity; its irrational tendency lies in the idea of continual interventions of God, each one leading to a further stage of development, in the institution of grace and of the Church and, finally, in that of predestination. Both rational and irrational tendencies are reconciled solely by means of an architectonic and rhythmical picture of the graded system on which the world is built. Thus the ascent of humanity and the ascent of the individual soul towards the Absolute End are constructed on architectonic lines.

The idea of Society, which is the result of the realization of the highest end, is also architectonic in its conception, since in it, not only does the individual pass through the particular phases, but Society also ascends from one plane to another through its graded social organization: from serfs to freemen and nobles and burghers, and thence to monks and priests, right up to the supreme positions in Church and State. This last point is very closely connected with the exclusively architectonic way of thinking, and must still be specially emphasized.

The graded social system and the scholastic habit of thought correspond to and condition each other. In both cases the individual parts are not independently related to the altruistic values and principles; they are related to them only through the medium of a whole, in which externally they are bound together in an architectonic system, and in which they share only in a very external modified quantitative manner. The purely architectonic unity of Society and culture is still further expressed in the fact that the stages of development of the individual, as of humanity, not only in length cohere merely externally, but that also in breadth the individual groups possess only an acquiescent, indifferent, purely external, modified relation with the meaning of the whole; that the whole alone realizes the idea of the Divine life-organism; that, however, particular classes and individuals have a very unequal share in the real ideal and the ultimate end, as indeed even the bliss of Heaven has its various phases and degrees. Transitions effected by means of miraculous intervention and purely quantitative relations with the ideal are made to square at all points with the idea of the harmony of the world, just as the social variety harmonizes with the unity of Society. There is no uniform moral ideal, which would imply the same formal goal for the training of each individual. There is, rather, a distribution of parts, classes, and services in an architectonic whole, which mutually complete and support each other, whose inner unity lies in the ecclesiastical authority, which relates the whole to the Divine Will, executes this Will, distributes the various parts, and assumes responsibility for the whole.

"The ordered variety of the ecclesiastical hierarchy is meant to repeat upon a higher plane, in the realm of grace, the harmonious variety of the natural order and of the order of the State. The variety of offices within the social organism, which in this respect is similar to the particular human organism, is a conditional necessity, and opens the way to the greatest possible number to take an active share in the public life of the Church. The gradation of the offices and duties belongs to the proper administration of the whole, and serves to adorn and beautify the Church."[123]

In other directions also the system contains obvious difficulties and obscurities, due to an artificial method of disconnecting and linking up ideas; the distinction between the natural and supernatural Love of God, the transformation of Neo-Platonic mysticism, which by an inward logic proceeds from the Spirit, into a radical miracle of the Church, is the one; while the uncertain view of Natural Law—now in an Aristotelian light, as a triumphant development of reason, and now in an ecclesiastical light, as an institution entirely corrupted by Original Sin—is the other. To that we must add the uncertainties of the "Doctrine of Perfection", which in itself ought to prescribe to every individual

[123] See p. 407.

the goal of the mystical ethic of grace, but which, owing to the fact that the average man finds it actually impossible to achieve this, only maintains an approximate standard, and ascribes the full ethic of grace to a special class, namely, monasticism, which can practise it vicariously, with the help of specially favourable means—or at least it suggests that this ideal can be more easily attained in the monastic state.

Taken as a whole, however, this system is undoubtedly a splendid and brilliant attempt to unite the different motives which go to make up human society: the social aims of this earthly life, and those which are religious, mystical, and universal. In his endeavour to preserve the independence of these various spheres of life, and also in his desire to maintain, in the ascent of the life-movement, the inner differences of the stages, while at the same time holding fast to an ultimate religious end, St. Thomas probably comes much nearer to the truth of life than the biological naturalistic constructions of modern sociology, with their collectivism, which represses the individual, and with their relativism, which finally tends to Monism.

At any rate, until the present day Thomism is the great fundamental from of Catholic social philosophy. The inconsistencies which it contains belong to life itself, and they are bound to emerge again and again, since alongside of the ordinary secular institutions an idea has arisen, an idea which will certainly never be allowed to die out, a universal, ethical, and religious idea, the idea, namely, of personality united with God, and of human society united with God, and this idea is struggling to create a society which will accord with its point of view, and it must aspire to carry out those ideas into the life of the whole, far beyond the circle of the particular religious community.

The mediaeval theory has certainly thought out the whole problem of the inconsistencies with keen insight, and just as plainly it has approximated to its own ideal.

If the Christian ethical ideal is to be maintained at all as the supreme aim, and is to be brought to universal recognition, it will have to incorporate within itself the natural forms of life, and the ethical ideals of this life, and this will never be possible otherwise than by means of the idea of an ascending development, which ascends from the values of the life of this world to those of the transcendent realm.[123a]

The particular way in which St. Thomas built up this system

[123a] Cf. my treatise, *Grundprobleme der Ethik, Z.f. Theol. und Kirche, 1902;* also the brilliant study of the Ethos of Dante by *Vossler: Dante, I, pp. 558-569.*

of thought was, however, dependent upon the character of the life and particular ideas of that period, in which the Idea of God was irrational and based on Will, and the different institutions and interventions were united with the logical and ethical need for unity only through an anthropomorphic architectonic world-plan, and by a purely architectonic method of connecting one stage with the next. It is not surprising that the criticism of the Scotists, and then, above all, of the Occamists, which followed the development of Thomism, distilled from it a pure indeterminism and a purely arbitrary conception of God, but it is equally clear that later on Catholicism reverted from this criticism to the Thomistic doctrine, with its ideas of continuity and transition.

The so-called Nominalist theology of the later Middle Ages undoubtedly rendered a real service by its penetrating criticism of this system of reconciliation, and by overthrowing this system it is manifest that the secular realm of life was allowed more scope; also a self-propagation of religious thought became possible which was freer and less restricted by intellectual considerations. From this point of view the theology of the Reformers developed out of the destruction of Thomism and the reinstatement of the absolute antithesis. In its place, however, they then had to strike out on a new line for the establishment of the ethics of the social order and of civilization. For Catholicism, on the contrary, this Nominalism only meant the destruction of the idea of compromise necessary to its idea of civilization without creating a new one. Nominalism resulted not merely in the destruction of dogma, but also, above all, in that of social ethics; while the stressing of the opposition between Reason and Revelation created a yawning gulf between Church and State.

SIGNIFICANCE OF THOMISM FOR CATHOLIC SOCIAL PHILOSOPHY

The further development, also, through Humanism, of those elements of antiquity which Scholasticism already contained, as in the case of a Nicholas da Cusa and a Thomas More, went farther and farther beyond the Catholic idea of a nature and civilization dominated and directed by grace, so that it became necessary for the Church to re-emphasize, in opposition to Humanism, all those elements in Thomism which helped to keep the balance true.[123b] This is why the Catholicism of the Counter-

[123b] See p. 408.

Reformation, in its work of reorganization, had to revert to the Thomist system of reconciliation and the Thomist ethic. In so doing, however, it also had to revert as far as possible to the Thomist presuppositions, which, at least in the shape of claims, were already present in the actual situation. This is why Catholicism always desires a renewal, at least in its main features, of the general political and social situation upon which it had erected its structure in the Middle Ages, and this is why it maintains, down to the present day, the philosophical and theological method of its architectonic logic. Modern Catholic social philosophy is still based upon both these premises, although to some extent it has modified and modernized the former. Down to the present day there corresponds to the metaphysic of the natural and supernatural graded structure of the universe a graded picture of Society, rank upon rank, and a quantitative graded morality of the particular classes in their relation to the absolute ideal; there corresponds to the task of an agreement and unification of these various ethical motives the demand for an authority which will control the whole, which will erect dogmatic and ethical propositions which will be clear and absolutely binding, removing from the individual the burden of making this adjustment, and dominating the common life in an authoritative manner.

Wherever Catholicism accepts the social doctrine of modern rationalism and individualism, and adopts the idea that all movement and vital unity is spontaneously generated from within, without any external authoritative law, and therefore without any power of compulsion, it there departs from its own traditional spirit, and the inevitable result must follow, in the shape of destructive reactions upon its metaphysic and its ethic.

That was proved very clearly during the period of the Enlightenment, when Catholic theology had accepted the new metaphysic of personality, as the result of the ethic and the social philosophy of Kant; when, however, the Catholic ideal of Society rebelled against this, the general metaphysical theories also were rejected.

To-day it is the significance of so-called "Americanism" and Modernism once again to prove in a striking way this close mutual connection; it will scarcely succeed by the adoption of the very varied modern ideas on natural philosophy, the philosophy of history, social philosophy, and metaphysics, where Thomism succeeded by the method of a simple and exclusive Aristotelianism.

The basis of modern life also, with its infinitely complicated practical conditions, is less able to adapt itself to a new extension of the Catholic Ethos of this kind than the social situation which existed in the time of St. Thomas was able to do.[123c] So far as one can see, Thomism will invariably conquer until it dies in the act of victory.

8. MEDIAEVAL SOCIAL PHILOSOPHY ACCORDING TO THE PRINCIPLES OF THOMISM

A fundamental idea which includes and integrates the whole of life had been discovered in this theoretical and ethical permeation of the ecclesiastical unity of civilization. The graduated structure of a realm of ends rising from plane to plane—from the sphere of the senses and of animal impulse to the plane of intellectual and social purpose, and thence again to the sphere of religious and supernatural ends; which embraces the sphere of Nature and the sphere of Grace, the social organizations outside the technically religious sphere, and the grace-imparting institution of the Church, the Primitive State, fallen humanity, and the future life; which embraces all this in the conception of the *Corpus Christianum*, or in the extended idea of the Church which takes in the preparations for it in Nature: this constitutes the fundamental idea and the plastic imaginative point of view, closely connected with metaphysics and a philosophy of history in which the differences and inconsistencies of life merge into a unity.

UNIFORMITY OF THE
FUNDAMENTAL SOCIOLOGICAL THEORY

With this uniformity of the idea of civilization, however, there now arose also the uniformity of the fundamental sociological idea, of the fundamental sociological theory, which expresses as a universal and theoretical ideal the common relationship of human beings to one another in the attainment of the absolute final end, and in the practical exercise of the intermediate ends which lead to this ideal.

Only now did men feel the need, and discern the possibility, of formulating the sociological fundamental idea of the ideal of the Christian Church as the centre and the norm of every possible valid kind of sociological structure, and also the need and possibility of constructing these social groups from this centre. What-

[123c] See p. 408.

ever cannot be logically constructed in this way is attributed to the influence of sinful corruption and hostility to the norm. But Providence, which works through the Law of Nature and its relation to the Kingdom of Grace, sees to it that on the whole all sociological formations issue in this direction, and also that all that denies this ideal, all the institutions which are tyrannical, oppressive, and enslaving, can be transformed into means whereby the good is encouraged and sin is restrained.[124]

Against those real disturbances and corruptions, however, which are produced by pure selfishness and unbridled passion, it suffices to use the sermon and the exercise of discipline, and to maintain the purity of the Faith and the power of the Church, whereby these particular disturbances naturally become at least exceptional, incidental events, which can be overcome, or otherwise must be endured, in humility, as the penalty for sin.[125]

The Primitive Church had no uniform social philosophy. From her point of view the social structure of the Church, and the social structure outside the Church, were separated by a wide gulf.

With the aid of the Stoics she learnt, it is true, to derive the secular social institutions from a central idea, the *Lex naturae*, and to this extent she recognized them to be appointed by God. Essentially, however, the Early Church still saw in them only the distorted form of the social order, clouded by sin, which through violence, law, capital punishment, war, private property, and trade contradicted the real idea, and which had accepted these features partly as a penalty and partly as a discipline for sin: at the same time she considered that the original ideal was largely obscured by paganism and human selfishness.

So far as the sociological ideal within the Church was concerned the situation was quite different; the following factors predominated within it: the authority of the priesthood, and the redemptive power of the sacraments, sanctification, self-denial, submission to the Church, and a love which knows no law and no avarice.

Thus both sides of life remained separate, and the theoretical identification of the *Lex naturae* with the Law of Moses only referred to the unity of the absolute Natural Law of the Primitive State with the Jewish-Christian Law, and served merely as a general method of pacifying men's consciences about the validity of the social formations outside the Church; this theory, however,

[124] See p. 409.
[125] See p. 411.

made it no easier to accept these institutions in their present concrete form, save only through patience, and a rather despairing submission to the course of this sinful world. That is why the two elements never agreed in a practical unity. That is also the reason why it was theoretically impossible to understand and control this structure from the standpoint of the sociological fundamentalism of the Christian Faith. In this respect Augustine's fluctuations are especially characteristic; on the one hand, he formulated the idea of the ascending series of ends, and the use of the earthly for the purpose of the heavenly; but, on the other hand again, in his doctrines of sin and predestination, he radically rejected and condemned the natural life of Society as it actually was, without, however, on that account in any way requiring a new and suitable intellectual theory of Society. Thus a uniform Christian social philosophy was impossible, a social philosophy which was divided between the Church and the *Lex naturae* did not agree with the claim of the Christian idea, to comprehend all from the standpoint of its absolute values, and to reject that which cannot be so understood; here, therefore, the inconsistency was complete.

The doctrine of the later Middle Ages, and especially that of Thomism, on the contrary, was able to construct a uniform social philosophy because it started from the idea of the actuality and necessity of a Christian unity of civilization. The preceding pages have shown how it was that Thomism was able to assume this unity of civilization as something natural and practical, and also how it was able to build up the theory on which it was based out of the conception of the hierarchy of ends. The vital factor in this doctrine is the new conception of the Law of Nature, in which the difference between the absolute Primitive State and the relative state of fallen human nature becomes less important, and in which the more positive emphasis is laid on aspects of healing and progress towards a higher ideal, than on the negative aspects of destruction and punishment. Whether the Fall had taken place or not, human beings would still have created social institutions, only this process would have been carried out in the spirit of love and voluntary submission and control, without the resistance of the senses to reason, and therefore without pain and without suffering. But, apart from the fact that their basic ideas would have been different, in reality the institutions which they created would still have appeared very similar to those which had actually come into being. The Law of Nature, therefore, is no longer identical with the Christian Law of Grace and the Golden

Age of the Stoics; it is only the natural preparation for, and preparatory form of, the mystical community of grace, which is understood in the sense of the Aristotelian doctrine of evolution, as the working out of the impulse of reason in natural terms.[126]

Naturally, therefore, it has deficiencies and limitations and externalities which must not be allowed to become stumbling-blocks, and, therefore, even in its clouded and relative form the Law of Nature can be related to the ethic of grace and to the Church. In its essence it is related to material welfare, and only to God as the principle of order and harmony which can be naturally discerned. It therefore needs education and discipline, law and regulations, the human application and development of principles.[127] The Kingdom of Nature becomes the portal of the Kingdom of Grace.[128]

At this point, however, there emerges a supreme interconnection of ends, which is common to both, and together with this a sociological fundamental theory which also is common to both, only modified in both spheres. From this fundamental theory a uniform social philosophy can and must proceed, which no longer assumes a different basis for the Church and for the world, but which deduces all the imaginable and possible social formations from one axiomatic basic ideal, and which applies the theory upon which the Church is based also in a graduated manner to the social structure which lies outside the Church. Only thus can one speak of a uniform Christian social doctrine, which also derives, estimates, and shapes the social institutions which lie outside the ecclesiastical sphere, from the sociological ideal which lies at the heart of the Church itself. Only thus does one attain that enthusiastic glow of feeling, based on the conviction that the Church alone holds in her hands the key of all social knowledge and the means of healing all social distress—as the modern Thomists, in face of the social crises and confusion of the present day, always triumphantly proclaim. But, even so, it is clear that this saving social doctrine of Christianity is a very complicated historical product, and that it is very far from being the simple and easy result of fundamental Christian ideas. A universal "Christian social philosophy" only became possible after the Ancient World had contributed largely from its own scientific store of ideas, and after actual historical developments had taken place which were of the utmost significance for Society at large.[129]

[126] See p. 411.   [127] See p. 412.   [128] See p. 412.   [129] See p. 413.

SOCIAL THEORY OF THOMISM:
PATRIARCHAL AND ORGANIC IDEA

In the foregoing pages it has been made clear that this sociological theory was composed of a complicated mass of ideas
borrowed from various directions, and also of actual historical
facts by which it was conditioned. The question now is to discover
the meaning and the content of this Christian fundamental
sociological theory, so far as it has been formulated, with all that
it implies. Sociologically considered, what is the fundamental
ideal of the Christian social doctrines, which, starting from the
Church as its basis, then assists the social institutions outside the
Church to come to their own full term of development, and in so
doing sets the tone of the whole of the social life of mankind in
accordance with certain standards and certain fundamental
sentiments? What is the spirit of Catholic Christian sociological
thought in general? What is it which makes it sure that even at
the present day, and particularly at the present day, it possesses
a universal remedy for all social ills?[130] In the endeavour to
answer this question, in point of fact, we shall trace the emergence
of essentially Christian ideas, but we shall see that this process was
dependent on the appropriation of many ideas from the idealistic
speculations of the Ancient World, and from many other sources.

The Gospel had developed a sociological fundamental theory
which one may describe as radical religious individualism, and the
religious universalism of love. That, however, did not directly
produce either a religious organization of its own, or a standard
for the social institutions outside the directly religious sphere.
Jesus applied this ideal in particular cases; everything else in the
general course of events He committed to His Heavenly Father,
who would realize the ideal in a universal way through the
coming of the Kingdom of God. The Gospel was not at all concerned with the question of "how" this was to happen. It was
only out of the worship of the Risen Lord that a new religious
community arose, which summed up both the individualism and
the universalism of Jesus, in the idea of a community for worship;
and in this community secured to each individual religious
equality, and the most intimate union with the other members
of the Body.

Since, however, this community developed within itself great
differences in dogma, priesthood, and sacrament, it was only
able to gather up the whole in the idea of a united organism,

[130] See p. 414.

within which each member has its honour and its purpose, and in which also each member must accept the function appointed to it for the welfare of the whole. Paul had already coined the famous and enduring formula which effectively expresses this idea—the essential being of this community for worship is an organism which includes various stages or functions, an organism in which all the members, united by a strong sense of solidarity, share in the purpose and meaning of the whole. Within such an organism many elements find expression: the value of the individual, the obligation towards a super-individual whole; various stages and functions and inner organizations are incorporated into the idea of the whole. On the other hand, the community itself is affected by the various differentiations and hindrances as well as advantages which result from the connection with social institutions outside the Church, and from natural differences. ·

From the outset the Christian social idea applied to these differences the conception of the Patriarchalism of love; it enjoined the voluntary acceptance of, and submission to, these differences, which were to be utilized by some as an opportunity for the exercise of charity and devotion towards their less fortunate brethren, and by others as occasions for displaying the virtues of trust, patience, and humility to those above them; by this means the voluntary relationships of submission and authority produced the peculiar ethical values of mutual personal relationships.

Here once again Paul has preceded us with his formulas. Mediaeval social doctrine now emphasizes both these ideas, the idea of the organism and the idea of patriarchalism, as the essential meaning of the fundamental theory.

The mighty organized structure of the Mediaeval Church, with its great main divisions into the three classes of priests, monks, and laymen, in which, further, the clergy were fully organized, in a well-articulated system of various ranks and grades, together with the contemporary classified structure of the general life of Society, combine to form the idea of a general organism which is composed of various classes and groups. The *Corpus mysticum* with its services and duties, and also with the honours and needs of the individual members, which show the relation of the part to the whole, becomes the theory of the conception of Society in itself, and each social group is characterized as a *corpus morale et politicum*, or as a *corpus mysticum*, in which individuals are always described as members of an organic whole.[131] At the same time, however, a voluntary mutual relationship of this kind between

[131] See p. 415.

all these parts and members, which, in particular instances, owe their position purely to compulsion, and theoretically contain a large element of non-liberty, which, moreover, are maintained in their position by the idea of a kind of caste-tradition—is only possible by laying great stress on patriarchal ideas. This patriarch-alism, however, is not given any special prominence in most of the presentations of the Catholic social ideal. It seems to be implied in the organic idea itself, which indeed for its part em-phasizes the variety of the groups and services, and in so doing requires a mutual adjustment of all the inequalities which the organism contains. Out of the organic idea, however, there still follows only the division of labour and service in general, and something which, it is true, is rational, necessary, and harmonious. But in addition to those inequalities which the conception of an organism requires there are some which far transcend the purpose of the harmonious unification of the members into one body—inequalities which are created purely by the supreme power of force, by the arbitrary power of positive law, by the privileges or accidents of Nature; there are differences of disposition and of destiny which can only be held to proceed from the inscrutable Will of God, and which cannot be explained in rational terms. All this is gathered up into the patriarchal conception, and is overcome by it alone, both in the spiritual and the ethical sphere.

Further, the continual exhortations to the lower classes to evince humility and gratitude, and to the ruling classes to exercise paternal care and love, go far beyond the demands which the merely organic idea needed to raise in the interests of mutual harmony. The demands, therefore, are also based always on passages from the Bible, especially from Paul and the proverbial Wisdom of the Old Testament. This idea is classically represented by the type of the Family, and from this it is transferred to the whole, as the idea of the organism spread from the *Corpus mysticum* of the Church to the rest of the social institutions.

From the very beginning, in the ethic of the Primitive Church, the original model of all social relationships was that of the domin-ation of the husband within the family over wife and children, and the willing subordination of the members of the family, as well as of the servants, to the authority of the housefather; the virtues of obedience, free self-conquest, reverence, and self-giving love, on the part of the latter, and the virtues of care for others, self-sacrifice, readiness to bear responsibility, on the part of the former, were exalted as the fundamental virtues of the closest and most intimate human relationships.

The mediaeval ideal of the Family remained the same; it laid very great emphasis likewise upon the authority of the husband. This element comes down from ancient Germanic times, and is a relic of the old military organizations; indeed, it can be traced back farther still, beyond that which had already been attained. It lies behind the conception of the Family in the Primitive Church, and is present in the modifications of the ideal contained in Roman, Hellenistic, and Jewish Society.

In this respect all that Christianity did was to modify from within this idea of male domination by its teaching about love and good will; it only established the principle, on the one hand, by voluntary submission, and, on the other, by stressing the duty of individuals to develop a right attitude in their relations with each other; externally, however, it permitted the conditions of authority and subordination to continue as they were before, although with important and increasing security for the individual personality of women, children, and servants.

The patriarchalism of natural authority gives place to the patriarchalism of love, with its emphasis upon voluntary subordination, and the duty of looking after the welfare of others. In so doing, however, the relationships themselves become softened and humanized. This sociological ideal of the Family as the original ideal of human relationships is applied to all the conditions of rule and subordination in general. Repeatedly we are reminded that Christendom is a great family, in which the virtues of the Family ethically hallow and glorify all the infinitely varied mutual relationships of humanity.[132]

The fundamental sociological theory, therefore, is expressed in those two ideas: the idea of the organism and the patriarchal conception of the Family. Further, both these ideas are very closely related to each other. Both are based upon and deduced from the fundamental Christian idea of the love of God and the love of man. The unity and solidarity of the organism arises first of all out of the idea of the community and of the Church, in which all the members are members of Christ or of the Body of Christ, and the various sections of the Church, the clergy, monks, laity—with their various functions—act as the complement of each other in mutual love, and in their common love of God, to form the united body of the Church, or the *Corpus mysticum*. This doctrine of the *Corpus mysticum* is, then, only extended and combined in theory with the Platonic and Aristotelian doctrine of the harmonious unity of the aim of Society, together with

[132] See p. 416.

the varying destiny and service of individual members and groups.

Thus the whole of Christian Society appears as an organism composed of groups and classes both from within and without the Church, inspired and shaped by the realization of the absolute aim of salvation, an analogy to the comprehension of various elements and groups in the sub-human and individual human organism. In so doing it takes its place in the graduated series of the cosmic realms of ends as the realm of organized human reason, as the stage from which the realm of reason is raised into the mystical unity of life. Above it there is, then, only the realm of immaterial spirit, or of the angels, which in its several choirs and inequalities is likewise organized on the lines of an organism.

Patriarchalism is to be interpreted and derived from the Christian idea of love in exactly the same way; the only difference is that here it is not a question of fusing the objective groups within the Church and within Society into an inclusive solidarity of love, but it is a question of the differences of inequality, as they are felt subjectively, in the shape of a sense of privilege or of injustice in the demands which the individual makes on life. Love banishes individualistic personal desires, and a position of privilege becomes an opportunity for service, evil is overcome by good, and those who act thus find their own lives broadened and enriched by the relations into which they enter through the unity of love which includes the whole. At the same time, however, the necessity for this patriarchalism only arises out of the conditions of fallen humanity, and it is peculiar to the Church Militant. In the Church Triumphant (as in the angelic spheres) the organic principle will again be supreme.

Although both these conceptions are closely connected with each other through their common basis in the idea of love, their functions within the whole system are very different; indeed, they are actually opposed.

The conception of the organism assumes the unity of human society in relation to an absolute goal—that is, with the Church and the salvation which it offers. Thus it means a unity in which is involved the recognition of the Church as the soul of the whole organism, in which, of course, the freedom of the Church and its dominant position is implied. This idea also implies the necessity for mutual consideration on the part of all the groups, estates, and authorities amongst themselves. Thus it constitutes an ideal of a complete social harmony, with the further implication that whenever this harmony, in actual fact, has been disturbed, it

ought to be restored. Finally, and above all, it means that each
member within the system possesses an end and a dignity of his
own, and this lays upon each individual the obligation to assist
every other member to enter into his spiritual inheritance where
it is necessary.

The organic idea, however, is also the active, formative critical
principle of Christian sociology, which on occasion can even
become revolutionary. Unjust institutions, which are not obedient
to the Law of God, may and must be altered; godless rulers must
be deposed or warned, and taught to amend their ways. The
"right of resistance" and of rebellion is a right of the Christian
conscience for the sake of love and of organic harmony—that is to
say, if it can be exercised without causing still greater general
disorder. The Church especially is justified in her struggle against
godless and insubordinate State authorities, and is therefore
justified in revolution. In so doing she is only maintaining the
uniformity of the Christian body. Also differences of rank, which
are otherwise so strongly emphasized, are lost sight of in this sense
of solidarity, and in relation to the final religious goal. The language of the doctrine of Society can then sound almost democratic,
and it can emphasize strongly the "Natural Law" Christian claim
of the individual for a share of the whole and of its goods.

In the Canon Law—that is, in the supreme law of the *Corpus
Christianum*, which is above all particular and class rights—all
have equal rights, and all are obliged to submit to the same
judicial procedure; this, of course, assumes their orthodoxy—
that is, their relation to the central end of the organism. It is a
beginning of the idea of subjective public rights.[133]

At this point, therefore, the individualistic naturalistic Law of
Nature links up with the Christian world of thought, and it
penetrates as deeply into it as it possibly can, in view of the
predominance of the organic idea of solidarity. It is only into the
conception of the Church itself that these individualistic Natural
Law elements do not penetrate. Within the idea of the Church
there exists only the absolute rule of the Pope; among his subjects
there is no co-operation at all; the individualism of the organic
system is here limited to the salvation of the soul, which is to be
conferred by the Church.

The Conciliar movement, however, then extended the organic
idea also to the system of Church government, in the sense of a
share in it being given to individuals, first of all to the bishops,
then also to certain classes of laymen. This extension of powers

[133] See p. 418.

was based upon the theory that the Church as a *societas perfecta*, as the epitome of Society, ought to realize the ideal of the organism in this sense. The Church, however, rejected this interpretation and extension of the organic idea.[133a] The Church cultivated an extensive personal individualism, but she did not permit this to penetrate into the sphere of Church government itself; she only used it, when necessary, against secular institutions which were hostile to God, and harsh and oppressive towards the Church.

If, however, in this direction the organic idea (that is, of the share and co-operation of the individual in the common values of life), makes individualism a vital force, summoning it to rationalize its claims in accordance with reality, in the other direction it proclaims an amazingly far-reaching solidarity, by the very fact that the recognition of these values, and the common effort to realize them in practice, does bind individuals closely together. From that point individualism veers towards Socialism. We need only add the further elements of Christian humility and brotherly love, together with the estimate of private property as a development which has a relative usefulness, but which is quite secondary, and to some extent always has to be removed—and the theory of a communism which will meet every kind of need is complete. This kind of communism has its permanent living example in the Religious Orders, and, finally, in the Church itself, but the guilds and the constitution of the courts also contain elements of communism. Such communism, however, must always be combined with the rights and the protection of the individual, and it must always recognize and defend useful private initiative; also it never serves the ends of merely material welfare, but it is always merely the basis of a *perfecta societas*, ensuring the higher ends of life. Thus it always remains a merely relative kind of communism, which only intervenes in case of need. Incidentally, however, from this standpoint the organic idea can still produce— along with the supernatural character and stability of the religious foundation of the whole—both strongly democratic and individualistic demands, and also socialistic and communistic demands, and in so doing it may cut very deeply into existing conditions. Both these tendencies are based equally upon the rational *Lex naturae* and upon the Ethos of revelation; in this respect, indeed,

---

[133a] On the extension of the individualistic and constitutional elements of the organic idea to the government of the Church, and on the theory of the Church as the *societas perfecta*, that is, as the sum-total of the sociological fundamental theory, see *John Neville: Figgis, From Gerson to Grotius. Cambridge, 1907, pp. 35–36.*

these tendencies finally coalesce; and their combination, in spite
of an external similarity, fundamentally distinguishes those conceptions from modern rationalist democratic individualism, or
even from Socialism itself.[133b]

On the other hand, the conservative, stabilizing aspect of the
system, which accepts actual conditions as it finds them, is due
to the patriarchal idea. Society is full of inequalities of every
kind, both in the Church and in the world. The equality which
does exist is exclusively religious, and even here the position of
clergy, monks, and laymen is very different. These inequalities,
however, are most evident in the relations between master and
servant, and in differences in property, official position, and the
various secular callings. In this respect it is the duty of every man
to remain within his own class, and to serve others gladly. The
Christian virtues are not progress and change, but the preservation of healthy organizations and contentment with one's present
position in relation to the whole. Resistance may only be offered
when the Christian conscience is injured and the practice of the
faith is hindered. In this direction the influence of Christian
sociology is conservative and traditionalist; indeed, in many
respects it has a directly quietistic tendency.[133c]

It was along this line, then, that the ideas about natural inequalities—talent and incapacity—and, above all, the theories
about the effect of sin, became important; this latter idea was
held to explain why man has to submit to despotic rule—it is a
punishment and a means of discipline; despotisms are regarded
as effected by God, as *causa remota*, just as much as systems of
government which have been reasonably established by means
of treaties and a plebiscite. From this point of view, then, the
ruling powers appear to have been appointed by the permission
and Providence of God. Politically this means that the ideas of
the Divine Right of Kings, and of the patriarchal-Christian duties
of education and example which belong to the ruling powers,
become important; these are the ideals which are developed in
the treatise *De regimine principis*.

To a greater extent than in the sphere of politics, however, this
idea gains significance within the social sphere itself. Here it

[133b] See p. 419.
[133c] The illustrations of this will be found below, in the description of the
conception of the calling, and of the question of the idea of equality; see also
the sections dealing with asceticism and with the architectonic nature of
development. The class idea appears everywhere as one of the most essential
elements in mediaeval thought in all its ramifications.

works in the direction of class stability, and encourages the idea of the supreme importance of the idea of social position. In addition to the protection of the individual, and the solidarity of mutual help within the framework of the class organization, it signifies pre-eminently order and stability in social life, contentment with existing circumstances, the cessation of the menacing struggle for existence by recognizing the existing classification of social groups. In close connection with this stability of the class organization there arises economic traditionalism, which secures a livelihood to each group, but which also maintains each group in that higher or lower station in life which is suited to it.[134]

The question, however, whether in any particular case the progressive or the stabilizing principle ought to be applied gives rise each time to a complicated exercise of casuistry. This process of casuistry arrives at a decision by considering the probable result and effect of a certain course of action upon the whole, and, in so doing, as far as possible it appeals to the Aristotelian ethic and doctrine of Society; yet every time ideas are utilized which in reality are logically developed from the fundamental idea of the Christian Church, or which at any rate could be made to conform to them.

This theory represents that peculiar mixture of active and militant, passive and quietistic elements, of legitimist and absolutist, and of democratic and individualistic points of view, of revolution from above and from below, of optimistic rationalism, and of a pessimistic sense of sin, which dominate the sociology of Catholic thought down to the present day. In order to understand the source of this peculiar blend of ideas less attention needs to be paid to the conjunction of various influences such as ideas from antiquity, from Germanic sources, from the Church and from the Bible, and more consideration should be given to the dual tendency of the sociological fundamental theory—to the existence, side by side, of the idea of the organism and the idea of patriarchalism.

This complexity and power of manifold application lies in the Christian idea itself as soon as it is applied to secular and social conditions; it is not merely the result of accidental historical confluences. All that does depend upon these accidental historical confluences is the form of the systematized theory and the scale of the social horizon.

The tensions and inconsistencies which are involved in the blending of these ideas are no serious difficulty for Catholic

[134] See p. 419.

thought, because in all these difficulties the final decision is made by the ecclesiastical authority, which refers each given case to the highest aim of the whole system, that is, to religion. It is this fact which explains the strongly casuistical and varying character of the decisions, upon which is based the possibility *temporum ratione habita* of meeting conditions with very divergent positive standards.

The various underlying tendencies connected with this theory, however, later on in the process of historical development have led away from Catholic doctrine in a very different direction, to emancipation and secularization, to modern developments of individual elements.

The constituent parts which represented the ideas of the organism, of individualism, and of Natural Law were joined with nascent Liberalism, while the patriarchal and positivist ideas were linked up with the purely realistic absolutist doctrine of sovereignty, whether in the form of the Machiavellian tyranny, or as we see it in religious guise in the doctrine of Divine Right.

Catholic sociology, however, in face of these modern one-sided developments, prides itself upon possessing the harmonious principle which balances all these different tendencies, and unites them all in the one fundamental religious idea. At the same time the impossibility of preserving this harmony without the continual intervention of authority, and the sense of the absolute necessity of a Divine central authority for a system which can only be organized from the religious point of view, is to Catholic sociology the proof of the intellectual necessity for the Divine authority of the Papacy which it asserts.

From that point of view it is quite plain, why, in spite of all the disturbances and progressive movements of the later Middle Ages, the Church has always returned to the doctrines of Thomism.[135]

Among these various opinions the Thomist ethic stands out as the real masterpiece of reconciliation. Further, it is evident that in reality this social doctrine contains a wealth of wise psychological observation, and a host of methods for the solution of difficult sociological problems, which the modern social doctrines are only able to meet with great effort.

A "Cosmos of Callings"

Both points of view, however, find a common ground, particularly in the idea which is so vitally important for the whole system, the conception of the "calling", of the *officium* or *minis-*

[135] See on this point the suggestions in *Th. Meyer: pp. 48 ff.*

terium which is allotted to the individual member in relation to the whole. The teaching of St. Paul and of the Early Church about remaining "in the calling to which one has been called" becomes all the more necessary when the differences of class and organization are regarded as *de Lege naturae*; it becomes, with the *Lex naturae*, together with the positions appointed by grace, the doctrine of the *officium* or *ministerium*, or of "vocation" within the whole.

Since men's capacities are unequal and none can influence the whole, and since the division of labour is the result of the inequality of human powers, the organization according to class and profession is not something which has been produced by sin and the perversion of the world, but something which has been willed by God in accordance with the harmony of the world, and in line with His purposes of Grace. It cannot be emphasized too strongly that this ethic has introduced into social philosophy, and into the whole sociological temper, an idea which was unknown in the Early Church. Quite obviously it contains the strong tendency to a positive valuation of "the world", to the incorporation of the existing situation into the cosmos of life-values, which is visible in the whole Thomist and later mediaeval system.

In the Gospel, labour and professional work were regarded from the point of view of the manual labourer and of the lower middle classes, which is familiar from the ethics of the Talmud, and which were common to the Hellenistic East. But under the expectation of the great transformation of the world which brooded over primitive times they did not receive a positive religious value; they belonged to a provisional state of life.

When the Church began to turn her attention to the world she then worked out mainly the ideal of the equality of the Primitive State from the purely religious idea of equality, and in so doing she glorified the new order of life and love which the Church had introduced, regarding existing inequalities as the result of the Fall. We must also take into account the state of Society in the Ancient World, in which, along with all the economic connections and organizations, the ideal of the citizen still always remained that of the private gentleman who is not directly concerned with the narrow business world. In this respect Christianity never entirely overcame the spirit of the ancient *Polis* (city-state). When, therefore, in the later Middle Ages the idea of "the calling" came to be recognized and accepted—carrying with it the implications of the value of the unequal positions of work and service for the whole system, as expressions of love, and as a duty and service to the whole, with the ethical value of a personal relation towards the whole—the reason for this, naturally, does not lie merely in the use of the Pauline idea of the organism, and in the example of the organic form of the ecclesiastical organization, but also in the actual form which mediaeval Society had assumed.

The underlying ideal of mediaeval Society was primarily that of the feudal system—with its corporations, its dependence, and its service; afterwards, however, probably it was mainly the ideal of the industrial town of the Middle Ages, with its cohesion in a system of organization, law, and the service of free labour. Not in vain does St. Thomas always lay stress on the town in his economic writings—on the town in which that system of service, cleansed from violence and brutality, was based upon free labour and personal service for the whole. This actual situation, through its incorporation into the religious and organic theory as "vocation", is idealized and rationalized—and perhaps the whole business is not so topsy-turvy as it might seem. It was not the Christian attitude towards work and an ecclesiastical movement for the emancipation of the serfs which produced this world of civil callings. In the first place it was the result of economic and political conditions, as will appear later. On the contrary, it was rather this achievement of the city in the cause of emancipation, in the division of labour, and in setting free those who had been enslaved, which essentially created the new positive conception of "the calling" as a rational constituent part of the social system.

Here also, however, the irrational patriarchal elements once more press their way into this rational system of "callings", which, under certain circumstances, makes a social programme possible; when this happens the pessimistic conservative and passive elements in the social ideas of the Early Church gain a strong, even though a modified, influence.

The duty and the position, namely, of the individual member still remain limited, in various ways, by pure positive law, by violence, and by accident, and the positions and duties which thus become unworthy and oppressive are also estimated as callings and services within which the Christian ought to remain.

To sum up these "irrational" elements which lead to a passive acceptance of the inequalities appointed by God: in the Family the ruling element is a male domination, which extends to the complete absorption of the wife's property by her husband, and the dominance of the male includes an extensive right of discipline; this state of affairs must be patiently endured as the result of the curse of sin. Again, the masses of the serfs have been bound to serve their masters since the Fall, and actual slavery persists throughout the Middle Ages, for as a result of the Fall labour has become punishment and pain; it is laid as an obligation upon different classes and callings, though in very different ways, for the claims on life are strongly differentiated according to class and position, so that, on the one hand, more freedom is permitted to those in the higher ranks of Society, while, on the other, no man may try to rise beyond the limits of his class, nor forsake the position or the calling which he inherits from his father. These elements engender a spirit of patience, of humility and suffering, which permeates the whole of life. It has no connection with the joy of fulfilling one's calling within the organic organization, but it is rather a passive acceptance of the results of the Fall, and of inequalities appointed by God.

Here also there is that combination of rational and irrational elements, of purposeful development and positive Divine appointment, of aspiring movement towards a goal, and a clouded atmosphere caused by sin and the penalty of sin, which we find in the whole of the mediaeval system. It is obvious that only a casuistic ethic of class and calling could find a way out of all these complications.[136]

COMPLEX CHARACTER OF THIS SOCIAL THEORY

While, however, very divisive tendencies are already connected with the union of these two ideas, each one of them also contains within itself a number of very varying motives, and in these complications there lie further difficulties, which it is the task of the social philosophy of the Church to overcome.

This fact comes out very clearly in connection with Patriarchalism. At first this theory contains nothing more than the doctrine of an essential inequality of mankind, which is based, in the last resort, upon the irrational appointment of God, whose Will ordains very varied and unequal situations; it contains, further, the idea of the inward ethical conquest of these inequalities by the idea of love, which, both in service and in care for others, everywhere gives itself freely and self-sacrificingly for the good of the whole and for the brethren. It is purely an ethical and religious sociological idea, which is directly involved in the ideal

[136] See p. 420.

of religious equality and of actual variety; in itself it can be applied to the existing inequalities both in a passive and a quietistic sense as well as in a reforming and purifying sense; the attitude is determined by the way in which the existing inequalities are regarded; either they are accepted simply as they are, or only those among them are recognized which are really based unchangeably and essentially in human nature and in historical development.

Further, however, Patriarchalism contains the theological idea of the Primitive Church, of a shaping of the inequality into differences of power and authority, of possessions, and of natural qualities, which is not the result of the inequality ordained by God in itself, but which is the result and the penalty of the Fall, since the passions introduced by the Fall—selfishness, lust of power, and sensuality—influence human conditions in opposition to the Christian and natural idea of social harmony.

In this respect Catholic social doctrine, even in its mediaeval form, in which certainly it has largely overcome the passive detachment of the Early Church, and has found a positive and organic relation with the natural social development, still prescribes to a great extent the virtues of patience and humility, the spirit of acceptance of the penalty for sin, and of willing suffering as an expiation for sin.

It is a Christian spirit of deliberate gloom which here makes itself felt; when it is combined with ascetic tendencies and practices it often goes to great lengths of self-depreciation, and loss of all sense of value; then it merges with all the pessimistic moods which lead to the renunciation of the world.

So far as the whole of social philosophy is concerned, Thomism pushes this spirit of self-depreciation far into the background, and lays great emphasis upon the positive attitude towards social organizations and aspirations and developments, but in the doctrine of sin and of the corruption of the world and of humanity this pessimism, with all its assumptions, is retained, incidentally, and in particular instances. From these particular points, when occasion arises, it can again and again penetrate far into the whole. It is doubly inclined to do this in the mediaeval doctrine which incorporates Aristotle, because this brings, even though in a very limited way, a third element into social philosophy—that of ethical Naturalism.

Thus those elements which from the Christian-Stoic standpoint of the Early Church appeared to be purely the punishment for sin and the corruption of the world, from the empirical-realistic and evolutionary-historical standpoint of Aristotelianism, seemed to be differences derived from Nature, based upon differences in talent and in psycho-physical characteristics, which divide mankind into ruling peoples and slave peoples, which divide callings into those which are noble and according to reason, and those which are merely servile, without reason and ignoble. For the aristocracy this leads to the point of view of the "lord and master" and the Divine Right of Kings, for the rest of the population to a position of dependence and service within the duties of one's calling.

However little in itself this theory corresponds to the Christian point of view, it was possible to base it partly upon the doctrine of the organism, which needs also less honourable functions within the organism, partly on the doctrine of sin, which can regard whole nations and classes as delivered over to punishment on account of sin, and partly on the idea of Providence, which permits powers to arise and which appoints rulers; in actual experience it has frequently had this effect. Even in a man of such deep ethical feeling as St. Thomas it is amazing to see how unquestioningly he accepts the Aristotelian point of view that the aristocratic and ruling classes are the logical result of Nature.[137]

The varied ideas which are bound up with the idea of the organism, however, part company almost more clearly still. In reality the Christian conception of the organism is thoroughly and characteristically different from modern "organic" ideas of Society.[138] In spite of incidental analogies with biology and Natural Law, it emphasizes pre-eminently that the social organism is a work of conscious intelligent creation, in which man certainly works out the Aristotelian instinct of reason, but in deliberate obedience to the Will. In this men have a share in the Divine Providence and government of the world which proceeds from reason and will, or, rather, in this process it is God who exalts men to co-operate and to have a conscious part in the carrying out of His Will.[139]

In the conception of the organism, therefore, it is less the formation according to law and evolution which is emphasized than that of the unity of the whole, which is foreordained to the members, and which is described as one which is appointed

---

[137] See p. 421.

[138] Examples of this in *P. Barth: Geschichtsphilosophie als Soziologie* and *Kistiakowski: Gesellschaft und Einzelwesen*. For the mediaeval thinker the biological illustrations meant very much less than they do now, since he knew nothing of the whole modern conception of Natural Law.　　　[139] See p. 421.

by reason and will. That is the essential element which is taken over from the thought of Aristotle.[140]

Then, however, the question arises: in what does this unity, fore-ordained for the individual, consist? It is the familiar difficulty of the organic idea of Society in the idealistic sense of Plato—that Society realizes an idea of harmony and of the supremacy of the highest spiritual values over Nature; it only does this, however, in general; in particular, it makes use of individuals for the realization of this ideal value, leaving it a matter of entire indifference whether each individual himself has an actual share in the value which is represented by the whole.

Aristotle shares this difficulty in spite of his opposition to the Platonic "Ideal Man", and in spite of his category of a specific collective unity of will, since to him the State is the realization of reason working itself out in fellowship, which realizes the ideal of legal harmony and order, but not a sharing of the individual as such in the values of reason; hence his aristocratic superior attitude towards mechanical professions, and peoples given over to slavery.[141]

Such a conception of the unity of the organism, however, although St. Thomas now and again seems to accept it, is completely impossible for the Christian-organic idea, according to which everything depends on the individual sharing in the value of the spiritual personal life which is to be realized through the whole.[142]

Since, however, on the one hand, the organic idea teaches the differentiated incorporation of individuals into the whole, and the unequal relation of the members to the purpose of the whole, while Christian individualism, on the other hand, requires that each individual shall have a share in the collective purpose: both the fore-ordained unity of the organism and the position of the individual towards the central aim of the organism became something quite different.

In the last resort the prescribed unity becomes the authority which inspires and directs the whole, which, according to the principles of distributive righteousness, appoints to each according to his position and in his measure, a share in the central value of the whole.

---

[140] For the emphasis upon unity in face of multiplicity and its connection with Aristotle, as well as with the ecclesiastical doctrine of authority, see *Gierke, III, 515 f.*; hence all the insistence upon unity and monarchy even in particular forms of social organization.

[141] See p. 421.   [142] See p. 422.

Thus each individual organism within the great system is regarded as directed and held together by one authority, since it rightly (that is, with consideration for the individual) realizes the specific end of the particular group, of the family, the urban community, the State, of the guilds and societies. Thus, with its central religious purpose the religious authority is exalted above the whole as the real soul of the whole of human society in all its degrees and groups; this authority in part allows the particular groups to realize their ends themselves, in part it intervenes in case of need, with its rectifying activity, implanting righteousness; above all, it directs and defines the whole itself in its fundamental conditions, in order that each individual in his own way, and in his own place, may find his own part which is in accordance with the eternal purpose.

An idea of reason which inspires development, and in so doing realizes itself, is replaced by authority, which, directly or indirectly, guides every individual towards the highest End of all; or, rather, the product of the reasonable entelechy and development of Society is only truly organized in the sense of righteousness by the supernatural authority, which, if it is left to reason alone, is always imperilled, even entirely apart from all the obscurity which has been caused by the Fall. In the last resort the "organism" is considered as the directing authority for the organizations created by natural instinct and understanding of the purpose of life towards the real and ultimate religious End, and this directive authority is the teaching and pastoral office of the Church, which reaches its highest point in the Papacy. For that very reason, too, the Conciliar movement was illogical when it tried to organize the hierarchy itself—the seat of authority—in terms of an "organism". The hierarchy directs the organism, yet it is not itself to be understood in an "organic" sense; this statement, however, shows most clearly that the actual organic idea has been discarded. The organic idea of unity is transformed into the idea of authority, which regulates the participation of individuals in the value of the whole, in harmony with the infallible authority, without allowing individuals to express an opinion in the matter. The problem is solved by confidence in and reverence for authority.[143] The relationship between the individuals who have been placed in very different positions by the organism still remains very unequal. For the attainment of the purpose of human life some individuals seem far more highly favoured than others. The "organic doctrine" of the Church met this difficulty, on the one

[143] See p. 423.

hand, by formulating the religious doctrine of vicarious oblations, which arose out of its conception of "merit" and of love, and, on the other hand, by a doctrine of perfection which allows for quantitative differences, but which does not on that account do away with the aim in principle.

Both these ideas have already been emphasized in the section on the estimate of mediaeval asceticism, and also in the description of the merely architectonic character of the idea of development. Here we now perceive their value and their function in the whole system, and their fundamental significance in Catholic social philosophy as a whole. Only in this form could an essentially Christian individualism become incorporated into a system which subordinates individuals to the restoration of a social unity organized within itself—a system which equally recognizes within this social unity the conditions of the natural life, with its enormous variety in the struggle for existence which has been effected by Nature and by History, with all its opposition to the supernatural ideal of the religious ethic of love. Thus the immense difficulty, essentially inherent in the Christian idealism of personality and of love, of producing a universal social ideal at all, has been overcome; the ecclesiastical authority takes all the institutions of Society under its administration, and ensures to the individual a just share in the central purpose; the equal participation of all in the objective value of the system is at the same time linked up with the moral achievement of the individual, and it is not a natural claim; beyond this it is sufficient for the individual to have a proportionate share in the *bonum commune* in things secular and sacred, according to his position within the organism; the individual's share in supernatural salvation is also different in proportion. As the ethic of development makes it possible to render radical Christian standards relative, and also connects relative ethical values with the Christian ideal, so the idea of "proportion" conquers the difficulties of the social relativism which is implied in the organic idea. Providence, the Church, and the world-reason which indwells the laws of social formation see to it that in any case this proportional equality within the organism is attainable through an authority which apportions justice rightly. Every instance of a real and complete separation from the objective value in general has its root in the guilt and evil will of the individual. If, however, this element of evil is ultimately ascribed to predestination, this opens up a sinister irrational background to which the Thomist system and contemporary Catholicism do not care to direct more attention

than can be helped. Rather, within the system the Divine Will is
only emphasized in so far as institutions and differences in general
are referred to it; this is done in such a manner, however, that
their contribution to the restoration of an organic whole is
emphasized more strongly than anything else. In spite of these
differences, however, it is possible for men to attain at least a
proportionate share in the absolute values of life and fellowship,
and this proportional participation is dependent upon the qualities of frugality and submission, as well as upon the individual's
care for others and the exercise of charity; through the manifestation of such qualities these differences are again swept away by
the Love of God which creates the whole organism.

If the real difficulty both of an idealistic religious social ethic,
and also of the Christian social ethic, lies in the fact that, on the
one hand, it only achieves the development of individuals by
promoting them to a share in objective values which are universally valid, and which bind them together in fellowship, while,
on the other hand, it is only able to secure, in an unequal and
defective manner, the share of the particular individual in these
objective values supported by the community in face of the
differences effected by Nature; the difficulty, however, is here
overcome by faith in the Law of Reason which satisfies everyone,
and is dominant in the social structure, by that authority which
carries out distributive justice, inspires the whole, and attains its
highest point in the central authority of the Church, while
individuals are satisfied with a merely proportionate share in the
absolute and relative values of fellowship; as this corresponds to
the individual's position within the organism, it will of necessity
be a variable quantity. Thus also the no less essential opposition
of the ethic of love towards the organizations of secular interests is
overcome, since the ethic of love in the highest sense is predominantly ascetic, and appointed to a particular calling and a particular class, while a lower standard of perfection is expected from
the laity; this perfection, however, does not cease to be perfect
in its own way, since the service rendered by the laity is also
directed towards the highest End of life. From this point of view
the idea of unity and yet of difference is extended right up to the
Church Triumphant; each degree and each calling has its particular reward and its special meed of bliss, and in Paradise
Beatrice teaches her poet that the fact that there are different
degrees of celestial bliss does not alter the fact that all
is joy.[144]

[144] See p. 424.

IDEA OF SOCIAL REFORM ABSENT FROM THOMISM

Thus out of manifold complications Catholic social philosophy again attains to an impressive unity. We might then imagine that a system of this kind would have a very deep influence upon practical social life. In actual fact that did take place very often, but never deliberately and systematically, in the shape of an ecclesiastical social reform. This points to a further characteristic feature of the social philosophy of Catholicism. The concentration of Christianity upon the inward, personal, and religious aspects of life was still predominant; this comes out clearly in the fact that even when the Christian unity of civilization had been restored, the only result was that the strongest resistance of all, the opposition of the independent secular powers, was broken down, and certain rights of the Church were established; there was still no idea of the need for a systematic transformation of the social order, subduing and moulding the natural basis of life. There was still no real understanding of the difficulties and complications which are inherent in the natural basis of life, and which hinder it from realizing ideal values. This social philosophy was, indeed, an all-embracing sociological system, but even at the height of its intellectual development it was not a programme of actual social reform. The Christian social doctrine of the Middle Ages was as far removed from being a programme of social reform as was the social teaching of the Early Church, although for different reasons.

While the Early Church accepted the social order of the Ancient World as something fixed and incapable of being reformed, and learnt to tolerate it, as the sinful corruption of the order of Natural Law, while it strove to heal its harmful effects by works of charity, the Mediaeval Church, on the other hand, believed firmly in the Divinely appointed harmony of Nature and Grace, and regarded the relative approximation of actual social institutions to the ideals of the Church as the natural, necessary, logical world-order, which, to be secured only needed the authority of the Church, and a constant renewal of the vitality of its religious principles. The centralization of the Church in the Papacy organized the Church as a religious hierarchy, incorporated the political powers into the structure, but, so far as economic life and social life in the narrower sense were concerned all was left to the Law of Nature. That was as far as the social transformation extended. To the Early Church social reform was too difficult, to the Mediaeval Church it seemed superfluous. The Mediaeval

Church idealized the actual situation and declared herself in favour of the true ideal, which was required both by reason and by revelation. The relative approximations and preparations which it discerned as already present in the actual existing situation it made absolute as the Law of Nature, and it then incorporated them into the ecclesiastical, intellectual process as the architectonic development of history. Even the exercise of charity was now left to the Religious Orders, to the corporations, and to the cities, and the Church confined herself to the consolidation of her own power, believing that if this were secured everything else would naturally fall into line. Social reform simply meant the struggle for the Church and for Natural Law. That, however, did not mean that Society was to be remoulded on the lines of radical Christian thought, but that a comparatively satisfactory situation was stabilized, and that the relative natural values of Society were exalted to the rank of the absolute supernatural values of the Church. There was no need for Christianity to transform the world; rather God rules the world in so far as it approaches the standard of the Church.

Hence modern Catholic social reform is also primarily a return to the principles of Christian Natural Law and of the dominion of the Church; it is opposed to the idea that new conditions require a new theoretical structure of social ideas, and it encourages the fight against the errors of Liberalism. Only quite recently has the Papacy come forward with pronouncements upon social and economic questions, after the modern world has demonstrated their difficult and complicated character. Its teaching on these questions, however, only consists in recalling Society to a conscious and systematic return to "natural" principles, in a world in which the times are out of joint.[144a] In itself the idea is the same as that of the Mediaeval Church; this theory does not capitulate, like the Primitive Church, to the power of the natural basis of life which is under the influence of sin; neither, however, like modern Idealism, does it seek to restore the highest ethical ideals of an unconditional value of personality, and of a free inward spiritual fellowship, by the subjugation of an antagonistic and difficult natural basis by means of human labour and insight, but it believes in the Divinely appointed harmony between the natural basis of life and the Christian and ecclesiastical superstructure as it was approximately realized in

[144a] This, above all, is to the credit of Leo XII, the "social" Pope; his mandates are behind all modern Catholic works of this kind. Cf. *Mausbach: Christentum und Weltmoral, p. 44.*

the great period of the Middle Ages, manifesting therein the great law of the Divine Government of the world. It claims that Liberal theories have destroyed the true understanding of Natural Law, and that the practice of Liberalism has sinfully disturbed the process of true Nature. What is required is the restoration of the true Natural Law and of the dominion of the Church, and Nature will again follow its harmonious course, completed and supported by charitable activity, and by the appropriate healing of the specific evils which have been produced by Capitalism and a machine age.[145]

CATHOLIC CONCEPTION OF LAW

Finally, this is also connected with the ultimate fundamental peculiarity of Catholic social doctrine; its peculiar conception of Law, which contrasts sharply with the modern doctrine of the creation of law by the will of the State. While the modern theory will only recognize law formally, as law, when it has been produced by the will of the State—even when it sanctions social and ethical ideas which it contained before the State was formed—and thus imparts to the modern State the unrest of a continually renewed attempt to transform ethical and rational demands into legal enactments, Catholic social doctrine conceives Natural Law as existing before the State, which binds it to a positive legal working out of the organic and patriarchal theories of Christian Natural Law. In so doing it is free to take into account variation in circumstances and in suitability, but it is still bound to consider that which it creates as the working out of the principles of Natural Law, and continually to improve them according to its insight into Natural Law. Here also that means that all that is essential is already in existence, has already been "given", that the course of Nature and of Providence of itself guides humanity into right knowledge, that the State, like all positive expressions of law, must order its life according to these principles, and that only from this standpoint do its laws attain their binding character.

This, however, means that no room at all is left for any idea of a great social transformation, which the State, by means of fresh legislation, might introduce for the moulding of new conditions. Nothing, then, remains save to have recourse to eternal and unchangeable principles, which can only be adapted to new conditions in their application to particular instances. This "Law of Nature" is no revolutionary, world-transforming theory, which has been newly discovered by human reason, like the Natural

[145] See p. 424.

Law of the Enlightenment, or the modern theories of the State and of Society; it is a conservative, organic, and patriarchal conception of the Law of Nature, which is under the protection of the Church, and is only entirely intelligible to the illuminated Christian reason, even although, in itself, it proceeds from pure reason. It is rather a rationalism which quiets the mind with accepted truths, which can be supported by definite proofs, than one of critical initiative and reform. The world order is based upon reason, it is true, but this basis is not human reason but Divine; it is objective, not subjective. That, too, only explains why it unites itself so easily with supernaturalism and with the ecclesiastical mysticism of grace.[146]

RETROSPECT AND FORECAST

From these two general characteristic features which have just been described two conclusions may be drawn: (1) We gain a final view of the universal social philosophy of Catholicism which arises out of Thomism and which permanently maintains its dominant position; (2) from this standpoint we gain a deeper insight into the essential nature of Christian social philosophy in general, into the possibilities of social philosophy which are contained in Christian thought, and thus we gain fresh light upon the course of their past and future development.

The Middle Ages created a Christian unity of civilization and a comprehensive Christian sociological fundamental idea. This unity of civilization, however, did not constitute a social reform in accordance with Christian principles; it simply meant the acceptance of relatively favourable actual conditions, and their fusion with the religious and ecclesiastical world into a harmoniously developed whole. This was made possible by the fact that the situation produced by the general conditions was not regarded as a fortunate historical accident, but as a logically necessary result of Nature; and the inherited conception of the moral Law of Nature was then applied to these politico-social conditions, and made the basis and the standard of all the positive legislation of the State. Thus the Natural Law which had been shaped by the actual situation was now united with the Ethos and the community-spirit of revelation, just as the teleological metaphysic of immortality became united with dogma. The structure which takes place in both cases of the ascent from Nature to Revelation has, however, its final cause in the Being of God Himself, whose nature it is to guide the world-process through Nature up to

[146] See p. 426.

Supernature by a process of evolution, which, in spite of the Fall, and even under the conditions of sin, still continues to develop.

If we regard this result as the culminating point of the previous historical development, then, in the simplest manner, the past is illuminated. As has been already pointed out, the Christian ethic, purely in itself, was the specifically religious ethic of a personalistic religious way of feeling; it was an ethic of love and holiness, of surrender to God in moral obedience, and union in God by means of a religious love of the brethren. From the standpoint of this ethic, nature and the natural motives were only the general bases of life, to be kept within the narrowest limits; where they transcend those limits they are considered the self-assertion of the earthly and finite self and the denial of love. It outlined, therefore, an ideal of personality purely consecrated to God and rooted in Him, and also the ideal of a community which overcomes all differences and all hardness purely through love; it was, however, quite conscious that this ideal can only be completely realized when there is a new heaven and a new earth. Thus from the outset it was opposed to any morality which was connected with the struggle of men with one another; its ideal of personality was expressed in courage and honour, and its ideal of the community in righteousness, an appropriate solidarity, and a reasonable limitation of spheres of interest. It held that human honour exists only in relation to God, and it could therefore renounce all claim to the honour which comes from men. The Christian ethic knew a spiritual unity which fused all contradictions in the molten fire of the Love of God, and therefore it was not concerned about "rights", and the struggle for "rights". It was thus able to assimilate the ideal of the monogamous family, but not that of the State, with its emphasis upon law, war, and tyranny, nor that of the economic struggle, with its emphasis on wealth, power, and possessions.

At all points the Christian ethic was opposed to an ethic which arose out of the struggle for existence, and it merely moralized that ethic by ennobling the fighting virtues, and by introducing ideas of solidarity and of law without discarding this ethic altogether. So far as it was concerned it aimed at the radical removal of the struggle for existence, in God, and the only conflict it recognized as lawful was the conflict for truth and love against selfishness and error. In any case, the Christian ethic everywhere transcended that relative position which merely moralized the struggle for existence, and reached out after the absolute ideal of love and holiness. It set itself deliberately to undermine the motives of the lower ethic, and to remove those conditions of life which increase the struggle for existence, and the moral endeavours which only attempt to modify it. Thus the Christian ethic was unable to influence the society of the Ancient World, whose political and popular morality everywhere bore the traces of its origin in an ethic of conflict, and the effort to limit the sphere of conflict; all it could appropriate from the Ancient World was the Stoic doctrine of Natural Law, which already, from its own point of view, had entered upon the same course of religious ideas; the Stoics had evolved both their ethic of personality and of human fellowship from the participation of mankind in the Divine Reason; on the other hand, they regarded the concrete world of the State and of Law as the obscuring of Reason by means of selfish and confused conflict. In so far as this ethic had achieved a relative valuation of social institutions, as they had evolved through the struggle for existence and the endeavour to control that conflict by ethical means, the Church appropriated this social doctrine of the Stoics, and, through the relative valuation of social institutions which this opened up, the Church came to terms with the social life of the Ancient World.

The Christian ethic, however, was still only able to adopt an attitude of toleration and endurance so long as the institutions and customs, established upon a basis of this kind, in their essence still bore the traces of the political struggle for power, of formalizing and legalizing law, of the economic competitive struggle. The fact that the late Roman Empire already began to adopt bureaucratic methods, and to introduce associations like guilds, meant a cessation of the struggle for existence with which the Christian ethic could come into closer contact; this, however, only took place to a very limited extent, and its practical effect was almost negligible. Now, however, the mediaeval world, with its extremely rudimentary idea of the State, with its feeble economic competition, in the absence of a strict and rational legal system, with its sparse population, and in the absence of that notive for conflict among the population due to migration on a large scale, with the erection of semi-communistic groups of people dependent upon personal service and mutual help, above all with the traditionalist regulation of the protection of the food supply, and the scope for industry and for consumption in the peaceful industrial town, created a way of life in which the struggle for existence was very largely regulated, and the formalistic legal standpoint was still largely undeveloped. The system of class and guild meant the preservation and the enfranchisement of individual initiative, united with the strongest limitation of its incalculable results, and with a very strong sense of personal solidarity. For the mediaeval world there is no State, either in the ancient or in the modern sense of the word, and therefore the specifically political lust of power is absent. Whenever the fighting instinct flares up naturally in wild adventures, and in private feuds, the ecclesiastical "peace of God" tries to extinguish it, or the Church diverts it into Holy Wars. The coarse brutality and cruelty of the Middle Ages appear to be the result of sin and personal disposition; they do not belong to the essence and structure of Society. These conditions formed a social situation with which the Christian ethic could make its peace. It was a compromise, for the struggle itself remained; it was only limited and regulated; the struggle itself, however, was regarded as "Nature", which is transcended by Grace. In a situation which already has done so much to limit and suspend the conflict, Grace can take part. The classification of Society in professional groups and guilds, together with a sparse population, constituted that cessation of the struggle for existence in which the natural requirements of life could still be satisfied, and the ascent to the ethic of sanctification and brotherly love was still possible.

With the non-political class organization of the society of the Middle Ages the Christian ethic at last became, in theory, a social ideal. Even yet, however, it still could not be evolved directly from its fundamental Christian ideas, for it was the ethic of Nature and not of Grace. Indirectly, however, it fused these conditions with its own ideal along the following lines: it revised the Stoic doctrine of Natural Law, which previously had served this end and completed it in the spirit of Aristotle; it began to lay less emphasis upon the absolute contrast between present conditions and the rational Primitive State, and more upon the relative reasonableness of politico-social developments; in the actual social situation, as it was now emerging, which had been freed from ancient paganism and its idolatry of the State, the Law of Nature and of Reason at last attains its full development, and the Church unites this ethic of reason with the ethic of revelation, as the double product of the one Divine Light.

This is the explanation of the mediaeval social philosophy which represents a Christian culture and a Christian Society, and yet does not mean that Society is based upon and moulded by directly Christian principles. This, however, also explains the later development of this social philosophy. It preserved, as long as it was at all possible, its guild character, and at the same time its unpolitical and economic traditional character. Here, in spite of all its own special characteristics, Lutheranism followed entirely in the track of Catholic social philosophy. Calvinism, on the contrary, found conditions in Geneva and in America which forced it to take an active part in modern social, political, and economic conditions, and correspondingly it transformed the whole Christian social philosophy and ethic; one main object of the following thesis will be to present a clear picture of this transformation within the sphere of Calvinism. Lutheranism and Catholicism are also obliged to face the facts of modern social development, the formation of gigantic modern States, the colossal increase in the masses of the population, the unleashing of the political struggle for power and of the economic competitive struggle, with the unlimited aspirations of Capitalism within the sphere of production, and with the release of individuals now only connected by the equality of the law. In this situation the old doctrine of social harmony and of the system of stages was no longer any use. Christian "social reform" was now necessary. Catholicism alone, however, took this Christian social reform resolutely in hand, for in its ideal of a society guided by the Church it possessed the impulse and the power for a reform of this kind, while Lutheranism, which was bound up with the State, was drawn helplessly into the whirlpool of the modern problems of Society. In this situation, however, Catholic social reform, theoretically and fundamentally, simply means a return to the Law of Nature, and that means to the unpolitical class society guided by the Church, in which the State has only utilitarian tasks, while the Church hopes to lead Society back to peace through the ideas of self-restraint and of group-solidarity which are involved in the "class" idea. In order to achieve this end nothing is needed beyond the supremacy of the Catholic idea and of its science of Christian Natural Law. All the advantages of capitalist production may be incorporated into such a system so long as they do not aim at being anything more than technical improvements in production and distribution.

Thus the modern Catholic social policy is a capitalistic re-generated programme of mediaeval class ideas, and it becomes consciously "reforming" because the harmony between Nature and Grace which has been disturbed can no longer itself restore the balance, but must itself again be restored, in much more complicated and much more difficult general conditions. Whether in so doing this programme is so directly opposed to the trend of

modern development as the Liberal doctrine of progress believes
may here be left an open question; when we reflect, however, that
in the present development there appear various tendencies for
the creation of new servitudes, monopolies, bureaucratic regulations, and that Liberal individualism can often only present itself
as an interim period between two periods of oppression, we can
then understand how it is that Catholic social philosophers think
that their social Natural Law still holds good to-day in spite of
Liberalism, and that there is a very great need—in face of these
coming periods of oppression—for the Christian spirit of the value
of the individual in the sight of God, and of reconciliation through
love; they believe that this is all the more necessary because
modern radicalism is about to derive morality once again purely
from the struggle for existence and its self-limitations, or even to
proclaim a struggle for existence apart from all morality, which
will describe the Christian morality of love as an attack upon all
the natural and best instincts of humanity: Catholic thinkers
claim that both types of the social ethic which Catholicism has
united in an intelligent way are on the verge of being severed in
the most harmful way; the fear is that the first natural type will
fall a prey to pure Naturalism, and that the coming time of
oppression will become a time of wild exploitation; it will only be
possible to reunite these types upon the basis of the Catholic
social philosophy of the religious union of mankind on the organic-
patriarchal, class-division on labour lines, propositions which are
certainly logical.[146a]

These characteristics represent the universal sociological ideal
of the ecclesiastical unity of civilization, the spirit of Catholic
social doctrine. From this standpoint it is easy to prove how the
great social institutions—especially those of the Family, the State,
and Society—could be controlled by the principles of a Christian
social philosophy. In each case they were special forms of the
realization of the fundamental theory, directed towards an end
of Natural Law, which it behoved them to strive to attain as
their special contribution to Society. Their Christian character
consists in the two following elements: (1) that the union between
the individual and the community which takes place within them
is conceived and moulded in the organic and patriarchal sense;
and that (2) the primary particular aim which is founded upon
their basis in Natural Law is placed in a fixed relation to the
central religious purpose, and thus with the all-embracing inclusive unity of the Church and of the ecclesiastical authority.

[146a] See p. 426.

THOMIST ETHIC OF THE FAMILY

The social philosophy of the Church now taught an entirely definite, logical theory of the rise and progress of social institutions along the lines of the evolution of history. The Family is the original and fundamental form of social life, which, according to Aristotle and the Bible, as the monogamous family is the first result of that Reason which forms men into communities; on account of its reproductive function, the Family is a specially hallowed example of what human life in fellowship ought to be, determining personal relationships by its own example. The community is constituted by the grouping together of families; for reasons which will be explained later on, St. Thomas regards the community essentially as an urban community, alongside of which, however, the village and farm communities are also naturally taken into account. Above the communes was the province, and then the Empire. The States are unlimited in number. St. Thomas and the later Middle Ages were not concerned with the question of the union of these States within the Empire. It is, of course, obvious why the Catholic social doctrine of the present day does not consider this question at all.

Finally, within the communes and the State there are the groups which are united by the ties of class and profession, and the corporations which are the supporters of social life in the narrower sense, and in which the characteristic corporate and class organizations of the Middle Ages are presupposed. The whole system, however, is gathered up in the Church, with its hierarchical organizations and its Religious Orders, which is thus, in the last resort, governed by the Pope, and through him by Christ Himself, the Lord of Christendom; this means that the reins of government are really in the hands of the clergy and the ascetics.[147]

A monographic presentation of this social structure would go far beyond the limits of the subject of this book. It would also have to deal with many peculiarities of the Thomistic doctrine due to the historical situation, and with its dependence upon its authorities, for in St. Thomas we are dealing to a large extent with purely academic theories. We will therefore emphasize only those points of view which are of permanent value.[148]

[147] See p. 427.
[148] For the relation between the merely academic doctrine and reference to the actual historical realities of the day, see the instructive observations of *Maurenbrecher*, who lays stress on the unconscious adaptations of Aristotle within this theory.

The Family is determined primarily by its own particular purpose in Natural Law, which leads quite naturally to monogamy, private property as the wealth of the family, and the right of inheritance, and it consists in the production and education of offspring—Malthusian scruples are still unknown. After all that has been previously described, it is obvious that the family group is of the organic and patriarchal character, whether it lives as a small family, or as a large united family, carrying on together a common business or industry; it is also natural that the servants form part of the patriarchal organization of the family. The dignity of the individual human being is thus relatively preserved by a whole series of customs or legal enactments; above all, it is maintained in the personal and ethical mutual relationship of love. The incorporation of the Family into the central religious purpose of the Church consists in this: so far as possible the purely sexual side is ignored, since the aim of marriage is limited solely to the rational reproduction of human beings, and thus of members of the Church; the wedded state itself becomes a symbol of the union of Christ and the Church. In both respects the ascetic limitation of the sex instinct is effective, since marriage becomes solely an institution for reproduction, and a symbol of the spiritual unity of love. In all other respects its sacramental character brings it under the ecclesiastical marriage law, which the Church tries to extend as far as possible in opposition to the civil marriage law; it is also greatly influenced by the widespread power of the confessional. Since, moreover, the Church penetrates the personal relationships within the family with the Christian virtues of love, raising these above their natural union to the religious union of love, the family becomes the original form of, and the preparation for, all social relationships, as we have already seen in the analysis of Patriarchalism.[149]

THOMIST ETHIC OF THE STATE

The purpose of the State—or, as it was more correctly described in the mediaeval sense of the word, the supreme authority—so far as Natural Law is concerned, is the maintenance of order and the peace of the country; this implies that it is the duty of the Government to create a setting within which it will be possible to carry out the peaceful exercise of one's vocation, the minimum at least of a legal morality, and the ideal of a justice which is both distributive and commutative. This means that the State has to see that each citizen has his share, according to his rank and position, in

[149] See p. 427.

the *bonum commune* of the State, or its material welfare, and that in matters of exchange, treaty negotiations, and the behaviour of individuals towards each other all takes place according to a strict legal standard and the exact correspondence between one service and another, between injury and compensation. Partly as an outcome of the inward impulse of reason, and partly as a result of intelligent arrangement, the form of organization which the State makes its own is the patriarchal and organic, with a decided leaning towards monarchy, in which alone the authority of the Government and the unity of the organism, formed on the pattern of the universe, are firmly established. The individual value of the members of the organism is, however, always to be expressed on the basis of the same idea of the organism. This takes place best in a mixed constitution; the idea that lies behind this is probably that of the representation of the various professional classes and their co-operation; in the mind of St. Thomas, however, this constitution is constantly confused with that of the meeting of the citizens in the Aristotelian city-state, and in his theory the connection with the concrete constitutional life of his day is very much reduced; as a result the Catholic theory is, largely, comparatively independent of feudal tenure and the feudal system; the relation between the public authority and subjective public rights is treated in a highly abstract manner. The right, and even the duty, of revolution exists wherever a tyrannical and selfish Government prevents the realization of the purpose of the State, on condition, however, that such a revolution will not do more harm than good. The detailed illustrations which St. Thomas gives reveal a very strong dependence upon mere book-learning, and as they are applicable neither to the mediaeval State nor to the modern world, they may be left out of account; his teaching on the origin of the State, on the relation between natural, positive, and international law, his view of the course of political history, his relation to the legal theories and legal sources of his own day, are merely of academic interest. The main point is that the purpose of the State is confined to utilitarian welfare and legal justice, the combination of the Divine authority of the power of the State with the subjective rights and claims of individuals, the importance of piety, loyalty, and the patriarchal temper for the political whole. Those are permanent features in the Catholic theory of the State.

The State is the organization of secular and legal interests, so far as this is necessary for a Christian society, of which, indeed, it only constitutes one element. It is the secular side of the same society of which the spiritual side is represented by the Church. It is thus easy to discern the relation of the State to the central religious purpose. This lies both in the emphasis upon the elements of love contained in the idea of the organism and of patriarchalism, which also make the State the preparatory school for the cultivation of a Christian disposition, and in the strict limitation of the purpose of the State to material interests and formal righteousness. Thus the conception of the political ideal as an independent ethical end, which is characteristic of the ancient and modern conception of the State, is not entertained; by every theory of the ultimate value of the religious end of life such an outlook must be viewed with grave misgiving. This purely utilitarian conception means, further, that the State is considered as detached from all intellectual, religious, and higher ethical interests, which the State only receives from the Church, and which must remain under the direction of the Church. The State may intervene whenever it will in the purely utilitarian side of life. Indeed, by fixing prices and by all kinds of regulations for the protection of the independence of each community it may have a profound influence upon economic life; but in the realm of the mind and the spirit the Church must be supreme.

The relation of States to each other ought to be that of members of the Christian family. War should only be permitted when it is waged for a just cause, provoked by the wrongdoing of others, and its aim ought to be the promotion of all that is good, and the prevention of evil. Further, wars are only permitted when they are official and ordered by princes; private wars and feuds are forbidden. The selfishness of nationality, moreover, does not yet come under consideration for the international unity of Christian civilization; the metaphysic of the Church does not yet permit the sense of nationality to arise. In the last resort the question of the justice of a war is decided by the supreme arbiter in all moral matters, the Church. Finally, and above all, the incorporation in the spiritual aim of life is expressed in the theory of the supreme dominion of the Church, which indeed only intervenes in purely secular matters when they are connected with spiritual interests; she, however, decides in a sovereign way, from her own standpoint, whether such a connection exists or not. The spiritual authority is the ruling and guiding spirit of the secular authority as well, just as God rules the organism of the world even when He leaves it to carry out its own laws. The main task here is that everywhere the true faith, and the Canon Law which expresses it, shall be dominant; compulsory conversions of Jews and unbelievers are, however, not permitted; in cases of stubborn denial, certainly, in the interests of the salvation of the rest, heretics are to be excommunicated, and then given over to the power of the State for punishment as harmful disturbers of Society. Believers are only allowed to be subject to unbelievers so far as external circumstances of law and authority make it necessary. Intercourse with unbelievers is only allowed in so far as it can awaken hope of conversion, otherwise so far as necessity commands it. Only through baptism does one belong to the order both of the State and of the Church, and for unbelievers baptism means naturalization in the Christian Society.

Further, if we take into account the guidance of the royal conscience by the ecclesiastical ideal, and remember the claim that the duty of princes is to train nations in virtue, then the incorporation of the State into the religious purpose, in spite of its independence on the side of Natural Law, becomes supreme. On the other hand, however, from a State which thus interprets its mission there is no cause to fear that any ethical motive will arise to prevent the absolute religious value of life from finding its fulfilment. The only differences which can possibly arise occur in connection with the extent and the relationship between the secular and the spiritual powers in the share they take in the common task; indeed, the whole vast conflict between the Empire and the Papacy was only a difference of that kind, so far as it was a question of theory and principle. The Thomist doctrine here represents, clearly and honestly, the entire supremacy of the spiritual authority, in which alone the purpose both of Reason and of Redemption is gathered up into a coherent unity.[150]

THOMIST ETHIC OF SOCIETY AND OF ECONOMICS

The Thomist doctrine of actual Society is much more incomplete and confused; further, it can only be regarded to a limited extent as typical of Catholic social doctrine. Certainly its main characteristic is typical, that is, that the whole organization of Society is based in Natural Law upon the necessity of labour, and upon the division of labour which that involves. In contrast with the Early Church, in which statements of this kind only occur incidentally, this assertion is something new. At bottom the Primitive Church had maintained the ancient ideal of the citizen living on his own income, looking down upon the artisan class, and had only required for the working classes the exercise of love and kindness; otherwise labour was only fully honoured in

[150] See p. 428.

the cloister. Now the mediaeval civil order is reflected in the social ideal of work and property, and a differentiation which is based solely upon labour. That leads (according to Natural Law) to the organization of class-groups and corporations engaged in the same kind of work, and also to the task of the authority which directs the society—a task which consists in this : On the one hand, the care of the preservation of those groups and the protection of their food supply, and, on the other hand, the restriction of individuals to their own class and to their work, in order that the social organization may not be disturbed.

In this expression of the doctrine of Society St. Thomas is thinking all the time of small, self-supporting, economically unified groups; this the sense in which he interprets the Aristotelian autocracy; instead of regarding the State, politically and ethically, as an end in itself, he places the security of a means of support which is not disturbed by unavoidable contingencies, in which, as far as possible, all needs are met by the economic unity itself, and in relation to the outer world all that is to be desired is a supplementary form of trade in which imports exceed exports. This might lead to a radical social system, based upon personal labour and upon a just wage, in which the most revolutionary results could only be avoided by the recognition of the right of inheritance based upon Natural Law in the continuance of personality through the family.[151] This system, however, adjusts itself quite naturally to the existing conditions, since labour is differentiated into physical, intellectual, and governing activity, since income must be regulated by social position, and since lack of liberty is accepted unquestioningly as the result of the Fall. At this point entirely different motives enter into the idea of the organization of Society based upon the performance of labour and the securing of a sufficient minimum of existence. Patriarchalism breaks through the simple fundamental theory, and the actual spirit of this social doctrine only becomes applicable to the agricultural labour of the peasants and the industrial work in the towns. The *domini saeculares*, or the ruling aristocracy, as well as the men of the contemplative and intellectual life, men of science and of the Church, are considered from a very different, and indeed a very aristocratic, point of view. Manual labour is left to the lower orders; this is in part an unavoidable concession to the natural conditions of Society,[151a] and in part it is due to the influence of the aristocratic outlook of Aristotelianism.

[151] See p. 428.
[151a] On these conditions of Nature see the very instructive work of *Michels: Die oligarchischen Tendenzen der Gesellschaft. Archiv. XXI.*

At this point we make the remarkable discovery, that, in contrast to the inclination of modern Catholicism towards the rural population and its specific Ethos, it is solely the city that St. Thomas takes into account. In his view man is naturally a town-dweller, and he regards rural life only as the result of misfortune or of want; the town of which he thinks is itself strongly agrarian, and supports its own life by a system of ordered exchange of goods with the surrounding country which is under its rule. This exclusive reference to the town can, however, scarcely be said to be explained merely by the accidental reason that St. Thomas, as an Italian and a member of a mendicant order, only knew town life, and that as the commentator of Aristotle his horizon was bounded by ideas of the city-state. For Aristotle prefers agriculture to industry, whereas St. Thomas describes agriculture as "dirty and miserable". Further, St. Thomas connects the Aristotelian contempt for industry merely with the dependent wage-earner, while he considers those business men who take part in municipal government to be full citizens in the Aristotelian sense of the word, all of which is contrary to Aristotle's meaning. All this points rather to the circumstance which has already been emphasized, that it was still only the mediaeval town, with its principles of peace, with its basis of free labour and corporate labour-groups, with its stronger intellectual interests, and its care and protection through its administration for everyone, which provided a fertile soil for Christian ideals.[152] Thus, while it is true that the limitation to the town is extremely one-sided, still the Thomist ethic makes clear in the city-ideal typical traits of the Catholic-Christian doctrine of Society, which also permit its application to the universal and to the whole. In particular, it is only from this standpoint, and not from the point of view of feudal Society, that the claim of the social theory is developed, that all income and all distinctions must be based upon the personal contribution of labour. That is a question of civic ethics, not of feudal ethics. St. Thomas, who is himself an off-shoot of the feudal nobility, ignores feudal tenure and the feudal system; everywhere, however, he assumes the class organization as a matter of course. Only he does not care to illustrate this from the feudal system. In this sense, too, the otherwise very one-

[152] For the significance of the town in Christianity, which first brought in a real Christian lay civilization with independent activity, see *Uhlhorn: Liebestätigkeit, II, 174, 201, 210*; in the town in particular did it become possible to replace the standard of birth by the idea of the calling (*325 f.*), likewise the idea of mutual supplementation (*404*), and the beginnings of a conscious social policy (*450*).

sided orientation of St. Thomas towards the city has its general
and typical significance for the Catholic social ethic. It is patriarchal within the limits of the necessary concessions to the unavoidable natural conditions of power and natural distinctions,
but it is in no wise feudal. It is bourgeois in the sense of the
agrarian-industrial town, with its settled organizations of labour,
and its clear proportion between labour and income.[153]

The detailed consideration of this subject is merely of academic
interest. Once again only those features of this civic idea are of
universal significance which reveal a capacity for universal application to the whole, and which reveal the spirit of this organization of labour and profit. On the one hand, the most important
point to observe is the positive value assigned to work, to profit,
to private property, and to the right of inheritance, coupled with
the admission that, in accordance with Natural Law, it is an
actual duty, both to oneself and to one's relations, to gain a sufficient measure of property, which will ensure the maintenance of
the family according to the standards of one's class. Since this is
based upon the requirements of Natural Law, i.e. with consideration for its suitability for production, the purely consumer's
standpoint of the Early Church has been discarded, and the
actual conditions of economic life are taken into consideration.

On the other hand, however, in contrast with the Capitalistic
Spirit, this is the traditionalist spirit (to use Max Weber's term)
of the whole idea of economics. It is expressed in the differentiation, according to rank, of the way of life, and in the
injunction to the political authorities, through a policy of
protection of food supply and of the regulation of prices to maintain for each individual the income according to his rank. It is
the standpoint of the conservation of food supplies, which is
closely connected with the maintenance of permanent professional
groups, in which the same trade or calling is handed on, without
variation, from father to son, through many generations.

It is further expressed in the doctrine of prices, or the *pretium
justum* regulating trade and barter, which objectively corresponds
exactly to the value of the wares, and which may include in
addition only that which is necessary for the life of the trader;
this very naïve economic theory does not say how such an objective value can be established; it is in touch with actual conditions
only through the admission of certain fluctuations, and through
the incidental recognition of subjective factors in fixing a price.

This traditionalist spirit is finally expressed in the well-known

[153] See p. 428.

doctrine of interest and usury, which is now based upon the Aristotelian doctrine of the unfruitfulness of money, and which contains a whole theory of money; fundamentally its intention is to obviate unjust exploitation, as well as dangerous mobilization of trade, to hinder the whole unaccountable effect of a production which goes on increasing indefinitely, emancipating itself from a limited circle of customers, and also to prevent men from gaining an income without labour. The extraordinarily complicated details and factors of these economic doctrines must here be left without further remark. The whole spirit of this way of thinking on economic matters may be summed up thus: property and gain are based upon the personal performance of work; goods are exchanged only when necessary, and then only according to the principles of a just price, which does not give an undue advantage to anyone; (this "just price" is best regulated by the Government), consumption is regulated (a) in accordance with the principle of moderation, which only permits the natural purpose of the maintenance of existence to be fulfilled, and (b) which makes room for a generosity which takes the needs of others into account; at the same time great differences in social position and in fortune, and therefore in the exercise of liberality, are fully recognized. It may be mentioned in passing that this spirit still exists, even when the capitalist system is recognized, with all that this involves of the unavoidable effect of the infinite subdivisions of the processes of labour, and the vastly enlarged sphere which has to be catered for under modern conditions. This spirit characterizes Neo-Thomism even at the present day. According to Ratzinger, the Christian social ideal which will heal the wounds of the world is still composed of the following elements: emphasis upon a certain amount of property for every member of Society; the means of gaining a living in accordance with one's social position; restraint and the limitation of production to the actual stimulus of the economic production of goods which are absolutely necessary; the renunciation of private gain arising out of speculation as a purely private undertaking; the closest possible connection between the possession of capital and labour; a willingness on the part of the owners of property and capital to make such a combination possible, even, when possible, at the cost of a personal sacrifice of chances of making money in association with others, or of their share in profits; and finally, alongside of these psychological elements, the enforcement of vigorous State regulations in order to carry through and maintain a social constitution of that kind.[154]

[154] See p. 428.

THIS SOCIAL IDEAL CONTROLLED
BY THE CHURCH

All this, however, refers merely to the ideal of Society from the point of view of Natural Law. Beyond that there is the ultimate religious purpose. The Christian connection with this ideal consists primarily in this: that the self-restraint, the sacrificial spirit, and all the traditionalism which are necessary if this system of Natural Law is to be maintained, can only really be produced with the aid of the Christian virtues of love, humility, and hope—a hope which is anchored in the real values of the future life. The heroic renunciations of monasticism were meant to strengthen this spirit by their example, and to preserve it for Society as the indispensable basis even of the natural forms of life.[154a]

Further, in addition to the positive value of work as the means of existence, it also appears as a beneficial method of asceticism, which destroys carnal ideas and prevents the distraction caused by sensual pleasure. As a result of the Fall, it serves also as an exhortation to humility. Labour is thus both a penalty and a means of salvation. Rightly understood, and exercised in this spirit, it is the means for the preservation of the physical existence of Christian Society, and to this extent, as well as property, it has been appointed by God as the necessary presupposition for the higher values of life. From the highest point of view, however, work does not merely preserve Christian society, but it preserves love, since commercial profits make it possible to support churches and monasteries, partly by means of fixed taxes, partly by voluntary gifts, since all that is not necessary for the maintenance of existence is placed at the disposal of brotherly love and charity. When poverty and distress require it, property is again regarded as belonging to the whole community; private property had only been permitted to develop from motives of convenience. Thus even the theft of St. Crispin is justified. At this point the familiar ideas of the Early Church reappear.

The new social doctrine, however, pours a great deal of water into the wine of the radical ethic of love. According to this ideal, not only does the duty of giving away only begin when possessions have passed the minimum limit needed for existence (which, indeed, varies very much according to social position), but it teaches that it is a direct duty first of all to ensure one's own maintenance, and that it is not allowable to endanger the foundations of the economic existence of the family by a generosity which

[154a] See p. 430.

threatens its own existence. For a man who himself belonged to a Mendicant Order, this was certainly neither worldliness nor legalism, but consideration for the conditions of economic prosperity. For those who renounce the world St. Thomas makes it very clear indeed that it is absolutely necessary for them to make an entire renunciation of all property, and he defends this position with great vigour against the ancient Orders. So far as life in the world is concerned, however, it is characteristic of St. Thomas that he recognizes that such a modification of the commandment of love is unavoidable; this recognition, like so much else, is a sign that we are in an entirely different world from that of the Early Church, that we now have before us a permanent Christian order of society, with its incorporation and sanctification of the natural basis of life. Charity is no longer the only social idea, which throws a bridge across the gulf between the equality of the Primitive State and the coming equality of love in heavenly bliss, thus bridging a world steeped in sin and destined to pass away.[155]

The main features of the mediaeval social philosophy are therefore clear, even in questions of detailed application. Both in its exclusiveness and in its comprehensiveness, as well as in its positive incorporation within the world, it stands out in clear relief against the indefinite, incomplete social doctrine of the Primitive Church, which never attained a clear idea of its attitude towards the world. In this, however, it also reveals its marked difference from the sociological idea of the Gospel. The Pegasus of absolute religious individualism and of the radical ethic of love is yoked to the plough of the social order, makes its fruitful furrows in a soil which is comparatively easy to cultivate, and only finally aspires after the regions of the supersensual life and of eternity. The new humanity of religious personality and of the fellowship of love in God has made a compromise with the old humanity of the struggle for existence, of force, of law, of war, and of violence, with the natural basis of existence.[156]

The compromise only became possible within the sphere of the mediaeval order of Society, which rose from the rejuvenescence of the whole social order in a semi-civilized economic system based upon agriculture, which to the earliest, very moderate beginnings of the higher political and economic differentiation and unification, and, in a decided preponderance of the personal element over the

---

[155] For details see *Maurenbrecher*; also *von Eicken, 488–547 f.*, and the work of *Funk*, which has already been mentioned; further, *Ratzinger: Volkswirtschaft*, and there is a great deal of material in *Uhlhorn: Liebestätigkeit, II.*
[156] See p. 430.

abstract and rationalistic elements, offered to the religious ethic easily accessible points of approach.[157] The theory of the Church, therefore, stabilized this situation by its conception of Christian Natural Law, which, again, the Church anchored firmly both in its scientific metaphysics and in its doctrine of revelation.

This theory is neither an ideology which annihilates and ignores the natural basis of life, nor is it a system of social reform which transforms and Christianizes the natural basis of life. This mediaeval social philosophy is a combination of faith in Providence and Rationalism, which regards the natural basis administered by reason as naturally ordained for the religious end: the actual practical conditions which made it temporarily possible for the Church to accept them in this way are transformed into an eternal Natural Law in the architectonic-historical-development meaning of this conception, and in so doing, for this purpose, in contrast with their real nature, they were still more considerably idealized. It is an open question whether, in reality, these are the only conditions which allow the Christian idea to obtain a tolerably possible realization. In any case, after these social doctrines had been destroyed in the fourteenth and fifteenth centuries, the Catholic Church again returned to these theories in the period of the Counter Reformation. After a further shattering experience in the eighteenth century the Church took them up afresh with some new adjustments, particularly in the direction of democracy, Capitalism, and the order of a modern State Church. To what a great extent these theories—at least in their main features, in the combination of Natural Law with morality and grace to form a united Christian Society—represent the only system of a Christian doctrine of Society which had been evolved until that time appears finally and pre-eminently in the fact that even Protestantism—the new form of the Christian idea which arose out of the religious crisis of the sixteenth century—was only able to establish a doctrine of society by reshaping and continuing this Catholic social philosophy. The social philosophy of Protestantism is also based upon the idea of Natural Law.

CATHOLIC SOCIAL PHILOSOPHY AND ITS
CONNECTION WITH HISTORY IN GENERAL

Now, however, as we approach the end of this section, we must inquire, on the other hand, to what extent the Christian ideal

[157] This has also been pointed out by *Uhlhorn*, *II*, *439 f.*, but also the darker side (*p. 441*); it consists in this, that as soon as the "natural order" failed, Society faced the social crises without any other guidance.

determined the social development of the Middle Ages after it had itself been effectively and even decisively influenced in its development of a social philosophy by the actual conditions of the life of the day.

This question is extraordinarily difficult and complicated, and in reply I can only offer some very modest suggestions. Yet, in spite of that, for the sake of completeness, they must be expressed with that brevity which befits mere suggestions. In so doing I do not take into account the well-known general civilizing influence of the Church, which, however, has an important sociological aspect. The Church was the teacher of art and science, of technical knowledge and organization, of administration and law; she was the continuation of the ancient culture. Here we are concerned solely with actual social influences, and only with those which are the direct result of intrinsically Christian religious ideas.

First of all, it seems to me unquestionable that the Church did succeed in basing Society upon the Christian conception of the family—that combination of the elements of authority with those of personality and individualism. To what extent the modification of the Patriarchalism of the ancient Germanic kind, and also of that of Roman law, may have been due to the cessation of the habit of reckoning everything in terms of military organization, the interest of the families in the destiny of the women who marry out of the tribe and of their children, the economic necessity of a settlement and a legal definition of the law regarding the wife's property—the strongest factor in effecting the intimacy and individual character of the family relationships was the ideal of the Church, with its emphasis upon the value of personality and upon love; at the same time, however, we cannot ignore the fact that the Church did help to establish the authority of the house-father. This Christian conception of the family, united with Jewish and Stoic ideas, still constitutes the foundation pillar of our social order. All reforms and emancipations in this sphere are faced by the fundamental question of how far they can move within the framework of this conception, or to what extent they desire to open up the future land of a completely new order of Society. The immense problem of sex ethics is here solved in a quite definite sense, which gave to the European peoples one of their chief characteristics, and which, to a certain degree, modern individualism knows how to assimilate; this ethic, however, is once more seriously menaced by modern economic conditions.[158]

[158] Cf. *Marianne Weber: Ehefrau und Mutter, pp. 200–278; Schmoller: Grundriss, I, 244–253*; also the article by *Gothein* which has already been mentioned.

Secondly, it seems to me a fact of the highest importance that, in the transition from the semi-anarchist feudal states and city-federations to the uniform bureaucratic modern sovereign State, the Church was an example of the only sovereign institution which governed through a vast body of officials, supported by unconditional obedience, and using a formal written law. Indeed, one might even say that the modern conception of the State, in which the will of the individual is united with a collective will which can be legally represented, which at the same time secures the inviolable personal rights of the individual, found its first method of orientation in the *Corpus mysticum* of the Church, and through this it is distinguished from the ancient conception of the State, in which the State is abstractly bound to observe the laws, and in which it was impossible to keep a clear line of demarcation between the collective will and the will of the individual. At least all these modern conceptions of the law of the State have grown out of the elements of a philosophy of the State which was bound up with the Church, and directed towards the collective will of the *Corpus mysticum*.[159]

Thirdly, however, and further, we may well believe that the whole of social thought and feeling in general has been deeply influenced by the idea of an objective fellowship with absolute values and truths. The historico-philosophical idea of an "objective spirit" is a transformation of the ecclesiastical unity of life, without the ecclesiastical means of fellowship. The Platonist State and Stoic cosmopolitanism were still only the preliminary condition for this idea. It was only the Church which practically effected a combination which first of all united the fellowship in absolute spiritual values, and through the very share of the individual in these personal values gave to the individual his own independent value. In this particular, Liberalism perpetuates in a secular form an idea which had first been realized by the Church, and it is very doubtful how far this ideal can be maintained against naturalistic reactions without any religious support at all. It is one of the chief arguments in Catholic apologetic that it is precisely the idealistic and humane demands of Liberalism which would find in the Church their strongest support. That there is a certain connection cannot be denied, even though at that time, and still

[159] This is the main idea of *Gierke, III*; also of *J. N. Figgis: From Gerson to Grotius*, which attributes the development of modern political thought to the idea of the Christian Society which is represented variously in Catholicism, Lutheranism, and Calvinism, with at the same time the influence of the Renaissance behind it all.

more to-day, the price of the support of the Church is a great loss of that idealistic individualism and of the mobility of its spiritual content.

Fourthly, we may say that the increasing modification of slavery, the weakening of the system of serfdom, the development of civic freedom out of the subject peoples collected in the towns, and thus the tendency towards the free industry of the guilds, together with the whole concentration of a nascent Capitalism on the organization of free labour, were at least partly conditioned by the religious ideal of personality and its practical realization in law. In contrast to the Capitalism of the ancient world, the newer Capitalism, with an intensive rural economy, cannot think in terms of slave plantations, of capital investments in State farms; neither is it mainly occupied with the overseas trade which is necessitated by a coast civilization. Rather it is obliged to follow trade and industry within the interior of the country; for this purpose it can only use free labour which can be educated to do work of good quality and may be vitalized by considerations of self-interest. Thus, from the outset, the newer Capitalism is in a totally different position from that of the ancient world; at the same time we may consider that the entirely new tendency of Capitalism towards free labour, and the specifically modern social problem of the relation of free labour (which has no capital) to rational-calculating capital, are affected by the ethical demand for the freedom of the individual.

The possibility that the new civilization with its exalted aspirations might fall back into a social system based on slave labour—a possibility which in itself was always present, and which was practically realized in America—was not excluded, however, merely by the political and economic structure which laid down the lines on which the new Capitalism was to move; rather it was excluded by the fact that this structure itself (alongside of the main reason, namely the influence of the constitution which certainly was endeavouring to secure the economic and finally, also, the legal independence of the unfree) was still in some way or another also conditioned by the work of the Church as she gained the rights of personality for the unfree. The Church never set this up as a legal demand, but in this connection here it always took into account positive law and the effects of the Fall; this, too, was the attitude of the Church right through the Middle Ages towards the slavery which lasted throughout that period. Indirectly, however, and from within outwards, and particularly in securing the position of the family, it seems very probable that

Catholic social philosophy was at least a contributory cause. Moreover, the freedom of the towns and the individualizing of the religious life are obviously linked together as influences which mutually affect each other. To this extent the unique character of modern economic development is still derived from the freedom and the rights of man which the Church proclaimed.[160]

The fact that the results of this Christian social philosophy have had a very dualistic effect is something which this phenomenon has in common with other great historical formations. In any case, Christian thought, down to the present day, has been engaged in the endeavour to remove or to limit the unfavourable results, and at the present time it sees in that one of its main tasks. Catholic social doctrine to-day, in the first place, works precisely along the same lines, and it is only the result of its whole development if—in the attempt to solve these difficult questions which have grown up with and out of its own system of thought— it wavers between the older methods of Patriarchalism and modern methods of an individualistic democratic order of labour; like the whole situation itself, both methods have grown, to a great extent, out of its own development and its own history.

Finally, two general points of view ought not to be overlooked. The social philosophy of the Catholic Church is based upon the idea of the ecclesiastical unity of civilization, and upon the victory of the universal Church over the territorial churches, from which it had taken over the conception of the penetration of the sacred and the secular; over these churches, however, it set up its new ecclesiastical culture and science as a centralizing system of Church law and Church policy. Emphasis has been laid, quite rightly, on the fact that it is only to this circumstance that we owe the unity of European civilization and its cultural foundations in the ancient world and in Christendom. The uniformity of Western civilization was preceded by the uniformity of the Church, and was provided by her with her own means of subsistence.[161] On the other hand, however, the education of the nations of Europe by the powerful unity of the Church means, also, an increasing inwardness and subjectivity of the emotional life, a personalizing of all the relationships of life, which finds its earliest magnificent expression in the time of the Religious Orders in the early Middle Ages, and then rises to a height in the city civilization and in the new Orders which corresponded to that, upon which, however, the unity of the Church was finally shattered.

[160] See p. 430.   [161] See *Ranke: Die Romanisch-germanischen Völker, Einleitung.*

Whatever the Ancient World and the Renaissance may have done for the intensification of individuality, Christianity, which, indeed, always included within itself both Stoicism and Neo-Platonism, has always been the strongest influence of all, and the really permanent attainment of individualism was due to a religious, and not to a secular movement, to the Reformation and not to the Renaissance.

If out of the natural anarchistic individualism of uncivilized humanity there develops the spiritual individualism of the autonomous personality, filled with objective values, and therefore representing an actual value of its own, then this ideal of modern sociological thought—at the same time, however, with all the difficulties which it contains—is an effect, not wholly, it is true, but still very largely, of mediaeval Christianity. Even as the fellowship idea of the "objective spirit" is closely connected with the mediaeval period, so also is the individual idea of "personality".

In the individualistic sect-movements, and, above all, in the Reformation, we shall see this idea break through its ecclesiastical Catholic shell, and more or less renounce the Catholic solution of the problems which it contains.[162]

It is, however, amazingly interesting to observe, that, with this emergence of religious individualism, and with this destruction of the old sociological organism of the sacramental and sacerdotal Church, there arises also anew for the renewed Christian individualism the whole struggle for a sociological organization of its own and for a relation to social conditions; and further, to note how by the removal of the incrustations of the Primitive Church and of the mediaeval hierarchical Church the former task is made extraordinarily difficult, while the latter finally has only become capable of solution by continuing and transforming in its main features the mediaeval solution of the problem.

9. THE ABSOLUTE LAW OF GOD AND OF NATURE, AND THE SECTS

REAPPEARANCE OF THE SECT-MOVEMENT

Before we can proceed to describe the great new developments of the Reformation we must consider the radical complementary

---

[162] See *Thode: Franz von Assisi; Neumann: Byzantinische Kultur und Renaissance-kultur; Brandi: Das Werden der Renaissance, 1908; Arnold Berger: Die Kulturaufgaben der Reformation, 1895.*

phenomenon, which existed alongside of both the Primitive Church and the relatively conservative social theory of mediaeval Christianity, with its recognition and incorporation of the life of the world.

The tendency towards conservatism was prepared by Paulinism, and it was continued in the combination of radical and conservative elements which was achieved in the Thomist social doctrine, in the form of a structure of Christian civilization upon architectonic-evolutionary-historical lines. The opportunity for this was provided by the new social situation which arose in the Middle Ages, while the Neo-Platonic doctrine of the graduated organized structure of the Spirit provided the theoretical method. In this system for the construction of secular social institutions the Stoic-Patristic theory of the *Lex naturae* was continued, but with it was mingled the politics and economics of Aristotle. Under these influences Paulinism was pushed far into the background. Inequality, State development, private property, and the rise of a dominant caste do not belong merely to the relative Natural Law of fallen human nature, but they are rooted already in the Natural Law, and in the Primitive State in general; it is only their particular compulsory form, and the pain which they involve, which they owe simply to the relative Natural Law of fallen humanity. Even alongside of Paulinism, however, there already existed a radicalism which was indifferent and even hostile to the world; it appeared in the form of the love-communism of the Primitive Church and in the Chiliast-Apocalyptic rejection of the world; similarly, Radicalism existed alongside of the social development of the Early Church which carried on the Pauline tradition in the Montanist and Donatist sects, and, above all, in monasticism. Under its influence, and with the aid of the rationalistic-individualistic Stoic doctrine of Natural Law, the great Fathers of the fourth century also proclaimed a Natural Law of communism, freedom and equality, while Augustine proclaimed an aristocratic Natural Law of the dominion of goodness.

The result of the first main section of this book was to bring out the fact that from the very beginning the social doctrines of the Christian Church had a dualistic tendency which caused them to flow in two channels. The strict law of the Scriptures, the radical Law of Nature, monasticism, and the theological theory of the Primitive State there revealed themselves as motives and expressions of a second radical tendency which accompanied the compromise of the Church.[162a]

[162a] See above, *pp. 161–164.*

In the central period of the Middle Ages, however, this second tendency broke forth afresh with extraordinary power. This took place precisely at the moment when the ecclesiastical unity of civilization and its inclusive attitude towards the world had become intellectually complete in Thomism.

In opposition to the modifications of the moral law of Jesus which compromised with the world-order, there arose the strict radicalism of the ethic of the Gospel, wholly directed towards self-conquest and brotherly love; it appealed both to the Divine Law of the Gospel and to the Natural Law of the Primitive State, which also was considered to have had no other ideal save that of holiness and generous love, an ideal which left no room for secular political and economic inequalities and cruelty. Since the Church, in its organization of a universal Christian society and of civilization, allowed no scope for these radical ideas, or, rather, was only able to tolerate them in the form of a special class, serving her own purposes, i.e. in monasticism, these ideals were forced to find a way of development alongside of the Church. The contrast between the radical law of the Scriptures and the way of life of genuine Christians which was measured by this standard, and the ecclesiastical ethic and social doctrine, with its relative and inclusive tendency, led to the formation of sects. Thus it was that the development of the sects alongside of the social doctrine of Thomism, which is the classic epitome of the ecclesiastical ethic, became the second classic form of the social doctrine of Christianity. Thus that element which could not be completely expressed within the ecclesiastical unity of civilization and of Society made a place for itself within the sects, whence it had a reflex influence upon the Church itself.

It is not my purpose at this point to present in detail the history of this development of the sects, which, to some extent, is still most obscure and complicated. This must be left to the detailed researches of ecclesiastical and social historians.[163] But it is absolutely necessary to make clear the general significance of this sect-movement for Christian social doctrine. For this adds a new feature to the presentation of these doctrines, a feature which had been latent from the very beginning, but which only now emerges clearly. When this element is carried over into the modern world it becomes still more important, for only then do we gain a conclusive insight into the sociological character of Christianity.

[163] See p. 431.

SECT-TYPE AND CHURCH-TYPE CONTRASTED

The importance of this element is the fact that at this point, alongside of the Church-type produced by Christianity in its sociological process of self-development, there appears the new type of the sect.

At the outset the actual differences are quite clear. The Church is that type of organization which is overwhelmingly conservative, which to a certain extent accepts the secular order, and dominates the masses; in principle, therefore, it is universal, i.e. it desires to cover the whole life of humanity. The sects, on the other hand, are comparatively small groups; they aspire after personal inward perfection, and they aim at a direct personal fellowship between the members of each group. From the very beginning, therefore, they are forced to organize themselves in small groups, and to renounce the idea of dominating the world. Their attitude towards the world, the State, and Society may be indifferent, tolerant, or hostile, since they have no desire to control and incorporate these forms of social life; on the contrary, they tend to avoid them; their aim is usually either to tolerate their presence alongside of their own body, or even to replace these social institutions by their own society.

Further, both types are in close connection with the actual situation and with the development of Society. The fully developed Church, however, utilizes the State and the ruling classes, and weaves these elements into her own life; she then becomes an integral part of the existing social order; from this standpoint, then, the Church both stabilizes and determines the social order; in so doing, however, she becomes dependent upon the upper classes, and upon their development. The sects, on the other hand, are connected with the lower classes, or at least with those elements in Society which are opposed to the State and to Society; they work upwards from below, and not downwards from above.

Finally, too, both types vary a good deal in their attitude towards the supernatural and transcendent element in Christianity, and also in their view of its system of asceticism. The Church relates the whole of the secular order as a means and a preparation to the supernatural aim of life, and it incorporates genuine asceticism into its structure as one element in this preparation, all under the very definite direction of the Church. The sects refer their members directly to the supernatural aim of life, and in them the individualistic, directly religious character of asceticism, as a means of union with God, is developed more strongly and fully; the attitude of opposition to the world and its powers, to which the secularized Church now also belongs, tends to develop a theoretical and general asceticism. It must, however, be admitted that asceticism in the Church, and in ecclesiastical monasticism, has a different meaning from that of the renunciation of or hostility to the world which characterizes the asceticism of the sects.

The asceticism of the Church is a method of acquiring virtue, and a special high watermark of religious achievement, connected chiefly with the repression of the senses, or expressing itself in special achievements of a peculiar character; otherwise, however, it presupposes the life of the world as the general background, and the contrast of an average morality which is on relatively good terms with the world. Along these lines, therefore, ecclesiastical asceticism is connected with the asceticism of the redemption cults of late antiquity, and with the detachment required for the contemplative life; in any case, it is connected with a moral dualism.

The asceticism of the sects, on the other hand, is merely the simple principle of detachment from the world, and is expressed in the refusal to use the law, to swear in a court of justice, to own property, to exercise dominion over others, or to take part in war. The sects take the Sermon on the Mount as their ideal; they lay stress on the simple but radical opposition of the Kingdom of God to all secular interests and institutions. They practise renunciation only as a means of charity, as the basis of a thoroughgoing communism of love, and, since their rules are equally binding upon all, they do not encourage extravagant and heroic deeds, nor the vicarious heroism of some to make up for the worldliness and average morality of others. The ascetic ideal of the sects consists simply in opposition to the world and to its social institutions, but it is not opposition to the sense-life, nor to the average life of humanity. It is therefore only related with the asceticism of monasticism in so far as the latter also creates special conditions, within which it is possible to lead a life according to the Sermon on the Mount, and in harmony with the ideal of the communism of love. In the main, however, the ascetic ideal of the sects is fundamentally different from that of monasticism, in so far as the latter implies emphasis upon the mortification of the senses, and upon works of supererogation in poverty and obedience for their own sake. In all things the ideal of the sects is essentially not one which aims at the destruction of the sense life and of natural self-feeling, but a union in love which is not affected by the social inequalities and struggles of the world.[163a]

All these differences which actually existed between the late Mediaeval Church and the sects, must have had their foundation in some way or another within the interior structure of the twofold sociological edifice.[164] If, then, in reality both types claim, and rightly claim, a relationship with the Primitive Church, it is clear that the final cause for this dualistic development must lie within primitive Christianity itself. Once this point becomes clear, therefore, it will also shed light upon the whole problem of the sociological understanding of Christianity in general. Since it is only at this point that the difference between the two elements emerges very clearly as a permanent difference, only now have we reached the stage at which it can be discussed. It is also very important to understand this question thoroughly at this stage, since it explains the later developments of Church History, in which the sect stands out ever more clearly alongside of the Church. In the whole previous development of the Church this question was less vital, for during the early centuries the Church itself fluctuated a great deal between the sect and the Church-type; indeed, it only achieved the development of the Church-type with the development of sacerdotal and sacramental doctrine; precisely for that reason, in its process of development up to this time, the Church had only witnessed a sect development alongside of itself to a small extent, and the differences between them and the Church were still not clear. The problem first appears clearly in the opposition between the sacramental-hierarchical Church conception of Augustine and the Donatists. But with the disappearance of African Christianity this opposition also disappeared, and it only reappeared in a decisive form after the completion of the idea of the Church in the Gregorian church reform.

The word "sect", however, gives an erroneous impression. Originally the word was used in a polemical and apologetic sense, and it was used to describe groups which separated themselves from the official Church, while they retained certain fundamental elements of Christian thought; by the very fact, however, that they were outside the corporate life of the ecclesiastical tradition— a position, moreover, which was usually forced upon them— they were regarded as inferior side-issues, one-sided phenomena, exaggerations or abbreviations of ecclesiastical Christianity. That is, naturally, solely the viewpoint of the dominant churches, based

[163a] See p. 432.   [164] See p. 433.

on the belief that the ecclesiastical type alone has any right to exist. Ecclesiastical law within the modern State definitely denotes as "sects" those religious groups which exist alongside of the official privileged State Churches, by law established, groups which the State either does not recognize at all, or, if it does recognize them, grants them fewer rights and privileges than the official State Churches. Such a conception, however, confuses the actual issue. Very often in the so-called "sects" it is precisely the essential elements of the Gospel which are fully expressed; they themselves always appeal to the Gospel and to Primitive Christianity, and accuse the Church of having fallen away from its ideal; these impulses are always those which have been either suppressed or undeveloped in the official churches, of course for good and characteristic reasons, which again are not taken into account by the passionate party polemics of the sects. There can, however, be no doubt about the actual fact: the sects, with their greater independence of the world, and their continual emphasis upon the original ideals of Christianity, often represent in a very direct and characteristic way the essential fundamental ideas of Christianity; to a very great extent they are a most important factor in the study of the development of the sociological consequences of Christian thought. This statement is proved conclusively by all those who make a close study of the sect movements, which were especially numerous in the latter mediaeval period—movements which played their part in the general disintegration of the mediaeval social order. This comes out very clearly in the great works of Sebastian Franck, and especially of Gottfried Arnold, which were written later in defence of the sects.

The main stream of Christian development, however, flows along the channel prepared by the Church-type. The reason for this is clear: the Church-type represents the longing for a universal all-embracing ideal, the desire to control great masses of men, and therefore the urge to dominate the world and civilization in general. Paulinism, in spite of its strongly individualistic and "enthusiastic" features, had already led the way along this line: it desired to conquer the world for Christ; it came to terms with the order of the State by interpreting it as an institution ordained and permitted by God; it accepted the existing order with its professions and its habits and customs. The only union it desired was that which arose out of a common share in the energy of grace which the Body of Christ contained; out of this union the new life ought to spring up naturally from within through the power of the Holy Spirit, thus preparing the way for the speedy coming of the Kingdom of God, as the real universal end of all things. The more that Christendom renounced the life of this supernatural and eschatological fulfilment of its universal ideal, and tried to achieve this end by missionary effort and organization, the more was it forced to make its Divine and Christian character independent of the subjective character and service of believers; henceforth it sought to concentrate all its emphasis upon the objective possession of religious truth and religious power, which were contained in the tradition of Christ, and in the Divine guidance of the Church which fills and penetrates the whole Body. From this objective basis subjective energies could ever flow forth afresh, exerting a renewing influence, but the objective basis did not coincide with these results. Only thus was it possible to have a popular Church at all, and it was only thus that the relative acceptance of the world, the State, of Society, and of the existing culture, which this required, did no harm to the objective foundation. The Divine nature of the Church was retained in its objective basis, and from this centre there welled up continually fresh streams of vital spiritual force. It was the aim of the leaders of the Church to render this basis as objective as possible, by means of tradition, priesthood, and sacrament; to secure in it, objectively, the sociological point of contact; if that were once firmly established the subjective influence of the Church was considered secure; it was only in detail that it could not be controlled. In this way the fundamental religious sense of possessing something Divinely "given" and "redeeming" was ensured, while the universalizing tendency was also made effective, since it established the Church, the organ of Divine grace, in the supreme position of power. When to that was added the Sacrament of Penance, the power of spiritual direction, the law against heretics, and the general supervision of the faith, the Church was then able to gain an inward dominion over the hearts of men.

Under these circumstances, however, the Church found it impossible to avoid making a compromise with the State, with the social order, and with economic conditions, and the Thomist doctrine worked this out in a very able, comprehensive theory, which vigorously maintained the ultimate supernatural orientation of life. In all this it is claimed that the whole is derived, quite logically, from the Gospel; it is clear that this point of view became possible as soon as the Gospel was conceived as a universal way of life, offering redemption to all, whose influence radiates from the knowledge given by the Gospel, coupled with the assurance of salvation given by the Church. It was precisely the development of an objective sociological point of reference, its establishment on a stable basis, and its endeavour to go forward from that point to organize the conquest of the world, which led to this development. It is, however, equally obvious that in so doing the radical individualism of the Gospel, with its urge towards the utmost personal achievement, its radical fellowship of love, uniting all in the most personal centre of life, with its heroic indifference towards the world, the State and civilization, with its mistrust of the spiritual danger of distraction and error inherent in the possession of or the desire for great possessions, has been given a secondary place, or even given up altogether; these features now appear as mere factors within the system; they are no longer ruling principles.

It was precisely this aspect of the Gospel, however, which the sects developed still farther, or, rather, it was this aspect which they were continually re-emphasizing and bringing into fresh prominence. In general, the following are their characteristic features: lay Christianity, personal achievement in ethics and in religion, the radical fellowship of love, religious equality and brotherly love, indifference towards the authority of the State and the ruling classes, dislike of technical law and of the oath, the separation of the religious life from the economic struggle by means of the ideal of poverty and frugality, or occasionally in a charity which becomes communism, the directness of the personal religious relationship, criticism of official spiritual guides and theologians, the appeal to the New Testament and to the Primitive Church. The sociological point of contact, which here forms the starting-point for the growth of the religious community, differs clearly from that upon which the Church has been formed. Whereas the Church assumes the objective concrete holiness of the sacerdotal office, of Apostolic Succession, of the *Depositum fidei* and of the sacraments, and appeals to the extension of the Incarnation which takes place permanently through the priesthood, the sect, on the other hand, appeals to the ever new common performance of the moral demands, which, at bottom, are founded only upon the Law and the Example of Christ. In this, it must be admitted that they are in direct contact with the Teaching of Jesus. Consciously or unconsciously, therefore, this implies a different attitude to the early history of Christianity, and a different conception of Christian doctrine. Scripture history and the history of the Primitive Church are permanent ideals, to be accepted in their literal sense, not the starting-point, historically limited and defined, for the development of the Church. Christ is not the God-Man, eternally at work within the Church, leading it into all Truth, but He is the direct Head of the Church, binding the Church to Himself through His Law in the Scriptures. On the one hand, there is development and compromise, on the other literal obedience and radicalism.

It is this point of view, however, which makes the sects incapable of forming large mass organizations, and limits their development to small groups, united on a basis of personal intimacy; it is also responsible for the necessity for a constant renewal of the ideal, their lack of continuity, their pronounced individualism, and their affinity with all the oppressed and idealistic groups within the lower classes. These also are the groups in which an ardent desire for the improvement of their lot goes hand in hand with a complete ignorance of the complicated conditions of life, in which therefore an idealistic orthodoxy finds no difficulty in expecting to see the world transformed by the purely moral principles of love. In this way the sects gained on the side of intensity in Christian life, but they lost in the spirit of universalism, since they felt obliged to consider the Church as degenerate, and they did not believe that the world could be conquered by human power and effort; that is why they were always forced to adopt eschatological views. On the side of personal Christian piety they score, and they are in closer touch with the radical individualism of the Gospel, but they lose spontaneity and the spirit of grateful surrender to the Divine revelation of grace; they look upon the New Testament as the Law of God, and, in their active realization of personal fellowship in love, they tend towards legalism and an emphasis upon "good works". They gain in specific Christian piety, but they lose spiritual breadth and the power to be receptive, and they thus revise the whole vast process of assimilation which the Church had completed, and which she was able to complete because she had placed personal Christian piety upon an objective basis. The Church emphasizes the idea of Grace and makes it objective; the sect emphasizes and realizes the idea of subjective holiness. In the Scriptures the Church adheres to the source of redemption, whereas the sect adheres to the Law of God and of Christ.

Although this description of the sect-type represents in the main its prevailing sociological characteristics, the distinctive significance of the sect-type contrasted with the Church-type still has a good concrete basis. (There is no need to consider here the particular groups which were founded purely upon dogma; they were indeed rare, and the pantheistic philosophical sects of the

Middle Ages merge almost imperceptibly into sects of the practical religious kind.[165]) In reality, the sects are essentially different from the Church and the churches. The word "sect", however, does not mean that these movements are undeveloped expressions of the Church-type; it stands for an independent sociological type of Christian thought.

The essence of the Church is its objective institutional character. The individual is born into it, and through infant baptism he comes under its miraculous influence. The priesthood and the hierarchy, which hold the keys to the tradition of the Church, to sacramental grace and ecclesiastical jurisdiction, represent the objective treasury of grace, even when the individual priest may happen to be unworthy; this Divine treasure only needs to be set always upon the lampstand and made effective through the sacraments, and it will inevitably do its work by virtue of the miraculous power which the Church contains. The Church means the eternal existence of the God-Man; it is the extension of the Incarnation, the objective organization of miraculous power, from which, by means of the Divine Providential government of the world, subjective results will appear quite naturally. From this point of view compromise with the world, and the connection with the preparatory stages and dispositions which it contained, was possible; for in spite of all individual inadequacy the institution remains holy and Divine, and it contains the promise of its capacity to overcome the world by means of the miraculous power which dwells within it. Universalism, however, also only becomes possible on the basis of this compromise; it means an actual domination of the institution as such, and a believing confidence in its invincible power of inward influence. Personal effort and service, however fully they may be emphasized, even when they go to the limits of extreme legalism, are still only secondary; the main thing is the objective possession of grace and its universally recognized dominion; to everything else these words apply: *et cetera adjicientur vobis*. The one vitally important thing is that every individual should come within the range of the influence of these saving energies of grace; hence the Church is forced to dominate Society, compelling all the members of Society to come under its sphere and influence; but, on the other hand, her stability is entirely unaffected by the fact of the extent to which her influ-

---

[165] For the special character of the mediaeval sects in principle, contrasted with the heresies of the Ancient World which were merely determined by dogma, see *Lechler, I, 42*. It is the nature of an association (*Verein*), *p. 54*. On the Donatist controversy as the original type of the whole sect movement, see *Kawerau, a.a.O.*

ence over all individuals is actually attained. The Church is the great educator of the nations, and like all educators she knows how to allow for various degrees of capacity and maturity, and how to attain her end only by a process of adaptation and compromise.

Compared with this institutional principle of an objective organism, however, the sect is a voluntary community whose members join it of their own free will. The very life of the sect, therefore, depends on actual personal service and co-operation; as an independent member each individual has his part within the fellowship; the bond of union has not been indirectly imparted through the common possession of Divine grace, but it is directly realized in the personal relationships of life. An individual is not born into a sect; he enters it on the basis of conscious conversion; infant baptism, which, indeed, was only introduced at a later date, is almost always a stumbling-block. In the sect spiritual progress does not depend upon the objective impartation of Grace through the Sacrament, but upon individual personal effort; sooner or later, therefore, the sect always criticizes the sacramental idea. This does not mean that the spirit of fellowship is weakened by individualism; indeed, it is strengthened, since each individual proves that he is entitled to membership by the very fact of his services to the fellowship. It is, however, naturally a somewhat limited form of fellowship, and the expenditure of so much effort in the maintenance and exercise of this particular kind of fellowship produces a certain indifference towards other forms of fellowship which are based upon secular interests; on the other hand, all secular interests are drawn into the narrow framework of the sect and tested by its standards, in so far as the sect is able to assimilate these interests at all. Whatever cannot be related to the group of interests controlled by the sect, and by the Scriptural ideal, is rejected and avoided. The sect, therefore, does not educate nations in the mass, but it gathers a select group of the elect, and places it in sharp opposition to the world. In so far as the sect-type maintains Christian universalism at all, like the Gospel, the only form it knows is that of eschatology; this is the reason why it always finally revives the eschatology of the Bible. That also naturally explains the greater tendency of the sect towards "ascetic" life and thought, even though the original ideal of the New Testament had not pointed in that direction. The final activity of the group and of the individual consists precisely in the practical austerity of a purely religious attitude towards life which is not affected by cultural influences. That is, however, a different kind of asceticism, and this is the reason for that difference between it and the asceticism of the Church-type which has already been stated. It is not the heroic special achievement of a special class, restricted by its very nature to particular instances, nor the mortification of the senses in order to further the higher religious life; it is simply detachment from the world, the reduction of worldly pleasure to a minimum, and the highest possible development of fellowship in love; all this is interpreted in the old Scriptural sense. Since the sect-type is rooted in the teaching of Jesus, its asceticism also is that of primitive Christianity and of the Sermon on the Mount, not that of the Church and of the contemplative life; it is narrower and more scrupulous than that of Jesus, but, literally understood, it is still the continuation of the attitude of Jesus towards the world. The concentration on personal effort, and the sociological connection with a practical ideal, makes an extremely exacting claim on individual effort, and avoidance of all other forms of human association. The asceticism of the sect is not an attempt to popularize and universalize an ideal which the Church had prescribed only for special classes and in special circumstances. The Church ideal of asceticism can never be conceived as a universal ethic; it is essentially unique and heroic. The ascetic ideal of the sect, on the contrary, is, as a matter of course, an ideal which is possible to all, and appointed for all, which, according to its conception, united the fellowship instead of dividing it, and according to its content is also capable of a general realization in so far as the circle of the elect is concerned.[165a]

Thus, in reality we are faced with two different sociological types. This is true in spite of the fact (which is quite immaterial) that incidentally in actual practice they may often impinge upon one another. If objections are raised to the terms "Church" and "Sect", and if all sociological groups which are based on and inspired by monotheistic, universalized, religious motives are described (in a terminology which is in itself quite appropriate[165b]) as "Churches", we would then have to make the distinction between institutional churches and voluntary churches. It does not really matter which expression is used. The all-important point is this: that both types are a logical result of the Gospel, and only conjointly do they exhaust the whole range of its socio-

[165a] See p. 435.
[165b] See my treatise: *Religion und Kirche, Preuss. Jahrb., 1895.* It would be an interesting subject of inquiry to find out to what extent the monotheistic universal religions (non-Christian) contain similar differences. It may well be supposed that similar phenomena occur within Islam.

logical influence, and thus also indirectly of its social results, which are always connected with the religious organization.

In reality, the Church does not represent a mere deterioration of the Gospel, however much that may appear to be the case when we contrast its hierarchical organization and its sacramental system with the teaching of Jesus. For wherever the Gospel is conceived as primarily a free gift, as pure grace, and wherever it is offered to us in the picture which faith creates of Christ as a Divine institution, wherever the inner freedom of the Spirit, contrasted with all human effort and organization, is felt to be the spirit of Jesus, and wherever His splendid indifference towards secular matters is felt, in the sense of a spiritual and inner independence, while these secular things are used outwardly, there the institution of the Church may be regarded as a natural continuation and transformation of the Gospel. At the same time, with its unlimited universalism, it still contains the fundamental impulse of the evangelic message; the only difference is that whereas the Gospel had left all questions of possible realization to the miraculous coming of the Kingdom of God, a Church which had to work in a world which was not going to pass away had to organize and arrange matters for itself, and in so doing it was forced into a position of compromise.

On the other hand, the essence of the sect does not consist merely in a one-sided emphasis upon certain vital elements of the Church-type, but it is itself a direct continuation of the idea of the Gospel. Only within it is there a full recognition of the value of radical individualism and of the idea of love; it is the sect alone which instinctively builds up its ideal of fellowship from this point of view, and this is the very reason why it attains such a strong subjective and inward unity, instead of merely external membership in an institution. For the same reason the sect also maintains the original radicalism of the Christian ideal and its hostility towards the world, and it retains the fundamental demand for personal service, which indeed it is also able to regard as a work of grace: in the idea of grace, however, the sect emphasizes the subjective realization and the effects of grace, and not the objective assurance of its presence. The sect does not live on the miracles of the past, nor on the miraculous nature of the institution, but on the constantly renewed miracle of the Presence of Christ, and on the subjective reality of the individual mastery of life.

The starting-point of the Church is the Apostolic Message of the Exalted Christ, and faith in Christ the Redeemer, into which the Gospel has developed; this constitutes its objective treasure, which it makes still more objective in its sacramental-sacerdotal institution. To this extent the Church can trace its descent from Paulinism, which contained the germ of the sacramental idea, which, however, also contained some very unecclesiastical elements in its pneumatic enthusiasm, and in its urgent demand for the personal holiness of the "new creature".

The sect, on the contrary, starts from the teaching and the example of Jesus, from the subjective work of the apostles and the pattern of their life of poverty, and unites the religious individualism preached by the Gospel with the religious fellowship, in which the office of the ministry is not based upon ecclesiastical ordination and tradition, but upon religious service and power, and which therefore can also devolve entirely upon laymen.

The Church administers the sacraments without reference to the personal worthiness of the priests; the sect distrusts the ecclesiastical sacraments, and either permits them to be administered by laymen, or makes them dependent upon the personal character of the celebrant, or even discards them altogether. The individualism of the sect urges it towards the direct intercourse of the individual with God; frequently, therefore, it replaces the ecclesiastical doctrine of the sacraments by the Primitive Christian doctrine of the Spirit and by "enthusiasm". The Church has its priests and its sacraments; it dominates the world and is therefore also dominated by the world. The sect is lay Christianity, independent of the world, and is therefore inclined towards asceticism and mysticism. Both these tendencies are based upon fundamental impulses of the Gospel. The Gospel contains the idea of an objective possession of salvation in the knowledge and revelation of God, and in developing this idea it becomes the Church. It contains, however, also the idea of an absolute personal religion and of an absolute personal fellowship, and in following out this idea it becomes a sect. The teaching of Jesus, which cherishes the expectation of the End of the Age and the Coming of the Kingdom of God, which gathers into one body all who are resolute in their determination to confess Christ before men and to leave the world to its fate, tends to develop the sect-type. The apostolic faith which looks back to a miracle of redemption and to the Person of Jesus, and which lives in the powers of its heavenly Lord: this faith which leans upon something achieved and objective, in which it unites the faithful and allows them to rest, tends to develop the Church-type. Thus the New Testament helps to develop both the Church and the sect; it has done so from the beginning, but the Church had the start, and its great world mission. Only when the objectification of the Church had been developed to its fullest extent* did the sectarian tendency assert itself and react against this excessive objectification. Further, just as the objectification of the Church was achieved in connection with the feudal society of the Early Middle Ages, the reappearance of the tendency to form sects was connected with the social transformation, and the new developments of city-civilization in the central period of the Middle Ages and in its period of decline—with the growth of individualism and the gathering of masses of people in the towns themselves—and with the reflex effect of this city formation upon the rural population and the aristocracy.

The Sect-type and the Law of Nature

Further, this also explains the differing attitude of the Church-type and of the sect-type to the idea of Natural Law, which had already long ago been merged with the Biblical idea of law as a unity which was natural to Christian feeling. The Church proves the rationality and universal validity of her moral law by deriving it from the moral Law of Nature, as it existed in its perfection at the dawn of the creation of humanity, and it is only exalted in the Church through the particular ethic which results from being endowed with the sacramental grace of supernature. But that is only of importance for the theory of apologetics. In practice the Church was unable to carry out that Divine and Natural Law, since it involved universal brotherhood and equality, and the absence of the State, of possessions, law, and the element of compulsion. The Church felt that in this sinful world this law could not be obeyed, and thus a conception of the Christian law in this sense would either condemn the Church to impotence or would drive it to revolution. So the Church decided to make this absolute Natural and Divine Law relative; in fallen humanity it is changed into the relative Natural Law of the order of the State and of Society, whose character of law, power, and force is both a penalty and also a remedy and a means of discipline for sin. The organ of redemption which dominates the world, can, however, adjust itself to this relative Law of Nature, since it incorporates its institutions as preparatory and lower stages, and dominates them in a uniform manner by means of the ecclesiastical central authority. The imperfections which remain are unavoidable, and are the results of the fallen state; they are blotted out by the

* I.e. under Hildebrand.—Translator's Note.

power granted to the Church of the forgiveness of sins, covered by the merits won by the special class of ascetics. Indeed, on the level of scientific theology and ethics the Church had already incorporated the secular social institutions into the absolute Natural Law itself, as a logical inference; the only office it left to the Fall was its transformation into the painful system of violence and compulsion, so that now the State, Society, and possessions all appeared to be directly justified both by God and by Nature.

In direct contrast with that position, however, the sects adopted an entirely different attitude towards Natural Law. They did not base their arguments upon learned patristic or Aristotelian researches into the Law of God, but upon the plain Law of Christ, or the Sermon on the Mount. When they feel it necessary to base this Divine Law more broadly upon a rational and universal foundation, they merely identify it with the Natural Law of the Primitive State, with the pure law of an uncorrupt Nature in which there was neither violence, law, war, the oath, nor private property. The sects rejected compromise with the world, and therefore also relative Natural Law. They had no conception of an architectonic scheme of Society and of the universe, with all the relative elements and gradual evolution which such a conception involves; for them absolute contrasts alone existed. By their appeal to the absolute and pure Law of Nature, however, they gave to their Biblicism a still deeper emphasis, an illuminating reason, and a passionate sentiment.

At the same time this conception of absolute Natural Law permits a good deal of variety of interpretation. It can include human inequality in position, calling, and influence, inequalities which can only be obliterated by love, in a communism of love which gives its all for the good of the whole. It can, however, also mean the equality and the equal rights of all individuals, and then it leads to democratic and communistic ideas. At all events the New Testament Divine Law, and the absolute Law of Nature, are both opposed to existing conditions. The more strongly, however, it is emphasized that these conditions are not only opposed to the Will of God, but also to Nature, the more men feel impelled to attack them, to attempt to reform, to improve, to create something new.

This end, however, can be obtained in various ways. There is the method of pure detachment from the world, and the attempt to realize the ideal in groups of men and women who amid suffering and endurance obey the Law of God. There is the method of peaceful and orderly reform, which desires to influence the authorities in Church and State in the direction of as close an approximation as possible of actual conditions to the ideal: in the case of the Church the ideal is that of poverty, and in the case of the State it is that of peace; if the Church fails to do her duty the method can then be tried of placing the responsibility upon the shoulders of the laity and upon the government of the State, urging them to introduce these reforms by force. Since from the standpoint of this ideal it is easier to reform the Church than the State, and since in order to reform the Church the help of the State is needed into the bargain, this reform on the lines of the absolute Law of Nature and the Scriptural Divine Law is directed by preference against the Church, and it becomes an ecclesiastical revolution. Where, however, the idea is also directed against the unnatural and ungodly conditions within the State and Society, it then develops into a democratic socialistic revolution, which does not shrink from violence, but justifies it by appealing to the Old Testament and to the Apocalypse. At the same time, all these forms of absolute Natural Law which, in one way or another, have thus been shaped, are closely connected with general social movements, or even with political and national movements. Sometimes the impulse comes from the ranks of the oppressed lower classes, who resolve to band themselves together to defend their own existence, and to gain a personal share in religion. Sometimes nationalistic tendencies, friendly to the State, promote the sect ideal, at least within the Church, with the aim of making the relation of the Church to a National State easier; in such instances, however, their ideas of Natural Law usually also colour their ideas of the State. And sometimes it is the social revolution of the later Middle Ages which claims the Law of God and of Nature as its ideal, and desires to set up a Christian order of society by force, for the satisfaction of its own interests.

Further, the fact that the sects swept away the idea of relative Natural Law altogether, substituting for it the idea of the absolute Natural Law which is regarded as identical with the Divine Law of the Bible, produced a number of important religious and theological results, which are typical of the sociological character of the sect-system and of its relation to the Church-system.

First of all, the Divine Law was no longer reduced primarily to the Decalogue, which was replaced by the New Testament, or the really Christian Law of God, the Law of Christ, or the Sermon on the Mount. It had been easy to unite the Decalogue with relative Natural Law, and since in the main the Christian moral law was reduced to the Decalogue, it was in general brought down to the level of that which was practically possible and could be carried out by the mass of mankind. The distinctly Christian element was only introduced by being added artificially to the superstructure, in the requirements of mysticism and ritual, and in the "Evangelical Counsels". The Divine Law of the sects, however, aimed at the specifically Christian element, not so much at the ethical temper of the Sermon on the Mount as at the examples which it gave of this spirit and the proof of this temper required by the New Testament. That certainly limits the New Testament idea, but it still maintains it, in its fundamental tendency, over against the broadening tendency of the Church.

Secondly: the institution by the sect of the absolute Law of God and of Nature as the sole authority, and the consequent removal of the whole idea of stages and of development, involve the most far-reaching consequences. They alter the whole outlook on life and the world, but these consequences were not perceived by the theology of the sects, which was mostly very simple. The relation between God and the world becomes much simpler and more intelligible. The intention and the Law of God are expressed, without a shadow of ambiguity, in the Bible and in the voice of pure Nature alone; this law needs no complicated doctrine. The moral demand is addressed to all men alike; there is no need of a graduation of perfection, according to various vocations. Creation does not descend through various stages, down to materiality, nor does creation thence mount again through stages, like some great work of art, from Nature up to Grace and Supernature. But creation places mankind immediately before the task of the realization of its ideal; and this ideal is here presented shorn of the quality of a mystical supernature, which elevates man's nature above itself.

In the literature of the sects there are no allusions to these things, yet this must have been the influence which caused the whole idea of the cosmic process of development to recede, in order to make room for the sense of a direct relation between God and the creature. On the other hand, this idea does not affect the vocational organization of Society, which is taken for granted in these circles, so long as they avoid communist democratic Socialism. Indeed, Wyclif in particular lays very great stress upon it. His translation of the Bible introduces into general use the word "calling" in its present-day meaning.[165c]

Since these sectarians belonged mainly to the lower classes in the towns, work and professional organization and the love of

[165c] See *Weber: Prot. Ethik., Archiv. XX, p. 40.*

labour seemed natural enough. The only element which has been
discarded is the incorporation into the process of development
from Nature to Supernature. To that must be added the third
element: the strong emphasis upon the idea of law. Catholicism
had for the conception of God two great main definitions: that of
supernatural absolute essence and existence, and that of law,
which governs the world of Nature and of Spirit. In it both these
ideas were not dialectically balanced, but they existed side by
side at the basis of its ideal of human society and of the world of
grace, continually changing and supplementing each other,
filling God's Natural and revealed Law with the redeeming
energy of grace, and in so doing it participates in the mystical
beatitude of infinite supernature. Since, however, in the thought
of the sects a mystical beatitude of this kind as the crown of the
graded structure disappears almost entirely, the conception of
law now becomes dominant; God's Being and Will constitute
His Natural and Revealed Law; the Bible is the Law-book of
revelation, identical with the Law-book of Nature. On the one
hand, this expresses the common character of the previous Christian
development of thought, which had only tried to combine both
these ideas in its conception of God; in the theology of the sects,
however, instinctively the only element which was retained was
the second element, the element of law. On the other hand,
however, it is still only the expression of emphasis upon personal
service, and the importance of the practical idea of morality.
Thus, in the theology of the sects the idea of law is substituted
for the idea of the Church as the organ of Grace and Redemption,
and this conception becomes its central feature. It is this conception of law which constitutes the essential truth and the
objective point of reference of these groups, and, in spite of all their
emphasis upon Grace, and even upon Predestination, this idea
still colours the whole system with a certain legal severity.

Once these main features of the sect-type are quite clear in our
minds, we can then perceive various differences within the
movement, which, owing to an inexact use of the term "sect", are
often thrown together indiscriminately, simply because these
groups have severed their connection with the Church. In the real
sense of the word the sect is a genuine sociological phenomenon—a
most exclusive form of fellowship, only the bond between its
members differs from that which unites the members of an
official Church. This term, therefore, cannot be applied to those
phenomena which contain no element of religious fellowship at
all, and which, at the most, produce changing groups due to

similarity of opinion, or the infection of suggestion. Thus we cannot apply the term "sect" to those purely enthusiastic and purely mystical phenomena in which there emerge the Neo-Platonic elements of the Mediaeval Church, or to those movements which are characterized by an entirely subjective and spontaneous excitement. In these instances we are dealing either with a purely individualistic emphasis upon direct communion with God, which is based upon the Inner Light, and in itself feels no need of fellowship; or with epidemic infections which are based upon the transference of strong passions from one person to another. While the sects base their fellowship objectively on the Revelation of Scripture, on the Law of God, and on its fulfilment controlled by the community, in itself mysticism has no fellowship-principle at all; its only idea of fellowship is intercourse between like-minded souls. Indirectly, however, the sect-type is also important for these phenomena; for as soon as they wish to organize themselves into a community they follow the example of the sect-type. Since the ecclesiastical objectivity of the sacramental institution is entirely excluded from their scheme, they also, in so far as they aspire after a permanent unity, must centre round these two points: a voluntary basis of membership, preserved by strict ethical behaviour. Even in these groups, in spite of their mysticism, and their doctrines of the supernatural Divine Substance, the moral law of Scripture takes the central position, and they build up their fellowship on the idea of Christ as their heavenly Master, their Lawgiver, and their Example, and on the principle of the fulfilment of the Law. The various phenomena then merge into each other: the sect can merge into mystical enthusiasm, and mystical enthusiasm can merge into the sect. But the structural principle itself, so far as it is present and logically worked out, is always derived from the sect-type, from the voluntary church, which always proves the state of grace of its members by practical verification in life and by holiness. When this does not take place these movements break up into casual groups of enthusiasts, who can, it is true, appeal to the enthusiasm of the New Testament, but which again and again, by the New Testament itself, are thrown back upon either the ecclesiastical institutional type or upon the voluntary community of the sect which observes the whole Law of Scripture.

These theoretical and general statements need to be interpreted by the history of the sect-movement; in this, however, I can only report on the researches of others, describing them from the point of view which has just been outlined. In so doing it will become plain that this method of interpretation is no artificial scheme pressed into service from the outside, but an interpretation which has arisen out of sympathy with the phenomena—an interpretation which only illuminates their inner coherence.

The Gregorian Reform and the Sect Movement

The point of departure for the development of the mediaeval sects[166] was the Gregorian reform and revolution within the Church. In both directions its influence was decisive: in the sphere of the development of the Church this influence was direct; in the sphere of sect-formation it was indirect. In this reform movement the canonical and universal Papacy rose against the seigniorial territorial Church in which all the interests of the feudal State were closely united with those of the clergy, and all the tasks and aims of the clergy with those of the feudal State, in which the task of Christianizing the people was in the hands of the great bishops, who were entrusted with all kinds of duties of government. Closely connected by ties of blood and by mutual interests with the nobility, surrounded by large groups of people dependent upon it both politically and economically, supplemented by a monastic system which was also fed by the aristocracy, and, where strictly Christian interests required it, exercising a compulsory reform from above downwards, this Church pressed heavily upon the lower classes and the inferior clergy, especially in France and Italy. In these circles, therefore, there arose a vigorous opposition to the seigniorial Church; in this respect it was the working classes of the towns who were most vocal. Already in the eleventh century in Italy and France these classes, together with the cities themselves, began to play a part, and to usher in the period of the great social movement, characterized by increase in population and the herding together of masses of people in the cities. They hate a Church which treats the inferior clergy like serfs, which exploits the manorial rights through its tithes, which uses the wealth of the Church not for the poor, but for the Church itself, or for the feudal requirements of the higher clergy—a Church which in every respect is the opposite of the poverty of the apostles, and which, in contrast to the Early Church, excludes the congregations from every chance of co-operation.

[166] On this point and the following section, cf. the extremely instructive and comprehensive articles by *Gioacchimo Volpe: Eretici e moti ereticali del XI al XV secolo, nei loro motivi et riferimenti sociali, Rinnovamento, 1907*, for June, August, and October.

Out of these elements Gregory's agitation created the Gregorian demagogy, and made an agreement with it against the autonomous seigniorial Church, while at the same time it was seeking to attain other ends, and was only utilizing the popular agitation for its own purposes. In the Lombard cities, and the so-called Patarini, this is quite obvious. Here the laity rose in passionate struggles against the married clergy, with their simony, and in the infinite confusion which followed, when this order of clergy, banished by the Pope, was prevented from carrying out its functions, and when in every city bishops and priests were fighting against each other, and when there was often no one to conduct a service at all, this lay movement greatly increased. The fact that the Pope decreed that the sacraments and orders of these simonist priests were not valid, meant that the Pope directly encouraged the laity to criticize the priesthood, and this renewed the situation which had prevailed during the struggle with the Donatists. It was inevitable that scepticism about individual priests should lead to scepticism about the office of the priesthood, that the superiority of the layman to the simonist priest should lead to independence of the priest altogether.

In this critical situation the excited laity was ripe to receive the inflammatory influence of an ancient sect, which was, it is true, in its dogma only semi-Christian, but which bore within its organization the sect-type of lay Christianity, and of criticism according to Scriptural and primitive Christian standards. This was the Gnostic-Manichaean sect of the Cathari, which spread from the East along the trade-routes and from the Byzantine enclaves of Italy, and thence pressed forward into the transalpine territories.[167] The more neglectful the feudal Church was in its pastoral care of the congregations under its jurisdiction, the more these congregations must have been inclined to listen attentively to the fiery propaganda of these sectarian apostles, and to note the examplary purity of these apostles in practical life. Their doctrine certainly was only partially Christian; it was a Manichaean dualism, combined with the harshest kind of asceticism based upon metaphysical arguments; it included the doctrine of the transmigration of souls, and it was supported by a Christology, interpreted in the docetic sense, and by the New Testament allegorically interpreted. These doctrines, however, were not the decisive element in the movement; it is even possible that they may have been to a great extent concealed; their main result was

[167] Cf. *Döllinger: Beiträge zur Sektengeschichte des M.A., 1890*, and *Tocco: L'eresia nel ME., 1884.*

to stimulate criticism of the doctrines of the Church, especially those relating to the hierarchy and the sacraments, to lead to a renewed interest in the Bible, and to the reawakening of the spirit of free lay discussion.

The most important aspect of this movement is its sociological side; it emphasized a lay Christianity, and the apostolate of the "perfect", who were poor and abstemious ascetics, who, in place of the ineffective sacraments of the Church, provided an effective confessional and absolution in the *Consolamentum*. This ritual act may seem to be a feeble echo of the institutional Church—(the effectiveness of the *Consolamentum* did not depend upon valid orders, but upon the "perfection" of the celebrant)—but, so far as propaganda was concerned, these *Perfecti* did not play a prominent part, and, in fact, the secret doctrines were often unknown. The effective elements in this movement were the free lay-preaching, the criticism of the Church by the laity, the intimate fellowship of the scattered members, the practical example of poverty, indifference towards the State and the ruling classes, the rejection of the official Church and of its priesthood, the refusal to swear in a court of law, or to have anything to do with the administration of justice, or with force, the abrogation of duties and tithes, the independent study of the Bible, and the habit of testing everything in Church life by the standard of the Primitive Church.

Towards the end of the eleventh century groups of this kind, which had probably already been influenced by the Cathari, spread through Upper and Central Italy, France, Flanders, Holland, and the Rhineland. They produced typical leaders like Peter of Bruys, Henry of Toulouse, Tamchelm the Fleming, Eudo of Stella. The terms in which the sects were described may be fitly applied to them. In Arnold of Brescia, particularly, we can trace clearly the process of transition from the Gregorian partisan and the mystical Dualist to a number of heretical groups which arose out of his ideals.

The further progress of heresy was connected with the rise of new classes and sections of the population, with the release of activity in the lower classes and in the towns. That is why at first they flourished chiefly in the South of France, in Lombardy, and in Italy, where the development of city-life was going forward with great strides. Thus Italy experienced its great period of religious and philosophical awakening, a period which was wedged in between two periods of religious indifference. It was at this time that, quickened by the general interest, the motives of Church and sect came into conflict with each other, and out of this clash of opinions there arose the Waldensians and the Franciscans, Bonaventura and Dante.[167a]

Only then did the Christian movement descend from the heights of aristocracy and of the landed nobility, from Kings and rulers down to the level of the people. The surplus population from the rural districts which came crowding into the towns were now aroused to take their own share in religious and ecclesiastical matters. As the official social theory of the Church—the organization of Society on professional lines—was in the real sense only borrowed from the ideal of the city, so also, on the other hand, the heretical movements also arose out of city-life, and there arose a sense of need for the religious activity of the laity, which had not been satisfied by the monastic reforms and founding of Orders in the eleventh and twelfth centuries (until the Mendicant Orders rose almost all the monks belonged to the rural districts and to the aristocracy). The newly developed activity, which was stimulated by the play of various forces, flowed also into the religious channel, under the dominating force of religious ideas. The result was that the laity began to take a vital part in religious matters, and, more or less under the indirect influence of the groups which have just been described, men sought to find their way afresh in the light of Primitive Christianity and of the Bible.

To some extent at least the Crusades also strengthened the sense of need for such a contact with Primitive Christianity; in part, however, along with other motives, they also arose out of Primitive Christianity itself. The Bible, and the New Testament in particular, had an increasingly wide circulation (especially when we remember that all was still in manuscript), and it was translated into the vernacular.

The vision of a new ideal world arose; gradually, as men gazed, it began to take definite shape before their eyes. And all that men had ever known or desired or imagined about the life of the Early Church was now gathered up in a picture of the most vivid colours: evangelical poverty and apostolic life, the fellowship of believers, and a living share in the Church; the priesthood as a characteristic of the community of believers as such, and almost an emanation from it; all laymen entitled to aid in the administration of the sacraments and to preach freely; a body of clergy content with voluntary gifts, not armed with secular weapons, and not promoters of discord among Christians. And as it is a youthful world of absolute ideas and feelings, many people loved to use startling and passionate expressions to describe it. They

[167a] See p. 436.

felt themselves seized by an irresistible passion to fashion their lives in all particulars according to the doctrine and the life of the Early Church; they believed that every Christian was under the strict obligation to live like the Apostles, i.e. to go through the world preaching the Gospel, and to edify the masses by their practical example.

Finally, like all dreamers and primitive folk (who lack the practical and the historical sense), they believed in the possibility of reforming Christian Society from within outwards, shaping it according to their own ideal, and according to that which had been laid down in Scripture."[168]

All this ferment of new life, however, was only forced into the channel of sect-formation by the Church herself. As soon as the Church felt tolerably sure of her own position, and she perceived the dangers of that connection with the social movement, she severed her connection explicitly with those democratic tendencies which were hostile to the Church which she had previously encouraged. In reality her absolutism was the direct opposite of those tendencies. She now formulated her terrible law against heresy, and drove all who opposed her into the arms of the sects. Above all, that independent lay Christianity was restricted, and the outlet which it still possessed in the ancient canonical election of bishops was closed; especially the right of examination which had been granted to the laity as a defence against simonist priests was withdrawn, and retained only by the Pope and the legates. As the influence of the Princes and the nobles had been withdrawn from the Church, so now the influence of the people was withdrawn. The sacraments again became entirely independent of the moral character of the priests. Laymen were also excluded from any share in the administration of Church property. The priesthood was clearly distinguished from the laity in dress, liturgical language, and way of life. The priests alone were now entitled to preach, and all co-operation of laymen in public services was forbidden. Theology (technically and scholastically) set itself in opposition to all popular literature, and law became a highbrow affair of the jurists.

The financial system which was now necessary for the newly centralized ecclesiastical system emphasized and strengthened the ecclesiastical taxes, and consumed the property of the poor, exactly as the previous seigniorial Church had done. The hated tithe, which could not be delivered to the simonist priests, was now demanded in full by the new Gregorian Church. In contrast

[168] *Volpe, June, pp. 668 ff.*

with the ancient feudal Church and the patristic Church of the Councils, the absolutist Church must have seemed (as, in truth, she was) something quite new. The necessity it felt to attain its ends by developing the whole juridical and political apparatus of a political administration which could interfere in all questions of law and of property, gave to all mystically inclined and interior souls the impression of a rigid externalism and worldliness.

Finally, we must add the chief point: it is clear that the Gregorian Reform was a complete failure so far as reforming the morality of the clergy was concerned. Its claims had aroused a spirit of severe criticism among the laity, but, in the light of this criticism the new body of clergy did not appear very different from that which had preceded it; in fact, the constantly renewed complaints about the clergy probably indicate that it was even worse than the earlier body had been. The absolute Papacy, which was in theory the source and the organization of everything, was now also made practically responsible, and this gave rise to endless criticism of the new system.

THE SECT-MOVEMENT IN SOUTHERN EUROPE: THE WALDENSIANS

The increasing radical movements of lay religion arose out of this hostility between a newly awakened Scriptural and ascetic piety, which itself had helped to build up the Church of the golden Middle Ages, and the result of this reform, and the exclusive attitude of the Church towards these movements, forced them to form themselves into sects. Thus there arose the most important and influential sect of all: the Waldensians. At first this was a Home Mission movement, with popular preaching carried on by missionaries in the apostolic way, who preached in the vulgar tongue, led lives of poverty, went to the least and the poorest among the people, and in everything obeyed the missionary instructions Jesus gave when He sent out the Twelve (Matt. x). When they were prohibited by the Church they became a sect, in which the fundamental idea was that of the religious equality of all believers—women as well as men—and in which, as among the *Cathari*, the Sacrament of Penance was administered by religious ascetics who travelled about from place to place, practising poverty, celibacy, and (in secret) the cure of souls. They threw over the doctrine of Purgatory, and the idea that human behaviour could influence life in Purgatory; they gave up indulgences and the Invocation of the Saints, swearing, fighting, and the shedding of human blood, capital punishment and war; each individual had to stand on his own feet, i.e. upon his own personal achievements and good works, i.e. upon his religious subjectivity. The Waldensian movement soon divided into two sections: the confederation of French nationality, and the more radical confederation of Lombardy, which entirely rejected priesthood and sacrament, ritual splendour and Church order, which linked itself up with the remains of local heresies.

Both groups expanded swiftly; the French "Poor Men of Lyons" confined their efforts to Southern France, while the Lombard movement spread beyond the Alps.[169] In their offshoots they became mingled with alien elements, most of all with that mystical enthusiasm (to which they were originally strangers) which, without the aid of Church or priest, realizes its Christian piety in mystic ecstasies, or with the militant ecstatic movements which were likewise outbreaks of a lay religion, hostile to the Church.

The followers of Ortlieb, the Joachimites, and the Brethren of the Free Spirit here mingled with the Waldensians, and we can trace these effects of a movement among the lower classes down to the beginning of the Hussite movement.[170]

The Franciscans, and other Movements in Italy

The original Franciscan movement was closely related with the Waldensian movement; St. Francis himself was possibly not free from direct Waldensian influences. The Poor Men of Lyons and the Poor Men of Lombardy correspond with the *Poverelli* of St. Francis of Assisi. The Franciscan movement belonged originally to the sect-type of lay religion. Here, however, the Church understood the situation, incorporated the new movement into her system, and made use of it precisely for winning back the endangered city elements of the population to the Church. Even so, however, the Franciscan Order with its lay associate members (Tertiaries) remained to a large extent a stimulus to lay religion, and to a mysticism which was indifferent towards the Church; and in its later struggles there arose in the "Spiritual" Franciscans a vigorous opposition against the ecclesiasticizing of the Order. They preached the ideal of the Primitive Church before Constantine and Sylvester, the ideal of the poor church, and of the apostolic life with service to the poor; their hatred of the hierarchy

---

[169] *Volpe* points out in several places that they spread especially in the circles of the weavers and in the woollen industry, i.e. in the circles in which production through handicrafts and home industries was most widespread, in which ideas of social reform are most at home, or even only in these circles; cf. also *Kautsky: Gesch. d. Sozialismus, p. 103.* [170] *Volpe, pp. 27, 24, 37, October, p. 296 f.*

increased more and more, and they split up into various sects and heresies. "In any case, they represent something new, movements of a democratic character directed towards aims which are both social and religious—*religious* explicitly and consciously, *social* only implicitly and uncertainly (for lack of social experience, and also because at that time even every material need sought to find its satisfaction in a religious transformation)."[171]

Most of these movements originally arose in Italy, which had been shaken by its violent struggles between the Curia and the Empire, the towns and the nobles, the clergy and the lay folk—in Italy where town-life had early begun to develop. Owing to the prevailing conditions, the nobility and the rural population, willingly or unwillingly, were soon also drawn into the heretical movements, which brought a fresh access of strength to heresy.

The watchword of the movement became "the Church"—the Church, that is, reformed in accordance with the Divine Law of the Gospel and the ideal of the Primitive Church—sometimes conceived only as a de-secularized sacerdotal Church, sometimes rather as a lay fellowship—and with this ideal there were combined heretico-mystical influences and apocalyptic prophecies. In the solitude of his monastery the Abbot Joachim, who had returned from the East, wrote his prophecies, in which he proclaimed the third Age, no longer an era of fear and servitude, of labour and of discipline, but an age of the Spirit and of freedom, of peace and absence of violence, of the humble and the poor, without social and class distinctions, without "mine and thine". In all this there emerged clearly the characteristic features of the Divine Law and of the Natural Law in the sense of the absolute Stoic-Christian-social doctrine, free from compromise. Caught up into the unrest of this critical time, these prophecies became a further important ferment within the sect-movement.

Then came the Flagellants, the Soccati, the Apostolic Brethren, the heretical "Spirituals", Fra Dolcino and Gerhard Segalleli. "There are no longer any Religious Orders, the Orders are hated and people do not want to be ruled; they desire the freedom and equality of the Primitive State."[172] "Simplification of life and of religious organization, a passion for the Early Church and a literal interpretation of Holy Scripture, an exact following of the word and teaching of Christ, a complete, and, likewise, a mechanical repetition of the apostolic life—that is, the common foundation upon which the different sects arise, with differences which can be extraordinarily great."[173]

[171] *Volpe, July, p. 26.*   [172] *Volpe, p. 72.*   [173] *Volpe, p. 73 f.*

Such is the great sect-movement of Southern Europe, with its various branches. Its fundamental element was its primitive Christian individualism aroused by the New Testament, breaking out in opposition to the materialized institutional Church, coupled with the co-ordination of individuals into groups for the practical performance of good works, combined with great indifference and hostility towards the world and its institutions of authority and property.

This sect-movement is that typical combination of religious individualism and moral rigorism which characterizes the sect-spirit; the rigorism holds fast to the Sermon on the Mount and the absolute Law of Nature, which indeed is in line with the whole radical Christian tradition, from the time of the Primitive Church and the Religious Orders. In all this the bond of fellowship is solely the "Law of Jesus", literally understood, and the institution, based likewise upon this law, of missionaries and apostles, vowed to poverty, who live only for the fellowship; the latter are often also priests, and are thus in the line of Apostolic Succession, but their qualifications and their influence are still held to be dependent only upon personal moral purity and austerity. The Pauline doctrine is almost entirely obscured by the Law of Jesus.

At the same time the Law of Jesus is conceived as identical with the Law of Nature, in the exact and complete meaning of the term, and as such it is usually thought of in the sense of a far-reaching communism of love, with its corresponding practical charity, and only now and again does it merge into democratic ideas of freedom and equality.

Alongside of these main currents there is also a second quite different element to be considered: that of mystical piety. This piety, which is influenced by Neo-Platonism and Averroism, only had an impulse towards fellowship according to the extent in which it came into touch with Waldensian and Franciscan ideas.

Finally, apocalyptic prophecy played its part in the whole movement. In the sect-movement, which was at first confined to small groups, this apocalyptic element held firmly to Christian universalism, as a miracle to be worked by God in the new age; with which, as the ideals of that new age, there were often combined the ideas of mysticism, freedom, and equality.

In the confusions of the *Trecento* this sect-movement drew Ghibellinism into its net, became entangled with the political situation, lost its original orientation, and finally it died out in all kinds of eccentricities and extravagances, leaving behind only an easily inflamed remnant of apocalyptic ideas. Humanism and the Renaissance, secular politics and the complete victory of the Curia, made an end of it, and since then in Italy and in Southern Europe the ecclesiastical institution has had nothing more to fear from a sectarian Christianity. That is one of the reasons why no movement on the lines of the German Reformation was ever possible in Southern Europe.[174]

WYCLIF AND THE LOLLARDS

In the North, however, in the fourteenth and fifteenth centuries, this Southern sect-movement was followed by a sect-movement which was just as thorough, the movement which centres round the names of Wyclif and Huss.[175] This movement differs from the Italian sect-movement in this respect: its influence was permanent, and, alongside of other movements of a more general character, it did a good deal to prepare the way for Protestantism. The Wyclif movement in particular had a decidedly strong influence in this direction. It also originated in opposition to the Papal absolutism, and its effects upon the political and economic situation both in the country at large and in the local parishes. From the fourteenth century onwards the civil authorities everywhere had begun to resist this ecclesiastical interference, and the English Monarchy had also initiated a very comprehensive policy of secularization. In this question Wyclif was on the side of the Government. Thus, in this instance, the primary motive was not a reaction among the lower orders, but national sentiment and the desire for political independence. The ideal upheld by Wyclif, however, was the ancient ideal of the "poor Church"—with its opposition to the spirit of the "world"—the Church before Sylvester and Constantine, the Church as it was when it was still in harmony with the law of God and with the Gospel. From his point of view a Church of this kind alone is in harmony with the religious ideal, and yet allows for an independent civil order.

Both these ideas, however, the ideal of the "poor Church", and independence of the secular authority, were combined in a theory which seems to me to be peculiar to Wyclif—a theory of Divine Law which had far-reaching implications. It was a very original

[174] On this question see *Volpe, October, p. 296 f.*
[175] On this point cf. *Lechler: J. v. Wiklif* (The first volume deals with Wyclif, and the second with Huss and the other reformers before the Reformation); *Buddensieg: J. Wiklif und seine Zeit, 1885;* on the relation between Wyclif and Huss see *Loserth: Huss und Wyclif. Zur Genesis der Hussitischen Lehre, 1884.* For the conception of the Church see in particular *Gottschick: Huss', Luthers und Zwinglis Lehre von der Kirche, Z. f. Kirch.-Gesch., 1886.*

interpretation of the Patristic teaching combined with Natural Law and Scriptural legalism; from time immemorial this group of ideas had combined the idea of the "poor Church" with that of the absolute Law of God and of Nature blunted by no compromise. Wyclif's new and skilful transformation of this ancient idea betrays the mind of the learned theologian; his movement therefore differed somewhat from Waldensian and Franciscan lay religion, which simply appealed to the Bible.[176] Wyclif opposed the accepted theory that "dominion"—whether spiritual or temporal—was derived from God through intermediaries. He held that the Divine Law of the Gospel (which he also conceived as identical with the Law of Nature) should be understood in this sense: the right to hold property and to wield authority is derived from God direct; this right, however, may only be enjoyed by those who observe God's moral law of love, humility, and self-control; it is a fief which is only granted to the vassal so long as he obeys the law of his lord. However, since the Church does not keep this Law, the State has the right to deprive her of her unlawful possession and to restore the ideal of the "poor Church", which exists solely for spiritual ends. In this theory Wyclif had no intention of attacking the property rights of the secular classes, since it would be impossible for them to disobey God's Law in the way which lay open to the priesthood. He considered that their property was legally connected with their secular functions, whereas the functions of the Church do not require the possession of earthly wealth—indeed, they rather exclude it. The primary aim of this conception of the *Lex Dei* or *Lex Christi* or *Lex Naturae*, obviously coloured by feudal ideas, was simply that of restoring the ideal of the "poor Church", and its radical social implications were not developed to their logical conclusion in the temporal sphere.[177] It is, however, very significant that in this strict conception of the *Lex Dei et Naturae* radical social consequences do emerge over against the whole existing order, even although at first they were only practically applied to Church property; more far-reaching consequences were inevitable. On the other hand, however, the habit of testing the Church by the *Lex Christi* also gradually led Wyclif towards the sect-type, so that in the end his ideas came to resemble those of the Waldensians, and the main features of the Franciscan movement.

From the time the schism broke out it is evident that Wyclif moved farther and farther away from his original ideal, which had been merely patriotic and ecclesiastical, towards a criticism

[176] See p. 437. [177] See p. 438.

of the idea of the Church itself, and to practical efforts on the
same lines, which he deduced likewise from God's Law. To him
the Church was no longer the institutional Church, imperilled by
schism and exploited by the hierarchy, but it is the number of the
elect. It is interesting to observe that it is a learned theologian,
the ornament of Oxford, who is arguing like this; in this theory,
however, there emerges quite definitely, so far as I know for the
first time,[177a] that influence of the idea of Predestination upon
sociological theory, which, at a later date, was to become so important[178] in Calvinism. The only influence of the idea of Predestination which had previously emerged lay in the fact that the
irrationalism of the Christian idea of God was expressed in the
idea of Predestination, and that from that standpoint individualism was determined in the sense of an essential inequality. Now,
however, the tendency of this idea to encourage individualism
appears from another point of view, in which it is interpreted as
the immediacy of the religious relationship, with a disintegrating
effect upon the idea of the Church as the ecclesiastical organ of
salvation. In this theory the idea of Predestination changes that
religious fellowship which is the effect of a centralized and united
hierarchical institution, with an unlimited power of radiating its
energies in every direction, into a strictly limited body of believers,
whose only law is that of the Bible, and who only recognize each
other by the practical ethical proofs of Predestination. The earlier
effect of the idea of Predestination is also clearly visible in Wyclif,
and distinguishes his conception of Christian social reform (as the
means of working out the principle of Predestination) from all
theories of an equalitarian democratic kind. In his teaching,
however, the second aspect of the idea emerges still more clearly,
since Wyclif's main interest lay not in social reform, but in that
which this presupposes, the reform of the Church. His main
emphasis, therefore, lay in the depreciation of the institutional
aspect of the Church, in order to exalt the individual and personal
immediacy of the soul's relationship with God—a relationship
which is the work of God, and not of the Church, and about
whose existence God, and not the Church, decides; he also laid
great emphasis upon the results of this theory in daily life, since
only thus does Predestination become visible, and only thus does
it fulfil its purpose.[179]

[177a] *Bezold*, however, in his book, *Die Lehre von der Volkssouveränität im M.A.*
(*hist. Zeitschrift, 1876*), suggests the names of *Durandus v. Pourçain* and *Lull* as
forerunners (*338 f.*); in their teaching, however, the idea of Predestination is
absent.   [178] See p. 439.   [179] See p. 440.

The practical proof of the truth of these theories ought to be in harmony with the Scriptural Divine Law—that is, it should lead to the spirit of detachment from the world, and from property, to very great strictness of life, and to a spirit of love, which expresses itself in service in every kind of position or calling within Christian Society—a spirit of love which makes everything common property. This, however, is tantamount to proclaiming the laity as the support of the religious community. This is why Wyclif gave the Bible in the vernacular, as the great fundamental law of the fellowship, into the hands of the laity, that they might use it for independent study and for independent criticism of the Church. The priesthood may still exist, but Wyclif would have it turned into a missionary body on the lines laid down in Matt. x, whose members are to wander up and down the country, in poverty and gentleness, proclaiming the Law of God. According to Wyclif, this kind of priesthood would have no character *indelibilis*, and finally even ordination may be omitted; there would be no hierarchy, and no organic-patriarchal system of stages and degrees—above all, no Papal Head. The Lord of the Church, that is of the elect, is Christ alone. This means, however, that the main pillar of the institutional Church has been destroyed, and that nothing has been put in its place. There is no idea of an independent new Church organization, but only of a reformation; there is here no idea of any social order in which State and Church exist side by side; the whole idea is that of an inclusive reform of Christendom, which will affect the State and Society. In all this, however, Wyclif does not visualize Christendom as an objective institutional Church, but as a fellowship of the elect, active in practical matters, guiding itself independently by the Law of the Scriptures, with no need of an objective priesthood, a fellowship which for the moment takes up the task of reform through certain individuals and groups, until the time of the general reformation shall come. That, however, means the dissolution of the institutional Church, and paves the way for the sect-type.[180]

Wyclif finally extended his criticism still farther, and undermined the second chief pillar of the institutional Church, the sacramental idea, even although he did not entirely destroy it. In the doctrine of Transubstantiation he deliberately rejected the central idea of the dominating position of the priest, and made the Eucharist a spiritual pleasure accompanying the physical, in which the priest was only the celebrant but not a miracle-worker.

[180] See p. 440.

He also criticized the other sacraments in the light of the Law of Christ, and discarded the sacraments of Penance, Confirmation, and Extreme Unction. He retained Baptism and the Lord's Supper, the Sacrament of Marriage, which in itself did not actually need a priest at all, and an emasculated form of priestly ordination. As part and parcel of this criticism. It is, of course, obvious that he also rejected the endless consecrations and blessings, pilgrimages, indulgences, fraternities, worship of the saints, pictures and relics, celibacy and the organic organization of the Church.

Wyclif did not undertake a positive organization of the elect, and their formation into an exclusive fellowship or group. He was satisfied, like St. Francis, with the organization of his missionaries, the Lollards. In this respect his ideas failed to come to a head. In them, however, there appear the characteristic effects of a return to the radical Law of the Bible, and to the Law of Nature, and towards an evangelical lay religion. Here, as in all other movements of this kind, this reaction takes the form of the individualism of the sect-type, with its radical detachment from the world—or, at least, a bare minimum of worldly possessions and pleasure combined with the highest possible degree of the communism of love. These views, welded into a coherent theory, then stand out in declared opposition to the institutional conception of the Church, and the ecclesiastical organic social doctrine with its spirit of compromise.

THE HUSSITE MOVEMENT

The Hussite movement was based entirely upon Wyclif's theories, although its development in various directions varied greatly. Huss himself was considerably less "advanced" in his views than Wyclif, but his work produced most radical consequences, combined with some characteristic forms of compromise. This movement developed to their logical conclusion both the radical ideas which were implicit in Wyclif's teaching—a church organization of the sect-type, and a thorough transformation of the general order on radical social lines.

In Bohemia the national opposition between Czechs and Germans, and the criticism of the hierarchy which was involved in the general spirit of hostility, had already led to several religious movements, and sectarian influences also were fairly widespread. Wyclif's ideas were thrown into this ferment; Huss adopted them, and became their prophet. "The Church, the community of the elect, in which the only valid law is the Law of God—the Papacy a mere historical development, and now actually in opposition

to the Divine Law, and thus anti-Christian, all ecclesiastical
authority dependent upon it, if it agrees with this law—everyone
under the obligation to resist false rulers; then the bitter criticism
of the conditions, particularly among the higher clergy and in
monasticism, of the evils wrought by the wealth and the worldly
dominion of the Church; the duty of governments to reform such
evils, the right of the laity to apply the Divine Law, even against
the hierarchy, and to avoid bad priests."[181] For these ideas of
Wyclif Huss died.

His martyr's death, however, kindled a flame which had great
results, both in the sphere of social development and in that of
Church History. For a long time this movement had a revolutionary effect upon the whole of Eastern Europe; it produced the
complete sect-type, and the revolutionary sense of the need to
realize an absolute Christian social order; both these elements
had a deep and enduring influence, which can be traced, possibly,
right down to the Anabaptist movement of the Reformation
period, and into the radical programmes of the Peasants' Wars.

In this revolution we can trace the influence of "evangelical"
ideas in three distinct groups which are characteristically different
from each other; the differences between these groups are significant both in their sociological effects in general, and for the
whole social influence of the Gospel.

The first group, the so-called Calixtines or Utraquists, preserved the conservative leading features of the teaching of Huss;
they became a schismatic institutional Church, which retained
priesthood and sacrament, and which only claimed the Cup for
the laity and the use of the vernacular in worship. They also
demanded that priests should lead a spiritual life according to
the Law of God. They looked to the nobles to fight for them
in order to gain the Reform of the Church, and also to protect
them. Ultimately and quite consistently, in return for certain
concessions, they were reconciled with the Church; severed from
its hierarchy and from Apostolic Succession, they realized that it
was impossible to maintain the institutional conception in the
Catholic sense. They possessed no basis on which they could have
formulated a new institutional conception in place of that of
Catholicism.[182]

The second group was that of the radical Hussites or Taborites,
who were driven by the ecclesiastical ban into armed revolution,

[181] See p. 440.
[182] This has been shown very well by *Gottschick* in his comparison between the
conception of the Church in the teaching of Huss and in Lutheranism.

and who were forced to form an independent organization according to the Law of God. In this group religious opposition was combined with nationalist hatred and the desire for a new national Church; alongside of the aristocracy, which stood for the pure Law of God, there were democratic movements among the peasants and lower classes in the towns. This altered the whole aspect of the movement: "The Divine Law alone is valid; there is none other; every layman has the right to judge and to proclaim both what this law is, and what may be contrary to it. According to this not only are Transubstantiation and the worship of the Host rejected, but also the worship of the saints, and of sacred pictures, the whole mass of ecclesiastical holidays, blessings and consecrations, the oath, Purgatory, and prayers for the dead, confession to a priest and indulgences, the sacraments of Extreme Unction and of Confirmation; in part also the specific difference between priests and laymen, and in any case between the ranks of the clergy. Their priests are not consecrated by bishops, but they are inducted by the congregations; they dispense Baptism and the Lord's Supper in the simplest form, and everywhere without churches and altars, without priestly vestments or liturgy, and all in the Czech tongue."[183]

All this shows very clearly the effects of the evangelical Divine Law, that is, of evangelical individualism, no longer controlled by any institutional idea, an individualism which utterly destroys the whole Catholic dogma of the Church, with all that it involves. Combined with that, however, the Law of God, in the sense of the absolute Law of Nature, and of the radical law of Christ, is applied to the whole of social life, and imposed upon the life of Society, no longer by princes and nobles, but by a community of Christian warriors for God.

This tendency towards violence was new. It could not be justified by appealing to the New Testament and to the Law of Christ, so there was now a reaction to the Old Testament, with its "holy" wars, and the forcible cleansing of Israel by righteous kings. Above all, however, this idea no longer represents Wyclif's conception of a law in which right and might correspond with Christian ethics, and with the loving service of the ruling classes for the whole, but with the Christian Natural Law of democratic freedom and equality. The idea of Predestination ceases to be effective, and the rationalistic-Stoic-Christian doctrine of equality is, as in the Gospel, deduced afresh from the Primitive State and

[183] Here, and below, farther on, I follow the excellent brief summary in *Müller: K.G., II, 44.*

transferred to the present time: "Those who break entirely with the world and with sin have the task of placing a new order alongside of it, which is not erected upon the Family and the State, upon property and dominion, but upon the Christian ideas of the equality of all in possessions and social relations . . . thus an effort is now made to get rid of private property, class distinctions, rates and taxes. The Luxemburg dynasty disappears, and is replaced by the Kingdom of God, i.e. in reality the rule of the sovereign people, which regards itself in all things as the instrument of God. These attempts certainly failed miserably, and the final result of the Revolution was only to strengthen the power of the nobility and to repress the other sections of Society. But the propagandist power of those ideals lived on in the hearts of the people."[184]

Thus in both directions: in the development of the sect-type, as well as in that of individualistic-communistic Christian Socialism—above all, in the proclamation of violence and of a Holy War—the main ideas of Wyclif and of Huss have been left far behind. K. Müller compares this situation, and rightly, with the contrast between the Independents and the Puritans[185]; it is actually an entirely parallel instance: the sectarian and radically social consequent of these ideas strides far ahead of the idea of a Christian society conceived from the standpoint of an ecclesiastical institution, after it had been repressed by the ecclesiastical system with its objective and relative point of view. At this point, therefore, it is relevant to ask: What were the actual concrete causes of these deviations and extremist developments?

Some thinkers regard them as a radical and logical development of the ideas of Wyclif. Others go farther back, and explain the development of this movement into the sect-type from the influence of Waldensian groups, which undoubtedly did exist in Bohemia; it is, however, certain that their influence upon the Taborites cannot actually be proved. Still more difficult and more important is the question of the origin of its equalitarian socialism, and of its revolutionary "right of resistance". That also might quite well be explained from the standpoint of Wyclif's predestinarian-aristocratic theory, although in itself this was an entirely different idea; if the revolutionary implications of this theory had been further developed from the point of view of the restoration of the true aristocracy and of its service of love for the community, the whole idea could easily have been diverted into the channel of radical democracy. In any case, the difference is

[184] K. Müller: K.G., II, 85.   [185] The same, II, 86.

fundamental. Others would find the explanation in Joachimite eschatology, with its ideas of an age of equality and freedom; some suggest the possible effect of early Slav communistic ideas, or of the transformation of the ideas of Wyclif in peasant and urban working-class circles into democracy, or of the effect of that natural communism which a long life in the army, with its constant travel, would produce.[186]

I can offer no opinion upon this problem of origins. All I wish to point out is the positive difference which exists between the equalitarian idea of the Christian Law of Nature, and the evangelical Law of God, which here becomes evident, and the love-communism of the Wyclif ideal of Society (conceived in an aristo-cratic and predestinarian sense), as well as between it and the realistic social philosophy of St. Thomas, which assimilates and subdues natural differences in its organic and patriarchal philo-sophy. In reality, at this point—to some extent indirectly—there emerges the Stoic-rationalist, equalitarian-communist conception of the Primitive State and of the evangelical Law, as it was taught by the great Fathers of the Church in the fourth century; we cannot doubt that there did exist some kind of continuity with Primitive Christian radicalism, even though it is clear that the causes of this Christian revolution were not theoretical ideas, but, in the last resort, practical conditions and social tendencies.[187]

The third group gradually drifted away from the Taborites, and finally formed the body known as the "Moravian Brethren". They upheld the same Wyclif-Franciscan ideal as the Taborites, but they rejected the method of force as un-Christian. Here, then, we see the emergence of the religious association or conventicle, which aims at realizing within its own circle, as far as possible, the ideal of love and holiness; so far as the world outside was concerned its aim was to withdraw from all contact with the State, and with force and secular power, and in a voluntary union to realize the evangelical Law of God, so far as the continu-ance of the world and of its organizations made that possible; in so doing equalitarian socialism was again discarded, and it was replaced by the spirit of the communism of love and practical charity, all of which presupposes private property and a secular calling. This was "the first great attempt of the lay world to realize a religious life which was not based upon a compromise

[186] See p. 441.

[187] The latter point is rightly emphasized by *K. Müller: II, 85,* and *I, 207;* only Müller does not lay stress on the difference between these ideas and the later official conception of the Natural Law taught by the Church, which indeed was very far from being identical with those Patristic doctrines.

with the world, a life which would not be content with formal
consecrations and a semi-morality, but one which took the whole
of life under its wing; it encouraged the withdrawal of earnest
Christians from the dangers of the world into close brotherly
fellowship, exclusive effort after personal holiness, in patience and
renunciation, in absolute peaceableness of spirit and unselfish-
ness."[188] Its founder was a layman, Peter von Chelzic, who refused
to have anything to do with any Wycliffite propaganda which
was supported by violence. Chelzic claimed that all Christians,
and not merely the clergy, ought to withdraw from all the sinful
activity of the world, especially from trade and public life,
with its lust of power and its spirit of compulsion. He held that
Christians ought to occupy themselves with agriculture and with
manual labour, and that when they are unjustly oppressed it is
their duty to suffer but not to resist. At this point Wyclif and Huss
were still nearer to the general doctrine of the Church about the
various degrees within the Church; they had summoned the
secular authority to intervene in order to reform the Church, and
they had regarded Christian Society as one in which Church and
State were both included and united in mutual influence upon
one another. The "Moravian Brethren", on the other hand,
severed the religious community from the State, and created a
society within Society. Thus, when the reform of Society as a
whole seemed an impossible ideal, Christian thought fell back
upon itself, increased the individualism of a merely religious
equality within its own circle, and filled it with the caritative social
ideal. This is a complete return to the social ideal of the Early
Church, after the Christian civilization of the Church had proved
itself to be a secularization and a refraction of Christian morality,
and the attempt to realize the absolute Law of Nature and of
God by violence had proved itself to be a bloody Utopia.

"The Church ought to be poor, without ornaments and ceremonies, without judicature, and free from all connection with
earthly power; its membership should be thoroughly voluntary,
its priesthood without preferment, and unlearnèd; it should serve
the people only by the Word, Prayer, and the Breaking of Bread,
and it should earn its livelihood by the work of its hands."[189]

---

[188] *K. Müller, II, 86.*
[189] *Ibid., II, 151.* When *Müller* adds: "These are the ideal of holiness of the
mediaeval Church, but viewed as the task of the whole community" (*p. 152*)
there ought to be added: "and without the lower and preparatory stage of the
secular morality of the relative Natural Law." In another passage (*Kultur d.
Gegenwart, I, vol. IV, p. 211,* and in the *K.G., II, 30*) the writer has emphasized
this point himself.

So long as there were priests who had entered the community from the Catholic Church the priesthood was no problem; when the good priests died out a bishop had to be consecrated from among the Waldensians, to whom they were closely related. In this retention of Apostolic Succession we see the last relic of the idea of the institutional Church. The discipline and education of individuals are, however, not exercised by the priest, but by the Church itself—a clear sign of the predominance of the sect idea. It should, however, be observed that the members of this sect belonged to the peasantry and the working classes; thus it also represents the affinity between sectarian and radical Christianity, and the outlook, the needs, and the conditions of life of the lower classes with their detachment from the wider world. A social ideal of this kind was only possible from the point of view of the lower orders; at the same time their craving for the realization of personality, by whatever cause it had been awakened, could only be satisfied in religious communities of this kind.

About the year 1500 a new party arose, originating from the upper classes, which protested against this narrow policy, and demanded a more positive attitude towards the world; it claimed the right of entrance into official life in the State, and freedom to swear in a court of law; the whole development closely resembled that which took place when primitive Christianity gradually entered the world of secular occupations. Thus the evolutionary process of these early days was again set in motion. Since, however, this sect was small and narrow, this development did not lead to that relative Christian ethic, which resulted when Christianity took shape as the Church within the ancient world. This sect merely remained a Dissenting body, somewhat more closely adapted to the world than hitherto.

The Hussite movement—the knowledge of which in German research is, indeed, very inadequate, while Czech sources are inaccessible—was certainly, primarily, merely a local movement; its historical influence, however, has been both extensive and profound; above all, its importance as a type for the whole branch of Christian social doctrine under discussion is immense. It displays the emergence of the sect-type out of a development of the ecclesiastical idea, which, under the influence of the Bible and of social conditions, had already strongly emphasized the individualistic and radical-ethical point of view which reduced the right of the world to exist at all to the barest minimum. There is here no idea of asceticism in the monastic sense of "mortification"; the ascetic tendency is expressed only in detachment from the

State, power, law, oath, war, wealth; that should be noticed by those who see in such features only the "Catholic corruption of Christianity into a system of asceticism", and not the continuance of the primitive Christian attitude to life.

Further, it is significant that in this Christian radicalism the peculiarly Christian ideas of love, and the purely religious individualism which includes secular inequality, are partly mingled with, and partly separated from, equalitarian individualism and its communistic-democratic result; it is evident that the latter is not an essentially Christian idea, but a rationalist idea which arose out of Stoicism, caught up by the democratic currents which arose out of the general course of social development; finding itself within an atmosphere impregnated with Christian ideas, it then seeks to justify its existence from the Christian Scriptures.

Finally, it is also characteristic of the Hussite movement that it finds it so difficult to achieve a Christian universalism. The only universalism it knows is the Chiliastic form, which holds that those who have been oppressed in this world will come into their own at the Final Judgment. Whenever this movement tries to exert the universalistic impulse within present conditions, there always arises alongside of that passive form of Christian piety, with its hope in the future life, the more aggressive kind, which believes that the end of the World has already come, and that therefore it is justified in having recourse to violence, which wages the Holy War of the Last Days with the authority of the Scriptural Apocalypse, or encourages revolution, which it justifies by borrowing social ideals and the idea of a "Holy War" from the Old Testament. All these features were repeated in the Anabaptism of the Reformation period, and in English Independency.

PEASANT RISINGS

Out of this complicated tangle of varied influences let us first of all study the equalitarian, and therefore the revolutionary, conception of the Christian Divine and Natural Law. This conception is that rationalistic reinterpretation of the purely religious equality taught by Jesus, which, under the influence of the great Church Fathers of the fourth century, had been completed, at least so far as the doctrine of the Primitive State was concerned, and which, later on, had again disappeared behind the predestinarian doctrine of Augustine and behind the doctrine (borrowed from Aristotle) of an inequality based on Natural Law. In the present state of our knowledge of these questions it is difficult to say what caused the reappearance of this doctrine. We saw that these ideas had already re-emerged in the teaching of Joachim and of Dolcino, in the latter in connection with the Peasant Rising of Val Sesia. These ideas were, naturally, always kept alive by the permanent Patristic tradition, by the democratic and republican elements of the *Corpus juris*, and by the religious theory of equality, which was also continually being renewed in an external social form in monasticism. In detail, of course, it was always in connection with particular events and external stimuli— chiefly democratic tendencies among the peasantry, and in the lower classes in the towns—which caused these ideas to break out and to be utilized to practical advantage. When this took place these ideas then found literary advocates, or rhetorical agitators, who placed at their disposal juridical and theological doctrines, or even ancient traditions of the sects, which then added their contribution to these movements. That such ideas were widespread, and that they were able to count upon general acceptance, is shown by the radicalism with which the famous *Roman de la Rose* (which belongs to the early part of the fourteenth century) proclaims these equalitarian democratic ideals as those of the Primitive State; it does not seem to matter very much that the specific connection with Christianity is lacking, for the Law of the Primitive State is regarded as equally the Christian Law of God.[190] In practice these ideas were expressed in the great Peasant Risings of the later Middle Ages, which are generally based upon the radical democratic equalitarian idea of Natural Law, combined with the ideas of Christian freedom and equality, and with the Law of the Primitive State.

The first cause of these Peasant Risings lay, of course, in the social and economic sphere. Sometimes they were due to the improvement of conditions among the dependent peasantry, which in England inspired the lords of the manor to try to reintroduce by force the state of serfdom, in order to supply their need for servants; sometimes they were due to the exploitation of the peasants through the burdens of war, as in France, sometimes, particularly in Germany, to other complicated conditions into which I cannot enter here. In so doing, however, to a great extent they absorbed the equalitarian and communistic conception of Christian Natural Law and made it their own; I cannot stay to explain how this came about. It is sufficient to know that the equalitarian socialistic democratic conceptions of Natural and Divine Law, as well as the Christian freedom which is based upon them, have not been developed, in any instance, out of

[190] See *von Bezold: Lehre von der Volkssouveränität, p. 340.*

the dialectic of purely Christian thought, but that they have been introduced through political and social revolutions; further, the only support which they find in tradition is in those elements of the Patristic ethic, which have not arisen out of the development of Christian thought itself. Whenever it is felt necessary to realize these ideas by violent methods, and the revolution needs a Christian justification, the Old Testament is always requisitioned in order to buttress the argument.[191]

On the other hand, those groups which arose out of the individualism of the sect-type, and out of the ideal of the subjugation of Society under the world-indifferent radicalism of the other-worldly ethic, and of the ideal of poverty, are far removed from this revolutionary spirit. This is a second form of development from the sect-type, which certainly mingles with the former, yet both these developments ought always to be kept distinct from each other; their relationship is like that of the Taborites and the Moravian Brethren, save that in both cases the peculiar opposition to the Church as such, which characterized the Bohemians, is lacking. Thus those experiments in communism which were made within the smaller exclusive circles of the Beghards and the Beguines, of the Brethren of the Common Life, and similar organizations, ought to be interpreted solely in the secondary sense. These movements were homes of refuge for the helpless and the solitary, for contemplative souls and for outcasts. In particular instances they sometimes became technical associations for production. In their essence, however, they did not represent the idea of a Natural Law which aims at reforming Society, but a group of the ascetic type of the communism of love which lives in detachment from the world. They do their part to revive lay religion and religious individualism, just as the mystics and the so-called pre-Reformation authors of religious tractates had done, but they had no idea of social reform. They correspond to the Primitive Christian type of the communism of love, which was quite harmless from the social and political standpoint.

Finally, however, it is not surprising that this religious individualism and the radicalism of the evangelical Divine law went still farther, extending its influence into the public life of the State and of the Church, and thus into the thought-world of the official institutions by which it was confronted. This was pre-eminently the case in the demand for a poor and purely spiritual Church, which immediately created a new basis for the relation between Church and State; this could not fail to introduce ideas of reform into ecclesiastical and juridical literature, since on all

[191] See p. 442.

hands the reaction had begun to stir against the universal claims of the Papacy.

As we have already seen, the domination of the world by the Church, and its universal guidance of social life, were based upon the fact that when this situation arose no actual State was then in existence; the idea of the State, therefore, was replaced by that of ecclesiastical unity and control; and all this was made possible by the simplicity of the social and economic conditions which then prevailed. When, however, national States arose, and a social life developed which could no longer be dominated and controlled so simply by the ethic of the Church, there then arose the crises of mediaeval Church History, and attempts to discover a new method of organization. The national States felt they must strive to influence the Church organizations within their territory, and in order to do this they proclaimed the power of the rights of the laity within the Church; to some extent, at least, the ideas of the sects were here quite useful, until the method of negotiations and concordats came to be preferred, and the ruling princes shared the ecclesiastical power with the Pope. On the other hand, however, the Church, which had assumed too heavy a burden, and which began to suffer under it, was severely shaken both externally and internally. The representatives of the ecclesiastical interest therefore had to try to create reform; in so doing they had to depend partly upon the laity, partly upon the ideal of the Church vowed to poverty and unworldliness; this led the Church nearer to the sect-ideal, at least in certain directions, until the strengthened centralization of the Church in the Papacy, and the habit of making concordats with ruling princes, practically made a final end of those reforms.

LITERATURE OF POPULAR SOVEREIGNTY

It was the jurists and theologians of the French Kingdom, and, relying upon them, the literary assistants of Louis of Bavaria, and among them again pre-eminently Marsilius of Padua in his famous *Defensor Pacis*, who first desired to attain the peace and reform of Christian Society by securing the authority of the State, and by leading the Church back to the Scriptural condition in which it was before Constantine. Here the resemblance to the early processes of Wyclif's thought is obvious.[192] Here, however,

---

[192] At a later date this analogy was expressed in the most decided fashion by Pope Gregory XI (*Riezler, p. 297*); John of Paris calls his statements "Waldensian", see *Haller: Papsttum und Kirchenreform, I, 1903, p. 74; Keller, pp. 102–113*, claims him for Waldensian influences.

the starting-point for securing the authority of the State is not the idea of a predestined endowment of power, but the general official doctrine of Natural Law. In relation to the State, therefore, the only fresh element is a greater emphasis upon the Natural Law and Aristotelian elements which it had in common with the Thomist theory. Positive law and the institutions of the Government arise from the will of the real legislator, the people, or its representatives; in the exercise of their functions these laws are bound by the will of the people; otherwise they are monarchical, like God's government of the world, that is, so far as they are consonant with reason. These very relative democratic statements only exceed the Thomist doctrine by a still stronger emphasis on Natural Law, and a more democratic conception of the same. On the other hand, however, they are considerably altered by the entirely different position which is now given to the Church in contrast to the State. According to the Divine Law, which here in itself is held to be identical with Natural Law, the Church is exactly like the State, which primarily proceeds from the agreement of all who share in it; the Church, therefore, is primarily identified with the whole body of the faithful, and, according to the special revelation of the Law of God in the Bible, its authority is limited to a purely spiritual dominion, exercised by a priesthood which is to be appointed, that is, to be presented for ordination, by the congregation. Thus it is the congregation which orders, controls and judges its priests. Among themselves the priests are all equal, and the bishops have only accidental privileges, that is, chiefly the right to ordain priests, in which the succession from Christ downwards is maintained.

The Papacy and the hierarchy is a disastrous and purely human institution set up by Constantine; in all cases where spiritual guidance and counsel are needed it should be used under the control of the secular authority. The duty of priests is to dispense the sacraments and to proclaim the call to repentance; in this matter, however, the Sacrament of Penance has merely a declaratory character, and is not "effectual", and the congregation must decide about each particular case. The sole standard is the Divine Law of the Bible; in case of doubt the decision rests in the hands of a General Council composed of all the faithful or of their representatives, to be called together by the secular power, as the representatives of the body of believers. In all secular matters, in legal affairs, and in the law of property the priests are dependent upon the secular authority which determines their number. Priests are called to lead a life of poverty in imitation of

Christ. Their right to inflict punishments, even on heretics, is limited to that of warning and threatening; the secular power will get rid of heretics who are harmful to the community.

The future life alone will see the external realization of the Law of God with its rewards and penalties; in this world the political Natural Law is dominant in the State, and in the Church the Law of God, in the form of the spiritual direction of souls, which, however, may never interfere with the law of the State.

It is clear that in all this the interests of the secular power are the paramount factor, and that the democratic principle of the congregation has been transferred from political Natural Law into the spiritual realm. In spite of the retention of the priesthood and of the sacraments, however, this idea reduces the institutional character of the Church in an amazing way, since the objective sacerdotal institution is changed into a community of the faithful, governing itself according to the Law of God, which, however, owing to the fact that the political power which represents the community everywhere acts in its name, becomes dependent upon the authority of the State. Even though there is here displayed no particular interest in the religious independence of the community, it is still undeniable that this whole theory proceeds out of the atmosphere of individualism, and of the pure Law of Christ, which the Franciscan programme of the "poor Church" and of lay religion diffused around it.[192a]

William of Occam, the second great literary advocate in these conflicts, taught a theory which was more definitely religious, and also more conservative from the ecclesiastical point of view. In his view both the spiritual and the secular authority are the heads of Christian Society, co-ordinated and appointed to work together, in which only in case of need would the Papacy have the right to interfere with a corrupt secular government, or, in the opposite direction, could it be maintained that a secular government would have the right to interfere with a secularized Church authority. The threat against the Franciscan doctrine of Poverty by John XXII, and the formalism of the Church absorbed in questions of policy, seems to him now to be such a case of need, and he calls upon the State and the laity to give their aid in this

---

[192a] On Marsilius and his predecessors see *Riezler: Die literarischen Widersacher der Päpste zur Zeit Ludwigs d. Bayern, 1874*; in my own opinion, *R.* modernizes Marsilius far too much and does not possess a sufficient acquaintance with the vital points in mediaeval social history. For the situation as a whole *Haller: Papsttum und Kirchenreform, I,* is very instructive; see also *K. Köhler: Staatslehre der Vorreformatoren (Jahrbb. f. deutsche Theol., XIX and XX).*

instance, since, finally, membership in the Church is determined
by faith alone, and not by the priesthood. Here again we see the
sectarian result of Franciscan lay religion; although such action
is only proclaimed as a temporary right, it leaves behind it permanent consequences:

"A Pope can err in faith and morals, and even a Council called
by him can err; the only other course to pursue is to call a general
Church Council which is based upon the community principle
and indirect elections, and which also does not exclude the secular
element; ultimately, indeed, women ought not to be excluded;
for in matters of faith there is no difference between priest and
layman nor between man and woman." The emergency law itself
which leads to such radical consequences is based upon the right
of equity, contained within the Law of Nature. St. Thomas had
already laid down that this right, in case of need, should and
ought to secure the fulfilment of the real intentions of the Law of
Nature, and of the Divine Law in opposition to the Positive Law.

Thus here also the individualizing tendency of religion approaches the sect-type, and together with this there arises also the
radical Christian Law of God and of Nature, emphasized sometimes more from the point of view of poverty and love, and
sometimes more from that of the equality of individuals.[192b]

Conciliar Theory of Reform

From the ecclesiastical side this was the legal teaching and
theology of the Conciliar Movement, which undertook to create
out of the ecclesiastical tradition itself a new principle of the
conception of the Church, since the great social Utopia of the
Papal universal civilization and universal dominion began to
decline on account of the result of its own approaching approximate realization.[193]

When the Conciliar Movement shifted the centre of ecclesiastical authority from the Papacy to the bishops and priests, it
did not directly discard the institutional conception; but to the
extent in which it made the laity the supporters of Christianity,
and the judges of the Church, in part, at least, it came very near
to the sect-type; while in the development of a democratic basis

---

[192b] For Occam see *Riezler, 249 ff.*, especially *260–262*. On the influence of
Marsilius and Occam, *ibid.*, *297 f.* The influence of Occam is naturally much
greater than that of *M.* The *Defensor Pacis* was only published in 1522. The
parallels between the Occamist theories and the doctrines of the sects, and
their connection with the theories of the radical minorities, are also emphasized
by *Haller: Papsttum und Kirchenreform, I, 81.*   [193] See p. 443.

it strengthened the individualistic-rationalistic elements of ecclesiastical Natural Law. Since the relative Natural Law of fallen human nature and the rigidity of politico-ecclesiastical organizations were being discarded, men felt the need for an absolute Natural Law. This might be sought either on the lines of Wyclif, in the purely Christian form of the absolute communism of love, and in the sacrifice of the elect, as possessors of right and might, for the whole, or in the rationalistic, individualistic equalitarian form, as it presented itself in the Stoic and Roman-juridical elements of the ecclesiastical intellectual treasure-house.

The whole movement rejected the doctrine of Wyclif without hesitation; all that then remained was the latter course, combined with the ideal of a purified priesthood, purely spiritual, and vowed to poverty, which, however, includes the right of the laity to examine and intervene for the purpose of purifying the Church, whenever the official Church fails in her duty. Lay religion, the Church as a community of believers, a Church characterized by poverty and spirituality, Natural Law: here all these elements are vitally connected with each other.

All this, however, since it could not even imagine in theory the abolition of the real root of the institutional conception in priesthood, sacrament and hierarchy, ultimately only issued in the victory of the hierarchy, which logically incorporates and centralizes the institutional idea; in union with the ruling princes, to whom the hierarchy conceded certain ecclesiastical rights, the hierarchy dealt the Conciliar Movement a fatal blow. But the ideas which had once been set in motion remained effective, and did their part to undermine the Catholic conception of the Church.[194]

Town Civilization and Individualism

Finally, we must not forget that the whole of the later Middle Ages, with the growth of an independent lay civilization in the cities, itself created a powerful competition with the previous world of thought, which had been controlled by the Church and particularly by the priests. Its first effect was naturally to limit the power of the ecclesiastical civilization; that, however, was followed by an increasing disintegration of the objective side of religion in general, as it was expressed in the institutional conception of the Church. It had this effect, almost involuntarily and unconsciously. Just as the development of city civilization in Italy produced sects, so also the later development of the cities in the

[194] See p. 443.

North had in its own way encouraged lay Christianity. The truth of this statement is stamped upon the literature of the later Middle Ages; the most famous example is the *Theologia Germanica*, a book which had a great attraction for Luther and for Protestantism. The popular religious movements of the later Middle Ages also presuppose a loosening of the ties of objective ecclesiasticism.[195]

Through all these movements, however, a sociological type of Christian thought was being developed, which was not the same as that of the sect-type; it was, in fact, a new type—the radical religious individualism of mysticism. This type had no desire for an organized fellowship; all it cared for was freedom for interchange of ideas, a pure fellowship of thought, which indeed only became possible after the invention of printing. In this type, therefore, the *Lex Christi* and the Law of Nature were no longer predominant. The isolated individual, and psychological abstraction and analysis become everything. All that is left of the *Lex Christi* is the example of Christ. This type, however, only attained its universal historical significance in the later Protestant Dissenters, and in their connection with Humanism. Therefore we will not deal with this question in detail until we reach the subject of the pure individualism of the Protestant Dissenters.

All these theories were not merely the logical outcome of thought; they were the result of conditions which had awakened the impulse to transform and re-create social life. Their basis was an actual change in the whole general situation, which alone really destroyed the whole fabric of the mediaeval world. We can only mention this in passing; the whole process has often been described. Political and economic interests freed themselves from the international control of the Church, and from its cramping economic ethic.

The State, which in its real sense was an unknown phenomenon in the Christian unity of civilization in general, arose out of the republican city organizations, out of the growing national feeling among the peoples, and out of the military-dynastic federations between different lands.

A nascent Capitalism, with its monopolies, its practice of credit, its associations for trade, and its home industries, destroys the moderate recognition of natural requirements, which were all that the simple ecclesiastical ethic had known. The transformation of the conditions of life which was involved in the growth of possessions, and in political independence, created a civilization

[195] Cf. *Karl Müller: K.G., II, 154–167; Gothein: Politische und religiöse Volksbewegungen vor der Reformation, 1878.*

of the senses which set aside the ecclesiastical principle of a love of the world which could be combined with religion.

The individualism developed by the Church, and the traditions of Stoicism and Neo-Platonism which she contained, seized on the aesthetic methods of differentiation and training of the personality alongside of methods which are purely religious, and thus bit by bit the inheritance of antiquity was again brought to light as the method of a supplementation and cultivation of individualism, in other than merely religious directions. As this developed the control of the Church declined. Literature, art, and science passed out of the hands of the Church into the hands of the laity. Above all, under these circumstances there arose, alongside of the continual renewals of the idea of the Church—alongside of the subjectivist groups and associations, and alongside of ecclesiastical and religious indifference—that third sociological type of Christian thought, which does not depend, like the Church, upon the institution, nor like the sect on the literal interpretation of the Law of God in the Bible, but which is an individualism which freely combines Christian ideas with all kinds of other elements, and which is either entirely unorganized, or else exists alongside of the Church and assumes its necessity for the mass of mankind. By this time it entered into contact with many humanistic groups, and since it had no sociological organization of its own, it had either no measurable and definite social influence or idea at all, or it created social Utopias, a free mingling of Christian and humanistic elements, literary *tours-de-force*, but not practical attempts at reform. Sir Thomas More's Utopia was the first of a whole series of free idealistic speculations. This type of idealism was to be swept away by the new wave of ecclesiastical life in the sixteenth and the seventeenth century, to return once more with the modern world.[196]

CONCLUSION AND FORECAST

It is only when we take all these factors into account that we can understand the reason for the disintegration of the ecclesiastical civilization. But whatever may have been the influence of these phenomena (which have been often described) in that process of disintegration, the conceptual and intellectual failure in the realm of thought (without which systems which are based on ideas are never really overcome) still proceeds from the disintegration of the essential ecclesiastical fundamental idea, that is, it was due to the influence of the sect-type, in which radical

[196] See p. 444.

individualism and the radical ethic of love combined against the church-type with its relative approval of civilization and the secularization of religious energies.

At the same time, for the whole question before us, it is extremely important to realize the significance of this opposition between these types; it is a great help in understanding not merely the disintegration of the mediaeval Christian unity of civilization, but it throws a great deal of light upon the nature of the Christian social doctrines, independently considered. This fundamental idea, which was expressed at the beginning of this section, has now been illuminated and illustrated, and in so doing its extraordinary significance for the understanding of these things has become clear. At bottom things are extremely simple, if we are willing to see them as they really are.

The Gospel itself presents essentially an ethical and religious ideal of humanity which has certainly very clear-cut social results. But the production of these results it leaves to the miraculous power of God, which, at the coming of the Kingdom of God, will set all things in order. The religious community for worship which arose out of the Gospel orders the life of the community with this future prospect in view. It also takes into account, however, the present situation which has to be endured for a time, and it here adopts a passive but conservative attitude towards existing conditions and organizations within its own circle, merely removing those results of the conditions which were not compatible with the new ethical ideal, so far as that was possible.

The priestly sacramental Church which developed out of this community preserved the absolute character of the Christian ideals in the central organization of the hierarchy, and made its practical standards relative, to the extent of recognizing in the institutions of the State and of Society the obscuring and modification of the Christian Natural Law of the Primitive State, which were rendered necessary by sin. From the attitude of passive toleration, and then of actual acceptance of the "world", the Church moved forward—after the ancient world had passed away—within the setting of the simpler mediaeval conditions of life, to an independent shaping and limitation of the institutions admitted by it to belong to the relative Natural Law, and it establishes in the Papal theocracy the Christian unity of civilization, in which the ethical ideal of the Gospel, with a certain amount of inevitable compromise, was reconciled with the world—and a ladder was created of ethical development, which rose from life in the world to the heights of mystical sanctification and brotherly love.

The Gospel, however, reacted against this materializing and relative tendency, with its radical religious individualism and with its absolute demands, which from the very beginning had never entirely adapted themselves everywhere to the ecclesiastical conservative process of development. In the sect, fellowship is expressed in personal piety and in ethical service, the radicalism of the ethical law of the Gospel was put into practice, and the concessions to relative Natural Law and fallen human nature were rejected. That led directly to the penetrating social consequences of the Gospel as the practical reform of Society, in which all ought to serve the ideal of the independent religious personality, and of unconditional brotherly love.

At first men hoped that this ideal would be realized naturally, as soon as the relative corrupt Church was reformed; then arose the hope of a miraculous Divine intervention and the Chiliastic dream; then, with the appeal to the Old Testament, men took to violence and brought in a Christian communism by force; ultimately these idealists withdrew once more from the world as a religious community which set up the Christian law in the centre of its own life, and tolerated secular institutions as the results of sin and as an alien environment, waiting for their hour of doom to strike.

This development of the Christian social doctrines continues through these contrasts. The Church is the principle of universalism and of Christian civilization, of intellectual freedom, of mobility and power of adaptation, but she binds herself to incarnate her Divine content in dogma and in the priesthood, limits her relative process to an exclusive degree, and claims external and exclusive dominion over the State and over Society, in order to ensure sufficient room for its inward effects of grace.

In so doing the Church was bound up with the general conditions which a theocracy of that kind and an ethic of that kind, which still always severely limited the life of the world, made possible. Since the Church is the freer principle, she is so only because at the same time she is more strictly bound up with the dogmatic-objective and ritual-institutional aspect.

The sect, on the other hand, is the principle of subjective personal truth and unity, and of the evangelical standards without compromise. At the same time the sect renounces universalism, which it can only restore by having recourse to force, which is contrary to all the Gospel standards, or it feels driven to take refuge in eschatology. On the other hand, however, in the sect the individual puts the Gospel into practice, also in its social consequences of radical individualism and of brotherly love, which is not hindered by any attachment to art or science, or indeed to culture in any form. The sect is the more mobile and subjective, the truer and more inward principle, because it is at the same time more exclusive and more powerful, and it is firmly based upon the literal interpretation of the Gospel.

A third type—that of a religious individualism which has no external organization, and which has a very independent attitude, with widely differing views of the central truths of Christianity— only emerges as a foreshadowing of coming developments in this interplay of Church and Sect.

In the modern world Christian social doctrines are in an infinitely difficult situation: on the one hand, Christianity is no longer undivided ecclesiastically, and it yet seeks the free spirituality and adaptability of the Church, without the binding guarantees of ecclesiasticism; while on the other hand, in spite of its position based on subjective conviction and a voluntary theory and vital ethical verification, it still cannot tolerate the radical lack of culture, the "conventicle-like" narrowness which is bound up with the social reform of the sect, and its literal interpretation of the Gospel.

It is neither Church nor sect, and has neither the concrete sanctity of the institution nor the radical connection with the Bible. Combining Christian ideas with a wealth of modern views, deducing social institutions, not from the Fall but from a process of natural development, it has not the fixed limit for concessions and the social power which the Church possesses, but also it does not possess the radicalism and the exclusiveness with which the sect can set aside the State and economics, art and science.

Full of the sense that to-day it still does represent the highest ethical ideals of humanity, it is still unable easily to formulate for itself the unwritten social programme which the Gospel contains, nor to apply it clearly to the conditions which oppose it. Gradually, in the modern world of educated people, the third type has come to predominate. This means, then, that all that is left is voluntary association with like-minded people, which is equally remote both from Church and sect.[197]

Alongside of this type the Churches are working with the ideals of past ages, in which they, as spiritual or actual rulers in the

[197] See p. 445.

State and in Society, were able to direct both according to their view of a Christian universal society.

Alongside of the Churches, however, there are the sects which build up a Christian society in exclusive Pietistic groups, which lead a strictly ethical life in an alien world.

It is only from the history of the Christian social doctrines that it is possible to understand this difficult situation, which is felt by every honest soul.

At this point in our inquiry we have been anticipating. But this anticipatory glance into the future throws a real light upon the whole. For the immediate historical questions also it makes the situation clear.

It explains the disintegration of the later Middle Ages, since in them that divergence of view began to appear. We can perceive also that the new formation of the Reformation which arose out of this great ferment was immediately confronted by this fateful question: Church or Sect?

It has deliberately held firmly to the church-type, and with that to the idea of a unified Christian civilization and a Christian order of Society. In so doing, the churches of the Reformation have preserved a fundamental feature of Catholicism, and to a great extent they have effected this with precisely the same methods which Catholicism had formed for this purpose.

But the sect-type also exerted a certain influence upon the thought of the Reformation, since in the Biblicism of the Reformers the germ of the sect-idea which the Bible contained began to stir and to make its presence felt. It conditioned both the inner tensions of its conception of the Church and of its ethic, as well as the breaking away of purely sectarian and mystical-individualistic groups. The new social doctrines of Protestantism can only be understood when it is realized that they are the direct outcome of the Christian social doctrines which had been developed during the Middle Ages.

NOTES TO CHAPTER II

[80a] (p. 204.) The reason for this defect is that St. Thomas himself developed his social theories in a purely literary scholarly manner from Aristotle, and in a purely ideological moral way out of the requirements of ethics, with a remarkable ignoring of the practical conditions, both political and social, by which he was surrounded—above all, that of the feudal system and the agrarian economy. But in reality this is only an illusion. His whole undertaking presupposes the unity of civilization as it had then become; his fundamental idea is based upon the theory of a social hierarchy, and his Aristotelian Natural-Law theory is actually to a great extent adapted to existing conditions, in connection with which the Law of Nature seems tolerably well adapted to the Christian ideal. All this seems to St. Thomas quite obvious. These obvious matters, however, need to be historically explained. That which is here offered is an attempt in this direction.

[84] (p. 208.) For the eagerness to press into the episcopate, especially on the part of the decurions who belonged to the old and well-to-do families, that is, of the urban officials who were responsible for the assessment, and whose office was compulsory and inherited, see *Löning: Gesch. des deutschen Kirchenrechtes*, I, *1878, pp. 148 ff.* In this way they tried to evade their exacting obligations. In general it was the wealthy classes which were most eager to enter the episcopate (*ibid., p. 152*). In order to combat this tendency, therefore, there were repeated State laws, attempts to limit the number of ecclesiastical offices, instructions to recruit the clergy from the ranks of the monastic orders.

[86] (p. 209.) For the transference of the disciplinary authority from the community to that of the bishop, and its transformation into a verdict passed in the name of God, and its effect on the relation to God and not to the community, see *Löning, I, pp. 254 ff., 265 ff.* Without the Sacrament of Penance there could be no real comprehensive discipline, also the result of the social boycott only gradually became attached to the excommunication by the Church. In Gaul there was the custom of a weekly private confession, with readiness to take over the penitential duties as a method for the spiritual discipline of the population; only then was there laid the foundation of the Sacrament of Penance, the real ecclesiastical method of domination (*Hauck: K.G. Deutschlands*, I, 275, and *Karl Müller: K.G.*, I, *1892, pp. 313–15*).

[87] (p. 212.) For both the last sections cf. (in addition to the third part of the first chapter) the excellent presentation of the subject by *Löning: Gesch. des deutschen Kirchenrechtes, I, 1878*, the first volume of which gives a very clear and able account of the post-Constantine Church. Cf. also in particular *chapter I, pp. 20–102*, and the sections about the share of the bishops in civil life and in the public administration of the law (*pp. 289–331*); a specially uncertain point in the system is the method of electing bishops; the early congregational principle and the new authoritative universal Church principle came into conflict, just as later on the uncertainty which surrounded the papal election before the office of cardinal had been created signified one of the weakest and obscurest points in the sociological system. Illustrations of the work done by the bishops for civilization, and their entry into social and public legal functions, from the Gallic Church in *Hauck: K.G. Deutschlands, I, 131 ff.;* for the opposition of the ascetics to this development (*pp. 76–80*) *Hauck* shows also how casual and external was this entry of the bishops into social and

political work; the real consequence of the Christian idea, as it then came to be felt, is represented by *Salvian, p. 70*, who requires, where possible, through the leaving of all possessions to the Church, the holding of property in common, and otherwise detachment from the world. He has no misgivings about the practicability of carrying out the material aspect of the question, and, on the other hand, this does not mean that the social policy of the bishops is established by granting that the realization of the Christian idea in life means a greater concern for the natural basis of life. On the two classes of bishops in the Gallo-Roman Church, the worldly political kind and the ascetic and genuinely Christian kind, cf. also *Löning, I, 120 ff.*

[87a] (p. 213.) For example, *Seeberg: Lehrbuch der Dogmengeschichte, II, 1898, p. 2*: "The spirit of the Greek Church had no mediaeval period; for it never advanced beyond the problems raised by Origen (?); that is to say, the Greek Church never had any St. Augustine. We can treat the whole mediaeval *D.G.* as the history of Augustinianism." I believe rather that the special character of the Middle Ages in the West in its politico-social development is the decisive factor also for its ethico-spiritual fundamental character. Over against the purely dialectical-ideological conception of the historians of Church and Dogma a little "Marxism" must be permitted here. Augustinianism forms only a specially important method for mastering the problems which arose out of this development, and that only finally in close connection with the help of Aristotelianism, which was quite alien to the thought of Augustine. The task of the following pages is to make this plain.

[89] (p. 218.) On this point cf. *von Schubert: Die Entstehung der Schleswig-Holsteinischen Landeskirche, 1895*, with a very valuable introduction on the significance of the Territorial Church period in Western Catholicism. The second volume of the *Lehrbuch der KG.*, by the same author, I was unfortunately unable to use. *Löning: G. d. deutschen Kirchenrechtes, II, 1878*, contains only the Merovingian Church, which, however, still forms the basis of the whole; here the whole chapter which deals with the public functions of the bishop is of importance (*pp. 220–275*); *Hauck's* magnificent *Kirchengeschichte Deutschlands* contains a remarkable amount of detailed material in the first three volumes. The *KG.* by *Karl Müller, I, 1892*, which lays a great deal of stress on the main features of the institutions, emphasizes the lasting significance of Charlemagne (*p. 353*, and especially *p. 359*): "There remained the union of Church and State, that of the institutions through which Christianity was really able to become the popular religion; and the Church after long centuries of labour was able to reach its goal within its borders. Charlemagne prescribed to the State the great new tasks of humanity, which the Germanic past had not known, and yet he did not essentially enlarge the group of duties which had to be discharged immediately by the State and its officials. For as he had learnt his task from the Church, which in that was to some extent the heir of the ancient Empire, so also he had left the fulfilment of its task in its hands, only placing it at his disposal, while at the same time for the same end he endowed it with a large number of powers in the State. Under his successors the remembrance of both in Church and State disappeared. In course of time the Church laid claim to those tasks and methods which it had disposed of as a Divine institution, and in so doing she set herself against the State. It is characteristic of the beginning of the new (that is, of the modern) day, that the State realizes once more that these ends are its own concern, and that it strives to carry them out in practice by means of its own methods through its own officials." For the continuance of the Carolingian basic ideas until the Gregorian Revolution, see *Hauck, III, 435,*

and even under Heinrich III, *p. 572*; for the canonization of Charlemagne through Barbarossa, see *IV, p. 264*. For the completely similar "interpenetration of Church and State" in England till 1066, see *Böhmer: Kirche und Staat in England, 1890, pp. 48–56.*—A view similar to that of *K. Müller* is taken by *K. Lamprecht: Deutsche Geschichte, II, 1892, p. 48*: "In reality, if we take a bird's-eye view of the closing mediaeval period, we see that it was Charlemagne who achieved the admirable feat of so uniting the interests of the Church and the world that it was only possible to sever this unity after centuries of severe conflict, from the days of Gregory to the time of Luther." *P. 49*: "The significance and importance of Charlemagne, and indeed of the Carolingian State, and of the Carolingian civilization in general, consisted precisely in this: that universally and dispassionately it began to gather up the very varied influences which affected the life of that day, and then began to combine them into that form which became the character of the mediaeval period . . . finally, the Church took over the work of reconciliation, and it is to the credit of Charlemagne that it was he who first of all obliged the Church to take up the position of a mediator in a permanent way." For the continuance of these fundamental features, "of this kind of endosmosis of Church and State" during the reigns of the Ottos, see *pp. 151 ff.*—For the similar conditions in France, which only lagged behind Germany at first, but which, after the unity of France had been effected, outstripped Germany in all cultural matters and finally also in the political sphere, see *Rambaud: Histoire de la civilisation française, I, 1901*, in which a magnificent systematic survey is given of all points affecting the history of civilization.—In this connection also we ought to mention *Uhlhorn's Liebestätigkeit*; Vol. *II* of this work describes the social and economic development of the Middle Ages as the background of Christian thought. *Uhlhorn* emphasizes the fact that Christianity had ceased to be mainly a religion of the town, and that this meant that charity was no longer a specially organized activity of the Church. The work of charity, stimulated in this direction by Charlemagne, became transformed into the social care of the Bishops and Abbots (*p. 61*) for the dependents upon their estates, and in the general service of the Empire, and, further, in the special organization of hospitals with widespread general social functions; the latter organizations then came into the hands of the monks, and also into those of special knightly and burgher Orders for the service of the sick and wounded. At the same time the social activity of the Church, i.e. of the executive authority of the Church, did not cease; it continued, along with the care of tenants and of political dependents, as *Hauck, IV, 52–55,* proves in opposition to *Uhlhorn. Uhlhorn* also emphasizes that fact that it was only in this way that Christianity was able to Christianize Society at all, in contrast with its aloofness from Society in the Roman world (*p. 5*), without, however, analysing the reasons for this change in greater detail; he simply says that the Germans "assimilated Christianity in a deeper way than the Greeks and the Romans could do, who had grown up in the atmosphere of paganism" (*p. 6*). The careful analysis of *Hauck*, however, proves that this cannot in any way be said to be true of the very eudaemonistic and legally coarsened Christianity before the time of St. Bernard. The reasons for this lie in the uncivilized character of the Germans, and in the establishment of the Church as the mediator of civilization through the Carolingian idea of the State.—*Hauck* gives illustrations of episcopal charity of this kind about Bernard of Hildesheim, *III, 396*; similarly, *pp. 410, 414, 438*. A sign of such care is the legal system of the bishop Burchard of Worms, who in the Name of the Trinity, and on a basis of agreement with all the groups under his rule, establishes a civil law and a system of penalties, which is designed, without respect of persons, to give also the poor the benefit of a good and just law (cf. *Gengler: Das Hofrecht des B. Burchard, 1859*). Under the Ottos nine-tenths of all market rights, together with trade rights and rights over the coinage, were in the hands of the bishops (*Lamprecht, IV, 99*). For England, see *Böhmer, p. 55*: "The aim was not only the outward prestige of the Church, but also the control and guidance of all classes of the Christian people" according to the "Law of God". In order to effect this, however, it was not desired to increase the separation between the two, but rather to effect a new and more intimate fusion between Church and State, and the clergy were required to evince as much ardour in carrying out the law of the land as in carrying out the "laws of God". But after the introduction of the monastic reform movement there was a still greater effort to dominate both public and private life with the spirit of religion" (*p. 60*).— This social activity for the public good consisted mainly in the fight against evil and injustice by means of a combined ecclesiastical and secular administration of justice, in the urgent endeavour to secure righteous dealing, in the administration of the civil law, in the establishment of schools, and in the healing of suffering in institutions for the service of the distressed. The real heart of the matter, the prophylactic shaping of political and social conditions, so that evil shall not arise, and which seeks the basis of a morally sound society primarily in a way of life which is sound and healthy from the legal, social, and economic point of view, is lacking. Thought about political and economic questions was still far too undeveloped to be able to see things in this way, and from the very outset there was no idea that all that is ethical and spiritual is dependent upon the nature of the natural basis of life.—The book by *von Eicken (pp. 169–307)* naturally considers this *endosmosis*. But it is precisely here that one sees the forced and untrue character of his presuppositions; he tries to explain dialectically the civilization of the Church directly from the nature of the "ascetic-hierarchical" idea. Hence he does not see in the Carolingian idea of civilization that which it really was: the welding together of secular and sacred interests, from which alone the civilization of the Church could proceed, the compulsion which the State exerted upon the Church in order to make her receive secular and social interests into her own life, but, on the contrary, he regards it from the point of view of a logical development as the first step in the absorption of the life of the world through the dialectic of the priestly ascetic ideal, which subordinates everything to salvation and to the Church. In reality, however, the very opposite was the case! The primary impulse here was given by events and not by theories. *Harnack: Dogmengesch.*, *III, 299*, accepts *Eicken's* arguments in general, but adds very rightly: "The Church, however, only developed her aggressive character after Charlemagne had shown her how the *Vicarius Christi* should reign on earth. Nicolas I learned from Charles I, and the Gregorian Popes learned from Otto I, Henry II, and Henry III, how the *rector ecclesiae* should exercise his office."

[90] (p. 219.) For this adoption of a new idea of the State and of the nature of royalty, cf. the illustrations in *R. W. and A. J. Carlyle: A History of Mediaeval Political Theory, pp. 214 ff.* Hence in the Carolingian period the patristic theories of the State recede, and in their place there arises a far more positive and active idea of the character of the State. At the same time the patristic formulas, when they are used, remain externally the same, but they appear rarely, and they have a new coefficient, until at the time of the Gregorian conflict they again come into frequent use (*p. 198*). Otherwise this idea retains the Stoic-Christian doctrines of the Primitive State and the original universal equality of

humanity, also the position with regard to slavery, the latter, however, is a good deal softened; the practice of enslaving non-Christian prisoners of war continues without question (*Hauck, I, 143, 532, 547; II, 89, 359*). The practice of turning freemen and serfs into slaves raises no scruples from the Christian point of view. All this is held to proceed from the Natural Law of the fallen State, and from the laws which it is the duty of the Christian to obey. To this extent everything was still going on on the old lines. But the rise of the State out of the condition of fallen humanity is regarded much more positively, in accordance with reality, and its Germanic origin, and now absolutely as a direct appointment of God; this point of view is considerably strengthened by the influence of the coronation ceremonies and the consecration of the Emperor. The Old Testament now begins to play its part, with its references to the anointing of David, whereas the Early Church, which regarded these things from the point of view of the New Testament, could only follow Paul in mere toleration of the State. Political social necessities found their justification in the Old Testament when the New Testament failed them (*ibid., pp. 216 ff.*).

⁹⁵ (p. 225.) This represents *Lamprecht's* view of the historical aspect of the subject; *Hauck* deals rather with the personal relations of individual Emperors and Popes, and with the personal qualities of Hildebrand (*III, 616*), with the idealistic glorification of the Papacy which was combined with the position of the Empire (*III, 537*), with the increasing popularity of the demand for the recognition of the Canon Law, which had been depreciated actually in Rome itself by the pre-Cluniac Popes (*III, 563*); he says that Henry III, who repeated Charlemagne's action with the opposite effect, was tragically self-deceived (*III, 542*).

⁹⁸ (p. 226.) Of these three dogmas the first two are usually left to the sphere of Church order and Church History, and the sacraments to the history of worship, by Protestant historians of dogma. *Harnack's* brilliant *History of Dogma*, which still dominates the research on this question, does, it is true, transfer the main emphasis from the sphere of dialectic development to that of psychological explanation. But we need to go farther on this line, and realize that it is precisely the modern sociological research and discoveries which here considerably enlarge the range of psychological conditions for the formation of thought. Church law and ritual need to be included in the history of dogma—at least so far as the Catholic Church is concerned—for in both these spheres there lie the chief roots of dogma. The worship of Christ and the Christian Sacrament of Holy Communion preceded the doctrine of Christ in the Early Church, and to a great extent conditioned it. The same holds good of the law of the Church. A purely intellectual conception of the Faith is much less important than people think. When the churches are studied sociologically, however, it is then precisely that it becomes plain that the cultus provides the real means of unity, and the system of law the form of unity; it is only natural that these fundamental sociological elements should be reflected above all in dogma, and that the purely logical theoretical speculative elements rather accompany the whole system as the special concern and interest of the theological experts. A purely intellectual religion in which worship and Church order are of merely incidental significance only came in with the rise of Protestantism; but Catholicism contains ritual and law as essential, and perhaps indeed as decisive, elements of religion; we shall see later on that the sociological element of cultus and law is developed much less fully within Protestantism. Catholic history of dogma, therefore, includes both these dogmas within its sphere (cf. *Schwane: Dogmengeschichte der mittleren Zeit, 1882*), and unites them with its

doctrine of the sacraments to form its complete ecclesiastical theory. This theory and the doctrine of sin and of grace are then said to constitute the decisive mediaeval promulgation of dogma in general; at the same time both groups are very closely connected, for the doctrine of the sacraments is only another aspect of the doctrine of sin and grace, it is only the doctrine of grace in its concrete form. On the other hand, the great theological and philosophical systems with which the Protestant history of dogma is mainly concerned, are merely attempts to unify and mediate the dogma of the Church, attempts to reconcile it with civilization and culture in general, or reflections upon dogma— in themselves they are not dogma at all. Of the three chief dogmas which have been named, the second, which is the one which gives modern Catholicism the most trouble, is only treated superficially by *Schwane*.

⁹⁹ (p. 229.) Cf. *Döllinger: Das Papsttum, 1892*, who (*p. 37*) says that from the time of the Pseudo-Isidorian Decretals the tendency towards the universal episcopate was the really decisive factor, and therefore lays the main emphasis on the fact that this was a great contrast to the view of the Early Church, and that only by a thorough correction of its traditions could it be shown to be historically correct. There is no doubt about the truth of the latter statement, but there is also no doubt that the Gregorian movement and the Pseudo-Isidorian Decretals also arise out of the very nature of the situation. *Schwane's* position is reconciling as far as possible (*pp. 494–579*) (in this section he presents the development of doctrine until 1215); he deals with the doctrine of St. Thomas (*pp. 539–547*), pointing out that the universal episcopate is, at least in theory, limited by the independent authority of the bishops, which is only directed by the Pope; in practice, however, in spite of this, the ruling authority of the Pope is universal and direct (*p. 542*). The idea of the universal episcopate is fully developed in the *Summa de ecclesia* of *Torquemada, pp. 567–574*. That, however, this was already the meaning of the Gregorian system is dealt with by *Hauck, III, 763–766*; the episcopate is *vicariae dispensationis munus, p. 764*. Cf. also *Hauck, IV, 164*, decision of the second Lateran Synod, 1139, that the Pope invests the bishops with their authority; and the opinion that while a see is vacant the episcopal authority returns to the Pope (*IV, 725*); the explicit declarations of Innocent III and the promulgation of his law book without the co-operation of the bishops, and the characteristic statement: "In tantum apostolicae sedis extenditur autoritas, ut nihil praeter ejus auctoritatem in cunctis ecclesiarum negotiis rationabiliter disponatur", (*IV, 729 ff.*) corresponding changes in the method of electing bishops. On the establishment of the universal episcopate, see also *Karl Müller: KG., I, 561*, and *Mirbt: Publizistik, 559–572*. On the Canon Law as the universal law of Christendom, see *von Eicken, 548–588*, who, however, here also exaggerates when he says that the spiritual law is the only logical form of law from the standpoint of the Church. It was always a question of the law of the State and the law of the Church alongside of each other, which indeed often caused friction. The theologians also emphasize explicitly that in this doctrine first of all there was attained the "unity of society" (*Schwane, 539, 547, 567*). Schwane himself says, *p. 535*: "The . . . history of the Papacy during the earlier part of the Middle Ages is not like the history of other human societies, and cannot be explained mainly from the physical, material, and intellectual energy of their supporters, but it presents the growth of a distinct idea, ever developing more richly, and under special and supernatural control and direction, which was instituted by Christ the Lord and incorporated in St. Peter, but which also lives on in the faith of the whole of Christendom, and in this faith it gains an ever clearer expression."

This is the idea of the priesthood and of the hierarchy. On this point, see *p. 518*: "The constitution is based upon the difference between the clergy and the laity, instituted by Christ Himself, or upon the hierarchy which He has Himself appointed as the support of the teaching, priestly [i.e. sacramental] and pastoral office and authority, since in the Church all the governing and saving power comes not from below, from the people, but from above, from Christ the Lord, and this grace is conferred either through a sacrament, directly from Christ Himself, or through the authoritative statement of the representative appointed by Christ, namely, through the supreme Head of the Church." The stages in the sociological process are quite clear : the mystical Christ, the priest-bishop, the diocesan bishop, the Papal bishop. It is also plain what measure of unification has been attained : the priesthood is based upon the sacraments and comes from Christ, the bishop and the Pope owe their authority to a positive declaration, and their ultimate source of authority is the Apostle-Prince Peter; all that is fully unified is the teaching and governing authority of the Pope, the sacramental authority belongs to the priest in virtue of his ordination, but it is controlled by the authority of the bishop, and he in turn is controlled by the Pope. This, however, is considered a sufficient basis for uniformity; the absorption of the sacramental authority by the Papacy was not necessary, and the complete absorption of the ruling and teaching authority was only attained by the Vatican, although in theory it was always required from the days of Gregory VII.

[100] (p. 231.) For the demand for freedom arising out of the demand for unity see *Hauck: KG., III, 766–769, 804, 835, 838.* In my opinion *Hauck* underestimates the logical necessity of the idea.—This is brilliantly treated by *Gierke: Genossenschaftsrecht, III, 515–545*, and also in a similar manner by *Hoensbroech: Moderner Staat und Römische Kirche, 1906.*—For the acceptance of Gregorianism in England, see the instructive book by *H. Böhmer: Kirche und Staat in England und in der Normandie im 11. und 12. Jahrh., 1899.* " 'Gregorianism' is the view that the Church ought legally to possess full autonomy, and the closely related dogma that the Papacy is divinely called to dominate the world." On the question of continuity he says : "Both meet us first of all within the sphere of the former Frankish Imperial Church. Pseudo-Isidore already demands the full autonomy of the Church, and the subordination of the laity to the clergy as a whole. Benedict Levita had already raised the question of the property rights of the founders and of the possessors of the churches in the property of the Church as a whole, and in Nicholas I there appears for the first time a Pope who desires to be not only the lord of the Church, but also the supreme ruler over all the kingdoms of this world, and who acts in accordance with this claim. Like the theocratic idea, so there arises also at the same time, as a result of the Carolingian Renaissance, also the hierarchical view of the relation between Church and State. But the political upheavals which took place after the ninth century, the attacks of the Normans and of the Saracens, the development of the German monarchy and of the great feudal dominions in France, and the subjection of the Curia to the supremacy of the nobility of Rome, acted as hindrances to the progress of the hierarchy. Only about the middle of the eleventh century were these "intervening authorities" either overcome or weakened, and at the same time the moral power of the hierarchy increased to such an extent that it was able to assert and realize the claims which had never been forgotten since the days of Nicholas I. In Germany this movement was supported by the Saxons and by a revolution among the princes, and in France by the strongly ecclesiastical bent of the ruling classes" (*pp. 1 ff.*). That

already in the Early Church the demand for autonomy produced the idea of theocracy also, but had no practical effect, is brought out by *Löning: Gesch. des deutschen Kirchenrechts, I*, and also above. For the doctrine of St. Thomas, that the secular authority was only indirectly controlled by the Church, through the control of all matters which refer to spiritual interests, see *Jourdain: La philos. de St. Thomas, I, 1854, pp. 423-428*. St. Thomas, however, also lays it down that in case of doubt the Church decides; cf. *De regimine principum, I, 15*, and *von Eicken, 377*.—For the theoretical view that⁴this demand for autonomy, and therefore of sovereignty, belongs to the nature of a religion which is based upon universal principles and truths, in contrast to the more limited cults of the Ancient World, and that such a religion, when it has developed into a church, must produce the demand for the supremacy of the Church and of the priesthood, cf. *K. Rieker: Der Ursprung von Staat und Kirche* in the *Festschrift für Emil Friedberg, 1908*, and *Troeltsch: Religion und Kirche, Preuss. Jahrb., 1895*. At this point modern Catholicism has greatly spiritualized its Church law; cf. *U. Stutz: Die kirchliche Rechtsgeschichte, 1905*. Modern Catholicism is distinguished from that of the Gregorian or mediaeval period by the fact that it renounces all claim to temporal power, and has become a purely spiritual cultural principle of progress; cf. *Ehrhard: Der Katholizismus und das 20. Jahrh., 1902*. But it still insists on the spiritual supremacy of the world, and in order to effect this it will scarcely be able to renounce the use of material methods altogether, at least in questions of education, and of those which affect the Church within the State. The mediaeval supremacy of the Pope was not merely a form of spiritual sovereignty over the world in the midst of widespread barbarism, when such civilization as there was, was most undeveloped, but it was the logical result of the idea which it will scarcely be possible to induce modern Catholicism to give up, as is rightly emphasized by *Hoensbroech*. The political aspect of the Catholic Church, about which so much complaint is made, and which, in its results, is so great a danger to the Church herself, is still the inevitable result of her whole sociological theory. Even in the spiritualized Church-order of the present day the practical result of the idea of the Church is the exercise of influence on the authority of the State through the Catholic democracy, in order that at least in the schools, and in the autonomy of the ecclesiastical administration, Catholic supremacy may be maintained. Even American Catholicism, which seems to be so completely severed from the mediaeval system, still seeks to gain control in municipal affairs, in order that, at least in popular education, it may have the State on its side; cf. *Houtin: L'américanisme*.

[109a] (p. 234.) Cf. *Schwane, 579-643*, whence one understands the central importance of these doctrines of cultus and dogma for the whole system of the ecclesiastical organism, together with the importance of the vast system of apologetics and hair-splitting scholasticism, which is in accordance with the importance of the object. Characteristically Hugo of St. Victor treated the whole of theology from the point of view of the sacraments (*p. 580*). On the continuity of this and the two former dogmas with the idea of the God-Man—that is, with the fundamental doctrine of the Church—see *p. 518*: "The fundamental dogma which has been mentioned (i.e. that of the unity of the hierarchy) is indissolubly connected with another: the dogma of the independence of the Church alongside of and above the State, because she is in herself a society which is self-contained, leading her own independent existence, which is based upon the God-Man as her Foundation and Chief Corner-stone, has charge of all that concerns the spiritual welfare of men, and is called to unite all men

and all nations within her embrace." The means of this dominion are the sacraments, and therefore it is only fitting, and in harmony with the whole idea, that they also, like the God-Man, should be composed of spiritual and sense elements. *P. 583*: "The healing of fallen humanity through the sacraments corresponds both to the physician, who is the Son of God manifest in the flesh, and also to the nature of that which is to be healed, which is composed both of body and soul." Also on *p. 589*: "That the form consists in the words of consecration is very characteristic of the Christian sacraments, because they are thus an image of their founder, the God-Man, in whom the personal Word of God, especially with a visible body, was hypostatically united with human nature." It is the ecclesiastical doctrine of Redemption, which combines very closely together the sacraments, the priesthood, and Christology in a unity of sense elements combined with that which is supersensible; in the East this doctrine developed in the direction of mysticism, while in the West it worked out along the lines of the training of the will, the ennobling of the will, of the impartation of spiritual strength, knowledge of sin, humility, and the control of the will of the individual and its guidance by the Church. Hence it comes to pass that with the Sacrament of Penance there is combined an immensely complicated system of jurisdiction. For the first rough method of jurisdiction, excommunication in the Gregorian sense, which involved a civil boycott as well, see *Döllinger: Papsttum, pp. 53 ff.*; even an unjust sentence of excommunication is greatly to be feared, and one who has been thus treated is not to be received (*p. 54*), according to Urban II and Gratian it is not murder to kill those who have been excommunicated, if it is done out of zeal for the Church (*p. 58*); according to Nicholas I and Gratian everyone who has been excommunicated is a heretic (*p. 59*); in the year 1337 half of Christendom was under sentence of excommunication, the episcopal officials excommunicated 10,000 souls at a sitting; in every parish there were thirty, forty, and even seventy persons excommunicated (*p. 81*); Gregory XI excommunicated into the seventh generation (*p. 82*). For the transition from this system of jurisdiction, which was connected with the penitential practices of the Early Church *in foro externo* into the far more effective system of the Sacrament of Penance, which was connected with confession and the practice of making satisfaction for sin, into the jurisdiction *in foro interno*, see *Loofs: Leitfaden zum Studium der Dogmengeschichte³, 1892, p. 258*. On the turning of absolution into a sacramental priestly act, see *K. Müller: Der Umschwung in der Lehre von der Busse im 12. Jahrh. Theol. Abhh.*, dedicated to *Weizsäcker, 1892*. To what extent this transformation is connected with the hierarchical tendency of the Church is not here examined; I can only venture on a surmise. Cf. also *K. Müller: KG., I, 574 ff.* with the closing sentence: "Otherwise during the Middle Ages among the laity the use of the Sacrament of Penance did not go much beyond the annual obligatory confession, unless there were special circumstances which caused it to be used somewhat oftener" (*p. 576*). The granting of indulgences was, however, connected with the preparatory Sacrament of Penance, and thus the extension of the practice of this sacrament also served to increase greatly the system of indulgences. The practice of penitence and confession was, however, only fully developed during the period of the Counter-Reformation.—On the difficulties and the significance of the doctrine of the sacraments for the final development of the conception of the Church, cf. *Mirbt: Publizität, pp. 424–446*.

[102] (p. 236.) On this international civilization, cf. *Hauck: KG. Deutschlands, III und IV; K. Müller: KG., I, 463–585; H. Reuter: Gesch. Alexanders III und der Kirche*

seiner Zeit, 1860–64; Böhmer: Kirche und Staat in England, pp. 405–411, according to Robert Pullen, *417*, and John of Salisbury, *421–426; Lamprecht: DG., Bd. III und IV; von Eicken: Geschichte und System der mittelalterlichen Weltanschauung, 1887; Rambaud: Hist. de la civilisation française, I, 308–458*. From the point of view of the sovereignty of the Pope, this civilization certainly had a strongly juridical and diplomatic character, which meant that on this side of things the Church was concerned only with the autonomy of the Church, the extension of the ecclesiastical jurisdiction over as many spheres as possible, the supremacy of the Pope in the Church, and the subordination in principle of the secular powers, without the implication that the ruling of the world according to the ethical standards of the Church was the direct motive and the actual effect. This undertaking of the Papal supremacy was bound up, however, with the international tendencies, especially those which emanated from France, the ascetic movements, the centralized developments of the Religious Orders, ecclesiastical law, the universities and theology, and thus this Papal supremacy constitutes at the same time the spiritual-ethical standard of a Christian civilization, and it thus justifies in its own eyes its compulsory methods. Further, it is implied that this supremacy of the Faith and of the Church brings also, as a matter of course, an ethical improvement and a higher standard of life. On the compulsory character of this civilization, see *Döllinger: Papsttum, 114–117; K. Müller: KG., I, 556–559, 588–592*, and, above all, *H. Ch. Lea: A History of the Inquisition of the Middle Ages, New York, 1888*; for the nature of this compulsion, which was not always direct, cf. *H. Reuter: Gesch. der Aufklärung im MA., 1875–77*.—The literary and ideal sources of these cultural ideas were Augustine, Gregory the Great, and Pseudo-Isidore, although to a great extent they were due first of all to the quite definite historical situation. But it would be an error to say, as *von Eicken* does, that this civilization was the direct result of the ideas expressed in the *Civitas Dei* of St. Augustine. In the mind of Augustine the *Civitas Dei* was not a spiritual and temporal unity of civilization; on the contrary, it was conceived as a purely ecclesiastical community, strongly opposed to the State and the interests of the State; indeed, in theory the Church is regarded simply from the point of view of the community of the "elect", and it is only in practice that it becomes identified with the sacramental objective Church. This spiritual point of view has no relation with the world, but alongside of it there is the *Lex Naturae*, which is recognized as the independent principle of the secular values of utility. When Augustine—especially in his writings against the Donatists—requires the consecration of the State by its service to the Church, his aim is essentially to claim the Imperial authority for the support of the Church against pagans and heretics. The name *Civitas Dei*, however, which leads so many to conclude that it means the life of the State organized by the Church (*Lamprecht* has gone very far astray on this point; cf. *DG. I, 307*: "The brilliant structure of a Christian State"!) does not mean this at all. Gregory was the first to take this idea of the *Civitas Dei* and de-spiritualize it, and finally it was identified with the sacramental priestly Church, combined, by means of a semi-Pelagian compromise, with the natural life according to the *Lex Naturae*; otherwise, in the absence of a strong Government, the Church took control of the secular life of the day so far as her own sphere was concerned, but this was not regarded as the duty of the Emperor controlled by the Pope. Cf. *Vossler: Dante, I, 395–400; Loofs: Grundriss des DG., 242–248*. Pseudo-Isidore goes farther, and in order to free the bishops from the authority of their metropolitans the universal monarchy of the Papacy was developed; this, however, does not yet mean the idea of an ecclesiastical civilization, but only the consequence of the development of the sacerdotal Church. This idea of civilization only arose out of the co-operation of the following influences: the new movement in favour of asceticism, the Gregorian constitutional idea and the Romance-Christian culture, the great international Orders, and the uniting of Christian Europe in the struggle against Islam; before this could take place, however, the aversion of Early Christianity to pagan civilization had to be overcome. This took place during the Territorial Church period, when the State was only half-civilized and the Church was comparatively civilized, and in any case far more advanced than the State, and when, in this situation, the Church began to develop still farther her own life and influence in the sphere of general culture. In literature dealing with the Middle Ages, in my opinion, this fact is not sufficiently emphasized, because it forms part of the assumptions of ordinary life; this point of view obtains also in the interpretation of the literature of the Early Church. Thus it can even come to pass that the impression may be created that the Middle Ages did not produce any kind of new ethical doctrine, as *Th. Ziegler: Gesch. d. Ethik, II, pp. 242 and 280*, suggests, whereas in reality the mediaeval period laid a new foundation, and therefore all its doctrines were affected by the changed point of view. For the fact that, although the tradition of the Early Church may seem to have been carried on, the whole world order had changed, see the very pertinent remarks by *Carlyle: Mediaeval Political Theory, I, 197 ff*. *Ziegler's* view, that it is possible to present a study of the mediaeval ethic without taking the concrete setting into account, is an error which has affected his whole work very seriously. It misses the whole point in the situation, and all he can say is to repeat continually the complaint that the Middle Ages were so Roman Catholic.—The rise of the brilliant spiritual world of France, and its union with the international supremacy of the Church, is a further problem of culture and of Church History which has not yet been sufficiently studied. In my opinion this was due in the main to the work of St. Bernard and the Mendicant Orders.

[103] (p. 237.) Thus *von Eicken: Geschichte, u.s.w.*, with certain limitations, also *Harnack: DG., III, 298*: "Christianity is asceticism and the Divine State." "Flight from the world, in the service of the world-dominating Church, and the domination of the world in the service of the renunciation of the world, this was the problem and the ideal of the Middle Ages." *Von Eicken* holds that Christianity itself is a product of the Gnostic-dualistic doctrine of Redemption of the Ancient World, which creates its personal Redeemer in Jewish-Christian Messianism and in the suffering God-Man who raises the world. I believe that in the previous pages of this present work I have made it plain that this is not true of Primitive Christianity on the ethical and social side, and also that this does not apply to the history of dogma. But, even if this point of view were right as a starting-point, it would still be impossible to argue that the Middle Ages as a whole can be interpreted from this standpoint. That a policy of world domination cannot logically be developed out of asceticism, has been felt by *von Eicken* himself, since he combines with asceticism the hierarchy (*p. 133*), which is the logical result, not of asceticism, but of the sacramental idea, and of the priesthood, and since he also admits that the hierarchy had adopted the Roman Imperial idea (*pp. 119 and 156*); the development of theocracy, however, was due entirely to the sociological consequence of the idea of the Church, with its conception of Truth and of the Sacraments; it was only the Papacy in its final form which looked back to the Empire, assisted, no doubt, by the feeling of Italian nationalism, and also by Humanistic ideas. The

defect of the able work of *von Eicken* is (i) that it regards the movement of ideas purely logically as the production of the whole by means of an all-embracing dialectic (cf. *p. 313*), whereas in reality the whole matter, first of all, should be regarded from the psychological point of view as the merging of various elements, which are only partially controlled by the dialectic which proceeds from the individual elements; (ii) that he formulates the fundamental Christian idea as asceticism without regarding the complicated and many-sided nature of the conception, without examining the varied motions and meanings of asceticism, and, above all, without noticing that the supernaturalism of Christian thought is always fused with the Hebrew faith in the Creation, and that in this combination in principle it asserted its own view against the dualism of Gnosticism and asceticism, and, finally, that the tendency to dominate the world which cannot be explained from asceticism itself is explained by the accident of the acceptance of the Roman Imperial idea, whereas it is precisely at this point that the predominating factor is not accident, but the logical result of the whole theory; in fact, the fundamental idea is not asceticism. The statement on *p. 354*: "This vigorous assertion of the interests of earthly existence forced the Church to allow these interests to have a certain amount of scope in economic life, and in the life of the family, and of the State; this was, however, in opposition to the strict logic of the system," is not true at all of the Church herself, and only applies to certain expressions of the ascetics themselves. The doctrine of the *Lex Naturae* (which will be described shortly) and its insertion into Christian thought, is denied by him entirely, especially the teaching of St. Thomas Aquinas, in spite of incidental quotations from his teaching which are never given their right value. A mass of varied quotations from all kinds of books does not assist us to attain an understanding of the mediaeval "world outlook", and, moreover, complaints about the moral corruption of the rulers are no proof of the "Divine State"; there are just as many complaints about the corruption of the Church. In the Christian idea itself, however, it is only the doctrine of Original Sin and the Devil which makes room for mortification; everything else is imported dualism, or religious excitement and exaggeration, or a means and a method for the achieving of religious concentration, as which, indeed, "asceticism" is alone recognized by the theory of the Church, cf. *Zöckler: Kritische Geschichte d. Askese, 1863.*

[106] (p. 241.) For the way in which monasticism became absorbed into the ecclesiastical system, see *Harnack: Gesch. des Mönchtums, p. 41*; numerous examples, first of the conflict between monasticism and the Church in the Gallic Church, then of the systematic subordination of monasticism under the bishops, and finally under the Curia, in *Hauck: K.G. Deutschlands.* The Waldensian and Franciscan movements, which are so closely akin to this whole development, throw a great deal of light upon this subject. For the relation between monks and priests according to Thomas A., see *Grabmann: Zur Lutherbiographie, Hist. Polit. Blätter, 1906, p. 111*: "Under the influence of Pseudo-Dionysius Thomas answers, the question, 'Who is in the state of perfection?' by saying that the bishops and the members of the Religious Orders are in the state of perfection and especially the bishops: the members of the Religious Orders, because through their vows they are under the obligation to be ever striving after perfection, and the bishops because they permanently exercise the pastoral office, and the bishops in particular because they are active in the pursuit of perfection (*perfectores*), while the monks are merely receptive (*perfecti*) (Ps. Dionysius), and because the active principle ranks higher than the

receptive element (*agens* and *patiens*) (Augustine)". . . . But when Thomas compares the position of the members of the Religious Orders with the priestly dignity and the sacerdotal character with reference to perfection, the priest takes precedence over the non-ordained monk. ". . . manifestum est excellere praeeminentiam ordinis quantum ad dignitatem, quia per sacrum ordinem aliquis deputatur ad dignissima ministeria, qui! us ipsi Christo servitur in sacramento altaris; ad quod requiritur major sanctitas interior quam requirat etiam religionis status."

[108] (p. 242.) Cf. *Zeller: Vorträge und Abhandlungen, I, 1865, Der platonische Staat in seiner Bedeutung für die Folgezeit.* The analogy between Christianity and Platonism here reappears from the point of view of the sociological effect of ethical religious thought. The predominance of religious and moral ideas leads to the predominance of the philosophers and priests, and, as soon as a uniform system of civilization shall arise, the supernatural character of the system can only be asserted in the form which will give to the actual religious ideals a definite position, while the secular tasks fall to the share of other classes in Society, but they are placed under the strict control of the religious and ethical ruling element. Because Christianity only developed into a unity of civilization in the Middle Ages, then only did the sociological comparison with Platonism become evident, whereas in the Ancient World, when the Church was confronted by a pagan world, the Stoic categories were called in to help. Here also we see clearly the close affinity which exists between Christianity and Platonism, and therefore the right they have to become more closely connected still. On the other hand, however, I do not think that we can ascribe this similarity to the fact, which *Zeller (p. 75)* seems to think possible, that the Church developed further the Platonist ideas which she absorbed along with various other ideas. The analogy is spontaneous.

[109] (p. 243.) For the idea of the organism with its mutual vicarious services, cf. *Uhlhorn: Liebestätigkeit, II, 96, 137, 255, 269*; here, for example, with reference to the sick: "Sufferers are in their own way as much justified as others; they form a class of their own, which is just as necessary for the whole, and serves the whole just as much as other classes in Society", namely, through vicarious sufferings and through the opportunity which they give to others to exercise mercy and charity to them. *Böhmer: Kirche und Staat*, according to Robert Pullen, *p. 419*: "As representatives of God, prelates take the highest rank in the universal human society which includes both the State and the Church, and they are, therefore, called to rule over both the other sections of Christendom, the monks and the layfolk." For the question of mutual oblations of a vicarious character in the attaining of merits, and in penitence within this system, see *Schwane: Dogmengeschichte, pp. 668–674*, especially *p. 669*: "Prayer, fasting, and almsgiving are very special ways of offering satisfaction, because their exercise requires a struggle against the senses, and therefore to some extent it is something irksome which is opposed to natural human desires. . . . If men are by nature members of a family, sanctified Christians are much more intimately bound together with all other Christians as members of the Body of Christ, so that both the good and the evil in an individual affect all the others. . . ." In this sense also the performances of the monks are to be understood; they are a vicarious realization of the ideal, through intercession and vicarious oblations; cf. *Grabmann: a.a.O., 104*. "That in such Contemplative Orders the spirit of the love of one's neighbour is increased, and that the prayer of intercession and the life of sacrifice practised in such monasteries is the Christian love of one's neighbour, can here only be suggested."—For the

division, and yet the unity, which under these circumstances is maintained, of the Christian ideal of perfection, see *Denifle: Luther und Luthertum*[2], *I, i, 133–181*, especially *179*: "The perfection of the Christian life consists precisely in this: that that commandment (of the love of God and one's neighbour) should be fulfilled as perfectly as possible, that is, so far as this is possible within the conditions of this earthly existence, and within the various classes and sections of Society." This is opposed by *Scheel* in his explanation of the translation of Luther's work *De votis monasticis, Luthers Werke, Ergänzungsband II, Berlin, 1905; Grabmann* again is opposed to *Scheel*, cf. his book: *Das christliche Lebensideal nach Thomas, Hist. Polit. Blätter, 1906, pp. 1–27, 89–114*, and *N. Paulus: Zu Luthers Schrift über die Mönchsgelübde, Hist. Jahrb. d. Görres-Gesellschaft, 1906, pp. 487–516.* We do not need to concern ourselves further with this controversial literature. From the purely historical point of view Catholic scholars are in any case right when they assert that the supposed uniformity of the life-ideal which Protestantism expects is not required by the official Catholic theory at all, that, however, in spite of this the Catholic theory does preserve the spirit of uniformity, and that it certainly does not regard asceticism as the only ideal of perfection. See *Grabmann, pp. 101 ff.*: "The fundamental error of the Protestants is this, that they have a totally wrong conception of the uniformity of the ideal of life. If we are dealing with the question of the uniformity of the Christian ideal of life we mean an essential unity, but not one which can be measured in a mechanical way (i.e. in a way which is the same for each individual). Within the specifically unified life-ideal it is possible to have a great deal of variety. But these differences and degrees do not mean that there is any real difference in the nature of the ideal itself. These forms of realization of the ideal again have their counterpart in Heaven (even Dante's Paradise knew ordered grades and degrees of bliss). Through obedience and chastity, or rather through the spirit of loving surrender to God which lies behind these virtues, the members of the Religious Orders have means at their disposal which enable them to reach a certain stage in the specific uniform life-ideal. But this does not mean that people living in the world cannot reach, by other means, exactly the same stage of perfection." *P. 99:* "The fact that the members of the Religious Orders are obliged by their vows to strive after perfection does not mean that other Christians are not under the obligation to strive after perfection also, since it is a familiar fact that it is possible to take a vow to do something to which one is already committed by the natural course of events. The pursuit of perfection is for every Christian not a matter of free choice but a duty. Both monks and nuns and lay people have to strive after perfection, only the Religious have a clearer path to follow." "The universal ideal is the love of God and man, but the ways of realizing this ideal are different. Asceticism is a specially advantageous method, only *accidentialiter* perfection consists in the Evangelical Counsels." "Although the monastic life is described as the 'better part', according to all the rules of logic it does not follow that the laity belong to a worse, or at least to an inferior, class (!) It does not even follow that the monastic life is the best for all" (*p. 100*). We must also note that these writers at the same time naturally admit the existence of numerous "unilluminated" ascetics and ascetic writers, that a class which is endowed with special means of attaining perfection only has meaning when it is part of a system which has other complementary aspects, and that the advantage of a method of perfection which, by its very nature cannot, and should not, be utilized by all, represents the difficulty of Christian supernaturalism in relation to secular values, and especially the fact that they are absolutely opposed by real asceticism. But it is right to assert that in this contradiction Catholicism ought not to be nailed down to the merely ascetic side of the contradiction, as though this were the only logical aspect of the problem. Catholicism is made up of the most heterogeneous elements (cf. *Harnack: Mission, p. 225*), as such great structures always will be. Thus we can only accept with great reserve Harnack's pronouncement in his *Mönchtum, p. 46*, that in the ascetic revival movements after Cluny within the Church there could be only one life-ideal and one ethic, that to this ideal all mature Christians, i.e. the clergy, were committed. Examples of the equal importance of secular morality in *Hauck, IV, 98 ff.*

110 (p. 245.) Cf. *Harnack: Mönchtum DG., III*, the sections on the *Geschichte der Frömmigkeit, 296–306 and 364–491*; *Vossler: Dante, I, 80–99*; *K. Müller: KG., I, 745–480*; for the eschatological and eudaemonistic motives for asceticism as merit and as penitence during the whole of the earlier period of the Middle Ages, see *Uhlhorn: Liebestätigkeit, II, 122, 158; Böhmer: Staat und Kirche, p. 38; Hauck: KG., II, 246, III, 346;* Charlemagne and monasticism, *II, 566, III, 342;* greater rigidity in the Roman asceticism, *IV, 320 ff.* For the period of St. Bernard the best authorities are still *Neander: Der h. Bernhard und sein Zeitalter², 1848,* and *Liebner: Hugo v. St. Viktor, 1832.* If we come to these works fresh from the customary view of "asceticism" of the Middle Ages, it is amazing to note how little ascetic or monastic these people are; the points they emphasize chiefly are the cultivation of the spiritual life, edification, knowledge of humanity, and self-knowledge, the awakening of the religious spirit, and along with that there goes a strong emphasis upon charity, which must take precedence of the joys of contemplation, and which assumes that the special calling of the monastic orders is to render service to the world; at the same time the secular way of life is not attacked, but it is assumed that it will be used in the true religious spirit; cf. *Neander, 41*: "The love to Christ which refers to the purely human element in Him, which Bernard regards as a stage from which the soul will gradually advance to the love of God for His own sake, which will include within it the love to all that is true and good." It is along this line that a mysticism heightened by asceticism can finally attain the religious transfiguration of the world and of humanity, as we see most plainly in St. Francis of Assisi. Or cf. *Neander, 46,* who is quoting St. Bernard: "As it is the purpose of the whole creation to glorify God, so this also is the aim of religious development: to will everything only for the sake of God. Such a spirit really means deification. Yet here below man can only live on these heights for isolated moments", that is, the deification of the secular sphere on earth only fails because the religious element has not sufficient force to penetrate it permanently. *P. 50:* "To him asceticism is a means, not an end." *P. 55:* "He began from the Christian point of view, that on account of the various standpoints and needs of humanity there must be various different forms and ways of living within the Church, without allowing this in any way to cause division, since the different members are united to each other through love. He here regards the different Orders (and their ascetic way of life), not as something in itself meritorious, but as a means of healing the various sicknesses of humanity, hence also they must be different." On the Franciscan movement, see *Thode: F. v. A. und die Anfänge der Kunst in Italien², 1904,* and *P. Sabatier: Vie de St F.⁴, 1894.* That the latter movement, in its religious nature-mysticism and its individualism, contained elements which tended to break up the ideas of the Middle Ages can here be left out of account; in any case, the ascetic and ecclesiastical idea ought not to be simply ignored

as *Thode* does. Very soberly, in fact from my own point of view too soberly, *Hauck* describes the influence of these movements upon the Church in Germany.

[112] (p. 251.) I came to realize the meaning of a combination of this kind through reading a small book by a Japanese Christian (*Utschimura: Wie ich Christ wurde, Stuttgart, Gundert*), which shows that the Christian ethic presents no special difficulties to a man who had grown up among feudal conditions, where there was a natural economy, and that it was felt to be related to the Confucian ethic, simply providing an increase of ethical energy through the love of God and the idea of Christ. The same Japanese almost loses his faith in Christianity, when he sees it in America and in Europe, where all the conditions of life are the exact opposite of Christianity, and where he only found it being really practised in small exceptional groups. Lafcadio Hearn, in *Kokoro*, puts similar sentiments in the mouth of one of his characters, a converted Japanese.—Further, the harmony between the Christian ethic and the class system of the Middle Ages is admitted to be the agreement of magnitudes which had an affinity for each other, but which still were only drawn together purely by the force of actual circumstances, and only later on realized that they were also connected in theory, by no less a man than *J. F. Stahl: Der christliche Staat, p. 5*: "Finally perhaps this may be a Divine effect, which shapes in a predetermined harmony among the Christian and especially the Germanic peoples, the fundamental organization which no race gives to itself, and which forms, both in its original disposition and in its maturity, an outward presentation and reflection of inward Christian relations. But that, as it is in part nearer to, and in part farther away from, the Christian religion, partly of necessity commanded by its spirit and partly freely penetrated by it, partly naturally and partly as a work of moral activity—all this together, as an indissoluble unity, it is, which, determining the State, makes it a Christian State." *P. 11 f.*: "Christianity manifests the meaning of the Divine order, which has arranged the variety of callings in social life, and has given to each its special consecration, and it urges man to be true to the calling he has received within this limited sphere, and Christianity manifests no less the consciousness that there is one element in humanity which is the same for all men because all are made in the image of God. . . . In the Middle Ages first of all did the Christian meaning of the 'class' system upon a Germanic basis first become conscious and living. The mediaeval period first made clear what a 'class' (*Stand*) was, That limitation to a special calling in life, and activity within a certain group, that state of being steeped in the idea of the special significance, strength, and the special moral obligations of this calling, whether it be knighthood and military service, or industry, or art, or any other calling at all, that affectionate care bestowed upon this calling, regarding it not merely as a means of earning money or of gaining political position, but as an end in itself, that intimate comradeship between the members of the same calling—these features of the Middle Ages present a picture of undying beauty." At the same time *Stahl* as a Protestant leaves out the idea of vicarious assistance, which, however, alone makes the merging into a unity possible, and the whole way of thinking is too strongly coloured with the point of view of the Lutheran conception of the "Calling".—Thus the intensive Christianization, which according to *Uhlhorn: Liebestätigkeit, II, 5 f., 7*, was only effected by the Middle Ages, and which he explains by referring to the emotional depth of the Germanic spirit, was still determined also by economic social conditions, and it is quite intelligible that a complete change in all these conditions would also entirely change the

Christianity of the Roman-German peoples in spite of their psychological disposition.

[113] (p. 253.) Here I must confine myself to a mere reference to the well-known literature on this subject which I have consulted. *Bücher: Entstehung der Volkswirtschaft*[4], *1904; Gierke: Genossenschaftsrecht, I; Schmoller: Grundriss der allgemeinen Volkswirtschaftslehre; Waitz: Deutsche Verfassungsgeschichte; Jellinek: Recht des modernen Staates*[2], *1905, 309–316; von Inama-Sternegg: Deutsche Wirtschaftsgeschichte; Lamprecht: Agrargesch.* (in the Middle Ages) *in HWB. der Staatswissenschaften*[2]*; Brunner: Quellen und Geschichte des deutschen Rechtes.* In the *Encykl. der Rechtswissensch.*[6] *hrg. v. Kohler; Lamprecht: Deutsche Geschichte, I–IV; Rambaud: Civilisation française;* and, above all, *Simmel: Die Philosophie des Geldes*[2], *1908,* in which the problem raised by the teaching of Marx, i.e. that the higher life of the spirit and the mind is absolutely determined by economic conditions, is treated in an extremely able way, with a great deal of valuable information, and apart from all materialistic presuppositions. That which *Kautsky: Gesch. des Sozialismus, I, i, pp. 35–39,* states is amazingly meagre, and a travesty of the real facts; all that is right is his statement that the ethic of the Church is certainly connected with a natural economy. The Church, which was originally a group animated purely by love, has become a political community, but she has always exercised her principle of love in a certain way through a kind of communism founded on a natural economy, and also through giving away surplus possessions, which the natural economy cannot use so long as it does not produce for markets or customers, but simply for its own immediate needs.— With reference to the money economy of the Middle Ages it should be added that a money economy does not of itself mean capitalism; for the conduct of wars, for fines, and for purposes of government money was absolutely necessary, and it was present; as a means of settling accounts it was used as a fiction. The fact that such money elements were present, which cannot be denied, does not mean, however, the presence of the results of the capitalistic use of money which have been described above.

[114] (p. 254.) For the Christianization of knighthood and chivalry, which during the period of the Hohenstaufen dynasty proceeded from the class of men, drawn from various sections of Society, who, being without land, attached themselves directly to the service of the Emperor and formed the chief military forces of the time; these men were called *Ministeriales* or *Dienstmannen,* and from the merging of this lesser nobility with the landed aristocracy, which receives its main characteristics from France, see *Rambaud: Civ. franç., I, 179 f.;* for the lay civilization of chivalry and its secular spirit, see *Lamprecht: DG., III;* for the entirely secular character of the Provençal chivalry, and the transformation of its poetry when these ideas entered the class of the burghers, in which love *(die Minne)* again became ethical and religious, and was then placed absolutely at the disposal of religious allegory and penetrated into Franciscan mysticism (it is from this view-point that we must understand Dante's Beatrice), see *Vossler: Dante, I, 486–501,* and *Die Philosophischen Grundlagen zum süssen neuen Stil., 1904;* this is at the same time a characteristic sign of the difference between feudalism and town-life. Knightly civilization, however, is always that point in mediaeval Christianity where, in reality, the compromise with an alien spiritual and ethical power which is contrary to the principles of Christianity is actually and obviously present. Of course, it is true that there have always been such compromises, and no religious ethic can avoid this difficulty. But it is important to note that these compromises do not lie in the recognition of the State, the Family, and economic life as such, as *von Eicken*

suggests, but in the recognition of the code of honour set up by chivalry, and in the spiritualization of the courtly forms of love-making.

[115] (p. 258.) Cf. *R. W. and A. J. Carlyle: History of Mediaeval Theory, I, Part IV, The Political Theory of the Ninth Century* ; *Reuter*, in his *Gesch. d. Aufklärung im Mittelalter*, draws attention to the elements which reveal the influence of the idea of Natural Law in a most able and understanding way, but unfortunately he treats them all from the wholly erroneous point of view of the *Aufklärung* (Enlightenment). Here, however, the only *Aufklärung*, that is, the discarding of the historical and miraculous element, to which the expression can really apply, was the movement of thought represented by the radical Averroistic sects. Abelard is entirely misinterpreted by *Reuter*. *Reuter*, like many theologians, does not understand that without having recourse to general necessities of thought Christianity could not have maintained its intellectual existence, and that without accepting the social philosophy of the Stoics in particular it would have been simply helpless when confronted with the problems of social life. No social doctrines can be evolved simply from the New Testament, and that which meets in Stoicism and Christianity is not a number of alien elements, but elements which are akin to each other and have grown up out of the same situation. These ideas have not been borrowed from an entirely foreign "ancient" way of thinking, as is often supposed by non-theological thinkers, with a faculty for making sweeping generalizations which is not admissible. Otherwise *Reuter's* book is extremely instructive, as a witness to the mass of material from antiquity which was incorporated in the life and thought of the Middle Ages.

[116] (p. 259.) For the leading part played by the Law of Nature in Abelard and in the *Decretum Gratiani*, see *Luthhardt: Gesch. d. chr. Ethik, I, 270 and 249*. When *L.* here adds, "this was the consequence of that setting aside by the Early Church of the importance of faith for ethics, and of the placing of faith and works side by side", as a Lutheran he forgets that Luther and Early Protestantism held the same views, for the same reasons as the Early Church and the Mediaeval Church, and very strongly.—On *St. Thomas Aquinas*, cf. the so-called *Summa contra gentiles*, and the great *Summa theologica* with its three parts, which in the *pars secunda* deals with ethics; see also the work of *Werner: Der h. Thomas von Aquino, II, 1859*, which gives copious extracts from the saint's works. *Rieter: Die Moral. des h. Thomas* I have, unfortunately, been unable to use. Indispensable for the understanding of Thomism is *Renan's* well-known book *Averroès et l'Averroisme, 1852*. In addition see the various histories of dogma and of Christian ethics which have already been named, as well as *Froschhammer: Th. v. A.* and *Jourdain: La philosophie de St. Thomas*, and *Janet: Histoire de la philosophie morale*. So far as the *Summa* is concerned, the parts with which we are here concerned are especially the treatises *De fine hominis, De virtutibus, De legibus, De justitia et jure*; further, the doctrines of the Primitive State, of sin, and of the opposition between the state of sin and the state of grace, which are scattered throughout the whole work. At this point also we must already mention works which deal with the social philosophy of St. Thomas: *J. Baumann: Die Staatslehre des h. Th., 1873*, a collection of translations and extracts from the writings of St. Thomas, which, however, fail to give due weight to the really vital connection with the fundamental theological doctrines, and therefore very incomplete; this writer also lays undue stress upon the commentary on Aristotle's *Politics*, which, according to *Thömes*, does not represent the views of St. Thomas at all, but is simply an account of the views of Aristotle himself, which St. Thomas, departing from the usual habits of mediaeval

commentators, distinguishes from his own opinion, and also *Baumann* does not
realize that the second part of this commentary was not written by St. Thomas
himself, which means that the sections between *p. 107* and *p. 166* do not count
(see *Thömes, 25–36*); see, further, *Feugueray: Essai sur les doctrines politiques de
St. Th.*, *1857*, very informative and able, only likewise overestimating the
commentary on Aristotle's *Politics*; this writer does not give the theological
doctrines their full significance (especially the doctrine of the Primitive
State); the book is also full of the erroneous idea that there is in existence a
great Christian system of politics of *égalité* and *fraternité* which corresponds to
the great principles of 1789, traces of which he claims to be able to discover
in St. Thomas, and in the writings of the ancient Fathers of the Church; the
whole outlook of Christian positivism and patriarchalism in social matters
which is connected with this conception of God and the doctrine of the Fall
of man is here underestimated; finally, see *N. Thömes: Commentatio literaria et
critica de S. Thomae: Operibus ad ecclesiasticum, politicum, socialem statum reirepublicae
Christianae pertinentibus, deque ejus doctrinae fundamentis atque praeceptis*—a Berlin
Dissertation of 1874, where the whole system of ideas and the situation of the
criticism of the sources, as well as the most important basic passages, are here
briefly and well described. In detail there is still room for several monographs.

117 (p. 260.) See the *Summa, I a, 2 ae, qu. 90*: "Principium exterius [alongside
of the inner one of virtue] movens nos ad bonum est Deus qui et nos instruit
per Legem (et juvat per gratiam)." This then leads to the fundamental
questions: "utrum lex sit aliquid rationis" and "de fine legis". Under the first
head the whole metaphysical-rational doctrine of law is developed; *qu. 91 a. 1*:
"Legem autem a Deo exire praesupponit (ut patet) legem ipsam in Deo esse."
The universal Law of Nature has reference to the end for which the world
was created; *qu. 90 a. 2*: "oportet, quod lex maxime respiciat ordinem, qui
est in beatitudine." This universal law penetrates the life of all creatures, and
reaches its summit in man in the conscious law of liberty; *qu. 91 a. 3*: "Etiam
animalia irrationalia participant rationem aeternam suo modo, sicut et
rationalis creatura; sed quia rationalis creatura participat eam intellectualiter
et rationaliter, ideo participatio legis aeternae in creatura rationali proprie
lex vocatur . . . in creatura autem irrationali non participatur rationaliter
unde non potest dici lex nisi per similitudinem. . . . Inter cetera rationalis
creatura excellentiori quodam modo divinae providentiae subjacet, in quantum
et ipsa fit providentiae particeps sibi ipsi et aliis providens. Unde et in ipsa
participatur ratio aeterna, per quam habet naturalem inclinationem ad debitum
actum et finem. Et talis participatio legis aeternae in rationali creatura Lex
Naturalis dicitur. Unde patet quod lex naturalis nihil aliud est, quam participatio legis aeternae in rationali creatura." From this share in the divine
law of reason human law proceeds, just as human thought proceeds from the
fundamental logical idea which flows forth from God; *qu. 91 a. 3*: "ita etiam
ex praeceptis legis naturalis quasi ex quibusdam principiis communibus et
indemonstrabilibus est quod ratio humana procedat ad aliqua magis parti-
culariter disponenda. Et istae particulares dispositiones adinventae secundum
rationem humanam dicuntur leges humanae." Then note especially the great
passage in *qu. 93–97*, in which the whole Law of Nature is derived from the
lex aeterna and is determined by its content. As his authorities for these doctrines
St. Thomas gives, in addition to Cicero and Aristotle, the other authors of
the Early Church with whom we are already familiar, naturally especially
Isidore and Augustine, whose Ciceronian definition of the State as *aliquis
rationalis coetus* he also makes his starting-point. Otherwise he proceeds upon

the assumption that the Bible contains the same doctrine in detail and explicitly. Here especially the famous passages from St. Paul (*Romans ii. 15*) always recur; but all the Old Testament passages which deal with the eternal Divine Law and the political examples from the Old Testament play an important part. The rationalism of Natural Law seems to be a thoroughly Scriptural doctrine; this naturally leads to an instinctive harmonizing of the Law of Nature and of Aristotle with the social and political conditions of the O.T.

[118] (p. 261.) While the doctrine of the Primitive State is restated under the influence of the Augustinian doctrine of grace, and the ancient doctrine of the perfect beginning of humanity or the Golden Age now becomes expanded in Christian dogma into the doctrine of a double perfection, of a perfection of reason and of the *bonum naturae* within its connatural limits (*imago Dei*), as well as of a perfection of the supernaturally imparted impartation of grace which transcends nature, or the substantial union with God (*similitudo Dei* or *donum superadditum*), the real nature of the Fall is no longer regarded as the loss of the "absolute Law of Nature", but as the loss of the mystical perfection imparted by grace due to the guilt of man. This loss, which is the basis of the doctrine of Original Sin, then first leads indirectly to the destruction of the *naturalis perfectio* or of the *bonum naturae*, and then only to the new conditions of fallen humanity, for the remaining *principia practica legis naturae*. They come under the condition of external conditions of life which have become more difficult, in which even the natural reason and judgment have become dimmed through Original Sin, in which reason and the passions have become divided, even in the sphere of the Law of Nature, which cannot be avoided in the nature of a humanity which the consciousness of guilt induced by Original Sin has altered, and which through the *donum superadditum* is no longer guaranteed and regulated in a supernatural way, but is left at the mercy of the natural perils of change and the passions of men (*Werner, II, 535 f.*). Hence far more emphasis is now laid upon the loss of the miracle of grace and the clouding of reason which is indirectly derived from this, whereas in the Early Church the predominating idea was the direct opposition which existed between the absolute Natural Law [which was held to be the same as the Christian ethic] and the sinful obscuring of the Law and the impotence of man to fulfil it. Hence in St. Thomas we find also that the doctrine of the relative Natural Law as the *remedium et poena peccati* is not developed in theory as much as in the Early Church. Also it is undeniable that the influence of Aristotle's evolutionary view of history, which, unlike the Stoic theory, has no conception of an absolute original perfection, but which teaches that Reason gradually makes its way through the mists raised by the senses and the passions, and in so doing produces the State, the Family, and Society, certainly tends to make it appear as though the *lex naturalis humana* were a natural product of evolution, not a mere modification of the perfect absolute Law of Nature. The old fundamental Stoic-Christian point of view still constantly reappears, however, as a natural presupposition, as, indeed, is only natural, seeing that the idea of *libertas* and *communis possessio* in the Primitive State was retained, and seeing that the whole idea of a perfect Primitive State is also quite natural from the point of view of Reason and a reasonable social order. The problem is discussed in principle under the title "*Utrum lex naturae mutari possit?*" *I a, 2 ae, qu. 94, a. 5*: "Isidorus dicit in lib. 5. Etymologiarum, quod communis omnium possessio et una libertas est de jure naturali. Sed haec videmus esse mutata per leges humanas. Ergo videtur, quod lex naturalis sit mutabilis. Sed contra est, quod dicitur in Decretis dest. 5 'naturale jus ab exordio rationalis creaturae

coepit, nec variatur tempore sed immutabile permanet'. Respondeo: dicendum, quod lex naturalis potest intelligi mutari duplicitur. Uno modo per hoc, quod aliquid ei addatur." Additions both to the Old Testament moral law and to human legislation are thus explained. "Alio modo potest intelligi mutatio legis naturalis per modum subtractionis, ut scilicet aliquid desinat esse de lege naturali, quod prius fuit secundum legem naturalem. Et sic quantum ad prima principia legis naturae, . . . quae diximus esse quasi quasdam conclusiones propinquas primis principiis, sic lex naturalis non mutatur, quin ut in pluribus sit rectum, quod lex naturalis habet. Potest tamen mutari in aliquo particulari et in paucioribus propter aliquas speciales causas impedientes observantiam talium praeceptorum." One of the first hindrances was the sinful condition of selfishness and the lust of power which necessitated new forms of law and new revelations of the Law of Nature. Thus capital punishment is explained as due to the new conditions of sin introduced by the Fall, after God had first brought death into the world as a punishment for sin. Above all, however: "Dicendum, quod aliquid dicitur esse de jure naturali dupliciter. Uno modo, quia ad hoc natura inclinat, sicut non esse injuriam alteri faciendam. Alio modo quia natura non inducit contrarium, sicut possemus dicere, quod hominem esse nudum est de jure naturali, quia natura non dedit ei vestitum, sed ars adinvenit. Et hoc modo communis omnium possessio et una libertas dicitur esse de jure naturali, quia scilicet distinctio possessionum et servitus non sunt inductae a natura sed per hominum rationem ad utilitatem humanae vitae, et sic etiam in hoc lex naturae non est mutata nisi per additionem." This *utilitas* is fitted to the conditions of the Fallen State, and the twofold point of view of the *lex naturae* . . . is that of absolute and relative Natural Law; cf. *Meyer: Die christlich-ethischen Moralprinzipien und die Arbeiterfrage⁴, 1904, p. 36.* It is here quite plain that early Stoic-Christian ideas are mingled with the Aristotelian theory of evolution, and that incidentally the latter holds the field. Further, for the original conditions in the Primitive State, and on the change in the idea of the absolute Law of Nature through the new moral and physical conditions of existence, see *Werner: D. h. Th., II, 503, 457, 536 f., 542 f. 460*, and also *1 a, 2 ae, qu. 98*: "Dicendum, quod in statu isto (the Fallen State) multiplicatis dominis necesse est fieri divisionem possessionum, quia communitas possessionis est occasio discordiae, ut philosophus dicit in II Polit. Sed in statu innocentiae fuissent voluntates hominum sic ordinatae, quod absque omni periculo discordiae communiter usi fuissent, secundum quod uniciuque eorum competeret, rebus quae eorum dominio subdebantur; cum hic etiam nunc apud multos bonos viros observetur." The Natural Law of the *libido* as of a change brought about (as a punishment) of the absolute Natural Law free from *libido* into a relative Natural Law, cf. *1a, 2 ae, qu. 91, a. 6*: "Sed inquantum per divinam justitiam homo destituitur originali justitia et vigore rationis, ipse impetus sensualitis, qui eum ducit, habet rationem legis, inquantum est poenalis et ex lege divina consequens hominem destitutum propria dignitate."—For Dante and these questions, see *Vossler, I, 417*; also *ibid., p. 388*, for Dante's view of the State in his *Monarchia*; Gerson's theory, in *Thömes, p. 106*, is exactly similar: (i) Jus cujuslibet creaturae: leges insitae omnibus rebus. (ii) Jus creaturae naturalis: lex proprie divina et lex proprie naturalis. (iii) Leges hominum viatorum: lex canonica et lex civilis (the law of the Church and the relative Law of Nature).

[119] (p. 262.) It cannot by any means be taken for granted that the Decalogue became the formula of the Christian moral law as it is to-day in our catechisms.

In the Early Church there was no fixed standard; there were only lists of virtues and offences, formal catalogues of the gifts of the Spirit, and beyond this the Augustinian formula of the double command of love, of the love of God in the narrower sense, and of the love of the brethren in God, according to the *Doctrina christiana*. The Decalogue only became popular through the use of the scholastic ethic, the practice of the popular preachers and of preparation for confession. Cf. *von Zezschwitz's Art.Katechetik in PRE²*. Through this, however, the equation of the Natural Law and the Decalogue gained both theoretically and practically a far higher significance; then also the material of the Decalogue could be interpreted and expanded out of the Natural Law. The Decalogue only became part of the Catechism at the Reformation, which indeed first created the Catechism. Previously there had been confession books for the unlearned, *speculum ecclesiae*, and similar works, in which the Decalogue, the doctrine of the sacraments, the *oratio dominica*, and the *symbolum* were placed together.—The *lex divina* of the Decalogue and of the Old Testament refer to the ends of reason within the life of this present world, and it is distinguished from the supernatural end of grace, and its *nova lex* which appeals purely to the general spirit and disposition of the believer, and not to isolated acts (*I a, 2 ae, qu. 91, art. 5*). Yet both are only distinguished from each other as *lex perfecta* and *lex imperfecta*, as laws which correspond to the stage which humanity has reached, in which the one points the way to the other, and indeed contains it already in germ. On the equation of the Decalogue and the Natural Law, see *qu. 98*, with the information that this law should only accidentally bring death and the knowledge of sin; on the contrary, that essentially it should educate and prepare the Church for the reception of grace. Here the Pauline-Augustinian Dualism of the Law and the Gospel, which was adopted by the Reformers later on, most clearly is broken through in favour of an ascending development including the ethic of this present world. *Qu. 98, a. 5:* "Dicendum quod lex vetus manifestabat praecepta legis naturae et super-addebat quaedam propria praecepta" (that is, the Jewish laws of ceremonial, etc.). *Qu. 98, a. 6:* "Lex vetus disponebat ad salutem quae erat futura per Christum . . . statim post peccatum primi hominis non competebat legem veterem dari; tum quia nondum homo recognoscebat se ea indigere de sua ratione confisus, tum quia adhuc dictamen legis naturae nondum erat obtenebratum per consuetudinem peccati. Oportebat hujusmodi auxilium quodam ordine dari, ut per imperfecta ad perfectionem manducerentur. Et ideo inter legem naturae et legem gratiae oportuit legem veterem dari." On the systematic character of the Decalogue as the epitome of the Law of Nature, *qu. 100*. The Decalogue virtually includes the whole of the Law of Nature (*a. 3*): "Utraque horum praeceptorum continentur in praeceptis decalogi. Nam illa, quae sunt prima et communia continentur in eis, sicut principia in conclusionibus proximis, illa vero, quae per sapientes cognoscuntur, continentur in eis e converso sicut conclusiones in principiis." On the other hand, however, the Decalogue is also identical with the Christian Law, and its two halves divide themselves into the Love of God and the love of the brethren; see the treatise *Expositio in duo praecepta caritatis et in decem legis praecepta*. We must not overlook the fact that this comparison had a good deal of effect; by constantly introducing the ideas of the Old Testament it distinctly affected the idea of the Law of Nature itself (cf. also the treatment of this question in the *de regimine principis*). The acceptance of the Aristotelian doctrine is also affected by it, in this way, that in it the conservative, anti-capitalistic features which are directed against indulgence and loss of self-control are emphasized. It is nowhere a pure Aristotelianism; it is always mingled with the ideas of the Bible. In detail, however, there is need of further research into this whole question of the reaction of these Biblical-Christian elements upon the conceptions and interpretation of the Aristotelian ethic; cf. *Feugueray, p. 204; Thömes, pp. 101 ff.*

120 (p. 265.) Law new and old, see *Werner, II, 571*; the formulation of the new mystical moral law (*Werner, II, 583*); the detailed interpretation (*Summa, 1 a., 2 ae., qu. 106–108*); the analysis of the New Testament Law in connection with Augustine, and how the latter appeals to the Law of Nature rather than to the Decalogue, *qu. 108, art. s.* See also the tractate *De fine, 1 a, 2 ae, qu. 1–5*, the key to the whole ethic, which, with Augustine, works from the conception of the "end" and incorporates into the Neo-Platonic, mystical Christian end of blessedness and the Vision of God, the Aristotelian end of social welfare, order and the full development of the intellectual and physical energies and capacities, subordinating them as an intermediate end, the attainment of which disposes and prepares the soul for the *finis ultimus.* See also *Heinrich: Lehrbuch der kath. Dogmatik, pp. 269 ff.*, see also *1 a, 2 ae, qu. 109 a., 3*: "Natura diligit Deum super omnia, prout est principium et finis naturalis boni. Caritas autem [that is, the sacramentally effected virtue of the *nova lex*, which contains within itself all the other mystical-supernatural virtues] secundum quod est objectum beatitudinis et secundum quod homo habet quandam societatem spiritualem cum Deo. Addit etiam caritas super naturalem dilectionem. Dei promptitudinem quandam et delectationem, sicut habitus quilibet virtutis addit super actum bonum, qui fit ex sola naturali ratione hominis." Hence, then, the morality of reason according to the Law of Nature has a natural reward, and the mystical morality of grace has a supernatural reward; there is a natural blessedness of the Natural Law and a supernatural of the law of Grace; *Werner, II, p. 519*: "Vita aeterna est quoddam bonum excedens proportionem naturae creatae, quia etiam excedit cognitionem et desiderium ejus. . . . Et inde est quod nulla creatura creata est sufficiens principium actus meritorii vitae aeternae [thus quite apart from sin, even from the standpoint of the absolute Law of Nature], nisi superaddatur aliquod supernaturale donum quod gratia dicitur [and this is true as well in the Primitive State as in the Fallen State]. For the ascent from the one to the other, see *Thömes, p. 58*: "Thomas hujus vitae bonae, nec solum illa, quae in eruditione animae sed illa quoque, quae in corporis bona condicione ceterisque rebus exterioribus ponuntur, multum ad beatitudinem 'imperfectam, quae in hac vita haberi possit' valere declaravit, sive ut 'praeambula vel praeparatoria', sive ut 'perficientia' sive ut 'adjuvantia extrinsecus' sive ut 'concomitantia'. Eam ob causam multam artem dialecticam magnumque studium in id consumpsit, ut rectum et verum hujus vitae bonorum faceret ordinem gradusque recte disponeret." Likewise *Feugueray, pp. 31, 37, 38.*—For the Augustinian interpretation of the ethic of the New Testament and its relation to this itself, see the observation in the first part, *p. 328*; I agree with the interpretation, that is, if the whole intellectualistic mystical and supernatural part is left out. In the ethic of the Gospel, too, the religious end is the centre which determines and organizes everything, only in it union with God takes the form of the union of the will of man with the Will of God in ethical obedience, and love of the brethren is the revelation and effect of the attitude of God towards man, especially in its ethical achievement, which, on the other hand, from the ethical achievement also leads to God, and to the true Will of God. To this extent I still hold to this point of view over against Harnack's objections (*Preuss. Jahrbb., March 1907*). On this point Protestantism is less clear than the

Augustinian ethic, since in part it places the Christian moral law in the Decalogue, and in part renounces formulas altogether and speaks only of the effect of faith. Precisely on that account also for Catholicism the problem of Christian ethics is this: how to combine the ethic which is derived directly from religion with one in which it is not possible to trace its origin in religion. Protestantism also was confronted with this problem and we shall see how many difficulties it caused. The scholastic-Augustinian statement of the problem itself is, however, in any case relevant, and harmonizes with the fundamental tendency of the Christian faith. On this point, see *F. J. Schmidt: Gottesliebe und Nächstenliebe (Preuss. Jahrbb., 1908, April No.)*, who expresses his own view on the difference of opinion between Harnack and myself and supports my contention. He does this, however, in a purely speculative way by deduction from the Christian idea. I, for my part, have taken up this position purely empirically from the Gospel, and only later when I was studying this question did I see how closely this interpretation is connected with the Augustinian-scholastic one, only apart from the mystical intellectualistic and sacramental features. *Schmidt* does not notice at all how his formulas coincide almost word for word with those of the Victorines, of St. Augustne and of St. Thomas. These analyses are easily underestimated in Protestant literature, and easily ignored entirely by non-theologicals; they contain, however, in reality much right feeling and acute insight.

[121] (p. 271.) For the graduated process of ascent, see *Werner, II, 507, 510 ff.*; cf. also *Baumann, 82; Feugueray, pp. 155 f., 193; Thömes, 72.* See also the preceding notes,—On the lack of any actual directly Christian policy and social reform, and the placing of all positive social construction, when this was required at all, on the plane of the principles of the Natural Law, and therefore on the sub-Christian level, *Feugueray, pp. 212 ff.*, speaks very truly. "The ideal of Christian Society as an end, and the successive realization of this ideal by suitable social action—this idea is in the minds of us all to-day. But one would search in vain for the least hint of such an idea in St. Thomas. It is, indeed, his great error that he cannot conceive of Christian politics at all. He does not see that Christianity has inaugurated a new civilization; he does not even know that the Christian principles of right and of justice are very different from the principles of antiquity, whether among the Gentiles or the Jews. It is true that he knew that the new law was far better than the old; he often compares the two laws, and he sees that the new law is higher, since its aim is not material and tangible, but noble and supernatural, since also it does not merely control the external actions of men, but the movements of their hearts ('cohibet manum et animam'), since it requires to be obeyed, not out of fear, but from love. This is the reason for the superiority of the new law, but so far as moral precepts are concerned, and the rule for external actions and the relations of men with each other, the new law has introduced nothing new at all; it has nothing to add to the ancient law. St. Thomas says plainly: 'Lex nova super veterem addere non debuit circa exteriora agenda' (*2 a, 2 ae, q. 108, a. 2*); and this ancient law, the Jewish law, he observes, was itself, so far as its ethic was concerned, simply the Law of Nature, the primitive law, so that in reality the moral law of humanity, according to St. Thomas, has not changed, and the Christian ethic does not differ from that of the ancient world; it does not differ, at least, save in the order of Grace in all that has to do with the salvation of souls; but in the order of Nature, for the precepts of justice, for ordering relations between men and nations, and, in consequence, for the principles of politics, Christianity and antiquity have one and the same

conscience . . . Christianity gives to man the means for eternal salvation, but its influence does not extend to the affairs of this life, and does not modify the temporal condition of men." This opinion is true of a good deal in Thomism ; but in it there is overlooked the inner difficulty of a Christian moulding of Society; and also the writer overlooks the amount of inner Christianization and harmonizing of the Natural Law with Christian thought which has taken place; even though this may have taken place very indirectly, still it must be taken into account. One has only to compare the Natural Law of the Enlightenment and the ancient doctrine of the State in order to see the difference. The Law of Nature is not a conception which only bears one meaning; it is also dependent upon the general way of thinking at any given period. The scholastic conception of Natural Law is, in fact, something which bears a strong impress of Christian ideas.

121a (p. 272.) Cf. my article: *Katholizismus und Reformismus* in the *Internationalen Wochenschrift, 1907*. For the relation between legalism and heteronomy to inward freedom and autonomy in this system, see *Gottschick: Ethik, 1907, pp. 63 ff.* From its teleological-mystical character there follows ultimately objectively freedom, but pedagogical considerations, the complicated nature of the Ethos and the demand for uniformity, often lead the individual to submit to authority and heteronomy. In any case the problem is far more complicated than Protestant controversialists usually admit. Catholicism naturally was also affected by other influences, to which its legalistic spirit and its stress on the acquisition of merit were also due.

121b (p. 274.) This does not mean that the modern conception of evolution would find no difficulties and problems in this sphere of thought. Certainly this conception is to-day, and most particularly to-day, one which contains the greatest difficulties, cf. *Bergson: L'évolution créatrice*. But this subject cannot here be pursued any farther. All that can be said is, that in any case, in the form of Thomism, these reconciliations and transitions do not spring out of an inner necessity of thought, but that they are posited in a purely anthropomorphic and arbitrary manner.

122 (p. 274.) On the idea of evolution in St. Thomas, see *Werner, II, 469 f., 518 f., 533, 547,* and the whole section on the various stages and their ends, *II, 295–317; Feugueray: pp. 131, 190 f., 193; Summa, I a, 2 ae, qu. 97 a.i:* "Humanae rationi naturale esse videtur ut gradatim ab imperfecto ad perfectum veniat." This applies also to the relation of nature to grace itself, whereby grace appears now as the perfection of nature, and now as a purely supernatural superstructure. *Qu. 106, art. 3:* "Non enim aliquid ad perfectum adducitur statim a principio, sed quodam temporalis successionis ordine, sicut aliquis primum fit puer et postmodum vir"; hence the process of revelation from the *Lex naturae* to the *Lex vetus*, and thence to the *Lex nova*.—The ultimately purely architectonic character of this idea of development is well brought out by *Gass: Gesch. d. christl. Ethik, I, 432, 324 f.*

123 (p. 276.) The connection between the scholastic-architectonic logic and the classified system which constituted the social reality is an idea similar to that expressed by *Simmel*, when he speaks of the connection between modern rationalism and relativism and a money economy and its social effects. This is an application of the Marxist idea of the dependence of the spiritual superstructure upon the social-economic substructure, which, if accepted with due precautions, seems to me to be a justifiable and illuminating idea. Naturally in so doing logic does not become a mere reflection and translation of economic-social conditions into supposed laws of thought, which then to the thinker

become transformed into apparently logical necessities. All thought, however, always possesses certain ideas which it takes for granted, which it regards as axiomatic. For real thought itself, however, these ideas are no axioms at all; when they are critically examined it is possible to break them up or to relegate them to a very secondary position without there being any need for the social substructure to be altered in the least. This way of thinking is, however, a consolation when we are confronted by unexamined ideas which seem perfectly natural, especially when they dominate practical life. The modern tendency to find mental satisfaction in measuring everything by a fixed rational standard, and the way it takes for granted that everything can be related to everything else, certainly receives from the apparently objective value of money, and the universal possibility of exchange which this involves, a strong psychological impulse to become a fixed habit of thought, whereas the purely logical process itself, when it only follows its own course, is not subject to these influences, and it then turns these accepted ideas into mere probabilities. The scholastic tendency to be satisfied with an external architectonic unity and to think that the needs of the value of the individual have been met when it has been assigned a quantitatively graduated share in the meaning of the whole, seems to me to be, in a similar way, under the psychological influence of the class and corporate social life in the State, Society, and the Church. Precisely on that account, therefore, the thought of the Middle Ages knew nothing of modern individualism which desires to give to each individual his direct share in the meaning of the whole. Of course this does not mean that in other directions the scholastic argument does not follow the logical-dialectical impulse pure and simple. Psychological influences of this kind also do not proceed solely from the social-economic sphere, as is shown by the influence of eschatology within scholasticism, in which, however, the social substructure made its appearance in the vicarious offerings, penitences, and wergilds of those days. I believe, however, that I have here shown that these psychological influences from the social sphere are very considerable, and that the Christian social doctrines of Catholicism are here determined by a psychological element of fact, not by the dialectic of Christian thought, whose individualism is here not satisfied, and also actually breaks away from it, as will be shown in the section on Protestantism.

[123b] (p. 278.) For this period, to which at present very little research has been given, and which especially on the side of its ethic and its social philosophy is still very obscure, see the beginnings of an understanding of the subject in *Hermelinck: Die theologische Fakultät in Tübingen vor der Reformation, 1477–1534, 1906*, and also my review *GGA, 1909*. For the ethic and social philosophy of Cusanus which was affected by Humanism, see, in addition to *Gierke, III*, the presentation of the subject by *Eucken: Beiträge zur Einführung in die Geschichte der Philosophie²*, *1906*; for the ethic of Sir Thomas More, which accepted entirely the universal Theism of the Renaissance, see the instructive study by *H. Dietzel: Beiträge zur Geschichte des Sozial. u. Kommunismus, Vierteljahrschrift für Staats- und Volkswirtschaft, V*. For the Thomism of the Counter-Reformation, the acceptance of the civilization of the Renaissance which this made possible, and the high civilization achieved by Catholicism in consequence, which at first far exceeded that of the Protestant countries, see *Gothein: Staat und Gesellschaft des Zeitalters der Gegenreformation (Kultur des Gegenwart, II, V, i.).*

[123c] (p. 280.) For the Catholicism of the Enlightenment, see *Ludwig: Weihbischof Zirkel von Würzburg in seiner Stellung zur theolog. Aufklärung und zur kirchl. Restauration, 1904/6*. It is here very evident that the Kantianism which

has penetrated the Catholic system in an amazing way shrinks primarily from the social ideal in which nature and grace are united in the universal supremacy of the Church. For modern conditions, cf. the extremely interesting book of *Abbé Houtin: L'américanisme. Quelques Lettres (1908)*, by *Loisy*, also shows repeatedly that the ideas of Thomism and of the Curia cannot be combined with the modern way of thinking on social questions, and with its metaphysical-ethical premisses. The attempts which have been made to allow modern Catholicism to accept modern social ideas alone without allowing them to influence dogma, ethics, or the philosophy of the Church, are illusions, and with good reason such merely social Modernists always finally end by becoming critical of dogma and philosophy also. It has not yet been proved to what extent a new system of Catholicism could be erected upon this basis. On this question see both the works of *M. Legendre* and *J. Chevalier: Le catholicisme et la société, Paris, 1907 (Collection des doctrines politiques publiée sous la direction de Mater, II)*, and *G. Tyrrel: Mediaevalism, London, 1908.* The former book is unimportant, the latter, however, is most interesting; it presents the reader with the ideal of an organic-evolutionary Catholicism, which is nothing less than the common spirit of Christianity working freely and inwardly in individuals, which, as religion, is distinguished from theology, and only as religion, not as theology, is Divine; hence in the fixed statements of the Church on dogma and ethics this religion only sees provisional dogmas of interpretation and therefore the latter cannot claim to have any right to be imposed on anyone by force; so far as the former is concerned they fall away completely; with this, then, it would be easy to adapt the claims of the Church to modern social life, as a free Church in a free State. There can be no doubt about the religious purity and the modern character of the whole conception, but in my opinion this would no longer be Catholicism at all, and in practice it would be quite impossible, without breaking up the unity of dogma, and with that the backbone of Catholicism. See also *Karl Holl: Der Modernismus, 1908*, whose judgment (*p. 41 f.*) seems to me to be absolutely to the point.

[124] (p. 281.) The sources for the following section are, in addition to his commentaries on the Bible and on Aristotle, the great *Summa*, which in the *secunda secundae* is especially concerned with ethics, the small *Summa*, whose third book deals with ethics, and the work entitled *De regimine principum*, of which, however, only the first book and part of the second can be regarded as having been written by St. Thomas himself. Also noteworthy are the works of *Jourdain, I, Janet I*, as well as the works which have already been mentioned by *Baumann, Feugueray, Thömes*, to whom should be added *Max Maurenbrecher: Thomas' Stellung zu dem Wirtschaftsleben seiner Zeit, 1898* (unfortunately, only the first volume has been published). Alongside of the Thomist writings themselves the works of the Neo-Thomists should always be studied as well, because they have made a systematic collection of the scattered material, and they bring out very fully its inner meaning in contrast to the very different modern spirit, and also because in their fight against the modern doctrine of Society they make very plain the historical importance of Thomism. Here we would make special mention of the very instructive work (already named) by *Theod. Meyer, S. J.: Die christlich-ethischen Sozialprinzipien und die Arbeiterfrage, 1904*, the first work appearing in the series *Die soziale Frage beleuchtet durch die Stimmen aus Maria Laach;* in the other works in this series, which deal with all kinds of modern social and political questions, it is possible to gain a good impression of the "spirit" which animates the Catholic Christian sociological thought of the present day; further see *Cathrein: Moralphilosophie. Eine wissen-*

schaftliche Darstellung der sittlichen, einschliesslich der rechtlichen Ordnung[3], *1899*, as well as *Ratzinger: Die Volkswirtschaft in ihren ethischen Grundlagen, 1881;* also *von Nostitz-Rieneck: Das Problem der Kultur, 1885.* Most of the works which deal with the Thomist doctrine of society and of politics have one defect, namely, that they do not take into account the ideal type of sociological thought which has been formulated in these works, or the fundamental theory of the sociology of Thomism, but they place the various doctrines alongside of one another, without attempting to reconcile them with each other. These theories, however, are in part those which are most dependent upon the history of the time and the least influential, in part, too, in their historically effective content they cannot thus be understood, but if that spirit is not felt they seem to be an eclectic blend of ideas from the Bible, the Fathers, Aristotle, Cicero, Seneca, the Canon Law and the conditions of the day, which *Janet* complains is all in great confusion. In reality, however, all this material forms part of a very able and consistent intellectual whole. *Von Eicken* should also be mentioned here, who certainly tries to present the whole mediaeval doctrine of civilization and of Society as one theory. But his treatment of the subject becomes an absolute travesty of the reality, since, in the most vigorous and doctrinaire way, he makes everything depend upon the conception of the world-domination of asceticism, and claims that in principle the Church did away with the Family, the State and Society altogether, and replaced all these group-forms by her own life. The only true ideal of the Church is supposed to be the ascetic Divine State as the sole form of social life, with the removal of the sex-life, of the State and sovereignty, of property and inequality. Although, in spite of this, the Church also uses the relative Christian Law of Nature, this is said to be due to the fact that the nature of the world with its opposing ideas has forced this upon the Church; and when the further objection is raised that the leading theologians derived this Natural Law from Christian thought, and gave it the most explicit recognition, the writer argues that this was due to a most unhappy lack of clearness of thought, which prevented the Church from ever coming to a clear understanding of the distinctive principles upon which she was based. All these arguments, however, are based upon false assumptions. On principle he does not attempt to explain the arguments of the theologians themselves, or of St. Thomas in particular, because he is convinced that he knows what these theologians do not know, and which they absolutely oppose—namely, that the world-supremacy of asceticism is the only fundamental Catholic idea, and that behind every effort to relate secular institutions with a religious value for life, there lies in wait the logical consequence of the ascetic domination of the world which denies the world, even when the religious expressions in question have themselves no suspicion of this. Instead of basing his study on the works of the great theologians, he prefers to amass a large number of individual characteristics which he pieces together like a mosaic, which are collected especially from monastic literature—that is, from the works of those who entirely renounce the world. This, however, produces a false impression of the whole subject, which, further, would make it quite impossible to understand the Catholicism of the present day and its social philosophy.—The section in *Gierke: Genossenschaftsrecht, III, 501-644,* which is entitled *Die publizistischen Lehren des Mittelalters,* refers to the whole mediaeval doctrine of Society, as well as to that of St. Thomas in particular; it is important to remember always that this general background forms an important complement to the thought of Thomism. There is also material to be found in *Gierke: Althusius und die Entwickelung der naturrechtlichen Staats-*

theorien, 1880.—On the situation in general, see *A. Ehrhard: Das Mittelalter und seine kirchliche Entwickelung, 1908.*

[125] (p. 281.) Cf. *Cathrein, II, 373.* "Naturally we shall only draw into the circle of our inquiry the societies which result necessarily out of the nature of mankind, and which alone are fit for and need to be the subjects of a philosophical inquiry, because they alone possess by nature a definite task and a definite organization. From the point of view of philosophy, the free societies are only regarded from the viewpoint of the general principles of law, which we have already made plain in the section on treaties and covenants (see above, *340 ff.*)." They are regulated according to the principles of the virtue of righteousness. At the same time, the observance of covenants which are not against righteousness is a duty of the *lege naturae.* This simplifies the Catholic doctrine of Society very much, and sets aside from the very outset a great mass of material, with which modern sociology is occupied, in order to find, not norms of Natural Law, but empirically based general conceptions of sociological relations. The fundamental and decisive idea is the gathering together into one of the natural and the normative, for which the Stoic doctrine of the Law of Nature and the Christian doctrine of Providence provide the foundation. At this point Catholic social doctrine comes into contact with its modern opposite, the biological-psychologically influenced social doctrine (on this see *P. Barth: Die Philosophie der Geschichte als Soziologie, I, 1897*), for which likewise that which is necessary for nature is also the normative, only that in the one instance nature is interpreted from the point of view of the normative, and in the other the normative is interpreted from nature. The modern epistemological idealism on the contrary creates quite other bases for social ethics, with its fundamental researches into the relation between the natural and the normative, between the psychological and the valid; cf. *Tönnies: Ethik u. Sozialismus, Archiv XXV.*

[126] (p. 283.) Cf. *Werne, II, 460 f.*, and *1 a, 2 ae, qu. 96, art. 3,* according to which even apart from the Fall a natural inequality of humanity in respect of spiritual and physical qualities would have been developed, and would have led to natural and necessary conditions of dominion on the part of some. Most striking of all in this connection is the change in the two main problems, which from time immemorial had held a predominating position, those of *property* and *slavery.* Here the Early Church and the Stoics denied that private property or slavery ever had any place within the pure Law of Nature; they regarded both as penalties for sin, and as means of curing the evil due to sin. St. Thomas, however, is now inclined, following Aristotle, to justify both under certain circumstances, from the point of view of evolution, through consideration for circumstances and utility, within certain limits also from the pure Law of Nature, without taking the Fall into account. It serves the development of humanity, he argues, if private property should arise out of the original negative communism; only its special forms are conditioned by the fallen state, though indeed Redemption again releases it for the use of all through the duty of love; see *Janet, I, 374–377,* and *2 a, 2 ae, qu. 57,* on Natural and positive Law, and *qu. 66, art. 2,* on private property. His views on slavery are similar, though they are expressed with more reserve; in the *Expositiones,* the commentary on the *Politics* of Aristotle, he accepts without question the argument of Aristotle, who bases slavery upon natural human inequality; in the *Summa, I, qu. 96, art. 3,* and *2 a, 2 ae, qu. 57, art. 3,* he declares that conditions of sovereignty are necessary from the point of view of Natural Law, and that they are not sinful; the slave-relationship, however, is a penalty for

sin, but within the conditions of the fallen state it is justified for the good
both of the slave as well as the master. At the same time he also says that
slavery is due to the law of nations, which is a natural law which takes concrete
circumstances into account without bringing in the idea of sin. See *Janet,
377–379;* on both points, see also *Maurenbrecher,* who rightly lays stress on the
inconsistencies in the teaching on slavery, while in that on property he lays
most emphasis upon the departure from the ancient teaching of the Fathers.
With regard to the third chief problem of the *Dominium,* that of political
sovereignty, it is clear from the above that this was held to have been part of
the pure Law of Nature, and that this view was still retained; it is only the
special compulsory form of the royal power which is due to sin, but as a means
of healing the evil of sin it is justified, *Janet. I, 398,* and *De reg. princ., II, 8 and 11.*

[127] (p. 283.) The limits of the Natural Law in the absolute as in the relative
state as the law of commands and of ends within this world, wherein it agrees
with the Mosaic Law, contrasted with the Gospel law of freedom, love, and
the supernatural-mystical end, see *1a, 2ae, qu. 107* and *108.* Both laws can be
differentiated "secundum quod una propinquius ordinat ad finem, alia vero
remotius: puta in una eademque civitate dicitur alia lex, quae imponitur viris
perfectis, qui statim possunt exequi ea, quae pertinent ad bonum commune;
et alia lex datur de disciplina puerorum, qui sunt instruendi, qualiter postmodum opera virorum exequantur", *qu. 107, art. 1;* here also the idea of
development.

[128] (p. 283.) The whole way of thinking which lies behind the ethical
teaching is that the absolute end of the *beatitudo* or *visio dei excedens facultatem
creaturae* can only be attained through a preparatory process of self-discipline,
and of the acquisition of merit through natural reason or the Natural Law.
These natural merits, effected by the freedom imparted to man, which are
also due to the share in the education of the world by God which is given to
man, and therefore ultimately to be referred back to the impulse of reason
divinely implanted in man, constitute the disposition and the preparation for
the reception of the virtues implanted by grace. Thus the whole process of
preparation comes under the control and guidance of the final religious end,
and thus of the Church, and, since this preparation is effected by the *Lex
Naturae,* all this also is included in this *Lex.* This, however, covers the whole
range of secular activity; *1a, 2ae, qu.94, art. 2;* the first is self-preservation with
all that this involves; the second refers to sex-relations and the education
(in the widest sense) of the coming generation. While both these are common
to man with all creatures *ex lege naturae,* the third is peculiar to the *lex naturae*
of humanity—namely, the ends of knowledge and the social combinations of
mankind. Since all this is referred to the absolute end, it is also referred to
the Church, and thus there arises a double conception of the Church, the
Church in the narrower sense, as the sacramental hierarchical institution,
and the Church in the wider sense, as the *respublica Christiana* or the *Corpus
Christianum* or the *regnum Christi*—that is, as the sum-total of life-relations formed
by the absolute purpose of grace. *Feugueray, p. 31,* remarks very aptly: "Everywhere grace is joined with nature, not in order to destroy it, but in order to be
added to it; and while it dominates nature it also exalts it. This distinctive
element also appears in the question of politics. Beyond and above rational
and philosophical politics there are the politics of theology, whose aim is not
to overthrow it, but to modify its conclusions and give it a different character.
The natural order of human society is thus completed and consummated in
the supernatural order." *Thömes* quotes (*p. 24*) from the *Commentary on Boethius:*

"Nec solum in spiritualibus, sed etiam in usu corporalium dirigit religio christiana et beatitudinem animae et corporis repromittit. Et ideo regulae ejus universales dicuntur, utpote totam vitam hominis et omne, quod ad ipsum quolibet modo pertinet, et continentes et ordinantes." At the same time it must be strongly emphasized that the expression "political" always means everything social in general, and not simply that which refers to the State, as St. Thomas says in the explanation of the Neo-Platonic graduated process of "virtutes purgati animi, purgatoriae et politicae: 'Est enim considerandum, quod ad politicas virtutes, secundum quod hic dicuntur, pertinet non solum bene operari ad commune, sed etiam bene operari ad partes communis sc. ad domum et aliquam singularem personam'." *Thömes: 72.* On the dualistic conception of the Church and the *regnum Christi*, see *Meyer, 65*: "From this point of view also the moral natural organism of human society is regarded, and as a glorious member, indissolubly connected, at the same time, with the supernatural social organism of the Christian Church, and thus incorporated into that magnificent world-harmony." On that, cf. *De reg. principum, I, 12.* Similarly, *p. 34*: "Whoever desires to take in hand the work of social reform should bear in mind that he is entering a sanctuary which is twice holy. It is hallowed by the foundation of nature, and it is again hallowed by the Divine Hand of the World-Redeemer who is the second Adam—also in the social sense—the regenerating principle of the whole social structure." Further, *St. Thomas: Summa, III, qu. 8, arts. 1 and 2*: "Genus humanum consideratur quasi unum corpus, quod vocatur mysticum, cujus caput est ipse Christus et quantum ad animas et quantum ad corpora." Further passages in *Gierke, III, 518*: "Countless times theologians and canonists use the word *ecclesia* in the sense of the whole body of humanity." *Vinc. Bellovacensis* speaks of "duo latera corporis unius". In the *Summa* of *Stephan Tornacensis* these words occur: "In eadem civitate sub uno rege duo populi sunt, et secundum duos populos duae vitae, duo principatus, duplex jurisdictionis ordo procedit"; the *civitas* is the *ecclesia*, the King is Christ, the peoples are the clergy and the laity, the two orders of life are the spiritual and the temporal, the *principatus* are the *sacerdotium* and the *regnum*, the two spheres of administration are the *divinum* and the *humanum*. At the same time a distinction is drawn between these two orders of life. "The mediaeval spirit is one in this, that it is convinced that the dualism cannot be final, but that all contradictions and inconsistencies must finally be lost in a higher unity." Passages which treat of this *ad unum reduci*, the *ordinatio ad unum*, the *unitas principii*, and on the basis of this argument of the unity and all-inclusive Christian valuation of life, see *pp. 519 ff.* Further, this is also the presupposition of the doctrine of the State which is opposed to the Curia, which only requires that within the system there should be a free agreement instead of the absolute control of the Church, *Gierke, III, 537–539.*

[129] (p. 283.) This is brought out very clearly in the historical sections of *Ratzinger's Volkswirtschaft*, which really only deals indirectly with the message of Jesus, since all that he says on this point is that humanity is hallowed by the fact that Jesus is the God-Man, and that work and the economic order are hallowed because He was a carpenter! Above all, the phrase *et cetera adjicientur vobis* is made to cover everything. According to *R.* it was only possible to begin with Paul. The patristic teaching also provided very one-sided and imperfect rules, owing to the fact that it grew up in a situation limited by the existence of a society wholly sunk in luxury and want. It was only in the Middle Ages that there was a classic period, to reach which, however, "a long, long way" had to be trodden, and to which the present day ought to return

while maintaining the fruits of the great progress effected by Capitalism, which ought to be controlled by the State, and simply made to serve the ends of really productive labour.

[130] (p. 284.) The consciousness of possessing a fundamental theory of this kind as a panacea for all social ills, characterizes the literature of the Neo-Thomist movement, see *Meyer, p. 5*: "The political questions have coalesced entirely with the social questions. But this solidarity lies much deeper than is generally supposed. It is in no wise based upon the surface of the external mutual influence of both these spheres, which are so closely connected with each other. Their real and their only foundation is no other than the indivisible unity of the whole moral order of the world. *P. 5:* "The solution of the social problem takes place upon the foundation of its unchangeable and holy principles, which form the natural basis for the whole social organism." *P. 6:* "The unchangeable idea and the essential basis of the social structure." *P. 7:* "The banner of invulnerable and wholesome principles . . . must be held high by the Church, and its priestly organs, the appointed teachers of morals and disinterested advisers of the Christian people." *P. 9:* "The Truth of God, inward harmony and order, that is, the eternal law of morality and of justice, is its (speaking of society) natural condition of life." *P. 23:* "The truth and the unchangeable necessity of a moral principle." *P. 28:* "The laws of social existence."—*Gierke's Genossenschaftsrecht, III*, really reaches its highest point in the manifestation of a fundamental theory of this kind. *P. 510:* "The development of the Roman-Canonist corporation theory came into touch at many points with the aspirations of the mediaeval spirit, which desired to understand in principle the Church and the State as a collective phenomenon, and thus to comprehend in a scientific manner the nature of human society in general. Although these endeavours began as far back as the days of the great Investiture controversy, it was only in the thirteenth century that they bore fruit in a formulated political theory. From that time forward these political doctrines were continued and developed in an unbroken process of development, and they became the supporters of the first independent philosophy of the State and of Law. And precisely for this reason they introduced an entirely new force into the history of conceptions of law. This result was due to the combined labours of various sciences. Theology and scholastic philosophy, political history and practical party politics, here came together in the same sphere with corporative jurisprudence. Although the various standpoints, aims, and methods were very unequal, and different from each other, here, as everywhere else, mediaeval science preserved a far-reaching unity and collective spirit. For, first of all, mediaeval society shared a common outlook upon the world, whose main principles were regarded by the mediaeval spirit not as an invention of its own, but as the revealed presupposition of human science. Thus men borrowed right and left from each other what they needed. . . . In this way the most varied elements from many different sources came to be combined together in one system: (1) The Holy Scriptures and their interpretation; (2) the patristic teaching, and, above all, the teaching of Augustine, about the Divine State, provided the specifically Christian features of the mediaeval doctrine of Society; (3) through the mediaeval legends of history and the popular views which they introduced there came in the Germanic ideas peculiar to the mediaeval spirit; (4) the reawakening of the ancient philosophy of the State, and, above all, of the Politics of Aristotle, which became the settled canon in these matters, was from the very outset in any case the standard for the scientific form of the whole doctrine; (5) and to

all these sources jurisprudence added an immense mass of the material of positive law which was treasured up in Roman and Canon Law and to some extent in the newer legislation of the Church." *Gierke* regards the nature of the order of Society which was thus constructed as the "organic idea"; he pays no special attention to the idea of Patriarchalism.

131 (p. 285.) On this question, cf. *Thomas: Contra Gent.*, *III*, *16–25*, the world order and all existence in general intended for God alone, *III*, *112–121*, the connection of the *Leges* given to man with an organic whole, directed towards the supreme aim of the love of God; on the starting-point and the type of the organic way of thinking in the *Corpus mysticum Christi*, see the *Summa*, *III*, *qu. 8*, and in particular the exposition of the passages which contain the parable of the Body (*Rom. xii and 1 Cor. xii*) in *Epist. ad Romanos*, *c. XII, lectio II*, and *ad Corinth I*, *c. XII, lectio 1–3*. The application of the organic idea in the Platonist and Aristotelian sense, as well as in the Scriptural sense, to human societies in general, and to the State in particular, *De reg. princ.*, *I*, *c. 1–3, 12.*— This subject is handled excellently by *Gierke: Genossenschaftsrecht*, *III* and *Althusius*. The general idea of the organism of the world, of humanity, of the individual sectional societies, of the Church, of the State, of the Family, and of all the social combinations in between, after the example of the animate universe, of the relation of body and soul, of the animal organism, of the Platonist microcosm according to which the macrocosm of the State is man on the large scale, and according to the specific Aristotelian doctrine, issues from a collective will flowing from reason, out of a special category, realizing definite ends for a definite purpose, see *Gierke*, *III*, *514–517*; the articulation within this organism on the basis of the inequality due to nature, and the division of labour to which this gives rise, with the relation of each member to the collective whole (*III*, *553–556*). An excellent summary in *Althusius, pp. 60–62*. There is similar material, though less complete, in *Maurenbrecher, pp. 29–38*. *M.* emphasizes that the argument for the necessity of the organism of Society in St. Thomas differs from that of Aristotle, in the latter it is the striving of reason, which only in the political community comes to its full exercise, and only in this self-activity of the reason of the community is the welfare of man achieved; in St. Thomas the reason is the necessity for the division of labour and the complementary system of callings and profits, which again plays no part in the theory of Aristotle. In this *M.* sees a different orientation of the organic idea from that of Aristotle, arguing that involuntarily St. Thomas has derived this idea from the social organization of the Middle Ages, which was always present to his consciousness. To Aristotle the Thomist interpretation would seem very materialistic. This is certainly true, but it is not the most important aspect of the question. The real example is the *Corpus Mysticum* of the Church, which, in accordance with the well-known Pauline parable, represents the division of labour through its different classes and callings. This is the idea which has been transferred with all its implications to the doctrine of society which we are considering; all the organic groupings are called technically *corpora mystica*, and even the organization of these secula *corpora mystica* are described as a hierarchy; see the references and quotations in *Gierke*, *III*, *518*, *546–553*; *Althusius*, *132–135*, *227 f*. The way in which this organic idea rose is a comparatively indifferent matter—whether through force and compulsion, the impulse of reason, or a social contract—since in all God effects the *causa remota*, and even the contractual origin was only conditioned by the impulse of reason, operative in the groups which thus came together under the guidance of God; indeed, even if the origin were due to force, this also

was under the control of Providence. See *Gierke, III, 568–581 556*; *Althusius, 63, 66*. The decisive element is this: that in actual fact all the various views and opinions about the question of the origin of the social groups always end in the idea of the organism, and its necessity from the point of view of the Divine Reason. Where the theories about the manner in which this idea of the organism arose took an independent line, and came to conclusions which differed from those of the temporal-spiritual organism, then the distinctive Catholic idea was left behind, and these theories tended to develop along the lines of modern thought, whether in the direction of the doctrine of sovereignty, or of the democratic Law of Nature; after the great thinkers of the sixteenth century, who were occupied with the doctrine of the State and of Society, the genuine Thomist ideal with some modernized alterations was again asserted afresh over against these modern theories. Cf. *Gothein: Staat und Gesellschaft des Zeitalters der Gegenreformation* in *Kultur der Gegenwart, II, 5.*— See also the brief but informative treatment of the subject by *Th. Meyer, 28–70*, and *Cathrein, II, 373–379.*

[132] (p. 287.) The patriarchal idea lurks behind all those expressions of opinion upon the organism which deal with Paul and the *Corpus Mysticum*, whereas the statements which are based on Aristotle (and indirectly on Plato) are only concerned with social necessities and requirements for the unity of the whole. Here, then, the purely ethical Pauline ideas are apparent, which only desire to reconcile the inequalities of real life with the religious equality of the children of God, and to overcome the former by ethical means, but which had no intention of establishing an organic theory of Society. Here the expositions of *Rom. xii* and *1 Cor. xii*, which have already been mentioned, are highly characteristic. The starting-point for such reflections is provided by the inequalities of mankind, which, in the view of St. Thomas, belong to the nature of humanity. On the one hand they are implied in the idea of the organism and of the division of labour, but there are also other reasons. (1) Also in St. Thomas there enters in the idea of the inscrutable Divine Will, which has placed human beings in the world, not, as in the sub-human sphere, as a unified species, but as individuals, each of whom has a special significance, and which further, through Predestination and Providence, has placed essential differences between them; *Contra Gent, III, c. 103:* "Sola creatura rationalis dirigitur a Deo ad suos actus non solum secundum speciem, sed etiam secundum individuum." But the differences which thus result from this are, in spite of the share which men take in the government of the world by God through reason, still conditioned by the Divine Providence: "Participat rationalis creatura divinam providentiam non solum secundum gubernari, sed etiam secundum gubernare. . . . Omnis autem inferior providentia divinae providentiae subditur quasi supremae. Gubernatio igitur actuum rationalis creaturae, inquantum sunt actus personales, ad divinam providentiam pertinet." This, however, produces strongly marked differences; *Lectio III ad Cor. I xii:* "Etsi membrorum distinctio sit opus naturae, hoc tamen agit natura ut instrumentum divinae providentiae." Hence Paul says: "unum quodque eorum in corpore"; but Paul adds: "et, sicut voluit, posuit Deus membra diversa," on which Thomas comments: "Nam prima causa institutionis rerum est voluntas divina secundum illud *Psalm 113* 'omna quaecunque voluit fecit'. Sic autem et in Ecclesia disposuit diversa officia et diversos status [this includes also the secular members] secundum suam voluntatem: unde et Ephes. I, ii, dicitur 'praedestinati secundum propositum ejus, qui operatur omnia secundum consilium voluntatis suae'." At the same time we must

remember that St. Thomas believed firmly in predestination; he pronounces free will as a form of carrying out the Will of God and evil as a *defectus*; *Contra Gent., III, 402*: "necesse est praedictam distinctionem hominum ab aeterno a Deo esse ordinatam." This implies that the positive Divine Will has a large sphere of action, even in matters which are not directly concerned with the salvation of mankind, although in the conception of God Reason is placed above Will: here is one of the most obscure elements in the Thomist system, the irrational aspect is neither in the conception of God nor anywhere else really set aside, although the system claims to be as rational as possible. (2) The differences are natural, as St. Thomas emphasizes everywhere, in which he follows Aristotle: "Illi qui intellectu praeeminent, naturaliter dominantur; illi vero qui sunt intellectu deficientes, corpore vero robusti, a natura videntur instituti ad serviendum." This natural inequality serves the purposes of order, which only becomes wrong when natural inequality is turned into an unnatural inequality by sin and passion: "inordinatio provenit ex eo, quod non propter intellectus praeeminentiam aliquis praeest, sed vel robore corporali dominium sibi usurpat, vel propter sensualem affectionem aliquis ad regendum praeficitur. . . . Hujusmodi autem inordinatio divinam providentiam non excludit, provenit enim ex permissione divina propter defectum inferiorum agentium, sicut et de aliis malis superius dictum est." (3) This leads to the argument that the inequalities which do not coincide with a just order are due to the Fall; this idea recurs constantly. (4) The ultimate reason lies in positive law, which in the form of government and of class privilege according to circumstances makes distinctions, which find their expression quite naturally in special claims on life, the desire to be honoured, and for a special share in the *bonum commune*. The doctrine of the *justitia distributiva* is of special interest in this connection; it is held that this regulates the share of the individual groups and persons in the *bonum commune* of society; *Summa, 2 a, 2 ae, qu. 61, a. 2*: "in distributiva justitia datur alicui privatae personae, inquantum id, quod est totius, est debitum parti; quod quidem tanto majus est, quanto ipsa pars majorem principalitatem habet in toto. Et ideo in distributiva justitia tanto plus alicui de bonis communibus datur, quanto majorem illa persona habet principalitatem in communitate. Quae quidem principalitas attenditur in aristocratica secundum virtutes, in oligarchica secundum divitias, in democratica secundum libertatem et in aliis aliter." In line with Aristotle this share in the goods belonging to the whole is to be in proportion to the individual's position in society. Hence the varied penalties for offences against various persons of high position; hence also "respect of persons" before the law is not only not contrary to righteousness, but it is even required by distributive righteousness (justice), cf. *ibid., qu. 62, de acceptione personarum*. The original illustration of such a position of dominance, conditioned by the force of nature, by the corruption due to sin, by the Divine order, and by human positive law, together with the ethical development in this relationship through the voluntary loving mutual relations within it, is the Family, with the *patria potestas* over the wife, the children, and the domestics; see *ibid., qu. 57, a. 4*: "utrum jus dominativum et jus paternum debeant distingui": the idea of law cannot be applied to the family relationship, since children and domestics belong inherently to the master, and are not persons who have an independent position apart from him, a characteristic which, in a modified form, is also applied to the wife; but in so far as the wife, the children, and the domestics are also regarded as human beings, they also have rights of their own: "ideo inquantum uterque (filius et servus) est homo, aliquo modo ad eos est justitia et propter hoc etiam aliquae leges dantur de his, quae sunt patris ad filium vel domini ad servum; sed inquantum uterque est aliquid alterius [that is, a part of the master himself], secundum hoc deficit ibi perfecta ratio. . . . Uxor autem, quamvis sit aliquid viri, . . . tamen magis distinguitur a viro quam filius a patre vel servus a domino . . . inter eos non est etiam simpliciter politicum justum, sed magis justum oeconomicum." These formulas come from Aristotle; for the actual social content, which they conceal, see the excellent observations of *Marianne Weber*, in her *Ehefrau und Mutter, 200–278*. The Christian-ethical transference of these legal relationships into the sphere of the freedom and love in Christ is revealed in the expositions of the Bible which have been already quoted, and in the tractates on the theological virtue of love and harmony, to which St. Thomas himself alludes (*ibid., qu. 80*), on the "virtutes justitiae annexae" and *qu. 81*: "de aliis autem hic enumeratis supra dictum est partim in tractatu de caritate, sc. de concordia et aliis hujusmodi." In this, however, the Family is the pattern for the ethical trans-formation of all conditions of force, superiority, and inequality; *De reg. princ., I, 1*: "Qui domum regit non rex, sed paterfamilias dicitur, habet tamen aliquam similitudinem regis, propter quam aliquando reges populorum patres vocantur." On the subject of the Family, including the domestics, as the source of all the overcoming of inequality through patriarchal-ethical ideas, see also *Th. Meyer, 70–142*, especially *p. 78*: "In this original social institution, which bears upon the face of it the traces of the ordering of the Hand of God, the organic inequality of the members appears as a fundamental law. This means, however, that this shows us the pattern of the Divine Plan for the whole formation of Society from the smallest beginnings up to the formation of a nation. For the further structure must inevitably follow the lines laid down at the beginning." The same emphasis is laid upon the family ideal as the patriarchal spirit of willing service and love extended to cover the whole of society by *Ratzinger*, in his *Die Volkswirtschaft in ihren sittlichen Grundlagen, p. 474*: "In the Family we find already the fundamental moral laws, according to which society could develop and ought to progress. These principles are love and freedom. Parental love cares for the helpless child, and after a long process of training and development the child is given a suitable sphere of activity in which he can move freely. Out of the love of the parents there arises the authority, the right, to influence the activity of the members of the family, to guide them into a definite direction and thus to confine them within certain limits. Since, however, this authority only issues from love, it is clear that freedom will not be limited more than the kindly forethought of the head of the family sees that it is necessary for the good of the whole. Love, authority, union on the one hand, freedom, justice, equality on the other hand, form the foundations of the social structure, of the family on a small scale, of Society on a large scale." *P. 406*: "All cannot have the same share to the same degree, Society is graduated rather on patriarchal and hierarchical lines; there will always be distinctions, high and low, rich and poor. But there is one thing which is not necessary, and that is that there should be, as there are to-day, those who are disinherited. Every human being can and ought to have his own share in the whole, according to his social position and the work which he renders."

[133] (p. 289.) On this point cf. *Feugueray* and *Baumann*, and in particular *Gierke*, where all these features are carefully gathered together, and are illus-trated from a very wide range of reading, which extends far beyond the litera-ture on St. Thomas himself. There also the Thomist passages are indicated;

on subjective public right, as the result of membership in the organism and the relation to the central end, see especially *pp. 553, 569–574, 595–599, 619–621,* the right of resistance, *624–626; Althusius, 138 and 275; von Eicken, 550 and 557.* Further illustrations of such democratic-individualistic views based upon the Catholic organic conception of Natural Law are provided by *Figgis: From Gerson to Grotius, Cambridge, 1907,* in which the development of the modern democratic idea of the Law of Nature from the ecclesiastical ideas is described in a very instructive way. How far modern Catholicism is in a position to enter into democratic-individualistic-rationalistic ideas is shown by the well-known *Spectator* Letters. From *Hitze: Kapital-Arbeit; Uhlhorst: Kath. u. Prot. gegenüber der sozialen Frage, 1887,* quotes thus: "Revolutions are deeds of the spirit, in them the moral element far exceeds the material. . . . It is a struggle between the historical forces and the rights of reason, a struggle between free personality and the rigidity of society, of the untrammelled, untamed spirit against the despiritualized form, of progress against stagnation, of the right which is being won against that which has been won, and since a peaceful reconciliation is not possible, the decision must be won by the sword, at the price of blood; this is almost a necessity of nature" (*p. 25*). All this, however, is conceived within the framework of the organic idea of Thomism. There it is said that there is a right to resist a tyrant, or a ruling authority which is not fulfilling its end of reason. It is a technical phrase taken from Aristotle's ethic. Those public subjective rights, however, are not granted by the State, or only made into rights by the recognition of the State, but they are to be understood in the light of the natural law of the organic idea, obligatory for the State and to be maintained by the Church; this is a fundamental difference from the modern point of view on the law of the State; cf. *Jellinek: System der subjektiven öffentlichen Rechte², 1905.* Hence there is nothing which modern Catholic literature opposes so hotly as the idea that the State has the right to create laws.

133b (p. 291.) For the communistic features, see below, in the discussion of the conceptions of property. It ought to be emphasized that this communism is always only relative in character, and to be introduced only in case of need. Further, the mediaeval period, with its lack of the individualistic-liberal-capitalistic economic order, and with the comparative domination of a communistic spirit in social actualities, did not need to emphasize it in principle. In the present-day reaction against the liberal economic order which has come into being in the interval, Catholicism now brings out its communistic elements, and lays stress on them in principle, and to this extent it comes very near to the Socialists, as *Uhlhorn: Prot. u. Kath.,* in a whole series of examples, notes, with proper Lutheran disapproval, *pp. 21–26;* see also *G. Wermert: Neuere sozialpolitische Anschauungen im Katholizismus innerhalb Deutschlands, Jena, 1885,* also the social pronouncements of Leo XIII. This Catholic communism is, however, always only relative, under the control of the Church, and aims at the social unity of certain classes, with a system of mutual support and self-limitation, that is, it remains within the framework of the class-organic idea; *Uhlhorn, pp. 22, 27, 9f.,* gives illustrations of this also.

134 (p. 292.) On the "traditionalist" character of the system, and the insistence on the duty of remaining within the traditional calling and position to which one has been assigned in society, the taboo on changing one's calling, with the possible exception of entering the monastic life, see *Maurenbrecher, 48, 50, 53, 89;* for the "traditionalist" character of economic thought in particular, in which the leading idea is the preservation for each individual of the basis of existence in accordance with one's class, and the guaranteeing of such a degree necessary

for existence (which may not be exceeded) through government and guild regulations, and which also stresses the need for frugality and contentment with little, see *Ratzinger: Die Volkswirtschaft in ihren sittlichen Grundlagen, 1881*; R. sees in the return to these principles, and in submission to government regulations founded on these principles—connected with Capitalism (which cannot be set aside) and with the division of labour—the Christian challenge to the social science of the present day. The mediaeval period "manifested this brilliant result of Christian civilization" (*p. 144*). Through sacrifice, i.e. through the renunciation of the freely calculating methods of production which belong to the Capitalist system, and the renewal of the patriarchal spirit, the society of the present day, which is on the edge of a precipice, must achieve this return to these principles (*p. 403*). On the traditionalist character of the Thomist doctrine of the calling, and of economics, see also *Max Weber: Die Prot. Ethik, etc., Archiv. XX, 20–26; XXI, 81–83*. On the patriarchal-conservative view of political matters see the tractate *De reg. princ.*, which only allows a right of resistance of a very limited kind with reference to a morally bad and godless Prince, but which otherwise exalts the religious Prince who fulfils his duty in the spirit of love, as the representative of God, and assures him that he will have a special place in heaven with a special reward; cf. the heaven of the princes in Dante's Paradise.

[136] (p. 296.) On this point cf. *Maurenbrecher, 29–38; Max Weber: Protest. Ethik. Archiv, XX, 36–42.* From this point of view ethics often become absolutely the ethic of the class and the calling or profession; see the analysis of the ethic of Anthony of Florence which is based upon St. Thomas in *Gass, I, 375–383*: "The ethic which was intended to be universal becomes immediately confined within the limits of a class morality, which continues to dominate it," "a conservative ecclesiastical system of ethics based upon routine, works, merits, obedience, and indulgences." "Excessive emphasis upon the merit of obedience," "a pedantic enumeration of the courtesies which one has to offer to one's superiors and to dignitaries."—For the contrast between this way of acting and that of the society of late antiquity see the great article by *Max Weber: Agrargeschichte (Altertum)* in the *Handwörterbuch der Staatswissenschaften*[3]; especially *p. 67*.—The Catholicism of the present day, with its deliberate emphasis upon culture also lays stress upon the idea of the calling. *Uhlhorn: Katholizismus und Protestantismus gegenüber der sozialen Frage, 1887,* thinks therefore that in this point modern Catholicism is "Lutheran" in its spirit, and that "the life of the world is regarded from a very different point of view from that of St. Thomas". But that is quite wrong. The ethic of civilization of St. Thomas according to the principle: "Gratia praesupponit et perficit naturam", contains all the principles of modern Catholicism. "The interpretation of the Thomist doctrine". *P. 11:* "It would be best of all if all men and women could become monks and nuns and lead a contemplative life. This is, however, impossible; it is a necessity for man to lead the active life instead of the contemplative, that is, that he must work, because otherwise he would starve. St. Thomas gives no higher place to work than this", is, it is true, a view which is held by very many Protestants, but it is positively false. It is based upon isolated expressions, which it uses as a basis for sweeping generalizations, in a quite inadmissible way; above all, it overlooks the fact that the Thomist system, taken as a whole, is precisely a cultural system, which, in its own day, was very modern. Every Catholic Congress, with its glorification of culture based upon Thomism, reveals this very plainly to those who wish to see.

¹³⁷ (p. 298.) See above, *Note 132*; and also *Maurenbrecher, 63–75*; in spite of the fact that he admits the universal duty of work, St. Thomas draws very clear distinctions; he distinguishes between mental and physical labour, and under the latter head he makes further distinctions, placing the aristocratic and noble callings far above those which are not noble, and those which are executed by men who are unfree. He places the dependent wage-earners, who do not take part in the municipal government and who probably were themselves originally not free, among the mechanics and dirty people; similarly, with his townsman's point of view, he places the peasants in a subordinate position; the unfree he often regards with the natural depreciation of Aristotle, even when he allows that they also are human beings with human rights. All this, however, is a concession to Naturalism which is in striking contrast with the fundamental ideas of Christianity. These ideas arise only too easily out of Patriarchalism, just as they often occur very easily among the Conservatives of the present day, however much they may lay stress on their Christian piety. See also *Feugueray, pp. 60–81*, who argues that this Naturalism is due to the psychology of St. Thomas, that is, that it arises from his doctrine of the effectuation of individualization through the physical elements of the organism. This would lead ultimately to predestination. This is right, but it is only one element in the intellectual process of Patriarchalism. That, further, predestination and Naturalism really come to the same thing, even though differently expressed, is rightly suggested by *Jodl, I, 167*, in agreement with *Feuerbach*. The form of expression, however, makes a great deal of difference; if it disappears, Patriarchalism easily develops into the masterful point of view which demands service from all; it was easier to make this mistake in the Middle Ages than it is to-day, since to-day we have not only the conservative Christian argument before our eyes, but also the idea of evolution in the Darwin sense.

¹³⁹ (p. 298.) Here, and in the following sections, I keep very closely to the very exact presentation of the organic idea in Thomism of *Th. Meyer: Die christlich-ethischen Sozialprinzipien, pp. 45–47, 78*. Man, as a reflection of God's Providence, takes his share in the creation of the State; it is not a work of the impulse of nature but of reason, the State is under the guidance of Providence and belongs to the organic type of world-unity controlled by the wisdom of God. See also *Gierke, III, 556, 629 ff*. St. Thomas emphasizes the *ratio constituens civitatem*.

¹⁴¹ (p. 299.) On this point see the remarkably instructive articles by *H. Dietzel: Beiträge zur Geschichte des Sozialismus, Z. f. Lit. und Geschichte der Staatswissenschaften, I. D*. quotes Plato: "We have given to each his portion, and thus have made the whole beautiful", and he adds: "this passage contains one of the most plastic and concrete formulations of the 'organic social theory' ", namely, in so far as it concerns the objective idea of the whole, and is not thinking of the value of the individual (*p. 394*). Thus we find also in St. Thomas passages in which he speaks of the *pulchritudo* or the beauty of the whole, as the meaning of the organic idea, and makes this the argument for the differences in position of the various members; *De reg. princ. 3*: "Non enim est pulchritudo in corpore, nisi omnia membra fuerint decenter disposita; turpitudo autem contingit, quodcunque membrum indecenter se habeat; *Epist. I ad Cor., Lectio I*; "Pertinet autem ad decorem et perfectionem ecclesiae, ut in ea diversa ministeria sint, quae significantur per ordines ministrantium, quod mirabatur regina Saba in domo Salomonis." *Ibid., Lectio III:* "Perfectio corporis non tota consistit in uno membro, quamvis nobiliori, sed ad ejus

perfectionem requiruntur etiam ignobiliora", and "Ita etiam [as in the organic body] in Ecclesia sine officio abjectarum personarum, puta agricultorum et aliorum hujusmodi, praesens vita transiri non possit, quae tamen posset duci sine aliquibus excellentioribus personis contemplationi et sapientiae deputatis, quae Ecclesiae deserviunt ad hoc, quod sit ornatior et melius se habens". This is the Platonist aspect of the social thought of Thomism which sacrifices the individual entirely to the realization of the idea. It is likewise the fundamental character of the idealistic doctrine of the State taught by Hegel; see the treatment of this point by *Dietzel* in his *Rodbertus*. See also the same author's article *Individualismus* in the *Handwörterbuch der Staatswissenschaften*. St. Thomas connects this idea with the idea of the glory of God. Cf. *Summa*, *I*, *qu. 65*, *art. 2*: "Aequalitas justitiae locum habet in retribuendo; justum est enim quod aequalibus aequalia retribuantur. Non autem habet locum in prima rerum institutione. Sicut enim artifex ejusdem generis lapides in diversis partibus aedificii ponit absque injusticia, non propter aliquam diversitatem in lapidibus praecedentem, sed attendens ad perfectionem totius aedificii quae non esset, nisi lapides diversimode in aedificio collocarentur, sic et Deus a principio, ut esset perfectio in universo, diversas et inaequales creaturas instituit, secundum suam sapientiam absque injustitia, nulla tamen praesupposita meritorum distinctione."

[142] (p. 299.) This inconsistency is raised everywhere by St. Thomas, since his conception of the member, of the *officium* and *ministerium*, still aims at giving each member a share in the whole and his ethic desires to establish a religious-ethical equality, in spite of all existing differences. This is the tendency of the whole idea of the Patriarchalism of love, and in it the organic idea finds its complement. See also *Meyer* in the section: "There is nothing more harmful especially for the inner social relations of the commonwealth than the misinterpretation borrowed from paganism of the fundamental organic character of society" (*pp. 57–70*). This is directed against the Platonist, Aristotelian, Hegelian conception of the organic idea, and emphasizes instead the idea of Christian individualism, which requires not the realization of an abstract idea, but that the individual shall have a share in the highest values of life. *P. 58:* "The Socialistic ideal of Plato which means death to freedom." "Both Plato and Aristotle lacked the same thing, namely, the Christian key to the full understanding of that (organic) principle, the right estimate of the personal dignity of man." *P. 61:* "The striking similarity between the neo-pagan and the ancient pagan conception and estimate of a principle which is not in itself a wrong one is in no way accidental. It is based upon its opposition to the Christian interpretation of the social organism which alone is true." *P. 63:* "The chief corrective lay precisely in the Christian consciousness, and particularly in the Christian estimate of the personal dignity of man. We need only listen to two main representatives of the specifically Christian social philosophy, St. Augustine and St. Thomas." How, however, such an individualism can exist along with the organic idea, neither *Meyer* nor either of the men whom he cites can say. In reality, as has been shown above, this idea cancels out the organic principle altogether, and the name only remains. Certainly we are here dealing with the most difficult point in social ethics; not the individual as such, but the individual who is filled with absolute ethical values has a value of his own, and each can only claim to aim at the attainment of these values; on the other hand, however, owing to the qualities given by nature, those values are not realized for and in all individuals, or at least they are not realized for and in all in the same way, so that all that can

be said with any certainty is that those values have a directive influence upon the whole, while numerous individuals are utilized simply as presuppositions and means. Thus every kind of social ethic fluctuates between the realization of the objective values in themselves, and the subjective share in them taken by individuals, with great concessions to Naturalism; cf. my remarks on the report by *von Schultze-Gävernitz*, in the *Protokollen des Ev. soz. Kongresses, 1907.*

[143] (p. 300.) For authority as the soul of the whole organism, see the *Summa 2 a, 2 ae, qu. 60, art. 3:* "Potestas saecularis subditur spirituali sicut corpus animae"; *ibid., I, qu. 96, art. 4:* "Quandoque multa ordinantur ad unum, semper invenitur unum ut principale et dirigens"; *Contra Gent., IV, 76:* "optimum autem regimen multitunidis est, ut regatur per unum . . . unitatis congruentior causa est unus quam multi"; *Summa, 2 a, 2 ae, qu. 10, a. 11:* "Humanum regimen derivatur a divino regimine et ipsum debet imitari". *Contra Gent., IV, 76:* "Manifestum est, quod, quamvis populi distinguantur per diversas dioeceses et civitates, tamen sicut est una ecclesia, ita oportet esse unum populum Christianum. Sicut igitur in spirituali populo unius ecclesiae requiritur unus episcopus qui sit totius populi caput, ita in toto populo christiano requiritur quod unus sit totius ecclesiae caput." *De reg. princ., I, c. 2:* "Manifestum est, quod unitatem magis efficere potest, quod est per se unum quam plures," that means the monarchical constitution of each organism. The original influence of the Aristotelian organic idea is here as plain as in the basing of the organic idea on the division of labour and of services, and as here the guiding principle is the original image of the *corpus mysticum*, so there it was the original image of the uniform ecclesiastical idea. On authority as the centre of the organism, see further *Gierke, III, 517–547, 560 f.,* and especially *p. 555*: "Finally, it came to be held that the nature of an organism required absolutely one unifying force, which as *summum movens* should vivify, guide, and set the standard for all the other forces; thus men came to formulate the statement that every social body needs a dominant section (*pars principans*); it is immaterial whether this is regarded as the head, the heart, or the soul of the whole. From the comparison of the ruler of the whole to the head there arose in many quarters even the idea that the monarchy was a natural institution, since there can be only *one* head; indeed, frequently men went further still, and declared that apart from union with the natural head the whole body and each member of the same was deprived of life altogether." This was applied particularly to the Pope in his position over the Church and over the *respublica christiana. Th. Meyer* writes in a similar vein, *p. 50*: "Authority, the essential controlling element in every form of society, which, as its soul, likewise conditions its unity"; *p. 66:* "Although, on the one hand, St. Thomas emphasizes rightly that the natural process of social development from the particular to the general, from the family to the community, and to the civic society, to this extent develops from below upwards, his teaching cannot be rightly understood, especially the ideal purpose of this wonderful spiritual organism, unless we stand in spirit at the central point of the whole world-order. From this point of view then do we see the question of authority in the right light, as the essential element in Society in essence and origin, in its aim and its task, in its relation upwards to God, and downwards to its inferiors and dependents. This light, however, shines with its illumination upon the inner relation of the organic parts to each other intended by the Creator and upon their relation to the whole. Indeed, to a great extent this truth even illuminates the principles of a sound political economy and of good administration." On that point, see also *Contra Gent., III, 1–3; IV, 23.* Hence in the organic

idea *Meyer* distinguishes the constitutive from the administrative organism, *p. 53*, the former is the Aristotelian idea, the latter is the Catholic idea, which is supported by the former.

[144] (p. 302.) Cf. the section on asceticism in this work; also the section which deals with the architectonic character of the thought of Thomism; a classical expression of this in Marsilius of Padua in *Gierke, III, 552*: "componitur (the organism) ex quibusdam proportionatis partibus invicem ordinatis suaque opera sibi mutuo communicantibus et ad totum." In St. Thomas, see the explanation of *1 Cor. xii, lectio III*, in which he says that the *activi* are necessary for the *contemplativi* "indigent enim contemplativi per opera activorum sustentari" and likewise the laity for the prelates, who could not exist without them. How the state of virginity exists as a complementary state alongside of the state of regular marriage, is explained by *Ratzinger: p. 94*: "Virginity, far from being as is said as a reproach, an institution which brings sterility into society, is rather a cause which maintains fruitfulness. The explanation of this apparent contradiction lies in its moral order, in the power of example, in the energy of sacrifice. The state of celibacy, through the greatest sacrifices, the most heroic renunciation, and the highest virtues, awakens the moral energy of those who are married, and thus helps to ward off the dangers which threaten the honour of the family and of marriage when the energy of sacrifice is wanting." On the quantitative inequality of perfection, that is, of the actual relation to the central purpose of the organism, cf. *Summa, 1 a, 2 ae, qu. 108, a. 4*: "Quod homo totaliter ea, quae sunt mundi, abjiciat, non est necessarium ad proveniendum ad finem praedictum, quia potest homo utens rebus hujus mundi dummodo in eis finem non constituat, ad beatitudinem aeternam pervenire. Sed expeditius perveniet totaliter bona hujus mundi abdicando et ideo de hoc dantur consilia evangelii." Thereby the natural tendency or disposition is the decisive element: "Praedicta consilia, quantum est de se, sunt omnibus expedientia, sed ex indispositione aliquorum contingit, quod alicui expedientia non sunt, quia eorum affectus ad ea non inclinantur." Here again the doctrine of predestination and the positing of the Divine Will are in the background. On the quantitative differences extending even into the blessedness of heaven, see *Contra Gent., III, 58*: "Quum finis proportionaliter respondeat his, quae sunt ad finem, oportet, quod sicut aliqua diversimode praeparantur ad finem, ita diversimode participent finem. Visio autem divinae substantiae est ultimus finis cujuslibet intellectualis substantiae. Intellectuales autem substantiae non omnes aequaliter praeparantur ad finem; quaedam enim sunt majoris virtutis et quaedam minoris; virtus autem est via ad felicitatem. Oportet igitur quod in visione divina sit diversitas, quod quidam perfectius et quidam minus perfecte divinam substantiam videant. . . . Idem ergo est, quod omnes beatos facit, non tamen ab eo omnes aequaliter beatitudinem capiunt."

[145] (p. 305.) On this point cf. *Ratzinger: Gesch. d. kirchlichen Armenpflege*, which treats the mediaeval period better than the corresponding work of *Uhlhorn, p. 247*: "By the close of the twelfth century the church system of poor relief, based on the regulations laid down during the Carolingian period (which was itself the transformation of the free system of the Primitive Church into one which came under the State) had almost everywhere come to an end; the parish took no trouble or responsibility for its poor any longer; the secular clergy no longer had any desire to undertake the work of poor relief. Ecclesiastical legislation, which was now exercised exclusively by the Popes (in contrast with the legislation of the Councils of the Early Church, which

regulated officially the system of poor relief), no longer regarded the relief of the poor as part of its activity, and the funds of the Church had entirely forfeited the character of a poor fund. It was only the regular clergy who did not forget their duties to the poor, and so long as there were monasteries they carried on works of charity. To the monasteries there was added a new factor, that of the confraternities and Orders, which drew their recruits from the ranks of the laity, and who took the place of an ordered ecclesiastical system of poor relief, in order that the decline of the latter might not be felt too acutely. Almost at the same time the life of the corporations in the towns was formed, the guilds were founded, and part of their duty was to care for the needs of their impoverished members. These are the elements which gradually came to the fore after the Crusades, and stepped into the place left vacant by the ecclesiastical system of outdoor poor relief, without being able to replace the latter. It was impossible for the monasteries to exercise that strict control which is necessary in this work of poor relief, if it is not to do more harm than good, and the confraternities and Orders confined their labours almost exclusively to the work in the hospitals. That which the congregation had done in the Early Church, with its pastor at its head, in the way of caring for the poor in their own homes, had now become an unattainable ideal. Henceforward certainly the reproach that the Church simply gave alms, but no real relief, was to a great extent justified." It is characteristic of St. Thomas that alongside of his presentation of the personal morality in the ascent from the natural virtues to the supernatural, and alongside of his social philosophy with its cosmos of the natural-supernatural organism, the question of a social reform, or even of a mission of the Church for the healing of social evils, does not arise at all; on the lack of any idea of social reform in his teaching, in this sense, see *Maurenbrecher, p. 49:* "In the thought of St. Thomas the way of life for everyone is determined by his class and position in society, into which he is born through the power of the inscrutable Will of Providence; no one ought to sink below the level of the class into which he is born; but to attempt to strive to rise above it is also forbidden. A social elevation of the lower classes, an "upward development of the masses" is, therefore, entirely alien to the thought of St. Thomas; his social ideal is thoroughly conservative; in this he was in harmony with the mind of his age in these matters." See also *p. 88 f.,* also *Feugueray, p. 213 f.; Uhlhorn: Liebestätigkeit, II, 448.* To what a great extent also modern Catholic social ideals are a return to the natural-supernatural harmony of society of the Middle Ages is shown by *Ratzinger: Die Volkswirtschaft, p. 325 f.* "The dignity and honour of poverty and of work, love of poverty and of simplicity of life even in the midst of wealth, co-operation and the levelling of distinctions between rich and poor through love and freedom (i.e. good will)", this is the social programme. In this there is a return to the Law of Nature, which then in these social forms works quite naturally the greatest possible well-being, *p. 323:* "The same ideas which lead a man to the heights of union with God also answer the questions of political economy: of the relation between rich and poor, of gain and the use of wealth, of labour and the profit gained by labour, etc. Christianity brings to those who accept and follow its teachings not merely the Kingdom of God, but everything else as well: prosperity, the balance between riches and poverty, progress in work and in dominion over nature, the freedom and equality of all in their origin and their aim, protection against degradation and exploitation through the brotherly spirit, and in the consciousness that all are the sons of the one Father in Heaven." This, however, can only be realized with the aid of the

Law of Nature, and its organic world of classes and callings. The modern tendencies of Catholic social philosophy, which accept the idea of the independent movement of modern society, and wish to make their theories independent of the Natural-Law doctrine of the Church, are for that very reason clear departures from the principle. Politico-social Modernism is no less contrary to the principle than is Modernism in the sphere of dogma and of the philosophy of religion, and it shares the same fate. Cf. *Loisy: Quelques lettres sur des questions actuelles, 1908*; who rightly emphasizes above all the politico-social opposition of the Church to the modern world, and cherishes little hope of the victory of a politico-social Modernism of this kind.

[146] (p. 306.) On this peculiarity of the mediaeval conception of law, see *Gierke, III, 609–627*, who also makes clear the great contradictions and complications which this contained, and still contains.—Also *von Nostitz-Rieneck, S.J.: Das Problem der Kultur (Erg.-H. zu Stimmen aus Maria Laach), 1885, p. 20 :* "The existing foundation of civilization consists first of all in the whole of material nature, and secondly it consists in the Law of Nature, the Natural Law of Society and the Natural Law for private individuals. And only because this basis is given and is firmly established, has the historical development of positive law a clear origin and a sure foundation." Here also is applicable that which applies to the whole of Catholicism, *p. 8.* "We follow two leaders, who always point out the same way : sound reason and the Christian view of the world." This can be applied only to a Law of Nature and a sound reason of a quite definite historical stamp, namely, with the stamp of Thomism. Cf. *ibid., p. 49 f.*, and also *p. 52:* "If, however, economic and spiritual progress is so great that new economic conditions and new forms of popular education are created, then the accepted order of society and law, or more accurately speaking, a part of its positive-legal enactments in private and in State law, will be no longer suitable for the situation."

[146a] (p. 311.) Here also there appears the extraordinary significance of the class idea. For the part it plays in modern Catholic social philosophy, see *Uhlhorn: Prot. u. Kath., p. 23*, in which he thus summarizes *Hitze: Kapital und Arbeit*: "What is desired is the strengthening of the Church, the weakening of the State. The idea of the State is so little operative that *Hitze*, for example, does not even take into account the fact that peasants, manual workers, and others are still primarily all citizens of the State. The State, according to his ideas, will be displaced by the class organizations or corporations which will then be formed, and in the State of the future, if one can even call that a State at all, which is envisaged by *Hitze*, the class organizations themselves will manage their own affairs independently through their own appointed representatives. . . . Meanwhile, since the way is being prepared for this desired class organization through a mass development of associations, and these associations quite naturally are under the control of the Church, and under the protection of St. Joseph, we can be under no illusions about what would happen to those affairs themselves, and how they would be ordered without the interference of the State. The aim is a Socialism controlled by the Church, a sacerdotal, or, to put it still more plainly, a theocratic Socialism." At the same time, however, we ought to realize that this Socialism is not based upon the idea of equality, but upon that of inequality, and just because it gathers together those who are equal into groups which are different and unequal in their demands upon life, does it need this class-group character, as *Ratzinger* points out continually. Further, this system of regulating society, in addition to the Socialistic concern for the welfare of the individual, also

means that each individual has to exercise a great deal of humility as a member of his class and his group; only thus is the spirit of competition banished, or rather it is limited to that which is useful and morally permissible. The class idea means a Socialism of groups which secures the means of existence, and secures humility and renunciation at the same time; see *Uhlhorn, p. 9:* "Look, for instance, at the proposals which *Hitze* makes for the raising of labour: factory labour is to be restricted, for certain products it would be forbidden altogether; ..." or read the work of *Parvin*, this genuine Catholic political economist, *Über den Reichtum*, in which the whole argument amounts practically to this, that the pursuit of business (which he regards simply as selfishness) should be greatly restricted, while he exalts renunciation as the highest, even if not the only, virtue. Or examine the methods proposed for remedying social evils in the historico-political papers. Above all, production is to be reduced. Associations are to be formed whose members will band themselves together to buy nothing which has been made in a factory, unless it serves to meet a real need, no piece of furniture for the house or article of clothing which is merely meant for ornament. The money which is saved in this way would then be given to monastic establishments, which also help to prevent further increase in the population." This last point is especially important; this social ideal presupposes the existence of a population which is quite moderate in size, as the first necessity, if competition is to be abolished.

[147] (p. 312.) For the fundamental theory in its effect upon the individual group, see *Gierke, III, 513 f., 544, 559, 640; Althusius, 60, 133 f., 232.* The superstructure in the family, parish, empire, Church, *Feugueray, 177, 142 f.; Gierke: Althusius, 227, 229, 241; Cathrein, II, 515, 520.* The class and corporate organization is everywhere rather assumed than developed on the lines of Natural Law. *Gierke* rightly lays stress on the fact that it is regarded as belonging rather to Natural Law than to positive law, *Althusius, 241;* it is, of course, actually based upon positive law through special privileges, etc., but that is still only the human carrying out of the Natural Law along the lines of expediency. In the famous proposal in *De reg. princ.* for the establishment of a kingdom or of a town the corporate organization according to class and profession, and even the special settlement of groups which are of the same kind is foreseen, *Baumann, 74 f.* Cf. also the passages in *Maurenbrecher, pp. 39* and *47*, in which the corporations and classes are held to be derived in part from nature and Providence, and in part from positive law, with at the same time the reference to the example of the angel choirs.—For the decline of the imperial idea, see *Gierke, III, 541–544.*

[149] (p. 313.) See *Feugueray, 177–186; Th. Meyer, 70–141; Cathrein, II, 380–447; von Eicken, 440–467.* According to *Gothein: Art. Agrargeschichte, II, Mittelalter u. Neuzeit,* in *Die Religion in Geschichte und Gegenwart, I, p. 247 f.:* "The marriage legislation, in which the co-operation of Church and State can be most plainly perceived, was immediately directed against the solidarity of the clan. It may be described absolutely as an emancipation of the individual, and especially of woman, a service which women have repaid a thousand times over by their loyalty to the Church. The establishment of marriage by the Church in the most flourishing period of the Middle Ages, which is also a time of the highest importance for the position of women, forms the corner-stone of the whole achievement: through it marriage according to the customs of the clan was permanently displaced." A further method of promoting the value of the individual was the freedom to dispose of one's possessions by will, a change which certainly was in the interest of the Church, *ibid., 248.*

[150] (p. 316.) Cf. *Feugueray, Baumann, Gierke*; also v. *Eicken, 356–436; Cathrein, II, 449–678.* Thus even the expressions of Aristotle which are meant in a political sense about the social nature of human reason, are understood by St. Thomas solely from the social point of view as assertions about the necessary economic supplementation of the callings within the State, which Aristotle, for his part, with his ideal of the full citizen and the man of private means, rejects; see *Maurenbrecher, 30 and 36*, which is at the same time an example of the "Aristotelianism" of St. Thomas.—Against the modern theories of the State, see the characteristic remarks by *Zirkel* in *Ludwig, II, 419:* "The Church has its source in Heaven, and has come down to earth, not in the territory of the State, but in the quite different sphere of the conscience. . . . The Church is occupied with working for the salvation of men, while the State cares for their material concerns."—For the struggle between the Empire and the Papacy, see *Hampe: Deutsche Kaisergeschichte, 1909.* For the way in which the Emperors were bound to observe the same ideal, and the claim simply to have a larger share in the government of the Christian society, which then naturally makes the imperial policy subject to that of the Pope, see *p. 19:* "But do the principles of a Christian ethical doctrine, to the extent in which they were exercised by Heinrich III, still harmonize with the requirements of a successful statesmanship?"

[151] (p. 317.) Thus the doctrine of property is treated quite independently and incidentally, as a question of Natural Law, without any connection with the doctrine of the division of labour and the differentiation of callings, where the questions of the communism of the Primitive State and of the right of property in the fallen State are discussed (*Maurenbrecher, p. 96 f.*). Instinctively, however, there must have been some feeling that there is a connection between these theories, since St. Thomas teaches that the formation of property developed out of the original customs of communism along the lines of Natural Law quite inevitably, and he teaches the same about the division of labour. Also the theory of the Natural Law of property, a feature new to the mediaeval Church and connected with the ideas of Aristotle (*Maurenbrecher, p. 104 f.*), is undoubtedly connected with the new value given to work, and to the different callings, which indeed St. Thomas supposes that he also derives from Aristotle. See also *M., p. 110.*

[153] (p. 319.) Illustrations of all this in *Maurenbrecher*, who, however, does not examine into the reasons why St. Thomas gives the town so much higher a position than the country.—It is always a striking fact that the mediaeval social doctrine of the theologians always ignores feudalism. It is only the Romantic-anti-revolutionary doctrine of the "Restauration" which comes back to it; see *L. von Haller* and *De Bonald.* Even then, however, it has not to-day penetrated thence into the real Catholic social doctrine, which gives the preference to democratic, peasant-agrarian, and bourgeois middle-class ideals.

[154] (p. 320.) On this point see especially *Ratzinger's Volkswirtschaft,* in its historical and systematic sections. On the *pretium justum* in St. Thomas, see *Brentano: Ethik und Volkswirtschaft in der Geschichte, 1901, p. 35 f.*; according to this St. Thomas made the permitted profits arising out of trade likewise dependent upon the degree of the necessities involved in membership of a certain class, and the subjective conditions of the formation of prices retained at least a restricted influence upon the objective *pretium justum*; thus here also there are concessions to that which cannot be avoided in actual practice.— The following work goes into the subject in closer detail: *F. X. Funk: Ueber die ökonomischen Anschauungen der mittelalterlichen Theologie, Z. f. ges. Staatswissenschaft,*

25. Jahrg., 1864. F. stresses the defectiveness, the incidental character, the limitations due to the period, and the specifically theological character of the expressions of St. Thomas, suitable for a confessor dealing with souls, and deals more fully with Antonio of Florence and Bernardino of Siena, but otherwise he does give the essentials about St. Thomas. He stresses the point that the knowledge of the productive nature of capital is probably present in his writings, and that in the question of the taking of interest this is expressed, thus that here also there is already in St. Thomas a definite move towards that which is actually necessary in practice, but that juridical authorities and Aristotelian theories prevented him from working through and finding a solution for the difficulties which this raised. He is also affected by the commands against usury in the Primitive Church and the supposed commands against it in the Bible. But he is on the way to make a distinction between usury and interest, or at least to understand it; only, since the Aristotelian theory, together with the positive law, forces him to it, he forms his own doctrine forbidding usury and interest (thus once more restricting this view), yet not without limiting clauses for the latter in the *lucrum cessans*, to which were added later the *damnum emergens* and the *periculum sortis*.—In similar vein is the book by *C. Jourdain: Les commencements de l'économie politique dans les écoles du moyen âge, Mémoires de l'institut national de France, Académie des inscriptions et belles lettres, Vol. 28, 1854. J.* sees in all this certainly only a very elementary way of thinking on economic matters derived from Aristotle, after previous complete indifference to economic matters as a whole: "Quelques notions sur la monnaie, des maximes sévères en matière de prêt, d'injustes préventions contre le commerce tempérées par les sentiments pour ses avantages sociaux" (*p. 24*), and fails to see in all this the expression of a mind—however imperfectly —acting genuinely and independently under the inspiration of the Christian spirit, in harmony with the fundamental principles of Christian thought. This spirit is clearly recognized and treated in detail based on St. Thomas by *Ashley: Englische Wirtschaftsgeschichte* (translated into German by *Oppenheim*), *I, 1896, pp. 129–167*; this writer points out very pertinently that these ideas were closely connected with the actual economic conditions, that is, with the personal relation between consumers and producers which existed almost everywhere, and the undeveloped condition of trade and finance; the latter at a stage of higher development, in spite of all the material advantages which it brings with it, is still full of moral dangers. This, in fact, is the very comprehensible fundamental and distinctive idea of Christian "economics", when, as in the case of St. Thomas, they are confronted with a life in which commercial intercourse is already a very complicated matter. The necessity for meeting the needs of life in a satisfactory way, and yet the need of avoiding the dangers of an economic egoism which comes to regard itself as its only end, is the general idea behind the whole scheme, and it seems to him that the mediaeval town provided the answer to this problem, at the stage of development which it had then attained. Of course it did not stay there, and out of the life of the town there has developed the modern administration of the State and modern Capitalism; this is why modern Catholic thinkers on economic questions turn more to the rural regions, and so far as the town is concerned try to restore some of the old corporations and associations. In other ways the Catholic ideal is not nearly so agrarian as the Lutheran conservative. This shows that Catholicism has a far larger world outlook, and also it is evident that the fact that the theories of St. Thomas were, to such a large extent, moulded by town-life, has also had an abiding influence upon

Catholicism.—The article *Th. v. A.*, by *F. Walther*, in *H. W. St.*[2], gives a very complete account, although much of it is drawn from *Maurenbrecher*. See also the brief account of St. Thomas, which studies his Patristic presuppositions, by *O. Schilling: Reichtum und Eigentum in der ethisch-rechtlichen Literatur, 1908.* This book, which contains a wealth of quotations, entirely confirms throughout the account which I have given of Early Catholicism in the first section of this work.

[154a] (p. 321.) Cf. with this the argument for the reintroduction of monasticism by *Zirkel: Ludwig, II, 164 f.*: "Monasticism is an idea which in isolated individuals developed in a higher degree attains a power through which they are able to overcome all the inclinations and impulses of human nature. This is the reason for the vows of poverty, chastity, and obedience. . . . Humanity needs a public manifestation of this way of life, in order to be reminded what can be done in the moral realm, and that the strongest passions are not invincible if they are treated with firm determination to overcome them. Within the State institutions of this kind are all the more desirable because all the other classes of men are so distracted, and taken up with their own occupations and duties, that it is good to have one class of men set apart to offer thanksgiving and adoration to God on behalf of the rest."

[156] (p. 322.) Here cf. the very characteristic expression of opinion about the communism of the primitive community: *Contra Gent., 135:* "Primus quidem modus, scil. quod de pretio possessionum venditarum omnes communiter vivant, sufficiens est, non tamen ad longum tempus. Et ideo Apostoli hunc modum vivendi fidelibus in Jerusalem instituebant, quia praevidebant per Spiritum S., quod non diu in Jerusalem simul commorari deberent. . . . Unde non fuit necessarium nisi ad modicum tempus fidelibus providere et propter hoc transeuntes ad gentes, in quibus firmanda et perduratura erat Ecclesia, hunc modum vivendi non leguntur instituisse." *Maurenbrecher* also notes other passages which are similar to this one, *p. 109.* This is a fundamental point of view; see below on the opposition to the teaching of the sects.

[160] (p. 327.) Cf. *E. Meyer: Die Sklaverei im Altertum, p. 39; Max Weber: Agrargeschichte (Altertum), p. 174 f.*, however, rejects this conception, and looks solely at the special conditions out of which the mediaeval town arose, which was established not for military ends but for economic purposes, under circumstances which made it necessary to aim at the furtherance of free labour alone. He points out also that the emphasis of the Church upon peace was also connected with this non-military-economic nature of the industrial town. Here it must certainly be admitted that the adjustment between the different classes of the unfree and the dependent, as well as the economic and legal growth of independence among the unfree and the half-free, was really based upon the transformation of the ownership of land from the single estate under the lord of the manor into a system of holdings for which rent was paid, and that also the handing over of dependents to the town where they could pay rent out of what they earned was one of the main causes of the rise of the towns. In spite of this, however, we can also take it for granted that Christian thought and the Christian Church also influenced this situation, and that in the town especially the realization of the idea of liberty was connected with the religious life of the towns. *Maurer: Gesch. d. Fronhöfe, II, 80–93,* attributes the softening influence to "custom", and says, *p. 90:* "The more that the position of the serfs improved the better it was for the unfree", but he gives no illustrations. In any case, the Church protected the marriage of the unfree and procured them the human rights of family life, and this naturally meant

a loosening of servile ties. *Maurenbrecher, 82; Langer: Sklaverei in Europa während der letzten Jahrhunderte des Mittelalters, Bautzener Gymnasialprogramm, 1891,* examines the subject in detail, and from the very outset this writer claims that the modification of slavery among the Germanic States was due to the influence of Roman Law and of Christianity, and also in the later developments in the direction of greater humanity in the treatment of slaves he believes that the influence of the Church was considerable. Further, actual slavery must be distinguished from the condition of those who were serfs, or free villeins (*Hörigenwesen*). Although the latter class, to a great extent, developed into freemen, who undertook free labour, slavery and the slave trade continued throughout the whole of the Middle Ages, and in principle it was never rejected by the Church. All the statements of theologians who claim that Christianity in the mediaeval period at least did away with slavery are based either upon crass ignorance or mendacious apologetics. Almost the very opposite is the truth. These slaves were usually non-Christians, and had been gained either in war or through trade; often, however, whole Christian towns, when they were captured by the enemy, were enslaved. In Spain slavery lasted until the eighteenth century, and thence was simply transferred to America. The modification of slavery in that land only consisted in substituting negro slaves for the natives of the country, to which people were accustomed in Spain and Southern Europe. Thus the modern negro slavery of America was directly connected with the Middle Ages, and, as long as it existed, it was justified by the same theological arguments. Where it ceased in Europe, this was due to political and economic conditions, never to its condemnation by the Church. Indeed, in Southern Europe, towards the close of the Middle Ages slavery absolutely increased, and the Church was not merely implicated in the possession of slaves, but it also inflicted the penalty of enslavement for all kinds of offences. The opinion above expressed refers only to serfs who became free or very nearly so. To what an extent matters of this kind are dependent upon economic developments, and how, before the growth of modern individualism, the Church could and would only have a relative influence upon this question, is shown by the fact that with the reversion to a natural economy after the sixteenth century in Germany there was again an increase in serfdom.

[163] (p. 330.) The only Church History which gives a connected account of these problems is that of *Karl Müller, I, 1892, II, i, 1902,* especially cf. *I, 207* and *II, 85 ff. Müller* sees in these sect-movements the penetration of monasticism and its ideals into the life of the laity, which begins in the thirteenth century and expresses itself in two ways: (*a*) as a violent form of Christian Socialism, and (*b*) as a patient, and often persecuted, community, living a life of detachment from the world. "In both tendencies the ascetic ideas and energies of the mediaeval Church force their way into the world of lay folk" (*II, 86*). At the same time he lays stress on the connection with the idea of the absolute Law of Nature, as this had been taught by the theologians of the fourth century. This argument does not meet the whole of the case, however, and occasionally the connection is the very reverse; monasticism represents the ecclesiastical aspect of tendencies which in themselves belong to a quite different sociological type than that of the Church, and which find their pure expression in the sects. The main problem is to find the connection between this world of thought and the Gospel itself, to which it always appeals, and whence it most certainly proceeds. Then there comes the question of the relation between the sect-type and the Church-type in general, as well as of

their common relation to the Gospel, whence both proceed. From the outset *Müller*, like most theologians, regards the Church-type as the normal type, and the sect-type as a secondary phenomenon, like monasticism and asceticism, out of the popularizing of which it is supposed to arise. I believe that here a specifically sociological inquiry into the inner structure of the conditions out of which both forms of fellowship arose would place a different construction upon the matter.—A connected account from the opposite standpoint given by *L. Keller: Die Reformation und die älteren Reformparteien, 1875.* Here the sect is regarded as the normal type, and everywhere, sometimes in rather a forced way, it is attributed to the Waldensians; while the latter are connected directly, through a very ancient tradition, with the Primitive Church. Because the sect-type is the normal, the nature of the sects is not interpreted in the light of the Church-type and of their common basis in the Gospel. Rather the Church-type is presented as the distortion of pure Christianity, and is reproached for its characteristics, while the toleration and practical ethics of the sects are emphasized; the lack of education among the sects is partly disputed, and the writer tries to prove how many sectarians have been cultivated people, and partly it is excused, owing to the wretched conditions under which many were forced to live, owing to the way in which they were persecuted. One great merit of this book is the emphasis upon the sect-type, but the actual description of the sects does not single out its salient characteristics; the whole description aims at a modern, tolerant, and ethically serious humanitarian Christianity, emphasizes only the voluntary and subjective position, but ignores wholly the literal law of the Scriptures, the radical Law of Nature, the tendencies to develop into fanaticism and Chiliasm, and this also means that the illiteracy of the sects is regarded from an entirely wrong point of view; it is an inherent part of their nature.—The brief allusions to the subject in *Luthardt: Gesch. der Ethik, I, 327–333* are entirely valueless; *Ziegler*, who finds no new ideas in the mediaeval ethic in general, ignores this movement entirely. The histories of dogma also give very meagre accounts; there are only a few casual observations in *Seeberg: Dogmengesch., II, 166–169. Loserth: Geschichte d. späteren Mittelalters, 1900,* has practically next to nothing on the subject, although he is supposed to be describing the dissolution of the "religious civilization"!—An informative summary of one part of the history of the sect-movement is given by *Lechler: J. v. Wiklif und die Vorgeschichte der Reformation, 1873.* Here, however, everything is regarded from the point of view of the Reformation, and the difference between the Scriptural emphasis of the sects on the Law of God and of Nature, and the Lutheran Biblicism of the comfort of grace and of Christ-mysticism is not emphasized; in reality, however, this difference is fundamental, as will be explained later on, and it constitutes the point at which the religious development of the Reformation differs from the sect-type.

[163a] (p. 333.) For this important distinction in the conception of asceticism which is capable of many interpretations and is very far-reaching, see above, *pp. 102 ff.* The asceticism of the Primitive Christian Church with its indifference to the world, and the ecclesiastical asceticism of late antiquity with its emphasis upon mortification, ought always to be differentiated. In Protestantism we shall see a new third conception of asceticism. In *Zöckler's* book on asceticism there are, unfortunately, few distinctions of this kind, and the great theme is treated in a very colourless way. But the usual Protestant polemic against asceticism also overlooks these distinctions, even when it is represented by men of the school of historical thought represented by *von Eicken* or *Viktor Hehn*.

[166] (p. 333.) For the following section I owe some of the most decisive elements in my point of view to the very instructive study of *Max Weber: Kirchen und Sekten in Nordamerika, Christl. Welt, 1906, pp. 558 ff., 577 ff.;* also see *Scheel: Individualismus und Gemeinschaftsleben in der Auseinandersetzung Luthers mit Karlstadt, 1524/25, Zeitschrift für Theol. u. Kirche, 1907*, and my work, *Religion und Kirche, Preuss. Jahrb., 1895.* As everywhere, so here also, in the background of my researches there is *Simmel's* conception of sociology as the science of the formal structural relations between the different forms of group-life.—Essentially the same point of view of the nature of the sects is taken by *Kawerau* in the article *Sektenwesen in Deutschland, Protest. Real-Encyklop.3 ed. Hauck.* Here the distinction is made between the sect with its voluntary basis of membership and its emphasis upon ethical strictness as the proof of the reality of its faith, and the Church, with its emphasis upon its institutional character ; at the same time the writer admits that the Church alone is a religion of the people and of civilization, while the sect represents a conventicle-type of religion coupled with ethical radicalism. The difference is, however, not examined in its ultimate reasons. But the sects of modern times, which have grown up within Protestantism, are also to a great extent very different from those of the Middle Ages, since the former, owing to the theological character of Protestantism in general, give more scope for doctrinal differences, and measure the ethical standard less by the Natural Law and the Divine Christian Law of the Sermon on the Mount than by the Protestant doctrine of the Calling. In point of fact, both characteristics, the voluntary and individualistic nature of the membership in the community on the one hand, and the radical Natural-Law Scriptural doctrine of the Law on the other, are not, in themselves, necessarily connected. The former is connected only with the rigid uncompromising ethical character of the proof of the reality of personal faith, which is based upon a real appropriation of salvation and on the union of all those who share this faith. That in the mediaeval sects this ethical proof consists in the observance of the Law of God and of the absolute Law of Nature must be explained by the fact that in the intellectual world of the Middle Ages the conception of Law was a fundamental constituent element, and that every new formulation always leads anew to the Law of Jesus and of Nature.—How close a combination of these two ideas is to the Message of Jesus can be proved by an examination of some quite modern radical programmes of reform. I will only remind the reader of the two books: *Paroles d'un Croyant*, by *Lammennais*, and *Sie Müssen*, by the socialistic pastor *Kutter* (*1904*). Here, Christian communism, the universal law of reason, and the rejection of all the ethical compromises of the Church, is clearly, in both cases, the decisive characteristic. If the Protestant sects are remote from communism and the absolute Law of Nature, the reason lies in this, that their emphasis on the centrality of the teaching of the Scriptures is based on the thought and outlook of Paul and not on the Message of Jesus, and that, therefore, in their acceptance of Paulinism they also have adopted his acquiescence in the secular order and its institutions. This does not mean, however, that they reject the ethical, anti-ecclesiastical radicalism, but they exercise it merely in the form of the ethic of the Calling. For the same reason the idea of the absolute radical-communistic Natural Law is alien to them; their idea of Natural Law, so far as they develop this idea at all, contains within itself the idea of the freedom of individualism, but not the equality of communism.—This contrast which has just been described has also been noted from a rather different point of view by *Ragaz* in his excellent work, *Das Evangelium und der soziale Kampf der Gegenwart, 1906.* See especially *p. 20 f:*

"It seems to me that the contradictory ideas which have here come to light may have been derived from one great antinomy, which runs right through the whole history of Christianity, and is indeed even older than Christianity itself. I would like to describe this contrast as that which exists between the quiescent and the progressive form of religion. In other words, it might be described as the difference between an aesthetic-ritualistic piety and an ethical-prophetic piety. Both streams may have taken their rise in the depths of the same mountain range, but they emerge from the mountains at different places, their waters are differently coloured, and they have a different taste. They arise, so far as this question is concerned, in the New Testament, but not at the same point; the one springs out of the thought of Paul and of John, and the other out of the Synoptic Gospels." Later on *R.* identifies the former tendency with the "Church", quite definitely, while, although he does not absolutely identify the latter with the "sect", he points to St. Francis, the Anabaptists, the development of Calvinism—that is, he actually is referring to the sect. To my satisfaction *R.* supports his argument by appealing to my presentation of *Protestantism* in the *Kultur der Gegenwart, I, 4,* and draws conclusions from that which I stated in that work, which were not so clear to me at that time as they are now. Only, the reason why the churches lower the standard of the Gospel is not so much a direct Quietism, or a quiescent attitude towards the life of the world, as it is the tendency to desire to dominate the nations and to maintain a unity of civilization, just as, on the other hand, the difficulty of carrying out those standards in practice leads to the effort to realize them within the narrower limits of small groups of a voluntary kind or to sects, to whom previously a universal society could only be conceived in the terms of Chiliasm, and therefore of violence.—Here, as in other places, the whole of this inquiry would have gained greatly if it had been possible to make some comparisons with the history of the Russian Church, and the Russian civilization and culture, if these matters were better known than they are. Here I can only indicate the articles by *Kattenbusch: Die Kirche in Russland* in the *Christl. Welt, 1908,* especially *pp. 730 ff.,* and also *Grass: Die russischen Sekten,* Vol. *I, 1907,* and the article by the same writer, *Die Bedeutung der russischen Sektenkunde für die Beurteilung von russischer Religiosität und Kultur,* in *Z. f. Religion und Geisteskultur,* published by *Steinmann, 1908, pp. 161 ff.*— Characteristic and instructive from the standpoint of Lutheran churchmanship on the sects is *Gottschick: Ethik, 1907, pp. 232 ff.*: "Essentially the sect consists in this, that it is the empirical representation of a community of nothing but awakened Christians, living apart from the world. This, at least, is its intention. Therefore it leads to a narrowing of Christian fellowship, which is contrary to the ideal of Christianity, for it not only denies that the Christian development has many stages, but it sets up special or even erroneous standards of the necessary characteristics of the Christian community; it further denies the universal calling of Christendom, i.e. that of bringing in the Kingdom of God through the development of history as the supreme force over the life of the world. For it regards the State, science, law, and art only as the "world" in the bad sense, and in the tense spirit of Chiliasm it renounces the effort to overcome the world through spiritual labour. In contrast with this idea, the characteristic sign, by which a Christian fellowship can prove that it is a "church", is this, that in the universal and historical spirit, on the one hand, it opens the door also to those who are learning to be Christians and offers a home to all Christian individualities, and thus it treats seriously the idea that the Christian community as a whole must precede the individual, and, on the other hand, that it organizes its legal system not in order to represent the community of the faithful, but rather as a system of the means for the cultivation and expansion of Christianity, and thus takes up the task of trying to permeate the spheres of life which God has ordained with the Christian spirit. In the exercise of this spirit the Church has gradually developed into the form of a church of the people or a national Church, that is, it has adopted a form by means of which the Church sets before herself the task of the education of the nations as a whole, and thus the individual does not enter into the Church by means of a voluntary decision, but rather he is born into it, by entering into the natural life of the nation which is under the educative influence of the Church. . . . These effective advantages compensate for the disadvantage, which is unavoidable, that in a Church which is thus ordered, elements of the 'world', in the bad sense of the word, penetrate into its life to a comparatively greater extent than into a sect. Not only on account of this comprehensiveness, but, above all, because of this its universal and historical ideal the great bodies of Catholic and Protestant churches claim to bear the name of 'Church'." With this description before us it is evident that the sect-type corresponds to the Synoptic message of Jesus, which is directed towards the future, gathers resolute adherents and pays as little attention to the "world" as possible, whereas the Church-type corresponds to the missionary faith of the Apostles and especially of Paul, which looks back to a religious possession of redemption, and to some extent accepts the "world". The difference between Jesus and Paul, expressed by *Wrede* (*Paulus, 1905*, with which I do not entirely agree, by the way), is also, from this point of view, the origin of different ideals and motives, which, consciously or unconsciously, remain separate all down the course of the history of Christianity. As the Scriptural argument for the superiority of the Church-type all that *Gottschick* can suggest is "the fact that in the New Testament the Christian character of the family goes beyond that of its individual members (*1 Cor. vii. 14*) and that Christ as well as Paul directs his efforts (i.e. his hope) towards the hope of the conversion of Israel as a nation". (*O. 233.*) The former point is certainly important, but it belongs to Paulinism, and characteristically on the question of Infant Baptism the Church-type and the sect-type have either separated or made their compromises. The second idea is, indeed, not conceived as connected with the Church, but as an eschatological Act of God.

[165a] (p. 340.) On account of their "asceticism" a large group of theologians is in the habit of describing the sects as a specifically Catholic phenomenon, although in so doing they are ignoring the central point of Catholicism—the hierarchy, the priesthood, the sacraments, and the objective nature of Grace. This takes place among those students who, in the school of Ritschl, have learned to regard the asceticism which is hostile to the world, "the monastic ideal of perfection", as the very essence of Catholicism, and who think that Catholicism was simply illogical and hindered by external difficulties from carrying out this ideal for all, whereas the sects do carry it out for all their members. With these theologians this idea is closely connected with their conception of the New Testament and of Protestantism; they regard the New Testament, namely, from its view of the Kingdom of God, as an ethico-religious unity of believers who trust in God and who overcome the world by their brotherly love; they look upon Protestantism as the discarding of the ideal of asceticism, and the return to a Christianity which asserts with joy the acceptance of the world, and of the duty of serving God within one's calling, by which it is related with the modern world. Thus *Brieger* (in his book *Die*

Reformation, in *Ullstein's Weltgeschichte*, *p. 198*) says, speaking of the mediaeval sects: "Only a very small minority broke away, possibly because the warmth of their religious feeling came up against cold decrees, their moral seriousness was hurt, and they longed for the Christian community of the apostolic period, from which the Papal Church with its worldly aims was as different as chalk from cheese. But even these renegades remained in agreement with the Church in their fundamental religious views. The sects of the Middle Ages, however many divisions they may represent, still bear without exception the stamp of the Catholicism of their day; indeed, they are its creation. . . . Only upon this soil could they grow at all." Thus *Möller-Kawerau: K.G.*, *III*, considers that the Anabaptists and the sects of the Middle Ages were the product of Catholicism because of their ascetic and legalistic tendencies. Thus *Ritschl*, in particular declared that the second great sect-movement of Protestantism, Pietism, was due to the incursion of alien Catholic standards of life. This whole argument, however, is fundamentally false. So far as Catholicism is concerned, I believe that in the previous pages I have shown that the characteristic feature of Catholicism is this: the union of asceticism and the life of the world, and the possibility of combining both these elements in the graduated structure of the Church, as the organ of grace. That the roots of asceticism were already present in the New Testament is to-day generally recognized as a fact which is closely connected with the recognition of the eschatological character of the New Testament. These ideas gave Luther trouble enough, and on this point *Brieger* gives it as his opinion that Luther did not read the New Testament in the historical sense (i.e. that he did not interpret it in the sense of liberty and acceptance of the world), but that he made the mistake of interpreting it literally! All this, however, shows that in the sect-movements of the Middle Ages, of the Reformation, of the Anabaptists, and of the Pietists, there were operating Scriptural, not Catholic elements, which alongside of the other elements of the New Testament which tended in the direction of the Church, the objective character of grace and the conservative adaptation to the world, have their own tendency and their own history. This is the sect-type, which everywhere accompanies the Church-type as a complementary movement, and which everywhere breaks through to the extent in which the main emphasis was laid upon the Synoptic Gospels and the "enthusiastic" sections of the New Testament. In this line of argument, too, the many-sidedness of the word "asceticism" is overlooked, to which allusion has already been made.

[167] (p. 352.) See *Vossler: Die göttliche Komödie, II, 28 ff.* From *Vossler's* work, which particularly in this volume is most original in treatment, we gain a very living impression of the extraordinary variety of the attitude of the leading nations towards the religious system of life of the Middle Ages. The seigniorial-Territorial-Church development was supported mainly by the German monarchy and Empire as well as by England; see *Hauck* and *Böhmer*. The great classical system of the central period of the Middle Ages was of French origin; hence the close connection between the country of France and mediaeval thought. Provence and Italy, apart from clerical circles, from the days of Gregory the Great fell into a state of increasing religious indifference, and they cultivated in a remarkable manner the remains of ancient Humanism. It was not until the twelfth century that the great religious period in Italy—which coincided with the development of town-life—began, which lasted till the fifteenth century. During this epoch, however, out of these conditions, the difference between the Church- and the sect-type was developed, and it was

precisely these contrasts which gave so much vitality to this period and so much significance. That there is a connection between the sect-movement in the North and that in the South is undoubtedly the case, but at present the evidence for this is insufficient.

[176] (p. 359.) Here Wyclif shares the accepted scholastic ideas of the Law of Nature and of God; see *Lechler*, *I*, *467*, and especially the passage from the *civili dominio*: "de quanto aliqua lex ducit propinquius ad conformitatem legis naturae, est ista perfectior. Sed lex Christi patiendi injurias propinquius ducit ad statum naturae quam civilis. Ergo ista cum suis regulis est lege civili perfectior"; this is the ancient distinction between the absolute and relative Law of Nature, whereby the former belongs to the Primitive State. When *Lechler* suggests that the later passage from *De veritate scripturae* "in tantum quod si lex aliqua dicit caritatem aut virtutem aliquam, ipsa adeo est lex Christi" means that the Natural Law is placed below the Christian Law, he is overlooking the fundamental identity between the absolute Law of Nature and the Christian Law of God. Wyclif is only asserting the absolute Law of Nature against the relative or civil law. The very fact that the Bible and Christianity are everywhere designated the "Law of God" by Wyclif shows that his whole intellectual outlook was coloured by the conceptions of the Law of God and of Nature (*Lechler*, *I*, *473*). Also the whole endeavour to set up the Bible as the sole authority and the source of the Divine Law means the assertion of the absolute and pure law against the relative Natural Law of the accepted order of Society and the compromises of the Church. Only gradually there developed out of this ideal of the Bible as the sole authority a dogmatic criticism of purely theological doctrines as well; this is an important distinction between this doctrine and the teaching of Luther; see *De civili dominio*: "Pure per observantiam legis Christi sine commixtione traditionis humanae crevit ecclesia celerrime, et post commixtionem fuit continue diminuta" (*Lechler*, *I*, *474*). Also in a similar vein: "Lex humana est mixta multa nequitia, ut patet de regulis civilibus, ex quibus pullulant multa mala; lex autem evangelica est immaculata" (*Lechler*, *I*, *475*). Thus the Bible is the "carta a Deo scripta et nobis donata, per quam vindicabismus regnum Dei" (*476*). It is the absolute Christian Law of Nature: the clergy should "uti pro suo regimine lege evangelica impermixte" or "Utilius et undique expeditius foret sibi (ecclesiae) regulari pure lege scripturae, quam quod traditiones humanae sunt sic commixtae cum veritatibus evangelicis ut sunt modo" (*477*). Hence "Lex Christi est medulla legum ecclesiae". "Omnis lex utilis sanctae matri ecclesiae dicitur explicite et implicite in scriptura." This, however, is also the Law of Nature in the whole life of Society: "Totum corpus juris humani debet inniti legi evangelicae tanquam regulae essentialiter divinae." The whole of Society ought to be and could be reformed according to the Law of Christ, and indeed solely from this point of view. This, however, cannot take place until the Church has been reformed; see *c. 44 v. Book I, De dominio civili*. To Wyclif the official theologian was "Doctor traditionis humanae et mixtim theologus" (*Lechler*, *I*, *477*), in which he was undoubtedly right. "Lex autem christiana debet esse solum lex Domini et immaculate convertens animas (to a Scriptural strictness and love) et per consequens recusari debet a cunctis fidelibus propter commixtionem cujuscumque attomi Antichristi" (*Lechler*, *I*, *478*). *Lechler* sees in this the Scriptural principles of the Reformation; such a point of view is, however, only possible where the mediaeval world of sociological ideas, with its emphasis upon Natural Law, is ignored; *Buddensieg* thinks of this still less. And yet this is the real key to the whole question! In the doctrine of the Reformers which starts

from the Pauline religion of grace the Scriptures contain the message of the grace of God and are the very opposite of a *Lex Christi*. It is precisely for that reason that the Reformers also have no feeling for the legal conception of the radicalism of the Early Church and for the reform of the secular order on these lines. This is its fundamental difference from the Wyclif movement, coupled with the retention of the Church-type.

[177] (p. 359.) The question why Wyclif did not deduce the radical consequences of this idea is very important for his doctrine. *Seeberg* simply says: "Naturally this does not mean(?) that the righteous are directly to take to themselves the possessions which have been unjustly seized by others. Rather the positive duties of life(!) are contained in the Gospel law" (*p. 168*). Passages which might throw light upon this dark saying are not indicated. The chief work, *De civili dominio* (now published in four volumes by *Poole, 1885 f.*), gives clear statements on the whole subject. Here first of all the *jus divinum* or *evangelicum* is stated to be the one absolute law which ensures to the righteous and the elect possessions in goods and in power as the gift of God, but it also lays upon the elect soul the obligation to use these possessions in the loving service of the whole, that is, in the communism of love. Only in this sense can we understand Wyclif's central expression *omnia bona communia* for the Primitive State and the state of redemption; in the spirituality of love and in the possession of the highest mystical good each special possession is common to all, in spite of all the actual differences in possessions effected by the grace of predestination: "dominium enim naturale propter sui spiritualitatem aliud non excludit" (*I, 126*). This is not meant at all in the sense of Stoic-rationalist individualism, but in the sense of a common spirit, which, in the service of the radical communism of love, uses all callings and offices, all possessions and all power for the good of the Christian Society; otherwise the classified social system still remains as before: the "vulgares", "saeculares domini" and the "sacerdotes". Along with the doctrine of predestination there is asserted as a fundamental idea the difference in callings, *ministeria et officia* (*Lechler, I, 531*), only they are placed unconditionally at the service of love, and this demand does not apply merely to one special class, that of monasticism (*Lechler, I, 582 ff.*), but to all Christians everywhere; of them all the Franciscan ideal holds good: "Pure naturaliter vel evangelice dominantes perfectissime dicunt atque verissime cum Scriptura, quod omnia bona mundi sunt singulorum nostri ordinis et tamen nihil habemus, civiliter in proprio et sic intelligit locutiones venerabilis ordinis fratrum minorum, qui sunt quasi nihil habentes secundum civilem solicitudinem et tamen omnia possidentes" (*I, 129*). Thus the differences are emphasized as Divine gifts, and yet in love they are no longer existent, even the differences between master and slave. "Quilibet christianus debet reciproce alteri ministrare, ergo et esse reciproce servus et dominus" (*I, 75*); and it is "regula indispensabilis christianae religionis, qua scimus quemcunque christianum, inquantum est donis Dei fertilior, in tantum debet esse aliis membris Christi servitute subjectior et per consequens magis servus" (*I, 77*). Apart from the slavery introduced by sin, this applies both to the Primitive State and also to the state of redemption: "Jus divinum est jus a solo deo institutum, per Christum verbo et opere explanatum ut lex evangelica" (*I, 125*), and this "jus divinum creatum est jus divinitus inspiratum; jus humanum [consisting in *jus canonicum* and *jus civile*] est occasione peccati adinventum". In itself it is the same point of view as in St. Thomas. But this human law is here rated at a much lower value than in the social doctrines of Thomism; indeed, it is regarded as an evil, which ought to be

removed from Christian Society, especially in the realm of Canon Law, which he regards as something quite artificial, and also from that of civil law, where it is granted only a very limited significance: "Ex istis incidenter patet divisio inter dominium naturale vel evangelicum et civile. Dominium quidem naturale est dominium divinitus institutum in primo titulo justitiae fundatum, quotlibet divites ex aequo compatiens, sed alienationem dominantis servata justitia non permittens. Dominium autem civile est dominium occasione peccati hominibus institutum, incommunicabile singulis et ex aequo multis dominis, sed abdicabile servata justitia" (*p. 126 f.*), this means, the Divine Law appoints to the righteous and elect soul a possession which cannot be taken away from him without injustice, which it is his duty to use absolutely in the service of love. On the other hand, the human law of the fallen State only secures to the individual a possession which is secured through compulsion, which only aids a few, and is not meant for the whole, which, precisely because this element of love is lacking, can be used for the whole in an external way through selling, for instance, and which can be taken away from him. This human law, however, means the removal or denial of love, and it is only justified to the extent in which it stems the tide of disorder and robbery, and retains within itself a relic of the Natural Law: "Unde supposito lapsu et cecitate proclivi bonis sensibilibus praecipue innitendi, necesse fuit leges et ordinationes humanas statuere, ne quilibet lapsus de bonis furtim caperet, quantumque voluntas indebite inclinaret" (*I, 128*). "Sequitur ergo, quod jus civile vel humanum, ut sapit justitiam, est jus ordinans idoneum ad custodiam temporalium pro utilitate rei publicae, ad refrenandum voluntates ipsam injuste dirrumpere et ad sagaciter ministrandum illa in necessitate temporum" (*I, 129*). This is the old idea of the relative Natural Law of the existing order as the *frenum et remedium peccati*. Wyclif, however, has no great opinion of this law; the *consensus populi* which determines it is unjust, "nisi praesupposita ratione, scil. quod persona dominans sit a Deo accepta ad illud officium; et per idem nulla principia juris civilis de successione hereditaria vel commutatione mutua terrenorum est justa nisi de quanto est legis naturae particula" (*I, 130*).—All this shows that the scholastic intellectual apparatus of the *Lex Naturae* has been to a great extent set aside in favour of the absolute Natural Law; but in this the idea of predestination has made the inequalities so firmly established that it is able to work in a conservative direction, so long as a special class can regard its *dominium* as just in essence, and administered according to the Will of God. Wyclif assumes this, with evident English self-satisfaction, of the secular classes (or estates); he only denies it for the clergy; therefore the revolutionary tendency is only directed against this class. In the background, however, there is the idea that the secular classes also ought to be tested by the Law of God, and that there ought to be a Christian ideal of Society according to the *Lex evangelii*; it will not be individualistic and communistic, but it will require a large measure of the voluntary communism of love. The revolutionary conclusions and the radical opposition of this whole theory to the social philosophy of Thomism are manifest.

[178] (p. 360.) This is an old Augustinian idea, which St. Thomas shared. But for St. Thomas the Church is the means by which, as a sacramental-hierarchical institution which imparts salvation, predestination is realized. Further, in view of the fact that it is impossible to tell whether anyone is in a state of grace or not, and that outwardly it is impossible to say whether in any particular individual the potency of salvation will be actualized or not, all are placed under the compulsory régime of sacramental observance, the non-elect as

well as the elect; it is felt that the difference will never be discovered till after death. This is the manner in which the doctrine of predestination is adjusted to the idea of the Church as an institution. It is only when this safeguard is removed that the doctrine of predestination reveals its tendency to destroy the conception of the Church. See the apt observations in *Gottschick: Huss'*, *Luthers und Zwinglis Lehre von der Kirche, Z. f. Kirch. Geschichte, 1886, pp. 352–356*.

[179] (p. 360.) Cf. *Lechler, I, 534*: Against the danger of despair about being in a state of grace: "Vivat ergo homo, quam plene sufficit, conformiter legi Dei et habeat perseverantem voluntatem in lege illa standi in vita, defensione et publicatione; et tollitur occasio desperandi." *435:* "Quilibet debet examinare vitam propriam, quousque non fuerit sibi conscius de mortali peccato. Istam ergo examinationem tractare diligentissime est necessarium cuilibet viatori, cum quilibet, sicut debet habere spem suae salvationis, ita debet credere absque formidine, quod sit in gratia gratificante." *P. 533:* "Non enim supponeret, quod sint tales [i.e. elect members of the true Church] nisi evidentia capta ex opere, quo sequerentur dominum Jesum Christum."

[180] (p. 361.) These consequences are emphasized by *Seeberg: Der Begriff der christlichen Kirche, I, 1885, p. 77 f.; Gottschick, p. 77*, however, says, with equal justice, that these conclusions were not actually drawn by Wyclif, but that what he did was to urge for the reform of the Church as a whole, while allowing priests and sacraments to remain in existence as institutional elements. The full force of these ideas is only felt "when the certainty of being of the number of the elect is regarded as something which is open to all. As soon as this certainty is reached, then the authority of external institutions disappears" (*p. 363*). In point of fact, however, Wyclif's opinions about the priesthood are somewhat uncertain and fluctuating, and he simply said that the sign of the elect was the practical reality of religion in their lives. The sect-type, of course, results from this way of thinking, but it was certainly not logically thought out.

[181] (p. 363.) Cf. *K. Müller: K.G., II, 79*. The starting-point here also is the Augustinian doctrine of predestination. "For it was precisely Wyclif's doctrine of predestination which, both in itself and in its conclusions, was destined to cause Huss to drift away from the teaching of the Catholic Church" (*Loserth, 59*). Otherwise the results of the idea of predestination appear less in Huss than in Wyclif, since Huss did not adopt the criticism of the sacraments, and he also held far more strongly the need for the priesthood. As to St. Thomas, so also to him, the priesthood and the Sacrament are the means by which the fact of predestination is realized in life, to which, in view of the fact that it cannot be established with any certainty whether any particular individual is of the number of the elect, the believer must hold fast. On this point see the excellent treatment of the subject by *Gottschick, p. 365*, especially *p. 366*: "Whereas Wyclif certainly seems to have justified elect laymen, if Christ calls and endows them, in undertaking priestly activity in the technical sense, Huss always assumed that there is a specific difference between the clergy and the laity" (*p. 366*). "The fellowship of the elect controlled by Christ ought to realize the Divine Law, whose content, if we wish to sum it up in one phrase, is 'the Franciscan ideal of life'" (*p. 368*). "The factors in which the Church makes itself felt, the sacraments and the sacerdotal administration, are the means by which the aim of preaching the message of Jesus is realized" (*p. 370*). "Huss was very far from holding a subjective view of fellowship which makes everything start from the individual; indeed, so far as the conception of the Church as the Body of Christ was concerned, he held that the individual is supported by the whole" (*p. 370*). "The union of the idea of predestination with that of the

Church did not lead Huss to depreciate the idea of the empirical Church (i.e. of the institution), but rather to put stress on the great need to try to make the Church conform to the Law of Christ." Thus the three estates in the Church, the *vulgares*, the *saeculares domini*, and the *sacerdotes*, ought to live according to the Law of Christ: "It is the duty of the first class to obey the commandments of God while doing the work which is permitted to them; the second class ought to use in God's service the power of force or of the sword which God has granted them in order to carry out the Law of Christ, and therefore they must both protect the servants of Christ and drive out the servants of the Anti-Christ; the third class, however, whose members are the representatives of Christ, ought as the soul of the Church to impart fresh life to her, through a life of detachment from the world wholly devoted to the following of Christ as closely as possible" (*p. 372*). It is manifest that here, still more than in the teaching of Wyclif, the Franciscan ideal of the Law of God has taken up into itself the class organization of the world. Criticism is directed only against the secularized hierarchy, with its wealth and its claims on the law, demanding that these should be transformed into poor servants of Christ according to Matt. x. Territorial churches, tended by pastors and priests according to the spirit and example of the Apostles, are his ideal, "about the limitation of which Huss certainly did not think any further" (*p. 393*). In so doing, however, it is clear that the elements of the institutional conception have been retained in the idea of the priesthood, the Sacrament, and the following of the Apostles. But, on the other hand, we may reply to *Gottschick* that these elements have been greatly shaken, and that the development into the sect-movement is not far away. As soon as the official priesthood is regarded as offending against the Law of God, and is therefore placed outside the Church of the elect; and when, on the other hand, the elect layman is placed outside the institution by being excommunicated; and further, as soon as, in both these instances, the Bible is given into the hands of the laity as the Law of God, in order that the clear distinction may be perceived between the mere *praescitus* and the *praedestinatus*, then true fellowship becomes something which is due to the understanding by the laity of the Law of God and to their agreement about it. The problem then is to effect the right agreement between these opinions, which ought to lead to the development of a priesthood in line with the true succession from the Apostles, which is also really religious and devout. This, however, means that the institutional conception is reduced to the furthest minimum, if the congregation has to choose its own priest from the existing succession. The Divine Law, however, which regulates the opinion of the laity, is in no way, as was later the "Word" in Lutheranism, the objective creator of fellowship, which arises simply out of subjective knowledge and insight into the Law of God. This—even although through being cast out of the Church—leads the way to the sect-type, and in actual practice this is what happened.

[186] (p. 366.) The two following writers suggest that the sect-type is due to the influence of the Waldensians, which is, of course, quite possible: *Preger: Ueber das Verhaltniss der Taboriten zu den Waldensiern des 14. Jahr. (Abhh. der hist. Klasse des Münchener Akad. d. Wiss., 1887)* and *Haupt: Die Sekten in Franken vor der Reformation, 1882. Volpe: September, p. 297,* agrees with these authors; *Loserth,* however, in reviews which are important in their bearing on the thought of Wyclif, *Gött. Gel. Anzz., 1889, p. 475,* and *ibid., 1891, pp. 140 ff.,* maintains that it is still impossible to prove these influences, and says that it is probable that the sect arose simply out of the logical consequences of the

teaching of Wyclif about the right of the elect to inquire and examine for themselves. This is possible. It seems impossible, however, to claim that the individualistic-communistic theories were derived from Wyclif. On this point I follow *K. Müller*, whose views are based also upon the work of *F. von Bezold: Zur Geschichte des Hussitentums* (which, unfortunately, I was unable to obtain for my own use). If these suggestions are correct, then the influence of the Wyclif movement in this respect can scarcely be regarded as a tenable position. It is not sufficient to say that Wyclif's doctrine of the definition of the Divine Law as the standard for the secular order also, proves this contention; for the conception of the Divine Law itself is different. What accounts for this I am unable to say. I believe, that in addition to a strong admixture of Chiliast ideas, there may be also Joachimite ideas present as well (see *Loserth's* otherwise very meagre sketch, *G. d. spät. Mittelalters, pp. 480 ff.*). *Müller* suggests ancient Slav communism; *Max Weber* tells me that he thinks that this is impossible, since this kind of communism, as "Hauskommunion", implied the patriarchal clan-type of family, and is constructed quite differently. *Weber* himself attributes this to the results of a widespread state of warfare, and the wandering life which this caused to so many people. The comparatively detailed sketch, based on *Palacky* in *Kautsky: Gesch. d. Sozialismus, I, 1, pp. 195–239*, suggests the "Beghards"; the work of *R. Zöllner: Zur Vorgeschichte des Bauernkrieges, 1872*, which essentially is based upon *Höfler: Geschichtsschreiber der hussitischen Bewegung, 1856–1866*, suggests the Beghards, Dolcinists, Italian Chiliasts, and old Slav communistic customs, and the communism of war. With reference to the violence which is incompatible with the whole thought of Christianity, we should note that here the Old Testament is called in to help, alongside of the Divine Law of the New Testament, as indeed the Old Testament often had to help out with the provision of a Scriptural basis for an argument for a secular ethic, and for social ideas. This supplementary part played by the Old Testament alongside of the New Testament, especially in questions of ethics and of social doctrines, needs a book to itself. This point will occur again and again in the section on Calvinism.

[191] (p. 371.) Instances of these democratic-communistic ideas are collected by *Kautsky* in his *Geschichte des Sozialismus, I, 1*; unfortunately they are often inaccurate, and the writer also reveals a complete lack of understanding of the religious motives and the differences between the various groups. To him the Christian communism of the Middle Ages is a poor example of a premature communism, due essentially to the ideas of the early Christian "slave community" (*Lumpenproletariat*) handed down through Christian literature, which, because it does not coincide with the stage of production which is still the ruling element in social life, and with the tendency to "development or evolution", is at the same time mystical, ascetic, politically impotent and the enemy of science, whereas the Socialism of the present day, which does fit in with the stage of production, is at all points the very opposite! A wealth of material, particularly on the South German peasant movements and the Taborites, is provided by *R. Zöllner: Die Vorstufen des Bauernkrieges*. For the English peasant rising of 1381, and its Christian-communistic programme, see *Kautsky: I, 1, pp. 183–195*. According to *Luce: Histoire de la Jacquerie², 1894*, the French *Jacquerie* did not contain any ideal elements of this kind. The thought behind the German movements is illuminated by the *Reformatio Sigismundi* (ed. *Böhm, 1876*), which, alongside of a relatively conservative ecclesiastical programme, still, in the interest of the slaves and the serfs, did assert the ideas of Natural Law and Christian liberty, i.e. the ideas of equality

and of the natural holding of all things in common (*Böhm, p. 48*). A summary of the German revolutionary-peasant movements is given by *Brieger: Ref. (Ullsteinsche W. G.), pp. 294–306*. Here there is everywhere evident the equation of the revolutionary demand with the Divine and Natural Law of the Primitive State, "when Adam delved and Eve span", while the element of force is justified by the example of the Old Testament.—How uncertain even otherwise competent theologians are in this sphere is shown by *Seeberg: D.S., I, 166 ff*. In all the different places in which *Seeberg* speaks of the Natural Law of the Middle Ages there is never any allusion to its varied elements, nor to the fact of the distinction between the absolute and the relative Natural Law, and, in particular, the deep inward necessity for the acceptance of this idea is not in the least understood.

[193] (p. 375.) That it was precisely the Avignon Papacy which completed the process of the centralization of the Church, and that this was expressed chiefly in the ecclesiastical system of finance, is rightly emphasized by *K. Müller: Kultur der Gegenwart, I, 4, 211*, and by *Haller: Papsttum und Kirchenreform*. The latter adds that this fiscal policy was a necessary by-product of centralization, since a sovereignty of this kind over the world costs money, like any other government. And it is well known that since the abolition or restriction of that older fiscal policy, the system of finance has always been a difficult point in the policy of the Curia.

[194] (p. 376.) *F. von Bezold: Lehre von der Volkssuveränität, pp. 351–358. P. 352:* "The transference of the Natural-Law construction of the State also to the Church." *P. 353:* "From the theses of Langenstein (1381) until the times of the Councils of Pisa and Kostnitz, which for us are incorporated in Gerson, the theory of the relation between the Pope and the Church passed through several stages until it forsook completely the sphere of existing institutions and of ecclesiastical tradition, and threw itself entirely into the arms of the doctrine of Natural Law [*von Bezold* evidently means of the absolute N.L., which, however, he does not distinguish from the relative N.L. of classical theology and ecclesiastical jurisprudence, which could quite well be combined with the state of the Church and of Society as it was apart from all idealism]." "The predominance of Divine and Natural Law finds in Gerson, as already was the case with Marsilius, its expression in the exaltation of equity as the supreme and unassailable legal court of appeal. Equity decides, without descending to legal quibbling, according to its own standard, its own simple feeling of right, whether and how this or that law is to be applied, changed, or abolished. A General Council then ought to act in harmony with this supreme law, and Gerson would entrust to such a Council indefinite powers." This "equity" (*Epikie*) is in reality only the right to assert the absolute Law of Nature against any deformations of the relative N.L., and of the positive law which is based upon it. Gerson argues thus (*p. 354 f.*) : "If the ecclesiastical authorities neglect their duty, this sacred duty is then laid on others even down to the peasants, yes, even to the most ignorant old woman in a parish." "For the unity, the peace, and the renewal of the Church", he exclaims, "not only the secular princes, but also the peasants and the workmen, and every believer down to the very least, must play their part, and even, if necessary, lay down their lives in order to save the flock as a whole, after the example of the ancients." He cites Cicero and Valerius Maximus as examples of the ancient civic virtue, which he desires to enkindle in the hearts of his Christian contemporaries for a spiritual republic. *P. 356:* "The Fathers of the Councils . . . themselves considered the possibility of utilising the energies of the masses for

the good of the Church." *Von Bezold* then speaks especially of Nicholas da
Cusa (*p. 357*): "In the Law of Nature which indwells human reason, every
binding determination of the positive law must originate. In this way an
isolated law is in closest connection with the inmost nature of man. Since,
however, by nature men are equally powerful and equally free, it is only the
collective body of humanity which possesses the constitutive authority to
create law." "Every government exists only because all willingly agree to
submit to it." He endeavours to interpret both the priesthood and the
monarchy along these lines. "All authority . . . is contained potentially within
the people, power both Christian and secular." "The Divine influence which is
certainly implied in all this, the *radius formativus*, is certainly left in the background." If we compare such statements with those of Thomism the difference
is startling. It is not the conception of Natural Law in itself which makes the
difference, but the way in which it is regarded and applied. The radical,
absolute Natural Law of the Primitive State stands out against the relative
Natural Law of the fallen State which justifies all existing institutions; and its
opposition to the latter is all the more intense because it is interpreted not in
the sense of natural inequality as in Aristotle and St. Thomas, but in the sense
of equality regarded from the Stoic-rationalistic point of view. And this conception of Natural Law can no longer claim to be the counterpart of the
Church-conception, since through the ideal of a purely spiritual Church and
the right of lay criticism by the standard of the Bible, it has meanwhile cut
away the pillars which supported the conception of the Church as an institution.
By the development of the Papacy in the past few centuries this has become
so greatly the sum total and final conception of the uniform and united organ
of salvation, that the suppression of the Papacy in Episcopalianism and in the
renewed system of Territorial Churches destroyed the fundamental conceptions
of the Church altogether. These theoretical efforts to destroy the idea of the
Church have always been only secondary elements in the great struggle of
Church reform, whose political importance is made plain in the interesting
work of *Haller*. "Thus, if these events form merely one chapter in the Christian
history of dogma, they are also at the same time no less, indeed still more, a
phase in the age-long struggle between Church and State, or, to put it more
accurately, between the Catholic Church and the nationalist State" (*Haller,
I, 479*). *Haller*, however, recognizes alongside of the motives of ecclesiastical
policy which proceeded from the English State Church system, also the
secondary elements of the destruction of the conception of the Church, since
he points to the "Pietism" of the demand for a poor Church (*p. 89*), and to the
influence of the *Defensor pacis* (*340 f.*), and above all to that of Occam(*p. 342f.*).
These secondary elements, however, went on working after the Councils—in
the renewed Papacy, in the Concordats, and in the Territorial-Church system—
had attained a result which satisfied the political demands of the day, but not
the religious criticism and the ideals of religious individualism.—For the
element of thought due to Occamism, and to the democratic conception of the
Law of Nature in the Conciliar Reform movement (see also *K. Müller: K.G., II,
65. 67f.*, and *K. Köhler, a.a.O.*). For the whole situation which formed the
setting for the theories which have been described above on *p. 413*, see *von
Bezold* in *Kultur der Gegenwart, II, V, 1* (a clear statement).

196 (p. 378.) Cf. *Dietzel: Beiträge zur Geschichte des Sozialismus* (*Z. f. Gesch. und
Lit. der Staatswissenschaften, II*). Here, on Sir Thomas More. For the new type
of an individualistic cultured Christianity, see, above all, the important works
of *Dilthey* in the *Archiv. f. Gesch. d. Philos., V and VI*. To what a large extent

the ideal of More is a new sociological type of religion is shown most clearly in the inquiry conducted by *Dietzel*: a common share in a universal Theism, evolved from Christianity and from the Stoics, combined with complete religious toleration so far as the views of the individual are concerned, and at the same time a distinct depreciation of worship and ritual.

[197] (p. 381.) This comes out very plainly in the *Evangelisch-soziale Kongress*, which is in itself so thoughtful and idealistic. Every time it meets, the effort is made to formulate its Christian Social ideas in a theological-ethical form, which will not be bound, like that of the sects, to the literal interpretation of the Bible, but which will express the "spirit of the Gospel", but which at the same time will not assert that the essence of religion is contained in the objective character of the Church as an institution, but which takes very seriously the ethical demands of the Gospel in the radical sense. In this, however, this movement has neither the sect community nor the Churches behind it; its supporters are solely individuals whose spirit is "Christian" in a free manner, but whose outlook is thoroughly in harmony with the modern elements in life. There is, however, no organized community in existence which embodies this "spirit"; in reality this spirit is always first of all produced by a church or a sect, and it is only when it has severed its connection with both these forms of religious life that it becomes simply the "spirit" of Christianity, which is a free principle, quite subjective in character, which, in the absence of any sociological basis of its own, finds it very difficult to do anything effective in social reform at all. At the same time this "spirit of Christianity" always experiences afresh the difficulties of coming to terms with the natural basis of human society. Its champions desire the spiritual interpretation of the Gospel, and the universality of a Christianity of the people, without the compromises of the Church and without concealing the purely Divine element in the institutional character of the Church. Its champions desire the ethical radicalism of a Society which is built upon the ideal of the Gospel, without the narrowness and pettiness of the sect. It is, however, impossible to carry the "spirit of the Gospel" into practice without some opportunistic restriction to that which is practically possible, and without the resolve not to allow the best to be the enemy of the good. Just as this situation is only intelligible in the light of historical development, so also, on the other hand, it throws a light upon the latter, where compulsory churches or revolutionary sects based upon the voluntary principle have taken the task in hand, and also for their part found it a very difficult and toilsome matter to make an adjustment to the natural basis of social life.

INDEX TO BOTH VOLUMES [1]

*As the Table of Contents is full and
detailed the index consists of names only.*

[1] Volume II. begins at p. 461.